D1455862

Dictionary of Personal Finance

Dictionary of Personal Finance

Joel G. Siegel, Ph.D., C.P.A.

Jae K. Shim, Ph.D.

Stephen Hartman, Ph.D.

MACMILLAN PUBLISHING COMPANY
New York

MAXWELL MACMILLAN CANADA
Toronto

MAXWELL MACMILLAN INTERNATIONAL
New York   Oxford   Singapore   Sydney

Macmillan Publishing Company
866 Third Avenue, New York, N.Y. 10022

Maxwell Macmillan Canada, Inc.
1200 Eglinton Avenue East, Suite 200
Don Mills, Ontario, M3C 3N1

Macmillan, Inc., is part of the Maxwell Communication Group of Companies

Library of Congress Catalog Card Number: 91-14276

Printed in the United States of America

printing number
1   2   3   4   5   6   7   8   9   10

Library of Congress Cataloging-in-Publication Data

Siegel, Joel G.
    Dictionary of personal finance / Joel G. Siegel, Jae K. Shim, Stephen Hartman.
        p.   cm.
    ISBN 0-02-897393-3 (hc)   ISBN 0-02-897394-1 (pbk)
    1. Finance, Personal—Dictionaries.   I. Shim, Jae K.
    II. Hartman, Stephen.   III. Title.
    HG151.S427   1992   91-14276
    332.024'003—dc20   CIP

The paper used in this publication meets minimum requirements of American National Standard for Information Sciences—Permanence of Paper for Printed Library Materials. ANSI Z39.48-1984.⊗™

DEDICATION

Roberta M. Siegel
Loving Wife and Colleague

Chung Shim
Dedicated Wife

Stephanie R. Hartman
Beautiful Daughter

Alan G. Hartman
Unbelievable Son

Contents

Preface

This dictionary is directed toward the public at large. The idea behind the *Dictionary of Personal Finance* is for the layperson, consumer, and professional to be able to read and comprehend terms and concepts continuously appearing in magazines (e.g., *Money, Personal Finance,* and *Changing Times*) dealing with money management, personal finance, and consumer economics. It is essential for the individual to know personal finance concepts and applications in order to achieve personal financial goals.

Personal finance and financial planning are the most important areas affecting individuals, as planning personal affairs is crucial to success in life. Hence, this dictionary will be a constant reference tool.

It covers all the areas and terms of personal finance. The topics include accounting, taxes, debt management, finance and investments, banking, housing, insurance, business law, career planning, retirement and estate planning, economics, and any other related fields. The dictionary includes the latest terminology and thinking.

The Dictionary of Personal Finance contains a host of practical applications, examples, illustrations, tables, graphs, and checklists to aid reader comprehension and use. In the Appendix are tables referred to in the text, such as those for discounting and compounding.

This dictionary can also be used as a supplement by students taking courses in personal finance in adult education programs, extension centers, and colleges and universities. It is also valuable for people who wish to study for professional certifications, such as Certified Financial Planner (CFP) and Chartered Financial Consultant (ChFC).

Acknowledgments

We wish to express our deep gratitude to Lloyd Chilton for his outstanding editorial assistance during this project. His input and efforts are much recognized and greatly appreciated.

Thanks also goes to Marson Salim and Meng-Chuen Wu for their assistance.

We would like to thank Bob Wilson, Jane Andrassi, and Patterson Lamb for their outstanding editing during the production stage. Their efforts are much recognized and appreciated.

About the Authors

JOEL G. SIEGEL, Ph.D., C.P.A., is a self-employed certified public accountant and professor of accounting and finance at Queens College of the City University of New York.

He was previously employed by Coopers and Lybrand, C.P.A.s, and Arthur Anderson, C.P.A.s. Dr. Siegel is a consultant to many clients in accounting and tax matters. He has acted as a consultant in accounting and finance to such organizations as Citicorp, International Telephone and Telegraph, United Technologies, American Institute of C.P.A.s, and Person-Wolinsky Associates.

Dr. Siegel is the author of thirty-five books and about two hundred articles on accounting and financial topics. His books have been published by Macmillan, Prentice-Hall, McGraw-Hill, Harper/Collins, John Wiley, Barron's, International Publishing, and the American Institute of C.P.A.s. His articles have been published in many financial journals including the *Financial Analysts Journal, Financial Executive,* and the *CPA Journal.*

In 1972, he received the Outstanding Educator of America Award. Dr. Siegel is listed in Who's Where among Writers and Who's Who in the World.

JAE K. SHIM, Ph.D., is professor of finance and accounting at California State University, Long Beach, and president of the National Business Review Foundation, a personal financial consulting firm. He has many client responsibilities in personal financial planning and is also involved in real estate investing. He received his Ph.D. degree from the University of California at Berkeley.

Dr. Shim has coauthored twenty professional books with Dr. Joel Siegel, including *Personal Finance, The Personal Financial Planning and Investment Guide,* and *Investments: A Self-Teaching Guide.* He has published many articles in professional journals.

Dr. Shim is a recipient of the 1982 *Credit Research Foundation Award* for his article on financial management.

STEPHEN W. HARTMAN, Ph.D., is a professor in the School of Management at the New York Institute of Technology. Dr. Hartman earned his Ph.D. from Syracuse University, writing his dissertation on New York State municipal finance.

Dr. Hartman has been a registered representative with a major brokerage firm, a personal finance adviser, author of a weekly personal investing column, and a member of public finance advisory boards. He was nominated as the comptroller candidate for Suffolk County, New York, and has held public office as a finance director for the town of Babylon.

In addition to coauthoring a business dictionary, he has written numerous articles, a Harvard Case Study, and research reports on many areas in finance. Dr. Hartman has extensive experience as a consultant to business and individuals in financial matters.

How to Use This Dictionary

The terms are in alphabetical order, using the word-by-word system. The entries are, for the most part, self-contained. The definitions are clear, understandable, comprehensive, and practical. All relevant information is included. Some terms require elaboration, which is provided by cross-referencing as indicated in small capital letters. Any important words that are included in the definition are italicized for emphasis.

If the definition of a term appears elsewhere, it is cross-referenced with *see*.

If an entry has more than one meaning depending on context or field, the definitions are numbered in the order of importance under the applicable field.

When a term is synonymous with another, that is indicated at the beginning of the definition by the word *or* followed by the synonym in italics.

Dictionary of Personal Finance

A

abandonment The voluntary giving up or surrendering of all rights, title, and possession of property with no intention of reclaiming it. The major test of abandonment is the voluntary intention to surrender or give up property. It results in the act of disposing of an ASSET which has no further value or use to the owner. Abandoned property can, in some instances, be considered a sale in which the normal rules of CAPITAL GAIN AND LOSS are applied.

Types of property that can be abandoned include CONTRACTS, copyrights, easements, inventions, leases, public offices as in resignation, patents, property, trade marks and trade names, and water rights. The term is also applied to a parent's desertion of children.

abatement
in general:
  1. To decrease in amount or value.
  2. Reduction on service charges.
taxation: Complete or partial cancellation of a tax levy or special assessment imposed by a governmental unit.
law: A temporary suspension or termination in a lawsuit.

ability to pay
business: A customer's ability to make payments to the vendor.
banking: A BORROWER'S financial ability to service the INTEREST and PRINCIPAL requirements of a LOAN agreement. Normally the ability to pay is determined by future earnings prospects. Those having a higher ability to pay would have a higher CREDIT rating.
labor relations: The ability of an employer to meet a union's financial demands.
bonds: The source of REVENUE pledged to service the BONDS. In the case of a corporate BOND, the source of revenue would be the earnings of the corporation. In the case of governmental BONDS, TAX revenues would determine the ability of the governmental unit to service the INTEREST and PRINCIPAL needs.

absolute liability A liability without fault that is imposed in some states when the activities of a person are considered inconsistent with public policy, irrespective of the fact that the action may not have been intentional or negligent. For example, if an individual owns a dog that bites someone, the owner of the animal is legally liable for any injuries sustained.

absolute sale A sale whereby the property passes to the buyer after the buyer and seller have agreed to the contract.

absusive tax shelter A LIMITED PARTNERSHIP that in the opinion of the INTERNAL REVENUE SERVICE is claiming illegal tax deductions. Typically, the tax shelter is "padding" the value of purchased property to generate overstated depreciation writeoffs. If the writeoffs are disallowed, the taxpayer is responsible for back taxes, interest charges, and penalties.

acceleration clause A clause in a CREDIT contract or MORTGAGE stating that if the BORROWER does not meet the payment schedule, all remaining payments may become immediately due and payable at once at the demand of the lender.

acceptance
  1. BANKER'S ACCEPTANCE
  2. Binding contract effected when one party to a business arrangement accepts the offer of the other. Acceptance may be implied or partial, oral or written, depending on the nature of the offer.
  3. DRAWEE'S promise to pay either a time

draft or sight draft. Typically, the acceptor signs his or her name after writing "accepted" on the bill along with the date. An acceptance of a bill in effect makes it a PROMISSORY NOTE: the acceptor is the maker and the drawer is the endorser.

accident The occurrence of an unpredictable event. Accidents can result in calamities having casualties, injuries, property damage, or loss. Accidents are sometimes referred to as acts of God. Insurance companies commonly INSURE against the effects of accidents.

An unavoidable accident is one that occurs despite the exercise of prudent care and diligence as compared to NEGLIGENCE.

airplanes: An airplane "accident" often involves a serious loss of life and extensive property damage. INSURANCE settlements resulting from these accidents can be extremely large. All the circumstances of an air accident are studied carefully to determine the mechanical condition of the aircraft, weather conditions, and the possibility that pilot error was a factor.

In recent years there have been intentional acts of sabotage causing several air disasters. These are not accidents in the true sense of the word since they were intentional actions.

automobiles: Upon the occurrence of an automobile "accident" the proper authorities as well as the INSURANCE COMPANY insuring the vehicle must be notified promptly. Automobile operators who abandon an accident scene without stopping can be found guilty of leaving the scene of an accident. They are termed "hit-and-run drivers."

maritime: An accident at sea is often referred to as an "accident of navigation." In these circumstances an investigation of the circumstances will focus on the sea conditions under which the ship was navigating to determine whether due diligence was followed.

accident insurance A type of HEALTH INSURANCE plan designed to pay a specific amount per day (e.g., $200) for a hospital stay resulting from an accident, and/or a specific amount for the loss of certain limbs or body parts (e.g., $5,000 for the loss of an arm).

accidental death and dismemberment insurance (AD&D) A type of HEALTH INSURANCE that pays a lump sum if the insured is accidentally killed in an auto accident or if he or she is hit by another car. The POLICY also pays a portion of the INSURED amount if the person loses part of the body such as a leg, an arm, or an eye. It may also pay disability income should the individual, become totally disabled.

accidental injury clause A clause in a HEALTH INSURANCE policy providing that so long as the result of a given action is accidental, coverage for an injury resulting from an accident will apply.

accommodation

1. A loan that does not require security or interest. An example might be a loan between members of the family or friends.

2. An insurer taking on a client because of personal rather than professional reasons, such as the possibility of getting other business.

accommodation endorser A person who endorses a PROMISSORY NOTE without obtaining benefit or compensation. It may be done as a favor to the borrower. The endorser's signature enables the debtor either to obtain credit or to obtain it at a lower interest rate. In the event the note is defaulted on by the maker, the endorser becomes liable. Such an ENDORSEMENT is common in banking. For example, a parent may act as an accommodation endorser for a child who needs credit.

account A record of the relationship and transactions between an individual and another party. The other party may be providing products or services. Examples are an individual's checking account at a bank and credit account at a retail store.

See also ACCOUNT BALANCE.

account balance Balance of an account at the end of a reporting period. The balance may be an asset or liability. Examples of asset account balances are the deposit balance in a SAVINGS ACCOUNT, MUTUAL FUND, or brokerage account. An example of a liability account balance is the unpaid balance on a credit card.

account exceptions

1. Objection of an individual to the accuracy of information included in his or her account, such as possible overcharges by a department store, bank, or brokerage firm.

2. Treatment of an individual that is different from the treatment of others considered to be in the same class, such as an insurance carrier's providing theft coverage to one homeowner in the neighborhood but not others, for special reasons (e.g., insured is a detective).

account executive Or, *registered representative*. A staff member of a BROKERAGE FIRM who provides financial recommendations and executes orders to buy and sell financial and/or real assets. The account executive acts as the client's agent. The account executive must pass certain examinations in order to be properly registered before he or she can practice.
See also BROKER.

account number Numerical designation of an account for identification purposes. The account number allows both parties to record and keep track of all transactions. Account numbers are assigned to bank accounts, mutual funds, and credit cards.

account reconciliation Adjusting the difference between accounts so that the figures agree. For example, you should analyze the difference between your checkbook balance and your bank account balance to reconcile items at the end of a period. Outstanding checks must be subtracted from the bank balance since the bank does not know at the present time of their existence. Bank service charges must be deducted from your checkbook balance when you find out about them from reading your bank statement. After the reconciliation is completed, the checkbook balance and bank balance must be in agreement. If not, an error is indicated in your records and/or the bank's records and must be corrected.

accountability The condition of being held responsible for one's action. Being accountable subjects one to full culpability for all actions, DEBTS, and conditions creating an obligation to perform the terms of an agreement or contract. Accountability can signify responsibility for TAX payments and or penalties, fines, or fees, as well as legal judgments.
See also LIABILITIES.

accretion

1. Growth in assets in acquisitions, mergers, multiplication or internal expansion. Examples are aging of wine, nursery stock, and livestock. It enhances the value of an ASSET in the natural course of events.

2. The process of land buildup because of the gradual accumulation of waterborne rock, sand, and soil.

3. An increase in value derived from an intended accumulation. An example is the increased value in a pension plan from accumulated PRINCIPAL contributions, and the INCOME thereon.

4. Adjustment of the difference between the FACE VALUE of a SECURITY (such as a BOND) and the price of the security bought at an original discount.

accrual An anticipation in accounting of future revenues or EXPENSES. Outlays and receipts are recognized in the period in which they actually take place instead of when payments are actually made or revenues received. This contrasts with CASH basis accounting, which records expenses and revenues at the time of cash payment or receipt.

A business having inventory, such as a manufacturer, must use accrual accounting. A service business, such as an attorney's or doctor's practice, has the option of using either the accural or cash basis of accounting.

accrual bonds BONDS that do not pay interest on a periodic basis but accumulate interest for payment when the bond is redeemed.

accrued dividend The typical DIVIDEND a company makes on its STOCK but for which the board of directors has not made a formal declaration. However, until the board of directors does make a formal declaration, an accrued dividend is not a legal obligation of the company, and if, in the opinion of management, the DIVIDEND should be reduced or not paid, management is free to make this decision. As opposed to an accrued dividend, a dividend formally declared but not paid is a dividend in ARREARS.

accrued interest
in general: INTEREST that has accumulated since the last payment date. It has been earned but not received.
real estate: INTEREST that accrues and will be paid when a piece of property is sold if the RENTAL INCOME from the property does not cover the MORTGAGE payments.

accumulated dividend An unpaid dividend due, typically to owners of cumulative preferred shares.

accumulation period The time period during which an annuitant makes premium payments to an insurance company.

acquisition
1. The purchase of an item such as an asset or good.
2. The attempt to acquire a controlling interest in another business.

acquisition cost
1. Price paid by an individual to buy merchandise, services, or assets. It equals the list price plus normal incidental costs to acquire the item, including installation.
2. Amount paid by a company to acquire another company. The expenditures include purchase price and legal fees.
3. A sales charge assessed by a MUTUAL FUND for purchase of a share of the fund. It is sometimes called FRONT END LOAD.
4. Purchase price and all fees required to acquire a property. For example, John purchases a duplex for $150,000 plus $6,000 in CLOSING COSTS. His acquisition cost is $156,000.

acquit
1. To release from an obligation.

2. To clear a person's name of a charge. An example is to set one free from an accusation of guilt by a verdict of not guilty.

across the board Including all, or almost all, of everything within a group or category. Examples are all employees receiving the same percentage raise from the employer, or almost all stocks rising in price on the same day.

action A legal term connoting a proceeding initiated by one party against another. An individual may, for example, sue another person or business entity for failure to meet a contractual obligation. The defendant is then notified by the court of the action seeking redress for the purported wrongdoing. If the defendant never responds to the suit, the plaintiff wins by default. Typically, the defendant responds and the case is decided through the judicial process.

action plan A strategy to be taken by an individual to accomplish some objective or purpose. An example is setting up a plan to start a new business.

active account Any type of account in which recurring activities occur. Such accounts include BOND accounts, CHECKING ACCOUNTS, STOCK accounts, and so on. An active account is a current account. An active account may have a high volume of activity.

If a BANK account has not been used for five years for a deposit or withdrawal, the MONEY may have to be transferred to the state, for example, as required by New York State law. The reason is that the DEPOSITOR may be deceased.

Some BROKERAGE FIRMS may charge a fee if there have been no transactions in an account for a period of time.

activity
account: The number of transactions occurring in a particular account.
personnel: The work accomplished in any given field of work commonly conducted by those who work in an entity.
securities: The volume of STOCK transactions

that occurs in a particular STOCK EXCHANGE at any given time. Active stocks trading in an EXCHANGE would have a higher degree of LIQUIDITY with a correspondingly smaller gap between the bid and asked prices.

activity charge Generally an activity charge, or service charge, is a payment for transactions occurring in an ACCOUNT. The net effect of an activity charge is to provide remuneration to the organization servicing a particular ACCOUNT. Normally activity charges are billed on a monthly basis.

banking: Charges made for DEPOSITS, withdrawals, or CHECKS presented in a CHECKING ACCOUNT.

utilities: Utilities, including electricity, gas, and water, commonly charged on the basis of the activity or units consumed for the account.

activity checking account The bank bases its service charge on the number of transactions in the account. For example, if a bank charges $.20 per transaction and you have 30 transactions for the month, the service charge will be $6.

actual authority The authorization given an individual to perform on behalf of the principal. *See also* AUTHORITY.

actual cash value (ACV) The replacement cost of an item less accumulated depreciation.

actual value
1. The proceeds received or to be received from the sale of property in an arms length transaction.
2. The book value of an asset equal to original cost less accumulated depreciation.
3. The discounted value of future cash receipts to be received from an asset.

actuals Physical commodities that may be bought. Examples are gold and soy beans. When the contract matures, the commodity may be delivered to the buyer. Many future contracts are closed out prior to the expiration date of the contract, and thus the transaction does not result in delivery.

actuarial calculation Mathematical projections of future events including ASSET APPRECIATION, earning power, and mortality in order to determine PREMIUMS, reserves, DIVIDENDS, INSURANCE, PENSION, and ANNUITY rates. Probabilities of future events are determined based on past occurrences by category.

Actuarial gains and losses will occur due to the difference between estimates and actual experience.

actuaries Experts involved in mathematical computations and analyses of risks and PREMIUMS for INSURANCE considering probability estimates.

ad valorem tax A tax levy imposed on property, typically based on a stated percentage of the property's value. The most common ad valorem tax is that imposed by states, counties, and cities on real estate. It can, however, be levied on personal property. Examples include PROPERTY TAXES, SALES TAXES, and EXCISE TAXES.

add-on charge (interest) The finance charge calculated on the amount financed for the term of the contract and added to the amount financed to determine the total payments. Under REGULATION Z, add-on interest is no longer permitted.

add-on clause
1. A clause that allows the lender to hold as SECURITY a number of items that are purchased over a period of time; the lender does not release the security interest on these items until the entire loan has been paid off.
2. A provision for adding new purchases to an existing installment contract.

add-on contract A clause in a CREDIT contract that states that if the BORROWER misses any payments, all the items under the contract can be repossessed, even though the payments may have already recovered the cost of some of the items.

add-on loan

1. A second loan taken out for a larger amount before the first loan is repaid. Taking out add-on loans is called FLIPPING. For example, assume that one's original loan of $10,000 has been repaid down to $5,000. The individual may decide to refinance the debt balance of $5,000 and borrow an additional $4,000 from the same lender. It may be a wise decision to increase an existing note at a lower interest rate.

2. A loan in which the interest is added to the original loan balance to determine the monthly payments.

See also ADD-ON METHOD.

add-on method A method of calculating interest by which the total finance charge is added to the PRINCIPAL amount; the sum is divided by the number of monthly payments to determine the amount of the monthly payment. For example, an individual takes out a $1,000, 12%, one-year ADD-ON LOAN. The finance charges on the loan would be $1,000 × .12 × 1 = $120.

To find the monthly payments, we add $120 to $1,000 and then divide the sum by the number of monthly payments to be made. This results in monthly payments of $93.33, calculated as follows:

$$\frac{\$1,000 + \$120}{12} = \frac{\$1,120}{12} = \$93.33,$$

which are much higher than the ones with the simple interest loan ($88.85 obtained from Table 5, Appendix A).

See also ANNUAL PERCENTAGE RATE (APR); SIMPLE INTEREST METHOD.

address of record Or, *legal address.* An individual's address where mail may be sent (e.g., contracts, notices).

adequacy of coverage Fully protecting against the risk of financial or other loss.

insurance: Adequacy of COVERAGE indicates that the potential for liability RISK is sufficiently INSURED. An individual should have sufficient INSURANCE coverage to protect against the hardships of loss and personal damage.

international trade: In order to protect against loss in international currencies, an exporter might buy a put option on the future value of a particular CURRENCY in order to protect against possible future currency loss in the country to which the export is occurring. Thus, the value of the CONTRACT would be protected since the put option would rise in value if the foreign currency fell.

stocks: Using market instruments to protect the investor against market risks. For example, a STOCK INVESTOR might buy a PUT OPTION for the same STOCK to protect against downside risk. Thus, if the STOCK should fall in price because of market activity, the put option would simultaneously rise in price thus protecting the investor against loss.

See also HEDGE.

adhesion contract A legal agreement containing standardized terms between a business and consumers dealing with the transfer of goods and/or services. The standard provisions in the contract must be accepted by consumers as is without change. Hence, the consumer has no other option but to agree with the terms or not do business with the seller. A standard warranty provision is a case in point.

ad hoc An activity occurring for a particular activity and not to be generalized to others. An AD HOC body is one convened for a particular purpose, the accomplishment of which causes it to cease its existence. AD HOC activities are unique and not formally sanctioned.

ad infinitum Unending. Without limit. To an infinite extent. An activity that continues without any foreseeable end.

adjudication order The formal giving or pronouncing of a judgment or decree in an action. An adjudication order signifies that all the claims against the litigants have been settled. A BANKRUPTCY adjudication of the bankruptcy court signifies that an individual is bankrupt and the property of the defendant is transferred to a trustee who will sell it and remit the proceeds to the CREDITORS.

adjustable life insurance Insurance coverage that may be changed by the policyholder as necessary depending upon changing circumstances. The policy owner may change the plan of insurance, premiums, and face value. For example, the insured may decide for financial reasons to modify the time period and amount of premiums to be paid.

adjustable rate mortgage (ARM) Or, *variable or flexible rate mortgage.* A MORTGAGE in which the interest rate is not fixed but changes over the life of the loan. Adjustable rate mortgages are often called ARMs. They often feature attractive starting interest rates and monthly payments. But there is the risk that payments will rise. There are pluses to ARMS:

1. Lower initial INTEREST (often 2 or 3 percentage points below that of a fixed rate) and lower initial payments, which can mean considerable savings. This means that ARMs are easier to qualify for.
2. Payments come down if interest rates fall.
3. Loans are more readily available and their processing time is quicker than for FIXED-RATE MORTGAGES.
4. Many adjustables are assumable by a BORROWER, a feature that can help when it comes time to sell.
5. Many ARMs allow one to prepay the loan without penalty.

There are also pitfalls to ARMS:

1. Monthly payments can go up if interest rates rise.
2. NEGATIVE AMORTIZATION can occur, in which the monthly payments do not cover all the INTEREST cost. The interest cost that is not covered is added to the unpaid PRINCIPAL BALANCE. This means that after making many payments one could owe more than was owed at the beginning of the loan balance.
3. The initial interest rates last only until the first adjustment, typically six months or

one year. And the promotional or tease rate is often not distinguished from the true contract rate, which is based on the index to which the loan is tied.

ARMs versus fixed rate

A borrower should consider a FIXED RATE LOAN over an ARM if he or she

- Plans to be in the same home for a long time. It pays to get an ARM if one is buying a starter home or expects to move or be transferred in two to three years.
- Does not expect INCOME to rise.
- Plans to take sizable DEBTS, like auto or educational loans.
- Prizes the SECURITY of constant payments.

checklist for ARMs

When shopping for an ARM (or for any other adjustable rate loan), the following checklist of questions to ask lenders is helpful:

- What is the initial LOAN rate and the ANNUAL PERCENTAGE RATE (APR)? What costs besides interest does the APR reflect? What are the points?
- What is the monthly payment?
- What index is the loan tied to? How has the index moved in the past? Will the rate always move with the index?
- What is the lender's margin above the index? The margin is an important consideration when comparing ARM loans because it never changes during the life of the loan. Note that Index rate + margin = ARM interest rate.

Example: An individual is comparing ARMs offered by two different lenders. Both ARMs are for 30 years and amount to $65,000. Both lenders use the one-year Treasury index, which is 10%. But Lender A uses a 2% margin, and Lender B uses a 3% margin. Here is how the difference in margin would affect the initial monthly payment:

	Lender A	Lender B
ARM interest rate	12% (10%+2%)	13% (10%+3%)
Monthly payment	$668.60 at 12%	$719.03 at 13%

- How long will the initial rate be in effect? Will there be an automatic increase at the first adjustment period, even if the index has not changed? What effect will this have on monthly payments?

- How often can the rate change?
- Is there a limit on each rate change and how will the limit affect monthly payments?
- What is the "cap" or ceiling on the rate change over the life of the loan?
- Does the loan require PRIVATE MORTGAGE INSURANCE (PMI) and how much does it cost per month?
- Is NEGATIVE AMORTIZATION possible?
- Is the loan assumable?
- Is there a PREPAYMENT PENALTY?

See also CREATIVE FINANCING; RENEGOTIATED RATE MORTGAGE (RRM); VARIABLE RATE MORTGAGE (VRM).

adjustable rate preferred stock (ARPS) Or, *floating rate* or *variable rate preferred stock*. PREFERRED STOCK that pays dividends that go up and down with the general level of interest rates. The prices of these SECURITIES are therefore less volatile than fixed-dividend preferred stock, and they may be a safe haven for investors. YIELDS obtained from adjustable rate preferreds may be lower than debt issues.

adjusted balance method A common method of computing finance charges by which the interest is determined using the balance remaining at the end of the billing period (ignoring purchase or returns made during the billing period). Interest is charged on the balance outstanding after it has been adjusted for payments and credits. This will result in lower interest charges than other methods such as AVERAGE DAILY BALANCE METHOD, PREVIOUS BALANCE METHOD and PAST DUE BALANCE METHOD. For example, assume that the monthly interest rate is 1.5%, which represents an annual rate of 18%. The previous balance is $400 and the payment was made on the 15th day of the month. The balance remaining at the end of the billing period is $100 ($400–$300), so the interest charge is $100 × 1.5% = $1.50.

adjusted basis A tax term of the cost or other taxable basis increased by capital expenditures or reduced by depreciation. An example is improvements made to a home, such as a new roof or electrical system, that increase the cost basis for the home for tax purposes, thus reducing the taxable gain when the house is sold.

adjusted gross income (AGI) A federal TAX term applying to the difference between a taxpayer's GROSS INCOME and adjustments to income. These adjustments include deductions for IRA and KEOGH PENSION PLANS, ALIMONY payments, and penalty on early withdrawal of savings.

Adjusted gross income is the taxpayer's income before taking either the standard deduction or itemized deductions, such as medical EXPENSES, state and local TAXES, INTEREST expenses, and contributions.

adjusted price Accrued interest is added to the price of a bond or note.

adjuster An insurance term applying to an employee of an insurance company or outside consultant to it who ascertains the reason for loss and estimates the amount of the insurable loss, if any. The adjuster may decide that the insured is not covered under the policy. The insured may retain his or her own representative, called a public adjuster.

adjustment

1. Change made to an account balance because of some happening or occurrence, such as a product defect.
2. In securities, modifying a contract for a STOCK SPLIT.
3. In insurance, the insurance company pays a claim to the insured.

administrative discretion The legal authority of an individual to act in a situation. An example is a tax official who evaluates the legitimacy of tax shelter credits taken by the taxpayer.

advance

1. An increase in the price of assets, such as

commodities, stocks, bonds, and so on.

2. Money given to an employee before it is earned or incurred, such as an advance against salary or a cash advance for travel expenses.

3. Prepayment for merchandise or services to be received or rendered at a future time. Some contracts require an advance before completion (e.g., construction project).

4. Transfer of funds from a lender to a borrower in advance on a LOAN.

advance bill An invoice received before merchandise has arrived. It may be asked for by buyers for tax documentation. The individual should not pay the advance bill until he or she is satisfied with the quality of the merchandise or service.

advance-decline (A-D) The ratio of STOCKS advancing compared to those declining. It is obviously more favorable to have more STOCKS advancing than declining. The general direction of the MARKET can be determined by the steepness of the advanced decline line over time. Minor day-to-day variations are insignificant. It is the direction over a period of time that is significant and important. An extremely steep A-D line is either bullish (favorable) or bearish (negative) depending on whether the line is increasing or declining.

The index may be expressed numerically (advances led declines by 4 to 1) or as a ratio (1,600 advances and 400 declines is an index of "4").

See also BEAR; BULL.

advance refunding An opportunity for one holding bonds due to expire shortly to exchange them for new bonds on favorable terms. This strategy is used by the U.S. Treasury to try to keep its bondholders from switching to other securities.

advancing market A market in which the AD-VANCE DECLINE line is strongly favorable, indicating that more STOCKS are advancing than declining. One theory holds that three consecutive days in which advances lead declines by 1,000 issues or more is a very BULLISH signal.

adverse possession Acquisition of land through prolonged and unauthorized occupation under an evident claim or right, in denial or opposition to the title of another claimant. Adverse possession is a statute of limitations that bars a legal owner from claiming title to land when the owner has done nothing to oust an adverse occupant during the statutory period. Courts of law are quite demanding of proof before they allow adverse possession. For example, the claimant must show proof that he or she has maintained actual, visible, continuous, exclusive, hostile, and notorious possession and be publicly claiming ownership to the property.

adverse selection In life insurance, an uninsurable applicant, or one with greater than average risk, wants to obtain a policy at the standard premium rate. The applicant may be in poor health or have a dangerous job. The insurance company will increase its standard rate for this type of policyholder or in fact not issue the policy. However, it is difficult to control adverse selection with group health policies.

advisory letters Any of a series of private financial newsletters written by financial "experts" primarily devoted to advice on STOCK MARKET and MUTUAL FUND investing, but also including advice on COMMODITY and MONEY MARKET fund investing. The advisory letters vary in their services; however, some may provide an 800 "hot line" where a subscriber can call to get the latest INVESTMENT advice, or the service may call the subscriber directly when it feels an INVESTMENT opportunity is particularly timely. In the case of commodity market, MONEY MARKET, and MUTUAL FUND letters, advice is often given on timing "switches" between commodities or funds, respectively, depending on MARKET developments.

Advisory letters are distinct from FINANCIAL ADVISERS in that they take no direct responsibility for investing and managing the client's PORT-FOLIO. Subscribers to advisory letters pay a

subscription fee that varies widely based upon the individual letter and any related services.
See also ADVISORY SERVICES; FINANCIAL ADVISER.

advisory services A fee-based investing service provided by financial specialists in several areas, including INSURANCE, STOCKS, and REAL ESTATE. Services may also include publications devoted to their INVESTMENT markets, INSURANCE strategies, or particular companies.

As with ADVISORY LETTERS advisory services take no direct responsibility for investing client PORTFOLIOS and limit their services to INVESTMENT advice based upon specific research.
See also FINANCIAL ADVISER.

affidavit A statement or declaration in writing, made under an oath before some officer (such as a NOTARY PUBLIC) who has the authority to administer the oath or affirmation. For example, in the case of affidavit of title, the seller (the affiant) identifies himself or herself and his or her marital status certifying that since the examination of title on the contract date there are no judgments, divorces, or bankruptcies, or unrecorded deeds, unpaid repairs, or defects of title known to him or her and that he or she is in possession of the property.

affirm To confirm, ratify, verify, and accept an item or event that can be terminated.

after date The period subsequent to the date appearing on a financial instrument such as a note, bill of exchange, or other credit instrument. For example, "payable 15 days after date" on a note dated January 5 means that payment is required on January 20.

after-hours dealing A stock transaction executed after the regular hours of the stock exchange. The transaction may be at a price different from the day's ending price. This trading usually occurs in the over-the-counter market.

after sight The period subsequent to the presentation of a financial instrument (e.g., note payable) for acceptance. For example, "after sight of 20 days after presentation" of a note on March 10 must be accepted on March 30.

after-tax cash flow CASH FLOW from INCOME-PRODUCING PROPERTY, less INCOME TAXES, if any, attributable to the property's income. If there is a TAX LOSS that can provide a tax saving from the shelter of income earned outside the property, that savings is added to the cash flow earned by the property. For example, a property generates $2,000 per year of cash flow. In the first year of ownership, depreciation and interest deductions provide a tax loss of $3,000. At a tax rate of 30%, the loss saves $900 ($3,000 × 30%) of income taxes. The after-tax cash flow is $2,900.
See also BEFORE-TAX CASH FLOW; CASH FLOW.

after-tax rate of return RATE OF RETURN after income taxes that an investor can keep out of the CURRENT INCOME and CAPITAL GAINS OR LOSSES earned from investments.

against the box Description of a transaction in which stock is sold short by the holder of a long position in the identical security. BOX means the securities are retained at the BROKERAGE FIRM for safekeeping. If stock is sold against the box, it is shorted; however, the seller *actually owns* the shares. The shares necessary to cover a sale against the box are typically borrowed from the broker. It is used to protect a long position in a stock against price depreciation. It is also used illegally to avoid taxes by recording the short sale as an actual sale while preserving the original long position in the stock.
See also SHORT SELLING.

age

1. The number of years old an individual is, information necessary to know for some reason, such as the retirement age for a particular job.

2. The period of time an individual has made use of something, such as an asset (e.g., automobile)

3. Aging an account, such as determining how long accounts receivable are outstanding, or how many days inventory has been held.

agency

1. The relationship between two individuals in which one is a PRINCIPAL and the other is his or her agent representing the principal in transactions with other parties. This relationship arises out of a contract, either expressed or implied, written or oral, wherein the agent is employed by the principal to do certain acts dealing with a third party.

2. A government body.

3. The capacity of buying and selling a security or property for a client.

agency issues BONDS, NOTES, and certificates issued by various federal government agencies that often pay a yield one-quarter of 1% higher than Treasury securities.
See also GOVERNMENT SECURITIES.

agent A person authorized by another, the PRINCIPAL, to perform or transact a service involving a third party. An agent generally performs a business-related service either for the private or public sector.

Agents have three basic characteristics:

1. They act on behalf of and are subject to the control of a principal.
2. They are not the principal.
3. They must follow the principal's instructions.

co-agent: Agents who share the principal's authorization to perform his or her best instructions.

exclusive agent: The only AGENT permitted to act for the principal in a particular territory or matter although the principal may act for himself.

general agent: One who is authorized to act for a principal in all matters concerning a particular business or employment of a particular nature.

independent agent: An independent business person contracting with a principal to achieve a particular outcome.

mercantile agent: Individuals employed for the sale of goods or merchandise. The two principal classes of mercantile agents are BRO-KERS and factors. Factors are sometimes referred to as commission agents or commission merchants.

private agent: An individual acting solely for an individual in the conduct of his or her private affairs.

public agent: A person appointed by a unit of the government or state for the purpose of representing the public on matters pertaining to the administration of public business affairs.

real estate agent: An individual primarily engaged in the sale or rent of REAL ESTATE for others. Real estate includes all types of property including vacant land, businesses, houses, and APARTMENTS.
See also TRANSFER AGENT.

aggregate amount The total or gross amount without adjustments.

demand: The total amount of goods and services demanded in the economy at alternative INCOME levels in a given period including both consumer and producer's goods, also referred to as total spending.

exercise price (AEP):

1. The gross amount that may be EXERCISED under the terms of STOCK OPTION contracts. The aggregate total exercise potential of the option CONTRACTS that makes up the AEP.

2. The STRIKE PRICE multiplied by the face value of underlying securities, in cases of TREASURY BILLS and notes of the Government National Mortgage Association (GINNIE MAE). The option value (STRIKE PRICE) represents a percentage of FACE VALUE.

income: Sum total of all INCOME without adjustment for inflation, TAXES, or certain types of double counting. The GROSS NATIONAL PRODUCT as the aggregate income of the nation.

indebtedness: The total of amounts payable to customers. The amounts due to customer CREDIT balances. Computing aggregate indebtedness is required by the SECURITIES AND EXCHANGE COMMISSION.

supply: The total amount of goods and services supplied to the MARKET at alternative price levels in a given period of time also, referred to as total output.
See also BROKER-DEALER; CALL; OPTION; PUT; STRIKE PRICE; TREASURY BILL; TREASURY NOTE.

aggregate indemnity   The total limit of coverage under all insurance policies for the covered loss for which the insured may be reimbursed. For example, the insured may have two health insurance policies; the total limit of coverage is provided by the primary policy in combination with the secondary policy.

aggregate limit   The maximum dollar amount of coverage in a health insurance policy, a property damage policy, or a liability policy. The maximum may be stated per occurrence or over the life of the policy. For example, the insured is responsible for an auto accident resulting in injury to two people of $175,000 and $125,000, respectively. Although the total damages are $300,000, the aggregate limit under the policy is assumed to be $275,000. Therefore, the insured must pay the balance of $25,000.

aggressive growth fund   Or, *maximum capital gain, capital appreciation,* or *small-company growth fund.* A type of MUTUAL FUND taking greater risk in order to yield maximum appreciation (instead of current dividend income). It typically invests in the stocks of upstart and high-tech oriented companies. RETURN can be great but so can risk. Aggressive investment strategies include leverage purchases, OPTIONS, SHORT SALES, and even the purchase of high risk stock.

agreement of sale   Or, *offer and acceptance, contract of sale, earnest money contract.* A written agreement between seller and purchaser in which the purchaser agrees to buy certain property and the seller agrees to sell it upon terms of the agreement. For example, Jeannette's broker prepared an agreement of sale to sell a home to David. Both principals signed it. The agreement states that the price of $100,000 is to be paid in cash at closing, subject to David's ability to arrange an $80,000 loan at a 10% interest rate.

air pocket stock   A stock that significantly declines in market price, typically after a bad report about the company in the financial news. An example was Bolar Pharmaceutical after the company admitted to falsifying information about its generic equivalent of the drug Dyazide. The price of the stock drops drastically because practically everyone wants to sell and there are only a few buyers. The plunge is similar to that of an airplane dropping in an air pocket.

aleatory contract   A contract giving more in benefits than the premiums paid by the insured. For example, after paying $5,000 in premiums, the insured may receive $200,000 because of the destruction of insured property. Most insurance policies are of the aleatory type. However, in most cases, the insurance company receives premiums in excess of benefits paid out to the public.

all-inclusive trust deed (AITD)   *See* WRAP-AROUND MORTGAGE (TRUST DEED).

all or none order (AON)
investment banking: An offering whereby the issuer retains the right to cancel the whole issue if an underwriting is not fully subscribed.
securities: A buy or sell order where nothing is to be done if the order cannot be completed in its entirety. However, the order will not be canceled unless the order is also marked FILL-OR-KILL ORDER (FOK).

all risk/all peril   A feature in an INSURANCE policy that covers each loss except for those specifically excluded by the policy. This is the broadest type of insurance that can be bought. For example, if an insurance policy does not specifically exclude losses from flood damage, the INSURED is covered automatically for such losses.
See also ALL-RISK POLICY; NAMED-PERILS POLICY.

all-risk coverage   *See* ALL-RISK POLICY.

all-risk policy A property insurance or other type of policy that covers ALL RISKS/PERILS except those specifically listed.
See also ALL RISK/ALL PERIL.

allied insurance risk Additional insurance to the principal risk. For example, additional lines to a fire insurance policy might be demolition, water damage, or increased cost of construction.

alligator spread An OPTIONS SPREAD that causes the customer to be "eaten alive" with COMMISSION costs to be executed. An alligator spread could be a series of PUT and CALL OPTION maneuvers that would be extremely unlikely to result in any profit for the customer.

Any OPTION transaction in which the commission costs are higher than potential profits.

allotment
labor: The assignment of wages to the dependents of an employee.
securities:
1. The distribution of securities on some basis to subscribers.
2. The apportionment or sharing of a new securities issue among underwriters.

allowance
marketing: The reduction in price or increase in quantity of a good or service that the seller gives the buyer. Allowance may be given in special sale, shrinkage, damage, and spoilage situations.
finance: Permission by the creditor that allows the debtor to deduct a specified amount in settlement of an existing account, such as because of a delay in receiving goods or quality problems with the merchandise.

alternative account A type of joint bank account of two individuals. Each person can withdraw funds, if need be.

alternative investment A type of INVESTMENT in which funds are placed in ASSETS that are riskier than savings in the bank, as neither principal nor income is guaranteed.

alternative minimum tax (AMT) A tax ensuring that a minimum amount of tax will be paid by high-income taxpayers who obtain significant tax savings by using certain tax deductions. Without AMT, some taxpayers may escape taxation completely. The AMT acts as a recapture mechanism, reclaiming tax breaks available to high-income taxpayers. A taxpayer's AMT is the excess of the tentative minimum tax over the regular tax. The AMT must be paid in addition to the year-end tax liability. Assume a taxpayer's tentative minimum tax is $60,000 and his or her regular tax is $45,000. Thus, the taxpayer must pay an AMT of $15,000 so the overall tax liability is $60,000. IRS Form 6251 is used to compute the AMT.

alternative order In investments, an order given to a broker to purchase or sell stock depending upon a specified alternative; also called an either-or order or a one-cancels-the-other order. Once the alternative is met, the order is executed. For example, there may be an integrated limit/buy stop order, wherein the purchase limit is less than the present market price and the buy stop is higher than the current market price.

amended tax return Changes in INCOME, deductions, or CREDITS that must be made to an individual TAX return, Form 1040, after it has been filed. Form 1040X, Amended U.S. Individual INCOME TAX Return, must be used to report these changes. The amended TAX return must be filed within three years after the date the original return was filed, or within two years after the date the tax was paid, whichever is greater. A return filed early is considered filed on the date it was due.

An amended return may require an additional payment of tax or a tax refund.

amendment Any addition or change in a legal document. When properly executed, it has the full legal force of the original document.

American classics index An index of 30 American classical stamps. It is equivalent to the Dow-Jones 30 Industrial Average for stocks.

american depositary receipt (ADR) A negotiable receipt representing ownership of shares
in a foreign company. It is traded on U.S.
securities markets and issued by an American
bank selected to retain the actual shares. ADR
is sold by brokers and registered by the SECUR-
ITIES AND EXCHANGE COMMISSION (SEC), which
means the companies issuing ADRs have to
publish ANNUAL REPORTS in English and use
standard accounting practices. But they are
still subject to FOREIGN CURRENCY RISKS. LI-
QUIDITY can also be a problem, because the volume of ADR trades is often small. Most ADRs
are traded in the OVER-THE-COUNTER (OTC)
market.

**American Stock Exchange market value in-
dex** An unweighted index of the AMERICAN
STOCK EXCHANGE (AMEX) stocks. It is computed
by adding all of the plus net changes and minus
net changes above or below previous closing
prices. The sum is then divided by the number
of issues listed and the result added to or
subtracted from the previous close. It is actually
more like an average than an index since it does
not have a base period.
See also MARKET INDICES AND AVERAGES.

amortization Payment of a loan on an installment basis. The term is usually associated with a
mortgage payment schedule. As a loan is amortized, the equity in the associated property is
increased. However, in the early years of a
mortgage, the majority of the payments are for
interest rather than principal.

For example, the payments on a 15-year
conventional $60,000 mortgage at 10% would be
$644.76. The first year's amortization of the
mortgage would have the following interest and
principal payments:

MORTGAGE AMORTIZATION SCHEDULE

Mortgage Amount	=	$60,000.00
Interest Rate	=	10%
Number of Years	=	15
Monthly Payments	=	$644.76

Payment	Principal	Interest	Balance
1	$144.76	$500.00	$59,855.24
2	$145.97	$498.79	$59,709.27
3	$147.18	$497.58	$59,562.09
4	$148.41	$496.35	$59,413.68
5	$149.65	$495.11	$59,264.03
6	$150.89	$493.87	$59,113.14
7	$152.15	$492.61	$58,960.99
8	$153.42	$491.34	$58,807.57
9	$154.70	$490.06	$58,652.87
10	$155.99	$488.77	$58,496.89
11	$157.29	$487.47	$58,339.60
12	$158.60	$486.16	$58,180.99

Interest for 12 Periods = $5,918.11

amortized loan A LOAN that is paid off in
periodic equal payments and includes varying
portions of PRINCIPAL and interest during its
term. Examples include automobile loans, mortgage loans, and most commercial loans. One
way to find the periodic payment is to divide the
principal loan amount by a Table 4 Appendix A
(Present Value of an Annuity of $1) factor.

Example 1: Kim Naomi has a 40-month
auto loan of $5,000 at a 12% annual interest rate.
She wants to know the monthly loan payment
amount.

Note that $i = 12\%/12$ months $= 1\%$ and
$T4(1,40) = 32.8347$ (from Table 4) Therefore,

$$\frac{\$5,000}{32.835} = \$152.28$$

So, to repay the principal and interest on a
$5,000, 12%, 40-month loan, Kim Naomi has to
pay $152.28 a month for the next 40 months.

Another way to determine the monthly payment is to use Table 6, Appendix A. This table
provides the monthly payment required to retire
a $1,000 installment loan for a selected annual
interest rate and term.

Example 2: Jerry takes out a $15,000, 12%,
48-month loan. He wants to determine the
monthly installment loan payment.

Using Table 6, he needs to follow these three
steps:

Step 1: Divide the loan amount by $1,000.

$$\$15,000/\$1,000 = 15$$

Step 2: Find the payment factor from Table 6, Appendix A, for specific interest rate and loan maturity.

The Table 6 payment factor for 12% and 48 months is $26.34.

Step 3: Multiply the factor obtained in Step 2 by the amount from Step 1.

$$\$26.34 \times 15 = \$395.10$$

His monthly installment loan payment is $395.10.

See also TIME VALUE OF MONEY; RULE OF 78.

annual exclusion Income that is not taxable to the recipient on the tax return, such as interest on municipal bonds and the proceeds from a life insurance policy.

annual percentage rate (APR) A true measure of the effective cost of credit. It is the ratio of the finance charge to the average amount of credit in use during the life of the loan, and is expressed as a percentage rate per year.

The lender is required by the TRUTH IN LENDING ACT (CONSUMER CREDIT PROTECTION ACT to disclose to a borrower the effective ANNUAL PERCENTAGE RATE (APR) as well as the finance charge in dollars. The borrower can then compare the costs of the loans for the best deal.

Banks often quote their interest rates in terms of dollars of interest per hundred dollars. Other lenders quote in terms of dollars per payment. This leads to confusion on the part of borrowers. Fortunately, APR can eliminate this confusion.

Presented below is a discussion of the way the effective APR is calculated for various types of loans.

single-payment loans

The single-payment loan is paid in full on a given date. There are two ways of calculating APR on single-payment loans: the simple interest method and the discount method.

(1) SIMPLE INTEREST METHOD. Under the simple interest method, interest is calculated only on the amount borrowed (proceeds). The formula for the simple interest method is

$$\text{Interest} = p \times r \times t$$

$$= \text{Principal} \times \text{Rate} \times \text{Time}$$

$$\text{APR} = \frac{\text{Average annual finance charge}}{\text{Amount borrowed or proceeds}}$$

Example 1: Kim took out a single-payment loan of $1,000 for two years at a simple interest rate of 15%. The interest charge will be: $300 ($1,000 $\times$ 15% $\times$ 2 years). Hence the APR is 15% ($150/$1,000). Under the simple interest method, the stated simple interest rate and the APR are always the same for single-payment loans.

(2) DISCOUNT METHOD. Under this method, interest is determined and then deducted from the amount of the loan. The difference is the actual amount the borrower receives. In other words, the borrower prepays the finance charges.

Example 2: Using the same figures from Example 1, the actual amount received is $700 ($1,000 − $300), not $1,000 to be paid back. The APR then is 21.43% ($150/$700). 21.43% is the rate the lender must quote on the loan, not 15%.

The DISCOUNT METHOD always gives a higher APR than the simple interest method for single-payment loans at the same interest rates.

installment loans

Most consumer loans use the add-on method. There are several methods for calculating the APR on add-on loans. They are (1) the actuarial method, (2) the constant ratio method, (3) the direct ratio method, and (4) the N-ratio method.

The ACTUARIAL METHOD is the most accurate in calculating the APR and the one lenders use most. It can be defined as interest computed on unpaid balances of principal at a fixed rate, with each payment applied first to interest and the remainder to principal. Since calculation by this method involves complicated formulas, annuity tables or computer programs are commonly used.

The CONSTANT RATIO METHOD is used to approximate the APR on an installment loan by the use of a simple formula, but it overstates the rate substantially. The higher the quoted rate, the greater the inaccuracy of the method. The constant ratio formula is

$$APR = \frac{2MC}{P(N+1)}$$

where

M = number of payment periods in one year
N = number of scheduled payments
C = finance charges in dollars (dollar cost of credit)
P = original proceeds

The DIRECT RATIO METHOD uses a somewhat more complex formula but is still easier than the actuarial method. It slightly understates the APR as compared to the actuarial method. The direct ratio formula is

$$APR = \frac{6MC}{3P(N+1)+C(N+1)}$$

The N-RATIO METHOD gives a much more accurate approximation of the APR than either the constant ratio or the direct ratio method for most loans. The results of the N-ratio method may be either slightly higher or lower than the true rate, depending on the maturity of the loan and the stated rate itself. The N-ratio formula is

$$APR = \frac{M(95N+9)C}{12N(N+1)\,(4P+C)}$$

Example 3: Assume Kim borrows $1,000 to be repaid in 12 equal monthly installments of $93.00 each for a finance charge of $116.00. The APR under each of the four methods is computed as follows (assume an annuity table or computer program gives an APR of 20.76%):

Actuarial method

The APR under this method is 20.76%, obtained from an annuity table or computer program.

Constant Ratio Method

$$APR = \frac{2MC}{P(N+1)}$$

$$= \frac{2 \times 12 \times 116}{1,000(12+1)} = \frac{2,784}{13,000} = 21.42\%$$

Direct Ratio Method

$$APR = \frac{6MC}{3P(N+1) + C(N+1)}$$

$$= \frac{6 \times 12 \times 116}{3 \times 1,000\,(12+1) + 116(12+1)}$$

$$= \frac{8,352}{40,508} = 20.62\%$$

N-Ratio Method

$$APR = \frac{M(95N+9)C}{12N(N+1)\,(4P+C)}$$

$$= \frac{12 \times (95 \times 12+9) \times 116}{12 \times 12 \times 13 \times [4(1000) + 116]}$$

$$= \frac{1,599,408}{7,705,152} = 20.76\%$$

These approximation formulas should not be used if there is any variation in the amounts of payments or in the time periods between payments—for example, balloon payments or extended first payment loans.

Note that some lenders charge fees for a CREDIT INVESTIGATION, a LOAN APPLICATION, or for LIFE INSURANCE. When these fees are required, the lender must include them in addition to the finance charge in dollars as part of the APR calculations.

Example 4: Bank A offers a 7% car loan if Kim puts 25% down. Therefore, if she buys a $4,000 car she will finance $3,000 over a three-year period with carrying charges amounting to $630 (7% × $3,000 × 3 years). She will make equal monthly payments of $100.83 for 36 months.

Bank B will lend $3,500 on the same car. Kim must pay $90 per month for 48 months. Which of the above quotes offers the best deal? (Use the constant-ratio formula.)

The APR calculations (using the constant-ratio formula) follow:

Bank A:

$$APR = \frac{2 \times 12 \times 630}{3000(36+1)} = \frac{15,120}{111,000} = 13.62\%$$

Bank B:

$$APR = \frac{2 \times 12 \times 820}{3500(48+1)} = \frac{19,680}{171,500} = 11.48\%$$

In the case of Bank B, it was necessary to multiply $90 × 48 months to arrive at a total cost of $4,320. Therefore, the total credit cost is $820 ($4,320 − $3,500).

Based on the APR, Kim should choose Bank B over Bank A.

See also ADD-ON METHOD; DISCOUNT METHOD.

annual percentage yield The true (effective) interest rate earned on an account that reflects the frequency of compounding.

annual-premium annuity An ANNUITY in which the annuity right is established by the payment of an annual PREMIUM for a given period.

annual report Reports prepared by companies at the end of the fiscal year. Contained in the annual report are the company's FINANCIAL STATEMENTS, president's letter, audit report, FOOTNOTES, supplementary schedules, and other explanatory data helpful in assessing the company's financial position and operating performance. The annual report is read by potential investors, shareholders, creditors, and other interested outside parties.

annual return The total yearly return from an investment.

annual yield: This is determined by computing a security's price change from the beginning to the end of the period. Annual yield computations also include all the security's annual INTEREST and DIVIDEND INCOME. The annual return may be expressed in dollars and/or percentage terms.

Example:

A STOCK is purchased at the beginning of the year for $5,000 and sold at the end of the year for $6,000. Dividend income received was $200.

Total Annual Return:

Difference in market price ($6,000 − $5,000) = $1,000
Dividend Income   +200
Total Return $1,200

Percentage Annual Return:

$$\frac{\text{Change in price} + \textit{dividend income}}{\text{Initial } \textit{investment}} = \frac{\$1,200}{\$5,000} = 24\%$$

Note: The total return may be negative. Assume in the prior example the stock was sold at the end of the year for $4,000.

Total Annual Return:

Change in market price ($4,000 − $5,000) = $−1,000
Dividend income   + 200
Total return $− 800

Percentage Annual Return:

$$\frac{\text{Change in price} + \textit{dividend income}}{\text{Initial } \textit{investment}}$$

$$= \frac{\$ - 800}{\$5,000} = -.16\%$$

See also ANNUAL STATEMENT.

annualize

1. To compute on an annual basis. For example, a $250 monthly return on a $30,000 INVESTMENT would be 30,000/(250 × 12) = 10% annual return.

2. To multiply taxable INCOME for part of a year by 12 and divide by the number of months involved, a procedure specified by the Internal Revenue Code. For example, if taxable income for 3 months is $20,000, it will be annualized as follows:

$$\$20,000 \times (12/3) = \$80,000$$

3. To place the terms of a CONTRACT on a fixed annual basis. Annualizing is common in financial forecasting.

annuitant An individual receiving an ANNUITY.

annuitize To contract, usually with an INSURANCE COMPANY, to receive payments at a preselected date for a predetermined period of time upon depositing a sum or MONEY or making payments over time. The contract is ANNUITIZED when the payments from the capital that has built up in the ANNUITY begins. The payments may be a fixed amount, or for a fixed period of time, or for the lifetimes of one or two ANNUITANTS, thus guaranteeing income payments that cannot be outlived.

annuity

1. A series of equal payments or receipts. With an ORDINARY ANNUITY, payments or receipts are at the end of the year. With an ANNUITY DUE, payments or receipts are at the beginning of the year.

2. In RETIREMENT PLANNING, a savings account with an insurance company or other investment company. The ANNUITANT makes either a lump-sum deposit or periodic payments to the company and at retirement, "annuitizes"— receives regular payments for a specified time period (usually a certain number of years or for the rest of his or her life). All the payments build up tax free and the amount is taxed only when withdrawn at retirement, a time when the annuitant is usually in a lower tax bracket. Although mostly sold by life insurance companies, annuities are really the opposite of life insurance: annuities pay off at retirement; life insurance pays off at death.

Annuities come in two basic varieties: FIXED and VARIABLE. Annuities can be for everybody. For young people, the vehicles are an excellent forced savings plan. For older people, they are tax-favored investments that can guarantee an income for life. Retirement annuities offer two main advantages:

- Interest is not taxed until the annuitant collects those monthly checks at retirement, when his or her tax bracket should be lower.
- Interest earned each year without a tax compounds the individual's wealth quickly.
- Unlike pension plans and IRAs, there are no limitations on the amount to be contributed to an annuity.

There are some pitfalls of annuities:

- They limit the annuitant's financial freedom. The annuitant cannot get his or her money back before age 59½. There are penalties for early withdrawals imposed by the IRS and the insurance company.
- The interest earned can be reduced by INFLATION or lag behind the return of other investments.
- Surrender charges are imposed if the annuitant decides to cash in the contract early.
- The so-called nonqualified annuities are annuities with the tax-deferral feature but which are paid for with after-tax dollars.

Qualified annuities, on the other hand, are used to fund such vehicles as INDIVIDUAL RETIREMENT ACCOUNTS (IRAs) and pension plans. In a qualified annuity, the contributions not only grow tax free but are also either tax deductible or not included in the annuitant's income.

annuity certain An ANNUITY that provides a specified amount of monthly income for a specified period of years without consideration of any life contingency. Payments are guaranteed for a fixed time period and are paid to either the INSURED or the insured's BENEFICIARIES.
See also LIFE ANNUITY, PERIOD CERTAIN ANNUITY.

annuity cost A cost, or accumulation, related to anticipated employee pension payments. It enables employees to satisfy the payment obligations of a pension annuity. The payments are accumulated in advance based on the employee's previous and current service.
See also ANNUITY; ANNUITIZE.

annuity due A term used by financial people addressing the amount of an ANNUITY paid at the start of each year during the life of an individual at a specified age contrasted with an ordinary annuity initiated at the end of the year. The annuity due payment is called an annuity obligation in advance as it is incurred on January 1 of a calendar year.

annuity rate The price of an ANNUITY, usually expressed as the sum required to purchase an income of some amount such as $500 or $2,000 a month for life.

annuity rent   A payment under an ANNUITY.

annuity rule   An income tax rule governing the way a pension benefit may be subject to tax.

annuity starting date   The date at which actual ANNUITY benefit payments begin to the ANNUITANT. The ANNUITY STARTING DATE, together with the size of the actual benefits desired, will determine the annuity COST.
See also ANNUITANT.

antedate   To assign a date that precedes the date a given instrument or legal agreement was actually prepared or executed. An example is insurance coverage that becomes effective prior to the actual issuance of the policy.

anticipated holding period   The time interval an individual expects to keep a financial or real asset. For example, someone may decide to buy and sell a stock quickly or to hold on to the stock for many years.

anticipatory breach   The breaching of a legal agreement prior to the time performance is required. For example, an individual may notify another party to a contract of his or her repudiation of it before the specified due date. An individual may be unable to carry out his or her obligations because of the inability to perform or may simply have changed his or her mind.

apartment (building)   A dwelling unit within a multifamily structure, generally provided as rental housing. An apartment building is a structure with individual apartment units but a common entrance and hallway. Apartments may vary in size from small, one-room bachelor unit to large, multibedroom units. Apartment buildings may be as small as a one-story duplex or as large as a high-rise building with hundreds of units and retail and office space.

apportionment
in general: A division or assignment according to some plan or proportion. For example, prorating some property expenses, such as insurance and taxes, between buyer and seller.

securities: The allocation of securities in a new issue among stockholders.
real estate: Partitioning of property into individual parcels by TENANTS IN COMMON.

apportionment clause   A clause that contains APPORTIONMENT.

apportionment statutes   State laws that allocate the burden of taxes among the BENEFICIARIES in the absence of a specific provision for apportionment in a WILL.

appraisal fee   A fee required for a professionally prepared estimate of the value of an asset (e.g., property, a collectible, or precious metal) by an independent expert.

appraisal of damage   Or, *assessment of loss, loss appraisal.* An evaluation of property loss. The APPRAISAL is typically conducted by a professionally trained appraiser, usually with the insurance industry. APPRAISALS of damage are most commonly done for insurance claims. They consider the quality and quantity of the items, age, value, and extent of damage.
See also ASSESSED VALUATION; ASSESSMENT.

appreciation
1. Increase in the worth of an item (such as real estate or a security). For example, an individual sold 100 shares of ABC company's stock for $55 per share; he bought the stock five years ago for $30 per share. The amount of appreciation was $2,500 [($55 − $30) × 100 shares].
See also CAPITAL GAINS OR LOSSES; RETURN; YIELD.
2. Recognition given, such as an employer bonus to an employee for good performance.

approval sale   A sale that is not finalized until the merchandise is accepted by the purchaser. Title will pass only when approval is given or when the goods are retained by the buyer for a reasonable time period or that period specified in the agreement.

approved list   A list of investments in which an entity such as a mutual fund or pension plan can invest. In some cases, a financial institution having a fiduciary responsibility may be restricted to certain types of investments. Investments having high risk may be omitted.

approximate compound yield A measure of the annualized COMPOUND growth of a long-term INVESTMENT.

appurtenant structures Something outside the property itself but considered a part of the property and adding to its greater enjoyment, such as the right to cross another's land (i.e., easement or right-of-way).

arbitrage Benefiting from the price differential between the same or comparable securities or commodities simultaneously trading on two different exchanges. The security would be bought from the exchange having the lower-priced security while at the same time selling the security on the higher-priced exchange.

arbitrageur A person engaged in ARBITRAGE.

area service manager Or, *zone representative*. A manager in charge of and having responsibility for a given segment providing services to consumers. An example is the manager of a service area in a retail business.

arithmetic average return A measure of RETURN over a single holding period or over multiperiods. When an investor holds an investment for more than one period, it is important to understand how to compute the average of the successive rates of return. There are two types of multiperiod average (mean) returns: arithmetic average return and the GEOMETRIC AVERAGE RETURN.

The arithmetic return is simply the arithmetic average of successive one-period rates of return. It is defined as

$$\text{arithmetic return} = 1/n \sum_{t=1}^{n} r_t$$

where n = the number of time periods and r = the single HOLDING PERIOD RETURN in time t. The arithmetic average return, however, can be quite misleading in multiperiod return calculation.

Example: Consider the following data showing that the price of a stock doubles in one period and depreciates back to the original price. Assume no dividends.

	Time periods		
	$t=0$	$t=1$	$t=2$
Price (end of period)	$50	$100	$50
HPR	—	100%	−50%

The holding period return for periods 1 and 2 are computed as follows:

Period 1 ($t=1$)

$$\text{HPR} = \frac{\$0 + (\$100 - \$50)}{\$50} = \frac{\$50}{\$50} = 100\%$$

Period 2 ($t=2$)

$$\text{HPR} = \frac{\$0 + (\$50 - \$100)}{\$100} = \frac{-\$50}{\$100} = -50\%$$

Therefore, the arithmetic average return is the average of 100% and −50%, which is 25%, as shown below:

$$\frac{100\% + (-50\%)}{2} = 25\%$$

See also MEAN.

arms length transaction Transaction entered into by unrelated parties, each acting in his or her own best interest. An example is a fair price determined between the buyer and seller of a house. It is assumed that in this type of transaction the prices used are the FAIR MARKET VALUES of the property or services being transferred.

arrearage Default on FUNDS due. Failure to pay an obligation at the due date. An example would be a loan payment that misses the due date. An arrearage ACCOUNT could be established that would be CREDITED when the payment or payments are made.

securities: Amount by which INTEREST on BONDS or DIVIDENDS on CUMULATIVE PREFERRED STOCK is due and unpaid. So long as the dividends on cumulative preferred stock are in arrearage, the dividends on COMMON STOCK cannot be paid.

arrears

1. At the end of a term. For example, interest on mortgage loans is unpaid at the end of a month.

2. Past due payments or other obligations. An example is CUMULATIVE PREFERRED STOCK DIVIDENDS that have been declared but have not been paid following their payment dates.

as if

1. Speculation, most commonly associated with INSURANCE, to demonstrate what the underwriting or reinsurance treaty results would have been in prior years if a new PREMIUM calculation had been in effect. A term referring to loss experience.

2. To examine what the financial results would have been if an alternative course of action had been taken.

as is

1. A term descriptive of secondhand or damaged goods sold without either an EXPRESS or IMPLIED WARRANTY by the seller. That is, the buyer shall accept delivery of goods in the condition found on inspection before purchase, even if they are defective or damaged. The term in effect warns the buyer to inspect the items carefully, as the burden of determining their condition falls on him or her.

2. Without guarantee, as the condition of REAL ESTATE.

ascending tops   A CHART pattern of a STOCK'S closing price over a period of time demonstrating repeatedly higher peaks. This upward movement is considered to be extremely BULLISH by CHARTISTS. The same analysis can be applied to the STOCK MARKET as a whole. A secondary consideration, but an important one, is the volume of TRADING. If the volume of trading expands near the peaks, this is considered a confirmation of the bullish action of the stock or stock market. See accompanying illustration below.
See also BULL MARKET.

ask price   *See* ASKED PRICE.

asked price   Or, *offering price, ask price, asking price.*

1. The price an investment (such as a security, commodity, or real estate) is offered for sale. It is usually the cheapest price at which one can purchase the investment.

2. For MUTUAL FUNDS, the current NET ASSET VALUE per share plus sales charges, if any.

assay   The ultimate test of a metal's purity, by chemical means—"the acid test," to certify that it meets the standards necessary for TRADING on a COMMODITIES EXCHANGE. This is particularly true of the PRECIOUS metals of gold and silver. For example, a 100 troy-ounce bar of refined gold must be assayed at a fineness of not less

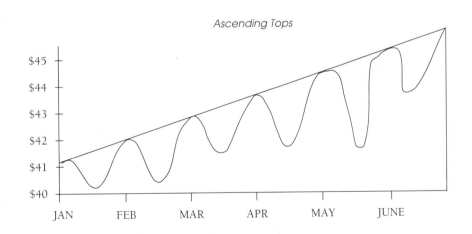

Ascending Tops

than 995 before the Commodity Exchange, Inc. (Comex) will allow it to be used in the settlement of a gold contract.

assaying The business of doing an assay of precious metals.

assessed valuation The value established by a government for PROPERTY TAX purposes. For example, an individual receives a statement indicating that in the judgment of the local tax assessor, the individual's property is valued at $80,000. If by law, properties in this jurisdiction are assessed at 80% of market value, the individual's assessed valuation would be $64,000 (80% × $80,000) and property taxes will be based on this ASSESSED VALUE.

assessment

1. To derive an appraised value for property.

2. Valuation placed upon property as a result of this process. For example, an individual owns a parcel of land assessed on the tax bill for $40,000. The TAX RATE is $1.00 per $100 of value. The tax assessment for the land is therefore $400.

3. A special tax levied by a municipality or association in the event of any repair or improvement such as for driveways and landscaping.

4. Damages paid in a lawsuit to the aggrieved party.

asset An economic resource that has future benefit and value. Assets are stated in dollar terms. Examples of ownership rights a person may have that constitute his or her assets are cash, automobile, boat, house, and furniture.

asset allocation The percentage of money in different investment types. For example, an investor's asset allocation could be 50% STOCKS, 30% BONDS, and 20% SAVINGS and MONEY MARKET FUND accounts. Each investor would have a different asset allocation mix depending on specific needs or aversion to risk. *See also* DIVERSIFICATION; MUTUAL FUND; PORTFOLIO.

asset-liability management Matching an individual's debt with his or her assets. Someone who is planning to buy a new car, for instance, would have to decide whether to pay cash, thus lowering assets, or take out a loan, thereby increasing debts (or liabilities). These decisions should be based on interest rates, earning power, liquidity, and one's comfort with having a certain debt level.

asset play A STOCK MARKET term used to indicate that a particular STOCK is an attractive INVESTMENT because its underlying NET WORTH is more than the price of the stock. For example, a SECURITIES analyst may recommend a company not because of good management but because it has significantly undervalued REAL ESTATE. Asset plays have been used as the basis for a LEVERAGED BUYOUT since it is possible to use the undervalued ASSETS of the target firm as COLLATERAL in obtaining LOANS for its purchase. Also, an acquirer can obtain valuable ASSETS of the acquired company at a low price.

assigned-risk pool A group of drivers who will have to pay relatively high AUTO INSURANCE PREMIUMS because, due to a variety of reasons, they tend to be more risky than other drivers.

assignment The conveying of any type of property by one party to another. An assignor conveys his or her TITLE to property to the assignee. The assignability of property relates to it being free of all claims and capable of being exchanged.

bankruptcy: In the case of BANKRUPTCY, an assignment of ASSETS can occur where all the ASSETS are assigned to the creditors for their disposal.

stock options: In the event a PUT or CALL OPTION is exercised, the Options Clearing Corporation will notify the STOCKBROKER that the holder's option has been exercised and the underlying STOCK is assigned by the BROKER.

stock and bond securities: STOCKS and REGISTERED BONDS are commonly assigned by simply filling out and signing the form on the back of the certificate. It is also possible to complete a separate stock or BOND assignment certificate to fulfill the assignment.

assignment of policy   The right of a party, the assignor, to allocate the benefits of particular INSURANCE POLICIES to a third party, the assignee. Marine insurance commonly uses assignment of policy to protect cargo for those having an insurable INTEREST. Thus, the assignee would have a risk involved, as in the case of a BANK financing the cargo. Normally, the assignment is done through an endorsement whereby the INSURANCE benefit rights are transferred. Property and casualty policies usually are nonassignable except if the insurance company has given its approval. However, in those cases where property and casualty insurance policies are deemed to be assignable, the beneficiaries are legitimate assignees.
See also ASSIGNMENT.

assignment of proceeds   An agreement to transfer monies to a third party. For example, an agreement may provide that an insurance company will pay a party other than the insured for a reimbursable loss.

assignment (wage)   Transfer of the right to collect WAGES from the wage earner to the creditor; a form of GARNISHMENT governed by a statute that provides relief for CREDITORS. Before such WAGE assignment occurs, a judgment must be entered at which time the affected individual has the right of reply.
See also ASSIGNMENT; GARNISHMENT.

assumable mortgage   A mortgage by which purchaser takes ownership of REAL ESTATE encumbered by an existing MORTGAGE and assumes responsibility as the guarantor for the unpaid balance of the mortgage.

assumption   A person agrees to assume the debts, commitments, or responsibilities of another. An example is a father agreeing to pay the remainder of his son's car loan.
See also ASSUMPTION OF MORTGAGE.

assumption clause   A clause in a MORTGAGE

that allows the owner of property to transfer the mortgage to a buyer.

assumption of mortgage   Takeover of MORTGAGE whereby a buyer agrees to accept the responsibility for the existing mortgage. The seller is not relieved of the obligation unless the lender agrees to release it. Many lenders require POINTS and increase the interest rate.

assumption of risk defense

1. An employee's willingness to assume the ordinary hazards of his or her occupation.

2. A DEFENSE used in a negligence action stating that the plaintiff was aware of a dangerous situation but still voluntarily exposed himself or herself to the hazard. In that case, the defendant should be relieved of any legal responsibility for the plaintiff's injury arising from that "known" dangerous condition.

assurance   The giving of a promise or guarantee to the receiver to instill confidence in the item. An example is a retailer's assuring the customer of the quality of a good or service provided.
See also INSURANCE.

at market order   *See* MARKET ORDER.

at order or better order   Instruction given by an investor to the account executive to buy or sell a stock at or above a predetermined price.

at par   Literally, "equal" to the nominal or face value of a SECURITY. The most common use of the term is in TRADING of BONDS where a bond trading at par is trading at a price equal to its FACE VALUE. However, if the bond or security should fall in price, it is trading at a DISCOUNT. Conversely, a bond or SECURITY trading above its PAR VALUE is trading at a PREMIUM. A bond would be selling at a discount or premium depending on such factors as the INTEREST RATE of the bond relative to the prevailing market interest rate, riskiness of the issue, and the maturity period.

at risk

investments: In business and INVESTMENT, a

term indicating that money is exposed to the possibility of loss. Thus, MONEY invested is at risk.

at the close An order to a STOCKBROKER to buy or sell a SECURITY in the final 30 seconds of TRADING. Because of the tumultuous trading that often occurs at the close, BROKERS never guarantee that these orders will be executed.

at-the-money The term used when the EXERCISE PRICE of an OPTION is equal to or near the current market price of the underlying stock.

at the opening A customer's order instructing a STOCKBROKER to buy or sell a SECURITY on its first opening price when the EXCHANGE opens for the day's business. If the order is not transacted, it is automatically canceled.

attachment A legal term of the writ authorizing the taking of property or rights due to a legal action. It is designed to safeguard the property possibly to satisfy a judgment in favor of the plaintiff in the action.
See also ATTACHMENT DATE.

attachment date The day the attachment of property under a court order takes effect.
See also ATTACHMENT.

attained age The age at which an individual may become eligible for a benefit or a liability. Some action at that age may be required. An example is an individual's retiring when reaching a specified age.

attestation clause A clause appearing at the end of a document, for example, a WILL, wherein the witnesses certify that the INSTRUMENT has been executed before them, and the manner of its execution.

attorney in fact A power of attorney giving permission for a lawyer to represent a client.

attorney of record An attorney whose name officially appears in permanent records or files of a case, or on the appeal or some document filed in the case, or on the appearance docket. It provides public notice of whom the attorney is representing in a particular case.

attorney-at-law Term indicating an attorney who has been admitted to practice law in his or her respective state and is authorized to perform both civil and criminal legal functions for clients. An attorney-at-law can perform the full range of legal functions including drafting legal documents, giving legal advice, and representing clients before courts, administrative agencies, boards, and other entities. In English law an attorney-at-law is referred to as a solicitor.

at-risk rules Rules permitting a taxpayer, for INCOME TAX purposes, to deduct losses only to the degree money is at risk of loss. At-risk amounts are restricted to the CASH INVESTMENT and the DEBT for which the taxpayer is personally liable. Thus, those portions of an INVESTMENT that are not AT RISK are not deductible.

If, for example, an individual loses $60,000 in a real estate INVESTMENT but invested only $50,000, then only $50,000 is TAX DEDUCTIBLE. However, there is an expansion of the AT-RISK amounts to REAL ESTATE only to include certain nonrecourse LOANS from qualified lenders.

attribution The assignment, permitted by the TAX law under certain circumstances, to one taxpayer of the ownership INTEREST of another. If, for example, the stock of Y CORPORATION is held 70% by a mother and 30% by her daughter, the mother may be deemed to own 100% of Y corporation. In this circumstance the ownership of Y STOCK is attributed to the mother. This can also be termed "direct" and "indirect" ownership as well as "constructive ownership."

audit Inspection of the accounting records and operations of a business, governmental unit, or individual by a trained accountant for the purpose of verifying the accuracy and completeness of all transactions and operations. An audit by a certified public accountant (CPA) determines the overall validity of financial statements.
correspondence audit: An audit conducted by the INTERNAL REVENUE SERVICE through the use

of the mail. Normally, the INTERNAL REVENUE SERVICE requests verification of a particular deduction or EXEMPTION through the completion of a form or the remittance of copies of records or other supporting materials.

compliance audit: A determination of the firm's compliance with specified organizational rules and regulations.

desk audit: A term normally used in connection with civil service procedures involving a review of the activities of a particular person filling a particular position to determine whether these activities fulfill the job classification responsibilities.

field audit: An audit by the INTERNAL REVENUE SERVICE conducted on the business premises of the taxpayer or in the office of the attorney or accountant representing the taxpayer.

financial audit: Examination of a client's accounting records by an independent certified public accountant to formulate an audit opinion. The auditor must follow generally accepted auditing standards. A careful evaluation of the internal control structure is necessary.

independent audit: An audit performed on an organization's records and procedures by an outside accounting firm.

internal audit: Investigation of an organization's procedures and operations by an internal auditor to assure that they conform to the organization's accounting and operating policies.

management audit: An evaluation of the efficiency and effectiveness of management.

tax audit: An examination of books, vouchers, and records of a taxpayer conducted by AGENTS of the INTERNAL REVENUE SERVICE.

audit (of returns) by Internal Revenue Service (IRS) An IRS examination of all or part of the tax return filed by the individual. The selection of returns for examination begins at the service centers. Returns can be selected by computer programs or by manual selection. The IRS uses the Discriminant Function (DIF) system, which involves computer scoring using mathematical formulas to select tax returns with the highest probability of errors. An audit usually concentrates on specific areas, such as charitable contributions and miscellaneous deductions. The taxpayer may be represented by any professional currently permitted to practice before the IRS, such as a CPA. An interview with a taxpayer must be suspended if the taxpayer requests the right to consult with a representative.

authority

1. One possessing power over others, such as a company manager who has the right to hire and fire.

2. One having the right to act, such as an attorney having the right to represent clients and make decisions on their behalf.

authorization The giving of a right to another to perform some act or function. An example is giving a financial representative such as a CPA or attorney the authority to act on your behalf.

automated teller machine (ATM) A computerized electronic device allowing customers to make specific transactions by the use of a plastic card that has ACCOUNT information recorded on it.

bank ATM: A computerized TELLER device located either inside or outside a BANK permitting customers, through the use of their ATM cards, to make deposits and withdrawals automatically from authorized individual accounts. ATMs operate 24 hours a day, seven days a week, and reduce the amount of floor traffic within the bank itself. They have found wide acceptance.

automatic extension The routine granting of additional time needed by an individual to do something. For example, taxpayers are granted an automatic extension of four months for filing tax returns (but not for payment of tax). This requires the filing of Form 4868, accompanied by the remaining estimated tax payment for the year. The application must be filed by the due date of the return.

automatic funds transfer The ability to transfer funds rapidly and accurately by use of modern computers and telecommunications systems without concern for distance. This ability, coupled with newer INVESTMENT vehicles developed by the brokerage industry, has brought with it the concept of automatic funds transfer.

Under the concept of the CASH MANAGEMENT ACCOUNT, developed and copyrighted by Merrill Lynch, when a SECURITY is sold in a customer's ACCOUNT, the proceeds are automatically transferred into an INTEREST-bearing MONEY MARKET ACCOUNT until the funds are called upon again for another purchase transaction.

The basic concept of automatic funds transfer is having the capability to transfer funds from one fund to the other without direct management.

automatic overdraft loan An agreement with a BANK that permits an individual to write checks in amounts larger than the funds in his or her CHECKING ACCOUNT with needed funds automatically borrowed from a preapproved CREDIT line. Of course, interest will be charged on the OVERDRAFT.

automatic premium loan *See* AUTOMATIC PREMIUM LOAN CLAUSE.

automatic premium loan clause A clause in LIFE INSURANCE providing that the premium not made by the GRACE PERIOD will be paid automatically with a policy loan borrowing from whatever CASH VALUES or dividends have accumulated. The INTEREST RATE is usually specified in the insurance contract. The main objective of this provision is to avert inadvertent lapse of the policy. This clause is strongly recommended since premiums can go unpaid under some circumstances, such as vacations or illness.

automatic reinvestment plan Or, *automatic* DIVIDEND *reinvestment.* Many MUTUAL FUNDS allow the stockholders to reinvest DIVIDENDS or capital gain distributions automatically into the purchase of more shares without paying a COMMISSION. The net effect of such a plan is to allow the dividends to COMPOUND over time. The INVESTOR, unless using this feature as part of a qualified retirement or other TAX-DEFERRED plan, will be taxed on automatically reinvested funds in the year they are CREDITED.

automatic transfer of savings (ATS) account A system that allows banks to offer customers automatic transfers from SAVINGS ACCOUNTS to CHECKING ACCOUNTS. These are essentially zero-balance checking accounts fed from savings accounts. The depositor earns interest until the funds must be transferred to cover the checks or to maintain a minimum balance.

automatic withdrawal A benefit of MUTUAL FUNDS allowing equal distributions to INVESTORS each month (or quarter) from DIVIDENDS and CAPITAL GAIN distributions. If the current earnings are not sufficient to meet the specified withdrawal amount, the fund will liquidate shares.

automobile bodily injury liability Insurance coverage for a driver or car owner who is legally responsible for bodily injury losses caused to others.

automobile insurance Insurance that protects an insured against two basic automobile risks:
liability coverage: Bodily injuries, property damages, and medical expenses to an individual and others when the insured is at fault. These coverages usually have certain limits. For example, $10/$20 limit would pay $10,000 for loss from bodily injury liability for any one person, or $20,000 for all persons involved in any one accident. Property damage liability is usually expressed as a single limit, such as $10,000 or $20,000, for any one accident.
physical coverage: Damage or loss of an individual's car due to fire, theft, or collision.

PREMIUMS for auto insurance vary from company to company, but all rates generally reflect the insured's age, sex, marital status, driving record, location, frequency of use, and car's age.

Example: Assume that John has a three-year-old car on which he is carrying the following auto insurance coverages: liability, 50/100/25; uninsured motorist, 15/30; collision, $50 deductible; comprehensive, $50 deductible. Recently, somebody who has no insurance ran into his car. John's medical costs totaled $5,400 and he lost 8 weeks' wages at $450 per week. Damage to his car totaled $4,000.

John's uninsured motorist section should cover both his medical expenses and lost wages. That reimbursement would be

Medical expenses	$5,400
Lost wages from accident:	
8 weeks @ $450	3,600
Total reimbursement	$9,000

Damage to his car will be covered by his collision section. The reimbursement would be

Repairs to car	$4,000
Less deductible	50
Total reimbursement	$3,950

automobile insurance plan Or, *assigned risk plan.* Arrangement that provides AUTOMOBILE INSURANCE to drivers refused coverage under normal procedures. This plan assigns a proportional share of the uninsurable drivers to each company writing auto insurance coverage in a state.

automobile liability insurance Or, *bodily injury and property damage liability insurance.* Insurance protection in case the INSURED is found negligent and hence liable for losses that others suffer because of bodily injury or property damage. This protection has certain limits. For example, $50/$100 limits would pay $50,000 for loss from BODILY INJURY LIABILITY for any one person, or $100,000 for all persons involved in any one accident. PROPERTY DAMAGE LIABILITY is specified as a single limit, such as $25,000, for any one accident.
See also AUTOMOBILE INSURANCE.

automobile medical payments insurance INSURANCE that will pay for the personal injury losses suffered by the driver of the insured vehicle and any passengers regardless of who is at fault.

automobile property damage liability Insurance coverage for a driver or car owner who is legally responsible for damages to the property of others.

available date The day an item or a person will be ready to meet some required function or activity. Examples are the date someone will be available to start a new job, and the date manufactured goods or services will be available for sale.

average balance account An account that assesses a service fee only if the average daily balance of funds in the account drops below a certain amount.

average daily balance The average daily balance is commonly used as a basis for (1) computing interest income for the depositors by banks and (2) calculating finance charges on credit cards (by lenders) or charge accounts (by retailers). The average daily balance on bank accounts is the average daily account balance a depositor keeps in his or her account for the month. It is the sum of the daily balances, divided by the number of days in the period. The average daily balance of credit cards or charge accounts is the average daily outstanding balance owed by a customer. It is calculated by adding up the outstanding balances owed each day during the billing period and dividing the sum by the number of days in the period.
See also AVERAGE DAILY BALANCE METHOD.

average daily balance method Method of computing finance charges by which the interest is applied to the AVERAGE DAILY BALANCE of the account outstanding over the billing period. This method does not reflect purchases or returns made during the billing period. The average balance is calculated by adding the balances outstanding each day and dividing the total by the number of days in the billing month. Payments made during the billing month reduce the average balance outstanding. The average daily balance method is less expensive than the PREVIOUS BALANCE METHOD and is widely used by stores that offer revolving charge accounts.

Example: Assume that the monthly INTEREST RATE is 1.5%, which represents an annual rate of 18%. The previous balance is $400 and the payment was made on the 15th day of the month. The finance charge under this method is computed below.

Average daily balance:

No. of Days	Balance		Weighted Balance
15 days	$400		$6,000
15 days	100		1,500
Total 30 days		Total	$7,500

Average daily balance $7,500/30 days = $250

$$\$250 \times 1.5\% = \$3.75$$

See also ADJUSTED BALANCE METHOD; PAST-DUE BALANCE METHOD; PREVIOUS BALANCE METHOD.

average indexed monthly earnings (AIME) An inflated-adjusted measure of career-average monthly wages. AIME is a concept used in Social Security to determine the size of retirement and other SOCIAL SECURITY benefits.

average share cost Actual cost of an investment used for INCOME TAX purposes. It is determined by dividing the total dollars invested by the total shares purchased. For example, if 100 shares of ABC company stock were bought for $4,500, the average share cost would be $45.

average share price

1. The average price of STOCK that was purchased at different dates.

Example: An individual purchased XYZ Company STOCK as follows:

Date	Number of Shares	Price/Share	Total
Jan. 6	1,000	$5	$5,000
June 2	200	$6	$1,200
Sept. 17	500	$4	$2,000
Total	1,700		$8,200

The average price equals

$$\frac{\text{Total cost}}{\text{Total shares}} = \frac{\$8,200}{1,700} = \$4.82$$

2. A calculation on a weighted basis of a basket of stocks indicating the mean SHARE price of those included. One popular measure, the Dow-Jones Average, includes 30 industrial stocks for the industrial index, 20 transportation stocks for the transportation index, and 15 public utility stocks for the utility index. A composite index, known as the Dow-Jones Average, is taken for all 65 stocks. There is also a Dow-Jones Bond Average measuring the average value of 6 groups of BONDS, and the Standard & Poor's Composite 500 index, which includes 425 industrial stocks, 50 utilities, and 25 railroads TRADED on the NEW YORK STOCK EXCHANGE.

average tax rate *See* EFFECTIVE TAX RATE.

average up A STOCK TRADER's strategy of buying or selling shares of STOCK as the price of the stock moves up.

stock purchase: The purchaser of stock makes an underlying assumption the stock will continue to increase and a program of continued purchases will lower the average COST per SHARE thus increasing overall profitability.

stock sale: The seller of a PORTFOLIO of STOCK seeks to maximize the benefit of a rising market by gradually selling shares as the MARKET increases; also known as selling into the market. This helps to ensure a steadily increasing sales price for the STOCK as a market rises, once again improving overall profitability.

An example of averaging up follows:

PURCHASES OR SALES OF XYZ CORP. STOCK

Shares	Price	Average Price
200	12	12.00
200	13	12.50
200	14	13.00
200	15	13.50
200	16	14.00

average yield basis Measure of the RATE OF RETURN on a series of INVESTMENTS over time. In SECURITIES, particularly in STOCK, DIVIDEND returns are calculated as a percentage of the purchase price of the stock; however, if the same STOCK has been purchased at varying prices over time, then the average YIELD basis is calculated on its TOTAL RETURN including DIVIDENDS as well as CAPITAL GAINS realized or unrealized.

See example below:

avoidance   Rendering null and void, refusing to honor, or avoiding the recognition of the terms of a contract. If an individual violates a WARRANTY agreement by not servicing at the proper intervals, then a company may render the warranty null and void and consider itself exempt from any liability.

avoidance of tax   Any lawful way by which a taxpayer seeks to lower his or her TAX LIABILITY. Examples are creating or seeking a TAX SHELTER or other TAX PLANNING opportunities such as ESTATE PLANNING. In contrast, TAX EVASION involves illegal methods to avoid paying TAXES.

AVERAGE YIELD XYZ STOCK

Purchase Date	Purchase Price	Quantity	Total Cost	Dividend Per Share	Total Dividend	Yield
Jan. 1	$15.00	300	$4,500.00	$1.50	$450.00	10.00%
Feb. 23	$18.00	200	$3,600.00	$1.50	$300.00	8.33%
Mar. 15	$23.00	250	$5,750.00	$1.50	$375.00	6.52%
Apr. 16	$19.00	500	$9,500.00	$1.50	$750.00	7.89%
June 25	$21.00	150	$3,150.00	$1.50	$225.00	7.14%
Aug. 14	$14.00	600	$8,400.00	$1.50	$900.00	10.71%
Sep. 16	$12.00	700	$8,400.00	$1.50	$1,050.00	12.50%
Total		2700	$43,300.00		$4,050.00	9.35%
Average Price/SHARE			$16.04			

12-MONTH AVERAGE YIELD INCLUDING CAPITAL GAINS AND DIVIDENDS

Sale Price	Purchase Cost	Capital Gain	Earned Dividends	Average Yield
$47,775.00	$43,300.00	$4,475.00	$4,050.00	19.69%

B

baby boom generation A term referring to those Americans born between the end of World War II and the 1960s when the veterans of World War II were in the family formation stage of their lives. The result was a tremendous surge in the birthrate: the intrinsic rate of natural increase went from 4.6 in the 1940–1944 period to a high of 21.1 in 1955–1959, declining to 8.2 by 1965–1969. The BABY BOOMER GENERATION created tremendous consumer demand in the economy, beginning with housing, as popularized in Levittown, New York, and including all types of consumer goods.

back charge An item that was previously charged to an account but remains unpaid. A monthly statement of charges sent to a customer, for example, will show both the prior and current months' charges.

back dating Dating any CHECK, document, INSTRUMENT or statement prior to the period when it is actually negotiated. Back dating does not affect the validity of the document.
mutual funds: A practice permitting a fund holder or potential fund holder to use an earlier date in order to INVEST a specified sum over a particular period of time to obtain a reduced sales charge. Back dating gives retroactive value to mutual fund purchases.

back-end load Or, *deferred sales charges.* A fee charged for redeeming MUTUAL FUND shares. These charges are intended to discourage frequent trading in the fund. Deferred sales charges are usually on a scale that reduces them each year until they disappear after a predetermined period of time.

back taxes TAXES that have not been paid on the date they were due or were underreported or omitted accidentally or intentionally from a previous TAX return. The taxing jurisdiction can demand back taxes in these circumstances, including the possibility of fines or penalties.

backup withholding A policy to assure that federal income tax is paid on earnings even though the recipient cannot be identified by a social security number. When a Form 1099 cannot be filed by a payer (e.g., bank, brokerage firm) because a social security number is lacking, 20% of the interest or dividends is withheld and remitted to the IRS. For example, if dividends earned are $800, then $160 ($800 × 20%) would be withheld. An account holder must fill out a federal W-9 form for the financial institution, stating that the social security number is correct and that he or she is not subject to backup withholding. Backup withholding is required per IRS Code Section 3406(a)(1)(c).

bad title A deficiency in TITLE that casts a "cloud" or a "shadow" on the TITLE and thus affects its transferability. Many things can affect a TITLE, including the lack of a necessary signature in a previous TITLE, an improper survey, an unsatisfied lien, or other claims to the property including governmental claims.

bail out
1. Action of an individual when he or she has financial difficulty that prompts him or her to sell a stock irrespective of price.
2. When the collateral for a loan is used as the basis for payment.
3. One entity giving financial aid to another. For example, the federal government gave a financial guarantee for loans to Chrysler Corporation.

bailee A person charging a fee to act as the guardian of objects for given purposes including safekeeping and maintenance. No transfer of

TITLE occurs in a BAILMENT and the net effect of the BAILEE is to retain temporary custody of the item or items in question. An example is a motorist, the BAILOR, who pays a fee to an automobile parking garage, the BAILEE, to park the car for a specific period of time expecting to have the automobile returned.
See also BAILOR.

bailor The individual who delivers CHATTEL for either repair or safekeeping to the BAILEE in the course of a BAILMENT.

bailment The delivery of items in TRUST by one person to another in exchange for a fee for a particular reason including safekeeping and/or repair. A bailment implies the existence of a contractual agreement, that after the bailment has been fulfilled the items in question will be returned in good order to the BAILOR. CHATTEL, or personal property, is the object of a bailment.
bailment for hire: A contractual agreement in which the BAILOR agrees to compensate the BAILEE for the performance of the bailment.
bailment lease: A contractual method for acquiring TITLE to an object only after a series of financial payments are made, which equals the original COST of the item plus the time value of the MONEY lent to the contractual purchaser. As long as the stipulated payments are made, the individual leasing the item may retain possession. An example is an auto lease with the right of purchase.
gratuitous bailment: The deposit of personal property solely for the benefit of the BAILOR and not lucrative for the BAILEE.
lucrative bailment: A bailment that takes place for a fee or other consideration to the BAILEE.

balance
1. Total credits less total debits in an ACCOUNT. An individual is better off having a CREDIT BALANCE than a DEBIT BALANCE.
2. In a general ledger, the equality between total credits and total debits of all accounts for a trial balance.
3. In a BALANCE SHEET, the total figure for assets always equals the total figure for LIABILITIES and owners' equity.
4. CREDIT BALANCE in a BANK ACCOUNT.
5. BALANCE on a LOAN.

balance sheet A statement of financial condition for a company at the end of a reporting period listing all the ASSETS, LIABILITIES, and the owners' or STOCKHOLDERS' equity. ASSETS indicate what the company owns while LIABILITIES are what the company owes. It is also called a STATEMENT OF POSITION. Assets less liabilities equals NET WORTH.
The accounting equation for a balance sheet is:

$$\text{Assets} = \text{Liabilities} + \text{Stockholders' Equity}$$

The balance sheet is classified into major groupings of assets and liabilities. These groupings include current assets, fixed assets, intangible assets, INVESTMENTS, current liabilities, and noncurrent liabilities.
The balance sheet is static and historical in form. The issuance of a balance sheet is required by the SECURITIES AND EXCHANGE COMMISSION in the United States and some other countries.
See also FINANCIAL STATEMENTS.

balanced (mutual) fund A MUTUAL FUND that combines investments in common stock and bonds and often preferred stock and attempts to provide income and some capital appreciation. Balanced funds tend to underperform all-stock funds in strong bull markets.

balancing The process of assuring that related information equals each other. Examples are assuring that the bank deposits per the depositor's records agree with those shown in the bank's records, and the adjusted checkbook balance equals the adjusted bank balance.

balloon
1. Balloon loan and payment.
2. Last loan payment when it is significantly more than the prior payments, also called partially amortized loan. For example, a debt agree-

ment might provide for a balloon payment when future refinancing is anticipated.

3. The final rental payment (including salvage value) for a leased property. The balloon payment is considerably greater than the preceding lease payments.

balloon clause A clause in an INSTALLMENT PURCHASE AGREEMENT or a MORTGAGE stating that the final payment will be substantially larger than all other payments.
See also BALLOON LOAN.

balloon loan Any loan with a final payment that is either (1) more than twice the amount of any one of the preceding six regularly scheduled payments or (2) due because a "call" provision is exercised by the lender. The TERM LOAN (or STRAIGHT LOAN) is a type of balloon loan.
See also BALLOON.

balloon-note mortgage A MORTGAGE that sets terms for only a short term, usually three to five years. At maturity, the entire balance of the loan is due and subject to full payment.
See also BALLOON LOAN.

balloon payment A final payment that is to be abnormally large, as compared to the other INSTALLMENT PAYMENTS.
See also BALLOON; BALLOON LOAN.

bank-by-phone account An account that allows an authorized user, with a touch-tone telephone and a password or security code, to access a bank's mainframe computer to perform certain functions. This access allows the account holder to check the account balance, transfer money from a money market account to the checking account, and (in some cases) to pay bills. Some banks may call this latter service "pay by phone." One can bank by phone using a telephone and actually speaking with bank employees.

bank card A card, generally made of plastic, with raised letters to facilitate machine processing, issued through a bank having an agreement with a major CREDIT corporation such as MASTERCARD or VISA entitling the holder to make credit purchases of a wide variety of merchandise and services. Depending upon the bank card agreement, fees include annual membership fees and monthly INTEREST charges. An individual should "shop around" among banks for the best arrangement as membership fees and interest rates vary.

Bank cards, also known as bank credit cards, are general purchase credit cards that can be used wherever in the world they are accepted. They are not backed up with specific COLLATERAL and rely extensively on the customer's past CREDIT HISTORY to determine whether he or she qualifies for their acceptance. Use of bank cards has greatly reduced the amount of CASH transactions while greatly increasing CREDIT sales.

bank credit The total financing an individual may obtain from his or her bank.

bank credit card A type of CREDIT CARD issued by banks that allows consumers to make purchases or obtain a CASH LOAN.

bank line Or, *line of credit*. A moral, not contractual, commitment by a *bank* to make a *loan* or loans, up to a specified total amount, to a borrower within a certain period of time. Since a bank line is not a legal commitment, it is not customary to charge a commitment fee. However, compensating balances, usually 10% of the bank line, and an additional 10% of an actual loan commitment may be required. A line the customer is formally notified of is termed an ADVISED LINE or a CONFIRMED LINE. On the other hand, a GUIDANCE LINE is internally set by the bank without notification to the customer.

bank loan A sum of MONEY lent to an individual (called a principal) for a particular purpose with a MARKET rate of INTEREST to be paid either over the life of the loan (*see also* AMORTIZE) or within a specified time. Each payment includes PRINCIPAL and interest. Bank loans take many forms. Loans can be made to a particular account through a CREDIT CARD or through direct payments. See example in table.
See also BANK CARD.

TWO YEAR AMORTIZATION OF A 5-YEAR $65,000 LOAN AT 10.5% INTEREST

Monthly Payment = $1397.11

Payment	Principal	Interest	Balance
1	828.36	568.75	64,171.64
2	835.61	561.50	63,336.03
3	842.92	554.19	62,493.11
4	850.30	546.81	61,642.81
5	857.74	539.37	60,785.07
6	865.24	531.87	59,919.83
7	872.81	524.30	59,047.03
8	880.45	516.66	58,166.58
9	888.15	508.96	57,278.43
10	895.92	501.19	56,382.51
11	903.76	493.35	55,478.74
12	911.67	485.44	54,567.07
13	919.65	477.46	53,647.42
14	927.70	469.41	52,719.73
15	935.81	461.30	51,783.92
16	944.00	453.11	50,839.92
17	952.26	444.85	49,887.65
18	960.59	436.52	48,927.07
19	969.00	428.11	47,958.07
20	977.48	419.63	46,980.58
21	986.03	411.08	45,994.55
22	994.66	402.45	44,999.89
23	1,003.36	393.75	43,996.53
24	1,012.14	384.97	42,984.39

Interest for 24 Periods = $11,515.03

bank rate

1. The interest rate a bank is paying on deposited funds.
2. The interest rate on a loan.

bank reconciliation

A term used when reconciling the differences between the BANK STATEMENT and the checkbook balance. The two balances should match. In other words, the checkbook balance must be the same as the bank balance at the end of the period. Reconciling differences relate to (1) items shown on the checkbook but not on the bank statement and (2) items shown on the bank statement but not on the checkbook.

To reconcile the BANK BALANCE:

1. Deduct outstanding checks (checks not cleared)
2. Add deposits in transit (not yet received at bank)

To reconcile CHECKBOOK BALANCE:

1. Deduct service charge
2. Add collections made by the bank.

Upon receiving the BANK STATEMENT, one should review each entry and check off, on the proper stub, each returned check. Add or deduct necessary items as illustrated below.

Example: John's BANK STATEMENT shows a balance of $348.50 on September 30, 19A. His CHECKBOOK BALANCE as of the same date is $277.00. Check #325 for $45.20 and check #333 for $29.30 are not enclosed with his statement. The bank has deducted a service charge of $3.00. The bank reconciliation follows:

September 30, 19A		September 30, 19A	
Bank balance	$348.50	Checkbook balance	$277.00
Less outstanding checks		Less service charge	3.00
#325 $45.20			
333 29.30	74.50		
Adjusted bank balance	$274.00	Adjusted checkbook balance	$274.00

bank secrecy

The bank's duty not to provide confidential information about a depositor. However, the bank may have to disclose such financial data in a legal action.

bank secrecy act

A federal law designed to uncover illegal activities. Under this law, banks are required to disclose certain information to the government about bank accounts. For example, the bank must report all cash deposits, withdrawals, and transfers of $10,000 or more to the Internal Revenue Service.

bank statement

A monthly statement listing all transactions affecting an individual's bank account. Items shown include bank service charges, checks drawn, deposits, automatic withdrawals, interest earned, and others. Included with the bank statement are canceled checks. A comparison should be made between the bank's records and the depositor's records to assure accuracy.

banker's acceptance (BA) A DRAFT drawn on a BANK by a corporation to pay for merchandise. The DRAFT promises payment of a certain sum of money to its holder at some future date. What makes BAs unique is that by prearrangement a BANK accepts them, thereby guaranteeing their payment at the stated time. Most BAs arise in foreign trade transactions. The most common maturity for BAs is three months, although they can have maturities of up to 270 days. Their typical denominations are $500,000 and $1 million. BAs offer the following advantages as an investment vehicle:
- Safety
- Negotiability
- Liquidity
- A yield spread several basis points higher than those of T-bills.
- Smaller investment amount producing a yield similar to that of a CD with comparable face value.

See also LETTER OF CREDIT.

bankruptcy (business) A situation in which the debt of a business exceeds the fair market value of its assets. It is also a court action under which a debtor may be discharged for unpaid debts, in whole or in part, and in which creditors receive distributions of assets from the debtor's property under the supervision of the court. CHAPTER 11 of the Bankruptcy Law provides for REORGANIZATION in which the debtor remains in possession of the business and in control of its operation, while the debtor and creditors are allowed to work together.

See also BANKRUPTCY (PERSONAL).

bankruptcy (personal) A legal process that is available for an individual who is overextended financially and is unable to pay his or her debts. Individuals can file for bankruptcy in order to seek to eliminate some or all of their debts legally.

Under CHAPTER 7 of the Bankruptcy Law, often called STRAIGHT BANKRUPTCY, the intent is to liquidate assets to pay the debts. Should this method be elected, the bankrupt can claim certain property as "exempt" and this property can be retained to preserve the basic necessities of life (such as a certain amount of equity in the home, an economical car, and personal clothing and effects.) Once a person has declared bankruptcy, he or she cannot be discharged from debts again for six years.

Under CHAPTER 13, often called WAGE-EARNER PLANS, the assets are not liquidated. Instead, interest and late charges are eliminated and arrangements are made to pay off some or all of the debts over several years.

Note that bankruptcy will not discharge all the debts. Debts that cannot be eliminated through bankruptcy proceedings include income taxes, child support, alimony, student loans, and debts incurred under false pretenses. Bankruptcy should not be taken lightly. One should be sure to consult an attorney on various decisions surrounding the issue and on how to get the greatest benefit from the new financial start.

See also BANKRUPTCY (BUSINESS).

bar chart Or, *histogram*. Graphical representations of statistical data using rectangular shapes showing frequency distributions. There is a vertical axis, Y, and a horizontal axis, X, which are labeled to illustrate basic concepts. The method allows comparison of concepts along a graduated basis of various concepts. (See p. 35.)

barbell portfolio Primarily a BOND SECURITY PORTFOLIO that distributes its BOND maturity dates around the normalized distribution concept found in a bell-shaped curve. On this basis there are fewer short- and long-term than medium-term bonds. The PORTFOLIO contains more intermediate bonds, 5 to 15 years, than short-term bonds, 1 to 5 years, or long-term bonds, those exceeding 15 years. The portfolio seeks to reduce short- or long-term RISK.

American versus Imported Car Sales

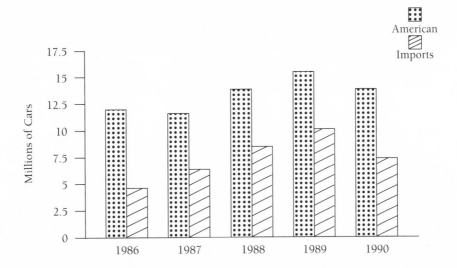

bargain and sale   The conveyance of property from one person to another for a consideration in the form of a sale. The term arises from the method of negotiation whereupon first there is a period of bargaining followed by a sale.

bargain and sale deed: The most commonly used form of REAL ESTATE DEED. There are two main types of bargain and sale deeds:

1. *With covenant*: The grantor of the deed promises that he has done nothing to hurt the TITLE to the property.
2. *Without covenant*: The grantor makes no warranty as to TITLE to the property.

If the real estate contract is silent as to the type of deed, a bargain and sale deed without covenant is granted.

bargain counter

1. In investments, a situation in which stocks are at lower prices than their assumed intrinsic worth because of a "bear" market.
2. Or, *bargain basement*. A physical location in a retail store where merchandise can be bought at very low prices.

Barron's Confidence Index   A corporate BOND index published weekly in *Barron's* following the trend in investor sentiment. It is the ratio of the average yield to maturity on best-grade corporate bonds to the intermediate-grade corporate bonds average yield to maturity.

The high-grade index is divided by the intermediate-grade index. An indication that stocks are heading higher is when the yield on the ten intermediate-term BONDS falls in comparison to the top ten, indicating more INVESTOR confidence.

barter   When individuals exchange products or labor and no cash is involved. For tax purposes, each party has to recognize income based on the fair market value of the product or service received. For example, a barter takes place when an electrician renders services to a retail store in exchange for furniture.

base pay   The regular salary of an employee excluding extra compensation such as overtime pay.

base rent   The minimum rent due on a lease with a percentage or participation requirement. For example, an individual with a small retail store in a mall rents space at $2,500 per month plus 10% of sales over $30,000 per month.

basic auto policy (BAP)   AUTO INSURANCE policy that provides coverage for both personal and business vehicles.

basic disability A term in a DISABILITY INSURANCE policy that describes the insured as unable to perform the duties of his or her regular occupation.

basic health insurance policy HEALTH INSURANCE that provides low levels of coverage for hospitalization, surgery, and other medical expenses.
See also MAJOR MEDICAL INSURANCE PLAN.

basic limits of liability Restrictions on financial and statutory LIABILITY that extend to an individual or corporation. The extent to which a party is exposed to an obligation, actual or possible loss, penalty, burden, or EXPENSE.
insurance: The extent to which one is legally exposed to risk. NO-FAULT automobile insurance pays the insured for injury or damage irrespective of who is at fault in an accident.
Limitation of Liability Act: Federal statute permitting ship owners to restrict cargo, passenger, employees, or harbor workers to the ship's value after a sinking or collision.
statute of limitations: Statute applying limitations to the claims of action in certain causes of action or criminal prosecutions. Actions must be brought within a specified period of time or the right to bring a suit elapses. Time limitations vary according to the governmental jurisdiction and the type of action.

basic price Or, *list price*. The usual published price of a good or service.

basis
interest rates: The stated INTEREST rate on a security.
Internal Revenue Service: The original COST plus out-of-pocket EXPENSE that must be reported to the INTERNAL REVENUE SERVICE when an INVESTMENT is sold and the capital gain or loss is calculated.
price: A rarely used odd-lot trading practice whereby the price is established by an exchange

floor officer at the end of a trading session for a buyer or seller of an odd lot when the MARKET bid and asked prices are more than $2 apart, or if no round-lot transactions have occurred that day. The customer gets the basis price plus or minus the odd-lot differential, if any.
yield to maturity: The yield to maturity of a BOND issued at face value.
See also YIELD TO MATURITY.

basis point A unit of measure for the change in interest rates for BONDS and NOTES. One basis point is equal to 1% of 1%, that is, 0.01%. Thus 100 basis points = 1%.

bear
investor: An individual believing the future prospects for a FINANCIAL MARKET are pessimistic, causing him or her to become defensive in strategy and sell, go short, or buy puts.
market: A BEAR MARKET is one that is falling over a period of time and for which the outlook is not promising.

bear market A prolonged period of declining stock prices; the bear's claws point down. Bear markets are unfavorable markets normally associated with investor pessimism, rising interest rates, economic slowdowns, or governmental control.
See also BULL MARKET.

bear raid An illegal trading act in which SECURITIES are sold SHORT below the last trading price in sufficient volume to depress the STOCK and result in a trading profit if the TRADE is closed. This can cause wild gyrations in a STOCK and is considered a form of STOCK manipulation. The SECURITIES AND EXCHANGE COMMISSION imposed the so-called up-tick rule mandating that stocks can be shorted only on the next up tick in the price of the SECURITY.

bear squeeze Security DEALER attempts that cause an increase in the price of STOCKS or commodities forcing short sellers to cover their sales by buying SECURITIES back. This action results in a squeeze on the SHORT sellers often incurring a financial loss for them.

bearer bond Or, *coupon bond*. A bond that does not have the owner's name recorded. Its coupons can be clipped and cashed by any holder since it is not registered in any specific name.

bearer (coupon) certificate Any SECURITY, although primarily a BOND, for which INTEREST is payable to the bearer of the interest coupon. These securities do not have the owner's name on their certificates nor are their names recorded on the company's registry. The holder, the bearer, of the coupon is entitled to the accrued INTEREST payment and the bond can be transferred without endorsement and a simple delivery.

The INTEREST coupons are usually numbered and dated as to when the payment is due. A formal announcement is made by the company as to when an INTEREST or PRINCIPAL payment will be made. Most American bonds are now registered bonds and the name of the owner appears on the certificate, whereas many international bonds still are of the bearer type.

bearer stock Any STOCK or SECURITY not having the name of the individual owner on the security or in the records of the corporation. The individual having custody of the stock owns it, and if there is no listed name, there is no requirement to sign it for transfer. Delivery is only needed to conclude the action. Bearer stock is discouraged today since it can be used as an illegal pass-through for MONEY.

bearish Expecting a decline in the price of a STOCK or the market in general.

before-tax cash flow CASH FLOW prior to deduction of INCOME TAX payments. For example, after deducting debt service of $15,000 from a NET OPERATING INCOME (NOI) of $20,000, David has a before-tax cash flow of $5,000.
See also AFTER-TAX CASH FLOW; CASH FLOW.

bellwether A STOCK or SECURITY that is widely held, usually by institutional investors, and indicates the general direction of the SECURITY MAR-

KET. E. I. Dupont & Co. and General Electric are examples of bellwether securities that give a general indication as to STOCK MARKET sentiment and are widely followed. The 20-year U.S. Treasury bond yield is an indicator of the direction of the BOND MARKET.

belly-up A generic phrase used to describe a company that has failed.
See also BANKRUPTCY.

beneficial interest The state of one who profits or benefits from a contract or property without retaining TITLE or ownership. A legatee or DONEE or other party directly benefiting from the ownership interests of others—for example, parties named in LIFE INSURANCE POLICIES, TRUSTS, and WILLS.

beneficial owner
property: The owner of a TRUST or the estate in equity who does not own the TITLE to the property that remains with the TRUST. One who has property rights with ownership. The TRUSTEE has a fiduciary responsibility to the beneficial owner and must manage the property in his or her best interests.
stocks: It is quite common for the STOCK of a client to be held by the BROKERAGE FIRM in STREET NAME. In this circumstance the beneficial owner of the STOCK is the client, but for safety, convenience, and COLLATERAL, in the case of a MARGIN ACCOUNT, the actual SECURITY is held in the name of the brokerage firm. Thus, the right of ownership is retained by the client even though the TITLE to the security is not in his or her name.

beneficiary designation An individual named to receive property, such as the beneficiary of a trust or a LIFE INSURANCE policy.

benefit period
1. In HEALTH INSURANCE, the duration of the period throughout which the health insurer will pay BENEFITS.
2. In DISABILITY INSURANCE, the maximum period of time for which benefits will be paid.

benefit-received principle The notion that tax assessments should be based on the degree to which taxpayers benefit from the goods and services paid by the taxes. Examples of this principle are social security tax and highway-user tax.

benefits in kind Merchandise or services of the employer that the employee may obtain at a discount. An example is a 20% discount on store merchandise given an employee of a department store.

bequest The giving of personal or real property pursuant to a will.

best buy A product or service that, in one's opinion, represents satisfactory quality at a fair price for that level of quality.

Best's ratings Annual ratings given to insurance companies by the A. M. Best Company to enable independent and objective judgments of financial stability and service to policyholders. The rating is also of interest to investors in insurance stocks. The highest rating is A+.

beta A measure of a security's VOLATILITY relative to an average SECURITY. Put another way, it is a measure of a security's return over time to that of the overall market. For example, if Paine Webber's beta is 2.0, it means that if the stock market goes up 10%, Paine Webber's common stock goes up 20%; if the market goes down 10%, Paine Webber goes down 20%. Here is a guide for reading betas:

Beta	What It Means
0	The security's return is independent of the market. An example is a risk-free security such as a T-bill.
0.5	The security is only half as responsive as the market.
1.0	The security has the same response or risk as the market (i.e., average risk). This is the beta value of the market portfolio such as Standard & Poor's 500 or Dow-Jones 30 Industrials.
2.0	The security is twice as responsive, or risky, as the market.

The following table shows examples of betas for selected stocks.

BETA VALUES FOR SELECTED COMPANIES (October and November, 1989)

Stock	Beta
Intel Corporation	1.55
International Paper	1.30
Corning Glass	1.15
Johnson & Johnson	1.05
Boeing	.95
Proctor & Gamble	.90

SOURCE: *Value Line Investment Survey,* (October and November issues, 1989), published by Value Line, Inc., 711 3rd Avenue, New York 10017.

Beta is nondiversifiable risk (systematic risk) resulting from forces outside the firm's control and therefore not unique to the given security. PURCHASING POWER, INTEREST RATE, and MARKET RISKS fall into this category. A particular stock's beta is useful in predicting how much the security will go up or down, provided financial analysts and investors know which way the market will go. Beta risk helps to analyze overall RISK and RETURN. Investors are compensated for this uncontrollable risk.

In general, there is a relationship between a stock's expected (or required) return and its beta. The following formula is very helpful in determining a stock's EXPECTED RETURN.

Expected return = risk-free rate + (beta × market risk premium) where the risk-free rate is the rate on a security such as a T-bill and the MARKET RISK PREMIUM equals the risk-free rate minus expected market return (such as Standard & Poor's 500 Stock Composite Index or Dow-Jones 30 Industrials).

The higher the beta for a security, the greater the return expected (or demanded) by the investor.

Example: Assume that the risk-free rate = 6%, and the expected return for the market = 10%. If a stock has a beta of 2.0, its risk premium should be 14%:

$$2.0 \times (10\% - 6\%) = 2.0 \times 4\% = 8\%$$

This means that an investor would expect (or demand) an extra 8% (risk premium) on this stock on top of the risk-free return of 6%. Therefore, the total expected (required) return on the stock should be 14%:

$$6\% + 8\% = 14\%$$

Better Business Bureau Local business-supported organizations designed to promote good business practices, assist the public in dealing with complaints, and provide useful consumer information. The Better Business Bureaus, which are loosely affiliated with a National Better Business Bureau, maintain information about local business firms and coordinate complaints and information with them.

bid and asked A term used in the OVER-THE-COUNTER MARKET to describe unlisted securities. Bid is the highest price an investor is willing to pay while asked is the lowest price a seller is willing to take. Together, the two prices represent a QUOTATION in a security or commodity. A spread is the difference between the BID PRICE and the ASKED PRICE for the security or commodity.

bid price
1. The price a buyer wants to pay, or "bid," for a particular security. It is the highest price offered by a dealer to buy a given security traded in the OVER-THE-COUNTER market.
2. The price per share that shareholders receive when they cash in (redeem) their shares.

big board A popular term for the NEW YORK STOCK EXCHANGE (NYSE). It is the biggest organized market. Companies listed on the Big Board are typically of higher quality than those listed or traded elsewhere.

bilateral contract A legal contract between parties who both agree to perform or not to perform some action.

bill Or, *charge; invoice*. A written statement regarding the terms of a contract and the partic-ulars, including COST and quantity, to purchase specific services and items. A general name for any receivable or payable accounts for goods sold, services rendered, or work done. In commercial usage a bill is a demand for payment.

The act of presenting a bill is billing.

bill payable: A merchant's term designating bills and promissory notes that are outstanding and awaiting payment. These are claims against ASSETS.

bill receivable: NOTES, drafts, CHECKS payable to one's benefit and for which the proceeds will be received.

bill of credit:
1. A guarantee for CREDIT granted to an international correspondent bank guaranteeing payment to a traveler.
2. A promissory note of the government issued upon its full faith and CREDIT intended to circulate as currency.

bill broker: One who negotiates purchases and sales of commercial paper.

bill of exchange: A three-party document in which one person, the DRAWER, instructs a second party, the DRAWEE, to pay a specified sum to a PAYEE. A form of a bill of exchange is a DRAFT and DRAFT ACCEPTANCE. A check is a demand bill of exchange. A bill of exchange can be paid immediately or at a future date.

bill of store: A customs document for exported goods that have been reimported to avoid customs duties. The bill of store must be presented to the customs authorities to avoid being subject to the same conditions and limitations applying to other foreign goods.

foreign bill of exchange: A document used in international TRADE by which the drawer requires the drawee to pay a sum of MONEY on a given date or when the goods reach the purchaser. The DRAWEE's signature on the bill of exchange constitutes his or her agreement to make payments.

bill of sale A formal instrument for the conveyance or transfer of title to goods and CHATTELS. It states that the goods have been paid for and that no outstanding loans exist on the personal property. This is the buyer's receipt that represents his or her ability to sell the property in the future. Unlike real estate, there is typically no registration requirement.

billing cycle The time between interim billings for merchandise or services, typically one month. It could also be the periodic mailing of customer statements within a month so as to allocate the work load efficiently.

billing date The last day of the month for which any transactions will be shown on a bank or retail credit card statement.
See also BILLING CYCLE.

bills outstanding Bills that have been received for goods or services but remain unpaid.

binder A temporary and symbolic payment of good faith obligating two or more parties until a final transaction occurs. Often, the binder is returned if the final agreement is not completed.
insurance: A written memorandum of the CONTRACT terms of INSURANCE that provides temporary insurance protection to the insured pending final acceptance by the insurance company.
real estate: A receipt for earnest MONEY or a deposit paid to secure the right to purchase a home for terms that have been agreed to. In REAL ESTATE a binder is a temporary deposit until the agreement goes to contract.

binding arbitration Term used in labor relations in which a neutral third party arbitrates a labor dispute by hearing the arguments of labor and management and rendering a judgment that the parties are committed to accepting. Binding arbitration may be voluntary or compulsory. It is voluntary if the parties have agreed to utilize the process; it is compulsory if a government agency requires them to accept arbitration.

An individual may enter a CONTRACT and agree that any dispute arising out of that contract will be settled through binding arbitration.

bi-weekly (mortgage) loan A bi-weekly accelerated mortgage reduction payment plan that will help a borrower pay off his or her current 30-year mortgage in approximately 20 years. These payment plans provide a dramatic build-up of equity, saving the borrower thousands of dollars in interest.

These plans do not change existing mortgages. The borrower is not reapplying or refinancing anything, so there are no points, no need for costly appraisals, and no credit constraints. Instead of making one monthly payment, the borrower makes a half-payment every 14 days. This schedule results in 26 half-payments yearly, or an extra monthly payment annually, achieving the following:

- The reduction the borrower will achieve on the loan more than doubles, even over the short term. For example, on an 11%, 30-year, $125,000 loan, after three years in the bi-weekly program the borrower would have $6,099 in equity available, as opposed to $1,891 if he or she had stayed on the regular monthly plan.
- The loan is also shortened if the owner keeps the property for the full term of the loan. A typical 30-year loan is completely paid off in little more than 20 years, with a saving of more than $142,000 in interest for every $125,000 borrowed.

Bi-weekly payment plans are offered by various firms hired to act as money managers to assist the owner. Once in the program, everything is automatic. Every 14 days an electronic wire transfer of half the monthly payment is sent from the owner's local bank or savings account. Then, after the second monthly half-payment, the funds are combined and the entire payment is transferred to the lender.

When shopping for a bi-weekly, there are five things to look for:
- A reasonable, one-time start-up fee
- Reasonable wire transfer fees
- A program that holds the borrower's funds in a major bank, not in a trust account or other privately controlled account
- A program that pays interest on all funds held
- Ability of the borrower to go off, and back on,

the program or to transfer at no additional charge.

blackout period   The period during which survivors are not entitled to Social Security income. This period begins when the youngest dependent child reaches 16 and ends when the survivors reach age 60.

blank check   A DEMAND DEPOSIT CHECK signed by the maker but having no designated amount. Normally, this is done so the DRAWEE can indicate the amount necessary. Obviously, this practice is risky. Anyone could CASH such a CHECK for whatever amount he or she indicates, provided sufficient funds exist in the CHECKING ACCOUNT, particularly as no drawee was indicated.

blank endorsement   The payee's signing of only his or her name to the back of a check. It transfers title to anyone carrying it at the time. It can be cashed by anyone.
See also RESTRICTIVE ENDORSEMENT; SPECIAL ENDORSEMENT.

blanket contract   An insurance policy applying to property of the insured at different geographic locations. This policy is especially suitable when property is moved among locations.

blanket insurance   A single INSURANCE POLICY that covers (1) two or more kinds of properties in two or more locations and (2) two or more kinds of properties in the same location. This type of insurance is suitable for such businesses as chain stores that are geographically distributed and also whose property is covered in a blanket manner. The insurance policy is allocated to the property items based on their fair market values.

blanket medical expense insurance   A HEALTH INSURANCE that covers medical expenses on an ALL RISK/ALL PERIL basis. Medical expenses are automatically covered unless a specific medical expense is excluded.

blanket mortgage   A single MORTGAGE or other ENCUMBRANCE that covers more than one piece of real estate. It is usually released only subsequent to the mortgage loan being fully repaid. A partial release clause can be included, however, in the original mortgage agreement that specifies how much of the loan must be repaid before a piece of property can be released.

blanket rate   The same rate for transportation charges for a delivery of merchandise to buyers within a particular locality.

blanket recommendation   Recommendation of a brokerage firm to its clientele either to buy or sell a given stock in an industry irrespective of the investor's goals or present portfolio.

blended rate   An INTEREST RATE that is higher than the rate on the old loan but lower than the rate offered on new loans. It is generally offered by the lender to induce home buyers to REFINANCE existing, low-interest rate loans as an alternative to assuming the existing loan. For example, Allison wants to sell a home to Christine. Christine can assume the existing loan of $50,000 at an interest rate of 9%. Christine could obtain a new loan at an interest rate of 13%. Allison's lender offers the alternative of refinancing the loan for $80,000 at a blended rate of 11%.

blind pool   A LIMITED PARTNERSHIP in which limited partners rely on the GENERAL PARTNER to select particular properties after the funds are put together. For example, each of 500 investors contributes $10,000 into a limited partnership. The general partner has not located the property to be purchased, so the investment money is said to be a blind pool.

blind trust   An individual gives permission to a third party to manage his or her finances. The individual leaves decisions to the fiduciary. This arrangement may be made, for example, when a possible conflict of interest exists. A blind trust would be appropriate for a politician who may make legislative decisions affecting an industry in which he or she owns an interest.

block
securities industry: A significant amount of

STOCK, usually more than 10,000 SHARES or any quantity worth over $200,000. Because of the impact of such a large number of shares on the MARKET during any one TRADE, special handling is often required by which the necessary buyers or sellers are prearranged. However, block trading has become more common as the volume of the STOCK EXCHANGE has increased with the greater presence of institutional participants. A block sale occurs only with previously issued STOCK.

banking: Large number of deposited CHECKS in a SAVINGS account along with a DEPOSIT slip.

block trading Or, *block transaction.* Trading of STOCKS in large amounts usually exceeding 10,000 SHARES. The presence of block trading often indicates institutional MARKET activity. *See also* BLOCK.

blow-off The climax of a substantial STOCK MARKET advance marked by extremely high volume often followed by a sharp price decline as TRADERS take profits.

blue chip

1. STOCKS issued by companies well known for high-quality products and services and their ability to make money and pay dividends. They have low risk and provide modest but dependable return. This term derives from blue chips in poker, which are worth more than red or white chips. The company offering the stock generally provides an uninterrupted track record of dividends and good long-term growth prospects. Blue chips are typically held as long-term investments. Examples are General Electric and Merck.

2. High-quality BONDS that are secure and stable in price and interest payments.

Blue Cross/Blue Shield A nonprofit organization offering HEALTH INSURANCE, mainly on a group basis. It is the nation's largest provider of HEALTH INSURANCE. Blue Cross is a hospital plan. Benefits provided by Blue Cross cover hospitalization expenses subject to some restrictions (for example, semiprivate room only). The member hospital sends the bills directly to Blue Cross for reimbursements. Blue Shield is a medical–surgical plan. The doctor sends the bills to the plan directly rather than to the patient. The patient is responsible for any difference between the doctor's fees and the scheduled rates.

Blue List A financial publication published daily listing bonds (primarily municipal bonds) and their market prices and yields. It is an excellent reference on the volume of tax-exempt securities in the secondary market.

blue sky laws A popular name for laws various states have enacted to protect the public against securities frauds. These laws include regulations over the licensing of BROKERS, registrations of new securities, and formal approvals by appropriate government bodies. This term originated when a judge ruled that a particular stock had about the same value as a patch of blue sky.

bodily injury liability loss A clause in AUTOMOBILE INSURANCE that protects individuals against losses from bodily injury. This coverage is usually given in a combination figure—the first amount is a limit per individual and the second amount is a limit per accident.

boiler room Source of high-pressure peddling over the telephone of stocks of dubious value and even fraudulent issues. A typical boiler room is simply a room lined with desks or cubicles, each with a salesman and telephone. The salesmen call what are known in the trade as sucker lists. Such recommendations are usually not suitable for a customer's account.

boilerplate Standard language found in CONTRACTS, INDENTURES, PROSPECTUSES, and the like. It typically appears in fine print.

bona fide In law, a Latin term meaning "in good faith," without fraud.

bond A legal instrument to obtain credit pledging direct assets and/or the full faith and credit of the issuing unit as collateral. A bond is a long-term debt obligation of the issuer. Bonds are typically stated in $1,000 denominations. All bonds provide for the repayment of the principal plus interest over a specified period of time known as its maturity date.

Bonds may be SECURED by collateral or be UNSECURED (debenture). A CONVERTIBLE BOND allows the owner to exchange it for other securities of the company at a later date under specified conditions. A REGISTERED BOND is registered in the name of the owner, whereas a BEARER BOND is unregistered and can be presented for payment by any bearer.

Bonds are issued by the federal, state, and local governments as well as private institutions. Bonds trade in a market and are subject to market variations in price. Subject to the terms and conditions of the bond itself, the interest rate is usually fixed at the stated rate on the face of the bond. If the general interest rates rise, the bond price will fall and sell at a "discount" to the market, adjusting the yield to maturity to approximately equal the current interest rate market. The discount is the difference between the lower price at which a bond may be trading and its higher face value known as the PAR value. If the market interest rates fall, the price of the bond will rise and could sell at a PREMIUM that is the difference between the higher price at which a bond may be trading and its lower face value.

bond anticipation note (BAN) Short-term municipal, state, or federal notes, backed only by the full faith and CREDIT of the issuer, in expectation of a long term BOND issuance. The PRINCIPAL and INTEREST of bond anticipation notes (BANs) are paid from the proceeds of a long-term BOND sale. BANs cannot be issued without a specific governmental authorization for a specific purpose, and governments cannot use BANs as a supplemental source of revenue by reinvesting the proceeds.

bond certificates Evidence of debt issued to investors who purchase bonds. The bond certificate includes the name of the ISSUER, TRANSFER AGENT, FACE VALUE of the BOND, INTEREST RATE, and MATURITY DATE.

bond conversion The process of exchanging BONDS having a CONVERTIBILITY option into SHARES of a company's common or PREFERRED STOCK. The timing of the conversion depends greatly on the conversion feature in terms of the expiration dates, general MARKET conditions, and the DIVIDEND rate on the common or preferred stock compared to the INTEREST YIELD on the BOND. Conversions are normally at the option of the investor; however, in certain cases it can be at the option of the company. This latter category is termed a forced conversion.

The effect of a BOND conversion is to turn DEBT holders into equity holders, thus reducing the overall debt of the company.

bond discount The excess of the FACE AMOUNT of the BOND (or PAR value) over the MARKET PRICE. On the other hand, when the market price of the bond exceeds its FACE VALUE, it is trading at a PREMIUM.

MARKET conditions are critical in determining the size of any bond discount or premium. When INTEREST RATES rise, the price of the bond falls to a discount, and when interest rates fall, the price of the bond climbs to a PREMIUM. Other factors in the MARKET affect bond prices. These include the supply of bonds at any one time, the demand for bonds by purchasers, the quality of the bonds, MATURITY DATES, CONVERTIBILITY features, revenue pledges, and so on.
See also BOND MARKET; BOND PREMIUM.

bond dividend A STOCKHOLDER DIVIDEND issued in BONDS rather than in CASH or SECURITIES. Such a DIVIDEND has the net effect of postponing CASH payouts to a later date while converting equity holders to DEBT holders. However, the bonds do have MARKET VALUE and can be sold at any time.

bond (mutual) fund A MUTUAL FUND that emphasizes safety and invests in BONDS. The portfolio may consist of various levels of quality of bonds depending on the particular objectives of the specific mutual fund. For example, there may be high-grade bonds, medium-grade bonds, or low-grade bonds (e.g., JUNK BONDS). There are three key facts about the bonds in any portfolio.

Quality: Check the credit rating of the typical bond in the fund. Ratings by Standard & Poor's and Moody's show the relative danger that an issuer will default on interest or principal payments. AAA is the best grade. A rating of BB or lower signifies a junk bond.

Maturity: The average maturity of the fund's bonds indicates how much an investor stands to lose if interest rates rise. The longer the term of the bonds, the more volatile is the price. For example, a 20-year bond may fluctuate in price four times as much as a four-year issue.

Premium or discount: Some funds with high current yields hold bonds that trade for more than their face value or at a premium. Such funds are less vulnerable to losses if rates go up. Funds that hold bonds trading at a discount to face value can lose most.

An investor should keep in mind the following guidelines:

- Rising interest rates drive down the value of all bond funds. For this reason, rather than focusing only on current yield, the investor should look primarily at total return (yield plus capital gains from falling interest rates or minus capital losses if rates climb).
- All bond funds do not benefit equally from tumbling interest rates. If interest rates will decline and the investor wants to increase total return, he or she should buy funds that invest in U.S. Treasuries or top-rated corporate bonds. The investor should consider high-yield corporate bonds (junk bonds) if he or she believes rates are stabilizing.
- Unlike bonds, bond funds do not allow the investor to lock in a yield. A mutual fund with a constantly changing portfolio is not like an individual bond, which one can keep to maturity. If the investor wants steady, secure income over several years or more, an alternative to funds would be to buy individual top-quality bonds or invest in a municipal

bond UNIT TRUST, which maintains a fixed portfolio.

bond house   A brokerage firm concentrating on the issuance and UNDERWRITING of BONDS. A bond house may have BOND BROKERS trading for their own accounts on the floor of the exchanges. Bond houses are critical in obtaining financing for corporations and governments, as they are involved in the entire transaction from the original development of the issue to the final marketing and sale. These transactions can be in the tens of millions of dollars or relatively small.

bond indenture   The lengthy, legal agreement detailing the issuer's obligations pertaining to a bond issue. It contains the terms of the bond issue as well as any restrictive provisions placed on the firm, known as RESTRICTIVE COVENANTS. The indenture is administered by an independent TRUSTEE. The terms of the bond may include the type of bond, amount of issue, COLLATERAL, and CALL PROVISIONS. Restrictive covenants may include a sinking fund requirement and maintenance of (a) required levels of working capital, (b) a particular current ratio, and (c) a specified debt ratio.

bond market

1. A generic term describing general MARKET conditions of the supply and demand for BONDS.

2. A relative term describing markets in which the SECURITIES and bonds of various concerns as well as governmental agencies are issued to obtain financing. Bonds are sold on the NEW YORK STOCK EXCHANGE, the AMERICAN STOCK EXCHANGE, and the OVER-THE-COUNTER MARKET. The market where bonds are exchanged are referred to as the SECONDARY MARKET and serve to furnish liquidity for the overall bond market.

bond premium

1. The amount by which the MARKET PRICE of a BOND exceeds its FACE VALUE (PAR VALUE). A bond selling at 105 is selling at a 5-point PREMIUM that reduces its YIELD TO MATURITY. The price of a bond moves inversely to MARKET INTEREST

RATES serving to adjust its YIELD TO MATURITY to the general MARKET rate of INTEREST. A BOND DISCOUNT occurs when a bond is selling below PAR.

Example: If an individual buys $10,000 in BONDS at 108, he or she will be paying $10,800 ($10,000 × 108%). The bond premium in this example is $800.

2. At the time of a bond sale, a bond premium results when the bond is sold at a price higher than its face value, which makes it a HOT ISSUE for the company.
See also BOND MARKET.

bond quotation Published investment information about a BOND including its CURRENT YIELD, daily volume traded, price, and net change for the day. The data for an IBM bond, shown below, illustrate how bond quotations are presented in the newspaper.

Bonds	Cur Yld	Vol	High	Low	Close	Net Chg
IBM 9⅜ 04	11.	169	84⅝	84	84	−1⅛

The column numbers immediately following the company name gives the bond coupon rate and maturity date. This particular bond carries a 9.375% interest rate and matures in 2004. The next column, labeled "cur yld," provides the CURRENT YIELD calculated by dividing the annual interest income (9 3/8%) by the current MARKET PRICE of the bond (a closing price of 84). Thus, the current yield for the IBM bond is 11%. This figure represents the effective, or real rate of return on the current market price represented by the bond's interest earnings. The "vol" column indicates the number of bonds traded on the given day (i.e., 169 bonds).

The market price of a bond is usually expressed as a percentage of its PAR (FACE) VALUE, which is customarily $1,000. Corporate bonds are quoted to the nearest one-eighth of a percent, and a quote of 84 5/8 in the above indicates a price of $846.25 or 84 5/8% of $1,000.

U.S. government bonds are highly marketable and deal in keenly competitive markets so they are quoted in thirty-seconds or sixty-fourths rather than eighths.

Moreover, decimals rather than fractions are used in quoting prices. For example, a quotation of 106.17 for a Treasury bond indicates a price of $1,065.31 [$1,060 + (17/32 × $10)]. When a plus sign follows the quotation, the Treasury bond is being quoted in a sixty-fourth. We must double the number following the decimal point and add one to determine the fraction of $10 represented in the quote. For example, a quote of 95.16+ indicates a price of $955.16 [$950 + (33/64 × $10)].

bond ratings Ratings that reflect the probability that a bond issue will go into default. They can influence investors' perceptions of risk and therefore have an impact on the interest rate. Bond investors tend to place more emphasis on independent analysis of quality than do common stock investors. Bond analysis and ratings are done, among others, by STANDARD & POOR'S and MOODY'S. Below is an actual listing of the designations used by these well-known independent agencies. Descriptions on ratings are summarized. For original versions of descriptions, see Moody's *Bond Record* and Standard & Poor's *Bond Guide*.

DESCRIPTION OF BOND RATINGS

Moody's	Standard & Poor's	Quality Indication
Aaa	AAA	Highest quality
Aa	AA	High quality
A	A	Upper-medium grade
Baa	BBB	Medium grade
Ba	BB	Contains speculative elements
B	B	Outright speculative
Caa	CCC & CC	Default definitely possible
Ca	C	Default, only partial recovery likely
C	D	Default, little recovery likely

Bond investors pay careful attention to ratings since they can affect not only potential market behavior but relative yields as well. Specifically, the higher the rating, the lower the YIELD of a BOND, other things being equal. It should be noted that the ratings do change over time and the rating agencies have "credit watch lists" of various types.

bond valuation The procedure of computing the price an investor should buy a bond for; with regard to the issuing corporation, the price it demands for the debt security. This process considers the COUPON INTEREST RATE, the life, and the degree of risk. The process of determining the value of a security such as common stock or a bond involves finding the present value of the security's expected future cash flows using the investor's required rate of return. Thus, the basic security valuation model can be defined mathematically as follows:

$$V = \sum_{t=1}^{n} \frac{C_t}{(1 + r)^t}$$

where

    V = intrinsic value or present value of an asset
    C_t = expected future cash flows in period $t = 1, \cdots,$
    n
    r = investor's required rate of return

The valuation process for a bond requires a knowledge of three basic elements: (1) the amount of the cash flows to be received by the investor, which is equal to the periodic interest to be received and the par value to be paid at maturity; (2) the maturity date of the loan; and (3) the investor's required rate of return.

The periodic interest can be received annually or semiannually. The value of a bond is simply the present value of these cash flows. Two versions of the bond valuation model are presented below:

If the interest payments are made annually, then

$$V = \sum_{t=1}^{n} \frac{I}{(1 + r)^t} + \frac{M}{(1 + r)^n} = I\,T_4\,(r, n) + M\,T_3\,(r, n)$$

where

    I = interest payment each year = coupon interest rate × par value

    M = par value, or maturity value, typically $1,000
    r = investor's required rate of return
    n = number of years to maturity
    T_4 = present value of an annuity of $1 (which can be found in Table 4)
    T_3 = present value of $1 (which can be found in Table 3, Appendix A)

Example 1: Consider a bond, maturing in 10 years and having a coupon rate of 8%. The par value is $1,000. Investors consider 10% to be an appropriate required rate of return in view of the risk level associated with this bond. The annual interest payment is $80 (8% × $1,000). The present value of this bond is

$$V = \sum_{t=1}^{n} \frac{I}{(1 + r)^t} + \frac{M}{(1 + r)^n} = I\,T_4\,(r, n) + M\,T_3\,(r, n)$$

$$= \sum_{t=1}^{10} \frac{\$80}{(1 + 0.1)^t} + \frac{\$1,000}{(1 + 0.1)^{10}}$$

$$= \$80\,T_4\,(10\%, 10) + \$1,000\,T_3\,(10\%, 10)$$

$$= \$80\,(6.1446) + \$1,000(0.3855)$$

$$= \$491.57 + \$385.50 = \$877.07$$

If the interest is paid semiannually, then

$$V = \sum_{t=1}^{2n} \frac{I/2}{(1 + 2/r)^t} + \frac{M}{(1 + r/2)^{2n}}$$

$$= \frac{I}{2}\,T_4\,(r/2, 2n) + T,\,M(r/2, 2n)$$

Example 2: Assume the same data as in Example 1, except that the interest is paid semiannually.

$$V = \sum_{t=1}^{2n} \frac{I/2}{(1 + r/2)^t} + \frac{M}{(1 + r/2)^{2n}}$$

$$= \frac{I}{2}\,T_4(r/2, 2n) + M\,T_3\,(r/2, 2n)$$

$$= \sum_{t=1}^{20} \frac{\$40}{(1 + 0.05)^t} + \frac{\$1,000}{(1 + 0.05)^{20}}$$

$$= \$40\,T_4\,(5\%, 20) + \$1,000\,T_3\,(5\%, 20)$$

$$= \$40\,(12.4622) + \$1,000(0.3769)$$

$$= \$498.49 + \$376.90 = \$875.39$$

bond yield The EFFECTIVE RATE OF RETURN on a BOND. Bonds are evaluated on many different types of returns including current yield, yield to maturity, yield to call, and realized yield.

current yield: The current yield is the annual interest payment divided by the current price of the bond. The current yield is reported in the *Wall Street Journal,* among others.

Example 1: Assume a 12% COUPON RATE on a $1,000 PAR VALUE BOND selling for $960. The current yield is

$$\$120/\$960 = 12.5\%$$

The problem with this measure of return is that it does not take into account the maturity date of the bond. A bond with one year to run and another with 15 years to run would have the same current yield quote if interest payments were $120 and the price were $960. Clearly, the one-year bond would be preferable under this circumstance because you would get not only $120 in interest, but also a gain of $40 ($1000 − $960) with a one-year time period, and this amount could be reinvested.

yield to maturity: The yield to maturity takes into account the maturity date of the bond. It is the real return to be received from interest income plus capital gain, assuming the bond is held to maturity. There are two ways to calculate this measure: the exact method and the approximate method.

the exact method:

Under the exact method, a bond's yield to maturity is the INTERNAL RATE OF RETURN on investment in the bond. It is calculated by solving the bond valuation model for *r*:

$$V = \sum_{t=1}^{n} \frac{I}{(1 + r)^t} + \frac{M}{(1 + r)^n} = I\ T_4(r,n) + M\ T_3(r,n)$$

where *V* is the market price of the bond, *I* is the interest payment, and *M* is the maturity value, usually $1,000. T_4 and T_3 are found in Appendix A, Tables 4 and 3, respectively.

Finding the bond's yield *r,* involves trial and error. It is best explained by an example.

Example 2: Suppose an investor is offered a 10-year, 8% coupon, $1,000 par value bond at a price of $877.60. The rate of return earned if the bond is bought and held to maturity is computed below.

First, set up the bond valuation model:

$$V = \$877.60 = \sum_{t=1}^{10} \frac{\$80}{(1 + r)^t} + \frac{\$1,000}{(1 + r)^{10}}$$

$$= \$80\ T_4(r,10) + \$1,000\ T_3(r,10)$$

Since the bond is selling at a discount, the bond's yield is above the going coupon rate of 8%. Therefore, try a rate of 9%. Substituting factors for 9% in the equation, we obtain

$$V = \$80(6.418) + \$1,000(0.422) = \$513.44 + \$422.0$$
$$= \$935.44$$

The calculated bond value, $935.44, is above the actual market price of $877.60, so the yield is not 9%. To lower the calculated value, the rate must be raised. Trying 10% we obtain

$$V = \$80(6.145) + \$1,000(0.386)$$
$$= \$491.60 + \$386.00 = \$877.60$$

This calculated value is exactly equal to the market price of the bond; thus, 10% is the bond's yield to maturity.

The approximate method:

$$\text{Yield} = \frac{I + (M-V)/n}{(M + V)/2}$$

here

    V = the market value of the bond
    I = dollars of interest paid per year
    M = maturity value, usually $1,000
    n = number of years to maturity

Example 3: Using the same data in Example 2,

$$\text{Yield} = \frac{\$80 + (\$1,000-\$877.60)/10}{(\$1,000+\$877.60)/2} = \frac{\$80 + \$12.24}{\$938.80}$$

$$= \frac{\$92.24}{\$938.80}$$

$$= 9.8\%$$

which came out to very close to 10%.

yield to call: Not all bonds are held to maturity. If the bond may be called prior to maturity, the yield-to-maturity formula will have the CALL PRICE in place of the par value ($1,000).

Example 4: Assume a 20-year bond was initially issued at a 13.5% coupon rate, and after two years, rates have dropped. Assume further that the bond is currently selling for $1,180, the yield to maturity on the bond is 11.15%, and the bond can be called in five years after issue at $1,090. Thus, if the investor buys the bond two years after issue, the bond may be called back after three more years at $1,090. The yield to call can be calculated as follows:

$$\frac{\$135 + (\$1,090 - \$1,180)/3}{(\$1,090 + \$1,180)/2} = \frac{\$135 + (-\$90/3)}{\$1,135}$$

$$= \frac{\$105}{\$1,135} = 9.25\%$$

The yield to call figure of 9.25% is 190 basis points less than the yield to maturity of 11.15%. Clearly, the investor needs to be aware of the differential because a lower return is earned.

realized yield: The investor may trade in and out of a bond long before it matures and obviously needs a measure of return to evaluate the investment appeal of any bonds he or she intends to buy and sell. Realized yield is used for this purpose. This measure is simply a variation of yield to maturity, as only two variables are changed in the yield-to-maturity formula. Future price is used in place of par value ($1,000), and the length of the HOLDING PERIOD is substituted for the number of years to maturity.

Example 5: In Example 3, assume that the investor anticipates holding the bond only three years and has estimated that interest rates will change in the future so the price of the bond will move to about $925 from its present level of $877.70. Thus, he or she will buy the bond today at a market price of $877.70 and sell the issue three years later at a price of $925. Given these assumptions, the realized yield of this bond would be

$$\text{Realized yield} = \frac{\$80 + (\$925 - \$877.70)/3}{(\$925 + \$877.70)/2}$$

$$= \frac{\$80 + \$15.77}{\$901.35} = \frac{\$95.77}{\$901.35}$$

$$= 10.63\%$$

Fortunately, a bond table is available to find the value for various yield measures. A source is the *Thorndike Encyclopedia of Banking and Financial Tables* by Warren, Gorham, and Lamont, Boston. Note that there are many financial calculators available that contain preprogrammed formulas and perform many yield calculations. They include Radio Shack EC5500, Hewlett-Packard 10B, Sharp EL733, and Texas Instrument BA35.

equivalent before-tax yield: Yield on a municipal bond needs to be looked at on an equivalent before-tax yield basis, because the interest received is not subject to federal income taxes. The formula used to equate interest on municipals to other investments is

$$\text{Tax equivalent yield} = \text{Tax-exempt yield}/ (1 - \text{tax rate})$$

Example 6: If the investor has a MARGINAL TAX RATE of 28% and is evaluating a municipal bond paying 10% interest, the equivalent before-tax yield on a taxable investment would be

$$10\%/(1 - .28) = 13.89\%$$

Thus, he or she could choose between a taxable investment paying 13.89% and a tax-exempt bond paying 10% and achieve the same results. *See also* RATE OF RETURN; YIELD.

bondholder An individual who has legal title to a corporate or governmental bond. He or she is a creditor because money was lent to the issuing entity. A bond may be registered in the name of the owner. If not, it is a BEARER BOND and the one holding it has the rights to it.

BONDHOLDERS are entitled to the PRINCIPAL and INTEREST on the bond. Bonds are a unit of DEBT for a company and bondholders have in bankruptcy a priority claim over the STOCKHOLDERS of the company.

bonus Additional CONSIDERATION, PREMIUM, or gratuity to which the recipient has no right to make a demand.

athletics: An additional incentive given to a professional athlete for agreeing to sign on with a particular team.

business: An addition to *salary* or *wages* often given at the end of the year without expectation of a direct return, such as a Christmas bonus or end of the year profit bonus. It serves as a token of appreciation for a job well done and to provide a continuing incentive for future effort.

insurance: A LIFE INSURANCE payment made by the INSURANCE company to the INSURED arising from the amount accrued in the form of investment returns.

bonus stock

common stock: STOCK given as an incentive to accept another form of SECURITIES, for example, stock given to investors in BONDS by a corporation. Such activities are unlawful in most states and the practice has been associated with the term "watered" and "discount" stock.

stock dividend: Bonus stock in Britain refers to a STOCK DIVIDEND issued by a company. Stock dividends serve to increase the total float of the stock.

book

In common usage, a bound and printed document that contains material consisting of words and concepts. A book is a printed literary composition.

book account: A detailed account of the DEBITS and CREDITS occurring in various transactions. A book account serves to give a detailed itemization of all transactions occurring over time.

books of account: Books in which business people normally keep a record of their business transactions. Books of account are normally part of an accounting system. In automated accounting systems accounting entries can be kept in a computerized system.

security floor trader: The record kept by a trading *specialist* of the buy and sell orders entered for a particular *security*. What the *specialist* does is match up the orders to maintain orderly transactions.

security underwriting:

1. Term used to give the INTEREST RATE indications on a pending SECURITY UNDERWRITING based upon INTEREST expressed for the issue by potential buyers.

2. It also applies to the record of activity for the members of the UNDERWRITING SYNDICATE whereby buy commitments are recorded to be balanced against supply of the offering.

book value

1. The net amount of an ASSET equal to the gross cost less ACCUMULATED DEPRECIATION. If an individual buys an automobile for $15,000 with a 10-year life and no salvage value and STRAIGHT LINE DEPRECIATION is used, the depreciation per year will be $1,500 ($15,000/10 years). The book value of the car at the end of the first year is $13,500 ($15,000 − $1,500).

2. In AUTOMOBILE INSURANCE, the value of a car based on the average current selling price of cars of the same make, model, and age.

3. The difference between total assets and total liabilities, less the value of the PREFERRED STOCK. This gives the book value of the common stockholders' EQUITY. Book value of the net assets of a company may have minimal or no significant relationship to their market value.

4. BOOK VALUE PER SHARE of a stock per a company's books based on historical cost. It may differ significantly from current MARKET PRICE per share. Book value per share of COMMON STOCK equals common stockholders' equity divided by outstanding common shares.

book value per share

The worth of each share of stock on the books of a company based on historical cost. Book value per share is usually less than the current market price per share. Book value per share equals:

$$\frac{\text{Total stockholders' equity}}{\text{Outstanding shares}}$$

For example, if a company's total stockholders' equity is $800,000,000 and there are 10 million shares outstanding, the book value per share is $80 ($800,000,000/10,000,000).

bookkeeping

The activity and profession of recording business transactions, including making entries in journals or on computerized entry systems. The recording of the financial activities occurring in the business are the basis for preparing the company's financial statements. The individual performing the bookkeeping activity is the bookkeeper.

boot
1. Any net cash or net mortgage relief a participant in an exchange might receive in addition to the actual "like kind" property. For example, in a 1031 TAX-FREE EXCHANGE, John exchanges his apartment complex worth $500,000 and receives Brian's land worth $550,000. John pays $300,000 cash and jewelry worth $200,000 to balance the values of properties exchanged. The cash and jewelry are BOOT.
2. In computers, the process of starting up a computer.

borrower One who receives CASH or other ASSETS from others with a promise to repay the PRINCIPAL and INTEREST by a certain date.

bottom line A term referring to the last line in an INCOME STATEMENT that reflects a firm's net income (profit) or net loss. NET INCOME equals revenue less total EXPENSES. The term NET is also used to describe the bottom line.

bottom price The cheapest price one will accept for an item or service.
auction: The upset price. The price below which the auctioneer cannot accept bids.
securities: A "firm" selling price. The lowest price at which a stockholder will sell a security.

bounced check Or, *not sufficient fund (NSF) check.* A check that has been returned for insufficient funds.

box A place where important records and documents are kept for safekeeping. It is usually referred to as a safety deposit box. Documents kept there may include stock and bond certificates, title to real estate, and a will.
See also AGAINST THE BOX.

bracket creep Moving into higher tax brackets as taxable income increases to adjust for inflation. Current tax law adjusts the brackets for inflation.

breach The breaking or violation of the law, legal or moral commitment, duty, or obligation either by commission or omission. Nonfulfillment of the obligations of an agreement or guarantee.

breach of contract Failure, without just cause, for one or both parties to carry out the terms of a contract. For a breach of contract to occur, there must be an unequivocal, decisive, and absolute refusal to perform the agreement.

When a breach of contract occurs, including the assured anticipation of a breach, the aggrieved party or parties may recover damages by entering a suit for such purpose. In these cases it is also possible to sue for performance when simple damage recovery is insufficient.

breach of warranty The failure to fulfill the terms of a promise or guarantee, whether expressed or implied, such as the failure to use normally expected materials. For example, an auto WARRANTY on a new car may be voided by the auto manufacturer if the purchaser fails to provide normal maintenance service.
real estate: The failure or falsehood of a promise or statement, or the nonfulfillment of a stipulation.

break In the SECURITIES industry, a significant and usually unexpected decline in the price of a particular SECURITY. If, for example, on the opening of its trading a STOCK is several points lower than the previous day's close, then it has suffered a break. It is also said to have GAPPED. Another term for a STOCK experiencing a break in prices is it has FALLEN OUT OF BED.

A break may occur when it is announced prior to trading that a company is under investigation by a governmental agency for fraudulent activities. A case in point occurred in 1990 with Bolar Pharmaceuticals when both the Food and Drug Administration and the SECURITIES AND EXCHANGE COMMISSION announced investigations of the company and the STOCK subsequently suffered a break in price from a high of 29 to below 9.

break-even

business: The level of sales where total revenue exactly covers total costs. Thus, zero profit or loss results.

securities: A security transaction in which the return only covers total transaction costs including brokerage fees.

real estate: Occupancy rate at which rental income generated by a property pays for operating expenses and debt service, leaving no NEGATIVE OR POSITIVE CASH FLOW.

break points The quantity purchase points at which the sale price of an item or commodity will be reduced. The greater the volume of purchase, the more break points are achieved, allowing greater pricing discounts. The reason for quantity discounts is that the unit COST for the supplier is lower as the number supplied is increased. For example, processing of orders and shipping costs per unit decrease with larger shipments.

breakout A term primarily applied to SECURITY analysis when a STOCK makes a significant upward or downward move from a prior trading range. A true breakout is always accompanied by heavy volume that confirms the direction of the STOCK. The size of the BREAKOUT is relative to the price of the security. For example, a stock normally trading in the 1 to 2 range breaks out if it moves to 3½ on heavy volume, whereas a stock trading at 120 has a breakout when it rallies to 125.

See also RALLY; RECOVERY.

bridge loan

1. Or, *swing loan.* A SHORT-TERM LOAN that is made in anticipation of permanent longer-term loans. The interest rate on the bridge loan is generally higher than on longer-term loans. An example is a temporary loan that is made to allow for a closing on the purchase of a piece of property before securing permanent mortgage financing.

2. A business loan that supplies cash for a specific transaction; repayment is made from

cash flows from an identifiable source. Usually, the purpose of the loan and the source of repayment are related; hence the term BRIDGE LOAN. For example, an advertising agency enters into a contract to produce a television commercial for the Apple Computer Corporation. The total contract will be for $300,000; however, the agency needs about $150,000 in financing to produce the commercial. The loan is a bridge loan since it supports a specific transaction (making the commercial) and the source of repayment is identifiable (completing it). Another example of a bridge loan would be dealer inventory financing; the loan would be paid from the sale of the inventory.

broad market

actively traded stock: A STOCK that is normally TRADED on high volume indicating a very liquid MARKET where large purchases or sales will not noticeably affect its price.

market: A MARKET having large volume and including many STOCKS such as the NEW YORK STOCK EXCHANGE.

broker A person dealing with others in the purchase and sale of property for a CONSIDERATION. A broker brings buyer and seller together. The broker typically does not obtain ownership to the property involved in the transaction.

business:

1. One who prepares contracts for a third party on behalf of his PRINCIPAL.

2. One who manages the purchase and sale of businesses for a commission.

securities: A licensed member of a STOCK exchange who is a representative of a brokerage firm and manages the purchase and sale of STOCKS, BONDS, and other SECURITIES for clients.

insurance: One who is licensed to deal with other INSURANCE agencies and companies to obtain INSURANCE COVERAGE for clients. INSURANCE BROKERS are licensed in the state or states in which they practice.

real estate: Individual licensed in a state to act as a middleman in the purchase and sale of REAL ESTATE.

broker (real estate)   A person licensed by a state to carry on any activities listed in the license law, for a fee, on behalf of both buyers and sellers of real estate. For example, a broker may be retained by a prospective buyer or tenant to find suitable property.

broker-dealer   A SECURITIES brokerage firm, usually registered with the SEC and the NEW YORK STOCK EXCHANGE, acting as a BROKER and DEALER. It acts as a BROKER when it buys and sells for its customers and as a DEALER when it buys for its own inventory with the likelihood of later sale to clients. Broker-dealers are required to state how they are serving in consummating a transaction.

brokerage fee   The payment charged by a BROKERAGE FIRM for transacting business for clients. In the case of a retail STOCK brokerage firm, the fee is determined by the size and price of the SECURITIES TRADED. As the size of the transaction increases, the fee charged is proportionately less. In an UNDERWRITING BROKER situation, the fee is a discount of the price received for bringing a SECURITY issue to MARKET.

brokerage firm (house)   Any firm acting as a BROKER or DEALER for SECURITIES on the various STOCK exchanges. Most firms in the United States are members of the NEW YORK STOCK EXCHANGE as well as others. When the firm negotiates and manages the purchase and sale of securities for clients, it is acting as a broker; when it is trading for its own accounts and selling to its clients, it is acting as a DEALER. One of the largest brokerage firms in the United States is Merrill Lynch Pierce Fenner & Smith, Inc.

See also EXCHANGE; MEMBER FIRM; STOCK EXCHANGE.

brokered CD (certificate of deposit)   CERTIFICATES OF DEPOSIT (CDs) purchased through a stockbroker. CDs also can be purchased through banks, savings and loan institutions, or credit unions. Although one can usually find a better rate at a local bank or savings and loan institutions, a CD purchased through a stockbroker offers greater liquidity without sacrificing federal deposit insurance. Brokered CDs, as they are known in the industry, have several advantages.

- Brokers typically do not charge a commission; rather, they collect a finder's fee from the bank.
- Brokered CDs are covered by the full $100,000 deposit insurance.
- Many brokers participate in the secondary market for these accounts, buying and selling them like stocks or bonds. This allows savers to cash out of their CD without paying an interest penalty—and to cash in on interest rate changes.
- Buyers may be able to get a better interest rate.

See also CERTIFICATE OF DEPOSIT (CD).

brokers' loans   Money borrowed by BROKERS from banks for various uses. It may be used by odd-lot dealers to help finance inventories of stocks they deal in; by BROKERAGE FIRMS to finance the underwriting of new issues of corporate and municipal securities; and to help finance the purchase of stock for customers who prefer to use margin rather than paying in cash.

bucket shop   An illegal operation in which the bucket shop operator accepts a client's money without ever actually buying or selling securities the client ordered. Instead, the operator holds the money, gambling that the customer is wrong. When too many customers are right, the bucket shop operator closes its doors and opens a new office.

See also BOILER ROOM.

budget   A FINANCIAL PLAN of activities expressed in monetary terms of the assets, debts, net worth, revenue, and expenses that will be involved in carrying out an individual's plans. Simply put, it is a set of projected or planned PERSONAL FINANCIAL STATEMENTS. A budget is used as a tool for planning and control. At the beginning of the period, the budget is a plan; at the end of the period it serves as a control device to monitor the individual's income and spending.

budget account A limited CHARGE ACCOUNT in which consumers must repay a specific amount of the charge within 30 days, then pay the remainder over a period of months.

budget charge account A British term for a retail CHARGE ACCOUNT that provides for CREDIT purchases.

budget deficit An excess of expenditure over income in a budget.

budget estimates The planned or projected figures of incomes and expenditures in a BUDGET during a certain period of time.
See also BUDGET; PERSONAL FINANCIAL STATEMENTS.

budget exceptions The deviations of the actual expenses or income from the budget figures of expenses or income. A detailed listing of exceptions may be made for each major item of expense or income.

budget mortgage A MORTGAGE that, in addition to principal and interest, requires monthly payments for property taxes and insurance. The money for tax and insurance payments is placed in an IMPOUND ACCOUNT (also called an ESCROW or RESERVE ACCOUNT). For example, Lori borrows $100,000 on a 20-year budget mortgage at 10% interest. Her monthly mortgage payment is $1,260, which consists of $965 principal and interest, $250 taxes, and $45 insurance.

budget summary A condensation of a budget document in which the major expenditure and revenue categories for the forthcoming budget are summarized. A budget summary is usually accompanied by a narrative explaining the major changes in the budget from the previous year as well as the overall rationale guiding the budget.

budget surplus An excess of income over expenditure in a budget.

budgeting
1. A process of estimating all income and expenses for a specified period.

2. A process of financial forecasting, planning, and controlling. It involves using a BUDGET to set and achieve short-term goals and ensuring that actual goals are in harmony with budgeted goals.
See also BUDGET.

bulge In investments, a material unanticipated temporary change in overall or specific security or commodity prices. A graph depicting prices shows a bulge.

bull An individual with a favorable outlook on the economy or the BOND, COMMODITY, and SECURITIES MARKETS. A person can also be bullish about a particular STOCK or SECURITY. A bull believes the MARKETS will go up and generally buys on the belief that he or she will profit as the MARKET rises.

bull market A prolonged advancing market that experiences a period of rising prices in securities or commodities; the bull's horns thrust upward. There is a high trading volume. Bull markets are favorable markets normally associated with investor optimism, economic recovery, and government stimulus.
See also BEAR MARKET.

bullion coins Any coins minted from pure gold or silver bullion. American gold and silver dollars are highly prized bullion coins. Many other nations mint gold bullion coins that are TRADED on a bullion exchange. The advantage of a bullion coin is that it is extremely liquid for trading purposes and easily verified.

bullish An expectation of an advance in the price of a SECURITY or the MARKET in general.
See also BEARISH.

bunching Concentrating taxable income and/or deductions in one or more years, usually done to put more taxable income in years with lower tax rates.

bundle of rights The various legal interests that owners have in their property. They are associated with having title, such as the right to occupy and use, sell, rent, expand, and grant easements.

business cycle The regular pattern of expansion (recovery) and contraction (RECESSION) in aggregate economic activity around the path of trend growth, with effects on growth, employment, and INFLATION. At the peak of the cycle, economic activity is high relative to trend, while at the trough (valley) of the cycle, the low point in economic activity is reached. The business cycle tends to have an impact on corporate earnings, cash flow, and expansion.
See also DEPRESSION; RECESSION.

buy in

securities: A transaction made when a SECURITY purchase fails because of a delivery failure and the purchaser or purchasing BROKER can obtain the SECURITIES elsewhere, charging the additional EXPENSE to the seller who failed to make delivery.

options: A method for terminating the responsibility to accept delivery of STOCK in which the option writer buys an option identical to the one he or she previously sold. This is also known as a closing purchase.

real estate: Purchase of property at an auction or TAX or mortgage foreclosure sale by the original owner or one with a previous INTEREST in the property.

government contracts: A strategy for obtaining future government work by submitting a low bid for a contract in the expectation that future modifications and other opportunities will more than compensate any short-term loss. It is a way of getting one's foot in the government contract door.

buy order

An order entered by the SECURITY DEALER with the investor's approval for the purpose of purchasing a SECURITY.

buy limit order: A buy order entered with a specific price to purchase a particular security. The INVESTOR is not obligated to pay more than the price limit, although he or she could actually pay less if the MARKET conditions favored a lower price.

buy minus order: Investor's instruction to purchase on down ticks in the MARKET PRICE or at last previous price if that is lower than the previous different price.

buy stop order: A customer's instruction that if the market price reaches or exceeds the buy stop limit, the broker is authorized to execute a MARKET buy order at the best obtainable price. Reaching or exceeding the stated price triggers the buy stop order converting it into a market buy order.

buy the book: The buyer's instruction to buy all the SHARES available in the floor trader's book as well as any that can be obtained from the crowd at the same price.

market buy order: Instruction to the BROKER by the customer to purchase a security at whatever price can be obtained in the open market.

buy-and-hold strategy

A long-term STOCK purchase strategy in which the investor makes purchases in quality companies over the years and ignores short-term trading patterns. The basic assumption is that a well-managed company will weather the storms and grow over the years. It is a rather passive strategy that does not require day-to-day stock management.

buy-back

reverse transaction: An agreement to sell an item with a pre-agreed reverse buy at a set price. This is illegal in some cases, and any short-term losses will be disallowed by the IRS under such an arrangement.

insurance: An agreement to rescind certain policy limitations on the INSURED if additional COVERAGE is purchased from the insurer.

production agreement: An agreement between two manufacturers by which the first gains control over the second's manufacturing output by agreeing to buy it first and then sell it back. Often this is merely a paper agreement to implement control by the purchasing company over the units produced by the second company.

international trade: An agreement by "X"

trading country to buy merchandise from the "Y" trading country in return for Y's agreement to purchase X's products.

buy-back agreement *See* BUY-BACK.

buy-down A cash payment to a lender to reduce a rate of interest on a loan a borrower must pay. The reduced rate may apply for all or a portion of the loan term. For example, a builder has a tract of homes for sale. In order to accomplish a sale of a house, the builder arranges for a buy-down loan with a lender to pay DISCOUNT POINTS so that the lender can offer a loan at a lower interest to the buyer. This can be done for the life of the loan at the cost of about 8 discount points for every point of interest rate reduction, or it can be done for a shorter period, such as the first three years of the loan term.

buyer's market A market condition in a particular industry (such as the housing industry) in which a buyer is in a more commanding position. This is the market with few buyers and many sellers. This means a buyer can negotiate prices and terms (such as quality assurance and closing dates) more to his or her liking and a seller who wishes to sell must accept them.

buyer's option
in general: Various choices offered to a buyer of an item or service at additional COST when negotiating the purchase.
real estate: An agreement by which a buyer, the optionee, is given the right, at his or her election, to purchase real property within a specified time at a specified price for a CONSIDERATION paid to the seller.

buying a loan portfolio An individual's investment in a loan portfolio of a FINANCIAL INSTITUTION.

buying long Buying SECURITIES in the hope that they will go up in value.
See also LONG POSITION.

buying on margin Buying BONDS, commodities, or STOCK through CREDIT extended by the BROKER to the customer in a qualified MARGIN ACCOUNT. MARGIN rules set by the Federal Reserve Board and the participating exchanges for SECURITIES generally require a ratio of 50% COLLATERAL to cover STOCK purchases. Margin rules for BONDS and commodities vary considerably. *See also* MARGIN BUYING; MARGIN PURCHASE.

buying power
personal: The amount of MONEY an individual has or has control of, enabling purchases to be made. In this sense, buying power refers to liquid ASSETS.
goods or services: The number of products or services that can be purchased by an individual.
money: The relative purchasing power of various currencies when compared to each other. Rating one currency based on its value with another international currency.
securities: The amount of CREDIT available for additional SECURITY purchases or short sales for an investor maintaining a MARGIN BUYING account with a BROKERAGE FIRM.
See also MARGIN PURCHASE.

buying range In investments, the price range in which security analysts recommend buying securities in a "bear" stock market. At the suggested prices, the securities may be a good buy because of anticipated future price increases. Security analysts at brokerage firms often note such situations in their analytical reports.

buyout The acquisition of a controlling INTEREST of a company's STOCK. A buyout can be previously negotiated or accomplished by a HOSTILE TENDER OFFER, resulting in the hot pursuit of the company in the SECURITY MARKETS.
leverage buyout: An action by which a group of entrepreneurs seeks to take control of the company through loans obtained using the target company's own ASSETS as COLLATERAL. The loan is repaid from operations of the target company or by liquidating the target company's ASSETS once acquired.

bypass trust An IRREVOCABLE TRUST created by parents to protect their ASSETS from outside claims, excepting ESTATE TAXES, in order to bequeath the largest amount possible of their ESTATE. In this type of a TRUST it is possible for the parents or parent to receive income from the

ASSETS placed in the trust during their lifetimes. The TRUST bypasses PROBATE upon the death of the parents.

C

cafeteria employee benefit plan A benefit plan allowing workers to select from a variety of FRINGE BENEFITS. For tax purposes, with minor exceptions, no amount shall be included in the gross income of the participant in this plan since he or she may choose among the benefits to be received.

California will A blank-form will that people can fill in themselves; it is legally valid if completed properly on a form that has been codified in state law.

call

1. Right to buy 100 shares (usually) of a specified stock for a limited length of time (until expiration).
See also CALL OPTION; OPTION.

2. Process of redeeming a BOND or PREFERRED STOCK issue prior to maturity.
See also CALL PROVISION.

call feature A feature in BOND issues allowing the BOND to be redeemed by the issuer prior to the expiration date. Call features are often found in corporate and municipal bonds.

A call feature becomes particularly important when a high rate of INTEREST is being paid and the MARKET rate of interest declines significantly. The call feature permits the issuer to refinance the issue by replacing it with a lower interest bearing issue.

Normally, bonds are not CALLABLE for at least ten years after they are first issued.

call loan

1. Or, *broker call loan*. A LOAN used by

BROKERS to finance purchases of securities. The rate is quoted daily in newspapers as a money market indicator.

2. A loan that may be "called" at any time by the lender or borrower.
See also BROKERS' LOANS.

call option The right (but not the obligation) to buy 100 shares of a specified stock at a fixed price per share, called the STRIKING PRICE, for up to nine months, depending on the expiration date of the option. The investor who has purchased a call option on a stock has the right to exercise the option at any time during the life of the option. This means that, regardless of the current market price of the stock, the investor has the right to buy 100 shares of the stock at the striking price (rather than the current market price). The downside risk of a call option is the loss of the entire investment if the company's stock price does not increase.

Example: On February 5, Mr. Guru becomes convinced that ITT stock, which is trading at $60 a share, will move considerably higher in the next few months. So he buys one call option on ITT stock with a premium of $2 per share. Since this call option involves a block of 100 shares of stock, it costs him a total of $2 times 100 shares or $200. The particular call he selects has a striking price of $65 and expiration date near the end of June. This action gives him for $200 the right to buy (1) 100 shares of ITT stock (2) at $65 a share (3) until near the end of June. If ITT stock goes up to $75 a share by the end of June, Mr. Guru would have the right to

purchase 100 shares for $6,500 ($65 × 100 shares) and to turn right around and sell them for $7,500, keeping the difference of $1,000, an $800 profit. This works out to 400% profit in less than five months ($800/$200 = 4 = 400%). However, if Mr. Guru is wrong and ITT stock goes down in price, the most he could lose would be his investment money, which is the price of the option, $200.
See also CALL; PUT OPTION.

call premium
bonds: The difference between the PAR VALUE of a CALLABLE BOND and its REDEMPTION PRICE when called. The redemption price usually has a call premium to remunerate the holder for loss of income and ownership.

There is a time value to the PREMIUM, and the nearer to the maturity date of the bond to the call date, the lower will be the premium, dropping to zero on the date of expiration.
options: The excess between the STRIKING PRICE of a CALL or PUT OPTION and the MARKET PRICE of the underlying SECURITY. The CALL PREMIUM is determined by the length of time left before the option expires, the correspondence of the striking price with the market price of the underlying SECURITY, and the VOLATILITY of the underlying STOCK itself. A highly volatile stock will cause correspondingly volatile price swings in the call.

Example: An underlying STOCK is selling at 42, and the 40 CALL OPTION, having three months before expiration, is selling at 5. The call premium is (40 + 5) − 42 or 3.
preferred stock: The difference between the PAR VALUE of a CALLABLE PREFERRED STOCK and its REDEMPTION PRICE when called. The redemption price usually has a call premium to compensate the investor for loss of INCOME and ownership.

call price   The contractual price at which a callable BOND or PREFERRED STOCK can be redeemed by the issuer. Generally speaking, the call price will reflect a PREMIUM, the CALL PREMIUM, to compensate the holder for the loss of ownership and income.

call provision   A provision of a BOND or PREFERRED STOCK issue that allows the issuer to redeem the outstanding securities before maturity by paying holders a premium above face value.

call value   The value of a BOND or STOCK CALL OPTION. Unlike a PUT OPTION, a call increases in value as the underlying SECURITY increases in value. A call option allows the holder to buy the underlying security at a contractually stated price.

Factors affecting the call value:
1. The price of the underlying security at the time the call is written.
2. The ability of the CALL to be exercised at a contractually agreed price, the STRIKING PRICE, as the underlying SECURITY rises in value.
3. The VOLATILITY of the underlying security.
4. The time value of the contract. The further away the expiration date is, the more time value will be added to the call value.

callable   A feature of a bond or preferred stock that permits a company to redeem all or part of its preferred stocks or bonds prematurely by paying a slight premium during a certain period if the price reaches a certain amount. This situation occurs when interest rates decline substantially.

callable bonds   BONDS that may be redeemed at the option of the issuing company prior to their stated maturity. A provision of the bond INDENTURE allows the issuer to retire bonds prior to maturity by paying holders a PREMIUM above principal.

cancel   To make null and void; to revoke or destroy; to rescind or set aside. To abandon; abolish; repeal; surrender; waive; terminate.
securities trading: To void a buy or sell order, price, or quantity. Cancel orders are normally executed very rapidly. They may or may not be accompanied by new instructions.

cancelable agreement   A provision in a contract permitting one or both parties to terminate the agreement on the occurrence of specified events. This is a CANCELLATION CLAUSE, which permits the agreement or contract to become null and void thereby allowing the parties to end their obligations. The reason for such a cancellation clause is to safeguard the interests of each participant in the event either is damaged.

cancellation
in general: Voiding a negotiable instrument by nullifying or paying it.
insurance: Prematurely terminating an insurance policy.
securities:
1. Voiding an order to buy or sell.
   See also GOOD-TILL-CANCELED ORDER.
2. Prematurely terminating a bond contract.

cancellation clause A clause in a contract that describes the terms under which coverage may be canceled. An INSURED or INSURER may cancel an insurance policy (such as a HEALTH and a PROPERTY AND CASUALTY INSURANCE POLICY) at any time before the date of expiration. Either party desiring to terminate the policy must send written notices of cancellation to the other party. The insurance company then should refund a portion of the premium as specified in the insurance contract.

canceled check A CHECK that has been paid to the payee and charged to the payor's account. The check is stamped paid and returned to the payor as documentation of payment. Canceled checks are retained by the bank and are normally mailed at the end of the month to the DEPOSITOR.

cap rate *See* CAPITALIZATION RATE.

capacity A credit standard judging the borrower's ability to repay the loan.
See also FIVE Cs OF CREDIT.

capital Material wealth used for the production of additional profits and wealth.
business: ASSETS invested in a business. Additional meanings include CASH in reserve, savings, SECURITIES, and other property of value. The NET ASSETS of a company.
See also BOOK VALUE; NET WORTH.

capital asset
fixed assets: A generic term referring to all fixed ASSETS of a business that can be DEPRECIATED, such as buildings, equipment, and furniture.
economics: A productive asset employed to create wealth that is consumed over time.
U.S. Internal Revenue Service (IRS): For TAXATION purposes the IRS defines capital assets to include most property one owns and uses for personal purposes, pleasure, or INVESTMENTS, for example, a house, furniture, car, STOCKS, and BONDS.

capital gains distribution INCOME for investors resulting from net long-term profits of a MUTUAL FUND realized when portfolio securities are sold at a gain. These profits from sales of securities are passed on by fund managers to shareholders at least once a year.
See also INCOME DIVIDEND.

capital gains or losses Any gain or loss from disposing of capital ASSETS that differs from the original acquisition price. There are two types of capital gains or losses for the purpose of the capital gain or loss tax. Long-term capital gains are those for assets held more than one year and all others are short term. Capital gains are net after all EXPENSES have been taken. Capital gains and losses are reported on Schedule D of IRS Form 1040.

capital growth An increase in the MARKET VALUE of an individual's investments or an increase in the NET ASSET VALUE (NAV) of MUTUAL FUND shares.

capital improvements Costs incurred from making changes in real property that enhance its value. Examples are replacing the roof, adding a room, and paneling the basement. These improvements increase the cost of the property for tax purposes.

capital markets The markets for long-term

(those with lives or maturities greater than one year) DEBT and corporate STOCKS. The NEW YORK STOCK EXCHANGE (NYSE), which trades the stocks of many of the larger corporations, is a prime example of a capital market. The AMERICAN STOCK EXCHANGE and the regional stock exchanges are also examples. In addition, securities are issued and traded through the thousands of brokers and dealers on the OVER-THE-COUNTER market.

See also FINANCIAL MARKETS.

capital stock Equity shares in a corporation issued to stockholders, including COMMON STOCK and PREFERRED STOCK.

capitalization rate Or, *cap rate* or *income yield*. A widely used method of determining the rate of return on a real estate investment, found by dividing the NET OPERATING INCOME (NOI) for the first year by the total investment. That interest rate that, when applied to the earnings of an investment, determines its appraisal or market value. The higher the cap rate, the lower the perceived risk to the investor and the lower the asking price paid. Whether a piece of property is overpriced depends on the rate for similar property derived from the marketplace. The method has two limitations: (1) it is based on only the first year's NOI, and (2) it ignores return through appreciation in property value.

Example: Assume that net operating income = $18,618 and purchase price = $219,000. Then, the cap rate is

$$\$18,618/\$219,000 = 8.5\%.$$

If the market rate is 10%, the FAIR MARKET VALUE of similar property is $18,618/10% = $186,180. The property may be overpriced.

See also INCOME APPROACH.

capping A FINANCIAL INSTITUTION's putting a ceiling on the interest rate that may be charged on a variable interest rate loan. For example, if a homeowner takes out a variable rate mortgage, the interest rate may be capped not to exceed 15%.

captive agent One having the sole privilege to sell in a territory. He or she may be paid a straight salary plus commission.

captive finance company A sales FINANCE COMPANY that is owned and operated by a maker of a "big-ticket" item such as an automobile. It is usually a wholly owned subsidiary whose objective is to finance consumer purchases from the parent company. An example of a captive finance company is the General Motors Acceptance Corporation (GMAC).

carat
1. Weight in units for valuable stones (e.g., diamonds). It is equal to 200 milligrams and divided into 100 "points." Thus, a 150-point diamond weighs 1.50 carats. Investment-grade diamonds should be at least one-half carat and preferably more than one carat in weight.
2. Karat. A unit of fineness for gold equal to 1/24 part of pure gold in an alloy.

career planning Any systematic attempt to arrange and determine one's work career. Career planning includes an assessment of the opportunities in the chosen vocation or profession as well as the educational requirements and other prerequisites, including any INVESTMENTS.

carrying charge
securities: The fee charged by a BROKER for carrying a customer's securities on MARGIN.
commodities: Or, *holding costs.* Expenses incurred because a business keeps inventories. These include interest on money invested in inventory, storage cost, insurance, and taxes.
real estate: Carrying costs, primarily taxes and debt service costs, of owning land before its development.
business: The seller's charge for an installment loan.

carrying forward balances
1. The transfer of a BALANCE in an ACCOUNT from the end of one time period to the beginning of the next time period. For example, the credit card balance due on April 30 is transferred to the next month's balance on May 1.

2. The noting of positive or negative balances from a completed budgeting time period onto the budget of the next time period.

carte blanche

1. A term connoting full authority to do something. An example is to give someone the full right and authority to fill in any amount he or she wishes on your CHECK. Another example could occur when your employer instructs you to buy whatever is needed for the office.

2. A retail CREDIT CARD (CARTE BLANCHE) having an annual membership fee. It allows the holder to charge a wide range of retail services wherever it is accepted throughout the world. Carte Blanche does not provide for installment payments, requiring all balances to be paid in full each month. In addition to providing for retail CREDIT purchases it also provides each card holder with airline, rental car, and lost baggage insurance.

cash

n.: Legal tender. Cash usually consists of paper MONEY, coins, negotiable instruments including CHECKS and BEARER BONDS and notes, MONEY ORDERS, and bank accounts.

v.: To convert any ASSET into paper currency and coins.

accounting: ASSET account on a BALANCE SHEET representing paper currency and coins or other negotiable money instruments.

cash a check To convert a DEMAND DEPOSIT CHECK into legal tender. When presenting a CHECK for CASH the back of the check must be endorsed to validate the transaction.

cash account An investor account that requires an initial deposit with a stockbroker and stipulates that full settlement is due the broker within five business days after a BUY or SELL ORDER has been given.

cash advance A loan that can be obtained by charging the amount to certain bank DEBIT or CREDIT CARDS. In addition to interest, a fee may be charged for taking out that advance based on a flat fee or a percentage of the advance.

cash and carry The practice by which a customer pays a retail store in cash for a good or service and either takes immediate delivery or arranges for delivery (at a charge).

cash basis budgeting BUDGET recordkeeping that recognizes income and expenses when cash is actually received or paid out.
See also BUDGET; BUDGETING.

cash before delivery (CBD) A condition in which the seller of goods requires the buyer to pay for them before taking possession. The seller may do this when he or she feels a risky or questionable buyer is involved. There may be a discount offered.

cash budget A personal budget for cash planning and control that presents anticipated cash inflow and outflow for a specified time period. The cash budget helps the individual keep cash balances in reasonable relationship to needs. It assists in avoiding idle cash and possible cash shortages. The cash budget shows beginning cash, cash receipts, cash payments, and ending cash. Examples of cash receipts are salary, interest and dividend income, and proceeds from sale of an asset. Examples of cash payments are purchase of car, investments in stocks, and payment of utility bills and rent.

cash discount A reduction in the COST of an item or service if the purchaser agrees to pay in CASH within a certain period of time. An example is a reduction from the cash price if the purchaser agrees to pay within 30 days AFTER PURCHASE.

Example: You buy an item for $1,000 on terms of 2/10, net/60. If you pay within 10 days you will receive a discount of $20, otherwise no discount may be taken. You are expected to pay within 60 days.

credit card sales: A cash discount made at the time of the sale by some merchants, at their own discretion, in place of charging a transaction to a credit account. CREDIT CARD companies usually charge the merchant a handling fee for all transactions and the merchant is simply reflecting the lower COST of a CASH transaction to the customer.

cash dispenser Or, *cash machine*. A computerized machine found in many locations used for dispensing CASH to clients who have a deposit account with the bank. The user inserts a plastic account card into the machine, which decodes it and credits or debits the customer's account. The device is capable of dispensing cash as well as receiving deposits. The advantages to the customer are that these machines operate 24 hours a day and are found in many locations. The advantage to the bank is that they help to reduce teller lines by servicing relatively simple transactions.
See also AUTOMATED TELLER MACHINES.

cash dividends A CASH distribution of a portion of the profits of a company paid out of retained earnings to the STOCKHOLDERS. Any such dividends are usually paid in the form of a CHECK by the company to the stockholder.

Not all public corporations pay cash dividends. Some may pay a STOCK DIVIDEND, whereas others pay no DIVIDEND. A dividend will not be paid until the board of directors of the company approves the payment.

There are two types of cash dividends. One is a REGULAR CASH DIVIDEND, which is a normally scheduled dividend, and the other is an EXTRA CASH DIVIDEND or a SPECIAL DIVIDEND, which is paid out of extraordinary income.

Example: You own 1,000 shares of XYZ Company, which declares a $.20 per share cash dividend. You are thus entitled to $200 (1,000 × $.20).

cash flow
in general:
1. The difference between what a business takes in for sales and services and what it lays out in expenses, taxes, and other costs that must be met. It is not the same thing as BOOK INCOME.
2. The stream of cash passing through one's hands before taxes. When one spends

more than one takes in, the individual has a NEGATIVE CASH FLOW. The opposite is a POSITIVE CASH FLOW. Examples of CASH INFLOW are salary income, dividend income, and sales of investments. Examples of CASH OUTFLOW are payments made for rent, utilities, clothing, entertainment, and purchases of assets (e.g., an automobile).
real estate: The amount of money available after subtracting all operating expenses and mortgage payments from rental income. For example, Harry acquires an apartment building with the first year of its operation shown below.

Gross rental income	$75,000
Less vacancy loss	5,000
Effective gross income	70,000
Less operating expenses	50,000
Net operating income (NOI)	20,000
Less debt service	15,000
Cash flow before taxes	$5,000

cash flow before taxes *See* BEFORE-TAX CASH FLOW; CASH FLOW.

cash flow calendar A budgeting device on which projected income and expenses are recorded for each budgeting time period in an effort to ascertain surplus or deficit situations.

cash flow statement A record detailing the sources of CASH receipts and the uses of cash payments during an accounting period. States where cash is coming from and where it is being put.

Cash flow represents the net profits to a given date plus every amount recorded as an EXPENSE that has not been disbursed. It represents the flow of money, also termed *capital flow*. It provides for the evaluation of financial sources and applications of the firm. A firm having cash expenditures exceeding expected cash receipts has a NEGATIVE CASH FLOW.
finance: An analysis of all the changes affecting the cash account during an accounting period.
investment: NET INCOME plus DEPRECIATION and

other noncash charges. Here cash flow is used as CASH EARNINGS. Investors are interested in cash flow because it gives an indication of the ability to pay dividends.
See also CASH BUDGET; INCOME STATEMENT.

cash loan A loan that gives a borrower cash to make purchases or to pay off debts.

cash management The task of earning maximum interest on all funds, regardless of the type of account in which they are kept, while having sufficient funds available for living expenses, emergencies, and savings and investment opportunities. Three basic tools of cash management are (1) a CHECKING ACCOUNT for monthly living expenses; (2) a small SAVINGS ACCOUNT for emergency cash; and (3) high-yielding, low-risk instruments (such as MONEY MARKET ACCOUNTS, CERTIFICATES OF DEPOSIT, and GOVERNMENT SAVINGS BONDS) for excess funds.

cash management account (CMA) A multipurpose account, offered through BROKERAGE FIRMS and other FINANCIAL INSTITUTIONS, that combines a CHECKING ACCOUNT, MONEY MARKET FUND, STOCK BROKERAGE ACCOUNT, CREDIT CARD, and DEBIT CARD into one account.

cash refund annuity An ANNUITY under which amounts yet unpaid to the annuitant are refunded to a beneficiary in a lump sum if the annuitant dies before receiving the original invested money.

cash sale
1. A sale paid for only with currency or check.
2. An exchange or transaction on the floor of the NEW YORK STOCK EXCHANGE that calls for delivery of the securities the same day rather than within the regular fifth business day delivery.

cash surrender value of life insurance Funds the INSURED will receive from the INSURER upon surrendering a CASH VALUE LIFE INSURANCE POLICY. The amount obtained is the cash value

provided for in the policy less a surrender charge and any outstanding loan and interest thereon.

cash value The accumulated portion of LIFE INSURANCE premiums as a savings feature that can be borrowed against or obtained as cash upon surrendering the insurance policy. It can be used as a source of LOAN COLLATERAL.
See also CASH SURRENDER VALUE OF LIFE INSURANCE.

cash value insurance LIFE INSURANCE that pays benefits upon the death of the insured and has a savings element that allows the payment of the benefits prior to death. The size of a cash value buildup varies from company to company. TERM LIFE INSURANCE does not have a cash value feature.
See also ANNUITY; NONFORFEITURE OPTION; WHOLE LIFE INSURANCE.

cashier's check A check that a financial institution draws on itself in exchange for an appropriate amount of money. It is thus a direct obligation of the institution. It is payable to a third party named by the customer. Some businesses or other payees will accept only cashier's checks rather than personal checks.

casualty insurance INSURANCE that protects a business or homeowner against property loss, damage, and/or bodily injury to a third party.
See also LIABILITY INSURANCE.

casualty loss Loss caused by damage, destruction, or loss of property as the result of an identifiable event that is sudden, unexpected, or unusual. It is covered by most CASUALTY INSURANCE policies and is tax deductible, with limitations and exclusions, to the extent that it is not reimbursed from insurance. For individuals only the unreimbursed loss in excess of 10% of ADJUSTED GROSS INCOME (AGI) less $100 is deductible—and that only if one can itemize deductions.

catastrophe policy A major medical EXPENSE insurance policy ($500,000–$1,000,000) designed to pay all medical expenses, above a certain DEDUCTIBLE amount, up to the limit of the POLICY.

cats and dogs
securities: A disparaging description of low-priced, highly speculative STOCKS with little hope of a strong future.
business: Items accumulating in inventory that have a very low sales turnover.

cause of action The circumstances giving an individual cause to seek judicial relief. A cause of action is some intrusion into a person's legal rights, including a breach of contract. A failure to discharge a legal obligation to do, or refrain from performance of, some act. Matter for which a lawsuit may be instituted. Unlawful violation or invasion of right.

caveat emptor A Latin saying for "let the buyer beware" before he or she buys. According to this concept, buyers purchase at their own risk in the absence of misrepresentations. This does not require the vendor to volunteer information. In recent years, however, the law requires the seller to disclose fully known defects in the product or service.

caveat subscriptor (venditor) Let the vendor beware. Without specific exemptions, the seller is liable for action on the part of the buyer for any alterations in the contract or warranty, whether explicit or implied. This is the basis for the consumer rights movement.

ceiling rate A controlled or administered price that is established for goods and services by a governmental agency usually during some period of extraordinary events. During World War II the Office of Price Administration set ceiling prices on items, which necessitated the imposition of rationing as the supply did not meet the demand.

A ceiling price is also termed price control.

certain period annuity An annuity that guarantees payment for the life of the BENEFICIARY as well as for a minimum specified period. In the event of the beneficiary's death prior to the expiration of the period, payments are continued to the beneficiary's heirs until the end of the period.

certificate A document attesting to the performance, or nonperformance, of an act. It can be official when issued by a formally constituted institution, including courts, educational organizations, governmental bodies, or religious organizations. Examples would include marriage certificates, diplomas, licenses, and property deeds. A certificate can also be issued between individuals, as in a simple bill of sale.

In the case of formal institutions, a certificate can have a formal seal either affixed to it or impressed on it, further adding to its authenticity.

certificate account A SAVINGS ACCOUNT in which the DEPOSITOR makes a commitment to the BANK to leave funds on deposit for a given time period. The advantage for the depositor is a commitment by the bank to pay a higher rate of interest.

certificate of deposit (cd) A TERM ACCOUNT or type of SAVINGS CERTIFICATE paying a slightly higher rate of interest than a passbook or other savings account. CDs generally require a minimum deposit and have maturities, commonly ranging from 32 days to 8 years. Deposits can range from $1,000 to $100,000. These savings certificates are often referred to as a "parking place," since investors can put their money there on a short-term basis until they find another investment that meets their long-term goals. There are no ceilings on rates. If money is withdrawn before maturity, there are usually interest penalties. CDs are insured up to $100,000.

Banks compete for deposits by offering attractive yields. To compare CDs, the depositor should look at the EFFECTIVE ANNUAL YIELD, which takes into account the effects of compounding. The figures in the table below indicate how much difference compounding can make on the rate of interest paid. For example, the annual return on a 6% CD with annual compounding is 6%, but the same CD with quarterly compounding could yield as much as 6.14%.

Banks calculate interest in various ways, so true YIELD varies widely on CDs with the same maturity and interest rate. Note that true yields are not always spelled out in bank advertising, but banks normally post the true yields inside bank offices, list them on window displays, or make them available over the phone.
See also BROKERED CD.

certificate of insurance   A document that outlines the benefits and policy provisions for individuals covered by GROUP INSURANCE.

certificate of release   A certificate relieving a person from liability. For instance, a finance company may issue a certificate stating that the borrower has fully paid the loan.

certificate of title   A lawyer's opinion (not a guarantee) of the status of a TITLE, which is attached to the ABSTRACT OF TITLE.

certificateless trading   The purchase of a security without receiving the CERTIFICATE. As an example, an investor buys stock on margin and the certificate is made out in STREET NAME and held at the BROKERAGE HOUSE.

certification
1. A written assurance by a responsible party of the correctness and reliability of a statement. As an example, an officer of a corporation might state in writing that specified criteria have been satisfied.
2. Written permission to do something, such as receiving a license or franchise to do business.
3. A statement by a governmental agency that a union may bargain for its employees.
4. Expression of an unqualified audit opinion on a company's financial statements by a certified public accountant (CPA).

certified check   Personal check that a bank guarantees to pay. The bank has already deducted the check amount from the depositor's account and is guaranteeing payment on the check. Some businesses will accept only this type of check from customers.

Certified Financial Planner (CFP)   Designation indicating an individual has passed examinations administered by the Denver-based College for Financial Planning. A Certified Financial Planner is one who has passed examinations in employee benefit plans, ESTATE PLANNING, insurance, investments, and taxation. The fees charged by a CFP range from a simple fee for his or her services to a commission on every investment product sold to the client.

The CFP is primarily concerned with personal, rather than corporate, FINANCIAL PLANNING. Due to the growing complexity of personal finance, there is an increasing need for the services the Certified Financial Planner provides.

NOMINAL & EFFECTIVE INTEREST PERIODS WITH DIFFERENT COMPOUNDING

Effective Annualized Yield in Percentages

Nominal Rate	Annually	Semiannually	Quarterly	Monthly	Daily
6	6	6.09	6.14	6.17	6.18
7	7	7.12	7.19	7.23	7.25
8	8	8.16	8.24	8.30	8.33
9	9	9.20	9.31	9.38	9.42
10	10	10.25	10.38	10.47	10.52
11	11	11.30	11.46	11.57	11.62
12	12	12.36	12.55	12.68	12.74

Certified Property and Casualty Underwriter (CPCU) An individual who is knowledgeable and authorized to assist in the underwriting of property and casualty insurance.

certified public accountant (CPA) Title awarded to accountants satisfying rigorous professional education (college degree majoring in accounting), examination (theory, practice, auditing, and law), and experience requirements (e.g., New York State requires two years). The CPA is licensed by the respective state to give an audit opinion on the fairness of a company's financial statements. Because of the CPA's accounting and financial knowledge, he or she may serve as a good financial adviser in personal financial planning decisions.

change of beneficiary provision A provision in a life insurance policy allowing the insured to change a beneficiary at will unless the beneficiary has been listed as irrevocable. In such a case, the beneficiary must state in writing his or her permission to make the change.

Chapter 7 A statute of the 1978 Bankruptcy Reform Act under which an individual's property is divided among creditors in satisfaction of his or her unpaid debts. As a general rule, any debtor subject to Chapter 7 is also subject to CHAPTER 11.
See also BANKRUPTCY (PERSONAL).

Chapter 11 A provision of the 1978 Bankruptcy Reform Act similar to CHAPTER 7, but for business firms.
See also BANKRUPTCY (BUSINESS).

Chapter 13 Or, *Wage-Earner Plan.* A court-approved and coordinated plan that pays off an individual's debts over a period of three years. It is a plan for the repayment of debts that allows a credit user in serious financial difficulty to pay off credit obligations without declaring BANKRUPTCY.
See also BANKRUPTCY (PERSONAL).

character A CREDIT standard judging the borrower's past record in repaying loans, among other factors regarding the credit worthiness of the borrower.
See also FIVE CS OF CREDIT.

charge
installment purchase: Term used to describe a CREDIT ACCOUNT purchase. The COST will be billed at a future date.
finance: The price for a product or service rendered.
accounting: A cost or EXPENSE allocated to a specific account.
criminal law: A formal charge filed by a complaint or indictment against a defendant.
jury: A judge's final statement to a jury in which the case is summarized and the relevant points of law the jury must observe are specified.
public charge: A person without means or who is not responsible. A public charge depends on public services for care and survival.

Chartered Financial Consultant (ChFC) A designation granted by the AMERICAN COLLEGE OF THE AMERICAN SOCIETY OF CHARTERED LIFE UNDERWRITERS in Bryn Mawr, Pennsylvania, for FINANCIAL planners who must pass a ten-course program and have three years' professional experience.

Chartered Life Underwriter (CLU) A designation granted by the AMERICAN COLLEGE OF THE AMERICAN SOCIETY OF CHARTERED LIFE UNDERWRITERS in Bryn Mawr, Pennsylvania, only to LIFE INSURANCE AGENTS who have specific experience or meet certain requirements and pass college-level examinations.

charting The technique used by TECHNICAL ANALYSTS to appraise the trends in volume and price of securities. In order to interpret charts, one has to detect buy and sell indicators. Some basic charts are line, bar, and point-and-figure. Charts reveal whether the market is in a major upturn or downturn and assist in predicting whether the trend will reverse. The technical analyst may see what price can occur on a given stock or market average. Also, charts aid in

predicting the magnitude of a price swing (see accompanying examples).
See also CHARTIST.

chartist A TECHNICAL ANALYST who charts the direction of securities and commodities to ad-

Line Chart

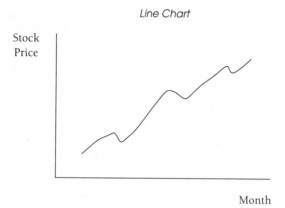

Bar Chart

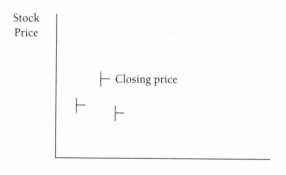

Point–and–Figure Chart

vise on buy, hold, or sell strategies. Chartists try to identify recurring past patterns as a predictor of future prices.
See also CHARTING.

chattel Personal (rather than real) property. Examples are furniture, jewelry, automobiles, and computers.

chattel mortgage A pledge of personal property, such as an automobile or furniture, to secure a NOTE. If the indebtedness is not paid according to the terms of the agreement, the holder of the mortgage has the right to obtain possession of the mortgaged property.

check card The holder of the card has a checking account. Such card is considered assurance to the retailer that the customer's check will be honored. It is usually used only for nominal charges.

check clearing The process of transferring funds from the bank, savings and loan association, or CREDIT UNION upon which the check was drawn to the financial institution that accepted the deposit.

check truncation The procedure whereby a depository institution keeps the canceled checks and sends only a listing of the month's transactions to the account holder, hence saving on processing and mailing of checks.

checking account A demand deposit; the bank withdraws funds and makes payment whenever demanded by the depositor, which is typically done in the form of writing a check.

chose in action A claim or debt that may be recovered by bringing legal action in a court of law. One has the right to sue another for a legitimate financial claim.

chose in possession Property held by an individual, such as an automobile.

churning A stockbroker's unethical behavior that encourages an investor frequently to buy and sell securities that result in large commissions for the broker.

civil court A state court in which numerous civil and criminal matters are resolved and a written record is made of the happenings.

claims adjuster Insurance specialist designated by an insurance company to investigate insurance claims, including an ASSESSMENT of whether a loss is covered and the dollar amount the company will pay.

claims ratio The percentage of PREMIUMS collected by an insurance company that are subsequently paid out to reimburse the losses of insureds.

clarity The degree of internal perfection of a gemstone or the degree to which a gemstone possesses irregularities that diffuse light and lessen its brilliance.

class action A legal suit initiated by one or more members of a large group of individuals for the benefit of all members of that group. As an example, a few investors may sue a company for losses incurred on the stock because of alleged false and misleading financial statements. Those investors, on behalf of all investors in the company, file a class action lawsuit to recover the losses.

classified stock A stock issue that is divided into two or more classes, carrying different rights and privileges.
See also TWO-CLASS COMMON STOCK.

classified taxation In property taxation, the classification of properties by use, with different tax rates assigned for each type. Some types of property may in fact be exempt from property taxes. For example, the county may impose a higher tax rate on unoccupied land than on land that has an office building on it in order to encourage occupancy.

clause In a contract, a provision describing some condition. An example is a paragraph in an insurance contract specifying an important matter such as coverage, exclusions, or termination rights.

clean hands
in general: Descriptive of forthright behavior with no dishonest intent. An example is the behavior of an inspector or purchasing agent in not taking bribes.
law: Descriptive of a plaintiff who has no record of improper behavior in the area in which he or she is charging the defendant. For example, if one brings legal suit against another for unfair competition, the legal action may be dropped if the plaintiff has in fact engaged in such practices.

cleaning deposit A nonrefundable fee paid to cover the painting and cleaning of a rental unit after a tenant moves out.

cleanup fund An element of coverage based on a "needs approach" in a family life insurance policy. Its purpose is to meet last-minute costs and those that occur after the death of an insured. Examples are probate fees and burial costs.

clear title A MARKETABLE TITLE. It is one free of clouds and disputed interests. Clear title is a requirement in order to convey a general warranty deed in a transaction.

Clifford Trust An inter vivos trust, established for a minimum of more than ten years, in which title to income-producing property may be transferred. An example is stock put in a trust by a father for a daughter. The daughter will receive dividend income from the trust for its entire duration. At the expiration of the trust, the father can reclaim the stock.

close a position
1. To sell a security and thus eliminate it from the investor's portfolio.
2. To eliminate a position in a commodities futures contract or option by offsetting the transaction.

close market When there is a narrow difference between the bid and asked prices of a security. A wide difference implies instability. A close market occurs in stocks having high volume.

close to the money A situation in which the strike price of a call or put option is near the "going" market price of the related security.

closed contract An agreement that *cannot* be modified by either party unless both consent. For example, an employer cannot reduce an employee's contractual salary unless the latter approves.

closed corporation A situation in which a company's shares are held by a few individuals, typically family members or management of the company. These shares are not available to the public.

closed park A MOBILE HOME park that requires the mobile home to be purchased from the park.

closed shop A company, or part thereof, that agrees to hire only members of the union.

closed-end account A credit account that permits a customer to use extended credit just once, typically for a specific purpose.

closed-end (mutual) fund A fund that operates with a fixed number of shares outstanding, which trade among individuals in secondary markets like COMMON STOCKS. That is, if one wishes to invest in a closed-end fund, he or she must purchase the shares from someone willing to sell them. In the same manner, in order to sell shares the brokerage house must locate a buyer. Transactions involving closed-end mutual funds are easy to arrange, however, since most of these funds are traded on the NEW YORK STOCK EXCHANGE or the OVER-THE-COUNTER market. A major point of closed-end funds is the size of discount or premium, which is the difference between their market prices and their NET ASSET VALUES (NAVs). Many funds of this type sell at discounts to the NAV, which enhances their investment appeal. An example of a closed-end mutual fund is Prudential Bache Securities' Global Yield Fund.
See also MUTUAL FUND; OPEN-END (MUTUAL) FUNDS.

closed-end investment company There is only one public issuance of stock for this company. The investment company's objective is to buy stocks in various entities. While treasury shares may not be acquired, shares are traded on the stock exchange at whatever the going market price is for the shares. Return is in the form of capital appreciation (depreciation) and periodic income.

closed-end investment trust *See* INVESTMENT TRUST.

closed-end lease A LEASE that involves monthly payments over a specified period of time. There is no charge at the end of the lease period. At the end of the leasing period, the lessor sells the leased item and bears any gain or loss from the entire transaction.

closed-end mortgage A type of MORTGAGE in which the property pledged cannot be collateralized for further loans.
See also OPEN-END MORTGAGE.

closely held corporation A CORPORATION that has only a few STOCKHOLDERS. It contrasts with a privately held corporation in that a closely held corporation is public although most of the shares are not traded.

closing The process of financially and legally transferring a house to a buyer; usually takes place in the office of the lender, an attorney, or an ESCROW company.

closing costs The fees paid by a home buyer in negotiating and financing the purchase of a home and paid at the CLOSING. Closing costs consist of loan application fees, loan origination fees, POINTS, TITLE SEARCH AND INSURANCE, appraisal fees, and other miscellaneous fees such as mortgage taxes and credit reports.

closing escrow The procedure of fulfilling all the conditions of the purchase and sale agreement. Once all the conditions have been met, the ESCROW AGENT prepares a summary of the monies received in escrow and the monies paid out of escrow, records the new deed with the County Recorder, and finally delivers a new deed to the buyer and the remaining funds from the purchase price to the seller. ESCROW is finally closed and official TITLE is given to the buyer.

cloud on title Or, a title defect. Any enforceable LIEN or claim that may bring into question the owner's title to the property. Such a cloud does not block the exchange of the property but may diminish its market value.
See also QUITCLAIM DEED.

club account A savings account in which a constant dollar amount is deposited periodically for a designated purpose, such as for ultimately buying a car. This special purpose savings account is typically issued with a coupon book. Interest is paid and there is usually a one-year maturity.

coinsurance A method by which the insured and insurer share proportionately in the payment for a loss. For example, in PROPERTY INSURANCE, it is a provision that requires policyholders to buy insurance in an amount equal to a specified percentage of the value of the improvements to their property.

coinsurance cap A limit placed on the amount of coinsurance in an insurance policy.
See also COINSURANCE.

coinsurance clause in homeowner's insurance policy A provision in a HOMEOWNER'S INSURANCE POLICY that limits the LIABILITY of the insurer. It provides that the insurance coverage must be at or above a stated percentage (usually 80%) of the replacement cost of the home before partial losses will be covered to the policy limit. This serves as an inducement for a homeowner to carry full coverage.

coinsurance factor A portion (such as 20%) of the expenses above the DEDUCTIBLE.

collapse
1. An unexpected and significant decline in prices of securities or commodities.
2. The BANKRUPTCY of a company.

collateral
real estate: Property given as security for a loan. If the borrower does not pay, the lender can usually seize the collateral.
securities: The legally required amount of cash or securities deposited with a brokerage firm to insure that an investor can meet all potential obligations. Collateral is required on investments with open-ended loss potential such as writing NAKED CALLS or PUTS.

collateral assignment The designation of an insurance policy's cash surrender value or death benefit as COLLATERAL for a loan. If the loan is defaulted upon, the creditor will cash in the policy and retain the balance of the loan with the remainder going to the BENEFICIARY. The ready assignability of life insurance makes it agreeable security to lenders.

collateralized mortgage obligation (CMO) Mortgage-backed, pass-through securities that separate mortgage pools into short- , medium- , and long-term time frames. CMOs are an outgrowth of the realization that simple Government National Mortgage Association (GNMA) or Federal Home Loan Mortgage Corporation (FHLMC, or Freddie Mac) mortgage-backed securities have uncertain durations (payback of principal and interest factor) because of the possibility of prepayment of the principal amounts remaining on the mortgages. By splitting mortgage pools into different time frames, investors now can buy shares in short-term (such as 5-year) or long-term (such as 20-year) pools.
See also MORTGAGE-BACKED SECURITIES.

collision insurance A form of AUTOMOBILE INSURANCE that pays for damage resulting from a collision or an object (e.g., rock) hitting the automobile.

collision (no-fault) coverage Insurance that covers damage to the insured's car whatever the reason, even when the other driver is at fault. The amount of coverage is equal to the lesser of the current wholesale value of the insured vehicle or the cost of repair, less any DEDUCTIBLE.

combination bond A bond supported by the credit of the governmental agency issuing it and by the income from the project (e.g., highway) financed by the security. An example is revenue bonds issued by the New York Triborough Bridge and Tunnel Authority.

commencement of coverage The date upon which insurance protection starts, normally occurring as soon as an insurance company has made a commitment. Prior to that time, the risk of loss belongs to the individual.

commercial paper A financial instrument issued to the public typically by large, financially sound corporations. It usually comes in minimum denominations of $25,000. It represents an unsecured PROMISSORY NOTE. It usually carries a higher yield than small CERTIFICATES OF DEPOSIT (CDs). The maturity is usually 30, 60, and 90 days. The degree of risk depends on the issuing company's CREDIT RATING. Commercial papers are rated by STANDARD & POOR's and MOODY's.

commercial property Property designed for business use, such as an office building, medical center, gasoline station, or motel, that carries a potential for profit. There is a risk to investing in commercial property but there is also opportunity for high return. The return comes in the form of net rental income and capital appreciation in price.
See also RESIDENTIAL PROPERTY.

commission
in general: Governmental regulatory agency, such as the Federal Trade Commission.
securities: The broker's fee for purchasing or selling securities. On the NEW YORK STOCK EXCHANGE, commissions average about 1% of the market value of the STOCKS involved in the transaction and approximately 1/4 of 1% on BONDS.
real estate: The broker's fee for buying or selling property for a client.

commission broker A broker who executes the investor's order for the purchase or sale of securities or commodities.

common stock Share in a public or privately held company. It is a security that represents an equity interest in a company. In the event of liquidation, common stockholders are paid after bondholders and preferred stockholders. The terms common stock and CAPITAL STOCK are often used interchangeably when the company has no preferred stock. A BOND, which is a DEBT issue, does not represent ownership.

The corporation's stockholders have the following rights and privileges:

1. *Control of the firm.* The stockholders elect the firm's directors, who in turn select officers to manage the business.

2. *Preemptive rights.* This is the right to purchase new stock. A PREEMPTIVE RIGHT entitles a common stockholder to maintain his or her proportional ownership by offering the stockholder an opportunity to purchase, on a pro rata basis, any new stock being offered or any securities CONVERTIBLE into common stock.
types of common stock

Stocks are classified into the following categories according to their special characteristics:
blue-chip stocks: Common stocks of high quality with a long and proved record of earnings and dividend payments. These stocks, often viewed as long-term investment instruments, have low risk and provide modest, but dependable, return. Examples include AT&T, Exxon, and Du Pont stock.
growth stocks: Issues that have a long record of earnings and dividends higher than for the economy as a whole as well as for the industry of which it is a part. Examples include high-tech stocks.
income stocks: Issues characterized by a higher dividend per share and dividend payout ratio. These stocks are ideal for investors who desire high CURRENT INCOME (rather than future CAPITAL GAINS) with little RISK. Examples are utility stocks such as AT&T and Consolidated Edison.

cyclical stocks: Stocks whose earnings and prices move with the BUSINESS CYCLE. Stocks of construction, building materials, airlines, and steel fall into this category.

defensive stocks: Stocks that tend to be less affected by downswings in the business cycles than the average issue. In other words, they are recession resistant. Utilities, soft drink, and consumer product stocks are examples.

speculative stocks: Stocks that generally lack a track record of high earnings and dividends and have uncertain earnings, but have the chance to hit it big in the market. Many of the new issues of oil and gas stocks and cancer-related pharmaceutical stocks are a sheer gamble. These issues are ideal for investors who are risk-oriented, hoping for a big return.

characteristics of common stock

The characteristics that make common stock an attractive investment alternative can be summarized as follows:

1. Common stocks provide an ownership feature, compared with fixed income securities such as BONDS, which do not.

2. Common stocks provide an income potential not only in terms of current income in the form of dividends but also in future capital gain (or loss).

3. Common shareholders can participate in the firm's earnings and lay claim to all the residual profits of the entity.

4. Common stock can be an inflation hedge if the total return from investment in common stock exceeds the rate of inflation.

5. Because a variety of stocks are available, as discussed above, the investor may choose from a broad spectrum of RISK-RETURN combinations for common stock investment.

common stock mutual fund A MUTUAL FUND that invests only in COMMON STOCKS of companies.

common stock valuation The process of determining the value of a common stock. It typically involves finding the present value of a stock's expected future income and capital gain,

using the investor's required rate of return as the discount rate. A pragmatic approach to valuing a common stock is to use the PRICE-EARNINGS (P/E) RATIO (or multiple).

Under this approach, estimated market price can be determined by the following:

Estimated earnings per share × estimated P/E ratio

Example: An investor expects the earnings for ABC Company to be $2,000,000, based on financial projections in a brokerage report and/or management's discussion in the ANNUAL REPORT. The company's tax rate is 34%. After-tax profit is therefore

$$\$2,000,000 \times 66\% = \$1,320,000$$

The company's P/E ratio was 10 and is expected to continue for the next year. Assume that the company's expected shares outstanding are 1,000,000. Estimated earnings per share is

$$\$1,320,000/1,000,000 \text{ shares} = \$1.32$$

Estimated market price = estimated earnings per share × estimated P/E ratio = $1.32 × 10 = $13.20

community property Property owned and held jointly and shared equally by husband and wife. It is acquired by both spouses during their marriage, irrespective of the wage-earning status of either spouse.

community property laws Laws providing that the property of deceased persons is distributed in a manner that assumes that property acquired during marriage is jointly owned and equally shared by the spouses no matter how much each contributed. Sixteen western states have adopted the community property doctrine.

See also COMMUNITY PROPERTY.

company car An automobile owned by the business but available to an employee for use.

comparative negligence A state law providing that when an accident occurs, negligence of a party is dependent upon his or her input to that accident. If two drivers are speeding, for example, their negligence to the accident is equal. In consequence, neither party would recoup damages from the other.

comparison shopping A process of comparing goods or services to determine the BEST BUY.

compensating balance The balance a borrower must maintain on deposit in a bank account, representing a given percentage of the loan. It is a deposit that the lender can use to offset an unpaid loan. The compensating balance is usually 10%. No interest is earned on this balance, which increases the EFFECTIVE INTEREST RATE on the loan. Assume an individual borrows $10,000 from the bank at 12% interest with a 10% compensating balance. The compensating balance is $1,000 ($10,000 × 10%), The effective interest rate is

$$\$1,200/(\$10,000 - \$1,000) = \$1,200/\$9,000$$
$$= 13.33\%$$

composite risk The combination of risks, such as business, inflation, market, and liquidity. This allows one to see the overall picture of risk. For example, a corporate bond may have a composite risk consisting of inflation risk, default risk, and interest rate risk.

composition A legal agreement that permits a debtor to remain in business. There is a discharge of part of the debt. The creditor receives a given percentage of the balance due in complete satisfaction of the obligation. Since a composition is a voluntary agreement between the parties, court costs are avoided. In addition, the company is not declared bankrupt.

compound interest The interest that accrues when earnings for a specified period are added to the principal, so that interest for the following period is computed on the principal plus accumulated interest. Interest is calculated on reinvested interest as well as on the original amount invested.
See also SIMPLE INTEREST.

comprehensive automobile insurance AUTO-MOBILE INSURANCE that covers losses resulting from theft of a car or from repairs if the car is hit by a falling object or damaged by fire, flood, or vandals—damage incurred other than by collision and rollover.

comprehensive (no-fault) coverage A provision that covers a variety of PERILS, such as glass breakage and losses caused by fire, theft, hail, water, flood, vandalism, riot, and accidents with birds and animals. Coverage limits are the same as for collision insurance.

comprehensive health insurance HEALTH INSURANCE that combines into one policy the protection provided by hospital insurance, surgical insurance, medical expense insurance, and major medical insurance.

comprehensive homeowner's liability insurance Personal liability insurance that provides coverage—as Part II of HOMEOWNER'S POLICY—on an all RISKS/ALL PERILS for personal acts and omissions by the policyholder.

comprehensive insurance *See* COMPREHENSIVE AUTOMOBILE INSURANCE.

comprehensive major medical insurance A HEALTH INSURANCE plan that combines the basic hospital, surgical, and physicians' expense coverages with major medical protection to form a single policy. The features covered vary among insurers.
See also MAJOR MEDICAL INSURANCE PLAN.

comprehensive personal liability insurance INSURANCE that provides the insured protection from liability losses that might arise out of any activity.

concession
1. A right to undertake and profit by a specific activity in return for services.
2. Reduced selling price to stimulate sales.

3. Permission or right, usually granted by a governmental unit, to use property for a specific kind of business in a given geographic region, such as a service station on a highway.

4. Per-share compensation for the investment banker's underwriting service in a new security issue.

condemnation A legal action involved in EMINENT DOMAIN where the government or other units take ownership of privately held real estate for public use (such as for schools, parks, streets, public parking, or public housing) regardless of the owner's wishes. The property owner must be paid the fair market value of the property taken from him or her.

condition precedent A CONDITION that must be met or action performed before something can take effect. For example, in most real estate sales contracts all payments must be made before the buyer may ask for transfer of title.

condition subsequent A condition that comes into being based on an action or event. For example, a contract between buyer and seller will only take effect if the seller is shown to have legal title to the property.

conditional commitment Agreement by a lender to provide loans to qualified borrowers within a specified time period but without specifically identifying those borrowers. An example is a commitment given by a bank to a real estate developer to provide mortgages to qualified borrowers.

conditional contract A contract providing performance based on the occurrence of a subsequent event. An example is an agreement to buy a car provided it satisfies your mechanic's testing of it.

conditional conveyance A situation in which collateralized property is held by a party until the loan is paid. A major condition is that the borrower make timely payments. If the loan is defaulted upon, the lender keeps the item.

conditional endorsement When an endorsement is made, the endorser makes a stipulation associated with it. An example is the endorser insists that the transferee cannot use the funds for one year.

conditional sales Sales made under a contract in which TITLE or security interest remains in the seller until the conditions of the contract have been performed by the buyer.

conditions
law: Provisions specified in a contractual agreement.
real estate:
1. Qualifications attached to an estate that, if they occur, will result in the defeat or enlargement of the estate.
2. Limitations imposed in a deed.
See also CONDITION PRECEDENT; CONDITION SUBSEQUENT.
insurance: Statements in an insurance policy that impose obligation on both the insured and the insurer by establishing the ground rules of the agreement. For example, the insured must pay the premium on time, notify the insurer immediately in the case of an accident, and cooperate with the insurer in defense of the insured in a liability suit.

condominium Ownership of a divided interest; for example, a home ownership arrangement in which the owner holds TITLE to a housing unit within a building or project, and a proportionate interest in the common grounds and recreational facilities.

confession of judgment A clause in a credit contract stating that if the lender sues the borrower for late payments, the borrower accepts guilt in advance, even if there is good reason for not paying.

conforming loans Loans that adhere to national guidelines of Freddie Mac and Fannie Mae, who buy the loans on the secondary market.

consideration
law: Anything of value given to induce entering

into a contract. It may be money, services, or goods. A valid contract must have sufficient consideration.

securities: The net amount received from the sale of securities equal to the selling price less transaction costs including brokerage fees and taxes.

consolidated liability plan Automobile liability coverage that establishes a specific dollar amount as the maximum that would be paid for all losses caused from a liability claim.

constant dollar plan The investment of a fixed amount of dollars in stocks at periodic times. When prices are low, more shares will be bought. However, when prices are high, fewer shares will be purchased.

constant payment loan A loan requiring equal periodic payments to pay off the loan after the last payment.

constant ratio method A useful method of quick calculation of the ANNUAL PERCENTAGE RATE of interest on a loan using the ADD-ON METHOD of calculating interest.

constructive receipt A tax law whereby income is taxable even though not actually received because the taxpayer in effect has constructively received it. Constructive receipt means the taxpayer is legally entitled to the money. For example, an interest coupon on a bond is taxable when the coupon matures, irrespective of whether it has been cashed in.

consumer cooperative The consumers own the seller. However, the company may also sell to the public at large. The net income is shared by the participants. A favorable characteristic of this cooperative is that because of group buying its members can buy merchandise at lower prices than would be available if they bought goods as individual buyers.

consumer credit Nonbusiness debt used by consumers for purposes other than home mortgages.

Consumer Credit Protection Act Or, *Truth in Lending Act.* Required disclosures by lenders to borrowers, such as unusual loan terms, effective interest rate, total interest, and total payments.

consumer durable A good that is expected to have a life in excess of three years, such as an automobile, an appliance, and furniture.

consumer finance company Or, *small loan finance company.* A nonbanking lender that makes secured and unsecured short-term loans to qualified borrowers. These companies do not accept deposits but rather obtain funds from their stockholders and through borrowing. They have higher ANNUAL PERCENTAGE RATES (APRs) than banks have, reflecting the risky nature of their loans.

consumer price index (CPI) An average of the prices of various goods and services commonly purchased by families in urban areas. It is frequently referred to as a COST-OF-LIVING INDEX. The CPI is published monthly by the Bureau of Labor Statistics of the U.S. Department of Labor. The so-called market basket covered by the index includes items such as food, clothing, automobiles, homes, and doctor fees. The CPI is the most widely used measure of the purchasing power of the dollar. Consequently, a provision that payments, rents, or wages rise in proportion to the rise in the CPI is written for Social Security payments and in many lease agreements and collective bargaining agreements. The CPI is widely used by an individual in monitoring INFLATION.
See also PRICE INDICES.

Consumer Product Safety Commission (CPSC) The federal agency that deals specifically with the risks of injury resulting from a wide range of consumer products.

contents replacement cost protection An optional feature available in some HOMEOWNER'S INSURANCE POLICIES that pays the REPLACEMENT COST of any personal property.

contingent beneficiary An individual who will become the BENEFICIARY if the original beneficiary dies before the insured. It is the policy-holder's second choice as beneficiary, dependent on the standing of the primary beneficiary.

contract of novation In law, substituting one acceptable party for another original party to a contract. It thus ends the old contract and begins a new one. The new contract has the same content but with a different party. An example is a parent's agreement to assume the debt of a child with the creditor's permission.

contract of sale A written agreement between a buyer and a seller in which the former agrees to purchase real estate property upon mutually agreeable terms.

contractual accumulation plan A formalized, long-term program to buy shares in an OPEN-END LOAD MUTUAL FUND.

contrarianism An investment philosophy based on crowd psychology, which urges investors to do the opposite of what the crowd is doing.
See also TECHNICAL ANALYSIS.

conventional loan A MORTGAGE LOAN that is not insured by a governmental body such as the VETERANS ADMINISTRATION. The loan is repayable in equal monthly payments, which include principal and interest. The interest rate is fixed over the term of the loan.

conventional mortgage A MORTGAGE that requires a large down payment, is typically available only to good credit risks, and has fixed monthly payments for the life of the loan. It typically has a 30-year period of fixed interest rates discharged on an amortized basis with equal monthly payments. It is neither insured by the FHA nor guaranteed by the VA.

conventional term life insurance *See* TERM LIFE INSURANCE.

conversion
securities: An interchange of one class of corporate security for another. For example, conversion of BONDS or PREFERRED STOCK for COM-MON STOCKS and the transfer from one MUTUAL FUND to another in a single family, called FUND SWITCHING.
foreign exchange: Switching from one currency to another using an exchange ratio.
real estate: Exchange of one real estate property for another.
insurance: Switching from short-term to long-term life insurance.

conversion charge A fee levied against an individual when he or she makes a transfer. For example, a MUTUAL FUND may charge a fee when the investor switches between funds, usually in a different family of funds.

conversion feature The right to transfer an item, account, or investment into another one. For example, a convertible bond has the feature of allowing the investor to convert that bond into stock at a later date. Another example is an insurance policy that allows the insured to switch from short-term to permanent life insurance.

conversion hedge A hedge in a foreign currency when delivery is taken at a later date to protect against a shift in the exchange rate. Assume a $10,000, six-month contract with a French company, payable in francs. To protect against a drop in the exchange rate, the investor may purchase a put on francs. If the price of francs goes down, the gain on the put will offset the loss on the contract.

convertibility A TERM LIFE INSURANCE feature that allows the policyholder to convert to a WHOLE LIFE policy without a medical examination or proof of insurability.

convertible A BOND or PREFERRED STOCK that may be exchanged by the owner for COMMON STOCK or another security, usually of the same company, in accordance with the terms of the issue.

convertible bond SUBORDINATED DEBENTURES that may be converted, at the holder's option, into a specified amount of other securities (usually COMMON STOCK) at a fixed price. They are hybrid securities having characteristics of both BONDS and common stock in that they provide fixed interest income and potential appreciation through participation in future price increases of the underlying common stock.

convertible preferred stock   PREFERRED STOCK that can be converted into common stock at the option of the holder.

convertible security   A PREFERRED STOCK or BOND that is convertible into COMMON STOCK of the issuing corporation at some stated ratio at a later date.

convertible term   A TERM LIFE INSURANCE policy that the insured may convert into a WHOLE LIFE INSURANCE policy.

convertible term insurance   A type of LIFE INSURANCE POLICY that allows the policyholder to convert a term policy to a CASH VALUE policy. It is at the option of the insured without the insured's having to prove evidence of INSURABILITY.

conveyance   To transfer title to real or personal property from one person to another. For example, a sales contract will document the sale of an item to a buyer.

cook the books   To falsify financial statements and records to misrepresent the operating results and financial health of an organization.

cooling-off ruling   A federal rule that provides a buyer with three business days in which to cancel a door-to-door SALES CONTRACT. It is the RIGHT OF RESCISSION.

cooperative
in general: An entity owned by members.
real estate: A corporation that owns housing units and whose tenants purchase shares of ownership in the corporation equivalent to the value of their particular housing unit.

cooperative apartment   Apartment building in which each TENANT owns a proportional share of the CORPORATION that owns the building.

coordination of benefits provision   A HEALTH INSURANCE provision requiring that benefits be coordinated among insurance carriers when the INSURED is eligible for benefits under more than one policy. This provision prevents the insured from collecting from the insurance companies more than the amount of his or her medical payments.

copayment clause   A stipulation in a HEALTH INSURANCE contract requiring that the INSURED pay a specific dollar portion of specifically covered expense items.

corner   Buying of a stock or commodity on a scale large enough to give the buyer control over the price. An investor who must buy that stock or commodity (for example one who is SHORT) is forced to do business at an arbitrarily high price with those who engineered the corner.

corporate bond   A DEBT SECURITY of a company. It represents an agreement that the face value (usually $1,000) of the loan will be repaid at maturity and that interest will be paid at regular intervals (usually semiannually). It is a corporate IOU, which is traded on major exchanges.

corporation   A form of business organized as a separate legal entity with ownership evidenced by shares of CAPITAL STOCK. The corporation continues to exist regardless of changes in its ownership. The corporation is formed by registering the ARTICLES OF INCORPORATION with the state authority, who returns it with a certificate of incorporation; the two documents together become a corporate charter. Corporations are taxed differently from SOLE PROPRIETORSHIPS and PARTNERSHIPS.
See also FORMS OF BUSINESS ORGANIZATIONS.

correction   In the SECURITIES markets a correction occurs when a STOCK or, indeed, the entire MARKET, moves downward, sometimes rather violently, after experiencing a general period of advancing prices. A true correction is then followed by a continued period of advancing prices, which distinguishes it from a major BEARISH turn in the overall direction of the stock or the market. See accompanying graph.

cosign To sign a NOTE on behalf of another person and, therefore, to guarantee payment. The cosigner becomes equally responsible for the loan if the borrower does not repay.

cost approach In REAL ESTATE, the principle that a buyer should not pay more for a property than it would cost to purchase at current prices for land, labor, and appraisals.

cost of living The cost to purchase those goods and services that are included in an accepted standard level of consumption.

cost-of-living adjustment (COLA) An upward adjustment to an employee's compensation or to SOCIAL SECURITY benefits to account for inflation. The adjustment is typically based on a price index such as the CONSUMER PRICE INDEX (CPI).

counterclaim A legal action by defendant against the plaintiff. It is a counter demand in litigation by the defendant. For example, if a plaintiff sues a defendant for $1,000,000, the defendant may in turn decide to sue the plaintiff for a similar amount. A counterclaim does not constitute an answer to the plaintiff's charges.

countercyclical (defensive) stock A stock of a company that maintains substantial earnings during a general decline in economic activity because its products are needed. Examples are food and entertainment stocks.

counteroffer An original offer to buy or sell answered with a simultaneous revised offer. For example, a buyer offers $100,000 for a house put on the market. The owner turns down the offer but submits a counteroffer for $125,000. Offers and counteroffers are not restricted to price but include such matters as financing arrangements and APPORTIONMENT of closing costs.

coupon Or, *coupon yield.* The interest rate printed on the BOND CERTIFICATE when it is issued. When interest is due, this coupon is clipped from the bond and presented to a designated bank for payment.

coupon bond *See* BEARER BOND.

coupon rate Or, *face rate; nominal rate.* The interest rate of a BOND as a percentage of the face value. It is printed on the COUPON of a bond.

coupon yield *See* COUPON.

creative financing Any financing arrangement other than a CONVENTIONAL MORTGAGE from a third-party lending institution. This form

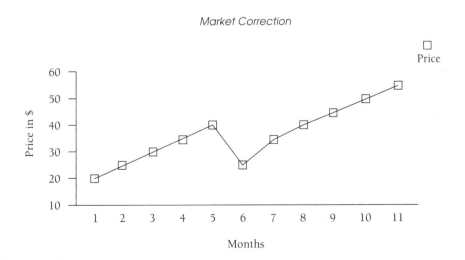

Market Correction

of financing is popular when the price of real estate is out of reach for many buyers. Creative financing devices include seller financing; owner carrying (OWC); BALLOON PAYMENT LOANS; WRAP-AROUND MORTGAGES; ASSUMPTION OF MORTGAGE; SALE-LEASEBACKS; LAND CONTRACTS; alternative mortgage instruments such as ADJUSTABLE RATE MORTGAGE (ARM) and SHARED EQUITY MORTGAGE (SEM).

credit

1. A purchase made on account by a consumer from a business.

2. Loan extended to business, individuals, or the government.

3. A form of trust established between a lender and a borrower.

4. In TAXATION, a dollar-for-dollar offset against a tax liability. An example of a tax credit is the child care credit.

credit application A form used to record information regarding a credit applicant's ability and willingness to repay debts.

credit bureau An AGENCY, typically established and owned by merchants and banks at the local level, that gathers credit information from its members and makes this information available for a specified fee to member creditors under the requirements of the FAIR CREDIT REPORTING ACT.

credit card A plastic card issued by a private business or commercial bank that allows the card holder to charge purchases at any store, oil company, or other business accepting it. The credit card may also be used to obtain a cash advance from the issuer.

credit card insurance INSURANCE that covers charges made on a lost or stolen CREDIT CARD. Under the CONSUMER CREDIT PROTECTION ACT, this insurance is no longer necessary.

credit card liability A liability for unauthorized use of a CREDIT CARD that occurs only if the card holder received notification of potential liability, accepted the card when it was first mailed, the company provided a self-addressed form to be used to notify them if the card disappeared, and the card was illegally used before the card holder notified the company of its loss. The liability is generally limited to $50 per card.

credit control sheet A form used to monitor the use of CREDIT, amounts owed, and to whom money is owed.

credit health and accident insurance INSURANCE purchased as payment protection for a loan in case the borrower is unable to meet the payments due to a disability or illness.

credit investigation Investigation of an applicant's credit history to compare it with information provided on the credit application.

credit life insurance A type of LIFE INSURANCE sold through lenders in connection with loans and charge accounts. It is usually decreasing term coverage since the coverage decreases at the same rate as the balance on the loan. It will pay the remaining balance of a loan if the insured dies before repaying the debt. Because the premium for credit life insurance is usually added to the loan and financed at the same rate, the insured ends up paying to insure not only the loan principal but also the INSURANCE PREMIUM and all finance charges.

credit limit A specified amount beyond which a credit customer may not buy on credit or borrow. It is the maximum outstanding DEBT on a CREDIT account.

credit overextension A condition under which excessive personal charges and debts cause extreme difficulty and possible inability to repay.

credit property insurance INSURANCE purchased to compensate the lender if property placed as security for a loan is destroyed.

credit rating A rating to help the lender determine whether a CREDIT applicant should be granted credit. It is based on the applicant's job

history, income, assets owned, credit history, and similar information. Many firms investigate and maintain credit records of individuals and businesses. Examples are TRW (for individuals) and Dun and Bradstreet (for businesses).
See also BOND RATINGS.

credit receipt Written evidence of merchandise returned and its sales price.

credit record An individual's credit history.

credit risk The chance of a loss through noncollection of a credit obligation.

credit scoring An objective method of evaluating a credit applicant's credit worthiness by assigning values to factors such as income, existing debts, job security, and credit history.

credit standard Criterion for qualifying for loans. Credit standards are traditionally judged by the FIVE Cs OF CREDIT.

credit union A depository institution formed as a cooperative having some common bond, such as the same employer, religion, union, or fraternal association. It is a mutual association owned by depositors. It draws together the deposits of its members and lends these funds out to other members or invests the money.

credit union share An investment (savings) in a CREDIT UNION in minimum amounts of $5 or $10 upon which interest is earned.

credit worthiness The ability and willingness to repay a debt; having a good credit history.

creeping inflation A gradual and continuous rise in the general price level, which is tolerable in the short term but may lead to sizable long-term price increases.
See also GALLOPING INFLATION.

crop insurance An insurance policy issued to farmers covering losses to crops.

crown loan A loan to the parents or children of the lender so that the income is taxed at the lower tax bracket of the borrower. These loans are subject to gift tax if they are not made at the prevailing interest rate.

crude rate of return A rough measure of the YIELD on amounts invested that assumes that equal portions of the gain were earned each year.

cumulative A type of PREFERRED STOCK. DIVIDENDS IN ARREARS must be paid before any future dividends are distributed to the common stockholders.

cumulative voting A voting procedure for corporate directors that enables a minority group of shareholders to obtain some voice in the control of a corporation. Normally, shareholders must allocate their votes equally among the candidates for the board of directors. Cumulative voting allows them to vote all their shares for a single candidate. For example, an individual holding 10 shares normally casts 10 votes for each of, say, 12 nominees to the board of directors. The shareholder thus has 120 votes. Under the cumulative voting principle he or she may vote this way or may cast 120 (10 × 12) votes for only one nominee, 60 for two, 40 for three, or any other distribution the voter chooses.

curb exchange The former name of the AMERICAN STOCK EXCHANGE, second largest exchange in the country. The term comes from the market's origin of trading on the streets of downtown New York.

currency futures contract The holder of the contract has the right to a specified amount of foreign currency at a later date. It is a legal obligation to perform, unlike an OPTION, which is the right to perform. There is a secondary market with standardized contracts. The contract is expressed in terms of dollars or cents per unit of the related foreign currency. The delivery date is typically one year or less. Trading units of different currencies follow:

Currency	Trading Unit
British pound	25,000
Canadian dollar	100,000
West German mark	125,000

current assumption whole life insurance
Variation of ordinary LIFE INSURANCE whereby present investment income and mortality experience are credited to the policy through the DIVIDEND, PREMIUM, or CASH VALUE structure.

current consumption   Consumption of consumer goods and services within one year.

current income   Money received from an IN-VESTMENT, usually on a regular basis, in the form of INTEREST, DIVIDENDS, RENT, or other such payment.

current income fund   A MUTUAL FUND whose investment objective is to produce high current DIVIDEND YIELDS on COMMON STOCKS.

current return   *See* CURRENT INCOME; CURRENT YIELD; RETURN.

current yield   The measurement of INVEST-MENT return that relates income to the market price. For a BOND, its annual interest divided by its current market price. For a COMMON or PRE-FERRED STOCK, the ratio of the annual cash dividend income received to the price paid by the investor. For example, a 12% coupon rate $1,000 par value bond is selling for $960. The current yield of the bond is

$$\$120/\$960 = 12.5\%$$

The problem with this measure of return is that it does not take into account the MATURITY DATE of the bond. A bond with one year to run and another with 15 years to run would have the same current yield quote if interest payments were $120 and the price were $960. Clearly, the one-year bond would be preferable under this circumstance because the investor would not only get $120 in interest, but also a gain of $40 ($1000 − $960) with a one-year time period and this amount could be reinvested.
See also BOND YIELD; YIELD TO MATURITY (YTM).

cusip number   A number assigned to a security, such as a bond or stock, for identification and recordkeeping reasons.

custodial accounts
minors: An ACCOUNT created for a minor by his or her parent or guardian through which all transactions are managed for the minor, who is not permitted to make transactions without the custodian's consent. Usually such an account is created either at a BANK or a BROKERAGE FIRM and the CUSTODIAN manages it until the child reaches majority age.

The TAX REFORM ACT OF 1986 curtailed the practice of shifting income to a minor for the purpose of reducing the grantor's TAX burden. Subsequent to the act, all gifts to minors under the age of 14 exceeding $1,000 are taxed at the rate of the grantor.
securities: A bank charged with the responsibility of managing the securities of a client. These responsibilities include purchasing and selling SECURITIES, receiving DIVIDEND and INTER-EST payments, and managing the client's ledger of accounts.
See also CLIFFORD TRUST; CROWN LOAN; UNIFORM GIFTS TO MINORS ACT.

custodian   Anyone having the responsibility of caring for and managing the property of another. An example is an individual's having the responsibility of managing a custodial account for a minor.
See also CUSTODIAL ACCOUNTS.

custodianship account for minors   *See* CUSTO-DIAL ACCOUNTS.

custody   The situation in which one person has another's assets and is charged with the legal management of those assets.
See also CUSTODIAL ACCOUNTS; CUSTODIAN.
children: Legal responsibility of a parent or guardian for managing all the affairs of a child or children as well as supervising and being responsible for their care and education. A custodial parent or guardian does not have to declare CHILD SUPPORT as income nor is it a TAX DEDUCTIBLE expense for the parent not having custody.
courts: The actual incarceration of a legal petitioner or the limitation of personal freedom for one in custody under his or her "own recognizance."

customers' man *See* REGISTERED REPRESENTATIVE.

customers' net debit balances Credit of stock exchange member firms made available to help finance customers' purchases of stocks, bonds, and commodities.

cyclical stock STOCK whose price movements tend to follow the BUSINESS CYCLE, improving its position when the economy is on an upswing and falling during times of decline. Stocks of construction companies, airlines, and the steel industry fall into this category.

D

daily high or low The TRADING RANGE of a SECURITY or Dow-Jones Averages in any one trading day. In the case of a security, the highest, lowest and closing prices are reported in financial services for the trading day along with the net change.

In the case of the Dow-Jones Averages (30 industrials, 20 transportation companies, 15 utilities, and the 65 stocks composite average), hourly INDEX prices, the opening and closing prices, the percentage change, the volume, and the high and low price for the trading day are reported.

daily interest
calculation: Term indicating that INTEREST on a BANK DEPOSIT or LOAN is being determined daily even though the amount may not be CREDITED or DEBITED until a later period of time, such as weekly, monthly, quarterly, or semi-annually.
compounding: A method of adding daily interest into the COMPOUNDING of a sum of MONEY. For example, if $100,000 were compounded at 10% interest for 365 days the total amount of interest earned would be $10,515.60, whereas if it were compounded just once for the year the total INTEREST earned would be $10,000 for a net difference of $515.60.
See also FUTURE VALUE.

damage deposit A fee paid to cover any physical damage beyond normal wear and tear or any economic damage such as failure to pay rent, caused by a tenant.

damages
injury or loss: A monetary restitution, which may be recovered either through insurance indemnification or by judicial settlement, for losses or injuries incurred either through an accident or illegal action.
compensatory: Financial settlement to compensate a victim of a personal injury or property loss. The intent is not to benefit from the injury or loss but merely to compensate for the damages incurred.
exemplary or punitive: Punishment for unacceptable or illegal conduct. Exemplary or punitive damages are primarily intended to deter future unacceptable acts. Such damages are awarded to the plaintiff in a legal action on an increased scale and are over and above the actual pecuniary value of the loss or injury.

data base A structured and sequenced table of facts and information for the purpose of future reference as well as to make summary reports.
computerized: Made accessible by computer. Modern computerized data bases have the capability of storing and sharing limitless information between computer systems, which can be calculated, indexed, searched, sorted, or reported in summary tables. Such data bases have the advantages of accuracy, instant calculations, and retrieval. Computerized data bases are in extremely wide use with applications in every field of endeavor.

date of issue

insurance: Date an INSURANCE POLICY is issued by an insurance company. The date of issue may not be when the insurance policy becomes effective.

In LIFE INSURANCE, date of issue is the date set forth in the policy itself.

debt: Date NOTES and BONDS become effective.

new issue: Date a new SECURITY will come to the MARKET and be issued for public sale.

date of record Date on which a STOCKHOLDER must own a STOCK in order to qualify for a declared DIVIDEND or STOCK RIGHT. The stockholder's name must appear on the official record of stock ownership by this date. The dividend will be paid on the payment date.

For example, a company may declare its intention to pay a 15 cent dividend on June 5 to the stockholders of record on May 8.

day of deposit to day of withdrawal (DDDW) account Or, *actual balance method*. A method of calculating the account balance on which interest is earned. Interest is calculated on the actual number of days the money is deposited in the account. When withdrawals occur, interest is earned for the number of days the money remained before the day of withdrawal.

Example: The following activities have taken place during the 90-day period:

Day	Deposit (Withdrawal)	Balance
1	$1,000	$1,000
30	1,000	2,000
60	(800)	1,200
90	Closing	1,200

With a 6% stated (nominal) interest rate, calculating interest under DDDW yields:

$$
\begin{align}
\text{(a)} \quad & \$1,000 \times .06 \times 30/360 = \$ 5.00 \\
\text{(b)} \quad & \$2,000 \times .06 \times 30/360 = \$10.00 \\
\text{(c)} \quad & \$1,200 \times .06 \times 30/360 = \underline{\$ 6.00} \\
& \hphantom{\$1,200 \times .06 \times 30/360 = } \$21.00
\end{align}
$$

See also FIRST IN, FIRST OUT (FIFO) METHOD; LAST IN, FIRST OUT (LIFO) METHOD; MINIMUM BALANCE METHOD.

day order Instructions to a STOCKBROKER that are valid only for the remainder of the trading day during which they were given to the broker.

day trading An investor buying and then selling a stock within one trading day. This may be advisable only when the security's price vacillates widely.

dead days Days appearing at the end of an interest period during which the bank will allow funds to earn interest even though they are not actually on deposit (typically a maximum of 10 days).

dead-end job A job or career having no further growth, SALARY increases, or promotions. The present job holder can advance no further than his or her present position. In such a circumstance, the job holder will have to determine whether he or she is satisfied with this eventuality or should seek a new position or career.

Most people become very discouraged when discovering they are in a dead-end position. Management should try to restructure dead-end positions to allow for career advancement recognition in order to prevent low morale and turnover and encourage higher productivity growth.

deadline The time by which an action is to be completed. For example, a STOCK must be TENDERED by no later than 12:00 A.M. May 1, 1991, in order to receive the TENDER OFFER price. After this deadline, all offers will be withdrawn.

deal A legally enforceable arrangement between two parties such as the seller and buyer for a product or service. There is mutual consent, and a bargain price may be involved.

dealer A person or a company that owns and offers SECURITIES. The dealer acts as a principal rather than as an AGENT. Typically, a dealer buys for his or her own account and sells to a customer from his or her own inventory, as distinguished from the BROKER who acts as the buyer's or seller's agent for a fee. The dealer's profit or loss is the difference between the price he or she pays and the price he or she receives for the same security. The dealer's confirmation must disclose to the customer that the dealer has acted as principal. The same individual or company may function, at different times, either as broker or dealer. For example, the specialist on the floor of the NEW YORK STOCK EXCHANGE acts as a dealer when buying or selling stock for his or her own account to maintain a market. The specialist acts as a broker when executing the orders commission brokers have left with him or her.

See also NATIONAL ASSOCIATION OF SECURITIES DEALERS (NASD); SPECIALIST.

dealer market   A MARKET in which only DEALERS participate for the purpose of later selling to the retail market. This market is usually characterized by high volume transactions. For example, when a new SECURITY issue is underwritten, the LEAD UNDERWRITER will seek participation from other UNDERWRITERS by asking them to buy a certain quantity of the NEW ISSUE. These participating underwriters will then sell the new issue to their retail clients.

dealer's spread   The COMMISSION or markup a DEALER makes when offering a new security. The commission is paid by the company offering the new STOCK rather than by the retail customer.

death benefit   The amount that will be paid under a LIFE INSURANCE policy upon the death of the INSURED. This is generally the face value of the policy plus any riders and minus any outstanding loans and interests applied against the cash value of the policy.

death rate   In INSURANCE, the probability that an individual will die at a given age.

debenture   Long-term unsecured BONDS. They are protected by the general credit of the issuing corporation. BOND CREDIT RATINGS are very important for this type of bond. Federal, state, and municipal government issues are debentures. SUBORDINATED DEBENTURES are junior issues ranking after other unsecured debt as a result of

explicit provisions in the indenture. Finance companies have made extensive use of these types of bonds.
See also BOND INDENTURE.

debenture market   *See* BOND MARKET.

debit card   A card issued for making electronic transfers of funds in stores, depository institutions, and other businesses in order to make transactions. These cards replace cash or checks by initiating automatic transfers of funds via computer systems. No cash or check is needed.

debit memorandum

1. Document issued by a bank to a depositor indicating that the depositor's bank balance is being reduced for reasons other than payment of a check, such as for bank service charges.

2. Form issued by a seller to a buyer indicating that the seller is increasing the amount the buyer owes, for reasons such as a previous error of the seller.

debt   Money or services owed to another in accordance with an agreement. The debtor may have to give collateral for a loan, such as a mortgage on his or her house. Principal and interest on the loan will have to be paid. Debt may either be short term or long term.
See also AMORTIZED LOAN; LOAN; MORTGAGE LOAN; STRAIGHT LOAN; TERM LOAN.

debt consolidation loan   A type of LOAN that combines all of an individual's debts into one large loan with small monthly payments. The idea is to pay off several smaller debts with varying due dates and interest rates and instead have one monthly payment, which is usually lower in amount than the payments on the other debts combined. The high rate of interest for the new loan greatly increases the total cost of the credit although the monthly payment may be lower than the sum of all the former payments.

debt securities   SECURITIES that serve as evidence to the existence of a debt, such as BONDS or NOTES as opposed to EQUITY securities, such as STOCKS, which manifest evidence of ownership.
See also FIXED INCOME SECURITIES.

debt service coverage ratio Ratio of monthly consumer debt payments to monthly take-home pay. This ratio helps a consumer determine how much debt to handle. The absolute maximum is 20%. This maximum limit includes payments due on CREDIT CARDS and personal, school, and car loans—but not MORTGAGES, HOME-EQUITY LOANS, or RENT.
See also CREDIT OVEREXTENSION.

debt-equity ratio Or, *debt to net worth ratio*. Method used in analyzing FINANCIAL STATEMENTS to determine the amount of financial protection for CREDITORS. The ratio equals total LIABILITIES divided by total STOCKHOLDERS' EQUITY. High ratios indicate high business RISK because of the need to pay high INTEREST costs relative to ASSETS. Creditors are reluctant to extend CREDIT to a highly LEVERAGED company.

The type of business a corporation is involved with affects the size of its debt-equity ratio. BANKS have high ratios, but their ASSETS are usually very liquid. Utilities also have higher ratios, but since they are part of a governmentally regulated industry, their rates can be adjusted to increase earnings.

BOOK VALUE is normally used to measure a firm's debt and equity securities in calculating the ratio. A more realistic measure, however, is MARKET VALUE since it adjusts to current MARKET conditions.

debtor One having a legal duty to pay a DEBT to another. The individual to whom the debt is owed is the CREDITOR. In BANKRUPTCY, the debtor is the subject of the proceeding.

decedent A person who has died.

deceptive practice legislation Laws enacted to prohibit deceptive trade practices. They cover door-to-door as well as mail-order selling.

declaration
insurance: A section of an INSURANCE POLICY that provides basic descriptive information about the insured person and/or property, the premium to be paid, the time period of the coverage, and the policy limits.

securities: An announcement to pay dividends as a result of the board of directors' decision.
See also DECLARATION DATE.
real estate: A legal record used to create a CONDOMINIUM. It encompasses the description of the property, common elements, individual ownership units, and what it is used for.

declaration date The day the DIVIDEND is voted and declared by the board of directors of a corporation. A dividend becomes a legal liability of the company on the declaration date.

declarations section of an insurance policy A section of an INSURANCE POLICY that contains the basic identifying details of the policy. It consists of the name of the policyholder, what is insured, the amount of insurance, the cost of the policy, and the time period covered by the insurance.

declining market A market in which there are more sellers than buyers, resulting in lower prices. Declining markets for real estate or securities may be caused by a recessionary business environment and rising interest rates.

decreased account An account in which the balance has been reduced, as by making a payment or returning merchandise.

decreasing term TERM INSURANCE in which the protection decreases over the life of the policy.
See also INSURANCE PROGRAMS; LIFE INSURANCE.

decreasing term life insurance A type of TERM LIFE INSURANCE that provides decreasing death benefits while the premiums remain constant.

decreasing term policy *See* DECREASING TERM LIFE INSURANCE.

decree The judicial decision in a litigated case, rendered by a court of law. For example, the court decision may require one party to a contract to carry out a specific condition under it.

deductible (of an insurance policy) The amount that an INSURED must pay on any insured loss before payment by the insurance company begins, usually on a per illness or per accident basis. The DEDUCTIBLE is paid by the insured or by another insurance policy in the event that multiple coverage exists.

deduction Those expenses allowed by the INTERNAL REVENUE SERVICE to be deducted from the individual's ADJUSTED GROSS INCOME (AGI). Allowable deductions include home MORTGAGE interest payments, state and local INCOME TAXES, charitable contributions, and employee expenses.
See also ITEMIZED DEDUCTIONS; STANDARD DEDUCTION.

deductions for adjusted gross income A tax computation in which certain tax deductible items are subtracted from the taxpayer's gross income to produce the adjusted gross income. These deductions, shown on Form 1040, include alimony payments, contributions to an individual retirement account (IRA) or Keogh pension plan, and penalties in the early withdrawal of savings.

deed A written document used to convey TITLE to real estate, when properly executed and delivered.
See also QUITCLAIM DEED; WARRANTY DEED.

deed in lieu of foreclosure A legal instrument that transfers real estate to the lender after the borrower defaults on his or her mortgage payments. The borrower should demand cancellation of the unpaid debt and a letter to that effect from the lender. This method relieves the lender of the inconvenience of FORECLOSURE proceedings and waiting out any required redemption periods. It is a voluntary act by both borrower and lender.

deed of trust (trust deed) A document that conveys title to a neutral third party (TRUSTEE) during the period in which the MORTGAGE LOAN is outstanding as security for DEBT.

deep discount bond A bond selling for a discount of 25% or more than its face value, usually because the coupon rate is lower than current YIELDS on newly issued bonds. A deep discount bond is sold when the issuing company is in financial difficulty. Its price appreciates faster as interest rates decline and falls faster as interest rates rise.
See also ORIGINAL ISSUE DISCOUNT (OID); ZERO-COUPON BOND.

deep-in-the-money Term used to describe the value of STOCK or index OPTIONS that differ significantly from the MARKET PRICE of the underlying SECURITY or INDEX. A CALL OPTION is deep-in-the-money if its STRIKING PRICE is much lower than the MARKET PRICE. Such a CALL could be WRITTEN or sold if a STOCKHOLDER of the underlying SECURITY is BEARISH on the STOCK and wants to protect the original INVESTMENT if the stock does indeed fall in price.

A PUT OPTION is deep-in-the-money if its STRIKING PRICE is significantly above the MARKET PRICE of the related security. This PUT would be desirable to sell by an individual who SHORTED the underlying stock and is anticipating that it may rise in price. The price increase of the SHORTED stock would be COVERED by the proceeds of the PUT option up to the STRIKING PRICE of the put.

Options that are deep-in-the-money have very little PREMIUM since their STRIKING PRICE is significantly different from the MARKET PRICE of the underlying security.

default Failure to meet the conditions of a LOAN contract (such as a MORTGAGE). It generally refers to the failure to meet the payments (INTEREST or PRINCIPAL, or both) as scheduled.

default charge Or, *penalty charge*. An additional charge generally calculated on an installment payment that is not paid when due.

default risk The likelihood that a bondholder will not receive the promised interest and bond redemption when due.

defeasance

contract: A specific act that causes a CONTRACT to become null and void.

corporate finance: A way to remove low INTEREST-cost LOANS from a BALANCE SHEET by securing higher interest-bearing SECURITIES to satisfy the LOAN payments. Such an action involves depositing the higher yielding securities in an IRREVOCABLE TRUST dedicated to redeeming the lower cost loan.

In a variation of the theme, a client could instruct a BROKER to perform a market purchase of an older outstanding BOND issue of a company and then exchange it for a SECURITY ISSUE that is later sold at a profit.

real estate: A MORTGAGE clause permitting the mortgagee to redeem the property after a DEFAULT. Thus, if the BORROWER defaults on the mortgage and agrees to pay the entire DEBT within the DEFEASANCE period, the property can be purchased by the borrower.

defendant

civil: The party against whom a judicial action is brought by a complainant for restitution of property or resolution of a complaint.

criminal: The accused.

defense insurance *See* AUTOMOBILE LIABILITY INSURANCE.

defense of suit against insured A clause in a LIABILITY INSURANCE CONTRACT in which the insurance company agrees to defend an INSURED in a lawsuit without merit. The insurance company agrees to pay the cost of litigation in addition to the liability COVERAGE of the POLICY. Thus, if a policy has a $250,000 liability coverage limitation and the legal costs are $75,000, the insurance company will pay the legal costs in addition to the $250,000 liability coverage.

defensive investment Any investment, domestic or foreign, undertaken principally to insure against loss rather than to make a profit. More often than not, such an investment is made in response to the actions of competitors. For example, in the 1970s the U.S. government was encouraging the domestic development of processes to produce petroleum from shale and coal. While such a synthetic fuel probably could never be produced as cheaply as natural petroleum from the Middle East, it represented a defensive investment to help ensure a source of supply.

defensive securities SECURITIES that have stable prices even in business downturns and market declines and provide a safe return on invested money. In other words, they are RECESSION-resistant. Examples are government bonds and stocks and debt of stable entities, including utilities and consumer products.

See also DEFENSIVE STOCK.

defensive stock Or, *countercyclical stocks.* COMMON STOCKS that tend to exhibit price movements contrary to the downward movements of the BUSINESS CYCLE. The prices of these stocks are expected to remain stable during contractions in business activity.

See also DEFENSIVE SECURITIES.

defer To postpone making a personal finance decision to a later time. For example, an individual may delay making an investment decision until he or she obtains advice from a tax adviser.

deferred annuity Or, *deferred payment annuity.*

1. An ANNUITY that begins fixed payments after a period of years.

2. An ANNUITY that does not begin to pay off until a specified time period elapses or an event such as a sixtieth birthday or retirement occurs.

See also ANNUITY; RETIREMENT AND PENSION PLANNING.

deferred annuity contract *See* DEFERRED ANNUITY.

deferred compensation *See* STOCK OPTION PLAN.

deferred contribution plan A method for an employer to add an unused profit sharing plan deduction (credit carryover) to a future contribution on a TAX DEDUCTIBLE basis. The employer's contribution to a PROFIT SHARING PLAN must be less than the annual 15% of employee compensation permitted under the Federal Tax Code.

deferred group annuity A group RETIREMENT PLAN consisting of lifetime income payments that commence after a future scheduled period of time and continue for life. A BENEFICIARY may receive additional payments after the death of the annuitant assuming the annuity is a REFUND ANNUITY in which the payments continue to be annuitized.

With a deferred group annuity, employee contributions are used to buy an annual paid-up single-premium deferred annuity. Added together these increments provide income payments at retirement to the annuitant or the annuitant's beneficiary.

See also REFUND ANNUITY.

deferred maintenance In REAL ESTATE, a type of physical depreciation resulting from lack of normal upkeep, such as broken windows and discolored paint, that adversely affects the value of a piece of property.

deferred payment annuity *See* DEFERRED ANNUITY.

deferred payments Payments to be delayed until a later time.

deferred premium life A LIFE INSURANCE PREMIUM that is not currently due. Payments are made on an installment basis other than annually.

deferred profit-sharing plan Profits a company pays to an employee TRUST during profitable years. Profits are normally distributed as a percentage of the employee's SALARY with 5% being the normal distribution formula. If the PROFIT-SHARING PLAN is QUALIFIED by the IRS, employee contributions are a deductible business expense.

The contributions are not currently taxable to the employee but are taxable at the time of DISTRIBUTION.

deferred retirement The RETIREMENT INCOME received by an employee electing to RETIRE after the NORMAL RETIREMENT AGE of 65 or 70. Depending on the deferred retirement plan, the size of the employee's retirement income may not increase.

deferred sales charges Commissions on LOAD and NO-LOAD MUTUAL FUNDS. Charges may range from 1% to 6% assessed on the investor if the shares are redeemed within a certain time period after purchase.

deferred vesting An employee's vesting of purchased PENSION rights subsequent to meeting specified conditions. These conditions include years of service with an employer, being a RETIREMENT PLAN member for a given period, or other requirements. Immediate vesting provides full pension rights when an employee initially begins the plan.

Under the rules of the EMPLOYEE RETIREMENT INCOME SECURITY ACT OF 1974 (ERISA) and the TAX REFORM ACT OF 1986, the two options are 100% vesting is required after five years, or 20% VESTING after three years of service, 40% at the end of four years of service, 60% at the end of five years of service, 80% at the end of six years of service, and 100% at the end of seven years of service.

deficiency An amount of MONEY below what is expected.
finance: When a person's liabilities exceed his or her assets.
income tax: An additional amount of money the IRS determines a taxpayer owes. Deficiency rulings can be appealed to the Tax Court.

deficiency letter
securities: Formal notification to a prospective issuer of new securities by the SECURITIES AND EXCHANGE COMMISSION that the offering PROSPECTUS is in need of revision or expansion. Such notices require prompt attention or the offering will be put in jeopardy.
income tax: A letter from the IRS informing a taxpayer of a tax insufficiency that needs to be remedied. The taxpayer has 90 days to file an appeal with the Tax Court.

deficit An excess of expenditure over income, resulting in insufficient funds that must be made up either by reducing savings or investments or through borrowing.

defined benefit pension plan An employee RETIREMENT PLAN that has a predefined RETIREMENT INCOME benefit formula with a variable contribution formula. The PENSION benefit formula usually is based on the worker's SALARY level as the RETIREMENT date is approached. Defined benefit pension plans are dependent on an adequate funding pattern to assure that sufficient funds are available to satisfy the promised benefits.

There are two types of defined benefit pension plans:

1. *fixed dollars:* Under this concept are the (a) UNIT BENEFIT approach having DISCRETE units of benefits being credited for years of service; (b) the LEVEL PERCENTAGE OF COMPENSATION in which all employees after a minimum age (usually 50) receive the same percentage of earnings after a minimum period of service (usually 20 years); and (c) the FLAT AMOUNT in which all employees receive the same total dollar amount of retirement benefits after they meet minimum requirements for age (over 50) and years of service (usually over 20).

2. *variable dollars:* There are two concepts in the variable dollar approach. (a) In the COST-OF-LIVING PLAN the dollar amounts of the pension are varied according to increases in the cost of living as normally measured by the CONSUMER PRICE INDEX (CPI), and (b) the EQUITY ANNUITY PLAN in which employee premiums purchase units in a VARIABLE ANNUITY plan; on the employee's retirement, these are converted to fluctuating RETIREMENT units consistent with the value of the underlying common STOCK PORTFOLIO.

defined contribution pension plan A PENSION plan in which employee contributions are fixed and benefits vary according to a formula. The formula may consider such factors as years of service, salary levels, and age. The organization benefits from a defined contribution plan be-cause it knows what its employee benefit costs will be; the employee benefits since there is no fixed RETIREMENT benefit, allowing for the possibility of future growth.

A defined contribution plan forces the organization to budget for continuous benefit payments, but it faces no future pension liability since most defined contribution plans are also FUNDED PENSION PLANS. Thus, employees are assured of receiving their benefits irrespective of whether the organization is in existence when they retire.

deflation A general decrease in prices. It is the opposite of INFLATION and distinguished from disinflation, which is a reduction in the rate of price increases. Deflation is caused by a reduction in the money stock of the economy.
See also INFLATION.

delayed delivery Delivery, by mutual consent of all involved parties, of the SECURITIES involved at a date later than the customary time, which is usually five business days after the TRADE DATE.
seller's option: a CONTRACT agreed to by both parties to a TRADE that allows for delayed delivery. This form of delivery is quite common in FUTURES trading.
See also DELIVERY DATE.

delayed (tax-free) exchange *See* 1031 TAX-FREE EXCHANGE.

delayed opening
securities: A delay in the start of trading in a particular SECURITY. A delayed opening normally occurs when there is an imbalance of buy and sell orders on a given security at the beginning of a trading day for any number of reasons. As the floor SPECIALIST cannot match up the buy and sell orders, the specialist requests permission from the EXCHANGE to delay the opening of trading of the STOCK until the orders can be matched.

A delay in the opening of a security can also occur when there is news pending from the company, and the president or chief executive officer of the company requests the exchange to delay opening trading until a public announcement is made. An example is an announcement of a pending TAKEOVER offer.

delayed retirement credit Incentives built into Social Security to encourage people to continue working past age 65.

delinquency Being in arrears in a payment on a tax or obligation when due.

delinquency charges clause A late payment charge that installment lenders impose if the payment is not made within a specified time period.

delinquent tax A TAX that is unpaid subsequent to the DUE DATE. Taxpayers owing delinquent taxes are usually penalized by the imposition of penalties, including interest as well as increased payments. In the most severe case, a legal JUDGMENT can be placed against the property in question. Additional penalties can include the possibility of imprisonment for the individual owing the taxes.

delisting Withdrawal of a particular SECURITY from trading on a SECURITIES EXCHANGE. STOCKS can be delisted when the company violates minimum standards of the exchange including failure to maintain a minimum NET WORTH, not having the required number of shareholders, or conviction of certain illegalities.

Of course, when a company is merged into another company or is no longer publicly TRADED, it will be removed from the exchange. This activity should not be confused with delisting in which the company's stock is not permitted to be traded because of nonconformance with basic exchange policies.

delivery The transfer of stocks from a seller to a buyer. The certificate representing shares bought in the regular way on the NEW YORK STOCK EXCHANGE normally is delivered to the purchaser's broker on the fourth business day after the transaction.

delivery date The date a seller is required to deliver something of value. SECURITIES trading has three kinds of delivery:

1. *cash:* Delivery occurs on the same day of the trade.

2. *regular way:* Delivery occurs in five trading days from the date of the original trade.

3. *seller's option:* The seller selects the date of delivery anywhere from 6 to 60 days.

delivery price
merchandise: The final price of a delivered item including delivery expenses, taxes, and any other special considerations.
futures trading: The price determined by the clearing house for futures deliveries. This also determines the amount needed in performance of the sale.

demand deposit A CHECKING ACCOUNT. Deposit from which funds can be withdrawn on demand and from which funds may be transferred to another party by means of CHECK.

demand loan Or, *demand note.* An obligation with no set maturity date, payable on demand by the lender. The interest is computed from the date of the loan to its repayment date.

demise
1. The giving or transference of an ESTATE by BEQUEST, charter, or CONTRACT for a period of time or life.
2. The making of a charter or LEASE for a period of years.

demising clause A CLAUSE found in a LEASE whereby the landlord (lessor) leases and the TENANT (lessee) takes the property.

demographics An analysis of housing needs, household size, ages, occupations, marital status, and other factors.

denomination The amount stated on the face of currency, stock, bonds. For example, a bond is usually issued in $1,000 denominations and the value of $1,000 will be inscribed on its FACE. This term corresponds to FACE VALUE or PAR VALUE.

dental insurance A type of health insurance to pay for dental care, typically including preventive expenses such as oral examinations, cleanings, and fillings, as well as treatment of dental injuries sustained through accidents.

dependent One who relies on the support of another person.
taxpayer: A dependent can be declared as a tax deduction on the tax return provided the taxpayer gave over half of the person's support.

dependent coverage Insurance protection that covers the dependents of a family.

depletion The physical exhaustion or using up of a natural resource, for example, a depleted coal mine or oil well. Depletion is an expense of the company.
accounting: The cost of depletion whereby depletion expense is debited and accumulated depletion is credited.

deposit
1. Money that the purchaser puts down to indicate his or her willingness to follow through with the PURCHASE AGREEMENT.
2. Funds placed in account and credited to the depositor.

deposit insurance INSURANCE on certain bank accounts provided by a federal agency. For example, a bank account is insured for $100,000 by the FEDERAL DEPOSIT INSURANCE CORPORATION (FDIC).

deposit or "earnest money" MONEY deposited with an individual for SECURITY for the performance of some contract. Deposit or earnest money can be forfeited if the depositor DEFAULTS on the terms of the CONTRACT.

deposit term life insurance A policy in which the premium (deposit) in the initial policy year is added to the regular term insurance premiums. The deposit will then earn interest. At a later date specified in the contract (e.g., 20 years), the policyholder can receive the deposit plus interest or may renew the policy without having to provide evidence of insurability. At the option of the holder, the deposit term policy may be converted to ordinary life or decreasing term life. In that event, the policyholder cancels the policy before the designated elapsed period (20 years in this case), and the deposit and interest thereon is forfeited. If the insured dies, the deposit and interest are added to the death benefit.

deposition A witness's testimony to a series of written questions or interrogatories, not in open court but in pursuance of a court order. A written word-for-word account is taken in all depositions. They are witnessed and intended to be used in civil or criminal actions.

Depositions are given under oath by a deponent outside the courtroom, often in an attorney's office.

depreciation
in general:
1. Cost of use as well as obsolescence of a fixed asset such as an automobile.
2. Charges against earnings to write off the cost, less salvage value, of an asset over its estimated useful life. It is a bookkeeping entry, not a cash expense.
real estate: The decrease in the value of property due to use, obsolescence, deterioration, normal wear and tear, or the passing of time.

depreciation base The recorded cost of a fixed ASSET that is to be recovered through DEPRECIATION excluding the asset's salvage value. For example, if an individual buys a car having an estimated life of 10 years and a salvage value of $2,000 for $15,000, the DEPRECIATION BASE is $13,000. Using the STRAIGHT-LINE DEPRECIATION METHOD, the depreciation on the car per year would be $1,300 ($13,000/10 years).

depressed market A state of affairs in a MARKET when the prices of products, services, or securities are in extremely poor demand, and characterized by depressed prices and trading activity. Supply exceeds demand in a depressed market.
See also DEPRESSED PRICE.

depressed price The MARKET PRICE of a particular good, service, or SECURITY is depressed because its related market is suffering from low prices and low demand. Trading activity is extremely low. Supply exceeds demand.
See also DEPRESSED MARKET.

depression A bottom phase of a BUSINESS CYCLE in which the economy is operating with substantial unemployment of its resources (such as labor), a depressed rate of business investment and consumer spending, and lack of public confidence. An example is the Great Depression of the 1930s. Depression is a much worse situation than a RECESSION. The economy is at a virtual standstill.
See also BUSINESS CYCLE; RECESSION.

descent When an owner of REAL ESTATE dies INTESTATE, having no enforceable will, the property descends, by operation of law, to the owner's inheritors.

devise A gift of REAL ESTATE by WILL or last testament. The individual obtaining the property is the DEVISEE while the person giving the property is the DEVISOR.

diagonal spread A PUT or CALL OPTION strategy in which the investor buys and simultaneously sells the same type of option; however, the STRIKING PRICES and MATURITY dates vary. The exact strategy depends on whether an individual is BULLISH or BEARISH on the underlying SECURITY. The immediate objective is to COVER at least part of the cost of the overall INVESTMENT STRATEGY by selling one expiration date of the same class of options to offset the LONG purchase of the other expiration date of the option.

Example: In a BEARISH diagonal spread call option strategy, the INVESTOR sells a near-term expiration date call option having a striking price near the MARKET PRICE of the STOCK while simultaneously buying a far-term OUT-OF-THE-MONEY call option with a further expiration date. The investor hopes the SHORTED near-term call option will expire if the market price of the underlying stock declines while HEDGING the strategy by being long on the OUT-OF-THE-MONEY call option if the underlying stock rises. Thus, if the market price of the stock rises, the OUT-OF-THE-MONEY call option would rise in value, offsetting the loss of the shorted near-term lower striking price call. The profit in the BEARISH diagonal spread is in the difference between the proceeds of the near-term call option less the cost of the far-term OUT-OF-THE-MONEY call option.

In the BULLISH diagonal spread strategy, the INVESTOR would sell a near-term expiration date OUT-OF-THE-MONEY CALL OPTION while simultaneously buying a far-term call option with a striking price near the MARKET PRICE. The hope is that the near-term out-of-the-money CALL OPTION will expire while the market price of the underlying stock rises just short of its striking price, HEDGING the strategy by being long on the out-of-the-money call. The sale of the near-term out-of-the-money CALL would help to offset, but not COVER, the purchase price of the far-term call and thus reduce the INVESTMENT risk. The profit potential is in the rise in value of the far-term call option after the near-term OUT-OF-THE-MONEY option expires.

It is never possible to SHORT the far-term expiration date option while buying a near-term

DIAGONAL SPREAD STRATEGY (BEARISH)

Purchase	Striking Price	Cost	Sale	Striking Price	Proceeds	Cost
2 October XYZ Calls	40	$400	2 July XYZ Calls	35	$800	($800–$400)
Net Proceeds		$400				

DIAGONAL SPREAD STRATEGY (BULLISH)

Purchase	Striking Price	Cost	Sale	Striking Price	Proceeds	Cost
2 October XYZ Calls	35	$800	2 July XYZ Calls	40	$300	($800–$300)
Net Proceeds		($500)				

option since the earlier expiration date of the purchased option would not provide COVERAGE for the shorted far-term option.

diamond
n. A precious stone used for jewelry. A diamond is graded on both purity and weight. Diamonds come in many shapes.

Diamonds have proved to be high return INVESTMENTS as well as INFLATION HEDGES.
adj. A REAL ESTATE term describing a piece of property, often a home. A piece of real estate described as a diamond is one requiring absolutely no initial repair or cosmetic work; it is in outstanding condition and appearance, which adds to its value and salability.

diary A daily written record of all developments, including meetings, conversations, and expenses.
expense diary: A daily written record of all expenses according to their purpose. For example, travel expenses by date and purpose are recorded including meals, lodging, mileage, public transportation costs, and telephone calls. A diary can be used as supporting documentation when one is attempting to prove expenses actually incurred. The INTERNAL REVENUE SERVICE requires or suggests that a diary be kept to support the TAX deductibility of promotion and entertainment, mileage allowance on a car used for business, and business deductibility for computer usage.

differential A difference in REVENUES and/or COSTS caused by an extraordinary event or circumstance.
securities: Amount paid to a DEALER or ODD-LOT

TRADER, for the completion of an odd-lot transaction. An odd-lot transaction is any purchase of shares that numbers fewer than a round lot, 100 shares. Normally the charge is one-eighth of a point or .125 cents per share, which is either added to the purchase price or subtracted from the sale price.
personnel: An extra amount added to a wage for working either in unusual conditions or nonstandard work hours. Anyone who works under these conditions is entitled to the wage differential. WAGE differentials often are the subject of collective bargaining agreements.
commodities: The PREMIUM or DISCOUNT paid for quality differences in selected commodities.

diminishing marginal satisfaction Conditions in which an individual, as he or she continues to use a good or service, finds it to be less satisfying.

Diners Club A travel, entertainment, and exclusive retail purchase CREDIT CARD. The Diners Club has a Club Awards program in which points are earned by making retail purchases that can be redeemed with items from a Diners Club merchandise catalogue. No-fee TRAVELERS CHECKS are also provided with an approved vendor.

The monthly bill must be paid in full upon receiving the statement. After six months, the Diners Club member may apply for a Club Plus Account in which extended CREDIT can be granted. An annual membership fee is charged.

direct damage
law: Damages that ordinarily arise from a violation of CONTRACT from which COMPENSATION may be recovered.

insurance: Damage caused from an INSURED PERIL, for example, fire, which is the PROXIMATE CAUSE of destruction to the structure of a building or its contents.

direct investment

1. Investment in a foreign corporation in which the investor has a controlling interest.

2. The purchase of an active ownership interest in a company, whether of a controlling or a substantial minority interest. This is contrasted with purchasing shares in a company and taking a nonactive posture.

direct liability

1. A confirmed financial LIABILITY on the part of a DEBTOR for any MONEY, objects, or services received. There are no extenuating circumstances as, for example, in an INDIRECT LIABILITY where an individual acts as a guarantor of another's direct liability.

2. A legal obligation resulting from an act of omission or commission. A liability can be imposed by a court of law on a defendant to the plaintiff in an action where damages are claimed and awarded.

direct ownership A type of ownership in which one or more investors have legal TITLE to an investment such as REAL ESTATE.

direct purchase A way of acquiring shares in an OPEN-END MUTUAL FUND, in which the investor simply orders and pays for the shares ordered plus any commissions. Contrasts with the role of a broker or financial service agent.

direct reduction mortgage (DRM) A fully amortized MORTGAGE requiring periodic payments that include both interest and partial repayment of principal. Typically, in the initial years of the loan the amount paid for principal is less and the amount paid for interest is more. This payment pattern gradually reverses in the later years. The periodic payment may include real estate taxes.

direct seller An INSURANCE company that sells its policies directly through salaried employees, mail-order marketing, or newspapers.

direct writing system A system for distributing INSURANCE without employing independent middlemen. The buyer deals directly with the insurer.

disability The inability, either in part or in whole, of the INSURED to perform duties related to his or her present occupation.

disability benefit Benefit that covers a PERIL in which a person is medically disabled, in whole or in part.

disability clause A clause in a LIFE INSURANCE policy that may contain either a waiver of premium benefit or a waiver of premium coupled with disability.

disability income exclusion An income tax provision under which a portion of a taxpayer's income is TAX EXEMPT in the case of disability.

disability income insurance A kind of INSURANCE that replaces a portion of the income lost in the event of disability.
See also DISABILITY INSURANCE.

disability income portion A portion of a DISABILITY clause under which the insured is entitled to a monthly income equal to $5 to $10 per $1,000 of the policy's face value.

disability income rider An amendment to a LIFE INSURANCE policy that provides coverage for payment of income to the policyholder in the event of DISABILITY.

disability insurance INSURANCE to provide regular cash income when an insured person is unable to work as a result of a covered illness, injury, or disease. Most disability payments are tax exempt as long as the individual policyholder pays the premium. The rule is that an adequate disability plan should provide at least 60% of the individual's current gross income. This figure is based on the assumption that some of the disability benefits will be tax free. If one owns a business or practice, he or she may need higher coverage to provide cash flow to cover business overhead.

disbursement   Payment in CASH or by CHECK in discharge of a DEBT or to pay an expense.
See also DISCHARGE.

disbursing agent   An institution that makes payment for another entity. An example is a trust department of a bank that pays the dividends of a company directly to stockholders.

discharge   Remove a financial obligation by making the appropriate payment in full.
mortgage: A MORTGAGE discharge is a document formally stating that a mortgage debt has been fully satisfied and is usually recorded in a local property deeds registry.

discharge of bankruptcy   An order whereby the BANKRUPT debtor is relieved of responsibility to pay his or her obligations. Although the debtor is no longer liable for discharged obligations, the bankruptcy will remain in his or her credit report for ten years.

discharge of lien   An order withdrawing a property lien subsequent to satisfaction of the claim through payment or other means.

disclaimer
accounting: Statement by an auditor not having sufficient evidence to form an AUDIT OPINION. For example, some uncertainty, such as a pending lawsuit, exists, which could seriously jeopardize the firm's profitability.
ownership: Giving up any ownership claim to property to which ownership was formerly asserted.
real estate: Renunciation of a claim to real property. For example, a piece of property becomes dilapidated and the absentee owner disclaims any ownership rights to the property.
warranty: Wording that specifically renounces any responsibility if certain circumstances occur; for example, the warranty on a camera is voided if the camera is submersed in water.

disclosure
accounting: All material and relevant information concerning a company's financial position and the results of operations, shown either in the financial statements or in the footnotes accompanying the statements. Disclosure usually contains information regarding the terms of major borrowing arrangements and the existence of large contingent LIABILITIES, contractual leasing arrangements, employee pension and bonus plans, major proposed asset acquisitions, accounting methods and changes in those methods used in preparing the financial statements, and other significant events including labor strikes, raw material shortages, and pending legislation or lawsuits.
The SECURITIES AND EXCHANGE COMMISSION (SEC) also requires special disclosures detailing any specific and unique developments affecting a company's financial position in Form 8-K. For example, a publicly TRADED company suffering an extreme disaster directly affecting its financial position should file this form.
new securities: Revelation by a company of all the pertinent financial and legal information concerning the company. Such information, which is included in the PROSPECTUS, is required by the SEC when a firm seeks to make a SECURITY or BOND public.
loans: Statement by the lending agency of the full amount of all the associated costs when making a LOAN. The TRUTH-IN-LENDING ACT (TILA), as amended in 1970, requires that CREDIT costs be expressed both in dollar amounts and in annual percentage terms based on the unpaid account balance. This act extends to the issuance, liability, and use of consumer CREDIT CARDS.

disclosure statement   A written statement of a borrower's rights under the TRUTH-IN-LENDING LAW and statement of all interest charges, which must be disclosed by a lender.
See also FULL DISCLOSURE.

discount
in general: Any price or CHARGE that is appreciably below that charged for comparable items or services.
business: A reduction in the amount given for prompt payment for an item. For example, if

payment is made within 10 days after purchase, a retail store offers a customer a 2% discount. The discount on a $500 retail purchase would be $10 ($500 × 2%).

A reduction in the unit selling price of merchandise due to a large quantity order.

bonds: The dollar or point difference between the price of a SECURITY and its redemption value. For example, a BOND having a FACE VALUE of $1,000 is selling at a $75 discount if its market value is $925.
See also BOND DISCOUNT.

securities: A description of a security selling at less than its face value but redeemable at face value. For example, ZERO COUPON BONDS are discount securities.

currencies: A term describing the relationship between two currencies. For example, the English pound may sell at a discount to the German mark.

news: The MARKET VALUE of a security reflects the impact of news having long-term consequences. For example, a company declares it is seeking protection under Chapter 11 of the Bankruptcy Code in order to protect itself from creditors.

The stock market as a whole may discount news by falling or rising on information concerning, for example, the general state of the economy. This is also termed "discounting the news."

bank loan: The deduction of INTEREST on a LOAN in advance.

cash: A method of reducing the price of an item or service in exchange for CASH payment.

Treasury bills: The practice of selling Treasury bills at less than FACE VALUE and redeeming them at full face value.

discount bond A BOND having a market price less than its face value. An example is a bond with a face value of $1,000 whose current market price is $980. Each year the bondholder receives interest on the face of the bond. The yield is determined based on the purchase price of $980 rather than the maturity value of $1,000. The discounted amount of $20 ($1,000

− $980) to be received at MATURITY is included in the yield calculation. *See also* BOND DISCOUNT; DEEP DISCOUNT BOND; ORIGINAL ISSUE DISCOUNT; ZERO COUPON BOND; YIELD TO MATURITY.

discount broker A STOCKBROKER who charges a reduced commission and does not provide investment advice.
See also FULL-SERVICE BROKER.

discount charge

1. In a new SECURITY offering, the UNDERWRITER will charge a discount to the company making the offering for its services in bringing the issue public. For example, if a company is issuing a STOCK to the public at $10 per SHARE and the discount charge is one-quarter of a point, the net amount raised for the new company is $9.75 ($10 − $.25). The discount charge also incorporates the basic commission a retail security client would normally pay when purchasing a security.

2. In banking, the BANK discount charge when a NOTE receivable is discounted at the bank before its MATURITY DATE. The bank discount charge equals

> Bank Discount Rate × Maturity Value of the Note × Period the note will be held by the bank.

> *Example*:

> A $1,000, six-month, 8% note is discounted at the bank after two months. The bank discount charge of 10% is computed below:

Face value of note	$1,000
Interest to maturity/	
$1,000 × 8% × 6½	40
Maturity value	$1,040
Bank Discount Charge =	
$1,040 × 10% × 4½	$34.67

discount house Or, *discount broker*. A securities BROKERAGE FIRM providing basic SECURITY transaction services to the public at a lower charge, or discounted COMMISSIONS. A discount house does not attempt to provide the same services a full-service and full-charge brokerage firm supplies.

Thus, a discount house normally does not provide INVESTMENT advice. A client is expected to perform his or her own independent SECURITY research.

discount interest *See* DISCOUNT METHOD.

discount loan A LOAN in which the whole interest charge is deducted in advance from the face value of a loan. The borrower receives the face value of the loan minus this deduction, which increases the EFFECTIVE INTEREST RATE on the loan. Assume an individual borrows $10,000 from the bank at a 10% interest on a discount basis. The effective interest rate is

$$\$1,000/(\$10,000 - \$1,000) = \$1,000/\$9,000$$
$$= 11.11\%$$

discount method A method of calculating interest by which the FINANCE CHARGES are calculated and then subtracted from the amount of the loan. The difference between the amount of the loan and the finance charges is then lent to the borrower.
See also DISCOUNT LOAN.

discount points An additional charge made by lenders on HOME MORTGAGES payable in cash at the time of the CLOSING. For example, if 2 points are charged on a $100,000 mortgage, the charge would be $2,000 ($100,000 × 2%). In comparison shopping for a mortgage, consideration should be given to both the INTEREST RATE and points (if any).

discount rate The amount charged member banks for loans from the FEDERAL RESERVE BANK.

discount yield The RATE OF RETURN on investments that are purchased below face value with the gain at sale or maturity representing interest

income for federal income tax purposes. For example, the annual discount yield on securities such as Treasury bills (T-bills) is calculated using the following formula:

$$\frac{P_1 - P_0}{P_1} \times \frac{360}{n}$$

where P_1 = redemption price (usually $10,000), P_0 = purchase price, and n = maturity in days. T-bills sold at $9,800 and maturing at $10,000 in 90 days have the following discount yield:

$$\frac{\$10,000 - \$9,800}{\$10,000} \times \frac{360}{90} = \frac{\$200}{\$10,000} \times 4 = .08 = 8\%$$

discounted cash flow A method of estimating the value or asking price of an investment such as a real estate investment, which emphasizes after-tax cash flows and the return on the invested dollars discounted over time to reflect a discounted yield. Under this method, the asking price or value of a real estate investment is the present worth of the future AFTER-TAX CASH FLOWS from the investment, DISCOUNTED at the rate of return required by the investor.

Example: An investor requires a rate of return of 10% on a piece of property advertised for sale at $150,000. He or she estimates that rents can be increased each year for five years. The investor expects that after all expenses he or she would have an after-tax cash flow in each of the five years, respectively, of $5,000, $5,200, $5,400, $5,600, and $5,800. The investor anticipates that this property can sell for $200,000 at the end of the fifth year. How much should he or she be willing to pay for this property?

The PRESENT VALUE table can be set up as follows:

Years	After-tax cash flow	Present value of $1 at 10%	Total present value
1	$5,000	.909	$4,545
2	5,200	.826	4,295
3	5,400	.751	4,055
4	5,600	.683	3,825
5	5,800	.621	3,602
Sell property	$200,000	.621	$124,200
Present value of property			$144,522

Using this technique the investor would be willing to pay $144,522 for the property.
See also PRESENT VALUE ANALYSIS.

discounting
   1. The process of finding the present worth of a future sum of money.
See also DISCOUNTED CASH FLOW; TIME VALUE OF MONEY.
   2. Advancing or lending money with a deduction of interest thereon.
See also DISCOUNT LOAN; DISCOUNT METHOD.

discretionary account   An ACCOUNT in which the investor gives full or partial written permission to an INVESTMENT ADVISER or BROKER to buy or sell securities at the adviser's discretion. Discretion can be limited to a specific SECURITY or group of securities. Investment advisers or BROKERS having discretionary accounts have complete latitude, unless specifically restricted, to choose the securities as well as their price and timing.

dishonor   Repudiating the payment or acceptance of a FINANCIAL INSTRUMENT such as a CHECK. For example, a BANK declines to CASH a check because of the account's lack of money.

disinflation   Slowing down of the rate of INFLATION. This condition usually occurs during a recession, when a lack of consumer demand prohibits retailers from passing on higher prices to consumers.
See also DEFLATION.

disposable income   Personal income left after taxes and other deductions from GROSS INCOME. It is the amount of take-home pay a worker receives after all deductions are withheld for taxes, insurance, union dues, and the like.

dissavings   An excess of spending over income. It occurs when one lives beyond one's means.

distribution
marketing: The movement of goods from the manufacturer to the consumer through wholesalers and retailers.

estate: The distribution of property to the legal HEIRS by the EXECUTOR of a properly drawn and executed WILL.
mutual funds: The payout by MUTUAL FUNDS and CLOSED-END INVESTMENT COMPANIES of realized CAPITAL GAINS on SECURITIES contained in the underlying PORTFOLIO.
securities: The sale of a large BLOCK of STOCK managed to prevent a fall in price of the SECURITY. A security distribution indicates to stock TECHNICIANS that the price of a particular security is coming under pressure and is about to fall in price.
economics: The allocation of national income throughout the population.
stockholders: A return of capital invested such as dividends to distribute part of the net income.

distribution period   The period of time between the date a stock DIVIDEND is declared by the board of directors of a company and the DATE OF RECORD when the STOCKHOLDER must officially own the STOCK to be entitled to the dividend.

diversification
   1. The spreading of investment money among many investment vehicles so as to reduce RISK. Diversification is also offered by the securities of many individual companies because of the wide range of their activities. Investing in a MUTUAL FUND will also accomplish diversification.
See also ASSET ALLOCATION; MUTUAL FUND; PORTFOLIO.
   2. Having different jobs or sources of income to protect against the loss of one.

diversified common stock fund   STOCK FUNDS, both CLOSED and OPEN, in which at least 75% of the assets are INVESTED in CASH, GOVERNMENT SECURITIES, SECURITIES of other INVESTMENT COMPANIES, and other securities. The guiding principle is to have no more than 5% of the management company's total ASSETS invested in the securities of any one issuer, and having no more than 10% of the voting securities of any issuing CORPORATION.

dividend

securities: A portion of the net income of a firm paid, at the discretion of the board of directors, to the STOCKHOLDERS OF RECORD. The most typical type of DIVIDEND is a CASH distribution; however, STOCK DIVIDENDS can also be made. Cash dividends are TAXABLE to the stockholder upon receipt, whereas stock dividends are not.

PREFERRED STOCK dividends have a priority claim by their owners over COMMON STOCK dividends.

insurance: CASH returned to an INSURANCE POLICYHOLDER by the insurance company. Insurance dividends are not deemed to be taxable by the INTERNAL REVENUE SERVICE as they are considered to be a REFUND of the PREMIUM paid.

dividend payout ratio

The DIVIDEND payment as a percentage of NET EARNINGS of a company. It equals dividends per share divided by earnings per SHARE. Generally speaking, newer and smaller companies pay a much lower percentage of earnings in dividends than larger, more mature companies. A company having a relatively large dividend payout ratio may have that much less CAPITAL for reinvestment purposes. Utilities commonly have high dividend payout ratios.

For example, if a company's net income is $1,000,000 and the CASH dividends are $100,000 with 25,000 common shares, the dividend payout ratio is

Dividends Per Share = $100,000/25,000 = $4
Earnings Per Share = $1,000,000/25,000 = $40
Dividend Payout Ratio = $4/$40 = 10%

dividend reinvestment plan

1. An investment plan that allows stockholders to acquire shares through reinvestment of DIVIDENDS, directly from the corporation and usually free of brokerage commissions. The shares may be available at a discount. In the case of public utilities, tax breaks are available on dividend reinvestment.

2. An option given by a MUTUAL FUND to reinvest dividends without a service charge.

dividend restrictive provision

A clause in a loan agreement or bond indenture placing a restriction on the amount of dividends a company can pay.

dividend yield

A ratio of DIVIDENDS per share divided by MARKET PRICE per share. A drawback of this ratio is the timing mismatch between the numerator, which is based on the DIVIDEND declaration date, and the year-end MARKET PRICE of the stock. For example, a $20 stock with a $2 dividend per share has a 10% dividend yield: $2/$20 = 10%.

divorce

The legal termination of a marriage. The agreement specifies the settlement rights of the parties. ALIMONY and/or child support may be involved. Alimony payments are tax deductible to the payor and taxable to the receiver. Child support payments are not tax deductible to the payor.

document

1. Anything printed, written, or otherwise noted that is relied on to record or prove something. Examples are wills, brokerage statements, and leases.

2. To substantiate an assertion by providing written or oral evidence to support it. An example are documents filed in a case against the spouse in a divorce action.

dollar-cost averaging

Procedure in which a constant dollar amount of stock or stocks is bought at regularly spaced intervals. The strategy represents time diversification. By investing a constant amount each time, investors buy more shares at a low price and fewer shares at a high price. The practice usually results in a lower average cost per share because the investor buys more shares of stock with the same dollars. The technique is advantageous when a stock price moves within a narrow range. If there is a decrease in stock price, the investor will sustain less of a loss than would ordinarily occur. If there is an increase in stock price, the investor will gain, but less than usual. There are some drawbacks to dollar-cost averaging: (1) The transaction costs are higher and (2) the strategy will not work when stock prices are in a continuous downward direction. Dollar-cost averaging is a conservative investment approach: It avoids the impulse buying that could occur when the investor is tempted to buy when the market is high or sell when the market is low. With the strategy a conservative stock may be purchased with relatively little risk, benefiting from long-term price appreciation. Further, the investor avoids buying too many shares at high prices. In a bear market, many shares are purchased at very depressed prices.

Example:

Date	Investment	Market Price per Share	Shares Acquired
6/1	$100,000	$40	2,500
7/1	100,000	35	2,857
8/1	100,000	34	2,941
9/1	100,000	38	2,632
10/1	100,000	50	2,000

The investor has purchased fewer shares at the higher price and more shares at the lower price. The average price per share is

$$197/5 = \$39.40$$

However, with the $500,000 investment, 12,930 shares have been bought, resulting in a cost per share of $38.67. At 10/1, the market price of stock exceeded the average cost of $38.67, reflecting an attractive gain.

donee   Individual receiving a gift or BEQUEST. A donee receives without first giving a CONSIDERATION. Person receiving a power, right, or interest.

donor
trust: An individual who devises a TRUST for a DONEE. A person acting as a GRANTOR.
gift: Person making a gift to an educational, community, or philanthropic organization.

dormant account
banking: An ACCOUNT in which there is no activity for a sustained period of time. When depositors move without notifying the bank or die leaving the estate uninformed about the account, the account becomes dormant. In many states, dormant accounts are publicly advertised, and if there are no verifiable claims made for the account, the MONEY reverts to the state.

For example, in New York after five years a dormant bank account reverts to the state. Before transferring the account to the state, the bank will give written notification of its intent to the DEPOSITOR. Of course, the depositor can later reclaim his or her money.

double bottom   A chart pattern used in TECHNICAL SECURITY ANALYSIS when a STOCK or STOCK MARKET drops to a certain price level and then

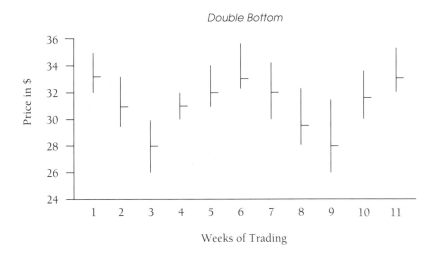

Double Bottom

Weeks of Trading

recovers, only to be followed by another drop in price to the same low. The bottom price is interpreted as a SUPPORT LINE for the stock or MARKET; however, if this support line is subsequently penetrated, then the analysis for the near term future would be very BEARISH (see accompanying chart).

double (treble) damages A damage award, often specified by statute, in which the actual damages awarded by a jury are doubled (tripled).

double indemnity rider An endorsement to a LIFE INSURANCE policy providing that if the INSURED dies by accident, as defined, twice the face amount of the policy will be paid to the BENEFICIARY.

double or triple indemnity An option of a LIFE INSURANCE policy under which payment of twice or three times the face amount of the policy in death benefits is made if the insured is killed in an accident.

double taxation Taxation of DIVIDENDS in which the federal government (1) taxes corporate profits once as corporate income and (2) taxes any part of the remaining profits distributed as dividends to stockholders as individual income.

double-digit inflation A yearly inflation rate of at least 10%.

double top A chart pattern used in TECHNICAL SECURITY ANALYSIS when a STOCK or SECURITY MARKET rises to a certain price level and then falls, only to be followed by a subsequent rise to the previous high price. This double high is interpreted as a RESISTANCE LINE for the stock or market; however, if this price resistance level is penetrated in future trading, then the interpretation for the near term future would be very BULLISH (see accompanying chart below).

Dow theory A theory of market analysis based upon the performance of the DOW-JONES INDUSTRIAL AND TRANSPORTATION stock price averages. The theory says that a BULL market is supposed to continue as long as one average continues to make new highs that are "confirmed" by the other. A reversal is signaled when one average does not confirm the other. A BEAR market is supposed to continue as long as one average makes new lows that are confirmed by the other.

Dow-Jones Industrial Average (DJIA) A price-weighted average of 30 blue-chip stocks, actively traded in the NEW YORK STOCK EXCHANGE. DJIA is calculated by adding the closing prices of the component stocks and using a divisor that is adjusted for splits and stock dividends. Stock splits and stock dividends increase the number of shares outstanding, leading to price decreases that bias the average unless

Double Top

Price in $

Weeks of Trading

they are taken into account. In mid 1986, this divisor value was 0.929, which is substantially less than 30. Examples of stocks included in the DJIA are General Electric, Merck, IBM, and Exxon.
See also MARKET INDICES AND AVERAGES.

down payment A partial payment of the purchase price that is required to be made at the time a purchase agreement is entered into. Normally, down payments are made in CASH. The down payment represents only a portion of the total cost.
See also EARNEST MONEY.

down reversal When the market prices of securities or commodities temporarily drop significantly while overall prices are increasing.
See also UP REVERSAL.

down tick Or, *minus tick*. A transaction of securities at a price below that in the preceding transaction. For example, if a stock has been selling at $23 per share, the next transaction is a down tick if it is at $22 ⅝.
See also UP TICK.

download A term used in TELECOMMUNICATIONS describing the transfer of a data file from one computer to another. The process requires a telephone connection between the two computers, a modem, and telecommunications software for both computers. Various telecommunication protocols are available to accomplish the downloading of data files. The data files can be either binary or text.

Depending on the software and the data transfer speed of the modems, downloading can transfer data at a very high rate of speed.

downside risk

1. An INVESTMENT RISK evaluation derived by estimating the total loss that could occur in a worst-case scenario. A variety of factors enter into such an evaluation including BOOK VALUE and NET EARNINGS as well as general MARKET conditions.

2. A company's RISK of loss in a downturn in business activity. For example, an auto manu-

facturer has downside risk in an economic downturn because it cannot slash its fixed costs, which results from the capital intensive nature of the industry.

dowry The amount of money, property, and other ASSETS a wife brings to her husband in marriage. The objective of a dowry is to ease the financial burden a husband assumes when entering the marriage.

draft
in general: A written order in which the first party, the DRAWER, instructs a second party, the DRAWEE, to pay a third party, the PAYEE.
See also CHECK.
bank draft: Drawn by one BANK on another.
clean draft: A DRAFT having no shipping documents attached.
documentary draft: One to which various shipping documents are attached.
sight draft: A draft payable upon presentation.
bill of exchange: Draft used in foreign transactions.
time draft: Payable on a specific date or time after presentation or demand.

drawee Individual to whom a bill of exchange or check is directed. For example, in a CHECKING ACCOUNT the BANK is the drawee, the person writing the check is the DRAWER or MAKER, and the person to whom the CHECK is written is the PAYEE.
See also BILL; DRAFT.

dread disease insurance policy A form of HEALTH INSURANCE that provides protection against medical expenses resulting from certain dreaded diseases such as cancer.

drive-in A facility leading from the inside of a business to the outside by which a motorist can have access to the goods or services the business provides. A typical example is the drive-in teller window in a BANK through which the motorist can conduct banking business from the comfort of his or her automobile.

drive other car (DOC) insurance A clause in AUTOMOBILE INSURANCE that protects an insured if his or her negligent acts result in bodily injury or property damage to a third party when the insured is driving a nonowned car on either or both (1) business activities and (2) personal activities.

dual earner household A family in which both the husband and wife are earning INCOMES that are combined for the needs of the household. Because of the rising cost of living and the implementation of AFFIRMATIVE ACTION, dual earner households are becoming very common.

dual listing
securities: A listing of a stock or bond on more than one exchange. An example is a listing of a multinational stock on both a domestic stock exchange and a foreign stock exchange.
real estate: A piece of property listed for sale with two real estate brokers.

due date In general, the date on which a legal obligation must occur. If the action does not occur on the due date, then it is PAST DUE. For example, federal INCOME TAXES have a due date of April 15.

due-on-sale clause A clause that permits the lender to require full payment of the MORTGAGE at the time the original buyer resells the property or effectively prohibits a new buyer from assuming the loan.

dunning letter Notices from a creditor that insistently demand repayment of debts from customers or borrowers.

duplex Two living units placed side by side in one building.

duplication of benefits Benefits in HEALTH INSURANCE for the same insured loss covered by two or more policies. In this case, each policy covers its proportionate share of the loss, or one policy becomes primary and the other secondary.

durable power of attorney A legal device allowing individuals to grant others general or specific powers for managing their finances.

E

each way Brokerage commissions earned on both the sale and purchase of a trade by the same broker.

early retirement RETIREMENT before NORMAL RETIREMENT AGE, commonly set at age 55 and 10 years of service. This decision results in reduced monthly benefits.

early withdrawal penalty A charge assessed against a holder of a fixed-term investment, such as CERTIFICATES OF DEPOSIT (CDs) if he or she withdraws the money before maturity. This penalty would be assessed, for instance, if someone who has a six-month certificate of deposit withdrew funds after four months.

earned income Any INCOME earned from labor or professional services as contrasted to income earned from passive sources such as INTEREST income and DIVIDEND income.
IRS: WAGES, SALARIES, and TIPS. Earnings from self-employment. Anything else of value you receive from your employer for services performed even if it is not TAXABLE (such as housing allowance or rental value of a parsonage for clergy members and meals and lodging for employees). Earned income is listed on Form 1040.

earned income credit In taxation, a special TAX CREDIT for some people who have at least one child and who have incomes below a certain dollar amount. The child must have lived with the taxpayer in his or her main home in the United States for more than half the year and the taxpayer's filing status must be married filing jointly, qualifying widow(er) with dependent child, or head of household. Special rules apply to each of these three filing categories.

earnest money Sum of MONEY given by the buyer to the seller at the time of purchase to indicate the buyer's willingness and ability to consummate the sale. If the sale is not completed because of the buyer's refusal or inability to complete it, then the earnest money is normally forfeited.

real estate: DOWN PAYMENT made by a purchaser of REAL ESTATE as evidence of good faith. Often the earnest money is deposited in an ESCROW ACCOUNT until the sale is completed.

earnest money credit A CREDIT toward the final purchase price for the amount of the EARNEST MONEY deposit. For example, if a parcel of land is being sold for $100,000 and an EARNEST MONEY deposit of $10,000 was given, then the amount due on completion of the sale is $90,000 ($100,000 − $10,000).

earnest money depository A BANK or TRUST COMPANY receiving and having CUSTODY of an EARNEST MONEY DEPOSIT.

real estate: An ESCROW ACCOUNT is normally established to receive an earnest money deposit after a properly drawn and established ESCROW AGREEMENT is achieved between the GRANTOR and the GRANTEE. The earnest money depository is the ESCROW AGENT.

earning asset
in general: An ASSET that earns some form of INCOME.
banking: An asset providing income. Examples include MORTGAGES and commercial loans.
investments: CAPITAL that produces income, for example, commercial REAL ESTATE.

earnings per share (EPS) In a publicly TRADED company, the NET INCOME divided by the total number of outstanding shares. EPS is probably the most important financial statistic for someone evaluating a company's financial position. For example, if a company has 1,000,000 shares outstanding and the NET INCOME is $10,000,000, the EPS is $10 ($10,000,000/1,000,000 shares).

Earnings per share is a very closely monitored indicator of the company's overall financial success. Earnings per share are reported annually and quarterly, and any change, or lack of change, is carefully noted. Comparisons with other companies' earnings per share are drawn to reach conclusions about the INVESTMENT value of the company. The overall MARKET VALUE of the STOCK is directly affected by the earnings per share of the company.

earnings report
in general: A term having the same meaning as INCOME STATEMENT or PROFIT AND LOSS STATEMENT.
report: A company report detailing the earnings for the trailing quarter in which yearly comparisons are usually made. Earning reports normally adjust for extraordinary items and any stock DILUTIONS that may have occurred in the interim.

earnings yield Or, *earnings-price ratio.* EARNINGS PER SHARE of a security divided by its MARKET PRICE. It is the opposite of the PRICE-EARNINGS RATIO. For example, if a company has an EPS of $10 and a market price per SHARE of $100, the earnings yield is 10% ($10/$100). The ratio is a measure of the YIELD on the stock. The higher the ratio, the better the yield.

easy credit Descriptive of period in which very few credit applications are rejected by the lender. This may be a result of ample money supply in the economy, lower interest rates, and/or loose qualification standards on the part of the lender.

easy money An increase in the amount of money available for business and individual spending as a result of reduction in the interest rate in the economy. Easy money tends to encourage investment spending and promote economic growth, which can be inflationary. *See also* TIGHT MONEY.

economic factor Economic conditions that can change and have an impact on one's investment portfolio, estate, or job status.

economic indicators Indicators that attempt to point where the economy seems to be headed and where it has been. Each month government agencies, including the Federal Reserve, and several economic institutions publish economic indicators. These may be broken down into six broad categories:

1. *Measures of overall economic performance.* These measures include GROSS NATIONAL PRODUCT (GNP), personal income, plant and equipment expenditures, and corporate profits and inventories.

2. *Price indices.* Price indices are designed to measure the rate of inflation of the economy. The CONSUMER PRICE INDEX (CPI), the best-known inflation gauge, is used as the cost-of-living index, to which labor contracts and social security are tied. The PRODUCER PRICE INDEX (PPI) covers raw materials and semifinished goods and measures prices at the early stage of the distribution system. It is the indicator that signals changes in the general price level, or the CPI, some time before they actually materialize. The GNP implicit deflator (a general price index of the components of GNP) is the third index of inflation that is used to separate price changes in GNP calculations from real changes in economic activity.

3. *Indices of labor market conditions.* Indicators covering labor market conditions are unemployment rate, average workweek of production workers, applications for unemployment compensation, and hourly wage rates.

4. *Money and credit market indicators.* Most widely reported in the media are MONEY SUPPLY, consumer credit, the DOW-JONES INDUSTRIAL AVERAGE, and the TREASURY BILL rate.

5. *Index of leading indicators.* This most widely publicized signal caller is made up of 11 data series: money supply, business formation, stock prices, vendor performance, average work-week, new orders, contracts, building permits, inventory change, layoff rate, and change in sensitive prices. They monitor certain business activities that can signal a change in the economy.

6. *Measures for major product markets.* These measures are designed to be indicators for segments of the economy such as housing, retail sales, steel, and automobiles. Examples are ten-day auto sales, advance retail sales, housing starts, and construction permits.

It is important to note that indicators are only signals. They tell an investor something about the economic conditions in the country, a particular area, an industry, and, over time, the trends that seem to be developing. *See also* INDEX OF LEADING ECONOMIC INDICATORS.

economic risk The chance of loss due to economic conditions. Economic RISKS include inflation risk, purchasing power risk, foreign exchange risk, and interest rate risk. *See also* RISK.

economics A science explaining the efficient use of scarce resources in manufacturing and distributing products as well as in rendering services. Economics is classified into MICROECONOMICS and MACROECONOMICS. Microeconomics is the study of the individual markets—for oil, agriculture, corn, and so on—that operate within the broad national economy, while macroeconomics is the study of the national economy as a whole, dealing with the "big picture," not details.

economy A system of manufacturing and distribution in a regional geographical area (e.g., South, Midwest) or country (e.g., United States). Poor economic conditions in a region can have a negative effect on an individual residing in that region because of, say, a loss of jobs and a lack of disposable income. On the other hand, one can prosper in a growing economy.

effective date The day a contract such as an

insurance policy, begins. After the effective date of the agreement, the parties are bound by it. Thus, the insured will receive reimbursement for damages after the insurance policy takes effect.

effective interest rate (effective annual yield)
1. YIELD TO MATURITY.
2. Real rate of interest on a loan. It is the nominal interest rate divided by the actual proceeds of the loan. For example, assume Eva took out a $10,000, one-year, 10% discounted loan. The effective interest rate equals

$$\$1,000/(\$10,000 - \$1,000)$$
$$= \$1,000/\$9,000 = 11\%$$

In this discount loan, the actual proceeds are only $9,000, which effectively raised the cost of the loan.
3. The EFFECTIVE ANNUAL YIELD, better known as the ANNUAL PERCENTAGE RATE (APR). Different types of investments use different compounding periods. For example, most bonds pay interest semiannually. Some banks pay interest quarterly. If an investor wishes to compare investments with different compounding periods, he or she needs to put them on a common basis. It is used for this purpose and is computed as follows:

$$APR = (1 + r/m)^m - 1.0$$

where

r = the stated, nominal or quoted rate
m = the number of compounding periods per year. For example, assume that a bank offers 6% interest, compounded quarterly; the APR is

$$APR = (1 + .06/4)^4 - 1.0 = (1.015)^4 - 1.0$$
$$= 1.0614 - 1.0 = .0614 = 6.14\%$$

This means that one bank offering 6% with quarterly COMPOUNDING, while another bank offering 6.14% with annual compounding, would both be paying the same effective rate of interest.

effective rate of return   *See* EFFECTIVE INTEREST RATE (EFFECTIVE ANNUAL YIELD).

effective tax rate   The average tax rate equal to the tax divided by taxable income. If the tax is $20,000 on taxable income of $60,000, the average tax rate is 33.33% ($20,000/$60,000).

efficient market   A controversial theory that a stock's price is the same as its investment value. In an efficient market, all data are fully and immediately reflected in the stock price. Price changes are as likely to be positive as negative. Thus, holders of this theory argue that it is useless to try to find undervalued stocks or to predict market movements. You cannot beat the market.

electrical funds transfer card   A system by which a CREDIT CARD user may receive money or conduct other financial transactions using an AUTOMATED TELLER MACHINE (ATM).

electronic funds transfer system (EFTS)   The computerized banking system for electronically transferring funds among sellers, buyers, and other parties with no need for writing checks. All transactions may be made using a debit card.

electronic terminals   AUTOMATIC TELLER MACHINES (ATMs) installed by many banks to handle routine bank customer transactions.

eligibility requirements
insurance: Essential requirements needed to qualify for certain types of INSURANCE. For example, only nonsmokers can qualify for reduced LIFE INSURANCE PREMIUMS.
pensions: Essential requirements needed to receive PENSION BENEFITS. For example, 20 years of employment service may be necessary for one to begin receiving PENSION BENEFITS.

elimination period   Or, *grace period.* A period that must elapse before an insured becomes eligible for coverage under an insurance policy.

emergency fund   Money set aside to be used in the event an unexpected, unfavorable event occurs. An example is a fund held in reserve in case of sickness.

emergency reserves   Funds set aside in case of an unforeseen event or emergency. For example, it is wise for a person to have some savings segregated in the event of disability.

eminent domain The right of government to seize private property for public purposes provided fair reimbursement is given to the owner. Land for schools, parks, roads, public parking, highways, and other social and public purposes are obtained this way. The legal proceeding involved in eminent domain is referred to as CONDEMNATION.

employee contract A legal agreement between the employer and employee specifying the particulars of the arrangement, such as employment term and compensation. The contract affords the employee protection in the relationship.

employee contributions Employee payments made for a contributory PENSION PLAN to which the employer also makes contributions.

Employee Retirement Income Security Act (ERISA) Federal legislation ensuring that private retirement plans are fair and secure. This law was passed in part to improve the chances that employees who are eligible for a pension actually receive those benefits. It also permits uncovered employees to establish their own individual tax-sheltered retirement plans.

employee stock ownership plan (ESOP) A stock bonus plan that encourages employees to invest in the company's stock, usually at a discount from the current market price through payroll deductions. Many plans defer delivering the stock to the employee until he or she leaves the plan or retires. This allows for the deferral of tax on the stock accumulation until a later year when the employee may be in a lower tax bracket. Because most of the funds are concentrated in the stock of one company, the plan does not provide any safety through diversification.

encumbrance

1. Any claim, right, LIEN, ESTATE, or LIABILITY that limits a clear TITLE to property. Encum-

brances include easements, mortgages, and judgment liens.

2. Debt secured by a lien on assets.

endorsement Or, *indorsement.* An endorsement is a written signature appearing on the back of a check or other FINANCIAL INSTRUMENT assigning and transferring property to another. To be effective, an endorsement must be for the entire instrument rather than just a portion.

conditional endorsement: An endorsement subject to the fulfillment of a special condition to be effective. For example, only upon the completion of contractually stated terms will the endorsement be effective.

financial instrument: A signature making CHECKS and other financial documents negotiable and transferable to a third party. The endorser's signature guarantees ownership of the INSTRUMENT and has the rights to assign it to another party.

full endorsement: Order by the endorser for MONEY to be paid to some named individual only.

endorsement in blank Or, *blank indorsement.* The simple affixing of an endorser's signature on the back of a NOTE or BILL without mentioning the name of any person for whom the endorsement is made. An endorsement in blank specifies no individual endorsee and may consist of a simple signature.

endorsement of payee In order to be NEGOTIABLE, ENDORSEMENT must be by the signature of the named PAYEE on the back side of the CHECK.

endowment Generally the permanent gift of MONEY or property to a specified institution for a particular purpose, for example, a gift of money to a university for the specific purpose of constructing a library facility.

Often an endowment may be a gift of money to be used as an investment vehicle to derive income for funding a particular activity. For example, a research foundation may be funded in whole or in part from the income of an endowment.

endowment insurance policy A CASH VALUE LIFE INSURANCE policy that assesses PREMIUMS over a specified period of time. At the end of that time, the cash value equals the face value, and the policy becomes endowed or fully paid up.

energy guide A label mandated by federal legislation informing consumers about the rates of energy consumption and related costs of automobiles as well as various appliances such as refrigerators, dishwashers, and air conditioners. By comparing the energy ratings of competitive products the energy guide helps consumers reach a more informed decision regarding their energy consumption COSTS.

energy labels *See* ENERGY GUIDE.

entrepreneurial profit
1. The net income earned by the hardworking owner of a business.
2. The financial reward for the serious and successful manager of real estate properties.

envelope system A method of strict budgetary control whereby exact amounts of money are placed into envelopes for specific purposes.

EPA mileage rating The result of mileage tests conducted by the ENVIRONMENTAL PROTECTION AGENCY (EPA) to determine the number of miles per gallon a car may be expected to get.

episode limits A clause in a HEALTH INSURANCE policy that specifies the maximum payment for health-care expenses arising from a single episode of illness or injury.

Equal Credit Opportunity Act (ECOA) A federal law making it illegal to discriminate when giving credit based on such factors as race, religion, marital status, and age. A lender must respond to credit applications within 30 days. If the application is denied, reasons must be given. The Federal Trade Commission is responsible for enforcing the provisions of the act.

equalizing dividend When the customary date of a dividend is altered, the shareholders will receive an extra distribution to make up for the delay. An example is when a dividend that is usually paid on July 1 is delayed to August 1.

equipment trust certificate A type of DEBT SECURITY used to pay for new equipment. Title to the equipment is held by a trustee until the notes are paid off. An equipment trust certificate is usually secured by a first LIEN of the equipment.

equipment trust obligation BONDS that are secured by certain types of equipment.

equitable distribution A fair division of property among relevant persons.

equitable owner The individual named to receive the benefit of property held in trust.

equitable remedy When an error as to an important matter in a contract has occurred, the injured party may receive protection from the court. This may result in rescinding the contract with monetary damages or requiring performance.

equity
1. An individual's NET WORTH.
2. In REAL ESTATE, the portion of an asset owned by an individual, that is, the market value of the property less any amount owned on the property.
3. In SECURITIES, the ownership interest in a specific security or group of securities.

equity buildup The increase of one's EQUITY in real estate resulting from a reduction in the mortgage loan balance and appreciation in the property's price.

equity of redemption The right to recover property during the FORECLOSURE period, such as an owner's right to reclaim his or her property within a year after foreclosure sale.

equity participation mortgage *See* SHARED EQUITY MORTGAGE (SEM).

equity REIT A type of REAL ESTATE INVESTMENT TRUST (REIT) whose investment money is directed toward the purchase of a portfolio of identified properties to be managed for the purpose of producing investment return through CURRENT INCOME as well as CAPITAL GAIN.

equity security A SECURITY that evidences ownership in a company, such as COMMON STOCK or PREFERRED STOCK.

equity trusts *See* EQUITY REIT.

equivalent bond yield Comparison of yields on BONDS with coupons and DISCOUNT YIELDS. For example, if a 10%, 180-day T-bill with a FACE VALUE of $10,000 costs $9,500, the equivalent bond yield is 10.67%, calculated as follows:

$$\frac{\$500}{\$9,500} \times \frac{365}{180} = 10.67\%$$

equivalent strategy Two strategies implemented differently but having the same profit diagram.

equivalent taxable yield What the return on a nontaxable security would be if it were taxable at an individual's tax rate. To compute the equivalent taxable yield divide the interest rate by the net of tax rate $(1 -$ the tax rate$)$. For example, assume a municipal bond that pays an interest rate of 7%. If one's tax rate is 28%, the equivalent rate on a taxable instrument is

$$\frac{.07}{1-.28} = \frac{.07}{.72} = 9.7\%$$

escheat The right of the state to take property when no one is legally qualified to inherit or make claim to the property of a deceased person.

escrow The arrangement in which a buyer puts a DEED and/or money into the care of a neutral third party (an ESCROW AGENT) to hold until certain conditions are fulfilled. After those conditions are met, the escrow agent releases the deed and/or money to the seller. The ESCROW is designed to benefit both parties involved. Escrow periods can be for any amount of time

agreed to by the parties who are buying and selling property. For example, a buyer of a home may insist that the seller place funds into an ESCROW ACCOUNT for unexpected repairs when the buyer actually moves into the home.

escrow account Or, *reserve account* or *impound account*. An account into which payment is made for specified expenses to ensure that funds will be available. An example is a special reserve account into which the lender places the borrower's monthly tax and insurance payments.

escrow agent The person placed in charge of an ESCROW. He or she is the AGENT of both parties until the conditions of the escrow are complied with by both the buyer and the seller and the escrow is closed.

escrow fees Those fees earned by the ESCROW AGENT for accumulating and keeping track of all the appropriate data from the various sources and for distributing these to the various parties.

escrow instructions Written proposals and acceptances regarding certain aspects of the transaction. The ESCROW AGENT must comply strictly with the original purchase and sale agreement.

estate The real and personal assets of an individual at the time of death. The distribution of the assets to the heirs is based on the WILL. If there is no will, the distribution is in accordance with a court order. It is a liquidation process. Court-supervised PROBATE achieves the following purposes: determines ownership of property; ascertains who is to receive the benefits; assures the proper transfer of property; and provides for the payment of debts and taxes.

The EXECUTOR of a will is the individual selected by the decedent during his or her lifetime to fulfill the terms of the will. Some functions of the executor are to manage property, collect estate assets, pay creditors, and distribute the remaining property.

In general, expenses applicable to settle a decedent's estate reduce the principal. Expenses to operate, preserve, and manage income-proucing property are charged against income.

estate building The accumulation of an individual's net worth over time. The ESTATE may grow from the increase in investments and savings and the return thereon.

estate in severalty Owned by one person, or sole ownership.
See also TENANCY IN SEVERALTY.

estate planning Deriving the most favorable tax effect for wealth that has been accumulated. This would assume that any inheritance is passed on to the BENEFICIARIES with the least amount given over to taxes.

The tax-planning aspects for ESTATES include the following:

- Determining what financial strategy could be developed, taking into consideration the particular assets being considered.
- The preparation of a WILL considering the tax and asset transfer ramifications.
- Tax effect, if any, of life insurance proceeds.

The gross estate includes all assets owned (e.g., stocks, bonds, real estate, cash accounts). Jointly held marital property is divided equally between spouses. The valuation of the assets is at the date of death or six months later at the option of the estate's executor.

ESTATE tax planning starts with computing the consequences of shifting property at some point in the future. Estate tax rates are graduated—the higher the incremental value of the estate, the higher is the incremental tax. To compute the estate tax, start with determining the gross estate (typically, the taxable estate plus adjusted taxable gifts). Subtract from that figure the allowable deductions, such as administrative expenses, debts, and the marital deduction. Then compute the tax. Subtract from the tax any credits allowable. Perhaps the most valuable credit is the unified credit. Like other credits, it is a direct reduction of the computed tax. However, because of its size ($192,800), it can allow some estates (those up to $600,000) to pass tax free. Note that the effect of the full unified credit may be diminished if the decedent made lifetime gifts that exceeded the $10,000 annual gift tax exclusion.

In the event there are children, the husband and wife can minimize estate taxes by having the spouse who dies first give children $600,000, which is exempt. The remainder should go to the surviving spouse as it passes tax free. When the other spouse dies, $600,000 of that spouse's estate is exempt to the children. In this manner, $1,200,000 of the estate passes to the children without tax. If the first spouse had given everything to the other spouse upon death, the initial $600,000 exemption would have been lost. Thus, the only exemption would have been the $600,000 passing to the children upon the death of the second spouse.

In 1990, the maximum estate tax rate is 50%. Federal estate taxes are paid with the filing of Form 706 (U.S. Estate Tax Return). The form is due nine months after the date of death. The state estate tax rate varies among states.

The executor will need certain information that should be made available to him or her, including documents and their location, list of assets and liabilities, and name and address of the testator's accountant, stockbroker, and insurance agent.

Example: You are single. When you die your funeral costs are estimated at $1,000. Your house is projected to have a fair market value of $300,000. There will be an outstanding mortgage of $50,000. Your personal property is estimated at $100,000. Debts are estimated at $60,000. Your IRA will be valued at $95,000. You are entitled to a pension benefit from your employer projected at $150,000. There is also a life insurance policy of $200,000. In your will there is a provision for a $5,000 gift to a charity. Administration expenses will be $6,000.

The following is your estimated net estate:

Gross Estate		
Home	$300,000	
Personal Property	100,000	
Pension Plans	245,000	
Life Insurance	200,000	
Total		$845,000
Less Allowable Deductions		
Funeral Expense	$ 1,000	
Administration Expense	6,000	
Mortgage and Debts	110,000	
Charitable Contribution	5,000	
Total Deductions		122,000
Net Estate		$723,000

estate-related costs The costs related to the transfer of an ESTATE.

estate tax A tax charged by the federal government or state on a deceased person's net worth that will be passed on to his or her heirs. The tax is paid by the ESTATE only rather than the recipients. The first $600,000 of property transferred is tax free. If the spouse is the sole heir, there is an unlimited exclusion. The estate is a separate taxable entity and is reported on IRS Form 1041.

estimated tax Quarterly payments for the estimated liability on taxable income that is not being withheld. To avoid a penalty for underpayment of taxes for the year, the taxpayer must either pay in during the year 90% of the estimated tax liability or 100% or more of the tax liability for the prior year.

even lot Or, *round lot*. A standard securities or commodities trading unit. For example, the standard New York Stock Exchange common stock TRADING UNIT is 100 shares, and most trades are in multiples of 100 shares.

eviction The action taken by a landlord to remove a tenant from leased property. This may be done because of a violation of the LEASE AGREEMENT such as for the tenant's failure to pay the rent.

evidence of title Documents, such as TRUST DEEDS, that manifest ownership.

excess major medical policy MEDICAL INSUR-ANCE that provides coverage over and above the benefits of a MAJOR MEDICAL POLICY.

exchange
1. Place where securities are traded, such as the New York Stock Exchange.
2. To give goods or services and obtain goods or services of equal value in return.

exchange acquisition Solicitation of sales requests by a BROKER so as to fulfill a purchase directive for a significant amount of stock. On the exchange floor, there is a matching of buys and sells.
See also EXCHANGE DISTRIBUTION.

exchange distribution A block trade made on the exchange floor between clients of a member firm. An investor needing to sell a significant block of shares in one transaction can get a broker to bunch together many orders. The securities go from the seller to the buyers in a single transaction. This transaction appears on the broad tape. The commission is paid to the broker by the seller only.

exchange members Approved and certified members of a STOCK EXCHANGE. Such members must purchase a "seat" on the exchange at a competitive MARKET PRICE. Exchange members are floor BROKERS representing one or more SECURITIES that they TRADE, with no COMMISSION, for security BROKERAGE FIRMS.

exchange of securities An agreement through which the securities of one company are exchanged for those of another company. This situation may occur in an acquisition of another company.

exchange privilege The right of a shareholder to go from one fund to another fund in the same mutual fund. Typically, the transfer is at no cost. The investor can move between funds based on changing needs and updated perceptions of investment opportunities and risks. For example, if the shareholder expects the stock market to drop, he or she may switch from a stock fund to a money market fund.
See also MUTUAL FUND.

exchange rate The ratio of one currency to that of another currency at a specified date.

exchange registered An adjective describing a BROKERAGE FIRM that is a member of an organized stock exchange.

excise taxes Broad-based tax imposed on the production and/or consumption of a wide range of domestic goods, services, or commodities as well as licenses in the form of license fees by the federal or state governments. For example, federal and state TAXES on cigarettes, which are justified as helping to discourage an unhealthy habit. Excise taxes are normally added to the total purchase price.

exclusion allowance That portion of an INSURANCE ANNUITY payment that may be excluded from TAXABLE INCOME. Under current law no more than 10% of an individual's total taxable income would be tax deferred under the exclusion allowance for ANNUITY PAYMENTS.

exclusions
gift tax: The amount a donor may transfer to another without tax consequences from the INTERNAL REVENUE SERVICE.
insurance: A provision in an INSURANCE CONTRACT that specifically denies COVERAGE under certain conditions. Such exclusions would include hazards considered to be so catastrophic as to be essentially uninsurable. Examples include any form of warfare or acts of God such as earthquakes or floods unless specific coverage was obtained for these hazards. Other areas excluded would be normal wear and tear that is expected as a result of the use of the product.
income tax: Portions of INCOME that are excluded from TAXATION because of specific exemption. For example, an IRA contribution would be excluded from total TAXABLE INCOME.

exclusive agency An exclusive grant of authority given to an AGENT or BROKER to sell within a specified MARKET or area. If a sale is made by any other BROKER during the period of the exclusive agency contract, the broker holding the exclusive agency is entitled to all COMMISSIONS in addition to the commissions payable to the broker effecting the transaction.

An exclusive agency contract does not preclude the principal from actively seeking to sell the property as well; however, the PRINCIPAL is precluded from employing another BROKER during the effective period of the exclusive agency CONTRACT.

exclusive insurance agent A person who represents only one insurance company.

exclusive listing A contract with a REAL ESTATE AGENT that lists the property with one agent for a set period of time, usually three to six months. *See also* EXCLUSIVE RIGHT TO SELL; OPEN LISTING.

exclusive right to sell An agreement with a REAL ESTATE AGENT that pays a COMMISSION to the agent even if the property is sold to a buyer found by the owner.
See also EXCLUSIVE LISTING; OPEN LISTING.

ex-coupon An issued bond that does not pay interest at the next interest date.
See also EX-INTEREST.

ex-dividend (XD) Without DIVIDEND. Typically a STOCK is trading ex-dividend four days prior to the RECORD DATE for the current dividend. This occurs because of the normal five-day settlement period for stock transactions. Normally the ex-dividend date occurs three weeks before the dividend is paid to SHAREHOLDERS of record. Persons buying a stock on or after the ex-dividend date are not entitled to the current period's dividend payment.

The price of the stock is automatically reduced by the size of the dividend payment on the opening of the ex-dividend trading date.

executed contract A contract whose provisions have been fully met.

execution
securities: Conducting a trade. An example is a broker's fulfilling a client's order to buy a bond.

law: The finalization of a contract that makes it valid.

executive insurance An insurance policy that pays the business for losses incurred when a "top" executive dies. The business is both the insured and beneficiary. Also included is reimbursement for costs incurred to search for a suitable replacement.

executor/executrix

executor: A male person chosen by a TESTATOR/TESTATRIX to administer and otherwise perform the terms of a will to an estate. These responsibilities include collecting and disposing of all properties as well as satisfying all legal obligations made against the ESTATE.

executrix: A female person appointed by a TESTATOR/TESTATRIX to administer and otherwise handle the conditions of a will to an estate. These duties include collecting and selling of all properties as well as meeting all legal commitments against the estate.

exempt income INCOME that is not subject to TAXATION. Examples include INTEREST payments from certain types of MUNICIPAL BONDS, student scholarships and fellowships used to pay tuition and course-related expenses, DIVIDENDS on veterans' LIFE INSURANCE, life insurance proceeds received because of a person's death, disability retirement payments (and other benefits) paid by the VETERANS ADMINISTRATION, workers' compensation benefits, insurance damages, and others for injury or sickness and child support.

exempt property Real estate that is not subject to property taxes. Property qualifying as exempt is owned by EXEMPT ORGANIZATIONS including charitable, governmental, and religious entities.

exemption A DEDUCTION permitted for reducing INCOME TAX liability. Exemptions are a reduction from the taxpayer's gross income.

There are two types of exemptions: personal and dependency. Within these two classes are five categories. These include exemptions for (1) individual taxpayers, (2) elderly and disabled taxpayers, (3) dependent children and other DEPENDENTS more than half of whose support is provided, (4) total or partial blindness, (5) a taxpayer's spouse.

exercise Taking advantage of the contractual right to purchase an underlying SECURITY.

convertible securities: Exchanging one security, CONVERTIBLE BOND, PREFERRED CONVERTIBLE STOCK, STOCK RIGHT, or STOCK WARRANT, for contractually stated SHARES of COMMON STOCK.

stock options: A PUT or CALL OPTION holder choosing to sell (put) or buy (call) the related SECURITY.

exhaust price The price at which a broker must sell a client's security that has dropped in market price. The security was initially purchased on margin, and the client is unable to provide money to satisfy the MARGIN REQUIREMENT.

ex-interest After the INTEREST. A debt SECURITY trading on or subsequent to the day interest is payable but before it is actually paid. An individual purchasing a debt security trading ex-interest will not receive the interest of the current period.

The price of the bond is automatically reduced by the size of the interest payment on the opening of the ex-interest trading date.

exit fees Or, *redemption fees.* Charges assessed upon redemption of MUTUAL FUND shares regardless of the length of time the investor has owned the shares.

expansion

personal: An increase in an individual's capabilities or resources.

corporate: An improvement in corporate sales, markets, or capital facilities.

economics: An improvement in the economy, such as indicated by increased production and manpower. Prosperity occurs when the economy is expanding.

expected return *See* EXPECTED YIELD.

expected yield The average of all the predicted RETURNS on an investment.

expenditure
v. Spending to buy ASSETS or satisfy an obligation. The EXPENDITURE may require the disbursement of CASH, exchange of property, or agreement to a future payment schedule.
n. An actual EXPENSE or amount paid to satisfy an expenditure. A COST that will bring future benefits.

expenditure sheet A listing of all expenditures by type that an individual has made such as for medical, entertainment, and transportation. The sheet helps the person think about what has been spent and possible areas needing cost reduction.

expense The result of using up a resource, depreciating a resource, or incurring a LIABILITY, for example, a contractual obligation, for the purpose of deriving revenue in the current period.
n. The COST of an item or service. In business, an expense is the *cost of goods sold* or services rendered.

expense record book Any book or log in which expenses are recorded as COSTS by date and purpose. An expense record book is intended primarily to be a convenient diary of current expenses to be used in helping to construct a full accounting of all expenses incurred by date and purpose at a later date.

experience rating A statistical technique conducted by an insurance company to determine a premium rate considering the past loss incidence of an insured group. Thus, insurance premiums are established on the basis of previous claim losses and cost experiences.

expiration The termination date in a contract or agreement. Examples are the maturity date of a CALL OPTION, and the date an insurance policy expires.

expiration notice Written or oral communication informing an individual that an expiration date is forthcoming or has in fact expired. Expiration notices may be given to individuals by insurance companies, landlords, and banks. An example is a landlord's informing a tenant in writing of the expiration date of the current lease.

explicit costs Costs that are clearly stated or shown. An example of an explicit cost to an individual is monthly rent.
See also IMPLICIT COST.

exposure Items owned and behaviors engaged in that expose an individual to the risk of financial loss.
See also AT RISK.

express contract A CONTRACT in which the parties openly agree in clear and distinct terms either orally, in writing, or both. An example is a marriage contract openly agreed to before a judge or minister and witnessed by all present.

express warranty A manufacturer's voluntary written WARRANTY that accompanies its product as an inducement to buy it.
See also IMPLIED WARRANTY.

ex-rights (XR) Without RIGHTS. A STOCK TRADES ex-rights on or after the ending date of a rights offering, entitling stockholders to purchase additional STOCK at a discount from the prevailing market price. After this date, the rights TRADE separately from the stock, and the purchaser of the stock is no longer entitled to the rights offering.

The price of the stock is automatically reduced by the convertible market value of the rights offering on the opening of the ex-rights trading date.

extended coverage Protection over and above that given by an INSURANCE POLICY or WARRANTY.

extended health insurance policy A policy that supplements the basic policy. It has large deductibles and high maximum limits. Generally it also requires the INSURED to pay a portion of the medical expenses.

extended term option A nonforfeiture option in LIFE INSURANCE that extends the term of coverage if premium payments are stopped, providing there is cash value available for this purpose.

extended warranty A service contract providing protection over and above that given by the WARRANTY available with a new product.

extension The granting of additional time to perform some act. An example is a bank's carrying a loan past the repayment date.

extension of time for filing The time period for filing a tax return extended beyond the due date. Individuals may automatically extend the filing of Form 1040 four months—from April 15 to August 15. The taxpayer must file Form 4868 requesting the extension by the date the tax return is due. The estimated balance of tax to be due must still be paid. Interest will be charged for understated estimated tax payments.

extension period The time period given in connection with prolonging an agreement between parties. Examples are a lender's giving a borrower three more months to pay the debt, and the landlord's giving the tenant one more month to make the rental payment.

extra An additional amount beyond what is agreed to or is customary. As an example, an employer gives the employee additional compensation for good performance.

extra dividend A DIVIDEND to shareholders on top of the customary dividend. Such a payment is made after an unusually profitable year. Some companies give the usual dividend in cash, and the extra dividend in stock.

eye care insurance A form of HEALTH INSURANCE designed to provide reimbursement for the expenses related to the purchase of glasses and contact lenses.

F

face amount Or, *face value*. The stated value of a BOND, NOTE, MORTGAGE, or other SECURITY on the actual INSTRUMENT. The face amount of corporate BONDS normally is $1,000; of MUNICIPAL BONDS, $5,000; and of federal government bonds, $10,000.

These securities often are issued as well as TRADED at either a lower value, DISCOUNT, or higher value, PREMIUM, than the FACE VALUE. However, the INTEREST due in the case of bonds, notes, and mortgages is calculated on the face amount of the issue rather than on the current DISCOUNT or PREMIUM in MARKET VALUE. For example, a federal Treasury bond with a face amount of $10,000 paying 9% interest would annually pay a total of $900 ($10,000 × 9% interest.

When bonds and notes mature, they are redeemed at the face amount. A security trading at the face amount is trading at PAR.

face interest rate The stated rate of INTEREST due on a BOND, NOTE or MORTGAGE. The face interest rate is calculated on the FACE AMOUNT of the SECURITY. The face interest rate may differ from the EFFECTIVE RATE and YIELD TO MATURITY depending on whether the security was purchased at a DISCOUNT or PREMIUM from the face amount.
See also DISCOUNT; EFFECTIVE INTEREST RATE.

face value *See* FACE AMOUNT.

face-of-note *See* FACE AMOUNT.

Fair Credit Billing Act (FCBA) A law designed to correct errors and abuses in credit billing and the handling of credit complaints. This act established time limits within which bills must be sent and complaints answered.

Fair Credit Reporting Act (FCRA) A law that regulates the use of credit information and allows consumers access to their own credit files. It is designed to force credit bureaus to keep only correct information about borrowers on file. It also requires a lender to explain how loan interest is calculated.

Fair Debt Collection Practices Act of 1978 A federal act that protects consumers against unreasonable collection practices.

Fair Labor Standards Act (FLSA) A 1938 federal statute establishing a minimum wage and a 40-hour maximum workweek. It also provided that employees be paid at one and one-half times their regular hourly rate when working overtime. The act also provided regulations for child labor, including the prohibition of such labor for children under the age of 16 in most occupations and up to the age of 18 in particularly dangerous employment.

fair market value The amount that could be received on the sale of an ASSET when there is a willing buyer and a willing seller for that asset.

fair program An insurance program sponsored by the federal government for individuals unable to get insurance through private carriers.

fall out of bed Vernacular term used in the STOCK market to describe a precipitous decline in the MARKET PRICE of a particular SECURITY.

falling out of escrow A situation in which one of the parties is unable to comply with the conditions of the purchase and sale agreement. For example, if the buyer is unable to obtain a loan by the time ESCROW was to close, the sale may become null and void.

family automobile policy (FAP) A standard form of AUTOMOBILE INSURANCE written to cover the insured and members of the family.

family group policy In INSURANCE a group discount rate given to the families of employees of an organization. The family group policy is in particularly widespread use for HEALTH INSURANCE when all members of the family have health care COVERAGE provided under one umbrella group rate for the organization.

There are three ways of paying for a family group policy. Depending upon the terms of employment with an organization, (1) the employee pays the full amount of the *policy,* (2) the organization pays the full amount, or (3) some combination is used whereby both the organization and the employee contribute to paying the INSURANCE RATE.

family income policy A life insurance policy giving additional income in the case of death of a parent of minor children. The policy includes a combination of ORDINARY LIFE and decreasing TERM INSURANCE. The BENEFICIARY will receive periodic payments until a certain date in the event the insured dies before the end of the stated date. If the insured is still alive at the specified date, he or she receives the face value of the policy.

family life cycle The stages in family life over time that may require a change in personal financial planning goals and strategies. The stages include single adult, young married, beginning parenthood, divorced parenthood, parenthood with older children, children having moved out, and retirement stage. The financial plan will vary depending on individual circumstances through life including age. For example, in the retirement stage, planning involves insurance and pension annuity programs.

family maintenance fund A fund designed to provide financial support to surviving DEPENDENTS until they are self-supporting.
See also LIFE INSURANCE; NEEDS APPROACH.

family of funds A group of MUTUAL FUNDS, all with different investment objectives, that are under the same management company. A shareholder can switch between the funds, sometimes at no charge as his or her investment objectives and perceptions change.

family trust Instrument used by a taxpayer who wishes to split his or her income with a family member, or to otherwise relieve himself or herself of tax liability on income from certain property, by conveying that property in trust for the family member. Thus, the taxpayer avoids tax on part of his or her income. The taxpayer must transfer the income-producing property and not just the income.

Farmers Home Administration (FHA) A federal agency that offers home financing to qualified individuals in low-income, rural areas.

federal agency securities DEBT INSTRUMENTS issued by U.S. federal agencies. Such agencies include the Federal Home Loan Bank, the Federal National Mortgage Association, the Federal Farm Credit Bureau, Tennessee Valley Authority, and others. While these AGENCY DEBT issues are not direct obligations of the U.S. Treasury, as authorized government issues they normally have a high CREDIT rating.

Federal Deposit Insurance Corporation (FDIC) The federal agency that insures bank accounts. Most commercial and all national bank accounts carry FDIC insurance up to $100,000. It is important to note that insurance is for each depositor and not for each account. If the amount held by one depositor exceeds $100,000, another account should be opened with a different bank, or additional deposits with the same bank should be made in another person's name.

federal estate tax *See* ESTATE TAX.

federal funds Reserve funds that depository institutions lend each other, usually on an overnight basis. Federal funds include other types of borrowings by these institutions from each other and from federal agencies.

federal garnishment law A 1968 federal statute limiting the amount of aggregate disposable earnings that can be deducted for any workweek from an employee. Under the Federal Garnishment Law, the maximum amount of a worker's

DISPOSABLE INCOME subject to GARNISHMENT is 25% or the amount by which his or her disposable earnings for that week exceed 30 times the federal minimum hourly wage, whichever is less. For example, if an employee has a weekly net paycheck of $400, the maximum amount that can be deducted for a garnishment order is $100, leaving the employee with a take-home pay of $300.

The Federal Garnishment Law tries to prevent unrestricted garnishment of WAGES to limit excessive CREDIT payments as well as to prevent loss of employment by the DEBTOR.

federal gift tax A federal TAX imposed on the transfer of MONEY or other property to another by gift. The donor is liable for the GIFT TAX and the tax is based on the FAIR MARKET VALUE of the property at the time of the gift. A parent may give $10,000 per year per child ($20,000 for parents electing GIFT-SPLITTING) without paying gift taxes.

Federal Home Loan Bank Board (FHLBB) The agency of the federal government that supervises all federal savings and loan associations and federally insured state-chartered S&Ls. It is a central bank in this industry. It also operates the FEDERAL SAVINGS AND LOAN INSURANCE CORPORATION (FSLIC).

Federal Housing Administration (FHA) A federal agency within the Department of Housing and Urban Development that provides financing opportunities for home buyers, especially those with little down payment funds or with a need for smaller monthly payments. It insures mortgage loans that meet its standard.

federal income taxes A U.S. government levy on the net earnings of an individual. The tax rate is typically graduated as earnings increase from one tax bracket to another. The tax rate depends on the taxpayer's status (e.g., married, single). Form 1040 is filed annually by April 15 with the Internal Revenue Service.

Federal Insurance Administration A federal

agency that sponsors crime insurance for families residing in crime-ridden areas.

Federal Insurance Contribution Act (FICA) A federal law applying to Social Security taxes and benefits. FICA taxes are withheld from employee wages and remitted to the government so funds will be available to pay retired individuals or their survivors. Both the employee and employer pay these taxes. The FICA tax rate and base wages subject to tax vary over time. Retirement benefits depend upon such factors as retirement age and contributions made. Retirement benefits will also change over time.

Federal National Mortgage Association (Fannie Mae) A privately owned and managed corporation that purchases mortgage loans originated by other lenders. FANNIE MAE issues STOCKS and SECURITIES to obtain funds for its purchase.

Federal Odometer Disclosure Law A 1972 federal law prohibiting the tampering with motor vehicle odometers for the purpose of altering a vehicle's true mileage setting. It prohibits the disconnection, resetting, or altering the odometer of any motor vehicle with the intent of changing the number of miles indicated on the odometer.

The thrust of the law is to ensure that odometers can be an accurate reflection of a motor vehicle's mileage to help the customer determine its MARKET VALUE.

Federal Reserve System The system, created by an act of Congress in 1913, made up of 12 Federal Reserve District Banks, their 25 branches, and all national and state banks (about 5,700 member banks) that are part of the system scattered throughout the nation. It is headed by a seven-member board of governors. The primary function of the board is to establish and conduct the nation's monetary policy. The system manages the nation's monetary policy by exercising control over the money stock. It controls the money supply primarily in three ways:

(1) by raising or lowering the reserve requirement; (2) by changing the DISCOUNT RATE for loans to commercial banks; and (3) by purchasing and selling GOVERNMENT SECURITIES, mainly three-month bills and notes issued by the U.S. Treasury. The system also serves as the central bank of the United States, and a banker's bank that offers banks many of the same services that banks provide their customers. It performs many other functions, such as setting MARGIN REQUIREMENTS, regulating member banks, and acting as fiscal agent in the issuance of U.S. Treasury and U.S. government agency securities.

Federal Savings and Loan Insurance Corporation (FSLIC) A defunct federal agency that insured deposits in savings and loan associations and similar institutions. It was an entity created to insure deposits and depositors against loss by insolvency of these federally chartered savings and loan institutions. Its duties have been largely assumed by the FEDERAL DEPOSIT INSURANCE CORPORATION (FDIC).

Federal Trade Commission (FTC) A federal agency responsible for thwarting unfair trade practices and guarding against monopolies.

Federal Unemployment Tax Act (FUTA) The federal and state governments require employer contributions to a governmental fund to pay unemployment insurance benefits to former employees who are not working. Some states (e.g., New Jersey) also require an employee to contribute into the fund.

federal withholding taxes Automatic employer DEDUCTIONS from an employee's SALARY for the payment of federal INCOME and SOCIAL SECURITY taxes. The deductions are remitted directly to the IRS and the SOCIAL SECURITY Administration or as otherwise directed by the IRS and the Social Security Administration.

FHA mortgage insurance Federal agency (FEDERAL HOUSING ADMINISTRATION) established in 1934 to insure MORTGAGES provided by FHA-approved lenders to help ensure a steady supply of mortgage MONEY on FHA-approved homes at reasonable rates. The basic intent is to make mortgages more desirable INVESTMENTS for LENDERS.

FICA taxes SOCIAL SECURITY taxes that are withheld by an employer from an employee's salary. The current Federal Insurance Contribution Act (FICA) TAX RATE (1991) is 7.65% to a ceiling of $53,400 in earned INCOME. FICA TAXES produce more tax REVENUE than corporate INCOME TAXES and are the second largest tax source after the personal income tax.

Social Security tax deductions are remitted directly to the Social Security Administration.

fiduciary An individual or institution responsible for holding or managing property owned by someone else. Examples are an executor, guardian, or trustee. A fiduciary must conduct his or her activities in a prudent manner.

fiduciary responsibility An individual transacting business, including INVESTING, receiving, and spending MONEY, for the benefit of another. Fiduciary responsibility may include the consignment of MONEY in a TRUSTEESHIP for a specified period of time for the custody and/or management of the same for the owner.

Those having fiduciary responsibilities toward others must maintain high ethical standards. Any violation of such a TRUST is guilty of ethical misconduct and can be sued for any damages.

Examples of those having fiduciary responsibility would include BANKERS, EXECUTORS, and lawyers.

file

1. A collection of data stored as records. Examples of files kept on individuals are employee personnel files, credit card account files, and bank records. A file may be kept in order of time, subject, alphabetical entry, or numerical entry.

2. Act of making formal submission of a document to an entity, such as the submission of a tax return to the INTERNAL REVENUE SERVICE.

filing status A category in which a taxpayer belongs when preparing a tax return. The four basic categories are single, married filing jointly, married filing separately, and head of household. The filing status affects the tax liability. For example, the tax for single individuals is higher than that for married ones filing jointly.

fill The execution by a broker of a client's order to purchase or sell a security. The order is satisfied when such security is supplied. A *partial* fill occurs if less than the amount of the order is supplied.

fill-or-kill order (FOK) A buy or sell order in the SECURITY and COMMODITY MARKETS by a client to the BROKER either to execute the order immediately at the specified price limit or to cancel it entirely. Although fill-or-kill instructions are normally buy orders, they can also be sell orders.

Fill-or-kill orders are useful for large quantity executions in which a MARKET ORDER could cause a measurable price change in the security or commodity being TRADED.

filtering down Situation in which, over time, a neighborhood is occupied by progressively lower-income residents.

final dividend

1. The end-of-year declared dividend. The year end of a company may be calendar or fiscal year.

2. The final installment of a LIQUIDATING DIVIDEND.

final expense fund Amount of life insurance needed to cover burial, probate, and other costs arising from death.

finance charge A charge for the COST of CREDIT. INTEREST and POINTS are the two most common forms of finance charges. POINTS (1 point = 1% of the total loan) are an upfront fee charged for the credit, whereas interest is charged over the course of the LOAN.

INTEREST charges as well as points add to the total cost of the LOAN, and under the TRUTH-IN-

LENDING ACT, all COSTS associated with a LOAN must be disclosed to the consumer prior to final acceptance.
See also CONSUMER CREDIT PROTECTION ACT; REGULATION Z.

financial adviser A professional who sells a particular financial and investment product, or who gives professional financial advice. The financial adviser may be knowledgeable in INVESTMENTS, TAX PLANNING, INSURANCE, ESTATE PLANNING, or similar fields.

financial analysis Application and transformation of financial data into a form that can be used to monitor and evaluate an entity's financial position, to plan future financing, and to designate the size of the entity and its rate of growth. Financial analysis includes the use of financial ratios and the analysis of cash flows.
See also FINANCIAL STATEMENT ANALYSIS.

financial assets Intangible investments—things you cannot touch, wear, or walk on. They represent an individual's equity ownership of a company, or they provide evidence that someone owes a debt, or they show an individual's right to buy or sell an ownership interest at a later date. Financial assets include common stock, preferred stock, savings accounts, money market certificates, Treasury bills, money market funds, bonds, and options.

financial future A contract to buy or sell a financial instrument at a given price in a specified future month. A relationship exists between the price of the contract and the interest rate of the underlying financial instrument. For example, as interest rates drop, the value of the contract increases. Examples of financial instruments used in financial futures contracts are Treasury bills, Treasury notes, GINNIE MAES, and certificates of deposit. Futures contracts may be used to speculate on interest rate changes and to hedge investment portfolios against adverse movements in interest rates. CURRENCY FUTURES, a form of financial future, are used to speculate in foreign exchange rates. These contracts are supervised by the Commodities Futures Trading Commission.

financial goals An individual's objectives in financial terms. Financial goals may be long term, intermediate term, or short term. For example, a person's goal may be to have $1,000,000 in savings at age 65 when he or she retires. Another financial goal is to have adequate funds to buy a house for about $250,000 by age 35.

financial independence A general term describing a self-supporting individual who is not dependent on any one source of financing and associated restrictions, and is able to pay all bills and expenses without help. For example, a financially independent wife having her own career and benefits is not dependent on her husband's INCOME to provide her support.

financial institutions and markets Institutions, such as BANKS, that serve as intermediaries between suppliers and users of funds. In general, they are wholesalers and retailers of funds. It is in the FINANCIAL MARKETS that entities demanding funds are brought together with those having surplus funds. Financial markets provide a mechanism through which the financial manager may obtain funds from a wide range of sources, including financial institutions. The figure on p. 120 depicts the general flow of funds among financial institutions and financial markets.

The financial markets are composed of MONEY MARKETS and CAPITAL MARKETS. Money markets (credit markets) are the markets for short-term (less than 1 year) debt securities. Examples of money market securities include U.S. TREASURY BILLS, federal agency securities, BANKERS' ACCEPTANCES, COMMERCIAL PAPER, and negotiable CERTIFICATES OF DEPOSIT issued by government, business, and financial institutions. The money market securities are characterized by their highly liquid nature and a relatively low default risk.

Capital markets are the markets in which

*General Flow of Funds through and between Financial
Institutions and Financial Markets*

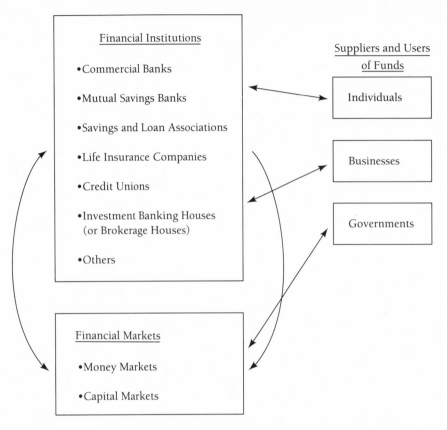

long-term securities issued by the government and corporations are traded. Unlike the money market, both debt instruments (BONDS) and equities (COMMON and PREFERRED STOCKS) are traded. Relative to money market instruments, those of the capital market often carry greater default and market risks but return a relatively high yield in compensation for the higher risks. The NEW YORK STOCK EXCHANGE, which handles the stock of many of the larger corporations, is a prime example of a capital market. The AMERICAN STOCK EXCHANGE and the regional stock exchanges are still another example. These exchanges are organized markets. In addition, securities are traded through the thousands of brokers and dealers on the OVER-THE-COUNTER (or unlisted) market, a term used to denote an informal system of telephone contacts among BROKERS and DEALERS. There are other markets that include (1) the commodity markets, which handles various commodity futures, (2) the foreign exchange market, which deals in international financial transactions between the United States and other countries, and (3) the insurance, shipping, and other markets handling short-term credit accommodations in their operations. A primary market refers to the market for new issues while a secondary market is a market in which previously issued, "secondhand" securities are exchanged. The New York Stock Exchange is an example of a secondary market.

financial intermediaries *See* FINANCIAL INSTITUTIONS AND MARKETS.

financial leverage A portion of an entity's ASSETS financed with DEBT instead of EQUITY and therefore involving contractual interest and principal obligations. Financial leverage benefits investors as long as the borrowed funds generate a return in excess of the cost of borrowing, although the increased risk can offset the general cost of capital. For this reason, financial leverage is popularly called TRADING ON EQUITY.
See also LEVERAGE; TRADING ON EQUITY.

financial loss Any loss of INCOME or ASSETS incurred by an individual or institution. Such loss could occur because of an accident, divorce, INVESTMENT loss, ill health causing absence from employment, lawsuit, or similar reasons.

The net effect of a financial loss is to impose a loss of wealth.

financial management records Any data, statements, receipts, financial reports, TAX RETURNS, or any other records of financial transactions documenting the financial performance of an individual or organization over a period of time. Financial management records should be as complete and accurate as possible, including dates and purposes of all transactions as well as who transacted them and with what effect.
financial information system: A systematic method of analyzing financial data for the purpose of assisting an individual or business in making sound financial management decisions. Sophisticated microcomputer software for financial management is available to help the individual or company keep as well as analyze financial management information accurately and systematically.

financial markets *See also* FINANCIAL INSTITUTIONS AND MARKETS.

financial needs approach A method for calculating LIFE INSURANCE needs that bases the amount of insurance protection on the goals, net worth, projected income, and expense figures of the insured.

financial performance A measurement of the use of and financial return on a company's or individual's financial ASSETS. For example, a MUTUAL FUND may advertise that if an individual had invested a certain sum of MONEY in the fund at a particular point in time, it would currently be worth $X.

Financial performance is a relative measure to other investments in order to determine the best use of assets.
See also PRESENT VALUE.

financial planner One who is engaged in providing PERSONAL FINANCIAL PLANNING services to individuals. He or she may be an independent professional or may be affiliated with a large investment, insurance, accounting, or other institution. Financial planners come from a variety of backgrounds and therefore may hold a variety of degrees and licenses. Currently, there are no state or federal regulations for the financial planning industry. However, some take specialized training in financial planning and earn credentials such as CERTIFIED FINANCIAL PLANNER (CFP) or CHARTERED FINANCIAL CONSULTANT (ChFC). Others may hold degrees or registrations such as attorney (JD), CHARTERED LIFE UNDERWRITER (CLU) or Certified Public Accountant (CPA).

To become a CFP, a designation conferred by the Institute of Certified Financial Planners (ICFP), a candidate must take a two-year course. The six parts of the course, each capped by a three-hour test, are the following: introduction to financial planning; RISK MANAGEMENT (INSURANCE); INVESTMENTS; TAX PLANNING and management; RETIREMENT PLANNING and EMPLOYEE BENEFITS; and ESTATE PLANNING. To become a CLU or ChFC, designations granted by the American College of the American Society of Chartered Life Underwriters, a person must pass a ten-course program and have three years' professional experience.

A handful of colleges award degrees and certificates in financial planning or "family financial counseling." Adelphi University offers a certificate in financial planning. Golden Gate

University offers master's degrees in both financial planning and services. The American College also grants a master's degree in financial services. Baylor, Brigham Young, Drake, Georgia State, San Diego State, University of California extensions, and other colleges offer certificates or degree programs with either a concentration or major in financial planning.

A financial planner may assist the client in the following ways:

1. Assess the client's financial history, such as tax returns, investments, retirement plans, wills, and insurance policies.
2. Help the client decide on a financial plan, based on his or her personal and financial goals, history, and preferences.
3. Identify financial areas in which the client may need help, such as building up retirement income or improving investment returns.
4. Prepare a financial plan based on the client's individual situation and discuss it thoroughly with him or her in plain English.
5. Help the client implement the financial plan, including referring him or her to specialists such as attorneys, investment counselors, bankers, and certified financial planners, if necessary.
6. Review the client's situation and financial plan periodically and suggest changes in the program when needed.

See also PERSONAL FINANCIAL PLANNING.

financial planning The process of developing and implementing plans to achieve financial goals.
See also PERSONAL FINANCIAL PLANNING.

financial planning software Personal finance computer programs that keep track of income and expenses by budget category, reconcile accounts, store tax records, figure net worth, track stocks and bonds, and print checks and financial reports. Some programs are sophisticated enough to generate a detailed, long-term personal financial plan covering planning for college education, investment planning, and retirement planning. Examples of financial planning software are "Dollars and Sense," "Managing Your Money," and "Sylvia Porter's Personal Financial Planner."
See also MONEY MANAGEMENT SOFTWARE.

financial position The financial health of a person or business entity as presented in the balance sheet. Financial position is typically expressed in terms of net worth (assets less liabilities).

financial responsibility law A state law mandating that the driver of an automobile must be properly insured so as to have sufficient funds to pay for losses arising from an accident. A minimum amount of automobile liability insurance is typically required.

financial risk

1. *personal:* The risk a person has of running into financial problems and/or incurring financial losses. An example is an individual who has most of his or her funds invested in JUNK BONDS.

2. *corporate:* Portion of total risk resulting from using DEBT. The greater the proportion of debt to EQUITY the firm has, the greater is its financial risk.
See also FINANCIAL LEVERAGE.

financial service business A business such as a bank or brokerage house providing services of a financial nature, to individuals.

financial skills An individual's abilities in handling personal financial matters. A business education, particularly the study of finance and/or accounting, will be of much help. Financial skills include mathematical and analytical abilities. To assist in planning, a person can retain a financial adviser such as a certified financial planner and certified public accountant.

financial statement analysis An approach used by investors to appraise the past, current, and projected financial condition and performance of a company. Ratio analysis is the most important type of financial analysis. It provides relative measures of a company's financial condition and operating performance. Horizontal analysis and vertical analysis are also popular forms. Horizontal analysis is used to evaluate the trend in the accounts over the years, while vertical analysis (common size analysis) discloses the internal structure of the entity. Vertical analysis reveals the relationship between sales and each income statement account. It represents the mix of assets that generate income and the mix of debt and equity financing. When using financial ratios, comparisons should be made of a company's ratios over the years to identify trends. In determining relative performance, comparisons should also be made between a company's ratios and industry norms (averages), as well as a company's ratios to competing companies in the industry. An example of a financial ratio of interest to an investor is dividend yield equal to dividends per share divided by market price per share.

financial statements (corporate) Reports containing financial information about a company. The required financial statements are balance sheet, income statement, and statement of cash flows. They may be combined with supplementary statements to show the financial position or operating performance of the entity. Financial statements are included in the company's annual report and filings with the Securities and Exchange Commission. *See also* BALANCE SHEET; INCOME STATEMENT; STATEMENT OF CASH FLOWS.

financial statements (personal) Financial reports prepared for an individual showing his or her financial well-being. A personal balance sheet (personal statement of financial condition) shows assets at estimated current values listed by order of liquidity and maturity without classification as current and noncurrent. Business interests representing a significant part of total assets should be shown separately from other assets. Only the person's interest (amount that person is entitled to) as beneficial owner should be included when assets are jointly owned. Liabilities are shown by order of maturity without classification as current or noncurrent. Income taxes are estimated on the difference between assets and liabilities and their tax bases. Taxes are based as if assets have been sold. A Statement of Changes in Net Worth is optional showing the major sources and uses of net worth. Comparative financial statements are also optional. Footnote disclosure should be made of the following: (1) individuals covered by the financial statements; (2) major methods used in computing current values; (3) nature of joint ownership of assets; (4) face value of life insurance; (5) nonforfeiture rights that do not qualify for asset inclusion (e.g., pensions based on life expectancy); (6) methods and assumptions used in computing estimated income taxes; (7) maturities and interest rates on debt; and (8) noncancellable commitments not reflected under liabilities (e.g., leases).

financial success How well an individual has done in monetary terms. Indicators of financial well-being are net worth and annual income. The perception of financial health will vary among individuals.

financial supermarket One-stop financial center that provides a variety of financial services to consumers. It typically combines the functions of a FINANCIAL INSTITUTION, INSURANCE company, BROKERAGE FIRM, and CREDIT CARD company. An example is the Sears Financial Network, which consists of Sears Savings Bank, Dean Witter, and Coldwell Bankers.

financial tables Tables found in most daily newspapers providing price, yield, volume, and other financial information on the securities and commodities markets. Extensive listings can be found in the *Wall Street Journal* and the *New York Times*.

financial tools Items to assist an individual in financial planning and analysis, such as time value of money tables and personal financial planning software.

finder's fee A fee paid to an individual or company for bringing the parties together in a business deal. The finder may also serve as a consultant until the deal is finalized. The fee may be a FLAT RATE, a percentage of the sale, or a percentage of gross margin. For example, finder's fees are paid in bringing a LENDER and BORROWER together or finding a customer for a particular service or good.

fire insurance—standard fire policy Also known as the 165–line policy because of the standard form used in most states. In order to complete the policy additional forms and endorsements must be added to cover numerous direct and indirect risks associated with the specific covered risk.

The Standard Fire Policy is found in SECTION I where the property coverage of most policies are listed, including HOMEOWNER'S and SPECIAL MULTI-PERIL.

There are four sections, listed below, in a Standard Fire Policy:
1. *declarations*—The listing of the description and location of property, INSURED amount, and name of INSURED.
2. *insuring agreements*—Stating the PREMIUM amount, the obligations of the INSURED, what must be done in the event of damage, and consequent claim.
3. *insurance conditions*—A description of what suspends or restricts the coverage, including any known change of hazards.
4. *exclusions*—Those hazards not covered under the fire INSURANCE policy, such as the standard exception of war-related events.

fire legal liability insurance A fire INSURANCE policy covering negligence when an INSURED'S fire spreads to another's dwelling causing property and/or personal damage. The injured party brings a negligent fire liability claim against the insured, alleging acts of negligence and omission resulting in the fire-related damage and injury to the plaintiff.

firm order A noncancelable order given to a BROKER by an INVESTOR for a SECURITY transaction. The TRANSACTION involves either buying or selling a security at a given price limit. Should the INVESTOR later renege on the order, he or she is liable for a suit.

first in, first out (FIFO) method A method for calculating the ACCOUNT BALANCE on which interest is earned. Under the FIFO (First In, First Out) method, withdrawals are first deducted from the balance at the start of the interest period and then, if the balance is not sufficient, from later deposits. The method works to the disadvantage of savers, since interest is automatically lost on money on deposit early in the interest period if it is withdrawn.

Example: The following activities have taken place during the 90-day period:

Day	Deposit (Withdrawal)	Balance
1	$1,000	$1,000
30	1,000	2,000
60	(800)	1,200
90	Closing	1,200

With a 6% stated (nominal) interest rate, calculating interest under FIFO yields

(a) $\$200 \times .06 \times 90/360 = \$\ 3.00$
(b) $\underline{\$1,000} \times .06 \times 60/360 = \underline{\$10.00}$
 $\$1,200 \qquad\qquad\qquad\qquad \$13.00$

See also LAST IN, FIRST OUT (LIFO) METHOD; DAY OF DEPOSIT TO DAY OF WITHDRAWAL (DDDW) METHOD; MINIMUM BALANCE METHOD.

first mortgage The original or senior MORTGAGE on a piece of property. Because of its precedence it has priority over all subsequent mortgages, and the mortgagee has precedence in payment in the event of DEFAULT.

first-party insurance Insurance coverage for an individual's own personal and real property.

fiscal policies Government spending and taxation programs.

fiscal year A business entity's accounting year other than on a calendar year basis. Due to the nature of its particular business, some companies do not use the calendar year for their bookkeeping. A typical example is the department store that finds December 31 too early a date to close its books after the Christmas rush. For that reason, many stores end their accounting year on January 31. Their fiscal year, therefore, runs from February 1 of one year through January 31 of the next. The fiscal year of governmental units usually runs from July 1 through the following June 30.

fit An investment term describing a situation in which a particular investment conforms to an investor's financial requirements and portfolio.

Five Cs of Credit Five elements used by lenders in evaluating a borrower's credit application:
1. Character (willingness to pay)
2. Capacity (cash flow)
3. Capital (wealth)
4. Collateral (security)
5. Conditions (economic conditions)

Character reflects a customer's integrity, and reliability in meeting financial obligations. The borrower's credit history indicates how reliable the borrower is in paying bills on time. Capacity looks at a borrower's earning power and/or cash flow. Capital analyzes a borrower's BALANCE SHEET (ASSETS and LIABILITIES revealing whether NET WORTH is positive or negative). Collateral refers to assets that can be secured and liquidated by the lender if a loan is not repaid. Finally, conditions mean economic conditions at the time of the loan and a borrower's vulnerability to business downturn or credit crunch. When much money is available, especially at low interest rates, it is much easier to obtain credit whereas in a credit crunch, many applicants would be rejected who would normally have been approved for credit.

Once the five Cs are analyzed, a borrower is assigned to a credit-rating category, which will determine the DEFAULT RISK premium for the borrower. Generally, the higher a customer's CREDIT RISK, the higher the loan rate.

fixed amount settlement option In insurance, choice given to a beneficiary of receiving a death benefit in equal installments until the insurance proceeds are exhausted. The option emphasizes the dollar amount per installment rather than the time period of installments.

fixed annuity *See* FIXED RATE ANNUITIES; VARIABLE ANNUITY.

fixed assets Any tangible ASSETS of a permanent nature such as a building, equipment, or furniture required for the usual activities of a business and which will not be consumed or sold in the immediate future. Fixed assets are necessary to conduct operations and therefore are not the object of sale. Fixed assets are usually referred to as property, plant, and equipment.

Fixed assets physically deteriorate over time, however, and can be DEPRECIATED as a COST of doing business.

fixed balance bonus account A savings account having an interest rate greater than the interest rate on a passbook account. A minimum balance must be maintained.

fixed benefits A nonvariable payment to a BENEFICIARY. For example, a fixed monthly PENSION payment of $2,000 to a retiree.

fixed charges Expenses such as bond interest, taxes, and royalties that an individual or a company must meet whether it has earnings or not.

fixed cost *See* FIXED EXPENSES.

fixed disbursements For a business or individual, EXPENSES that have to be paid regardless of activity. Examples include insurance PREMIUMS, rent or MORTGAGE payments, TAXES, and utilities. The costs of the actual EXPENDITURE items may vary over time, but the obligation to make the expenditure is fixed and cannot be avoided.

fixed dollar annuity ANNUITY in which the amount of monthly benefit does not change. *See also* FIXED ANNUITY.

fixed expenses The costs that remain the same regardless of activity. Examples are RENT, INSURANCE, and PROPERTY TAXES.

fixed income INCOME that does not change over time. Examples would include income derived from fixed interest rate BONDS, PENSIONS, or ANNUITY INCOME. People living on a constant income suffer a loss of buying power during INFLATIONARY periods when the real value of their earnings drop.

fixed income investment An INVESTMENT that promises to pay a specified amount of INCOME on a periodic basis. *See also* FIXED INCOME SECURITIES.

fixed income securities SECURITIES such as PREFERRED STOCKS and BONDS that offer purchasers a fixed rate of return. Government, municipal, and corporate bonds pay fixed interest income, while preferred stock pays a fixed dividend.

fixed interest rate INTEREST RATES or CHARGES that do not vary over time. For example, a FIXED RATE MORTGAGE contract specifies the interest payments to be made over the life of the mortgage and the payments, therefore, do not vary. *See also* FIXED RATE AND PAYMENT MORTGAGE.

fixed investment fund A MUTUAL FUND issuing SHARES to INVESTORS placing the monies in a predetermined list of investments—usually in fixed proportions.

fixed maturity *See* MATURITY DATE.

fixed period option settlement In insurance, the beneficiary's choice of receiving the proceeds of a death benefit in the form of income for a specified period (e.g., 10 years). The number of payments are fixed. An example is an income benefit of $2,000 per month for 60 months, totally $120,000.

fixed premium The same level premium payment each period to an insurance company.

fixed price A price for services or merchandise that does not take into consideration changes in COSTS that may occur between the time of sale and delivery. A fixed price indicates to the buyer that there will be no additional costs at the time of delivery of the good or service.

fixed rate and payment mortgage Or, *conventional mortgage.* A LOAN secured by real property featuring a fixed periodic payment of PRINCIPAL and INTEREST over the life of the MORTGAGE. All FIXED PAYMENT MORTGAGES are fixed rate and payment mortgages.

fixed rate annuities Annuity for which the INSURANCE company guarantees principal plus a minimum rate of interest. If an individual has little tolerance for risk, the fixed annuity is an ideal investment. In buying a fixed annuity, two interest rates are often used. One is the minimum guaranteed rate, which applies for the duration of the contract. The other is the "current" rate of interest, which reflects market conditions. *See also* ANNUITY; RETIREMENT AND PENSION PLANNING.

fixed rate certificate A certificate of deposit that has a constant rate of interest over its term. An example is an 8%, one-year certificate of deposit.

fixed rate loan A type of loan on which the interest rate does not fluctuate with general market conditions. Fixed rate loans include fixed rate mortgage (CONVENTIONAL MORTGAGE), consumer installment loans, and fixed rate business loans. Fixed rate loans tend to have higher original interest rates than flexible rate loans, such as an ADJUSTABLE RATE MORTGAGE (ARM), because lenders are not protected against a rise in the cost of money when they make a fixed rate loan.

fixed rate mortgage A MORTGAGE LOAN that is

at a set, specified interest rate for the lifetime or maturity of the mortgage.
See also FIXED RATE LOAN.

fixed return An investment that provides a constant return over its life. An example is a note that pays a fixed interest rate each period. Also, fixed income securities generally provide fixed returns to investors.

flat

securities: Securities on which interest and perhaps PRINCIPAL may not be paid. BONDS of bankrupt railroads and INCOME BONDS that need not pay interest when there are no earnings are traded flat.

real estate: A building that houses one household on the first floor and another household on the second floor.

flat dollar deductible A clause in INSURANCE policies that specifies a certain amount to be subtracted from any loss before payment is made.

flat market A securities market in which prices are basically moving horizontally and that often is associated with low volume.

flat rate

specific price: A fixed price that remains the same regardless of the quantity purchased or other related factors.

mortgage: A level payment MORTGAGE as in a FIXED RATE AND PAYMENT MORTGAGE.

loan: A rough indicator of INTEREST not considering whether the LOAN is held to its MATURITY.

insurance: A fixed PREMIUM that is unaffected by the INSURED'S loss record.

banking: A fixed rate that is charged to a DEPOSITOR'S CHECKING ACCOUNT if the BALANCE falls below a certain minimum level.
See also VARIABLE COST.

flat yield The return on debt or equity securities that does not include capital appreciation. It equals the annual return (interest income or dividend income) divided by the cost of the investment.

flexible budgeting An estimate of income and/or costs based on different projections (e.g., hours worked). For example, an individual can budget his or her costs depending on various levels of expected income. The greater the income, the more that can be spent.

flexible expenses An individual's costs of living that can be altered at will, such as the amount spent on entertainment. There is more flexibility for luxuries than for necessities.

flipping Taking out a second LOAN for a larger amount before repaying the first loan.
See also ADD-ON LOAN.

float

banking: MONEY held by a BANK in unpaid CHECKS. Also uncashed DEPOSITS that have been CREDITED to depositors' ACCOUNTS.

securities: The number of public SHARES issued by a CORPORATION.

bonds: Vernacular term meaning to issue and place in circulation.

floater endorsement An addition to a policy that itemizes specific item(s) for insurance protection under the endorsement.

floater policy PROPERTY INSURANCE that provides ALL-RISK coverage, except for exclusions, for the personal property item in question.

floating rate bonds A DEBT INSTRUMENT having a variable INTEREST RATE tied to a MONEY MARKET rate of interest or to the current interest rate on U.S. Treasury bonds. Normally, the rate is adjusted every six months.

The purpose of a floating rate BOND is to make the issue more attractive to INVESTORS who fear making a long-term commitment and missing an upturn in interest rates. It also ensures that the bond is less likely to TRADE at a DISCOUNT.

flood insurance INSURANCE that protects property from losses caused by floods and mudslides provided that the property is located in areas eligible under the National Flood Insurance Act of 1968.

floor
securities:

1. The actual trading floor area of the STOCK EXCHANGE where securities' trading occurs among BROKERS and TRADERS. Exchange rules allow only members to TRADE on the floor.

2. The price below which a STOCK must be sold, as in a SELL STOP ORDER. If the price penetrates the floor price, it will be "stopped out."

lower limit: The lowest amount of something, as in a MINIMUM WEIGHT, that must be observed.

floor broker A registered member of a stock exchange who transacts orders for clients on the floor to buy or sell any listed stock. A floor broker is distinguished from a FLOOR TRADER, who trades securities as a principal for his or her account, rather than for clients.

flower bond Or, *estate tax anticipation bond.* A type of U.S. government bond that can be used at its present value to pay estate taxes provided the decedent was its owner.

fluctuation
prices: Short-range changes in prices or INTEREST RATES that occur, usually on a daily basis in the case of SECURITIES.

In SECURITIES, a fixed fluctuation must occur between the bid and ask prices, depending on whether an individual is buying or selling a security.

economy: The changes occurring in the normal up and down cycles of the economy.

flurry An unanticipated and often intense increase in TRADING VOLUME of a STOCK often occurring on news concerning the underlying company or related developments. Flurries of trading activity are often as brief as they are intense.

follow-up action An activity occurring after an event and directly related to it. For example, a letter from the IRS indicating that a taxpayer is about to undergo an audit of his or her past tax returns would require the taxpayer to make a follow-up call or visit to his or her accountant to assure that everything is in order.

footnotes Explanatory notes following a FINANCIAL STATEMENT explaining certain financial statement figures and other essential matters necessary for a reader to understand a company's financial position. Examples of items covered in footnotes include disclosure of accounting methods, pending lawsuits, PENSION PLAN LIABILITIES, tax considerations, and any other matters that may directly affect the company, including possible mergers and acquisitions.

forecast
in general:

1. An individual predicting his or her future financial situation by preparing a forecast. Examples are forecasting future CASH receipts and cash payments in the form of a CASH BUDGET, and the preparation of a listing of future EXPENSES.

2. An attempt to predict future financial events based upon current data. Using electronic spreadsheets, many "what if" scenarios can be developed using various statistical methodologies in which possible courses of action can be tested in view of known data.

Forecasting is always problematical because past known relationships may not be applicable in the future where new relationships may develop.

business: Projections of future sales, revenues, earnings, financial position, and related information based on known sales and earnings information as well as developing population patterns, product developments, and related information.

economics: A branch of economics known as ECONOMETRICS in which data are extrapolated and simulated to correspond with current reality to develop a possible future pattern.

foreclosure A legal process whereby the owner of property is deprived of all legal rights and interests therein. It results from a DEFAULT on the part of the mortgagor in paying a MORTGAGE LIEN or taxes against the property.

In a foreclosure, the CREDITOR takes custody of the property through a court order and the property is sold at auction. The proceeds of the auction sale are used to pay the mortgagee any remaining BALANCE on the MORTGAGE, and to satisfy back TAXES due. The remainder is distributed to the original owner of the property.

foreign currency futures A contractual commitment to buy or sell a specified amount of a foreign CURRENCY by a predetermined date and rate of exchange. These futures are used to speculate on movements in international currencies as well as to HEDGE international contractual commitments that are to be redeemed in a particular foreign currency. Currency future contracts represent large sums of money that can be secured for a relatively small deposit. Small MARKET PRICE changes can represent significant differences in the value of the contract.

In the United States, foreign currency futures are traded on the Financial Instrument Exchange (FINEX), a division of the New York Cotton Exchange, the International Monetary Market (IMM) at the Chicago Mercantile Exchange, and the MidAmerica Commodity Exchange (MCE).

foreign exchange rate The price of one currency in terms of another as of a particular date. For example, 1 American dollar may be equivalent to 125 yen in Japanese currency while 1 American dollar may be equal to $.85 cents in Canadian currency. The foreign exchange rate changes daily.

forfeiture Loss of rights, ASSETS, or property as a result of the nonfulfillment of some obligation or condition. In some instances, forfeiture mandates a formal judicial action whereas in others the nonfulfillment of a contractual obligation is sufficient to cause a forfeiture.

For instance the loss of a LEASE can result from the failure to pay the current rent due. *See also* DEFAULT; FORECLOSURE.

forms of business organizations The manner in which a business is organized. There are three basic forms of business organizations: (1) the SOLE PROPRIETORSHIP, (2) the PARTNERSHIP, and (3) the CORPORATION.

A sole proprietorship is a business owned by one individual. Of the three forms of business organizations, sole proprietorships are the greatest in number. This form has several advantages:
- No formal charter required
- Minimal organizational costs
- Profits and control not shared with others

The disadvantages are
- Limited ability to raise large sums of money
- Unlimited liability for the owner
- Limited to the life of the owner

A partnership is similar to the sole proprietorship except that the business has more than one owner. Its advantages are
- Minimal organizational effort and costs
- Freedom from governmental regulations

Its disadvantages are
- Unlimited liability for the individual partners
- Limited ability to raise large sums of money
- Dissolution on the death or withdrawal of any of the partners

There is a special form of partnership, called limited partnership, in which one or more partners, but not all, have limited liability, up to the amount of their investment, to creditors in the event of failure of the business. The general partner manages the business. Limited partners are not involved in daily activities. The return to limited partners is in the form of income and capital gains. Often tax benefits are involved. Examples of limited partnerships are in real estate and oil and gas exploration.

A corporation is a legal entity that exists apart from its owners, better known as stockholders. Ownership is evidenced by possession of shares of stock. In terms of types of businesses, the corporate form is not the greatest in number but the most important in terms of total sales, assets, profits, and contribution to national income. The advantages of a corporation are
- Unlimited life
- Limited liability for its owners

- Ease of transfer of ownership through transfer of stock
- Ability to raise large sums of capital

Its disadvantages are

- Difficult and costly to establish, as a formal charter is required
- Subject to double taxation on its earnings and dividends paid to stockholders

See also LIMITED PARTNERSHIP.

formula timing The buying and selling of SECURITIES based on an INVESTMENT methodology that times such decisions with various indicators, depending upon the theoretical methodology. For example, some INVESTORS may turn BULLISH and begin buying STOCKS when the SHORT INTEREST RATIO is extremely high on the theory that everybody who is going to sell has already done so. Others may time their decisions based on the highs and lows of various securities.

fortuitous loss A loss that happens by chance or accident, not by the intention of the insured. Insurance policies provide coverage against losses that occur only by chance or accident. For example, life insurance will not pay a death benefit if the policyholder commits suicide within the GRACE PERIOD (such as the first two years) after the purchase.

forward market A MARKET in which transactions occur for future delivery. Examples include the COMMODITY, foreign CURRENCY, and STOCK and BOND futures markets. These markets are also called FUTURES EXCHANGES as they deal with future delivery.

401(K) (salary reduction) plan Or, *salary reduction plan*. A company-sponsored retirement program that allows an employee to defer up to $7,000, under current tax law, of the employee's gross salary withheld and invested in stocks, bonds, or money market funds. This amount is indexed for inflation using the CONSUMER PRICE INDEX. The employee's contributions and all earnings arising therefrom go tax free until withdrawn at the request of the employee or until the employee retires or leaves the firm.

Typically, the employer provides a choice of investment types into which the funds may be placed while earning tax-deferred returns. Additionally, many employers offer matching contributions. Under current tax law, the $7,000 limitation of annual deferrals to 401(K) plans applies only to an employee's elective deferrals —not the employer's matching funds. The employee's contributions plus the employer's may total, annually, the lesser of $30,000 or 25% of earnings. These contributions plus the current reduction in income taxes usually make a 401(K) salary reduction plan an excellent long-term investment.

fourth market Trading activity that takes place directly between buyer and seller of SECURITIES without the assistance of a broker, eliminating sales commissions. Buyers and sellers are usually large institutional investors, such as INSURANCE companies, MUTUAL FUNDS, or pension funds. The fourth market is aided by computers, such as a computerized subscriber service called INSTINET, an acronym for Institutional Networks Corporation. Among its subscribers are a large number of mutual funds and other institutional investors linked to each other by computer terminals. The system permits subscribers to display tentative volume interest and bid-ask quotes to others in the system.

fractional share Anything less than a full share of STOCK. Fractional shares may be required when there is a STOCK DIVIDEND or SPLIT or a DIVIDEND REINVESTMENT PLAN. When fractional shares are sold, they are sold as ODD LOTS by an ODD-LOT DEALER.

free checking account A CHECKING ACCOUNT for which no monthly fees, DEPOSIT, or CHECK cashing fees are charged. Normally, however, higher BANK fees will be charged for checks returned because of insufficient funds, CASHIER and CERTIFIED CHECKS, TRAVELER'S CHECKS, and related bank fees.

free riding A fraudulent investment practice of placing orders to buy securities with numerous brokers and paying for profitable transactions but not unprofitable ones.

fringe benefit Compensation beyond a salary, given to employees of an organization at no COST to the employees. Fringe benefits can include paid holidays and vacations, GROUP HEALTH AND LIFE INSURANCE, PENSION PLANS, and subsidized cafeterias. Fringe benefits are extremely expensive for organizations and they may exceed salaries up to 40%. Fringe benefits are the only form of COMPENSATION that is not directly TAXED by the government.

front-end load Initial sales commission at the time of the purchase of MUTUAL FUNDS. Administration and management fees continue to be charged annually regardless of whether a fund is a front-end load, BACK-END LOAD, (a charge when funds are withdrawn), or NO-LOAD.
See also LOAD FUND.

front-end loss An investment or activity that has losses at the beginning of a period and then later may start to generate profits. An example is a real estate venture that may have significant losses in the first year because of high start-up costs.

frozen account An ACCOUNT in a bank from which no WITHDRAWALS may be made without explicit permission from an authorized court of law. Frozen ACCOUNTS often occur after a DEPOSITOR dies or when the true owner has to be determined.

full disclosure
in general: A requirement to present all material information relevant to a certain matter.
securities: The SECURITIES ACT OF 1933 calls for full disclosure of new securities. To receive approval from the SECURITIES AND EXCHANGE COMMISSION (SEC), the applicant must provide the SEC with economic and financial data relevant to the company and the new offering. It does so in the form of a PROSPECTUS.
insurance: The insured is required to provide all pertinent information to the insurer for a policy to be issued.

real estate: A broker is required to present all known facts about the financial and physical condition of the subject property.
banking: A lender is required to disclose to borrowers the true cost and terms of loans.
See also TRUTH-IN-LENDING ACT.

full replacement coverage A type of INSURANCE policy condition under which an insured has the right to be indemnified for lost property without any reduction for DEPRECIATION.

full replacement policy A HOMEOWNER'S POLICY that will replace, rebuild, or repair damaged property for up to the maximum of the policy, which is set at a value equal to what is estimated as the cost of replacing the property.

full-service bank A BANK offering a full range of financial services to the public as distinguished from other BANKS whose charters restrict their range of services. The latter category includes SAVINGS BANKS and other special purpose banks. The services provided include CHECKING and SAVINGS ACCOUNTS, consumer and commercial loans, and TRUSTEE and SECURITIES services.

full-service broker A BROKER providing a wide range of services to clients. Unlike DISCOUNT BROKERS, full-service brokers provide buy and sell advice on STOCKS, BONDS, OPTIONS, COMMODITIES, and MUTUAL FUNDS. A full-service broker may offer research services, ASSET MANAGEMENT ACCOUNTS, tax shelters, and limited PARTNERSHIPS as well as allowing participation in new SECURITY issues.

A full-service broker will typically charge higher COMMISSIONS than a discount broker.

full trading authorization Or, *full discretionary account*. Permission given to a BROKER by a customer for a third party, such as an INVESTMENT ADVISER, to execute buy and sell orders in his or her account. In addition, funds or stocks may be withdrawn from the ACCOUNT.

full warranty A WARRANTY to cover all aspects of a product or service in the event of a breakdown or other interruption. There is full and complete service during the period of the warranty. Under the terms of a full warranty, any aspect of a product or service that does not meet manufacturers' specifications will be repaired or otherwise corrected. Warranties can vary in terms of whether they cover all parts and labor or just parts, for example, and no labor.

It has become fairly common practice to offer extended full warranty protection as an added COST for many products. For example, many car manufacturers offer an extended full warranty on their cars for an additional charge.

full-managed fund A MUTUAL FUND or INVESTMENT COMPANY authorized by its bylaws to INVEST in several different types of investments. Depending upon MARKET conditions, it can invest in different combinations of COMMON or PREFERRED STOCK, BONDS, and other SECURITIES. This type of a fund is also known as a GENERAL MANAGEMENT TRUST or INVESTMENT COMPANY.

full warranty
in general: A guarantee by a seller to a buyer to COVER all aspects of the quality of an item including parts and labor.
insurance: A written declaration by an INSURED to an INSURER that a particular condition does or does not exist that will materially affect the insurance policy premium and coverage terms. For example, in a FIRE INSURANCE policy, the insured issues a written statement declaring that there are operational fire detectors on each floor of the building.
warranty: Any written declaration of an existing factual representation.

fully paid policy In INSURANCE, a whole LIFE INSURANCE POLICY with limited payment terms for which all the PREMIUM payments have been made. For example, a 25-payment policy is completely paid for after 25 payments, and no future PREMIUM payments need to be made. A fully paid policy remains in effect for the life of the INSURED.

fun money Personal disposable monies that

are not essential for the day-to-day living of an individual and are expendable. Fun money can be spent for any desire one might have and not jeopardize the individual's financial viability.

fund
asset: An ASSET that has been restricted or earmarked for a particular reason. For example, a couple may have provided for the education of their children by setting aside money in an education fund established in a BANK.
trustee: CASH, stock, or other property placed with a TRUSTEE for the purpose of financial management as set forth in a formal agreement, including an endowment fund for a college.
mutual fund: A reference to a MUTUAL FUND.

fund switching The practice of moving ASSETS from one type of a MUTUAL FUND to another within the same family of funds to take advantage of timely investment opportunities. For example, one might move money from a fund specializing in American EQUITIES to a fund investing primarily in a specific foreign country when the comparative opportunity for an increased INVESTMENT return became greater in the foreign country.

fundamental analysis Analysis of INVESTMENT prospects for a particular security or an equity market that would consider the present state of the economy, the prospects for particular industries, current Federal Reserve MONEY MANAGEMENT practices, including the DISCOUNT RATE, and other related indices. The company's FINANCIAL STATEMENT would be thoroughly analyzed. Fundamental analysis, in short, attempts to consider all relevant pieces of investment information including earnings, DIVIDENDS, and PRICE EARNING RATIOS before reaching an investment decision.

This type contrasts with TECHNICAL ANALYSIS (charting) in which the primary investment consideration would be the INVESTMENT chart position in terms of price and/or volume of a particular STOCK or MARKET.

funded pension plan An INVESTMENT PLAN in

which the financing for the PENSION has already been committed, and the plan's financial viability is not tied to the financial viability of the sponsoring employer.

funding

1. Providing the necessary financial resources to carry out a particular activity.

2. Refinancing a DEBT prior to its MATURITY; also termed REFUNDING.

3. Putting money into INVESTMENTS or another type of reserve fund to provide for future PENSION PLANS.

future consumption

1. An expected purchase or use of goods or services at a later date to meet the consumer's needs and wants.

2. A statement that is expected to have a future benefit, such as a politician's promising to lower taxes if elected so that he or she may receive votes.

future return RETURN (earnings and capital gain) on investment expected for a future period of time. Future return, not historical or past return, is the one that determines the current value of an investment.
See also EXPECTED YIELD.

future value

1. The valuation of an asset projected to the end of a particular time period. An example is projecting what an individual's house will be worth in ten years.

2. The value of a particular current sum of money that grows at a compound interest rate after a given number of years. Using the compound amount (future value) tables (Table 1 and Table 2, Appendix A), one can determine the amount that will be accumulated in a pension plan or the future sum in a bank account. The future value is the opposite of the PRESENT VALUE.
See also TIME VALUE OF MONEY.

futures contract A CONTRACT to buy or sell a given commodity on a future date for a predetermined price. It requires delivery of a specific quantity of a commodity to the buyer of the contract at the date of expiration. The contract specifies the amount, method, quality, valuation, month and means of delivery, and commodity exchange to be traded in.

futures market Or, *futures exchange*. The commodity market that trades FUTURES CONTRACTS. It is a self-regulating body whose aim is to decide the conditions for acceptance of members, their trading terms, and their behavior in trading. Examples are Amex Commodity Exchange, the Commodity Exchange, Inc. (COMEX), the New York Mercantile Exchange, the Chicago Board of Trade, and the Chicago Mercantile Exchange.

galloping inflation/hyperinflation Extremely high rate of INFLATION.

garnishment An official proceeding whereby an individual's property, SALARY, or other ASSETS are attached and used to pay a DEBT or other legal obligation. Normally, the practice of GARNISHMENT orders an employer to withhold part of the disposable SALARY payments of an employee for payment to the court until the legal obligation has been satisfied.
See also FEDERAL GARNISHMENT LAW.

general damages Damages that cannot be quantifiably measured, commonly referred to as "pain and suffering." A court may estimate such damages and reimburse the aggrieved party.

general lien The right a CREDITOR acquires through a court proceeding to the ASSETS of a DEBTOR until a legally qualified DEBT has been satisfied.

general mortgage bond A BOND collaterized by a BLANKET MORTGAGE on a company's property, often subordinated to specific mortgages against certain properties.

general obligation bond A MUNICIPAL BOND that has the payment of the bond interest and principal backed by the FULL FAITH AND CREDIT of the issuing government. The backing is from general tax revenues of the issuing governmental unit.

general partner

1. A partner who has unlimited liability for partnership debts in the event the partnership fails. In an ordinary partnership, all members are general partners. The partners share in the profits.

2. The managing partner of a limited partnership who is fully accountable for partnership affairs.

generalist

1. An individual with numerous diverse abilities and interests.

2. An employee with many varied job responsibilities.

generation-skipping transfer The transfer of assets to a generation more than once removed from the transferrer. An example is the gift of property from a grandparent to a grandchild.

geometric average return A measure of return over a single holding period or over multiperiods. When an investor holds an investment for more than one period, it is important to understand how to compute the average of the successive rates of return. There are two types of multiperiod average (mean) returns: ARITHMETIC AVERAGE RETURN and geometric average return.

The arithmetic return is simply the arithmetic average of successive one-period rates of

return. The arithmetic average return, however, can be quite misleading in multiperiod return calculations.

A more accurate measure of the actual return generated by an investment over multiple periods is the geometric average return. The geometric return over n periods is computed as follows:

$$\text{Geometric return} = \sqrt[n]{(1+r_1)(1+r_2)\ldots(1+r_n)} - 1$$

Since it is cumbersome to calculate the nth root (although there is a formula for approximation), we will illustrate only the two-period return calculation ($n = 2$).

Example: Consider the following data where the price of a stock doubles in one period and depreciates back to the original price. Assume no dividends.

	Time periods		
	$t=0$	$t=1$	$t=2$
Price (end of period)	$50	$100	$50
HPR	—	100%	−50%

The holding period return for periods 1 and 2 are computed as follows:

Period 1 ($t=1$)

$$\text{HPR} = \frac{\$0 + (\$100 - \$50)}{\$50} = \frac{\$50}{\$50} = 100\%$$

Period 2 ($t=2$)

$$\text{HPR} = \frac{\$0 + (\$50 - \$100)}{\$100} = \frac{-\$50}{\$100} = -50\%$$

Therefore, the arithmetic average return is the average of 100% and −50%, which is 25%, as shown below:

$$\frac{100\% + (-50\%)}{2} = 25\%$$

Obviously, the stock purchased for $50 and sold for the same price two periods later did not earn 25%; it clearly earned zero return. The geometric average return provides a correct return.

Note that $n = 2$, $r_1 = 100\% = 1$, and $r_2 = -50\% = -0.5$. Then,

Geometric return $= \sqrt[2]{(1+1)(1-0.5)} - 1$

$$= \sqrt[2]{(2)(0.5)} - 1$$

$$= \sqrt{1} - 1 = 1 - 1 = 0\%$$

See also MEANS.

gift certificate A document representing a certain value bought from a business, such as from a retail store or restaurant, to give to another to use to obtain merchandise, food, or services at no charge. As an example, a husband buys a wife a $200 gift certificate to use for shopping at a clothing store.

gift giving See FEDERAL GIFT TAX.

gift inter vivos The transfer of property from a donor to donee during the former's lifetime, without consideration.

gift splitting Division between parents of a gift to a child to avoid taxation. For example, each parent gives a child a gift of $10,000; thus $20,000 is passed on to the child without tax.

gift tax A tax levied on the transfer of money or property made without consideration. The donor pays the tax based on the fair market value of the property at the transfer date. A parent may give a child up to $10,000 per year tax free. Gifts between spouses are unlimited.

Ginnie Maes DEBT SECURITIES sponsored by the GOVERNMENT NATIONAL MORTGAGE ASSOCIATION (GNMA). The purpose of the Government National Mortgage Association is to provide funding for high-risk MORTGAGES for high-RISK BORROWERS, usually in areas approved for government building projects that have no other funding sources. The government AGENCY also offers guarantees for MORTGAGES issued by others, including COMMERCIAL BANKS, MORTGAGE BANKS, and INSURERS.

GINNIE MAES are guaranteed by the U.S. government and therefore have a high CREDIT rating.

glamour stock Any STOCK, or group of stocks, that are extremely attractive to investors at any point in time. These stocks normally have a higher P/E RATIO than other stocks and can be quite volatile.

GNP (gross national product) deflator A weighted average of the price indices used to deflate the components of GNP. Thus, it reflects price changes for goods and services bought by consumers, businesses, and governments. The GNP deflator is found by dividing current GNP in a given year by constant (real) GNP. Because it covers a broader group of goods and services than the CONSUMER PRICE INDEX (CPI) and the PRODUCER PRICE INDEX (PPI), the GNP deflator is a very widely applied price index that is frequently used to measure inflation. The GNP deflator, unlike the CPI and PPI, is available only quarterly—not monthly. It is published by the U.S. Department of Commerce.
See also PRICE INDICES.

goal An objective an individual desires to accomplish within a prescribed time period. An example is a person wanting to become a millionaire by the age of 50.

goal dates The dates an individual sets for himself or herself to accomplish desired personal objectives. Examples are setting January 1, 2000, or before to buy a new house, or having sufficient savings to retire at age 60.

goal setting Establishment by an individual of the steps necessary to accomplish a desired objective. As an example, an individual who wants to buy a house at age 25 sets salary and savings guidelines to accomplish this goal.

gold bars The actual metal itself smelted into bars weighing 400 troy ounces (11.3 kg) held by central banks and TRADERS. In the United States, gold futures are traded on the Commodity Exchange (CMX). The Canadian Maple Leaf and the American Gold Eagle are one troy ounce gold coins that also are actively traded.

gold bugs A vernacular term given to individuals who believe gold is the only true repository of monetary worth and feel all national currencies should be backed up by gold bullion. Gold bugs ideologically believe in the value of gold as a constant monetary standard and view gold as an INVESTMENT HEDGE against the possibility of economic collapse or INFLATION.

gold bullion The actual metal smelted either into coins or gold bars. The standard for measuring the weight of gold is the troy ounce. *See also* GOLD BARS.

gold certificate A CERTIFICATE used as currency for governments backing their CURRENCIES with gold entitling the holder, upon demand, to the entire value of the certificate in gold bullion. The certificates are used in place of actual gold coins.

The United States recalled its gold certificates in 1933. Today it has a currency that is not backed by gold and is "free floating."

gold coin A pure gold coin minted by any of several governments and largely used for gold trading purposes. Examples include the South African Krugerrand, weighing a whole ounce, as well as the Canadian Maple Leaf and the American Eagle, which each weigh a troy ounce.

gold mutual fund A MUTUAL FUND that invests in gold stocks. An example is Lexington Gold Fund.

golden handcuff A method of retaining employees in an organization through the use of STOCK OPTIONS and PENSION PLANS that make it impractical for them to leave without suffering a significant financial loss. Golden handcuffs have been found to be particularly useful in start-up companies seeking to retain highly qualified personnel.

golden parachute agreement A very lucrative contract giving a senior corporate executive monetary or other benefits if his or her position is lost because of an acquisition by another company. Examples include bonus, severance pay, and stock option.

good delivery Minimum necessary requirements for a STOCK CERTIFICATE to be transferred and delivered from one owner to another. The conditions include having a certificate in good condition, having the right signature in the proper location, valid ownership, and all necessary documentation. If any of these conditions is unfilled, the transaction represents *bad delivery* and the shortcomings must be corrected.

good faith (goodwill) In the carrying out of a transaction, indication that each party will be ethical and fair and will act without malice or deception. Good faith implies honest intentions and observance of the concept of reasonableness.

If deception did occur without prior knowledge, the transaction, conducted in good faith, is still valid. For example, if a property deed is transferred to another in the course of a good faith sale, and it later becomes evident that a prior owner had not properly signed the certificate, the sale is still valid.

Contrary to good faith is bad faith, where one of the participants knowingly commits fraud or deception. Should this fraud be proved, the transaction is rendered invalid.

good-till-canceled order (GTC) A customer's order to buy or sell SECURITIES at a particular price. The order to the broker remains in effect until it is either executed or canceled. *See also* FILL-OR-KILL ORDER.

goodwill
personal: The good name and reputation an individual enjoys.
corporate: The additional value accruing to a company because of its favorable public reputation, customer relations, and other intangible factors that give the company a measurable competitive edge.
accounting: The intangible ASSET that has tangible value at the time of the sale of a company. The purchase price of a company is equal to net asset value plus goodwill. For example, if the net assets of company XYZ are $5,400,000 and its

goodwill is $600,000, then the purchase price would equal $6,000,000. Goodwill is an intangible asset AMORTIZABLE over 40 years.

government bonds Obligations of the U.S. government, regarded as the best grade issues in existence.
See also U.S. SAVINGS BOND.

Government National Mortgage Association (GNMA) Government-owned corporation, nicknamed GINNIE MAE. GNMA issues primarily pass-through securities. These pass through all payments of interest and principal received on a pool of federally insured mortgage loans. GNMA guarantees that all payments of principal and interest will be made on the mortgages on a timely basis. Since many mortgages are repaid before maturity, investors in GNMA pools usually recover most of their principal investment well ahead of schedule. Ginnie Mae is considered an excellent investment. The higher yields, coupled with the U.S. government guarantee, provide a competitive edge over other intermediate-term to long-term securities issued by the U.S. government and other agencies.
See also MORTGAGE-BACKED SECURITIES.

government (agency) securities Or, *agency securities*. Securities issued by U.S. government agencies, such as the FEDERAL HOME LOAN BANK (FHLB). Most of these securities are not secured by the federal government, unlike TREASURY SECURITIES.

go-go fund *See* PERFORMANCE FUND.

grace days The days at the beginning of an interest period during which a bank will allow funds to earn interest even though the funds are not actually on deposit.

grace period
insurance: The 30-day period after the due date allowed on LIFE AND HEALTH INSURANCE policies that maintains the policy coverage although the premium has not yet been paid.
banking: The time period in days in which savings deposits or withdrawals can be made and still earn interest from a given day of the interest period.
credit: The number of days between the billing date on a credit card or charge account statement and the date when finance charges begin.

graded vesting An employee's vesting in a pension plan taking into account such factors as age, service years, salary, and others. An actuarial formula is used.

graduated lease A LEASE that provides for a varying rental rate. Rental rates are determined based on periodic appraisals or tied to an annual CONSUMER PRICE INDEX (CPI). This type of lease is used largely in long-term leases. For example, a 7-year graduated lease may call for annual rent increases of 4 percent.

graduated payment mortgage (GPM) A special type of FIXED RATE MORTGAGE (CONVENTIONAL MORTGAGE) in which the monthly payments are lower in the early years of the loan than they are in the later years.

graduated tax *See* PROGRESSIVE TAX.

graduated wage A salary structure of a business, encompassing incremental salary levels dependent upon such factors as employees' years of service, performance, and type of job.

grandfather clause A stipulation in a new law or regulation exempting those already a part of the existing system from its effects. A grandfather clause permits those already participating in an activity about to be restricted to continue their present activities and association. For example, if an individual is currently piloting a boat without a newly required license, a grandfather clause may permit the individual to continue as before.

In certain cases, a modified grandfather clause may allow a certain period of time to elapse before compliance with the newly imposed conditions is required.

grantor
legal: An individual deciding to give property or creating a trust.

investments: An options trader who executes a call or put option order and receives a premium for the transaction.

graveyard market A bear market in which investors who sell their securities will suffer huge losses, while potential investors remain on the sidelines until things look brighter.

greater fool theory An investment strategy in which a person pays a known "high" price in the expectation that another person (fool) will pay an even higher price.

green shoe A clause in an underwriting agreement stating that in the event of exceptional public demand, the issuer will authorize additional shares for distribution by the syndicate.

gross earnings Unadjusted personal income for the individual INCOME TAX. GROSS EARNINGS includes all earned INCOME such as WAGES, salaries, and tips; all taxable INTEREST and DIVIDEND INCOME; taxable refunds of state and local INCOME TAXES; income from ALIMONY; business income; CAPITAL GAIN OR LOSS as well as capital gain distributions; other gains or losses; total IRA distributions; all PENSION and ANNUITY income; all income from RENTS, ROYALTIES, PARTNERSHIPS, ESTATES, and TRUSTS; unemployment compensation or INSURANCE income; and SOCIAL SECURITY benefits.
See also ADJUSTED GROSS INCOME.

gross estate The value of an individual's assets before deducting liabilities, taxes, and estate-related expenses. The gross estate includes stocks, bonds, real estate, and personal possessions.
See also ESTATE; ESTATE PLANNING; ESTATE TAX.

gross income The total of all income (before deductions) that is subject to federal taxes. Certain types of tax-exempt income are excluded from gross income. Examples of gross income are salary, interest income, dividend income, capital gains, and taxable pension withdrawals.

gross income multiplier A method of determining the price to pay for an income-producing property by dividing the asking price (or MARKET VALUE) of the property by the current gross rental income.

Example: Assume that current gross rental income is $23,600 and the asking price is $219,000; the gross income multiplier is

$$\$219,000/\$23,600 = 9.28.$$

A property in a similar neighborhood may be valued at "8 times annual gross." Thus, if its annual gross rental income amounts to $23,600, the value would be taken as $188,800 (8 × $23,600). This approach should be used with caution. Different properties have different operating expenses, which must be taken into account in determining their value.
See also GROSS RENT MULTIPLIER.

gross lease A LEASE in which the lessor pays all operational expenses including TAXES, utilities, INSURANCE, and maintenance. A gross lease typically is a short-term lease and is the common lease arrangement. Because of its short-term nature, a gross lease normally makes no provision for future rent increases.

As an illustration of a gross lease, a LANDLORD of an office building pays all the INSURANCE, maintenance, TAXES, and utilities out of the tenant's gross rent receipts.

gross national product (GNP) The current MARKET VALUE in dollars of all final goods and services produced in the economy in a given period. GNP is normally stated in annual terms, though data on it are compiled and released quarterly. It consists of personal consumption expenditures, gross private domestic investment, government spending, and net exports (exports minus imports).

gross profit margin Ratio of gross profit divided by net sales. A high gross profit margin is a positive sign as it shows that the business is earning an attractive return over the cost of its merchandise sold.

gross rent multiplier (GRM) The ratio of the selling price of property to its gross rental income. It is a popular INCOME METHOD that is used to appraise an income-producing property. For example, if the selling price of property was $350,000 and the gross rental income generated was $50,000, the GRM would be 7.

ground lease A long-term lease (such as 30 or more years) of land alone.

group clinic A type of health maintenance organization (HMO) in which a group of physicians offers services from a single hospital-clinic located in the same general area as the patients who are members.

group disability insurance DISABILITY INSURANCE that is sold collectively to an entire group under one policy.

group enrollment card A document signed by an individual eligible for group insurance as notice of his or her desire to participate in the group plan. If the plan is contributory, the card gives the employer authority to deduct contributions from the employee's pay.

group health insurance HEALTH INSURANCE that is sold collectively to an entire group of individuals under one policy.

group insurance INSURANCE provided employees by their employer. Group insurance is also available through unions and associations. It may be more desirable than individual insurance for three reasons. First, it is cheaper. Second, the employer often provides group insurance as a fringe benefit for employees. Third, it may cover a person who would be uninsurable. Employers usually share the cost with employees. The most common forms of group insurance are LIFE INSURANCE, ACCIDENT INSURANCE, and HEALTH INSURANCE.

group life insurance LIFE INSURANCE that is sold collectively to an entire group under one policy.
See also GROUP INSURANCE.

growing equity mortgage (GEM) A MORT-

GAGE on which the interest rate remains fixed but the payments are scheduled to rise, causing the loan to be paid off much faster than would otherwise be the case.

growth To increase financially in size and wealth. For example, an individual may experience financial growth in his or her net assets over a certain period of time.
See also GROWTH AND INCOME FUNDS; GROWTH FUND; GROWTH RATES; GROWTH STOCK.

growth and income fund A MUTUAL FUND that seeks both current DIVIDEND income and CAPITAL GAINS. The goal of the fund is to provide long-term growth without much variation in share value. An example is Fidelity Investors' Growth and Income Fund.

growth fund A MUTUAL FUND that seeks to maximize its return through CAPITAL GAINS. It typically invests in the stocks of potential companies that are expected to rise in value faster than inflation. These stocks are best for an individual desiring steady growth over a long-term period but feeling little need for income in the meantime. An example is the T. Rowe Price Capital Appreciation Fund.

growth rate
in general: The percentage change in EARNINGS PER SHARE, dividends per share, sales, market price of stock, or total assets, compared to a base year amount.
securities: The compounded yearly rate a security appreciates (depreciates).
See also TIME VALUE OF MONEY.
economics: The periodic growth rate in GNP of the economy, stated in percentage terms over the prior quarter. The growth rate typically signifies the state of the economy—expansion or detraction.

growth stock A stock of a young company with little or no earnings history. However, the company shows sales and earnings increasing faster than the average for its particular industry and for the general economy. A growth stock is

risky since capital APPRECIATION is speculative. An example is a HIGH-TECH STOCK.
See also COMMON STOCK.

guarantee insolvency fund A fund established to guarantee payment of INSURANCE benefits in case the insurer becomes insolvent.

guaranteed account A savings account that is assured by a third party with regard to payment. An example is a parent's written guarantee of a child's account.

guaranteed bond A BOND in which the INTEREST and PRINCIPAL or just interest are guaranteed by another organization. Railroad BONDS, when the railroad has leased the road of another and the security holders of the leased road require assurance of INCOME in exchange for control of the property, are often INSURED by an outside organization. MUNICIPAL BONDS are, in some instances, backed by the MUNICIPAL BOND INSURANCE ASSOCIATION (MBIA) for an additional fee. If the guarantor's CREDIT rating is stronger than that of the original issuer, then the guaranteed BOND assumes the CREDIT rating of the guarantor.

Parent-subsidiary relationships may also be used to guarantee a bond that is issued by a subsidiary.

guaranteed dividend
securities: A periodic STOCK DIVIDEND assured by a third party. For example, the stock of the FEDERAL NATIONAL MORTGAGE ASSOCIATION TRADES on the NEW YORK STOCK EXCHANGE and it pays a DIVIDEND on YIELDS from MORTGAGES guaranteed by the federal government.
insurance: NONPARTICIPATING LIFE INSURANCE sold by LIFE INSURANCE COMPANIES in which a portion of the payment coupons represent a DIVIDEND that is redeemable on payment. This type of INSURANCE is also termed a guaranteed dividend policy or a GUARANTEED INVESTMENT POLICY.

guaranteed insurability A CASH VALUE LIFE INSURANCE feature that allows the policyholder to purchase additional cash value insurance at predesignated intervals and standard rates without providing proof of INSURABILITY.

guaranteed investment contract An arrangement whereby an insurance company guarantees a rate of return for a limited time period, typically five to ten years, to be applied to the amount invested.

guaranteed minimum annuity *See* ANNUITY CERTAIN.

guaranteed period annuity *See* ANNUITY; STRAIGHT LIFE (PURE) ANNUITY.

guaranteed renewability option An option available with TERM LIFE INSURANCE policies that eliminates the need to provide INSURABILITY when the policy is renewed.

guaranteed renewable policy A policy that is always renewable as long as the PREMIUMS are paid, although the company can raise the policy's rates.

guaranteed security A stock or bond that is backed as to its face value and/or interest by an entity other than the issuer, such as an insurance company.

guardian One having the legal authority to take care of another as a parent; one acting as an asset administrator for an individual who is judged to be incompetent because of mental or physical impairment.
testamentary: Individual appointed as a child's guardian in the parent's will.
general guardian: One having the general care responsibility for an individual and his or her estate.
special guardian: Individual having limited authority of a guardian. For example, a special guardian may have no authority over the assets of an estate but must nurture and care for a child.

H

hammering the market Hard and consistent selling, including SHORT selling, of the STOCK MARKET. When a market is being "hammered" the volume rises and the stock indexes drop precipitously. For example, in October 1987 the NEW YORK STOCK EXCHANGE suffered a one-day "hammering" and dropped over 500 points on extremely high volume.

handling charge Charges incurred in a transaction or purchase related to the actual COST of the exchange.
banking: Transaction charges for CHECKS cashed, returned checks, or TRAVELER'S CHECKS as well as other general bank account management fees.
securities: An extra CHARGE for dealing with FRACTIONAL SHARES and other small transactions.
transportation: A CHARGE made when unusual attention must be paid in shipping certain types of dangerous, extremely fragile, or toxic cargoes.

hard dollars Actual payment made by a client for brokerage services. For example, a broker

may charge a client a flat fee of $500 for developing a personal financial plan.
See also SOFT DOLLARS.

hardening market
in general: A situation in which prices of items are starting to increase.
investments: An upward movement in securities prices.
insurance: Greater selectivity by insurance companies in issuing policies. When this occurs, there are usually higher premiums.

hazard Any situation that affects the probability that losses or PERILS will occur.

hazard insurance INSURANCE that lenders require borrowers to carry in order to protect the lender's financial stake in a house. It protects against risks such as storms or fires.

hazard reduction Action by the INSURED to reduce the probability that a loss will occur.

head and shoulders A CHART pattern for a STOCK or STOCK MARKET in which the highest point of the stock, or stock market, is preceded

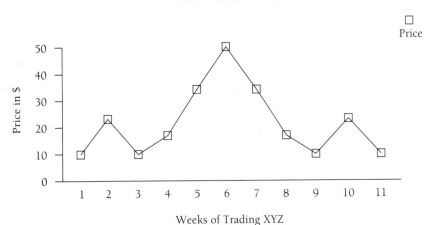

Head & Shoulder Chart

□ Price

Price in $ / Weeks of Trading XYZ

and followed by intermediate highs. When the pattern is graphed, it has the characteristic look of a head atop a pair of shoulders, hence the name. It is considered BEARISH when a head and shoulder formation is completed and moves to the right shoulder. According to classic chartist interpretations, the next leg would then be down.

However, an inverted head and shoulder formation is considered to be BULLISH since the completion of the chart's right shoulder normally precedes an upward movement (see chart on p. 141).

head of household An individual providing more than half the financial support of a relative living in his or her household during the course of a year. According to IRS rules, qualifying individuals include parents, grandchildren, adopted children and stepchildren, unmarried and married children, and any other relative.

If you qualify as a head of household under IRS rules you pay a lower tax than those who are single, but a higher tax than a married couple filing a joint return.

health insurance INSURANCE that provides protection against financial losses resulting from illness, injury, and disability. In general, any insurance program covering medical expenses and/or income lost owing to illness or accidental injury. For most people, health insurance is provided by the employer as a major fringe benefit. Otherwise, individual policies can be purchased. Policies can include any or all of the following coverages:

- Hospitalization—covers hospital room and board, medications, tests, and services
- Surgical—covers operations
- Medical—covers visits to the doctor's office and diagnostic laboratory tests
- Major medical—covers expenses that exceed the dollar limit of the basic coverage
- Comprehensive—includes all of the above
- Dental—covers most dental expenses
- Prescriptions—pays for prescribed medication

Usually health insurance requires COINSURANCE and COPAYMENT. A coinsurance clause requires the insured to pay a proportion of any loss suffered, usually 20% to 25%. A variation of coinsurance, a copayment clause, requires the insured to pay a specific dollar portion of specific covered expense items (e.g., prescription drug coverage). The following formula determines the loss that will be reimbursed when there is a deductible and a coinsurance clause:

Reimbursement = (1 − coinsurance percentage) (loss − deductible)

Example: Don bought health insurance with a $100 deductible per hospital stay and a 20% coinsurance requirement. If the hospital bill is $2,225, his reimbursement will be calculated as shown below:

$$\text{Reimbursement} = (1 - .20)\,(\$2,225 - \$100)$$

$$= .80(\$2,125)$$

$$= \$1,700$$

health maintenance organization (HMO) A medical organization consisting of a group of hospitals, physicians, and other health care personnel who have joined together to provide necessary health services to its members. Major emphasis is on preventive medicine. Members pay an annual fee for the service.

health risk

1. The risk an individual faces in losing assets and income because of illness and disability.

2. Assessment by an insurance company of an applicant as too risky to give medical insurance because of the applicant's medical problems, such as cancer.

heavy market A situation in which supply is significantly more than demand, resulting in a drop in prices of goods or services.

hedge Any strategy used to offset an INVESTMENT risk. While a perfect hedge would eliminate all investment RISK, it would also eliminate any possible INVESTMENT gain.

stocks: In STOCK INVESTMENT, there are several possible hedges. An investor having a LONG POSITION in a stock can follow several strategies. First, the INVESTOR could buy a PUT OPTION that could be EXERCISED should the STOCK fall. For example, if the stock is purchased at $50, the investor could hedge the position by also purchasing a $50 PUT OPTION. If the stock fell to $40, the PUT could be EXERCISED and the stock sold at $50. The expense would be the COMMISSION COST of buying the PUT OPTION and EXERCISING it as well as the STRIKING PRICE PREMIUM.

However, if the STOCK stayed at substantially the same price, or rose in price, the investor would lose the COST of the put option plus the purchase COMMISSION.

Another alternative is to sell a CALL OPTION to COVER the downside RISK for the amount received from the OPTION. However, if the stock fell lower than the option proceeds, then the investor would incur the loss. Additionally, if the stock APPRECIATED more than the STRIKING PRICE of the CALL OPTION, the option would be exercised, with the investor incurring a stock appreciation OPPORTUNITY COST.

Another HEDGE technique for an INVESTOR seeking to preserve CAPITAL GAINS against any possible loss is to SELL SHORT AGAINST THE BOX by shorting an equal number of SHARES of a stock that is owned LONG.

inflation: Investors seeking to insulate themselves against INFLATION have sought investment hedges in REAL ESTATE and gold since both ASSETS tend to rise in value during inflationary periods.

international trade: International commercial transactions in which monetary fluctuations that can have a significant impact on the value of the contract can be hedged by either buying or selling the futures of the currencies involved. For example, if you sell a product to an international company that expects payment in that nation's currency, the value of the transaction can be hedged by selling the CURRENCY'S FUTURES.

See also EXERCISE.

hedge fund A MUTUAL FUND that HEDGES its risk by buying or selling options to protect its positions against MARKET RISK. For example, a fund specializing in government DEBT SECURITIES may hedge its position by selling CALL OPTIONS against its position to protect it against downside RISK.

Contrary to popular opinion, a hedge fund constructively uses options to protect investment positions and is pursuing an extremely conservative INVESTMENT philosophy.

hidden clauses Purposely vague contractual language that may lead an unsuspecting purchaser to incur obligations or RISKS that are not readily apparent.

hidden load An annual undeclared charge by a MUTUAL FUND of 1% to 1.25% annually, used to pay marketing and distribution fees.

hidden tax A TAX placed on items without the consumer's awareness of its presence; the consumer considers it to be a part of the product's total cost. For example, an import tax imposed on a good is simply passed along to the consumer as a part of the total cost. The tax is imposed prior to its final sale.

hidden values Values that are undervalued on a BALANCE SHEET because of an accounting convention or because of a management policy; also called hidden ASSETS. For example, REAL ESTATE may be valued at its original purchase price rather than its current APPRAISED value.

high

in general: A relative term describing APPRECIATED prices or values compared to similar items or ASSETS at any MARKET point.

securities: The greatest price for a STOCK or DEBT instrument in a particular trading period or during its history of being publicly TRADED. Annual SECURITY TRADING RANGES showing the high and low price are published in the daily price quotations.

high coupon The interest rate on a debt security is high compared to the maturity amount of the instrument.

high current income fund A MUTUAL FUND whose investment objective is to produce relatively high cash DIVIDENDS to its owners. An example might be a fund that invests in high-yielding utility stocks. Most generally, this term has been applied to JUNK BOND funds over the past several years.

high flyer A vernacular term describing a STOCK that has APPRECIATED very rapidly in price, often beyond justification in terms of current or anticipated earnings. The prices of high-flying STOCKS are usually extremely VOLATILE and high in comparison to others in the same industry classification.

high-grade security STOCKS and BONDS having very high INVESTMENT quality RATINGS, usually A or better, by the three major SECURITY rating services: Fitch's, Moody's, and Standard & Poor's. The investment RATING is reached after considering the corporation's assets, LIABILITIES, quality of earnings, DIVIDEND record, and management as well as other factors.

Government bonds are rated based on the unit of government, types of government guarantees, the REVENUE and DEBT of the governmental entity, and previous CREDIT HISTORY. While the federal government consistently has the highest rating, state and local bonds also have high ratings assuming their CREDIT HISTORY and particular types of revenue guarantees are substantial.

high-tech stock The STOCK of companies involved in advanced technology fields, such as biotechnology, robotics, or computers.
See also COMMON STOCK; GROWTH STOCK.

hobbies and collectibles Tangible investment vehicles that include rare coin collecting (numismatics), stamp collecting (philately), paintings, ceramics, and furniture.

hold
banking: The practice of retaining an ASSET in an account until an item is collected or a LIABILITY is satisfied. For example, a PASSBOOK LOAN requires the amount of the LOAN to be held in a SAVINGS ACCOUNT until the loan has been satisfied.

securities: The practice of a long-term INVESTOR to buy and retain a security over an extended period of time; this allows the earnings of the company to grow, resulting in a concomitant increase in the STOCK'S MARKET VALUE.
See also BUY-AND-HOLD STRATEGY.

holder-in-due-course The federal ruling that provides protection for consumers holding a defective product that was purchased under an INSTALLMENT CONTRACT from a merchant who then sold the contract to a third party.

holder of record The person whose name is recorded by the issuing company or TRANSFER AGENT as the purchaser and owner of a SECURITY at a particular time. This is important for DIVIDEND declarations, which are always given to the holder of record at a particular date.

holding company A corporation organized for the objective of owning stocks of one or more corporations and controlling their policies and management. A parent-subsidiary relationship often exists. Holding companies control many subsidiaries in widely different business areas.

holding cost of a house The cost of a house plus any expenses related to the final settlement that are not tax deductible plus any expenses related to property improvements.

holding period The time interval for which an investor holds an investment. The return on a given investment depends primarily on this period of time. If an investor holds a security for more than one year and then sells it, there is a long-term capital gain or loss for tax purposes.

holding period return (HPR) The TOTAL RETURN earned from holding an investment for the HOLDING PERIOD of time. It is computed as follows:

$$\text{HPR} = \frac{\text{Current income} + \text{Capital gain (or loss)}}{\text{Purchase price}}$$

For example, consider the investment in stocks A and B over a one-year period of ownership:

	Stock	
	A	B
Purchase price (beginning of year)	$100	$100
Cash dividend received (during the year)	$10	$15
Sales price (end of year)	$108	$98

Combining the CAPITAL GAIN return (or loss) with the current income, the total return on each investment is summarized below:

Return	Stock	
	A	B
Cash dividend	$10	$15
Capital gain (loss)	8	(2)
Total return	$18	$13

Then the HPR is

$$\text{HPR (stock A)} = \frac{\$10 + (\$108 - \$100)}{\$100} = \frac{\$10 + \$8}{\$100}$$

$$= \$18/\$100 = 18\%$$

$$\text{HPR (stock B)} = \frac{\$15 + (\$98 - \$100)}{\$100} = \frac{\$15 - \$2}{\$100}$$

$$= \$13/\$100 = 13\%$$

In the case of a MUTUAL FUND, the return is distributed in three ways: DIVIDENDS, CAPITAL GAINS distribution, and price APPRECIATION. The ANNUAL RATE OF RETURN, or the holding period return (HPR) in a mutual fund is calculated incorporating all these three, as follows:

$$\text{HPR} = \frac{(\text{Dividends} + \text{distributions} + \begin{matrix} \text{capital} \\ \text{gain} \\ \text{beginning NAV}) \end{matrix} \; \begin{matrix} \text{(ending NAV} - \\ \\ \end{matrix}}{\text{Beginning NAV}}$$

where NAV equals net asset value and (ending NAV − beginning NAV) represents price appreciation. Assume that a mutual fund paid dividends of $.50 and capital gain distributions of $.35 per share over the course of the year, and had a price (NAV) at the beginning of the year of $6.50 that rose to $7.50 per share by the end of the year. The holding period return (HPR) is

$$\text{HPR} = \frac{(\$.50 + \$.35 + (\$7.50 - \$6.50))}{\$6.50}$$

$$= \frac{\$1.85}{\$6.50} = 28.46\%$$

See also MUTUAL FUND; RETURN.

holding the market An attempt to stabilize the falling price of a security that is being sold in abundance. Purchase orders are entered into to accomplish this objective. While this is against the law, an underwriter of a new issue may do this to STABILIZE the price. This practice must be approved by the Securities and Exchange Commission.

holdover tenant A tenant who remains in possession of leased property after the expiration of the lease term who can be evicted or given a new lease.

holographic will A WILL that does not satisfy all the formal requirements of a valid will.

home banking A TELECOMMUNICATIONS method of doing ordinary consumer banking using either a home computer, modem, and telephone line or a television with an interface device and a telephone connection. Home banking allows the DEPOSITOR to get up-to-the-minute information on ACCOUNT BALANCES as well as to pay bills. While home banking is still in its infancy, its future seems assured as telecommunications and computers gain consumer acceptance.

home equity credit line loan *See* HOME-OWNER'S EQUITY ACCOUNT.

home inventory A person's possessions at his or her residence, such as furnishings and jewelry. A listing of items and their costs is suggested in order to obtain adequate insurance protection and as documentation for insurance reimbursement in case of loss.

home loan *See* MORTGAGE; RESIDENTIAL MORTGAGE.

home warranties Warranties given by builders, sellers, and real estate agencies that protect home buyers from certain defects in a home as specified in the contract.

home-office deduction An INCOME TAX DEDUCTION for business expenses applying to a part of an individual's home ONLY if that part is exclusively used on a regular basis. There are several guidelines for qualifying for the deduction:

1. It should be the principal place of business for a trade or business.

2. It should be a place of business in which patients, clients, or customers are met and dealt with in the normal course of a trade or business.

3. It should be used in connection with a trade or business, if it is a separate structure not attached to the home.

EXPENSES may also be deducted for a space within the home if it is the ONLY fixed location of a trade or business. The space must be used on a regular basis to store inventory from the trade or business if selling products at retail or wholesale.

If the space in the home is used on a regular basis in the provision of day-care service, the business expenses may be deducted even though the same space is also used for nonbusiness purposes.

homeowner's equity account CREDIT LINE offered by BANKS and BROKERAGE FIRMS allowing a homeowner to tap the built-up EQUITY in his or her home. Interest paid is deductible as mortgage interest regardless of how proceeds are used (up to $100,000 debt).

homeowner's fee An amount established by the (condominium) homeowner's association that pays for such things as maintenance of common areas and facilities, repairs to the outside of any unit (paid for by all), REAL ESTATE TAXES on the common areas, and FIRE INSURANCE covering the exterior of the buildings.

homeowner's forms 1–8 (HO-1–HO-8) *See* HOMEOWNER'S INSURANCE POLICY.

homeowner's general liability protection INSURANCE that covers situations in which the homeowner or renter is legally liable for the losses of another.

See HOMEOWNER'S INSURANCE POLICY.

homeowner's insurance policy A type of PROPERTY INSURANCE policy designed for various risks of homeowners. Coverages include losses to the dwelling, other structures on the insured's property, unscheduled personal property, additional living expenses, personal liability, theft, and medical payments to others.

In determining insurance needs, the best figure to use is the replacement value, the cost required to rebuild, excluding land. An insured's minimum protection should be 80% of replacing the house. If the insured fails to meet the replacement cost requirement, the amount of reimbursement for any loss will be calculated using the following formula:

$$R = L \times [I/(RV \times 80\%]$$

where R = reimbursement payable, L = the amount of loss less deductible, I = amount of insurance actually carried, RV = replacement value.

Example: Linda has a home with a replacement value of $100,000 and suffers a $50,000 fire loss. She insured her home for $80,000. The amount of insurance reimbursement is

$$\$50,000 \times [\$80,000/(\$100,000 \times 80\%)] = \$50,000$$

types of homeowner policies

Seven different types of homeowner policies have been designed to meet the needs of buyers. Each is briefly described below.

homeowners-1 (HO-1): Known as the basic coverage, HO-1 offers protection against 11 of the 18 major property-damage perils—for example, fire, windstorm, hail, vandalism, explosion, lightning, riot, and smoke. Losses from these perils may be limited in the amount of coverage. The policy provides protection from the three liability exposures—comprehensive personal liability, damage to other peoples' property, and medical payments.

homeowners-2 (HO-2): Known as the broad form, HO-2 offers broader coverage than HO-1 in that HO-2 covers all of the 18 major perils that cause property damages—for example, falling objects, collapse of buildings, freezing of plumbing. It also provides protection from the three liability exposures.

homeowners-3 (HO-3): Often known as the special form, HO-3 provides all-risk coverage on the dwelling itself. ALL-RISK coverage on the dwelling means that if a loss is not excluded in HO-3, it is covered.

homeowners-4 (HO-4) renters: HO-4 is designed for people who are renting an apartment or a home. It insures renters' personal property on the same basis as HO-2.

homeowners-5 (HO-5) comprehensive: HO-5 is the most comprehensive coverage you can buy. Obviously, it is much more expensive than other forms.

homeowners-6 (HO-6) condominium: This is very similar to HO-4 except that it is designed for condominium renters, not owners.

homeowners-8 (HO-8): HO-8 is designed for owners of older buildings that have been remodeled and would have replacement costs high in comparison with replacement costs for similar homes. This particular form differs from other policies in that the coverage is on an actual cash value basis rather than on a replacement cost basis.

homeowner's no-fault medical payments protection   INSURANCE that will pay for injuries to visitors regardless of who was at fault for the loss.
See HOMEOWNER'S INSURANCE POLICY.

homeowner's warranty (HOW) program   A builder's ten-year guarantee that his or her workmanship, materials, and construction are up to established standards. The HOW provides reimbursement for the cost of remedying specified defects.

horizontal spread   Or, *calendar spread*. The purchase and sale of an equal number of OPTION contracts having the same STRIKING PRICE but with varying maturity dates. The purpose of the

horizontal spread is to offset the RISK of the furthest option contract by selling a nearer term option CONTRACT.

HORIZONTAL SPREAD

	Debit	Credit
Buy 5 XYZ July 60 striking price Call Options @ $600 per contract	$3,000.00	
Sell 5 XYZ April 60 striking price Call Options @ $300 per contract		$1,500.00
Net Cost	$1,500.00	

The purchased option contract with the furthest expiration date covers the shorted near-term option contract. It is never possible, therefore, to COLLATERALIZE a far-term option contract with a near-term option contract.

hospital income policy   An insurance policy that pays the insured a fixed amount of income for days spent as a patient in the hospital. It is partly intended to supplement lost wages. For example, the policy may provide for a benefit payment of $100 per day for each day hospitalized, not to exceed 180 days.

hospitalization insurance   A kind of HEALTH INSURANCE that provides reimbursement for hospital, surgical, and medical expenses incurred in connection with hospitalization.

hot issue   A new (IPO, Initial Public Offering) SEC-registered public offering having higher demand than supply when coming to market. It therefore sells at a PREMIUM price.

hot stock   A STOCK having a great deal of INVESTOR interest with subsequent high trading volume and rapid increases in price. For example, a publicly traded company announces it is about to be taken over by another company at a substantially higher price than the current market price. Under these circumstances, the stock experiences a very rapid rise in price together with heavy trading volume.

hotchpot The addition of assets of one who dies so as to distribute them ultimately to the beneficiaries.

house call *See* HOUSE MAINTENANCE REQUIREMENTS.

house confinement A customer's ACCOUNT maintained and managed by the BROKERAGE FIRM PARTNERS rather than an employee; also called house ACCOUNT. Usually, such accounts are large favored institutional or corporate accounts that receive individualized attention.

house maintenance requirements Minimum EQUITY requirements established by a BROKERAGE FIRM before additional equity is required from the customer. If the additional equity is not forthcoming within the allotted time, COLLATERAL will be eliminated from the customer's ACCOUNT.
See also MAINTENANCE MARGIN REQUIREMENT.

house poor Or, *property poor*. A family buying a home that costs more than they can afford.

housing affordability index A standard established by the National Association of Realtors to measure consumer ability to afford to buy a home. An index of 100 means a family earning the national median income has exactly enough MONEY to qualify for a MORTGAGE on a median-priced home. Some experts maintain that every one-point increase in the home mortgage INTEREST RATE results in 300,000 fewer home sales.

housing code A federal, state, or local set of structural building requirements that must be met in order to receive interim or final certification by the appropriate governmental level. Normally, housing code enforcement is done at the local level; however, many states have uniform housing codes to which all local municipalities must adhere. In addition, FHA-financed housing must satisfy certain building code requirements.

The housing code includes such areas as electrical wiring, insulation, plumbing, and roofing.

housing ownership records Records kept evidencing ownership of the house and the contents therein.

human capital The human resources involved in any organization. Human capital, just like financial CAPITAL, must be developed through the INVESTMENT of capital, time, and work. Normally, human capital can be developed through training programs in which skills can be improved, learned, and updated.

Human capital is the most important ASSET of any organization. Human capital represents a storehouse of knowledge and productive talent that is not represented in accounting because of its quantification difficulty.

human life value approach In INSURANCE, the methodology used in determining the value of an individual's life in terms of his or her earnings devoted to family support. The human life value approach considers the future value of a wage earner's INCOME devoted to supporting his or her family derived from the number of years of expected earnings prior to retirement. For example, a 30-year-old married male WAGE EARNER having two children and an MBA degree working in a major *corporation* could have a useful career of 40 years. If the employee were earning $35,000, and could reasonably expect a 5% raise every year, then 40 years of his earning potential would be equivalent to $4,227,992 of which at least $2,500,000 could be devoted to raising the family.

hybrid security A SECURITY that possesses features of both COMMON STOCK and a corporate BOND. An example is PREFERRED STOCK. It is like common stock in that it represents equity ownership and is issued without stated MATURITY DATES. It is also like a corporate bond in that its DIVIDEND is fixed for the life of the issue.

hypothecation The pledging of SECURITIES as COLLATERAL for a LOAN.

I

identified shares In taxation, the matching, in a given stock, of shares sold to shares bought when these are purchased on different dates. This matching is needed to determine the gain or loss on sale, and whether the gain or loss is short term or long term. If the shares are not identifiable, the first shares ''in'' are considered the first shares ''out.''

illiquid
1. The lack of sufficient LIQUID ASSETS, like CASH or MARKETABLE SECURITIES, to pay short-term debt.
2. The inability to convert an investment to cash on short notice without a large capital loss.
3. A condition in which current liabilities exceed current assets.

immediate annuity An ANNUITY that is purchased with one premium and whose payments begin immediately.

immediate or cancel order A customer's LIMIT ORDER to a security BROKERAGE FIRM to buy or sell immediately a significant quantity of a SECURITY, qualified by requiring that the portion of the order that cannot be filled at the LIMIT PRICE will be canceled.

immediate pay annuity See IMMEDIATE ANNUITY.

impaired credit A decline in the credit standing of a customer, and as such, the seller's credit line is restricted.

implicit costs Or, *opportunity cost*. The return foregone from an alternative use of time or facilities. For example, if an individual goes to the health spa on Tuesday night instead of working overtime and earning $60, the monetary return foregone is $60.
See also EXPLICIT COSTS.

implied condition A provision, even though not specifically stated in an agreement, known to the parties as an important element. For example, the buyer expects to receive goods meeting the seller's claims as to quality and use.

implied contract A contract arising from actions of those affected but not necessarily communicated in writing or orally. For example, it is assumed that a trustee will perform his or her duties in accordance with the responsibilities assumed.

implied warranty A WARRANTY in effect whether expressed individually or not. It is mandated by state law. It provides that products sold are warranted to be suitable for sale and will work effectively whether there is an EXPRESS WARRANTY or not.

impulse buying Unplanned retail consumer buying motivated by a whim or a spur-of-the-moment impulse. Impulse buying is a strategy exploited by many retailers. For example, newspapers are strategically placed at the checkout counter of a store.

in and out
securities: Description of the action of an OPTION or STOCK TRADER who purchases and quickly sells OPTIONS or STOCKS with the purpose of making rapid profits. An in and out TRADER has a very short-term time perspective.
insurance: A PREMIUM for fire INSURANCE for which the COVERED RISK is located in or out of a building. Since the property is susceptible to the risks of a building sometimes, a special in and out rate reflecting this condition is developed for the coverage required. For example, a bus is housed in a garage for maintenance and repairs during only part of its useful life.

in escrow The period in which the ESCROW AGENT informs both the buyer and the seller as to what documents or funds need to be deposited with the escrow agent in order to fulfill the conditions of the purchase and sale, and in which the parties collect the items requested. These items include such things as funds to cover mortgage insurance premiums, TAXES, HAZARD INSURANCE, and TITLE INSURANCE. Title insurance indicates that no one else has an ownership right to the property, confirmation that the seller has obtained an adequate loan to cover the purchase price, there has been an inspection of the property for termites, and the seller's original deed to the property has been obtained.

in the money A term describing the EXERCISE PRICE of a CALL OPTION that is less than the current MARKET PRICE of the related STOCK. For example, a 50 call option on a stock selling at 53 is in the money. A 50 PUT OPTION on a stock selling at 48 would also be in the money.

There are two reasons for buying or selling in the money options. First, if an INVESTOR is selling a COVERED PUT or CALL OPTION, more money would be realized giving greater downside price protection on the underlying stock. Second, in the money, options TRADE with less PREMIUM since they are not trading at the EXERCISE PRICE, causing their prices to move more directly with MARKET PRICES.

inactive stock An issue in which there is a relatively low volume of transactions. Volume may be a few hundred shares a week or even less. On the NEW YORK STOCK EXCHANGE most inactive stocks are traded in 10-share units rather than the customary 100.

incentive fee A payment given to an individual as an incentive to participate in some undertaking, such as a company's offering a consumer compensation to join a test market group.

incentive pay
1. Salary paid in consideration of other than hours worked. For example, wages may be tied

to units produced as an indicator of productivity.
2. A bonus paid to employees who meet a production quota within a prescribed period of time.

incentive stock option (ISO) A STOCK OPTION granted to employees under an option plan providing a more favorable tax treatment than qualified stock options. Employees receive the privilege of buying a specified number of shares in the company's stock at a given option price over a designated time period. ISOs are taxable at ordinary rates when the shares are sold by the employee. Thus, there is no tax when the ISOs are granted or exercised.

includable income A tax term applying to income that an individual must report as taxable income, such as interest income and dividend income on corporate securities. An example of nonincludable income (not subject to tax) is interest income on municipal bonds or proceeds received from a life insurance policy.

income
1. MONEY, received during a time period, that increases the total ASSETS of an individual or company if not spent. Such money can be realized as the result of INVESTMENTS, employment, or the sale of products or services.
2. Factors such as COMMISSIONS, gifts, INTEREST, and RENTS.
3. An excess of REVENUES over expenses and losses for an accounting period (NET INCOME). *See also* GROSS INCOME.

income approach Or, *capitalization approach.* In real estate, one of the three methods of the appraisal process generally applied to income-producing property, based on the expected future income from the property.

$$\text{Market value} = \frac{\text{Expected annual income}}{\text{Capitalization rate}}$$

For example, a rental property is expected to provide future annual income of $40,000. The capitalization rate is 10%. Market value equals

$$\frac{\$40,000}{.10} = \$400,000$$

The other two methods of real estate appraisal are the MARKET COMPARISON APPROACH and COST APPROACH.

See also CAPITALIZATION RATE.

income averaging A method of computing INCOME TAX LIABILITY by averaging the current year's income with that of the prior four year's income. It is designed for taxpayers whose annual taxable income varies widely. In effect, the excess of current taxable INCOME over 120% of average taxable income of the prior four years is taxed as if the excess had been received in five equal installments. The TAX REFORM ACT OF 1986 abolished income averaging.

income bond Or, *reorganization bond*. A bond that promises to repay principal at a set date but will pay interest only when earnings are available. Often the issuer promises to add any unpaid interest to the face amount of the income bond when it is paid off.

income deduction Certain nonoperating expense items appearing on a company's INCOME STATEMENT used in calculating NET INCOME for an operating period. These are noncontrollable expenses and include such items as INSURANCE PREMIUMS, INTEREST EXPENSE, and TAXES.

income dividend A distribution, to the shareholders of a MUTUAL FUND, of interest, dividends, and gains on sale of securities. Investment expenses are subtracted in determining the distribution.

income exclusion rule INCOME excluded from TAXATION including (1) INTEREST payments from TAX EXEMPT government BONDS, (2) returns of CAPITAL from ANNUITIES and PENSIONS, (3) DIVIDENDS on veterans' LIFE INSURANCE, (4) life insurance proceeds received because of a person's death, (5) amounts received from insurance because of the loss of use of a home, (6) child support, (7) welfare payments, (8) disability retirement payments paid by the Veterans Administration.

income fund A MUTUAL FUND whose primary objective is CURRENT INCOME and that seeks a PORTFOLIO of PREFERRED STOCKS, high-quality BONDS, and BLUE-CHIP STOCKS with consistently high DIVIDENDS.

income in respect of a decedent Income earned by a taxpayer prior to death but received by and taxed to the taxpayer's HEIRS.

income insurance Or, *disability income insurance*. INSURANCE that provides protection against the loss of future income.

income portfolio A portfolio of securities with the purpose of generating high current income (e.g., interest income, dividend income) instead of growth. However, depending on the overall market for debt and equity securities, price appreciation (or depreciation) may have a material effect. Securities providing fixed income are typically bonds and preferred stock.

income producing property Or, *investment property*. Real property used by an entity as INVESTMENT potential or as an income producer generally by being leased or rented.

income property REAL ESTATE purchased to be leased to TENANTS to generate INCOME in the form of RENT receipts.
See also INCOME PRODUCING PROPERTY.

income replacement In disability insurance, payment by the insurance company to the disabled insured of a monthly benefit that replaces a percentage or all of lost earnings.

income splitting
 1. The sharing of income among individuals. An example is two individuals splitting a sales commission.
 2. In taxation, a situation in which husband and wife compute their taxes on the joint return, assuming 50% of their taxable income was earned by each.

income statement Or, *profit and loss statement*. A FINANCIAL STATEMENT reporting the firm's operating performance and showing the elements used in arriving at the NET INCOME, including sales, cost of sales, operating expenses, income from operations, income before TAX, income before extraordinary items, and related items. Unlike a BALANCE SHEET, an income statement summarizes a financial period, normally a quarter. The income statement for the year must be included in the ANNUAL REPORT of the firm.

income stock A STOCK that pays a high CURRENT YIELD and has a good record of earnings and DIVIDEND payment over a period of years. *See also* COMMON STOCK.

income tax A government levy on the taxable income of an individual. The taxable income equals the gross income less deductions and exemptions. The tax rate is graduated, increasing as taxable income goes from one tax bracket to another. Tax rates also depend on the status of the taxpayer (e.g., married, single). Income tax may be paid to federal, state, and local governments.

income yield *See* CAPITALIZATION RATE.

incontestability clause A provision in a life insurance policy providing that once the insurance is in effect for two years, the insurer cannot void the policy due to a concealment or misrepresentation made by the insured at the time of application. For example, if one marks "no" to a question of whether the insured has high blood pressure when in fact he or she does, this denial will not cancel the policy after two years. But if there is a misstatement as to age, the premium would be retroactively adjusted upward.

incremental (marginal) tax rate The next higher tax rate when an individual's TAXABLE INCOME increases to the next tax bracket. It is the percentage of tax paid on one's last dollar of taxable income.

indemnification *See* INDEMNIFY.

indemnify
1. To agree to compensate for a loss or damage experienced by a person. The indemnifier may be an insurance company or employer.

2. A legal principle that determines the amount of the economic loss reimbursed for destroyed or damaged property.

indemnity approach
1. An INSURANCE POLICY seeking to protect an INSURED against future loss or to prevent the legal consequences of any contingent LIABILITY.
2. Making whole the harm after a sustained loss. The indemnity approach does not seek to have the insured make a profit, but merely to restore the person to his or her original financial position.

indemnity benefits HEALTH INSURANCE benefits paid in specified dollar amounts as listed on the benefits table.

indemnity income policy An INSURANCE policy that pays INCOME to the INSURED during hospitalization.

indenture
real estate: A contractual understanding detailing the legal interests and liabilities between two or more individuals as in a LEASE or MORTGAGE.
securities: A formal agreement, also termed a DEED OF TRUST, between a BOND issuer and BONDHOLDER detailing (1) the type of bond, (2) amount of the issue, (3) collateralized property (unless a DEBENTURE), (4) COVENANTS, (5) WORKING CAPITAL and the CURRENT RATIO, and (6) call privileges or redemption rights. The indenture also provides for a TRUSTEE for all holders of the BOND issue.

independent agent In INSURANCE, one representing several insurance companies who scrutinizes the MARKET for the best place for a client's insurance business. The independent agent has his or her own records and is not directed by any one company, paying all agency expenses from the COMMISSIONS derived from securing insurance clients.

indeterminate premium life insurance A NONPARTICIPATING form of LIFE INSURANCE POLICY in which the first few PREMIUMS will be lower than the later premiums; however, a maximum ceiling on future premiums is guaranteed. Premiums are adjusted to reflect the insurance company's anticipated mortality experience rate, INVESTMENT return, and expenses. If these factors are lower in cost than originally anticipated in the initial premiums, then future premiums will be reduced. However, if the COSTS are higher than originally projected, then the premiums will be increased, but not more than the guaranteed maximum.

index

1. A statistical yardstick expressed in terms of percentages of a base year or years. For instance, the Department of Commerce's CONSUMER PRICE INDEX (CPI) is based on 1982–1984 as 100. In April 1990, the index stood at 128.9, which meant that the CPI that month was almost 29% higher than that in the base period. An index is not an average. The index differs from an average in that it weighs changes in prices by the size of the companies affected. The STANDARD & POOR'S INDEX of 500 stocks calculates changes in prices as if all the shares of each company were sold each day, thus giving a giant like General Motors its due influence.
See also MARKET INDICES AND AVERAGES; PRICE INDICES.

2. In REAL ESTATE, the basis for setting an ADJUSTABLE RATE such as the one-year Treasury bill average, three-month CERTIFICATE OF DEPOSIT (CD) rate, or prime rate.

index arbitrage The purchase of a STOCK-INDEX FUTURE in one market and sale of the stocks that constitute that INDEX in another market, or vice versa, in order to profit from temporary price differences in the two markets. Index arbitrage is the most widely used form of PROGRAM TRADING.

index bond A bond in which the principal and/or interest will be paid, taking into account the change in purchasing power of the dollar or foreign currency. The bond may be linked, for example, to the consumer price index or to the exchange rate of the British pound. The purpose is to assure that the lender receives the real value of money at the payment date. For example, if price levels rise, the rate of bond interest is adjusted accordingly.

index fund A MUTUAL FUND that has as its primary objective the matching of the performance of a particular stock index such as the STANDARD & POOR'S 500 COMPOSITE STOCK PRICE INDEX. An example is Vanguard's Index 500 Fund.

index lease A rental agreement in which the tenant's rental is based on a change in the price of some measure, such as the CONSUMER PRICE INDEX.

index of leading economic indicators The series of economic indicators that tend to predict future changes in economic activity; officially called *Composite Index of 11 Leading Indicators*. This series is the government's main barometer for forecasting business trends. Each of the series has shown a tendency to change before the economy makes a major turn—hence, the term "leading indicators." The index is designed to forecast economic activity six to nine months ahead (1982 = 100). This series, published monthly by the U.S. Department of Commerce, consists of the following:
average workweek of production workers in manufacturing
Employers find it easier to increase the number of hours worked in a week than to hire more employees.
initial claims for unemployment insurance
The number of people who sign up for unemployment benefits signals changes in present and future economic activity.
vendor performance
Vendor performance represents the percentage of companies reporting slower deliveries. As the economy grows, firms have more trouble filling orders.

percentage change in prices of sensitive crude materials

Rises in prices of such critical materials as steel and iron usually mean factory demands are going up, which means factories plan to step up production.

contracts and orders for plant and equipment

Heavier contracting and ordering usually lead economic upswings.

stock prices

A rise in the COMMON STOCK index indicates expected profits and lower interest rates. STOCK MARKET advances usually precede business upturns by three to eight months.

percentage change in business and consumer credit outstanding

Change in the amount of money spent by consumers and businesses.

money supply

A rising money supply means easy money that sparks brisk economic activity. This usually leads recoveries by as much as 14 months.

new orders for manufacturers of consumer goods and materials

New orders mean more workers hired, more materials and supplies purchased, and increased output. Gains in this series usually lead recoveries by as much as four months.

residential building permits for private housing

Gains in building permits signal business upturns.

change in inventories

Expected higher sales means that companies will build up inventories. Rises usually lead upswings by up to eight months.

These 11 components of the index are adjusted for INFLATION. It is rare that these components of the index all go in the same direction at once. Each factor is weighted. The composite figure is designed to tell only in which direction business will go. It is not intended to forecast the magnitude of future ups and downs.

See also ECONOMIC INDICATORS.

index options CALL or PUT OPTION contracts purchased and sold on the Standard & Poor's (S&P) 100 Index, STANDARD & POOR'S (S&P) 500 INDEX, Major Market Index, International Market Index, Computer Technology Index, Oil Index, and Institutional Index. Essentially, the INVESTOR is RISKING a specified amount of MONEY, the price of the OPTION contract, on the possibility that the selected INDEX will move up, in the case of the CALL OPTION, or down, in the case of the PUT OPTION, sufficiently for the investor to make a profit by selling the option prior to the EXPIRATION DATE of the contract.

All options are short term in nature and the time value of their premiums depreciates over their life. Thus, index options are an extremely SPECULATIVE INVESTMENT, but do not have as much leverage or risk as a FUTURE CONTRACT.

See also CALL OPTION; FUTURES CONTRACT; PUT OPTION.

indexation The assignment of escalator clauses to long-term contracts so that wages, incomes, SOCIAL SECURITY payments, and even the tax system can be readjusted automatically in order to prevent INFLATION from distorting real income or other real values. In this way an individual's gains are not taxed away, thereby reducing real income. An escalator clause is a provision in a long-term contract tying these payments to a comprehensive measure of price-level and COST-OF-LIVING changes. The consumer price index and GNP deflator (implicit price index) are the measures most commonly used for indexation. Indexation may be partial or comprehensive. For example, assume that an employee's income goes up by 5% while prices go up by 5%. The employee has no more purchasing power than before, although the income tax will rise because a higher income will push him or her into a higher tax bracket. Indexation can avoid this situation by correcting the income for inflation.

See also INFLATION; PRICE INDICES.

indexed life insurance A policy whose face value changes in conformity with the change in a related price index. For example, the consumer price index may be the basis of the death benefit to keep up with inflation. The insured may have the option of having the index apply on an automatic or optional basis.

indexed loan   A long-term loan in which the principal, interest, or maturity is tied into a specific index. Thus, periodic adjustments will be made to conform to the change in the related index. An example is an ADJUSTABLE RATE MORTGAGE.

indexing method   A technique of calculating SOCIAL SECURITY benefits that revalues previous wage earnings in terms of current wage levels by multiplying each year's income by an index factor announced annually by the Social Security Administration.
See also INDEXATION.

indirect (group) ownership   A type of ownership in which a group of investors appoints a TRUSTEE to hold legal title to a real estate investment on behalf of all in the group.

individual account   A bank account registered in the name of a person.

individual health insurance   HEALTH INSURANCE that provides protection directly to an insured and his or her family.

individual practice association (IPA)   A type of HEALTH MAINTENANCE ORGANIZATION (HMO) in which physicians offer services from their regular offices to HMO members. Generally, these physicians also see patients who are not HMO members.

individual retirement account (IRA)   A tax-deferred retirement savings plan that individuals set up themselves. The maximum annual contribution is $2,000 or the amount of compensation earned, whichever is less. A married couple may contribute up to $4,000 if each of them earns $2,000 (up to $2,250 if he or she has a nonworking spouse). The IRA is a qualified individual retirement plan whereby the saver's contributions not only grow tax free but are also either tax deductible or not included in his or her income.

It is important to remember that under the TAX REFORM ACT OF 1986, however, a person who is covered by an employer's retirement plan, or who files a joint return with a spouse who is covered by such a plan, may be entitled to only a partial deduction or no deduction at all, depending on the ADJUSTED GROSS INCOME (AGI). The deduction begins to decrease (that is, the allowable deductions are reduced $1 for each $5 increase in income) when the taxpayer's income rises above a certain level; it is eliminated altogether when the income reaches a higher level.

Specifically, the deduction is reduced or eliminated entirely depending on the taxpayer's filing status and income as in the table below.

Example: A single worker with an adjusted gross income of $30,000 would be able to deduct an IRA contribution of

$$\$2,000 - [(\$30,000 - \$25,000)/\$5 \times \$1] = \$1,000$$

If an individual is not covered by an employee retirement plan, he or she can still take a full IRA deduction of up to $2,000, or 100% of compensation, whichever is less.

individual retirement account (IRA) rollover   A provision of the IRA law that allows employees receiving lump-sum payments from their company's pension or profit-sharing plan

If filing status is:	Deduction is reduced if AGI is within range of:	Deduction is eliminated if AGI is:
Single, or Head of Household	$25,000–$35,000	$35,000 or more
Married–joint return, or Qualifying widow(er)	$40,000–$50,000	$50,000 or more
Married–separate return	$0–$10,000	$10,000 or more

because of retirement or other termination of employment to roll over the money into an IRA investment plan within 60 days. Furthermore, current IRAs may themselves be transferred to other investment options within the 60-day period. Through this type of rollover, the IRA fund continues to accumulate tax deferred until the time of withdrawal.
See also INDIVIDUAL RETIREMENT ACCOUNT (IRA).

individual tax return A tax return filed by a person rather than a corporate entity. The standard tax return is Form 1040, which consists of various schedules such as Schedule A (itemized deductions), Schedule B (interest and dividend income), Schedule C (self-employment income), and Schedule D (capital gains and losses).

industrial revenue bond A TAX-EXEMPT BOND issued by a municipality to finance plants and facilities that are then leased to private industrial enterprises. The subsequent LEASE payments are used to service the debt. This strategy is intended to attract new industries to the area.

inflation A general increase in the price level. When inflation is present, a dollar today can buy more than a dollar in the future. Although the causes of inflation are diverse, a frequent source of inflationary pressures is the excess demand for goods and services, which pulls product prices upward—DEMAND-PULL INFLATION. Rising wages and material costs may lead to the upward pressure on prices—COST-PUSH INFLATION. Furthermore, excessive spending and/or heavy borrowing due to a BUDGET DEFICIT by the federal government can be inflationary. All of these sources may be intermingled at a particular time, making it difficult to pinpoint the cause for inflation.
See also PRICE INDICES.

inflation endorsement A provision in a property insurance policy that automatically adjusts coverage based on a construction cost index in the region. An example is an automatic adjustment to the coverage on one's house to reim-burse the insured based on replacement cost in the event the house is destroyed by a fire.

inflation hedge An INVESTMENT made to protect against the loss of buying power produced by INFLATION. Traditionally, two favorite inflation HEDGE investments are gold and REAL ESTATE. Both normally appreciate in value during inflationary periods. The STOCK MARKET can also be an INFLATION HEDGE, but typically only during periods of hyperinflation (high inflation). Another inflation hedge includes variable rate MONEY MARKET funds that increase their rate of INTEREST as INTEREST RATES increase.
See also HEDGE.

inflation rate A measure of the rate of change in prices. Two key measures include the CONSUMER PRICE INDEX (CPI) and the PRODUCER PRICE INDEX (PPI). A more precise measure of price changes for the overall economy is the implicit price deflator index of the GROSS NATIONAL PRODUCT.

inflation risk The RISK that the value of property will not increase at least as rapidly as the rate of INFLATION.
See also PURCHASING POWER RISK.

inflationary spiral An economic period characterized by extremely rapid increases in prices normally followed by an economic recession. For example, in the United States, the end of the 1970s was a period marked by extremely high INFLATION caused in part by large petroleum price increases, followed by an economic recession in 1982.

inflexible expenses Uncontrollable or fixed EXPENSES that must be made regardless of economic circumstances. Such expenses include INSURANCE PREMIUMS, home MORTGAGES and INTEREST payments, and utility expenditures.

information return A return filed with the Internal Revenue Service for which no tax liability is imposed. Examples are Form 1099, Form W-2, and Form 1065 (partnership return). There is a penalty for the failure to file an information return.

inheritance Any portion of an ESTATE acquired INTESTATE or through a BEQUEST made by a WILL or other final testament. Inheritances include MONEY and other property left by the DECEDENT. Inheritances occur within a line of family descent.

inheritance tax A state TAX levied on the value of assets received as the result of an INHERITANCE. Unlike the Federal Estate Tax, the inheritance tax is charged on the value of the property actually received by the HEIR rather than the value of the entire ESTATE left by the DECEDENT.

initial margin See INITIAL MARGIN REQUIREMENT.

initial margin requirement A legal requirement that an investor having a margin account with a brokerage firm must pay a specified percentage of the purchase price for stocks or bonds in cash. The remainder of the purchase price is on credit. There must also be a minimum amount of money invested to open the margin account initially. Under REGULATION T of the Federal Reserve Board, the initial margin is $2,000 plus 50% of the purchase price or 50% of the proceeds of a SHORT SALE.

initial price The first offering price of an item.
auction: The initial item price at the beginning of an auction.
securities: The first price of a STOCK after all buy and sell orders have been received and matched.

initial public offering (IPO) A corporation's first offering of STOCK to the public. It is typically an opportunity for the present investors, participating venture capitalists, and entrepreneurs to make big profits, as for the first time their shares will be given a market value reflecting expectations for the company's future growth.

injury independent of all other means An injury covered in a medical insurance policy that is independent of a prior injury.

inside information Privileged information obtained regarding material business results and pending SECURITY transactions that will not be made public until a certain date. Taking advantage of inside information for the purpose of making a profit is illegal.

insider Those having direct access to privileged information regarding the activities of a business that could have a material affect on the MARKET evaluation of the company should any transaction occur utilizing the information. Insiders include anyone having a direct involvement with the company, such as managers, members of the board of directors, attorneys, auditors, or printers.

The term is relative to one's access to private business information at any time and can include members of the public should they have direct access to any such information.
See also INSIDE INFORMATION; INSIDER TRADING.

insider trading Buying or selling by INSIDERS of SECURITIES listed on a STOCK EXCHANGE; also called INSIDE DEALING. All such TRADES must be reported to the SECURITIES AND EXCHANGE COMMISSION (SEC) within ten days of the end of the month in which they transpired. Inside trades that occur on the basis of INSIDE INFORMATION are illegal.
See also INSIDE INFORMATION; INSIDER.

insolvent Any person or company incapable of meeting current LIABILITIES because of insufficient assets. Insolvency usually precedes BANKRUPTCY; in the latter case a court-appointed administrator develops a FINANCIAL PLAN to help the debtor meet CREDITOR payment demands. Insolvency is distinguished from illiquidity in that in illiquidity there are sufficient ASSETS to meet creditor demands, but they are not in a CASH form.

installment credit A type of consumer credit in which the consumer pays the amount owed in equal payments, usually monthly.

installment loan A LOAN that is repaid in a series of periodic, fixed scheduled payments rather than in a lump sum. It is usually associated with the purchase of durable goods and services such as autos and appliances.

installment premium annuity contract A method of purchasing an ANNUITY through periodic payments. It contrasts with an annuity purchased by a single premium.

installment purchase agreement Or, *collateral installment loan; chattel mortgage.* A credit agreement that specifies the obligations of both the purchaser (or borrower) and the seller when a purchase transaction is being financed on an installment basis. The seller retains TITLE, and the agreement consists of four elements: a SALES CONTRACT, a SECURITY AGREEMENT, a note, and an INSURANCE agreement.

installment refund annuity An ANNUITY under which amounts yet unpaid to the ANNUITANT are refunded to the BENEFICIARY in installments in the event the annuitant dies before receiving the original cost of the annuity.

installment sale
in general: A sale in which periodic cash payments will be made over time. This is distinguished from a sale involving immediate and full cash payment.
real estate: A method of selling and financing property by which the seller retains title but the buyer takes possession while he or she makes the installment payments. The tax on the gain is paid as the mortgage principal is collected.

installment sales contract See INSTALLMENT SALE.

installments certain annuity See ANNUITY CERTAIN.

instrument A written document, such as a CONTRACT, DEED, WILL, LEASE, MORTGAGE agreement, or BOND, that provides rights and obligations for the parties concerned. An INSTRUMENT gives formal notice of an agreement, creating rights and duties for the affected parties, such as a contractual commitment. An instrument serves as evidence of the terms agreed to.

insurability Conditions and circumstances under which a particular RISK can be insured by an INSURANCE company. The INSURABILITY of a risk is defined by standards developed by an insurance company.

insurable interest A relationship with an individual or thing that is the basis of an insurance policy. An individual with an insurable interest can obtain a financial advantage from preserving the insured person or item. An example is a wife who has an insurable interest in her husband.

insurable title A property TITLE that meets clear ownership requirements as set forth in an ABSTRACT OF TITLE. An insurable title is one that does not contain any contingent LIABILITIES or prior unresolved ownership claims.

insurance A CONTRACT in which one party agrees, for a stipulated fee, to INDEMNIFY another for specified risks. The party agreeing to indemnify the other is called the INSURER and the party seeking insurance is termed the INSURED. The basic principle of INSURANCE is to pool the COVERAGE among a wide number of insureds susceptible to the same risks. Insurance risks are measured using the principles of probability to determine an adequate insurance PREMIUM.

There are several categories of insurance, including accident insurance, air travel insurance, ANNUITY insurance, automobile insurance, casualty insurance, FIRE INSURANCE, key man insurance, LIFE INSURANCE, malpractice insurance, marine insurance, mortgage insurance, product LIABILITY insurance, social insurance, term insurance, TITLE INSURANCE, and unemployment insurance.

insurance agent An INSURANCE company representative who solicits the business of insurance clients. The actions of an insurance AGENT, including representations of information, knowledge, and any wrongful acts, are the responsibility of the insurance company being represented by the insurance agent. Any notices given by an INSURED to an agent are equivalent to notifying the insurance company.

insurance agreement *See* INSURANCE POLICY.

insurance broker One acting as a middleman between the INSURANCE company and the INSURED. An insurance BROKER seeks business from the public as a free agent and places the insured with a company selected by the INSURER or the BROKER if there is no selection. An insurance broker is the AGENT for the insured although the broker could simultaneously be the agent for the insurer for certain purposes. Whereas an INSURANCE AGENT is tied to a particular insurance company, an insurance broker is an independent middleman not directly connected with any company. An insurance broker, in this respect, is a free agent.

insurance claim An INSURED'S request for INDEMNIFICATION from an insurer for an insured risk. An assertion by an insured for the right to payment for a loss incurred from an insured peril.

insurance commissioners Elected or appointed officials on a legally constituted INSURANCE COMMISSION, usually a state body, who have jurisdiction over the chartered INSURANCE companies operating under their purview. Insurance commissioners are charged with the responsibility of reviewing all related insurance company activities as well as insurance charters to protect the interests of the INSURED as well as the public.

insurance contract *See* INSURANCE POLICY.

insurance coverage INDEMNIFICATION categories and limits for PERILS INSURED against.

insurance dividend A sum of MONEY distributed to participating LIFE INSURANCE POLICYHOLDERS as a refund of a portion of the PREMIUM paid reflecting the overall experience record of the POLICYOWNER group. Since insurance DIVIDENDS are interpreted as a return of premium, they are not deemed to be taxable by the IRS. Policyown-

ers have a variety of options with insurance dividends.
See also PARTICIPATING DIVIDENDS; PARTICIPATING POLICIES.

insurance policy An insurance contract in which INDEMNIFICATION terms and PERILS covered as well as the PREMIUM terms are specified. The insurance policy is the basic written document containing the principal terms.

insurance premium The amount an INSURANCE company charges the INSURED for INDEMNIFICATION against specified perils. INSURANCE PREMIUMS are calculated on the basis of risk of loss for INSURED PERILS. Rates are established by class of insured and individual experience record. For example, a female automobile driver aged 25 living in a large metropolitan area will be in a rate class with similar female individuals. An insured with no losses will get the best rate for his or her class of insured compared to an insured with a high experience rate.

The periodic cost of the insurance is calculated by unit of insurance times the number of units purchased.

insurance programs Instruments that provide a vital means of meeting the financial objectives of individuals. The type and amount of insurance depends on the age, assets, income, and needs of an individual. Insurance is basically "replacement": LIFE INSURANCE provides income lost at the death of the wage earner; DISABILITY INSURANCE assures income when the insured is not able to work full time; HEALTH INSURANCE covers medical bills; and homeowner's/casualty policies pay most of the costs of theft, accident, or fire.

life insurance

Life insurance is the most important tool of ESTATE PLANNING and one of the most valuable aids to FINANCIAL PLANNING. There are two basic types of life insurance policies—TERM INSURANCE and WHOLE LIFE INSURANCE. All other kinds of policies are variations on one or more of the two basic types.

1. TERM INSURANCE: Term insurance is protection that insures the individual's family for a specified period of time. It pays a benefit only if the insured dies during the period covered by the policy. It provides for a level premium rate for the set period after which the policy ceases and becomes void, except when renewed or changed to some other form of policy. It is the cheapest form of life insurance because it provides the most coverage for the least money.

2. WHOLE LIFE INSURANCE (CASH VALUE INSURANCE OR STRAIGHT LIFE INSURANCE): Whole life provides insurance protection by the payment of a fixed premium throughout the lifetime of the insured. However, in addition to death protection, whole life insurance has a savings element called "cash value." As the policies mature, they develop cash values representing the early surplus plus investment earnings. There are many variations of whole life insurance: universal life, variable life, SINGLE PREMIUM WHOLE LIFE, adjustable life, and adjustable-premium life.

Characteristics of term insurance:
- Protection is provided for a specified period of time
- Initial premium is low
- Policy may be renewable and/or convertible
- Premium rises with each new term
- Insured or dependents get nothing back if insured survives the term
  Characteristics of whole life insurance:
- Protection is provided for life
- Premium is fixed
- Cash value grows
- Initial premium is higher than for term insurance
- Insured or dependents always receive benefits
- Whole life is available as universal, variable, single premium whole life, adjustable life, and adjustable-premium life
- Policy should be purchased with the intention of keeping for life or for a long period of time

disability insurance

Disability insurance provides a regular cash income when an insured person is unable to work as a result of a covered illness, injury, or disease. Most disability payments are tax exempt as long as the individual policyholder pays the premium.

health insurance

For most people, health insurance is provided by the employer as a major fringe benefit. Otherwise, individual policies can be purchased. There are three kinds of medical or health insurance: basic hospitalization, basic medical/surgical, and major medical.

property and liability insurance

Property and liability insurance is important to an individual's personal financial security. A person can be successful in the job, investments, and the like, and yet be almost destroyed financially by an accident, disaster, or lawsuit for which he or she does not have adequate property and liability insurance. It is wise to carry such insurance to protect family assets and future income from a catastrophic event.

See also PERSONAL FINANCIAL PLANNING.

insurance rate   *See* INSURANCE PREMIUM.

insurance record   Experience rate of claims and losses. The insurance record is used in predicting future losses and in developing insurance PREMIUM rates based on the EXPECTATION OF INSURED LOSS.

insurance reporting services   An independent service that evaluates and rates insurance companies and types of services offered.

insurance settlement   The receipt of proceeds from an insurance policy according to its terms, which may be in the form of either one payment or periodic payments.

insured   The individual INDEMNIFIED against specific PERILS in an INSURANCE POLICY. The INSURED may also contain others not specifically named within an insurance policy such as family members or others in a FIRE INSURANCE policy. GROUP INSURANCE policies may include many individuals as the insured.

insured account   An ACCOUNT at a BANK, BROKERAGE FIRM, or CREDIT UNION whose ASSETS are

INSURED by a federal, state, or private insurance organization. All DEPOSITS up to $100,000 in a commercial bank are insured by the FEDERAL DEPOSIT INSURANCE CORPORATION; credit union accounts are insured by the NATIONAL CREDIT UNION ADMINISTRATION; and brokerage ACCOUNTS are insured by the SECURITIES INVESTOR PROTECTION CORPORATION.

insured pension plan A funded pension plan in which contributions are used to buy annuities contracts.

insurer An INSURANCE company or insurance UNDERWRITER that issues an ACCOUNT to INDEMNIFY the INSURED. An insurance policy is a legally enforceable contract issued for a stated PREMIUM by an INSURER to an insured assuming the risk of loss for stated PERILS.

intangible assets ASSETS either lacking physical substance or representing a right granted by the government or another company. They include GOODWILL, patents, trademarks, tradenames, copyrights, and franchise fees.

integrated software A software package that combines numerous applications in one program. There are two or more modules that interact. Integrated packages can move data among several programs with common commands and file structures. In effect, multiple applications are in memory simultaneously. An integrated package is advisable when identical source information is to be used for varying purposes and activities. For example, *Framework* lets a user do word processing, outlining, telecommunications, graphics, data base, and spreadsheets and save each as a frame that can be incorporated into other frames.

interest

1. Amount charged by a LENDER to a BORROWER for the use of MONEY. INTEREST RATES are normally expressed on an annual basis. The total interest = principal × interest rate × period of time. For example, the interest on a $20,000 loan at 9% for 10 months = $20,000 × 9% × $10/12$ = $1500.

2. EQUITY ownership of an individual or company in a business property expressed in percentage terms or in dollars. For example, if an investor owns 100,000 SHARES of a company having 1,000,000 shares outstanding, the INVESTOR has a 10% ownership interest.

interest-adjusted cost index (IACI) A measure of the cost of LIFE INSURANCE that takes into account the interest that would have been earned had the premiums been invested rather than used to buy insurance. This index should be made available by insurance agents. If the agent is not willing to supply the value for this index, the policy should not be bought. Generally, the lower the index, the lower the cost for a given dollar amount of insurance protection. Certainly, policies with a positive index should be avoided.

Example: Norman is considering the purchase of a $100,000 CASH VALUE policy. His annual premiums will be $1,664. The policy will have a cash value at the end of 20 years of $35,008. Total dividends accumulated for the 20 years will be $9,300. The interest rate used is 5% and total dividends adjusted for 5% amount to $12,719. Then the 20-year, interest-adjusted cost index is calculated, step by step, as follows:

Step 1: Accumulate annual premium
at 5% deposited at the beginning of
each year for 20 years
$1,664 × 34.719* (Appendix A,
Table 2—Future Value of an
Annuity of $1) $57,772.42

Step 2: Accumulate total dividends at
5% compounded annually to end of
20th year and subtract $12,719   −$12,719.00
                               45,053.42

Step 3: Subtract cash value at end of
20th year   −35,008.00
                               $10,045.42

Step 4: Divide by 34.719, which is
what $1 deposited at the beginning
of each year in a 5% compounded
account will grow to in 20 years.
The result is the amount that
would have to be saved to reach
the sum derived in Step 3 $289.39

Step 5: Divide the number of
thousands of the policy's face
amount, in this case, 100, to
compute the annual
interest-adjusted cost per $1,000 of
face amount $2.89

The insured may use this figure to compare similar cash value policies from other agents and companies. If possible, policies with a positive index should be avoided.

   *Note that the value 34.719 here is the Table 2 value for 21 years at 5% less 1 (35.719 − 1). The reason for calculating this way is that the deposit is made at the beginning of the year, not the end of the year.

See also LINTON YIELD; NET COST METHOD.

interest-adjusted cost method A method of calculating the cost of LIFE INSURANCE that uses the INTEREST-ADJUSTED COST INDEX (IACI).

interest-adjusted net-payment index (IANPI) *See* INTEREST-ADJUSTED COST INDEX (IACI).

interest deduction The tax deductibility of interest paid by the taxpayer as shown on Schedule A (itemized deductions) of Form 1040. For example, under current tax law, there is full deductibility for interest paid on a home mortgage. However, interest paid on a credit card balance is not deductible.

interest option The POLICYHOLDER of a life insurance policy keeps the dividend earned with the insurance company to accumulate and earn a guaranteed minimum rate of interest. A BENEFICIARY can also leave the death proceeds with the insurance company to accumulate interest. The earned interest is subject to tax.

interest rate The cost of using money, stated as a rate per period of time, typically one year. An example is a 12% annual interest rate charged by the lender to the borrower on a loan.

interest rate futures contract A contract in which the holder commits to take delivery of a specified amount of the applicable debt security at a subsequent date. Typically, it is no more than three years in maturity. Futures may be in Treasury bills and notes, COMMERCIAL PAPER, CER-

TIFICATES OF DEPOSIT, or others. Interest rate futures are stated as a percentage of the par value of the related debt obligation. The value of the contract is directly tied to interest rates. For instance, if interest rates rise, the value of the contract decreases. If the price of the contract drops, the purchaser of the contract suffers a loss while the seller gains. A change of one basis point in interest rates results in a price change. The holder of the interest rate future typically does not take possession of the financial instrument. The contract may be used to hedge or to speculate on future interest rates and security prices. A speculator will find a FINANCIAL FUTURE attractive because of its potential significant return on a minimal investment from the low deposit. However, interest rate futures contracts are very risky.

interest (rate) risk Possibility that the MARKET VALUE of an asset will change adversely as interest rates change. For example, when market interest rates increase, the prices of fixed-income securities such as bonds drop.
See also RISK.

interest sensitive policy A life insurance policy that is credited with interest currently being earned by insurance companies on those policies.

interim financing A temporary source of financing on a short-term basis until a long-term financing source may be arranged. An example is a BRIDE LOAN made to a new company until a stock issue can be floated.

in the tank A slang term meaning that market prices of securities are down significantly.

intermediary An individual having the ability to make or assist in making financial decisions for others. Intermediaries include AGENTS, advisers, BANKS, BROKERS, or FINANCIAL INSTITUTIONS aiding or assisting others in various financial transactions for a fee. Intermediaries specialize in various financial areas of INVESTMENT and offer their clients a wide range of professional investment advice.

internal rate of return (IRR) Real effective annual return on an investment. It equates the cash invested with the present value of cash returns from an investment. For example, the YIELD TO MATURITY (YTM) on a BOND is the IRR. The IRR can be easily computed by using any financial calculator on the market.

internal revenue code Federal statutes defining the INCOME TAX law. The Internal Revenue Code is extremely detailed and covers all aspects of the income tax law.

international fund A MUTUAL FUND that invests in the STOCKS and BONDS of CORPORATIONS traded on foreign exchanges. These funds make significant gains when the dollar is falling and foreign stock prices are rising. Some funds invest in many overseas markets while others concentrate on specific foreign areas. Examples are T. Rowe Price International Stock Fund, T. Rowe Price Europe Fund, Fidelity Pacific Basin Fund, and Fidelity Canada Fund.

interval ownership *See* TIME SHARING.

inter vivos trust A TRUST formed between living people, such as a mother and daughter.

intestacy The state or condition of dying without a WILL.
See also INTESTATE.

intestate An individual who dies without leaving a WILL and having unknown intentions in terms of distributing the ESTATE. Under such circumstances, a court administrator is normally appointed to act as an EXECUTOR in distributing any ASSETS.
See also EXECUTOR/EXECUTRIX.

intestate decedent Individual who dies without leaving a WILL.
See also INTESTACY; INTESTATE.

intestate distribution The distribution of an ESTATE made for an individual who died without a WILL. Normally, a court-appointed administrator acts as an EXECUTOR in making the final distribution based on state law.

See also EXECUTOR/EXECUTRIX; INTESTACY; INTESTATE.

intraday An occurrence during an individual day. In the STOCK MARKET, the term is often used to refer to trading occurring in a day in which a new intraday high may occur for a STOCK, only to close at a lower price. The daily listing of price quotes for STOCKS is an example of the INTRADAY PRICE RANGE.

intrinsic value

1. The natural value of an item. For example, land is worth its resale value.

2. A theoretical "true value" of something after detailed analysis. The value may be determined by incorporating relevant information in a model. An example might be the theoretical "real value" of a company based on financial analysis, which may be different from its book value or market value.

inventory checklist

1. A list of items on hand owned by an individual, such as cars, furniture, and clothing.

2. A list of records retained of what is owned by a person, such as the deed to a house and the title to a car.

investigative report Any report prepared as the result of inquiry and research. The CREDIT RATING of a company or an individual will be determined as a result of an investigative credit report. An ABSTRACT OF TITLE is an investigative report on the TITLE history of a piece of property in which any title defects will be reported.

investment

expenditure: An EXPENDITURE made to acquire property or other assets for the purpose of producing revenue. For example, the purchase by an individual of an APARTMENT house for the purpose of deriving REVENUE and value APPRECIATION.

securities: Investing either long or short term in SECURITIES for value appreciation as well as DIVIDEND income.
See also CAPITAL ASSET.

investment adviser A person or company that advises others, for compensation, on how to get the maximum investment return on their assets; also called investment counselor. Investment advisers having 12 or more clients must register with the SECURITIES AND EXCHANGE COMMISSION (SEC), which enforces the Investment Advisors Act of 1940 designed to safeguard the investing public from dishonest investment activities.

investment asset Any ASSET purchased for the purpose of value APPRECIATION, including the possibility of earning additional INCOME. Examples of INVESTMENT ASSETS include STOCKS and BONDS, REAL ESTATE, antiques, jewelry, and rare paintings.

investment banker One that underwrites and offers new SECURITY offerings to the public. Normally, the INVESTMENT BANKING division of an investment firm or BANK will purchase the entire security offering from the CORPORATION and offer it to the public.

In large security offerings, several investment bankers will form a SYNDICATE to spread the RISK as well as to provide additional marketing capability. The lead investment banker heading the syndicate (called the originating house) will have its name mentioned first in the PROSPECTUS as well as in the newspaper advertisement, the TOMBSTONE, with the others mentioned afterward in descending order of importance to the syndicate.

investment climate The general economic, INVESTMENT, and psychological conditions, at any point in time, having an affect on an investment's success or failure. Economic conditions include INTEREST RATES, unemployment, DISPOSABLE INCOME, and other ECONOMIC INDICATORS as well as conditions unique to a particular industry. For example, a period of surplus oil would have a depressing affect on crude oil prices, which could contribute to lower profits for oil producing companies.

During boom periods, crowd psychology becomes very instrumental in causing INVESTORS to buy REAL ESTATE, STOCKS, and other suitable investments because investors fear they will miss "the bandwagon." During a recessionary period, a fear mentality may develop, discouraging individual investment commitments.

investment club A group of individuals joining together for the purpose of sharing SECURITY investment ideas. Normally, an INVESTMENT CLUB develops a pool of CAPITAL contributed by its members, which is subsequently invested in SECURITIES. Additional MONEY is also contributed at monthly or quarterly intervals, depending on the wishes of the members. INVESTMENT decisions are made through a vote of the membership.

investment company A company owning a diversified PORTFOLIO of SECURITIES that are professionally chosen and managed on the basis of certain investment criteria. The most common type of investment company is the MUTUAL FUND.
See also REAL ESTATE INVESTMENT TRUSTS (REITs).

investment counsel A financial adviser on investments to individuals with responsibility of making investment decisions. The fee for such a service may be a flat fee or hourly rate.

investment features The qualitative and quantitative characteristics of a particular type of investment. These features include dollar investment, rate of return, degree of risk, maturity period, and tax status. For example, attributes of a stock relate to the likelihood for income and growth in market price.

investment grade Descriptive of highly rated BONDS that are purchased by institutional investors because they are very marketable, and hence carry less risk. STANDARD & POOR's considers investment-grade items to be from AAA through BBB-minus whereas MOODY's considers them to be rated from AAA to Baa-3.
See also BOND RATINGS; JUNK BOND.

investment in default Any INVESTMENT that either goes into DEFAULT or already is in default at the time of the investment. A company in default would normally seek protection from its CREDITORS by declaring BANKRUPTCY. BONDHOLDERS would have the first claim on any ASSETS of the firm. Such a company would not pay any DIVIDENDS until it came out of bankruptcy.

If the INVESTOR believes the company has long term viability, an investment in default could be very profitable assuming sufficient time is allowed for the company to recover from its default condition.

investment income Or, *unearned income.* Passive INCOME derived from any of several financial INVESTMENTS. Investment income includes ANNUITIES, CAPITAL GAINS, DIVIDENDS, INTEREST, OPTION PREMIUMS, RENTS, and royalties. Under current law interest paid on a MARGIN ACCOUNT can be used to offset any investment income.

investment life cycle The period of time between acquiring an investment and disposing of it. A good way to measure the return from an investment is over its entire life. For example, if an investment was bought on January 15, 19X1, and later sold on January 15, 19X3, its life cycle is two years.

investment management An individual either managing his or her own investments or having a professional do it. The management of investments includes consideration of risk, return, maturity, liquidity, and so on. In deciding on investment choices and changes, one has to take into account the individual's financial situation, age, and goals.
See also INVESTMENT PLANNING; MUTUAL FUNDS.

investment objective Individual financial objectives determining subsequent financial INVESTMENT decisions. For example, a younger man may have a certain DISPOSABLE INCOME that he wishes to INVEST for the purposes of growth. He is willing and able to absorb any loss in CAPITAL that may result. Suitable investments would include investments in growth companies paying a minimal DIVIDEND.

An older person seeks to preserve CAPITAL as well as to maximize INCOME. Suitable income would include any of several secure, highly rated investments including high-quality BONDS, MONEY MARKET funds, and utility STOCKS paying a stable dividend.

investment philosophy A general term describing one's view of the best INVESTMENTS to make for maximizing individual INVESTMENT OBJECTIVES. For example, the investment philosophy of some INVESTORS may be that REAL ESTATE has far more investment potential and security than STOCKS or BONDS.

Other elements of investment philosophy include the timing of investments and the degree of acceptable RISK. Others may be significantly affected by fundamental economic conditions while still others may rely extensively on CHART positions in making investment decisions.

investment planning The process of formulating an INVESTMENT strategy based on an individual's goals and financial characteristics. Investment planning should aim at arriving at a good mix of RISK and reward. It should first outline the types of investments available, including their RETURN potential and riskiness. It should take into account the general risks of investing including those related to stock market price variability, INFLATION, and MONEY MARKET conditions. Investing is an integral part of all PERSONAL FINANCIAL PLANNING. Realistically, it can be done only with money left over after paying expenses, having proper INSURANCE, and making pension contributions. The person with CAPITAL has a wide choice of investment options.
types of investments

Investments can be classified into two forms: fixed dollar and variable dollar. Simply stated, fixed-income investments promise the investor a stated amount of income periodically. These include corporate BONDS and PREFERRED STOCKS, U.S. GOVERNMENT SECURITIES, MUNICIPAL BONDS, and other savings instruments (SAVINGS ACCOUNT, CERTIFICATE OF DEPOSIT). On the other hand, variable-dollar investments are those in which neither the PRINCIPAL nor the INCOME is contractually set in advance in terms of dollars. That is, both the value and income of variable-dollar investments can change in dollar amount, either up or down, with changes in internal or external economic conditions. These include COMMON STOCKS, MUTUAL FUNDS, REAL ESTATE, VARIABLE ANNUITIES, and other tax-sheltered investments.

factors to be considered in investment planning decisions
Consideration should be given to safety, return rate, stability of INCOME and DIVIDENDS, and LIQUIDITY.

security of principal: The degree of risk involved in a particular investment. There should not be a loss of part or all of the initial investment.

rate of return: The primary purpose of investing is to earn a return on the investor's capital in the form of interest, dividends, rental income, and capital APPRECIATION. However, increasing total investment returns would entail greater investment risks. Thus, YIELD and degree of risk are directly related. An investor has to choose the priority that fits his or her circumstances and objectives.

stability of income: When steady income is an important consideration, bond interest or stock dividends should be emphasized. This might be the situation for retired people or individuals who need to supplement their earned income on a regular basis with income from their outside investment.

marketability and liquidity: The ability of an investor to find a ready market to dispose of the investment at the right price.
See also PERSONAL FINANCIAL PLANNING.

investment risks The possibility of a CAPITAL LOSS as well as the incurring of legal liability as the result of an INVESTMENT. For example, a person's direct investment in a business either as an ACTIVE or SILENT PARTNER could result in loss of the original investment CAPITAL as well as a lawsuit for negligence or other legal matter.

investment software A computer program keeping a record and analysis of investments in shares, cost, and income. Some packages have price and dividend history of companies. Comparisons may be made of market averages and indices. The program updates the market value of the securities, shows unrealized gains or losses, presents accumulated dividends, and so on. Some packages reveal the tax effects of investment decisions. Examples of investment software are *Dow-Jones Market Microscope, Stockpak II,* and *Value/Screen Plus.*

investment trust An INVESTMENT COMPANY that uses its CAPITAL to invest in various investment vehicles. There are two principal types: the closed-end and the open-end investment company. The shares in closed-end investment trusts are readily transferable in the open market and are bought and sold like other shares. Capitalization of those companies is fixed. Open-end funds sell their own new shares to investors, stand ready to buy back their old shares, and are not listed. Open-end funds are so called because their capitalization is not fixed since they issue more shares as people want them.
See also MUTUAL FUNDS; REAL ESTATE INVESTMENT TRUSTS (REITs).

investor One who puts MONEY at RISK for any of several purposes, including INCOME, profit, and/or CAPITAL GAINS. The two basic types of INVESTORS are individual and institutional. Institutional investors, such as PENSION FUNDS and insurance companies, control billions of dollars of ASSETS making a profound impact on the economy and the STOCK MARKET.

invoice A bill, prepared by a seller of merchandise or services, that is presented to the purchaser. The invoice itemizes all purchases with the amount that is owed.

IOU A letter of DEBT written to the LENDER indicating "I owe you" a specified sum of MONEY to be paid at a certain date. The debtor must sign the letter to make it effective. If it is witnessed, it may be enforceable as a CONTRACT.

ironclad contract   A legal contract that will be very difficult to break.

iron law of risk and return   The direct positive relationship between RISK and RETURN. *See also* RISK-RETURN TRADE-OFF.

irrevocable   Something that cannot be taken, returned, or revoked. For example, an irrevocable TRUST is created by an individual's giving his or her ASSETS to a TRUST administrator.

irrevocable living trust   An irrevocable TRUST formed among living persons normally for the purpose of transferring property or other ASSETS.

irrevocable trust   A TRUST that cannot be broken without the express permission of the BENEFICIARY.

IRS private letter ruling   A resolution from the IRS of a taxpayer's problem or question. A taxpayer formally writes the Internal Revenue Service about a tax matter or problem he or she is having and asks the IRS for its opinion regarding the problem. The written reply to the question by the IRS resolves the issue.

IRS regulations   Treasury Department Regulations representing the government's interpretation of the Internal Revenue Code. The regulations are published in the *Federal Register*.

IRS rulings   Income tax rulings made by the INTERNAL REVENUE SERVICE regarding specific applications of the INTERNAL REVENUE SERVICE CODE. They are administrative rulings, having the force of law, that can be appealed in the federal courts.

issue
1. Floating a new public or private securities issuance, such as stocks and bonds. The issuer may be a corporation or governmental agency.
2. Stocks and bonds that are to be or have been sold.

issue limits   The maximum insurance coverage that the insured may obtain for a particular risk. For example, the insurer may place a $10,000,000 ceiling on malpractice insurance for a practicing accountant.

itemized deductions   A reduction in ADJUSTED GROSS INCOME for individual taxpayers. Items allowed to be deducted from adjusted gross income include medical EXPENSES, INTEREST, casualty losses, contributions, state and local income and real estate TAXES, and miscellaneous expenses. Some of these itemized deductions have limitations associated with them. For example, INTEREST on a MORTGAGE is deductible, but interest on a CREDIT CARD account is not. Medical expenses are DEDUCTIBLE only if they exceed 7.5% of adjusted gross income.

itemized nonbusiness expenses   *See* ITEMIZED DEDUCTIONS.

J

job jumper   Or, *job hopper*. An individual who changes jobs frequently, usually in the hope of improving career opportunities. Research does not demonstrate that job jumpers are any more successful than others staying with an organization over a sustained period of time.

Being termed a job jumper can be detrimental to one's career and job opportunities as employers may be reluctant to employ such an individual for fear he or she may leave soon.

joint account   A BANK or BROKERAGE ACCOUNT to which two or more people have equal access rights. There are two types of joint accounts:

1. One in which all parties must approve any transactions including signing CHECKS, buying or selling STOCKS, or withdrawing MONEY.

2. One in which any party has authority to make transactions in the account without needing the approval of the other parties to the account.

joint and several account Bank or brokerage account owned jointly by two or more people. Joint accounts can take two forms: (1) The first type requires all signatures on all checks (or approval of brokerage transactions), or (2) the second type allows any one owner to write checks (or approve brokerage transactions). One advantage of the joint account is that it lowers the service charges. Furthermore, the account has the rights of survivorship, which, in the case of a married couple, means that if one spouse dies the surviving spouse, after meeting a specified legal time requirement, can draw checks on the account. When opening a joint account it is important to specify the rights preferred.

joint and several liability A legal concept in which two or more individuals have an obligation that can be enforced against them by joint action against all members and against them as individuals, hence several liability or responsibility. For example, a CREDITOR can demand full repayment from any and all of those who have borrowed. Each BORROWER is liable for the full DEBT, not just the prorated share. For example, Kathy and Norman are GENERAL PARTNERS. The PARTNERSHIP borrows $50,000 from a bank agreeing to JOINT AND SEVERAL LIABILITY. Upon DEFAULT, the bank can collect the remainder of the $50,000 from either party.

joint liability A form of liability in which two or more parties have mutual responsibility for any legal exposure that may occur as a result of the terms of the agreement. Each member of a joint liability agreement SHARES mutual responsibility for all the consequences of the agreement.

joint ownership Ownership of REAL ESTATE or any other form of property in which at least two people have equal ownership. Upon the death of any of the members of the joint ownership, the property goes to the survivor(s). For example, a husband and wife may jointly own a home. *See also* JOINT TENANCY.

joint return The INCOME TAX status for married individuals filing a single joint income tax return. A husband and wife may file a joint return even if only one had INCOME or if they did not live together all year. However, both persons must sign the return and both are responsible. This means that if one spouse does not pay the tax due, the other may have to. In general, those filing jointly pay less tax than they would if they filed separately.

joint savings account A bank SAVINGS ACCOUNT to which two or more individuals have equal access. *See also* JOINT ACCOUNT.

joint tax return *See* JOINT RETURN.

joint tenancy A form of property co-ownership of two or more persons to whom real or personal property is deeded and who together have an undivided interest in such property as a whole. In the event that one of the JOINT TENANTS dies, the survivor(s) gets the property.

joint tenancy account An account in which each owner has access to the savings account and both are responsible separately and collectively for deposits and withdrawals.

joint tenancy with right of survivorship JOINT TENANCY requiring that upon the death of a joint tenant (one owner), the surviving TENANT automatically becomes the sole owner of the property.

joint will A WILL, executed jointly by two or more persons, having reciprocal provisions made in consideration of each other and signed by all the parties. The intention is to have the common disposition of all properties, normally jointly owned, to a third or more parties.

joint-and-last-survivorship annuity *See* JOINT-LIFE AND SURVIVORSHIP ANNUITY.

joint-life and survivorship annuity An ANNUITY that continues making payments as long as one of two or more ANNUITANTS is still alive. In the case of a husband and wife, should the husband die, the wife will continue to receive benefits, often at a reduced rate, for the rest of her life. It is not possible to outlive the benefits.

joint-life and survivorship insurance LIFE INSURANCE COVERAGE for two or more individuals with the death benefit paid to the last of those INSURED. PREMIUMS are lower for joint-life and survivorship INSURANCE than life insurance coverage for a single person since the likelihood of paying a death claim at the end is less.

judgment
in general: A final opinion on some matter formed after consideration of all known evidence.
accounting: An accountant's opinion regarding a set of financial facts as well as the implications they could have.
law: An official judicial decision on a matter brought before the court in which the rights and claims of all the parties have been considered. A judicial judgment includes a conclusion regarding facts found or admitted by the parties, followed by a decision or sentence of the law. The law's last word in a judicial matter.
real estate: A court decree placing a financial indebtedness on another to satisfy a claim. For example, Jones defaults in his lease obligations to Smith, and the court places a judgment against Jones upon completion of a judicial action initiated by Smith.

jumbo certificate of deposit A CERTIFICATE OF DEPOSIT having a minimum denomination of $100,000. Such certificates of deposit normally earn a higher INTEREST RATE than those of smaller denominations, but do not enjoy the coverage of the FEDERAL DEPOSIT INSURANCE CORPORATION.

Jumbo certificates of deposit are purchased and sold by CORPORATIONS, governments, large institutions, PENSION FUNDS, and INSURANCE companies.

jumbo loans Loans that differ from conforming loans because they are in excess of the conforming amount and reflect each lender's own guidelines.

junior mortgage bond A BOND whose priority of claims is lower than that of SENIOR MORTGAGE BONDS.

junk bond A high-yield BOND with a speculative credit rating of Ba and below by MOODY'S INVESTMENT SERVICE or BB and below by STANDARD & POOR'S. Junk bonds are issued by companies without long track records of sales or earnings, or by those with questionable credit strength. They have been a key to financing TAKEOVERS in recent years. They generally are more volatile and have a high DEFAULT RISK but pay higher YIELDS than INVESTMENT-GRADE BONDS.

K

Kelly Blue Book A source listing the wholesale and retail values of used cars. The book may be purchased or used at a library.

Keogh pension plan (HR-10) A tax-deferred retirement plan established by the Self-Employment Individual Tax Retirement Act of 1962 (HR-10) under which self-employed persons have the right to establish for themselves and their employees retirement plans that permit them the same tax advantages available to corporate employees covered by qualified pension plans. The contributions are tax deductible, and earnings are tax deferred until withdrawn.
See also RETIREMENT AND PENSION PLANNING.

key indication series *See* INDEX OF LEADING ECONOMIC INDICATORS; ECONOMIC INDICATORS.

kickback Or, a *payoff*.
finance: Occurs when sales finance companies reward dealers with CASH for discounting installment purchase paper through them.
government or business: A clandestine payment to an individual in government or business for favorable treatment or business CONTRACT.
labor relations: The illegal practice of requiring employees to return to the employer a portion of contractually determined wages as the price for obtaining a job.

kiddie tax The tax obligation for children under the age of 14 who must pay tax on investment income exceeding $1,000 at their parents' highest marginal tax rate. This requires the filing of IRS Form 8615.

killing
prevention: An action resulting in the stopping or prevention of some activity. For example, the BUDGET director killed the project because of a lack of funds.
stock market: Making a significant gain on a STOCK MARKET INVESTMENT that resulted from an unusual combination of chance and timing.

Krugerrand A BULLION COIN from South Africa that contains one troy ounce of gold.

L

labor laws Any of a series of federal and state laws regulating the labor market and general working conditions. These laws include the Minimum Wage Act, child labor laws, the National Labor Relations Act (Wagner Act), National Labor Relations Board, the Labor Management Relations Act (Taft Hartley Act), as well as applicable state legislation.

lagging indicators The economic indicators that follow or trail behind aggregate economic activity. There are currently six lagging indicators published by the government: unemployment rate, business expenditures, labor cost per unit, loans outstanding, bank interest rates, and book value of manufacturing and trade inventories.
See also INDEX OF LEADING ECONOMIC INDICATORS.

land contract Or, *contract for deed; installment sales contract.* A method of creative financing in real estate that enables the seller to

finance a buyer by permitting him or her to make a down payment followed by monthly payments. However, TITLE remains in the name of the seller until the MORTGAGE is paid off.
See also CREATIVE FINANCING.

land trust A trust agreement relating to real property. The real estate is managed by a trustee for the benefit of a beneficiary.

landlord An individual who owns property and rents it to TENANTS.

lapse
v. To pass slowly from one state to another. For example, the patient lapsed into a comma.
n. The loss and termination of a right or a privilege because of nonperformance of a needed activity within a certain period of time. For example, failure to pay an INSURANCE PREMIUM causes the INSURANCE POLICY to lapse, becoming null and void.

lapsed option An OPTION that expires because the holder fails to EXERCISE it within the required period of time. For example, an employee of a company may have an option to purchase company STOCK at a MARKET discount, but fails to make the purchase before the EXPIRATION DATE.

large loss principle Insuring against very high risk and significant losses, such as from a catastrophe. The occurrence of a severe loss will result in substantial dollar loss requiring protection through an insurance contract. The more the possible exposures, the more closely losses will match the probability of loss. In effect, a large number of insureds, each paying a modest premium, can guard against a few catastrophes that will be inflicted upon some.

last in, first out (LIFO) method A method by which banks calculate interest on depositors' account balances. Under the LIFO method, withdrawals are first deducted from the most recent deposits and then from the less recent

ones, and so on. This method does not penalize depositors as much as the FIFO method does, but it is still not a fair representation of actual funds on deposit during the period.

Example: The following activities have taken place during a 90-day period:

Day	Deposit (Withdrawal)	Balance
1	$1,000	$1,000
30	1,000	2,000
60	(800)	1,200
90	Closing	1,200

With a 6% stated (nominal) interest rate, calculating interest under LIFO yields

$$\text{(a) } \$1,000 \times .06 \times 90/360 = \$15.00$$
$$\text{(b) } \frac{\$200}{\$1,200} \times .06 \times 60/360 = \frac{\$2.00}{\$17.00}$$

See also FIRST IN, FIRST OUT (FIFO) METHOD; DAY OF DEPOSIT TO DAY OF WITHDRAWAL (DDDW) METHOD; MINIMUM BALANCE METHOD.

late charge A CHARGE assessed for a late loan payment. For example, a mortgagor must pay a $25 late charge to the bank for failure to make a MORTGAGE payment at the scheduled time.

law of large numbers A statistical concept holding that as the number of units in a group increases, predictions about the group become increasingly accurate. This is the mathematical foundation of insurance, which states that the larger the group of objects under one's management, the smaller the variation between actual and probable losses.

lawful money MONEY that is LEGAL TENDER and sanctioned by the government.

layering A combination of insurance policies with each adding an additional layer of coverage above the limits of the preceding policy. For example, policy X adds $50,000, then policy Y adds $75,000, and then policy Z adds $125,000, for a total coverage of $250,000. In some cases, an individual may have to take out several policies from different insurance companies to obtain the total needed coverage.

layoff A situation in which an employer suspends an employee for a limited or unlimited time period. A layoff usually results from adverse economic conditions for an employer.

leading economic indicators *See* INDEX OF LEADING ECONOMIC INDICATORS.

learning curve A curve depicting the productivity of a manufacturing process over time. In the initial stages of the learning curve, the productivity of the manufacturing process is lower than in the later stages because the manufacturer is learning how to resolve problems occurring in the process that reduce overall productivity.

After the producer learns how to deal with the obstacles, the manufacturing process can be done more quickly and inexpensively and with a higher quality output. Resources are used more productively and better manufacturing methods are developed.

lease A contract in which the lessee pays rent to the lessor for the use of real property for a designated period of time. Examples are the tenant's lease of an apartment and the rental of a car.

lease agreement A contractual agreement between a lessor and a TENANT for the use and possession of property for a certain period of time at a certain cost.
gross lease: A total figure for the lease of the property from which the LANDLORD must pay all taxes, utilities, insurance, and other expenses.
month-to-month lease: A form of tenancy in which there is no formal LEASE agreement between the landlord and the tenant. Normally, the landlord must give a one-month notice prior to canceling the lease.
net lease: A lease in which the tenant is required to pay all the related property costs including INSURANCE, TAXES, utilities, and others.

lease option An agreement stated in the lease giving the tenant the right to renew the LEASE for a stated period of time upon the expiration of the original lease. Most lease options include the LANDLORD'S right to increase the rent upon exercising the option.

leaseback Or, *sale and leaseback.* A transaction in which property is sold to a buyer with the agreement that the seller will have the OPTION to lease the property back from the new owner. There are many benefits to this type of a transaction. The original owner of the property receives the CASH value for the property (which may be needed because of financial conditions) and is not required to move, while the new owner has an assured tenant.

The net effect is similar to a LOAN with the property serving as COLLATERAL. Any profits are either amortized, in the case of a CAPITAL LEASE, or spread in proportion to the rental payments in an OPERATING LEASE. Losses are recognized immediately.

leg down A downward price trend of a security or commodity depicted on a chart. See illustrative chart.
See also LEG UP.

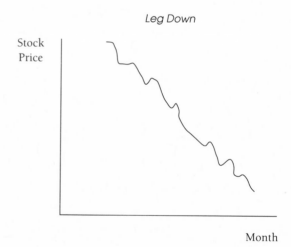

Leg Down

leg up An upward price trend of a security or commodity depicted on a chart. See illustrative chart.
See also LEG DOWN.

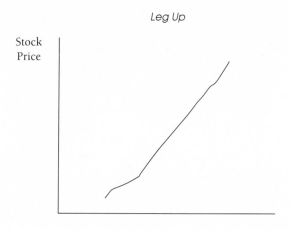

Leg Up

Stock Price

Month

legacy A gift by WILL of personal and real property.
absolute legacy: An unconditional and immediate gift.
conditional legacy: The BEQUEST of a gift depending upon the occurrence or nonoccurrence of a specific event. For example, the BENEFICIARY will receive the gift upon becoming employed or married.
contingent legacy: A LEGACY dependent upon the passage of time. For example, a particular gift is given to a minor "at the age of 21." A contingent legacy is dependent upon a predetermined event occurring.
specific legacy: A specific bequest for a beneficiary. For example, a particular beneficiary is designated to receive a particular piece of furniture.

legal liability
1. An obligation with specific terms and conditions requiring an individual to pay money or provide future goods or services.
2. Legal responsibility of a person for his or her acts or failure to act. Examples are the legal responsibility of a doctor for malpractice, or a homeowner's failure to clean up a sidewalk, causing injury to another.

legal list An acceptable list of investments in which a regulatory body allows an institution to invest. For example, pension funds, life insurance companies, and savings banks may not be permitted to invest in certain risky companies.

legal opinion An attorney's opinion regarding a specific matter; it has no binding effect.

lemon law Or, *lemon protection.* A law passed by several states guaranteeing a full refund of MONEY from a dealership to automobile purchasers who buy a new automobile that subsequently has major unresolved mechanical difficulties. If the purchaser can demonstrate that he or she has brought the car to the dealership a specific number of times to have a problem resolved with no satisfaction, then, under the lemon law, the consumer would qualify for a full refund from the dealer.

lender An individual who lends MONEY to a BORROWER at a specific INTEREST RATE to be repaid within a finite time period.
See also LENDING AGREEMENT.

lending agreement A contractual agreement that specifies to the borrower the terms of a loan including payment dates, INTEREST CHARGES, total cost of the LOAN, late payment charges, and any other related features.
See also TRUTH-IN-LENDING ACT.

letter of credit (LC) An INSTRUMENT written by a BANK guaranteeing the CREDIT of a third party for a certain period of time up to a specified sum of MONEY to a seller of goods. Essentially, a letter of credit substitutes the bank's credit for that of the named individual and serves as a form of negotiable instrument. Letters of credit are used extensively in international dealings.
commercial letter: A letter of credit used by a merchandise purchaser. It is sent to a local bank where the transaction is to occur, enabling the seller to present his bill of sale to the bank for payment.
confirmed letter: A form of a letter of credit by a local bank guaranteeing payment for a seller's draft if the bank that issued it fails to honor it.

export letter: A letter of credit sent to a seller or exporter informing him or her that a CREDIT has been established in his or her favor by a foreign bank and agreeing to honor the draft for the merchandise.

import letter: A letter of credit issued by a foreign bank to a local seller of merchandise allowing the seller to draw a draft on the foreign bank for the shipment of the merchandise.

letter of intent

in general: A document between two or more parties stating a desire to take or not take certain actions, often subject to the occurrence of a prior action. For example, a BANK may agree to make a loan subject to the determination of a satisfactory CREDIT RATING for the borrower. Normally, all letters of intent are written.

mutual fund: A commitment by a MUTUAL FUND shareholder to make, over a 13-month period, further INVESTMENTS of a specified sum of MONEY in order to qualify for lower sales fees.

letter of last instructions An informal memorandum containing suggestions or recommendations for carrying out the provisions of a will.

letter stock Or, *letter security.* A STOCK or BOND issued by a company before being registered with the SECURITIES AND EXCHANGE COMMISSION. When a company sells securities directly to the public, it can avoid registering them if the INVESTOR writes a LETTER OF INTENT stating that his or her purpose is to buy the security as an investment rather than to sell it.

The necessity of writing a letter to investors for purchasing this form of security is the origin of the names LETTER SECURITY, LETTER STOCK, and LETTER BOND.

level charge A charge or fee that does not vary over time.

level commission: A fee structure for INSURANCE AGENTS to ensure that their charges do not vary from one year to the next. This is done to promote higher quality service after the first sale of a policy.

level debt service: A provision found in a municipal charter requiring municipal DEBT payments to be approximately equal every year. Equal payments facilitate less complicated and more accurate budget projections.

level premium: A level and unchanging INSURANCE PREMIUM regardless of any change in risk.

level term insurance: An INSURANCE POLICY in which the COVERAGE amount stays the same over the entire length of effectiveness of the policy.

level term insurance TERM LIFE INSURANCE that provides a level FACE VALUE through increasing PREMIUMS.
See also INSURANCE PROGRAMS.

leverage

in general: The use of borrowed money to magnify potential RETURNS. It is hoped that the investment through leverage will earn a rate of return greater than the after-tax costs of borrowing.
See also FINANCIAL LEVERAGE.

securities:

1. The ratio in an investment of dollars controlled to dollars invested. Buying a stock on MARGIN, for example, allows an investor to borrow up to half the price of the stock. The ratio of dollars controlled to dollars invested in that case would be 2:1.

2. The practice of putting a larger sum at RISK than one has in hand by using MARGIN LOANS, WARRANTS, or PUTS and CALLS. These tools multiply one's chances of gain or loss as the market moves.

leverage fund Or, *leveraged investment company.* An OPEN-END MUTUAL FUND permitted by its charter to borrow funds from a BANK or other source.

dual purpose investment company: An INVESTMENT COMPANY or MUTUAL FUND issuing both income and capital SHARES. Income SHAREHOLDERS receive DIVIDENDS and INTEREST payments, whereas the capital SHAREHOLDERS receive all CAPITAL GAINS from INVESTMENTS.

leverage in real estate investing Use of OTH-ER PEOPLE'S MONEY (OPM) in an effort to increase the reward for investing. To many people, it means RISK. In reality, using leverage in real estate investing is an exciting way to earn big YIELDS on small dollars. When one is building real estate wealth, leverage will help the investment grow quickly without involving too much risk. High-leverage investing in real estate is especially powerful when inflation is in full swing because property values rise faster than the interest charges on the borrowed money. To show the full power of high-leverage investing, examples are given below.

Example 1: Gail pays a seller $100,000 cash for a piece of property. During the next 12 months, the property appreciates 5% and grows in resale value to $105,000. The $5,000 gain equals a 5% yield on her investment. But suppose she had put down only 10% ($10,000) in the property and mortgaged the balance. Now, her return on investment leaps to an astonishing 50% ($5,000/$10,000)! Viewed another way, since she put down only $10,000 on $100,000 worth of property, she actually controls an asset ten times the value of her actual cash outlay. This means 5% × 10 times = 50%. (In this example, for simplicity, we have omitted mortgage interest costs as well as the return on the $10,000 she would have invested somewhere else, plus any rental income she would have earned from the property).

Example 2: Instead of putting 100% down ($100,000), Gail put down 10% ($10,000) and bought nine more pieces of property, each costing $100,000, and each bought with 10% down ($10,000). Again assume that they appreciate at the rate of 5%. Her wealth increases $5,000 per piece × 10 pieces = $50,000—all in one year. Tying up her wealth in one property ($100,000) cost her $45,000 ($50,000 − $5,000). Conversely, spreading her funds over more properties and leveraging the balance would multiply her earnings ten times.

The lower the amount of cash invested, the higher her return (from value appreciation and/or rental income). On the other hand, the larger her cash investment, the lower her return. Also, a higher appreciation will greatly increase earnings on her leveraged investment.

pitfalls of high-leverage real estate investing

High-leverage real estate investing sounds good but this practice can destroy investors. An investor must be aware of the following:

• Remember that property values can go down as well as up. Some types of real estate in some parts of the country are experiencing value declines. Examples are Texas, Arizona, and New York.

• Select the property carefully.

• Anticipate a rising market resulting from a lower mortgage rate or a high inflation rate before jumping into a high-leverage world.

• Look out for NEGATIVE CASH FLOW. Income from highly leveraged property may be insufficient to cover operating expenses and debt payments. Do not overpay for property and underestimate costs. Buying for little or nothing down is easy. The difficult part is making the payments. Try to avoid negative cash flow (losses are tax deductible, however).

• Watch out for DEFERRED MAINTENANCE, which can create lots of problems down the road. One can avoid hidden costs and potential future expenditure by bargaining for a fair (or less than market) price and reasonable terms. In any case, over-repair is poison to the high-leverage investor.

See also LEVERAGE.

leverage stock STOCK bought on MARGIN with borrowed MONEY. The theory of leveraging stocks is that twice as much stock can be controlled with the same amount of MONEY, offering twice as much APPRECIATION potential.

Of course, should the stock decline in price, the losses would be twice as great.

leveraged buyout (LBO) A TAKEOVER of a company using borrowed funds. In the classic leveraged buyout, the ASSETS of the target company are used as COLLATERAL to finance the TAKEOVER by the raider (potential acquirer). The

CASH flow of the target company is used to repay the loan. At times, the LBO may be used by management to take the company private, so it is not publicly held, to prevent a raider from using the LBO against them.

Of course, it is possible for the raider to use his or her own ASSETS to COLLATERALIZE a loan in an LBO attempt against another company. In any event, the SHAREHOLDERS of the target company are always offered a PREMIUM price to induce them into selling their shares to the raider.

leveraging Using borrowed MONEY to control an INVESTMENT. The advantage of leveraging is that a small amount of EQUITY can be used to create a larger rate of return. The RISK is that leveraging can substantially increase the RISK of loss in the event the investment is unsuccessful.

liabilities A very broadly defined term implying legal or financial responsibilities to others.

corporate: An amount of MONEY owed by one company to another or unearned revenue requiring the performance of future services. Examples of corporate liabilities include accounts payable, accrued expenses payable, and BONDS payable.

legal: An obligation one is legally bound to perform immediately or in the future.

life insurance: Future benefits obligated to the POLICYHOLDERS and their BENEFICIARIES. INSURANCE COMPANIES are required by state law to maintain sufficient reserves to meet any liability claim made against them. The CASH surrender value of a LIFE INSURANCE company's policies is also considered part of the liabilities.

personal: An amount of MONEY owed or services to be provided based on advance payment received (e.g., a retainer). Examples of liabilities to an individual include TAXES payable, loans payable, CREDIT CARD balances, and a MORTGAGE payable.

liability exposure The extent to which one is at a liability RISK in any matter. The amount of damages or legal LIABILITY for which one could be responsible.

primary liability: A liability in which one is directly responsible. For example, if one were to fall on a homeowner's front step and sustain injuries, the homeowner would bear primary liability responsibility for any damage claims or other legal liability.

secondary liability: Contingent claims for which one could be liable if the primary obligator fails in his or her responsibilities.

liability insurance The INSURANCE to protect against the liability the insured becomes legally obligated to pay due to bodily injury, property damage, or professional liability or libel. The two categories of liability insurance are (1) personal exposures liability and (2) professional liability. Personal exposures liability is for acts or omissions that result in lawsuits against an individual for bodily injury and/or property damage to a third party. Professional liability is the liability created when an individual with professional training claims expertise in a specialized area greater than the layman. In liability insurance, the insurer agrees to indemnify the insured for financial indebtedness that the insured might owe a third party as well as legal expenses incurred for his or her liability.

liability risk *See* LIABILITY EXPOSURE.

license A legal document given by a regulatory agency to conduct some activity subject to prescribed terms. Typically, a fee is charged. Examples are a marriage license and driver's license.

lien A claim of a party, typically a creditor, to hold or control the property of another party to satisfy a debt or liability. It permits the creditor to liquidate the property that serves as collateral in the event of a DEFAULT. A MORTGAGE would create such a lien upon property in the event of default.

life annuity *See* ANNUITY.

life annuity, period certain *See* ANNUITY.

life annuity with no refund (straight life) *See* ANNUITY.

life care center   A home complex for the aged that takes care of their needs.

life cycle

1. The movement of a person through the different stages of life from birth to death.

2. The movement of a product or business through the stages of development, growth, expansion, maturity, saturation, and decline.

life-cycle costs

personal: The costs for an individual that change over the life cycle. For example, a major COST in young parenthood is buying a home. Later in life, a major cost is the college education of the children.

corporate: Costs associated with the development of a product from inception though the four stages in the life cycle: introduction, growth, maturity, and decline. In the early introduction and growth stages, costs are extremely high as intensive capital investment occurs and marketing and management strategies are developed and tested. In the maturity stage, per unit costs diminish as the earlier INVESTMENT brings its reward, and in the decline stage, per unit costs increase once again as increases in productivity and marketing bring diminishing profit returns as per unit COSTS escalate.

life-cycle planning

personal: The planning needed by individuals during their life cycles, such as a young married couple without children, a married couple with children, a married couple after the children have left, and retired people. Each stage in the life cycle requires different personal financial planning. For example, an older person is concerned with planning RETIREMENT.

corporate: The management strategies developed as a product moves through the four product life cycles: introduction, growth, maturity, and decline. As a product enters each stage of its life, new management challenges must be resolved through successful life-cycle planning.

life estate   A freehold interest in an ESTATE,

limited to the duration of the life of the grantee or other stipulated individual. Upon the demise of the grantee, or other stipulated individual, the estate reverts to the GRANTOR. For example, the U.S. government granted former President Eisenhower and his wife, Mamie, a life estate at their Gettysburg Farm as a historical site. Upon their deaths, the property reverted to the U.S. government as a historical landmark.
See also LIFE TENANT.

life expectancy   The average number of years a person is expected to live based on actuarial tables. The life expectancy for females exceeds that of males. The insurance plan or retirement plan is dictated by an individual's average life expectancy.
See also INSURANCE; RETIREMENT AND PENSION PLANNING.

life goals   Personal goals that one desires to accomplish during his or her lifetime. The ability to accomplish some of the goals depends partly on financial success. An example is to put one's children through college.

life income option   A provision in an insurance policy providing annuity payments for the rest of the annuitant's life.

life insurance, creditor rights   The protection afforded by state law to beneficiaries providing that the proceeds from life insurance cannot be attached by creditors of the insured and/or BENEFICIARIES.

life insurance policy   Insurance coverage against death of a person with payment going to a named beneficiary, typically another family member. The insured pays a periodic or lump-sum premium, and on his or her death, the face value of the policy (less any loans against it) is payable to the beneficiary. Some policies provide for living benefits to the insured during his or her lifetime, such as cash surrender value or income payments.

life insurance trust   A trust that is set up and names the beneficiary of the grantor's life insurance policy. When the insured dies, the trust is obligated to make payment of the life insurance proceeds as provided for in the agreement.

life-style The pattern of living an individual chooses. An individual's life-style is highly dependent on the amount of DISPOSABLE INCOME available. Those living beyond their means need to resort to increasing their personal DEBT to finance their life-style.

life tenant The grantee who is the TENANT of a LIFE ESTATE. Upon the death of the tenant, the ESTATE reverts to the grantor. For example, President Eisenhower and his wife, Mamie, were life tenants of the Gettysburg Farm LIFE ESTATE granted by the U.S. government. Upon their deaths, the property reverted to the U.S. government as a historical landmark.
See also LIFE ESTATE.

lifetime reverse mortgage A MORTGAGE plan that provides senior citizens who are house-rich and cash-poor a healthy cash flow from the EQUITY in their homes, with no requirement for repayment of any kind during their lifetimes. The terms are that borrowers retain TITLE and are not required to pay back the loan as long as they continue living in their homes. Once the home is no longer the primary residence—usually due to the death of the borrower—the estate typically sells the home and repays the loan, with the balance of the proceeds of the sale going to the estate. The loan is a nonrecourse loan, meaning that there is no recourse to the borrower or to the estate if the selling price of the home fails to cover the amount of principal and interest due. Of course, the loan cannot exceed the value of the home in any case.
See also REVERSE ANNUITY MORTGAGE (RAM).

limit
securities: A LIMIT ORDER by which a specific price is placed on either buying or selling a SECURITY.
insurance: A term indicating the maximum extent of COVERAGE granted as well as areas that are excluded from coverage.

limit move Up and down price limits placed by the commodity exchanges on all COMMODITY FUTURES trading. If a commodity future makes a limit move, it has moved either "up" or "down" its price limit, whereupon trading is closed in the commodity future until the next trading day.

limit order An instruction to execute an order for a stock only at a particular price or better. The BROKER continues the order until a given date or until the customer terminates it. Assume an investor places a limit order to buy at $20 or less a stock now selling at $22. If the stock goes up to $30, the buy order will not be executed. If the stock falls to $20, the order will immediately be executed.

limit or market on close In this SECURITIES instruction, a floor BROKER seeks to buy or sell a SECURITY at a set price, and if this is not achieved during the trading day, the order becomes a MARKET order on the close of the day's trading. This strategy is useful for individuals who must buy or sell a security on a particular day and wish to do so at a predetermined price; however, the market on close order ensures that the TRADE will be completed, at whatever the MARKET PRICE is, within the same trading day.

limitation
1. Exceptions and limits of insurance coverage including the maximum amount of insurance available under a policy.
2. The greatest amount allowed subject to a restraint. For example, an individual's job performance may be limited by his or her education.

limited liability
business: The principle that financial liability in a business or STOCK investment does not extend beyond the original investment. A CORPORATION and LIMITED PARTNERS enjoy limited liability. GENERAL PARTNERS and SOLE PROPRIETORS have UNLIMITED LIABILITY.
law: Any illegal or contractually restricted obligation.

limited partner A member of a PARTNERSHIP whose liability for the debts of the partnership is restricted to the member's investment. A limited partner is not allowed to participate actively in the management of a partnership.
See also GENERAL PARTNER; LIMITED PARTNERSHIP.

limited partnership (syndicate) A type of PARTNERSHIP in which the LIMITED PARTNER is legally liable only for the amount of his or her initial investment. Typically there are two classes of partners: the GENERAL PARTNER (usually the organizer), who operates the SYNDICATE and has unlimited financial liability; the LIMITED PARTNERS (the investors), who receive part of the profits and the tax-shelter benefits but who have no voice in the management of the business. The sponsor or general partner manages the partnership and uses the cash of the limited partners for ventures such as gas or oil exploration, real estate, or equipment leasing.

limited pay life insurance LIFE INSURANCE that allows premium payments to cease sometime before the insured become 100 years old.

limited payment policy An insurance policy in which the scheduled premium payments are for a specified limited period (e.g., five years) after which time they stop.

limited payment whole life insurance policy A type of WHOLE LIFE INSURANCE policy that offers coverage for the entire life of the insured but schedules the premium payments to end after a limited period, usually 10 or 20 years. The beneficiary receives the proceeds only at the death of the insured.

limited warranty A written WARRANTY that fails to meet the conditions of a full warranty in one or more respects. For example, a limited warranty granted by an appliance manufacturer may be limited to the parts, but not the labor, in repairing an appliance.

line
1. A bank commitment to lend funds to a borrower up to a specified amount over a specified future period.
2. An insurance term describing the maximum liability the insurer assumes for a particular item.
3. The major activities of a company, such as products.

line of credit The maximum preapproved amount that a person can borrow without completing a new CREDIT APPLICATION.

Linton yield The rate of return that an insured will earn on the cash value accumulated under a CASH VALUE LIFE INSURANCE policy. To calculate the Linton yield, the annual premium for an equivalent amount of a DECREASING TERM policy is subtracted from the cash value insurance annual premium. This "extra" premium is then compared to the cash value (plus dividends for participating policies) that would be accumulated after a given number of years (e.g., 5, 10, 20) to determine an annual rate of interest at the end of the given time period.
See also INTEREST-ADJUSTED COST METHOD.

liquid Descriptive of the condition in which an individual has adequate cash and near-cash assets to meet current debt.

liquidated damages An amount of money specified in a contract as compensation to be paid if the contract is not satisfactorily consummated. An example is an offer to buy real property that includes a statement to the effect that once the seller accepts the offer, if the buyer fails to complete the purchase, the seller may keep the buyer's deposit (the EARNEST MONEY) as liquidated damages.

liquidating dividend A distribution of a company's paid-in-capital rather than out of retained earnings. Thus, a liquidating DIVIDEND is not really a dividend because it is a distribution of CAPITAL and not from accumulated earnings. Since it is in effect a withdrawal of the capital investment, a liquidating dividend is *not* taxable to the recipient. Liquidating dividends are more common with utility STOCKS.

liquidation

in general: Conversion of ASSETS into MONEY.

business: The breaking up and selling of a company and its assets for cash distribution to its creditors and then owners. Chapter 7 of the Federal Bankruptcy Code covers a forced liquidation.

stocks: In the event of an unmet MARGIN CALL, a BROKERAGE FIRM would liquidate a sufficient amount of the client's SECURITIES to meet the cash MARGIN requirement.

See also PREFERRED STOCK; MAINTENANCE CALL.

liquidation period In INSURANCE, the period of time during which an ANNUITANT receives benefits from an ANNUITY policy. In a STRAIGHT or LIFE ANNUITY, the payments cease upon the death of the ANNUITANT, whereas in a refund annuity due to the annuitant's premature death, an additional amount representing the difference between the purchase price and the amount paid out during the annuitant's life will be paid to the ESTATE.

liquidity

1. The immediate convertibility of various assets into cash without significant loss of value. For example, a person's holding of marketable securities is more liquid than his or her house.

2. A person's ability to meet current liabilities when due. This ability may depend upon a person's current assets and expected future cash flow. It may be important for a person's assets to be sufficiently liquid to meet financial near-term commitments and to take advantage of new investment opportunities.

liquidity of assets ASSETS that can be readily converted into CASH without any loss of PRINCIPAL. For example, SEC-registered STOCKS trading on the NEW YORK STOCK EXCHANGE can easily be sold for a CASH settlement. The concept of liquidity is crucial to many INVESTMENT strategies.

stocks: The ability to sell STOCKS without materially affecting the price of the SECURITIES. A highly liquid market can easily absorb the sale of securities without materially affecting the MARKET PRICE.

liquidity ratio The ratio of LIQUID ASSETS divided by current debt. A low ratio indicates that the individual has a liquidity problem and may be unable to meet his or her debt obligations at a near-term date. The individual may have to take steps to improve the situation, such as consolidating several loans into one with a longer maturity date, or taking on a part-time job.

list price A manufacturer's suggested retail price for an item. Many items can be bought at a cost below the list price.

listed firm Or, *listed security.* Any firm whose stock is approved by the SEC and traded on any of the recognized stock exchanges such as the NEW YORK STOCK EXCHANGE (NYSE) and the AMERICAN STOCK EXCHANGE (AMEX). The term also indicates that the STOCK meets the ongoing minimum listing qualifications. Stocks that do not meet the exchange's minimum qualifications are delisted.

listed option A call or put option that has been approved for trading on an exchange.

listed securities STOCKS and BONDS traded on an organized security exchange such as the NEW YORK STOCK EXCHANGE (NYSE) and the AMERICAN STOCK EXCHANGE (AMEX). They are distinguished from unlisted securities, which are traded in the OVER-THE-COUNTER (OTC) market. Listed securities must meet various criteria regarding number of stockholders, number of shares owned by the public, market value of each share, and corporate earnings and assets.

listing agreement A contract permitting a REAL ESTATE AGENT to list a property exclusively and/or with a MULTIPLE LISTING SERVICE and specifying the commission rate and time period of the agreement.

listing broker A licensed REAL ESTATE BROKER who obtains a listing of property for sale.

living benefits of life insurance Life insurance benefits that the insured can obtain while still alive.

living trust A TRUST that is effective and operating during the person's life.

load (sales charge) A sales commission charged to purchase shares in many MUTUAL FUNDS sold by BROKERS or other members of a sales force. Typically, the charge ranges from 4% to 8.5% of the initial investment. The charge is added to the NET ASSET VALUE (NAV) per share when the offer price is determined. Not all MUTUAL FUNDS have a LOAD. It is important to note that the absence of a sales charge in no way affects the performance of the fund's management and ultimately the return on investment.

load (mutual) fund A MUTUAL FUND sold to the public that charges sales commissions, usually called a FRONT-END LOAD, when shares are initially purchased.

loading Additional costs added to an installment contract reflecting administrative costs, commissions, risk, interest costs, points, and other charges.
insurance: Adding the cost of AGENT COMMISSIONS, TAXES, and associated administrative costs to the cost of an INSURANCE POLICY.
open-end mutual funds: Adding to the SHARE price the amount necessary to offset selling costs.

loan A legal transaction in which a lender places property, often MONEY, in the possession of a BORROWER, who has the obligation to repay the property plus INTEREST within a specified time period.

All loans create DEBT having four characteristics. (1) A lender pays MONEY or lends property to a BORROWER. (2) The borrower's ACCOUNT is CREDITED with the amount of the transaction from which the borrower withdraws funds. (3) The loan is formalized in a CREDIT or loan agreement. (4) The debt can be forgiven through repayment of the borrowed property within the agreed time frame. Loan examples include loans for automobiles, commercial and consumer use, and MORTGAGES.

loan amortization The systematic repayment of the loan principal and interest. For example, on 1/1/19X1 a $100,000 loan is taken out at 10% interest payable over three years at year end. The annual loan payment is $40,209. A loan amortization schedule is shown below.

loan applications A form filled out by a BORROWER providing personal and financial information used by the lender in assessing borrower RISK. Information requested usually consists of the following: (1) borrower's name, (2) borrower's address, (3) amount and type of loan, (4) description of COLLATERAL, and (5) employment and financial data.

loan commitment An agreement by a lender to lend MONEY to a BORROWER. A loan commitment usually includes the amount of MONEY to be lent, the INTEREST RATE that will be charged,

SCHEDULE OF LOAN AMORTIZATION

Year	(a) Payment	(b) Interest (10%)	(c)=a−b Reduction of Principal	(d) Carrying Value
1/1/X1				$100,000
12/31/X1	$40,209	$10,000	$30,209	69,791
12/31/X2	40,209	6,979	33,230	36,561
12/31/X3	40,209	3,656	36,553*	0
	$120,627	$20,635	$99,992	

*Difference due to rounding.

and the time period for which the loan commitment is valid.

loan fund An institutional fund available to make LOANS, usually to employees. Any INTEREST earned from the loans is accrued in the fund for subsequent LOAN availability. In certain loan funds, only the accrued interest can be lent to BORROWERS.

loan origination fee The lender's charge to the borrower for doing all the paperwork and setting up the MORTGAGE LOAN, such as credit checks, APPRAISAL, and TITLE expenses. For example, the lender approves a $100,000 mortgage loan with a 1% loan origination fee. The loan origination fee is then $1,000.

loan-to-value (LTV) ratio The ratio of the loan principal (amount borrowed) to the property's fair market value or sales price. For example, on a $100,000 home with a mortgage loan principal of $80,000 the ratio is 80%. The LTV ratio on a CONVENTIONAL LOAN is 80%. Home mortgages at more than an 80% LTV ratio generally require PRIVATE MORTGAGE INSURANCE (PMI).

loan value
in general: The amount of MONEY a LENDER agrees to lend on pledged COLLATERAL.
securities: The amount of MONEY a BROKER can lend to an investor on MARGINABLE SECURITIES. If the MARGIN RATE is 50%, then for a PORTFOLIO of STOCKS qualifying as marginable worth $20,000, the broker can lend $10,000.
insurance: The ceiling an INSURED can borrow against his or her life insurance contract. For policies having a CASH SURRENDER VALUE, the amount that can be borrowed equals the surrender value. The policy serves as COLLATERAL.
See also MARGINABLE SECURITIES.

local taxes Income taxes paid by an individual to the state or county in which he or she resides.

location A place or position where something is kept, such as where personnel files are re-tained, or the safe deposit box in which important records are kept for safekeeping.

locked-in vesting An employee who has vested in a contributory pension plan. The employee should not receive funds from the plan until retirement. To do so results in an IRS charge.

long Signifying ownership of securities, indicating that the investor has bought a particular investment instrument. For example, ''I am long 100 IBM'' means I own 100 shares in that company. This term is the opposite of being SHORT on an investment.

long bond
ownership: Term indicating a DEBT SECURITY owned outright by an INVESTOR who can transfer the TITLE to others upon a sale.
maturity: A BOND having a MATURITY of ten years or longer. Such long-term bonds generally have a higher YIELD than short-term bonds as the longer maturity increases the MARKET RISK of the bond.

long position In SECURITIES, indicating that the INVESTOR owns securities outright and can sell and transfer their TITLE at any time.

long term
equities: A period exceeding one year. Under IRS rules, SECURITIES held more than one year qualify as long-term assets.
bond maturity: A period exceeding ten years.

longevity pay SALARY or WAGE increases given in recognition of long-term employment: the greater the length of service, the higher the longevity pay. In certain cases, longevity pay may also include bonuses. The purpose of longevity pay is to increase the motivation of long-term employees.

long-term capital gain or loss Under IRS rules, a period exceeding one year. However, under current tax law LONG-TERM CAPITAL GAINS AND LOSSES typically have the same tax consequences as SHORT-TERM CAPITAL GAINS AND LOSSES. However, the Tax Reform Act did not change the limited offset of long-term capital losses against ordinary INCOME.

long-term goals A relative term; however, long-term goals are generally five years or more depending upon the circumstance. For example, an individual is developing long-term goals when his or her planning extends beyond five years. Examples of an individual's long-term goals are a successful professional career (e.g., becoming vice-president of a company, putting children through college, and having sufficient RETIREMENT savings).
See also LONG-TERM PLANNING.

long-term investor One who INVESTS for a period exceeding five years. For example, a long-term investor may choose an investment PORTFOLIO to prepare for RETIREMENT in ten years.

Many long-term investors choose conservative investments, such as BLUE-CHIP STOCKS, federal securities, or municipal tax-free bonds.

long-term planning Planning for five years or more. Long-term planning seeks to improve one's future status through current and intermediate term actions. An example of a long-term plan that will be accomplished in steps is to be a multimillionaire at age 65.

loss-control activities Activities designed to prevent or minimize losses. An example is insuring property properly.

loss-of-income insurance
insurance: COVERAGE included in property insurance that provides for the loss of income resulting if a PERIL such as fire severely damages a place of business, forcing employees out of work.
In *disability insurance:* COVERAGE for lost INCOME is provided in the event a severely disabling illness or injury occurs, preventing the insured from being gainfully employed.
Social Security: Workmen's compensation insurance is provided under SOCIAL SECURITY Insurance for employees sustaining work-related injuries that impair their ability to be gainfully

employed. Social Security also provides supplementary RETIREMENT benefits for those retiring from employment.

loss prevention A program of RISK reduction, implemented by many organizations, emphasizing safety management and procedures. The intent of such programs is to reduce the severity and frequency of losses in the workplace.

A loss prevention program may consist of safety meetings, bonuses given to employees for the implementation of safe procedures, signs, and warning devices. An organization having a good employee safety record normally receives lower workmen's compensation premiums.

loss ratio An insurance term connoting the degree of losses based on the insurance premium paid, typically determined on an annual basis. It equals

$$\frac{\text{Claims paid and claims to be paid}}{\text{Premium}}$$

loss reduction A risk-management approach to emphasize safety so as to reduce the number and severity of possible losses. As an example, an employer promises a cash award to the worker with the best safety record for the month.

low-balance method A method of determining interest on a SAVINGS ACCOUNT balance whereby interest is paid on the lowest balance on deposit in the account during the interest period.
See also MINIMUM BALANCE METHOD.

low grade A quality rating meeting minimum qualifications. A low-grade quality rating is a poor one.
securities: SECURITIES are rated as to quality by underwriting houses including Fitch's, Moody's, and Standard & Poor's. A low-grade security would be one rated B or lower. D indicates default.

A low-grade DEBT SECURITY will be forced to pay a higher rate of INTEREST because of the high risk associated with it. Low-grade equity issues are normally not kept in the portfolios of institutions investing large sums of MONEY in securities.

low-load fund A MUTUAL FUND that charges low sales commissions on the purchase of its shares, such as 1% to 2%.

low par A one- or two-dollar PAR VALUE for a COMMON STOCK.

lump sum A single payment for an entire amount as opposed to many payments made over time.
See also LUMP-SUM PAYMENT; LUMP-SUM DISTRIBUTION.

lump-sum distribution A single one-time payment for something rather than many payments made over time. For example, upon RETIREMENT an employee may receive a single lump-sum distribution of his or her PENSION benefits.
See also LUMP SUM; LUMP-SUM PAYMENT.

lump-sum payment
1. A one time payment made by an entity as a settlement for something. For example, an INSURER may make one payment rather than periodic payments to an INSURED to settle a policy. A LIFE INSURANCE company may make a lump-sum payment to a beneficiary on the death of the insured.
2. A one-time expenditure to buy something. For example, an individual may pay CASH for the full price of an automobile rather than paying for it with an INSTALLMENT LOAN.
See also LUMP SUM; LUMP-SUM DISTRIBUTION.

luxury tax Tax charged on purchases of "luxury" items. Under current tax law, there is a 10% federal luxury tax on cars selling for more than $30,000, furs and jewelry selling in excess of $10,000, and private boats selling above $100,000.

magnetic ink character recognition (MICR) A magnetic coding imprinted on checks and deposit slips to speed up the check and deposit clearing process.

Magnuson-Moss Warranty Act of 1975 The act that regulates express written WARRANTIES. One of the objectives of the act is to prohibit written warranties from limiting the IMPLIED WARRANTY to a shorter period than that covered by the written warranty. Before passage of this act, many written warranties contained clauses that relieved the seller of an implied warranty. However, the seller can still avoid an implied warranty by the selling of the product "as is."

maintenance call A notice by a BROKERAGE FIRM informing a SECURITIES client with a MARGIN ACCOUNT of insufficient EQUITY in the ACCOUNT to meet brokerage or industry rules. The mainte-nance call will require additional sums of MONEY to be promptly deposited or securities in the account will be LIQUIDATED to meet the call.

maintenance fee
banks: The fee some banks charge for maintaining an INDIVIDUAL RETIREMENT ACCOUNT (IRA) or Keogh pension plan at the bank.
securities: An annual fee charged by some brokerage firms to SECURITY clients for the administrative costs of maintaining securities held in the account. Maintenance fees are also charged for INDIVIDUAL RETIREMENT ACCOUNT (IRA), and KEOGH PENSION PLANS.

maintenance margin requirement Or, *minimum maintenance; maintenance requirement.* The minimum percentage EQUITY an investor must maintain in a STOCK or BOND purchased using borrowed funds, as required by the NEW YORK

STOCK EXCHANGE (NYSE), the NATIONAL ASSOCIATION OF SECURITIES DEALERS (NASD), and brokerage firms. The NYSE and NASD both require a maintenance margin equal to 25% of the market value of securities in margin accounts. Many brokerage firms require more—typically 30%.

See also INITIAL MARGIN REQUIREMENT; MARGIN BUYING; REGULATION T; SHORT SELLING.

maintenance requirement *See* MAINTENANCE MARGIN REQUIREMENT.

major medical insurance plan A type of HEALTH INSURANCE plan designed to supplement the basic coverages of hospital, surgery, physician's expenses, and health-care costs. After the limits of a BASIC HEALTH INSURANCE POLICY have been exhausted, major medical takes over medical expenses in excess of those covered by the basic plan. It is used to finance medical costs of a more catastrophic or long-term nature on a blanket basis. There may be a lifetime limit. For example, if the lifetime limit is $300,000 and a policyholder expends $50,000 of coverage in a given year, the lifetime limit would be down to $250,000.

See also GROUP HEALTH INSURANCE; HEALTH MAINTENANCE ORGANIZATION (HMO).

making a market The act of a SECURITY DEALER who maintains firm bid and asked round lot quotes for publicly traded SECURITIES as part of his or her obligation to maintain an orderly market. Such a dealer is termed a MARKET MAKER in the OVER-THE-COUNTER MARKET.

managed account A SECURITIES account managed by a BANK trust department or INVESTMENT ADVISER having FULL DISCRETIONARY AUTHORITY to buy and sell securities based on INVESTMENT judgments.

management

1. Individuals in charge of an organization who make the key decisions. They may be referred to as managers, supervisors, executives, or bosses.

2. The planning, organizing, and controlling of affairs and activities. An example is proper planning of work by an individual to accomplish his or her objectives.

management fee

securities: A charge against the ASSETS of a SECURITY PORTFOLIO for their management. In the case of an OPEN-END MUTUAL FUND, the management fee is also reflected in the selling cost of the security, whereas in the case of an INVESTMENT ADVISER or bank trust department, the management fee is usually a percentage of the assets.

real estate: A flat charge to maintain property, collect rent, and perform bookkeeping functions.

management risk

1. The financial or legal RISK an owner has in operating a company. For example, the owner could be sued for defective products causing injury to an individual.

2. The risk the owner of a company has when making strategic operational decisions that could directly affect the company's future. Since there never is sufficient information, time, or resources to make decisions, there is always an element of RISK.

manipulation

psychology: Controlling the behavior of others through guile and deceit.

securities: Any control exercised by an individual or group to affect directly the MARKET PRICES of SECURITIES. One method involves artificial trading between two or more people at the highest possible price to attract bids from other traders for the purpose of achieving a short-term profit.

Spreading incorrect rumors is another method creating possible major short-term price movements. A successful rumor can have a very powerful market effect, allowing the rumormonger to achieve potentially significant short-term profits.

Any attempt to manipulate directly the price of SECURITIES traded in the STOCK MARKET is illegal and is subject to criminal penalties.

manufactured housing Partially factory-assembled housing units designed to be transported in portions to the home site, where finishing of the building requires another two to six weeks.

See also MOBILE HOME.

margin

securities: Partial payment made by the customer when he or she uses credit to buy a security, the balance being advanced by the broker. The Federal Reserve Board determines margin requirements.

real estate: The difference between the INDEX a lender uses to adjust ADJUSTABLE RATE MORTGAGE (ARM) rates and the interest rate the lender actually charges the borrower. The ARM interest rate is the sum of the value of the index and the MARGIN.

commodities trading: Deposits required by commodities exchanges.

margin account An account created by a securities broker that allows an investor to purchase approved stocks or bonds on credit. The stockbroker lends the margin purchaser the money while retaining custody of the stock as collateral. This is a form of leverage that magnifies the gains and losses from a given percentage of price fluctuation in the securities.

The MINIMUM OR INITIAL MARGIN REQUIREMENT —the lowest margin on which stocks or bonds can be purchased or sold short—is established by the Federal Reserve Board as authorized by the Securities Exchange Act of 1934. However, the New York Stock Exchange establishes the minimum margins that must be maintained by retail traders.

Currently the New York Stock Exchange requires a 50% margin. Therefore, $50 would be needed to buy $100 in stock. If the stock were to fall, the broker would require that additional money be deposited in the account to provide additional security. This is known as MARKING THE MARGIN ACCOUNT TO THE MARKET. While this action does protect the broker, it can accelerate stock selling in a down market as traders seek to raise cash in order to cover their margin accounts.

The main purpose of margin requirements is to prevent excessive speculation in the stock market. Margin requirements are changed infrequently. Tightening margin requirements would reduce speculation in the market by requiring greater cash to be applied to any securities' purchases.

In futures trading, a margin is a deposit put up by an investor when buying a contract. In the event the futures price moves adversely, the investor has to provide additional funds to satisfy the margin requirements.

margin buying (margin trading) Buying securities on credit. An investor opening a margin account signs a margin agreement, similar to an agreement signed to obtain a bank loan. This document states the annual rate of interest, its method of computation, and specific conditions under which interest rates can be charged. The Federal Reserve Board sets rules specifying the minimum percentage of the purchase price that a margin customer must pay in cash, known as an INITIAL MARGIN REQUIREMENT. This requirement is currently at least 50% of the current market value of the security. (Some securities may not be purchased on margin.) A 60% margin requirement means that 100 shares of a stock selling for $200 a share can be purchased by putting up, in cash, only 60% of the total purchase price, that is, $12,000, and borrowing the remaining $8,000. The stockbroker lends the margin purchaser the money at interest, retaining custody of the stock as COLLATERAL. This is a form of LEVERAGE that, whether used in a long position or a short position, magnifies the gains and losses from a given percentage of price fluctuation in securities.

margin call A regulation imposed by the broker that requires the margin investor to put up more funds if an investor's equity in a margin account declines below a minimum standard set by an exchange or by the firm.

margin purchase *See* MARGIN BUYING.

margin rate The amount of cash COLLATERAL needed to buy STOCK in a MARGIN ACCOUNT. Under FEDERAL RESERVE Regulation T, stock INVESTORS are permitted to borrow up to 50% of the price of a stock in a stock MARGIN ACCOUNT, but they do not have to pay what they borrow until the stock is sold. Regulation T is subject to modification at the discretion of the Federal Reserve.
See also MARGIN; MARGIN BUYING; MARGIN PURCHASE; MARGIN REQUIREMENT.

margin requirement The amount that must be paid by the investor when purchasing securities on credit.
See also INITIAL MARGIN REQUIREMENT; MAINTENANCE MARGIN REQUIREMENT; MARGIN BUYING.

marginable securities Stocks and bonds that may be bought on MARGIN. The Federal Reserve Board publishes a list of approved marginable SECURITIES that can include any STOCK, CONVERTIBLE BOND, WARRANTS, or RIGHTS issued by companies and listed on stock exchanges, as well as those trading OVER-THE-COUNTER. In order for a security to be considered marginable by the FEDERAL RESERVE Board, the issuing company must meet certain financial criteria.

marginal analysis A method under which the added (marginal) benefits derived from a decision are compared with the extra (marginal) costs associated with that decision. If added benefits exceed extra costs, one should accept the decision. For example, suppose an individual wants to choose between two automobile insurance policies that differ with respect to coverage and cost. In deciding between the two, it is not necessary to look at the total coverage and total premiums of each. He or she should compare the extra coverage with the extra premium. The decision should be made on the basis of whether the more comprehensive policy is worth the extra cost.

marginal benefits *See* MARGINAL ANALYSIS.

marginal cost The change in total COST relative to overall volume. For example, if one more unit of output costs $25, then the marginal cost is $25. Generally speaking, as activity increases, economies of scale result and the LEARNING CURVE principle is effective. However, as activities continue to increase, then marginal costs begin to rise as management limits are reached.

At the point of optimum output, marginal cost is equal to average total unit cost (see accompanying chart).

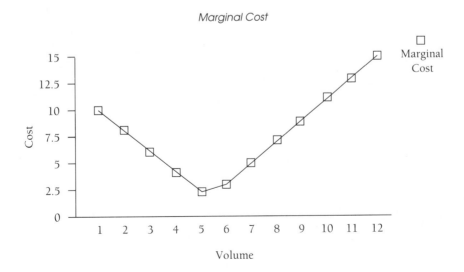

Marginal Cost

marginal tax rate The rate paid on the last dollar of taxable INCOME. For example, under current tax law there are three TAX brackets in 1990 if one's filing status is single:

  15% on taxable income not exceeding $19,450
  28% on income more than $19,450 but not exceeding $47,050
  33% on income more than $47,050 but not exceeding $97,620

If a single taxpayer's income equals $60,000, the total taxes paid will be $14,919.00.

First $19,450 of taxable income at 15% = $2,917.50
Next $27,600 of taxable income
  ($47,050−$19,450) at 28% = $7,728.00
Remaining $12,950 at 33% = $4,273.50
  ($60,000−$47,050)
Total $14,919.00

The tax rates of 15%, 28%, and 33% are marginal tax rates while the average tax rate is 24.9% ($14,919/$60,000).

marital deduction A TAX DEDUCTION permitted for transferring property from one spouse to another as permitted under the FEDERAL GIFT TAX for lifetime transfers as well as the FEDERAL ESTATE TAX for testamentary transfers for a DECEDENT.

marital deduction trust A TRUST used in ESTATE PLANNING designed to gain the maximum benefit of the MARITAL DEDUCTION by dividing the property in half. Under this arrangement, one-half of the marital ASSETS are transferred to the marital deduction TRUST while the remaining ASSETS are placed in another trust for the primary purpose of escaping taxation.

marital tax rate TAX RATE paid by married couples on the last dollar of taxable income. For example, under current tax law there are three tax brackets if the filing status is married filing jointly:

  15% on taxable income under $32,450
  28% on income more than $32,450 but less than $78,400
  33% on income more than $78,400 but less than $162,770

If a married couple's joint income (with one spouse working) equals $80,000, and they are filing jointly, the total taxes paid will be $18,261.50.

First $32,450 of taxable income at 15% = $4,867.50
Next $45,950 of taxable income
  ($78,400−$32,450) at 28% = $12,866.00
Remaining $1,600 × 33%
  ($80,000−78,400) = $528.00
Total $18,261.50

In this example, the average marital tax rate on $80,000 taxable income is 22.8% ($18,261.50/$80,000). Married filing jointly offers a significant tax advantage over married filing separately since the break points for 15%, 28%, and 33% are only half as much as married filing jointly:

  15% on taxable income under $16,225
  28% on income more than $16,225 but less than $39,200
  33% on income more than $39,200 but less than $123,570

Thus, for a married taxpayer earning $80,000 filing separately, the total taxes paid will be $22,330.75.

First $16,225 of taxable income at 15% = $2,433.75
Next $22,975 of taxable income at 28% = $6,433.00
  ($39,200−$16,225)
Remaining $40,800 × 33%
  ($80,000−$39,200) = $13,464.00
Total $22,330.75

For the married taxpayer filing separately the tax rate on $80,000 taxable income is 27.9% ($22,330.75/$80,000) or 5% higher than for a married taxpayer filing jointly.

market Or, *marketplace.* Any public place where products or services are bought and sold in an open and free manner.

  1. A place where buyers and sellers come together for the purpose of transacting business trade.

  2. *v.* To sell or develop a good or service for the purpose of meeting a specified demand.

  3. The supply and demand for a given good or activity at any point in time.

4. A recognized SECURITIES MARKET, such as the NEW YORK STOCK EXCHANGE.

market analysis

finance: Research on the STOCK MARKET and individual SECURITIES as well as DEBT SECURITIES to determine future trends and directions. There are two schools of MARKET analysis. These are technical and fundamental analysis.

See also FUNDAMENTAL ANALYSIS; TECHNICAL ANALYSIS.

marketing: The study of various markets and their existing clients to determine their potential and existing needs. This research includes all aspects of a market, including the psychology of the marketplace, prices, monetary variables, seasonality and timing, the demography of the market's clients, competitiveness, and so on. The objective of this type of market analysis is to forecast and, if possible, control trends and develop goods and services to take advantage of opportunities. Or, *market research.*

market bottom or top

In investments, the lowest or highest price for a market index in a specified time frame.

market breadth

An analysis of the STOCK MARKET's performance by comparing the number of STOCKS that rose as opposed to those that fell. The greater the number of stocks that went up as opposed to those that fell, the more BULLISH is the indicator. Conversely, the larger the number of stocks falling as opposed to those rising, the more BEARISH is the indicator.

market if touched order (MIT)

An instruction to buy or sell a security or commodity once a predetermined market price occurs, at which time it translates into a MARKET ORDER. For example, a stock is currently at $50 per share. An investor may place an order to buy at $45 per share. When the market price drops to $45, the stock is bought at whatever market price exists when the order is executed.

market indices

See MARKET (STOCK) INDICES AND AVERAGES.

market (stock) indices and averages

Market gauges used to track performance for STOCKS and BONDS. In theory, an average is the simple arithmetic MEAN while an index is an average expressed relative to a preestablished market value. In practice, the distinction is not quite that clear. There are many stock market indices and averages available. Each market has several indices published by Dow Jones, Standard & Poor's, and other financial services. Different investors prefer different indices. Indices and averages are also used as the underlying value of index futures and index options.

dow-jones averages

Dow-Jones averages are the most widely used and watched market indices published by the *Wall Street Journal.* The Dow-Jones Industrial Average (DJIA) is one of the four stock averages compiled by the *Journal.* This average consists of 30 large companies and is considered a "blue-chip" index (stocks of very high quality). The DJIA represents about 20% of the market value of the New York Stock Exchange (NYSE) stocks. There are three other Dow-Jones averages: the transportation, composed of 20 transportation issues, the 15 utilities, and a composite of the total 65 stocks. The DJIA would be a simple average of 30 blue-chip stocks but when a firm splits its stock price, the average must be adjusted in some manner. In fact, the divisor is changed from time to time to maintain continuity of the average. The Dow-Jones averages are designed to serve as indicators of broad movements in the securities markets. The Dow-Jones Composite, also called *65 Stock Average,* combines all three Dow-Jones averages.

barron's indices

Barron's, which is also a publication of Dow Jones, compiles Barron's 50 Stock Average and an index of low-priced securities that meets the needs of small investors. Barron's also publishes a weekly average called Barron's Group Stock Averages covering 32 industry groups.

standard & poor's indices

Standard & Poor's Corporation publishes several indices, including the two most widely used—the S&P 400 Industrials and the *S&P 500-Stock Index*. The S&P 400 is composed of 400 industrial common stocks of companies listed on the New York Stock Exchange and the S&P 500-Stock Index consists of the 400 industrials and utilities and transportation stocks. They are used as broad measures of the market direction. They are also frequently used as proxies for market return when computing the systematic risk measure (BETA) of individual stocks and portfolios. The S&P 500 Stock Index is one of the U.S. Commerce Department's *Index of 11 Leading Economic Indicators*. This index represents some 80% of the market value of all issues traded on the NYSE.

The Standard & Poor's 100 Stock Index consists of stocks for which options are listed on the CHICAGO BOARD OPTION EXCHANGE (CBOE).

value line average

The Value Line Average is a simple average of 1,685 companies from the NYSE, AMEX, and the OVER-THE-COUNTER market.

other market indices

Different exchanges publish their market indices. The NYSE publishes a composite index as well as industrial, utility, transportation, and financial indices. The AMERICAN STOCK EXCHANGE (AMEX) compiles two major indices—the AMEX Market Value Index (AMVI) and the AMEX Major Market Index. The National Association of Securities Dealers also publishes several indices to represent the companies in the over-the-counter market. It publishes the NASDAQ OTC composite, insurance, industrial, and banking indices.

wilshire 5000 equity index

The index is published by the Wilshire Associates of Santa Monica, California, and represents the market value of 5,000 NYSE, AMEX, and over-the-counter issues.

bond averages

Barron's publishes an index of 20 bonds, 10 utility bonds, and 10 industrial bonds as an average of the bond market. Dow Jones publishes two major bond averages—the Dow-Jones 40 Bond Average, representative of six different bond groups, and the Dow-Jones Municipal Bond Yield Average.

mutual fund averages

Lipper Analytical Services compiles the Lipper Mutual Fund Investment Performance Averages. It publishes three basic fund indices for GROWTH FUNDS, GROWTH-INCOME FUNDS, and BALANCED FUNDS.

market letter Or, *investment letter*. A letter or brief statement sent to SECURITY INVESTORS by BROKERAGE FIRMS and MARKET authorities, often for a fee, giving an expert market analyst's point of view about current market conditions suggesting particular INVESTMENT strategies, often including specific buy and sell recommendations, to follow. Some market letters, such as the Granville Letter, have issued recommendations causing spectacular advances or declines in the stock market.

Market letters are only advisory in nature and take no specific responsibility for directly managing an investor's ASSETS.

market maker In investments, a DEALER, floor BROKER, or SPECIALIST who maintains a MARKET for SECURITIES by buying and selling them into his own ACCOUNT and then reselling them to clients. It is the responsibility of a market maker to try and maintain an orderly market in often volatile conditions as well as to guarantee liquidity.

See also MARKET SPECIALIST.

market-on-the-close order An order to buy or sell SECURITIES at the MARKET as near as is practical to the close of trading. Often this type of order is issued if a LIMIT DAY ORDER was unsuccessful and the TRADE must be completed before the end of the trading session.

market opening In investments, the time at which TRADING first starts. Trading may not begin simultaneously for all securities as there may be an imbalance of buy or sell orders and the FLOOR BROKER is trying to match up the orders with available securities.

market order A customer instruction on the STOCK EXCHANGE to buy or sell a SECURITY or securities at once at the highest MARKET PRICE. The order is unconditional and the BROKER has the obligation to execute the instruction in an orderly manner meaning that the market order, assuming there is sufficient trading volume in the SECURITY, will result in a price that is within the bid and asked range.

market price Generally, a price of a good or service determined through competitive forces in a fair, open, and free market.
securities: The bid or asked price of a SECURITY at any time.
See also MARKET VALUE.

market rate for savings bonds The rate that SERIES EE AND HH SAVINGS BONDS will pay if held to maturity. The rate is 85% of the latest six-month average rate on five-year TREASURY SECURITIES.

market rate of interest
1. The rate of INTEREST on DEPOSITS and other INVESTMENTS resulting from demand and supply conditions in the MONEY MARKET. Market rates may be found in the financial pages of newspapers.
2. The current rate of interest institutions are asking on loans. The market rate of interest is influenced by several factors, including the DISCOUNT RATE, PRIME RATE, market demand for money, current availability of CAPITAL to lend, and borrower's financial condition.

market risk The change in an EQUITY or DEBT SECURITY'S price resulting from changes in the STOCK or BOND MARKET as whole, regardless of the fundamental change in the company's financial condition or operating performance. The RISK may be due to economic and/or political uncertainties.

market specialist In SECURITIES, a member of a STOCK or commodities exchange who represents a specific security or group of securities. His or her responsibility is to maintain an orderly MARKET during particularly turbulent periods by buying and selling securities into his or her own account and providing liquidity. The market specialist also maintains ''the book'' where all buy-and-sell orders are entered and matched together to make a sale.
See also MARKET MAKER.

market technicians In SECURITIES, those who adhere to the technical analysis school of market analysis. Market technicians perform technical analysis whereby future security price movements are based on past price fluctuations. Adherents to this field of thought anticipate that past price patterns will reproduce themselves in the future, allowing elaborate technical analyses of current price movements to be projected into the near and intermediate term.

Market technicians disregard fundamental analysis and examine market charts exclusively to detect patterns foretelling future price movements. The various STOCK price patterns that market technicians analyze are termed TECHNICAL INDICATORS.

market timing The analysis of the appropriate time in which to buy or sell an INVESTMENT. Market timing is based on many variables, including current prices, economic conditions, seasonality, and governmental policies. For example, there may be a timing risk when choosing to buy a SECURITY trading at an all-time high. On the other hand, it may be a good time to buy a security at its 52-week low because it may be undervalued.

market value The fair or true price of a product or service in an open and free competitive market. Many factors enter into determining market value, but supply and demand are critical elements. Market value is dependent on an unending supply of information.
See also MARKET PRICE.

market value policy Management policies developed to support the market value of its equity and debt securities. There are many alternative policies management might choose, including selling certain subsidiaries and distributing the proceeds to the SHAREHOLDERS, raising the DIVIDEND, or streamlining the company in order to increase profits.

marketable security

personal: Any SECURITY, including STOCKS, BONDS, COMMERCIAL PAPER, and TREASURY BILLS, that are actively traded on a MARKET and can be quickly transferred into CASH.

corporate: A security that the company intends to hold for one year or less and that can be easily sold. Marketable securities are presented on a company's BALANCE SHEET at the lower of cost or MARKET VALUE.

marketable title Title that is free from reasonable doubt as to who the owner is. It is the title that a reasonable buyer, informed as to the facts and their legal importance and acting with reasonable care, would be willing and ought to accept. The buyer might want to locate a title insurance company that will insure the title as being marketable. If the defect is not serious, the insurance company will accept the risk.

markdown

securities:

1. Amount subtracted from the selling price when a customer sells securities to a dealer in the OVER-THE-COUNTER market. Had the securities been purchased from the dealer, the customer would have paid a markup, or an amount added to the purchase price.

2. Reduction in the price at which the underwriters offer MUNICIPAL BONDS after the market has shown a lack of interest at the original price.

3. Downward adjustment of the value of securities by banks and investment firms, based on a decline in market quotations.

business:

1. Reduction in the original retail selling price, which was determined by adding a percentage factor, called a MARKON, to the cost of the merchandise. Anything added to the markon is called a MARKUP, and the term markdown does not apply unless the price is dropped below the original selling price.

2. In retail, reduction in selling price.

markup *See* MARKDOWN.

Mastercard A CREDIT CARD issued through a BANK. There are over 3,000 banks worldwide that issue Mastercard, and each bank determines the INTEREST RATE to be charged, the annual fee, if any, and any other charges or fees. This credit card can be used anywhere in the world for credit purchases wherever merchants agree to accept it.

matched and lost In investments, when two orders of the same quantity and price for the sale of a stock goes to the exchange floor at the same time. In this instance, a toss of the coin indicates which order will be used.

matured endowment The ENDOWMENT time period that the face value of a LIFE INSURANCE POLICY is payable to the insured.

maturity

1. The period when a financial obligation such as a LOAN, MORTGAGE, or BOND matures and must be paid. The ORIGINAL MATURITY is the time period from the effective date of issue to the MATURITY DATE.

2. A term describing a stage of growth of a company. The maturity stage of growth describes a company that has passed through the inception and growth stages and is now well established, has good CREDIT, and is a major factor in its market segment.

3. An individual who has matured in a personal sense. Typically, a person matures with age and experience.

maturity date The due date for any DEBT INSTRUMENT when the PRINCIPAL must be paid. *See also* MATURITY.

maturity value The amount to be received on the MATURITY DATE of a financial instrument. It may be a lesser amount (e.g., bond bought at a premium) or a greater amount (e.g., bond bought at a discount) than the initial cost. Maturity value usually refers to the face value of a bond or note. Assume a 10-year, $10,000 bond is bought at 98% (a discount). Thus, the initial investment is $9,800. At the end of the tenth year, the maturity value of $10,000 will be received. Hence, the investor's gain is $200, which is subject to tax in the tenth year.

meal expense deduction An INCOME TAX deduction from ADJUSTED GROSS INCOME for employment-related meal expenses. Food and beverages are not DEDUCTIBLE unless (1) the EXPENSE is directly applied to the performance of the taxpayer's trade or business, and (2) sufficient documentation exists. The DEDUCTION is not permitted unless it is for the actual discussion of business-related matters. Additionally, the EXPENSE cannot be extravagant as defined by the INTERNAL REVENUE SERVICE.

mean A simple arithmetic average of amounts. It is calculated by adding all values in the sample divided by the total observations.
See also ARITHMETIC AVERAGE RETURN; GEOMETRIC AVERAGE RETURN; MOVING AVERAGE.

mechanic's lien A claim placed against property by an unpaid workman or material supplier. A sale of the property can be forced to recover the money owed. To be entitled to a mechanic's lien, the claimant must have provided the work or materials pursuant to a contract with the landowner or his or her representative. The legal rationale behind the mechanic's lien is that the labor and materials supplied enhance the value of the property and therefore the property should be security for payment.

median The median is the middle value when the numbers in the data set are arranged by order of importance. The median is the midpoint in a range of values.

Medicaid A form of public assistance for health-related expenses for aged, blind, and disabled individuals and families with dependent children falling below a certain minimum income level. It is referred to as Title XIX of the 1965 amendments to the SOCIAL SECURITY ACT. Medicaid is jointly administered and sponsored through the federal and state governments.

medical expense deduction An ITEMIZED DEDUCTION for nonreimbursed medical expenses exceeding 7.5% of adjusted gross income. Included under the expense are doctor's bills, the cost of medicine, laboratory tests, and hospital costs.

Medical Information Bureau A computerized system accessible to life and HEALTH INSURANCE companies who are members. It keeps health histories on file for INSURANCE applicants and is accessible by telecommunications. The Medical Information Bureau makes it possible for one company located, for example, in New York, to receive a medical history on a health insurance applicant who had previously applied for health insurance in Des Moines, Iowa.

The basic intent of the Medical Information Bureau is to guard against fraud on the part of applicants.

medical insurance *See* HEALTH INSURANCE.

medical payments Payments made to medical doctors, dentists, laboratories, and pharmacies for health care. Medical expenses are tax deductible over a specified amount (7.5% of ADJUSTED GROSS INCOME under current tax law). They are reported on Schedule A of Form 1040. For example, if a taxpayer's adjusted gross income was $40,000, and his or her medical payments were $4,000, the taxpayer could deduct only $1,000 ($4,000 − $3,000).

medical payments coverage of auto insurance Coverage under an AUTO INSURANCE POLICY that pays for all reasonable medical expenses caused by an accident, such as surgical, medical, X-ray, dental, ambulance, hospital, nursing, funeral, and other related expenses. It applies to the insured, the spouse, relatives living at home, and other passengers in the insured car. The insured, spouse, and relatives are also covered if they are struck as pedestrians by another vehicle. Liability limits are stated on a per-person basis.

medical payments insurance *See* MEDICAL PAYMENTS COVERAGE OF AUTO INSURANCE.

Medicare A program enacted under Title XVIII of the SOCIAL SECURITY Amendments of 1965 providing medical benefits for those 65 years of age and over. Medicare COVERAGE is also available for those under 65 years of age who are disabled and have been receiving Social Security disability benefits for the past 24 months. The program is funded through Social Security taxes.
See also MEDICARE, PART A; MEDICARE, PART B.

Medicare, Part A The first part of the MEDICARE program by which retired employees over the age of 65 who are currently receiving SOCIAL SECURITY benefits also qualify for hospital insurance COVERAGE. It pays 80% of all allowable hospital costs. In addition, the first day of hospital admission has a substantial DEDUCTIBLE amount.
See also MEDIGAP INSURANCE.

Medicare, Part B The second part of the MEDICARE program, by which retired employees over the age of 65 who are currently receiving SOCIAL SECURITY benefits are provided supplementary MEDICAL INSURANCE COVERAGE on a voluntary basis for physicians' services. It pays 80% of all allowable physician costs.
See also MEDIGAP INSURANCE.

medigap insurance Private HEALTH INSURANCE to cover all or part of the 20% of hospital and medical costs not covered by Medicare.
See MEDICARE; MEDICARE, PART A; MEDICARE PART B.

meeting of the minds An agreement of all parties to the terms of a CONTRACT. In order for there to be a meeting of the minds there must be
1. An offer and acceptance
2. An evaluation of the property under consideration
3. A financial consideration
4. Financial and related terms

member firm A SECURITIES BROKERAGE FIRM having at least one member who belongs to a major stock exchange such as the NEW YORK STOCK EXCHANGE. By exchange rules, the membership must be held by an individual and not a firm.

microeconomics The study of the individual units of the economy—individuals, households, firms, and industries. It zeros in on such economic variables as the prices and outputs of specific firms and industries, the expenditures of consumers, wage rates, competition, and the markets.
See also ECONOMICS.

millage rate Property TAX RATE whereby each mill represents $1 of TAX assessment per $1,000 of assessed property value. For example, a house in Rolling Hills is assessed at $150,000 and the millage rate is 25 mills. The tax ASSESSMENT for the home would be $3,750 ($150,000 × .025).

minimum balance checking account A specified dollar amount or a minimum balance that must be maintained in the account at all times. If less is maintained, the amount will be assessed a monthly service charge.

minimum balance method Or, *low balance method*. One of four methods by which banks calculate interest on depositors' account balances. The other three are FIFO (first in, first out), LIFO (last in, first out), and DDDW (day of deposit to day of withdrawal). The minimum balance method pays interest on the minimum balance in the account. This method, which discourages withdrawals, is the most unprofitable for the depositor.

Example: The following activities have taken place during a 90-day period:

Day	Deposit (Withdrawal)	Balance
1	$1,000	$1,000
30	1,000	2,000
60	(800)	1,200
90	Closing	1,200

With a 6% stated (nominal) interest rate, calculation of interest under the minimum balance method yields

$$\$1,000 \times .06 \times 90/360 = \$15.00$$

See also FIRST IN, FIRST OUT (FIFO) METHOD; LAST IN, FIRST OUT (LIFO) METHOD; DAY OF DEPOSIT TO DAY OF WITHDRAWAL (DDDW) METHOD.

minimum maintenance *See* MAINTENANCE MARGIN REQUIREMENT.

minimum payment On a consumer CHARGE ACCOUNT, the amount of money that must be paid on the balance to maintain the account in good standing. The minimum payment is designed to discourage reckless charge account spending, and to assure that the cardholder is still financially capable.

minimum period guarantee annuity An ANNUITY that guarantees a minimum period of INCOME payments whether or not the ANNUITANT lives to receive them. Assuming the ANNUITANT lives during the minimum guarantee period, it is an income for life. Should the annuitant die during the guarantee period, the balance is paid to a BENEFICIARY.

minor's account A BANK SAVINGS ACCOUNT in the name of the child and the parent for which the child has DEPOSIT and withdrawal privileges. The child must be old enough to sign for the account.

Normally, with a minor's account there are no minimum deposit requirements or charges assessed. However, as soon as the child becomes of legal age (18 years of age in most states), all normal minimum deposit requirements and charges apply.

mispricing An item that is not priced correctly, such as a food item at a supermarket that has an overstated marked price. A consumer should check unreasonable prices before paying for the merchandise.

misstatement of information The falsification of information provided in an agreement or document (e.g., insurance policy, employment application) by the applicant. Examples of misstatement may include age, job experience, and health. Such misstatement may void the contract or require an appropriate adjustment to it. For example, an employer may fire an employee for deceit. If age has been misstated, an insurance company may adjust the coverage and premiums, taking into account the correct age of the applicant.

mixed account A brokerage account having both owned and borrowed shares. When securities are owned, it is referred to as a LONG position. When securities are borrowed, it is termed a SHORT position.

mixed deposit A deposit at a bank containing both cash and checks.

mobile home A premanufactured dwelling, often made of metal, which is placed either on a minimal or no foundation. Mobile homes are usually located in mobile home parks with other mobile homes. An advantage is the ease of moving the home around.

mode The mode is the *most commonly occurring* value in a data set. It is a meaningful statistic only when a particular value clearly occurs more frequently than any of the others.

model unit A typical house, apartment, or cooperative used as a sales campaign device to show how the actual unit bought will probably look in design and construction. An example is a model home.

modified life insurance An ordinary life insurance policy in which the beginning-of-year premiums are less than typical while the later-year premiums are more than typical.

monetary assets ASSETS held in CASH, marketable securities, ACCOUNTS receivable, or CHECKS that can easily be converted to cash. Property, machinery, and inventory are nonmonetary assets.

monetary indicators ECONOMIC INDICATORS that tell about money and credit market conditions. Most widely reported in the media are MONEY SUPPLY, consumer credit, the DOW-JONES INDUSTRIAL AVERAGE, and the TREASURY BILL rate.

money

1. CURRENCY and coins that are designated as legal tender by the government. Money retains its value because individuals are willing to receive it in exchange for merchandise or services provided. The value of money can be affected by the rate of INFLATION, which cheapens its worth. The value of money relative to other currencies is determined by the international monetary exchange markets.

2. In effect, CASH.

money income   INCOME that is measured only by the current value of MONEY. It does not take into account the rate of INFLATION.

money management   A branch of personal finance and FINANCIAL PLANNING. It studies management of money in general, covering banking, credit management, consumer loans, BUDGETING, and tax savings.
See also PERSONAL FINANCIAL PLANNING.

money management software   Computer programs that can keep track of income and expenses by budget category, reconcile bank accounts, store income tax records, figure an individual's net worth, and print checks and financial statements. Examples of money management software are "Dollars and Sense" and "Managing Your Money."
See also PERSONAL FINANCIAL PLANNING SOFTWARE.

money market   The marketplace in which short-term securities are traded.
See also FINANCIAL INSTITUTIONS AND MARKETS.

money market account   *See* MONEY MARKET DEPOSIT ACCOUNT (MMDA).

money market certificate   A type of CERTIFICATE OF DEPOSIT issued by BANKS, SAVINGS AND LOAN ASSOCIATIONS, MUTUAL SAVINGS BANKS, and CREDIT UNIONS. They have six-month maturities and pay interest at a maximum rate set equal to the rate paid on the most recently issued six-month TREASURY BILLS.

money market deposit accounts (MMDA)   A federally insured MONEY MARKET ACCOUNT offered through a depository institution, such as a BANK, CREDIT UNION, or SAVINGS AND LOAN ASSOCIATION. It usually pays a higher interest rate than a traditional PASSBOOK SAVINGS ACCOUNT, since it earns interest at rates competitive with MONEY MARKET FUNDS. If the account balance falls below the minimum deposit required, the interest rate drops to that of a traditional passbook account.

money market (mutual) funds   A open-ended MUTUAL FUND that pools the deposits of many investors and invests exclusively in short-term debt securities (maturing within one year) such as U.S. government securities, commercial paper, and certificates of deposit. These funds provide more safety of principal than other mutual funds since NET ASSET VALUE (NAV) never fluctuates. Typically shares are quoted at $1 each. (Each share has a net asset value of $1.) Through a unique accounting treatment, all returns are paid as interest so the share price does not change.

The yield, however, fluctuates daily. Examples are Fidelity Spartan Money Market Fund and Merrill Lynch CMA Money Fund.

Money market funds have the following advantages:
- They are no-load.
- A minimum deposit in these funds can be as little as $250. If an investor wants to buy short-term securities, a minimum purchase is at least $10,000.
- The fund is a form of CHECKING ACCOUNT, allowing the investor to write checks against his or her balance in the account, although there may be a usual minimum withdrawal.
- Interest is earned daily.
- These funds can be used as a "parking place" in which to put money while waiting to make another investment.

The disadvantages are the following:
- The deposit in these funds is not insured as it is in a federally insured deposit in banks.

• Money market funds can be risky when they invest heavily in commercial paper that does not get the top two credit ratings by Moody's and Standard & Poor's.

See also SUPER MONEY MARKET FUNDS.

money order A money INSTRUMENT, bought from BANKS, the post office, and telegraph and express companies, that can be readily converted into cash by a payee. Normally, money orders are purchased by those who do not have a CHECKING ACCOUNT. Money orders are purchased expressly for the purpose of paying a DEBT or to transmit funds upon the CREDIT of the issuer.

One advantage of a money order is that the payee does not have to wait for it to clear as would be the case with a traditional check. The name of the PAYOR and PAYEE are shown on the face of the money order.

money purchase plan A pension annuity is acquired by giving a specified payment (typically based on salary) at regular intervals.

money supply The total supply of money in the economy, consisting of (1) CASH in circulation, (2) DEPOSITS in savings and CHECKING ACCOUNTS. There are several measures of the money supply including M1, M2, M3, representing cash in circulation, CHECKS, and SAVINGS ACCOUNTS. L represents longer term assets such as Treasury obligations, Treasury BILLS and BONDS, and high-grade commercial paper.

monitoring the portfolio The process of supervising the financial performance of an investment PORTFOLIO in order to make buy or sell recommendations regarding certain INVESTMENTS to achieve a maximum financial return on the total assets. The investment return of certain investments could be higher than others, and unless the portfolio is continuously monitored, these opportunities cannot be utilized.

monitoring unexpended balances The process of overseeing funds that have been allocated but have not yet been spent. For example, an uncashed CHECK in a CHECKING ACCOUNT would cause the ACCOUNT to have an artificially high BALANCE unless the outstanding check were accounted for.

It may be possible in a budget to appropriate unexpended balances, which have not been encumbered, for another purpose.

monopoly Or, *cartel*. A situation in which all production and distribution is totally dominated by one firm or group of firms colluding. In this situation, consumers and suppliers are at an extreme disadvantage since the monopolist can dictate price as well as demand for supplies.

Antitrust legislation, including the Sherman Anti-Trust Act, the Clayton Anti-Trust Act, and the Robinson-Patman Act have been passed to prevent the rise of abusive monopolies. The FEDERAL TRADE COMMISSION is an independent regulatory agency charged with the responsibility of administering ANTITRUST legislation.

monthly investment plan (MIP) An investment strategy whereby an INVESTOR invests a particular sum of money each month in an INVESTMENT. In SECURITY investments, this is a form of DOLLAR COST AVERAGING and assumes that the long-term direction of the investment is up. The investor is able to reduce the average unit cost of the investment with increased financial returns. Many MUTUAL FUNDS have a monthly investment plan available for investors.

monthly review An appraisal of performance done at the end of each month by an individual. Examples are an investor's examining his or her monthly brokerage statement, or an employer's evaluating an employee's quality of work. A variance may be determined between expected performance and actual performance to uncover areas of inefficiency or efficiency. Means of corrective action may be necessary to correct problems.

month-to-month lease A month-to-month tenancy, which can be terminated at any time by either party with proper notice.

Moody's Investor Service A FINANCIAL SERVICES COMPANY owned by Dun & Bradstreet and located in downtown Manhattan. Moody's is probably one of the best-known investment rating services, with Standard & Poor's being the other. Moody's rates corporate as well as governmental SECURITIES with ratings ranging from AAA for highest investment quality to D for default.

mortality rate Or, *death rate*. Deaths per 1,000 population. The mortality rate is broken down by age, race, and sex. For the total population in the United States, the death rate has been gradually declining to approximately 8.6 deaths per 1,000 population. There is a significant difference in the mortality rate between males and females with the male mortality rate being 9.4 while the female is 7.9, reflecting the longer life span of women.

mortgage A long-term LOAN secured by property. The borrower, the mortgagee, pledges not only the property but also his or her personal CREDIT to repay the LOAN. If the mortgagee DEFAULTS on the loan, the property can be FORE-CLOSED by the mortgagor in repayment of the loan. The mortgagee retains use of the property during the terms of the loan.

The terms of mortgages vary widely. There are first, second, third, and even fourth mortgages. All mortgages, other than the first, are termed junior mortgages since they are subordinate to the terms of the first mortgage.

There are fixed-rate payment mortgages (conventional mortgages), adjustable rate mortgages (ARMs), and EQUITY LOANS in which the property's unused equity is pledged as COLLATERAL. The usual time period of a mortgage ranges from 15 to 30 years. These are private mortgages that are not insured by a unit of the government.

ARMs tie their INTEREST RATES to the financial MARKETS, and the interest rates can be adjusted within the limits specified in the mortgage agreement. Many mortgages have limits to the actual size of the change in the interest rate from year to year as well as the upper limit that may be charged.

The longer the length of the mortgage, the more total INTEREST would be paid although monthly payments would be lower. Additionally, longer mortgages have higher interest rates since the mortgagor bears a greater INVESTMENT RISK with a longer mortgage. The following table compares a 30-year, $60,000 mortgage at 10% interest with a 15-year, $60,000 mortgage at 9.5% interest.

MORTGAGE PAYMENTS

| | 30-Year 10% Mortgage | | | |
Principal	Interest Rate	Years	Monthly Payment	Total Payments
$60,000.00	10.00%	30	$526.54	$189,555.46
Total Interest	$129,555.46			

| | 15-Year 9.5% Mortgage | | | |
Principal	Interest Rate	Years	Monthly Payment	Total Payments
$60,000.00	9.50%	15	$626.53	$112,776.27
Total Interest	$52,776.27			

| | Payment Difference Between 15-Year and 30-Year Mortgage | | |
Difference	Monthly Payment Difference	Total Payment Difference	Total Interest Difference
15–30 year	$99.99	$76,779.19	$76,779.19

The federal and state governments also play a role in the mortgage market. There are Federal Housing Administration insured mortgages, and G.I. mortgages guaranteed under the Serviceman's Readjustment Act of 1944 whereby the VETERAN'S ADMINISTRATION guarantees for a LENDER a percentage of the mortgage loan up to a maximum amount.

The FEDERAL NATIONAL MORTGAGE ASSOCIA-TION (FNMA), established in 1938, is the largest single supplier of funds for residential housing. The GOVERNMENT NATIONAL MORTGAGE ASSOCIA-

TION (GNMA), also established in 1938, guarantees borrowings by private mortgage lenders. The Federal Home Loan Mortgage Corporation (FHLMC) was established in 1970 by the Emergency Home Finance Act and purchases residential mortgages.

The following is an example of a mortgage amortization schedule:

MORTGAGE AMORTIZATION SCHEDULE

Mortgage Amount	$60,000.00
Interest Rate	10%
Number of Years	15
Monthly Payments Are	$644.76

Payment	Principal	Interest	Balance
1	$144.76	$500.00	$59,855.24
2	$145.97	$498.79	$59,709.27
3	$147.18	$497.58	$59,562.09
4	$148.41	$496.35	$59,413.68
5	$149.65	$495.11	$59,264.03
6	$150.89	$493.87	$59,113.14
7	$152.15	$492.61	$58,960.99
8	$153.42	$491.34	$58,807.57
9	$154.70	$490.06	$58,652.87
10	$155.99	$488.77	$58,496.89
11	$157.29	$487.47	$58,339.60
12	$158.60	$486.16	$58,180.99

Interest for 12 Periods = $5,918.11

A mortgage has a number of advantages over other DEBT instruments, including favorable interest rates, less financing restrictions, and extended maturity dates for loan repayment. For PERSONAL PROPERTY, such as an automobile, the LIEN is called a CHATTEL MORTGAGE.
See also AMORTIZATION; PREPAYMENT CLAUSE; OPEN-END MORTGAGE; PURCHASE-MONEY MORTGAGE; ACCELERATION CLAUSE; SUBORDINATION CLAUSE; BLANKET MORTGAGE.

mortgage banker An individual or company that originates MORTGAGES and collects payments on them. The mortgage banker usually sells these mortgages to long-term investors and obtains service fees for the loans. The mortgage banker is a major originator of FHA- and VA-INSURED MORTGAGES and also plays a substantial role in the CONVENTIONAL MORTGAGE markets.
See also MORTGAGE BROKER; MORTGAGE SERVICING.

mortgage bond A BOND secured by a real asset by the issuing firm. In case of DEFAULT, the BONDHOLDERS may FORECLOSE on the secured property and sell it to satisfy their claims. There are two types: SENIOR MORTGAGE BONDS, which have first claim over proceeds from liquidating pledged assets, and JUNIOR MORTGAGE BONDS.

mortgage broker An individual or company that obtains mortgages for others by finding lending institutions, insurance companies, or private lenders. The mortgage broker sometimes makes collections and handles disbursements. The mortgage broker is usually compensated in the form of a percentage of the amount financed.
See also MORTGAGE BANKER.

mortgage interest deduction Federal tax deduction allowed for INTEREST paid or accrued within the taxable year for a home MORTGAGE. Mortgage deductions can be made on the principal home so long as the mortgage does not exceed $1 million if the owners are filing jointly, or $500,000 if they are married filing separately. On mortgages taken out after October 13, 1987, on the main home other than to buy, build, or improve the home, the taxpayer is limited to $100,000, or $50,000 if married filing separately. The latter mortgage can be used to pay off credit card bills, buy a car, or pay tuition costs.

For those taxpayers having a second home, the dollar limits apply to the total mortgages on both homes.

mortgage life insurance An insurance policy that will pay off the balance of the mortgage in the event of death of the wage earner.

mortgage loan *See* MORTGAGE.

mortgage payment tables Handy tables available to determine the monthly MORTGAGE PAYMENT, which consists partly of PRINCIPAL repayment on a loan and partly of interest charges.

It is determined through a LOAN AMORTIZATION type of formula. These tables contain monthly payments for virtually every combination of loan size, interest rate, and term. Table 5 (Monthly Mortgage Payments) of Appendix A provides selected combinations for $10,000 fixed-rate loans.

Example: Sylvia wants to find the monthly mortgage payment on a $95,000, 10%, 30-year mortgage. Using Table 5, she needs to follow the three steps:

Step 1. Divide the amount of the loan by $10,000 (that is, $95,000 ÷ $10,000 = 9.5)

Step 2. Find the payment factor for a specific interest rate and loan maturity. The Table 5 payment factor for 10% and 30 years is 87.76

Step 3. Multiply the factor obtained in Step 2 by the amount from Step 1

$$\$87.76 \times 9.5 = \$833.72$$

The resulting monthly mortgage payment would be $833.72.

mortgage points *See* POINTS.

mortgage pool A collection of residential MORTGAGE LOANS that are packaged together as a mortgage pool and sold in the SECONDARY MARKET to INVESTORS. Companies having mortgage pools hope to earn a short-term profit while using the proceeds to make additional mortgage loans available to homeowners.

mortgage rate The INTEREST RATE charged on a MORTGAGE LOAN.

mortgage REIT A type of REAL ESTATE INVESTMENT TRUST (REIT) that does not own property but provides short-term financing for construction loans or for permanent MORTGAGE LOANS for large projects.
See also REAL ESTATE INVESTMENT TRUSTS (REITs).

mortgage servicing The supervision and administration of a MORTGAGE LOAN after it has been made. This involves such things as collecting the monthly payments; keeping accounting, tax and insurance records; and foreclosing default loans. A MORTGAGE BANKER, not a MORTGAGE BROKER, services the loans.

mortgage trust *See* MORTGAGE REIT.

mortgage-backed securities A share in an organized pool of residential MORTGAGES. Some are pass-through securities whose principal and interest payments are passed through to shareholders, usually monthly. There are several kinds of mortgage-backed securities. They include the following.

GOVERNMENT NATIONAL MORTGAGE ASSOCIATION (GNMA—GINNIE MAE) SECURITIES: GNMA primarily issues PASS-THROUGH SECURITIES. These pass through all payments of interest and principal received on a pool of federally insured mortgage loans. GNMA guarantees that all payments of principal and interest will be made on the mortgages on a timely basis. Since many mortgages are repaid before maturity, investors in GNMA pools usually recover most of their principal investment well ahead of schedule. Ginnie Mae is considered an excellent investment. The higher yields, coupled with the U.S. government guarantee, provide a competitive edge over other intermediate-term to long-term securities issued by the U.S. government and other agencies.

FEDERAL HOME LOAN MORTGAGE CORPORATION (FHLMC—FREDDIE MAC) SECURITIES: Freddie Mac was established to provide a secondary market for conventional mortgages. It can purchase conventional mortgages for its own portfolio. Freddie Mac also issues pass-through securities—called participation certificates (PCs)—and guaranteed mortgage certificates (GMCs) that resemble bonds. Freddie Mac securities do not carry direct government guarantees and are subject to state and federal income tax.

FEDERAL NATIONAL MORTGAGE ASSOCIATION (FNMA—FANNIE MAE) SECURITIES: The FNMA is a publicly held corporation whose goal is to provide a secondary market for government-guaranteed mortgages. It does so by financing its purchase by selling DEBENTURES with maturities of several years and short-term discount notes from 30 to 360 days to private investors. The FNMA securities are not government guaranteed and are an unsecured obligation of the issuer. For this reason, they often provide considerably higher YIELDS than TREASURY SECURITIES.

COLLATERALIZED MORTGAGE OBLIGATIONS (CMOs): CMOs are mortgage-backed securities that separate mortgage pools into short-, medium-, and long-term portions. Investors can choose between short-term pools (such as 5-year pools) and long-term pools (such as 20-year pools).

Mortgage-backed securities enjoy LIQUIDITY and a high degree of safety since they are either government-sponsored or otherwise insured.

mortgagee clause A clause in PROPERTY INSURANCE specifying that in the event of loss, a MORTGAGEE may receive first reimbursement under the policy.

most active list A list of the most actively traded stocks. They are shown in the *Wall Street Journal* under the heading "Most Active Issues." The determinant of which STOCKS make the most active list is the actual trading volume. It is not uncommon for stocks to TRADE several million shares in one day.

moving average An average that is updated as new information is received. The average is calculated on a fixed period and showing trends for the latest interval. With the moving average, a series of calculations is made by taking the arithmetic MEAN of a consecutive number of items, then discarding the first item and adding the latest item, and continuing the process so that the number of items in the series remains constant. For example, a 14-day moving average price of a security includes prices for the past 14 days. Each day, the oldest price is dropped from the average and the latest day's price is included in the calculation. Moving averages are useful in assessing prices that fluctuate frequently (and seasonally).

moving expenses Expenses incurred by a person and his or her family—whether the individual is a salaried employee or self-employed—when he or she moves to a new place of work in a different location. Income tax regulations allow one to deduct such expenses, both direct and indirect, from TAXABLE INCOME, within legally fixed limits.

moving expense deduction A deduction from ADJUSTED GROSS INCOME of employees and self-employed individuals for moving costs. The Internal Revenue Service specifies a minimum distance and minimum period of employment required for such expenses to be allowable. While direct costs (e.g., moving furniture) are not restricted in amount, indirect costs (e.g., house-hunting costs) are subject to certain limitations.
See also MOVING EXPENSES.

multiple earnings approach Or, *multiple-of-income approach.* An approach in LIFE INSURANCE that involves estimating the funds needed to replace the income lost due to a premature death by multiplying the annual income of the person involved by the number of years the income will be needed by dependent survivors. Under this method, one simply multiplies his or her gross annual income by some selected number. Some experts suggest that life insurance should equal 5 to 10 times the annual gross income. This rule of thumb, however, may not always be appropriate because no two families are exactly the same. The amount will vary with family needs, goals, net worth, future expenses, income, and life style requirements.

For example, Lynne has a gross annual income of $30,000. If the multiplier is 5, life insurance coverage should be

$$\$30,000 \times 5 = \$150,000.$$

See also NEEDS APPROACH.

multiple indemnity clause A provision in a LIFE INSURANCE policy that provides for a doubling or tripling of the face value in the event the INSURED dies as a result of an accident.

multiple listing   A book containing the real estate listings of many area agents.

multiple listing service (MLS)   An information and referral network among REAL ESTATE AGENTS that pools all properties offered into a common offering list. If a sale results, the LISTING BROKER and the selling broker split the COMMISSION. The members of a MLS receive the advantage of greater sales exposure, which, in turn, means a better price and a quicker sale.
See also MULTIPLE LISTING.

multiple of gross income rule   A rule of thumb a LENDER uses to determine a borrower's housing affordability. The rule states that the housing price should not exceed roughly 2½ times a family's gross annual income. For example, a borrower's annual gross income is $40,000. The maximum price he or she could afford for a house is

$$2.5 \times \$40,000 = \$100,000.$$

See also 35-PERCENT RULE.

multiple-peril insurance   Business and personal PROPERTY INSURANCE that covers the insured property for multiple perils. It combines into one policy numerous types of property insurance.

multiple retirement ages   Manner in which an employee can retire without reduction in benefits; EARLY RETIREMENT, NORMAL RETIREMENT, and DEFERRED RETIREMENT.

municipal bond insurance   INSURANCE POLICIES issued by private INSURERS to guarantee MUNICIPAL BONDS in the event of a DEFAULT. The insurance can either be purchased by the issuing governmental entity, in which case the BOND becomes a AAA issue, or by the individual INVESTOR. The insurance provides that the bonds will be purchased from the bond investor at PAR value.

The major portion of municipal bond insurance is written by two firms. The first is the Ambac Indemnity Corporation (previously named the American Municipal Bond Assurance Corporation), and the second is the Municipal Bond Insurance Association (MBIA). The former is a private corporation while the latter is a pool of private insurers.

Municipal governments issuing insured bonds have the highest investment rating because of lower RISK, but their YIELD is consequently lower when compared to other comparable uninsured municipal bonds. However, for those investors willing to TRADE safety for higher yield, they remain attractive investments.

municipal bonds (MUNIES)   BONDS issued by local governments and their agencies on which interest is excluded from federal income taxation. Interest is also exempt from state income taxation in the state of issue.
See also GENERAL OBLIGATION BOND; INDUSTRIAL REVENUE BOND.

municipal bonds (tax-exempt) fund   A MUTUAL FUND that aims at earning current tax-exempt income by investing solely in MUNICIPAL BONDS.

municipal note   Or, *bond anticipation note* (BAN). A short-term municipal DEBT obligation having a maturity of two years or less secured by the jurisdiction's full faith and credit.

municipal securities   *See* MUNICIPAL BONDS.

munies   *See* MUNICIPAL BONDS.

mutual
1. A type of INSURANCE firm in which policyholders are legally the shareholders (owners) of the firm.
2. MUTUAL FUND.
3. MUTUAL SAVINGS BANK.

mutual company   *See* MUTUAL.

mutual fund custodian   A COMMERCIAL BANK or TRUST COMPANY that provides safekeeping for the SECURITIES of a MUTUAL FUND. The CUSTODIAN often performs the administrative work of the fund as a TRANSFER AGENT including making payments to and collecting INVESTMENTS from SHAREHOLDERS.

mutual funds Investment companies that invest in various investment instruments. Mutual funds are popular investment vehicles that represent ownership in a professionally managed PORTFOLIO of securities. There are major advantages, listed below, in investing in mutual funds.

1. *Diversification.* Each share of a fund gives an investor an interest in a cross section of stocks, bonds, or other investments.
2. *Small minimum investment.* An investor with a small amount of money (as little as $25 or $50) can achieve diversification through the large number of securities in the portfolio. A handful of funds have no minimums.
3. *Automatic reinvestment.* Most funds allow investors to reinvest dividends automatically as well as any capital gains that may arise from the fund's buying and selling activities. Funds typically do not charge a sales fee on automatic reinvestments.
4. *Automatic withdrawals.* Most funds will allow shareholders to withdraw money on a regular basis.
5. *Liquidity.* An investor is allowed to redeem the shares owned.
6. *Switching.* An investor may want to make changes in his or her investments. His or her long-term goals may remain the same, but the investment climate does not. To facilitate switching among funds, such companies as Fidelity Investors and Vanguard Group have introduced "families" of funds. The investor may move funds among them with relative freedom, usually at no fee.

net asset value (NAV)

The value of a mutual fund share is measured by net asset value (NAV), which equals

$$\frac{\text{Fund's total assets} - \text{liabilities}}{\text{Number of shares outstanding in the fund}}$$

Example 1: For simplicity, assume that a fund owns 100 shares each of General Motors (GM), Xerox, and International Business Machines (IBM). Assume also that on a particular day, the market values below existed. Then NAV of the fund is calculated as follows (assume the fund has no liabilities):

(a) GM—$90 per share × 100 shares	=	$ 9,000
(b) Xerox—$100 per share × 100 shares	=	10,000
(c) IBM—$160 per share × 100 shares	=	16,000
(d) Value of the fund's portfolio		$35,000
(e) Number of shares outstanding in the fund		1,000
(f) Net asset value (NAV) per share = (d)/(e)		$35

If an investor owns 5% of the fund's outstanding shares, or 50 shares (5% × 1,000 shares), then the value of the investment is $1,750 ($35 × 50).

There are three ways to make money in mutual funds. NAV is only one of the three. NAV indicates only the current market value of the underlying portfolio. An investor also receives CAPITAL GAINS and DIVIDENDS. Therefore, the performance of a mutual fund must be judged on the basis of these three, which will be discussed later.

types of mutual funds

Mutual funds may be classified into different types, according to organization, the fees charged, methods of trading funds, and their investment objectives. In OPEN-END FUNDS, investors buy from and sell their shares back to the fund itself. On the other hand, CLOSED-END FUNDS operate with a fixed number of shares outstanding, which trade among individuals in secondary markets like common stocks. All open- and closed-end funds charge management fees. A major point of closed-end funds is the size of discount or premium, which is the difference between their market prices and their net asset values (NAVs). Many funds of this type sell at discounts, which enhances their investment appeal. Funds that charge sales commissions are called load funds. No-load funds do not charge sales commissions.

LOAD FUNDS typically perform no better than NO-LOADS. Many experts believe investors should buy only no-load or low-load funds. They should have no trouble finding such funds that meet their investment requirements. The prospectus contains such information as the fund's investment objectives, method of selecting securities, performance figures, sales charges, management fees, and other expenses.

Depending on their investment philosophies, mutual funds generally fall into ten major categories:

- *Money market funds.* Money market funds are mutual funds that invest exclusively in debt securities maturing within one year, such as government securities, commercial paper, and certificates of deposit. These funds provide a safety valve for many investors because the price never changes. They are known as dollar funds, which means investors always buy and sell shares at $1 each.

- *Aggressive growth funds.* Aggressive growth funds go for big future capital gains instead of current dividend income. They invest in the stocks of upstart and high-tech oriented companies. Return can be great but so can risk. These funds are suited for investors who are not particularly concerned with short-term fluctuations in return but with long-term gains. Aggressive growth funds are also called maximum capital gain, capital appreciation, and small-company growth funds. An example is T. Rowe Price Capital Appreciation Fund.

- *Growth funds.* Growth funds seek long-term gains by investing in the stocks of established companies that are expected to rise in value faster than inflation. These stocks are best for investors who wish steady growth over a long-term period but feel little need for income in the meantime. An example is Fidelity Magellan Fund.

- *Income funds.* Income funds are best suited for investors who seek a high level of dividend income. Income funds usually invest in high-quality bonds and stocks with consistently high dividends. An example is Axe-Houghton Income Fund.

- *Growth and income funds.* Growth and income funds seek both current dividend income and capital gains. The goal of these funds is to provide long-term growth without much variation in share value. An example is Washington Mutual Investors Fund.

- *Balanced funds.* Balanced funds combine investments in common stock and bonds and often preferred stock, and attempt to provide income and some capital appreciation. Balanced funds tend to underperform all-stock funds in strong bull markets. An example is Phoenix Balanced Fund.

- *Bond and preferred stock funds.* These funds invest in both BONDS and PREFERRED STOCK with the emphasis on income rather than growth. The funds that invest exclusively in bonds are called bond funds. There are two types of bond funds: bond funds that invest in corporate bonds, and municipal bond funds that provide tax-free income and a diversified portfolio of municipal securities. In periods of volatile interest rates, bond funds are subject to price fluctuations. The value of the shares will fall when interest rates rise. An example is Nicholas Income Fund.

- *Index funds.* Index funds invest in a portfolio of corporate stocks, the composition of which is determined by the Standard & Poor's 500 or some other market index. An example is Fidelity Spartan Market Index Fund.

- *Sector funds.* Sector funds are funds that invest in one or two fields or industries. These funds are risky in that they rise and fall depending on how the individual fields or industries do. They are also called specialized funds. An example is Franklin Utilities Fund.

- *International funds.* International funds invest in the stocks and bonds of corporations traded on foreign exchanges. These funds make significant gains when the dollar is falling and foreign stock prices are rising. An example is Putnam International Equities Fund.

how to read mutual fund quotations

Below are quotations of mutual funds shown in a newspaper.

Funds	NAV	Offer Price	NAV Chg.
Acorn Fund	30.95	N.L.	+ .38
. . .	. . .	. . .	. . .
American Growth	8.52	9.31	+ .05

In a load fund, the price you pay for a share is called the offer price, and it is higher than net asset value (NAV), the difference being the commission. AM Growth is a load fund. As shown above, American Growth has a load of $0.79 ($9.31 − $8.52), or 8.49% ($0.79 ÷ $9.31). Acorn Fund is a no-load fund, as "N.L." indicates. In a no-load fund, the price you pay is NAV.

In the case of a closed-end fund, below is a typical listing shown in a newspaper.

Funds	NAV	Strike Price	% Diff
Claremont	35.92	29⅜	−18.2
. . .	. . .	. . .	. . .
Nautilus	34.41	34½	+0.2

In "% Diff" column, negative difference means the shares sell at a discount; positive difference means they sell at a premium.

performance of mutual funds

Generally, mutual funds provide returns to investors in the form of (1) change in share value (or net asset value), (2) dividend income, and (3) capital gain distribution. The return for mutual funds is calculated as follows:

$$\frac{(\text{dividends} + \text{capital gain distributions}) +}{(\text{ending NAV} - \text{beginning NAV})}$$
$$\text{beginning NAV}$$

Example 2: Assume XYZ mutual fund paid dividends of $.50 and capital gain distributions of $.25 per share over the course of the year, and had a price (NAV) at the beginning of the year of $8.50 that rose to $9.50 per share by the end of the year. The return is

$$\frac{(\$.50) + \$.25) + (\$9.50 - \$8.50)}{\$8.50} = \frac{\$1.75}{\$8.50} = 20.59\%$$

In assessing fund performance, investors must also resort to the published BETA of the funds in order to determine the amount of risk involved. Beta is a measure of risk based on the price swings of a fund compared with the market as a whole, measured by the Standard & Poor's 500-stock index. The higher the beta, the greater the risk.

Beta	What It Means
1.0	A fund moves up and down just as much as the market.
>1.0	The fund tends to climb higher in bull markets and dip lower in bear markets than the S&P index.
<1.0	The fund is less volatile (risky) than the market.

Betas for individual funds are widely available in many investment newsletters and directories. An example is VALUE LINE INVESTMENT SURVEY.

mutual fund ratings

Investors can get help in selecting mutual funds from a number of sources, including investment advisory services that charge fees. More readily available sources, however, include *Money, Forbes, Barron's,* and *Personal Finance. Money* has a "Fund Watch" column appearing in each monthly issue. In addition, it ranks about 450 funds twice a year in terms of fund performance and risk. *Forbes* has an annual report covering each fund's performance in both up and down markets. *Value Line Investment Survey* shows the make-up of the fund's portfolio beta values. Information about no-load funds is contained in the *Individual Investor's Guide to No Load Mutual Funds* (American Association of Individual Investors, 612 N. Michigan Ave., Chicago, IL 60611).

In summary, investors should not choose a fund only on the basis of its performance rating. They should consider both performance and risk (beta).

how to choose a mutual fund

What mutual fund to choose is not an easy question and there is no sure answer. It will be advisable to take the following steps:

1. Develop a list of funds that appear to meet investment goals.
2. Obtain a PROSPECTUS. The prospectus contains the fund's investment objectives.

Read the statement of objectives as well as the risk factors and investment limitations. Also request the Statement of Additional Information, which includes the details of fees and lists the investments; a copy of the annual report; and the most recent quarterly report.

3. Make sure the fund's investment objectives and investment policies meet investment goals.

4. Analyze the fund's past performance in view of its set objectives, in both good markets and bad markets. The quarterly and annual statements issued by the fund will show results for the previous year and probably a comparison with the S&P 500. Look at historical performance over a five- or ten-year period. Look for beta figures in investment newsletters and directories. Also, read the prospectus summary section for per-share and capital changes. *Money, Forbes,* and other investment periodicals publish semiannual or annual performance data on mutual funds.

5. From the prospectus, try to determine some clues to management's ability to accomplish the fund's investment objectives. Emphasize the record, experience, and capability of the management company.

6. Note what securities make up the fund's portfolio to see how they look. Not all mutual funds are fully diversified or invest in high quality companies.

7. Compare various fees (such as redemption, management and SALES CHARGES, if any) and various shareholder services offered by the funds being considered (such as the right of accumulation, any switch privilege within fund families, available investment plans, and a systematic withdrawal plan).

See also BETA.

mutual insurance company An INSURANCE company that is owned by its policyholders and operates on a nonprofit basis.

mutual savings bank A SAVINGS BANK whose depositors are the owners. They are found primarily in the northwestern United States.

N

NADA Used Car Guide A monthly automobile guide, known as the blue book, published by the National Automobile Dealers Association. It lists three different values, including average automobile retail prices, average automobile loan values (principally used by banks), and average automobile trade-in or wholesale value. There is an annual subscription fee for the publication. Values published in the guide are the result of nationwide surveys of auto auction sale results.

NADA has a membership of approximately 20,000 new car or truck dealer franchises in the United States. NADA was established in 1916.

naked Any unhedged SECURITY position that exposes an INVESTOR to RISK. For example, a CALL OPTION writer who does not own the underlying STOCK is assuming the risk of having the stock increase in value with the resulting increase in the value of the call option. As the call option is worth more, there is a greater possibility that the call will be exercised. This exposes the call WRITER to a potential loss situation.

An individual who owns a security outright is also naked in that he or she is exposed to downside risk.

naked option

1. A CALL OPTION that is sold without owning the underlying SECURITY. Should the security

move up in price, the OPTION price will also increase. In that event, there is a possibility that the CALL will be EXERCISED resulting in a loss for the call WRITER.

2. A PUT writer who is not SHORT the underlying security. Thus, if the underlying security should fall in value, the put will increase in price. In that event, there is a greater possibility that the put will be exercised resulting in a loss to the put writer.

named-perils policy An INSURANCE policy that specifically names the perils covered. *See also* ALL RISKS/ALL PERIL.

narrow market

1. In investments, a SECURITY having relatively few SHARES outstanding with a small number of INVESTORS. This type of a security normally has low volume and is subject to wide price movements as it is TRADED in this narrow market. The market is not capable of managing higher trading volume, as the impact on prices would be exaggerated.

2. A security trading with a very small difference between the BID AND ASKED prices.

National Association of Securities Dealers (NASD) A self-regulatory organization that has jurisdiction over certain broker-dealers who handle OVER-THE-COUNTER (OTC) securities. The NASD requires member BROKER-DEALERS to register and conduct examinations for compliance with net capital requirements and other regulations.

National Association of Securities Dealers' Automatic Quotations (NASDAQ) A subsidiary of the NASD that facilitates the trading of approximately 5,000 most active OTC stock issues through an electronically connected network.

National Credit Union Administration A federal agency that insures deposits in all federal and many state-chartered credit unions.

National Credit Union Association (NCUA) *See* NATIONAL CREDIT UNION ADMINISTRATION.

National Flood Insurance Program INSURANCE COVERAGE providing reimbursement for damage caused by floods to personal and business property, authorized under the National Flood Act of 1968. The act creates a property insurance pool in which property insurance companies with ASSETS over $1 million or more may become members either as RISK BEARERS (issuing their own policies) or as NONRISK bearers (normally issuing a SYNDICATE-type POLICY as needed by the insurance pool). The objective of the National Flood Insurance Program is to provide reasonable flood coverage.

There is a three-year waiting period before the insurance becomes effective.

National Foundation for Consumer Credit An organization that sponsors nonprofit credit counseling centers in many areas.

national health insurance A nationwide governmental health insurance program. Unlike Great Britain and some other nations, the United States does not have a national health insurance program. It does provide Medicare Parts A & B providing hospital and medical service care for the retired and Medicaid for the disadvantaged and for retirees falling below a specified INCOME level. However, the average American must seek private HEALTH INSURANCE COVERAGE to provide for hospital and medical services. The largest private medical insurer is Blue Cross/Blue Shield. *See also* MEDICARE; MEDICARE, PART A; MEDICARE, PART B; MEDICAID.

National Highway Traffic Safety Administratiton (NHTSA) Created by the National Highway Traffic and Motor Vehicle Safety Act of 1966 to establish safety standards for motor vehicles and motor vehicle equipment. The objective is to protect the public from unreasonable RISK of injury resulting from automobiles. The Energy Policy and Conservation Act and

Clean Air Amendments of 1970 also gave it authority to set standards for fuel economy and emissions.

This federal agency is responsible for establishing fuel economy standards and regulating the safety performance of new and used motor vehicles and their equipment, including tires. The agency also investigates auto safety defects and requires manufacturers to remedy them including the possibility of ordering recalls.

nearest month The expiration month of a commodity future or option contract. For example, assuming an option has expiration dates in September, December, March, and June, the nearest month would be June for a trade made in May.

needs Those items that are essential for existence or fulfillment, such as food and shelter.

needs approach An approach for determining LIFE INSURANCE needs that considers the financial resources available in addition to life insurance and the specific financial obligations a person may have. The idea is first to add up the total financial needs and then to deduct accumulated assets. The approach considers the following funds:

1. Emergency and administrative funds— funds for the costs of final illness, funeral and burial bills, probate costs, uninsured medical costs, debts, and estate taxes.
2. Special fund—fund needed for other specific needs, such as educational expenses and paying mortgages.
3. Retirement fund—additional money set aside to support one's spouse and dependents.
4. Family income fund—fund to support surviving dependents until they are self-supporting.

The figure below illustrates the use of the needs approach to help estimate the amount of life insurance to buy.

HOW MUCH LIFE INSURANCE?

		Sample Entries
(1) Funding Needs		
1. Emergency and Administrative Fund	$ 15,000	
2. Special Fund	125,000	
3. Family Income Fund	80,000	
4. Retirement Fund	60,000	
Total Needs		$280,000
(2) Available Resources		
1. Savings	$30,000	
2. Investments	60,000	
3. Life Insurance		
a. Group Insurance	50,000	
b. Social Security	500	
Total Resources		($140,500)
Life Insurance Gap		$139,500

Life insurance is not a static product. Family needs may change; family income might vary; family size may alter. Therefore, basic insurance needs can vary over time. It is wise to reassess coverage periodically in keeping with the changes that occur in one's life.

negative amortization Increase in the outstanding loan balance that occurs when the MORTGAGE payment does not fully cover the required interest charge on the loan. This situation generally occurs under INDEXED LOANS for which the indexed rate change may not affect the periodic debt service payments.

negative carry A situation in which the return rate on a security is less than the interest rate on money borrowed to finance the purchase. For example, if an investor borrows at 13% to buy a bond yielding 11%, a negative carry situation exists.
See also REVERSE LEVERAGE.

negative cash flow
in general: A situation in which a business spends more money than it takes in within a given time period. This is an unfavorable situa-

tion that may result in liquidity or solvency problems.

real estate: A situation in which operating expenses and mortgage payments exceed rental income. For example, David acquires an apartment building within the first year of its operation; it shows a *negative cash flow* of $8,000:

Gross rental income		$60,000
Less vacancy loss		5,000
Effective gross income		55,000
Less operating expenses		40,000
Net operating income (NOI)		15,000
Less debt service		
Interest	20,000	
Principal payment	3,000	23,000
Negative cash flow		$8,000

negative yield curve A condition in which interest rates on short-term debt securities are higher than interest rates on long-term debt securities.
See also POSITIVE YIELD CURVE.

negligence An act resulting from the omission of prudence that a reasonable person would exercise in a particular situation. A legal delinquency resulting when an individual fails to pursue a considerate and responsible course of action.
contributory negligence: The failure to provide prudent care, resulting in an injury.
criminal negligence: The failure to render proper care, resulting in the killing of an individual (manslaughter).
gross negligence: The intentional failure to take legally due and proper care, having a serious personal or property outcome.
ordinary negligence: Any situation in which an individual fails to exercise proper responsibility, resulting in an outcome that has a seriously detrimental effect.

negligent action This is "actionable negligence" or "negligence in law" that occurs from nonobservance of the law.
See also NEGLIGENCE.

negotiable
1. Any readily transferable INSTRUMENT.
2. A registered SECURITY that has an ASSIGNMENT and a power of substitution signed by the registered owner, either on the certificate or by an accompanying STOCK or BOND power.
3. A price that can be bargained about and further adjusted.
4. A matter that is resolved between two or more parties through discussions in which common interests are redefined. For example, broker commissions are now negotiable and clients may seek to negotiate the rate of COMMISSION being charged.

negotiable instrument Any INSTRUMENT that can easily be CONVERTED into CASH.
For an instrument to be negotiable it must meet certain criteria:
1. It has to be signed by the maker.
2. It cannot have conditions.
3. It must promise to pay a certain sum of MONEY.
4. It must be payable on demand by the BEARER or to the order of a named party.
5. It cannot contain any other promise or restriction.
See also NEGOTIABLE.

negotiable order of withdrawal (NOW) accounts Equivalent to CHECKING ACCOUNTS paying interest on the funds on deposit. While interest is paid at the passbook rate on regular NOW accounts, no interest rate ceiling exists on SUPER NOW ACCOUNTS.

nest egg An amount of MONEY put aside and saved by an individual for a serious purpose, such as RETIREMENT, purchase of a home, or an emergency. Such money is also termed "serious money" and is invested conservatively.

net
1. The amount remaining after all DEDUCTIONS have been subtracted.
2. The NET amount of the PROCEEDS of a sale, taking into account the acquisition cost and any additional INVESTMENTS made. For example, an

individual purchases a home for $75,000 and ten years later sells it for $150,000. Additionally, the homeowner invests an additional $25,000 in home improvements. The net profit = $150,000 − ($75,000 + $25,000) = $50,000.

3. The difference between plus amounts and minus amounts, or the difference between additions and subtractions.

4. The NET INCOME OR LOSS of a business.

5. A term used to describe a network.

net after-tax gain The gain after the tax effect has been considered. For example, if the gain on the sale of a stock was $3,000 and the individual is in the 28% tax bracket, the net gain is $2,160 ($3,000 × .72).

net asset value (NAV) The value of a MUTUAL FUND's total assets less any debt, divided by the number of shares outstanding. It is a fund's share price.
See also MUTUAL FUNDS.

net change In investments, the change in the day's ending market price of a stock relative to the prior trading day's ending price.

net cost method Or, *net payment method*. A method of determining the actual cost (not the price paid) of a LIFE INSURANCE policy. It adds the total of all PREMIUMS and subtracts any accumulated cash value and accrued DIVIDENDS. Unlike the INTEREST-ADJUSTED COST METHOD, it does not consider the TIME VALUE OF MONEY. This is computed for a specified point in time during the life of the policy. If the net cost is negative, it means that the policy will pay for itself. For example, John is considering the purchase of a $100,000 CASH VALUE 20-payment policy. His annual premiums will be $1,664. The policy will have a cash value at the end of 20 years of $35,008. Total dividends accumulated for the 20 years will be $9,300. The net cost of the policy after 20 years is shown below:

Net cost = ($1,664 × 20) − $35,008 − $9,300

= −$11,028

= $33,280 − $35,008 − $9,300

= −$11,028

net current assets A person's current assets less current debts. Current assets are those that have a life of one year or less, such as cash and marketable securities. Current liabilities are those due within one year, such as a six-month bank loan.

net earnings The employee's take home wages after all required and optional deductions are subtracted from the gross salary. An example of a required deduction is FEDERAL WITHHOLDING TAX. An example of an optional deduction may be amounts contributed as union dues.

net estate The assets minus liabilities and deductions of the estate.
See also ESTATE; ESTATE PLANNING.

net federal estate tax payable The amount of ESTATE TAX payable to the federal government after all credits are subtracted.

net income Or, *net profit*. Revenue less all expenses. The bottom line is the key measure to a company's operating performance for the period.
See also NET LOSS.

net income multiplier A method of determining the price of INCOME-PRODUCING PROPERTY. It is calculated as

Purchase price/NET OPERATING INCOME (NOI)

For example, assume that NOI = $18,618 and the asking price = $219,000. Then the net income multiplier is

$219,000/$18,618 = 11.76

NOI is the gross income less allowances for vacancies and operating expenses, except DEPRECIATION and DEBT payments.
See also GROSS INCOME MULTIPLIER; GROSS RENT MULTIPLIER: CAPITALIZATION RATE; INCOME APPROACH.

net lease Or, *triple net lease*. The lessee pays not only a constant rental charge but also expenses on the rented premises, including maintenance.

net long-term gain In taxation, the excess of total long-term gains less long-term losses on the sale of capital assets (e.g., stocks, bonds). Long-term classification is for any capital asset held one year or more. This is reported on Schedule D of Form 1040.

net loss The excess of total expenses over sales.
See also NET INCOME.

net operating income (NOI) GROSS INCOME of a rental property less allowance for vacancies and OPERATING EXPENSES, except DEPRECIATION and DEBT repayments.
See also CASH FLOW.

net payment index The measure of cost of a CASH VALUE LIFE INSURANCE policy. It adds a policy's premiums and subtracts dividends and cash value. The index does not consider the TIME VALUE OF MONEY.
See also NET COST METHOD; INTEREST-ADJUSTED COST INDEX.

net profit margin Ratio of net income to net sales. It reveals the entity's ability to generate profit at a given sales level. One can use the ratio to appraise a company's operating efficiency and pricing strategy.

net rental The rental charge on leased premises including property expenses and taxes.

net short-term gain In taxation, the excess of short-term gains less short-term losses on the sale of capital assets (e.g., stocks, bonds). Short-term classification is assigned for any capital asset held for less than one year. This is reported on Schedule D of Form 1040.

net transaction A securities transaction in which a fee or commission is not charged for the seller and buyer. For example, no commission is charged the buyer when purchasing a new issue. If the stock is offered at $30 a share, the investor pays that exact or issue price.

net worth
1. The difference between total ASSETS and total LIABILITIES.
2. A measure of personal or family wealth determined by subtracting total debts from total assets.
3. The owner's EQUITY.

net worth statement *See* FINANCIAL STATEMENTS (PERSONAL).

new high/new low A listing published in the *Wall Street Journal* and other newspapers summarizing those companies trading on the NEW YORK STOCK EXCHANGE that have reached the highest or lowest prices of the year.

new issue The first public offering of a STOCK or BOND issue. A PROSPECTUS normally accompanies most new issues that details the financial and business aspects of the company disclosing information vital to the success of the issue.

For a new issue to TRADE on the STOCK EXCHANGE, it must have received approval from the SEC.
See also INITIAL PUBLIC OFFERING, SECONDARY DISTRIBUTION.

news ticker Or, *wire*. A news medium employed in BROKERAGE FIRMS that transmits late breaking MARKET information including CORPORATE earnings reports and news developments, government rulings, trading figures, and economic data.

New York Stock Exchange (NYSE) Or, *Big Board*. The largest and most respected organized SECURITIES EXCHANGE; it handles a majority of the dollar volume of securities transactions and a high percentage of the total annual share volume on organized securities exchanges. Its listing requirements are the most restrictive. For example, for a company to be listed on the NYSE for the first time, the corporation must have 2,000 stockholders owning 100 shares and its aggregate market value must be at least $18 million.

New York Stock Exchange Index A daily index of stock prices that includes all the stocks traded on the NEW YORK STOCK EXCHANGE. *See also* MARKET INDICES AND AVERAGES.

nifty-fifty Fifty stocks most favored by institutional investors. The mix of this group is constantly changing, although companies that continue to produce stable earnings growth over a long time tend to remain favorites of institutional investors.

night depository An area provided by BANKS where DEPOSITORS can make DEPOSITS, including CHECKS and CASH, directly into a vault within the bank.

no-load No sales charge or commission. *See also* MUTUAL FUNDS.

no-load (mutual) fund A MUTUAL FUND that does not charge a sales commission. Sales strategy includes advertisements and toll-free (800) telephone orders, so that an investor buys shares directly from the fund rather than through a broker, as is the case in LOAD MUTUAL FUNDS.

no par Or, *no par value stock.* A STOCK that does not have a PAR or stated value assigned to it. There is no value stated on the STOCK CERTIFICATE. When the stock is issued, the company credits the CAPITAL STOCK account for the entire amount received.

nominal income The value of income expressed in current dollars. No adjustment is made for changes in the PURCHASING POWER of the dollar.

nominal interest rate
1. The STATED RATE OF INTEREST on a DEBT security or LOAN. It may not be the true rate earned. In the case of BONDS, the terms nominal interest rate and COUPON RATE are synonymous. The interest received on a bond investment equals the nominal interest rate times the face value of the bond. For example, on an 8%, $10,000 bond, the investor would receive annual interest income of $800 ($10,000 × 8%).

See also EFFECTIVE INTEREST RATE.
2. The interest rate without adjusting for INFLATION.
See also REAL INTEREST RATE.

nominee An individual or business entity in whose name financial or real property is transferred. For example, bonds may be held in a STREET NAME registered to the brokerage firm (nominee) even though the investor is the real owner.

noncallable A BOND or PREFERRED STOCK that cannot be called or paid off at the option of the issuer. The MARKET VALUE of a noncallable issue would be higher than a CALLABLE issue since the INVESTOR has confidence that a particular YIELD can be "locked in" until the issue expires, rather than facing the RISK of being called, usually after the first five years, at any time.

noncancelable A provision normally found in a HEALTH INSURANCE POLICY whereby the policy cannot be canceled because of an illness or accident, providing the PREMIUMS are current.

noncatastrophic loss A loss that is not caused by a catastrophic event such as nuclear explosion, war, and hurricane. Losses arising from catastrophic occurrences are not typically covered by private insurance.

noncontestability clause A provision found in an INSURANCE POLICY guaranteeing that the INSURED may not be deprived of COVERAGE if untrue, inaccurate, or fraudulent information is discovered by the INSURER. In most cases the provision is effective after a specified period, two years in most states, and the insurer must act prior to this period in order to contest the insured effectively.

noncontributory pension plan A PENSION PLAN under which the employee does not make any contributions.

noncumulative A feature that does not allow the unpaid DIVIDENDS of a PREFERRED STOCK to accumulate.
See also CUMULATIVE.

noncumulative preferred stock A PREFERRED STOCK for which the DIVIDENDS do not accumulate if they are unpaid. This contrasts with the CUMULATIVE PREFERRED STOCK for which the dividends do accrue when the dividend is unpaid.

nuncupative will A WILL given orally by a TESTATOR, often in his last sickness, before a sufficient number of witnesses and later reduced to writing. An oral will testified to by witnesses for proof. Nuncupative wills are invalid in certain states and are valid in others only when specific restrictions are met.

nondiscretionary trust A TRUST in which the TRUSTEE is unable to have any discretion in making the DISTRIBUTIONS to BENEFICIARIES.

noneconomic spending Wasteful expenditures that are not related to quality, price, or family consumption needs.

nonfinancial assets ASSETS in the form of physical property, such as REAL ESTATE, cars, boats, and PERSONAL PROPERTY.

nonforfeiture clause A clause in an INSURANCE policy that contains the insured's settlement options if he or she defaults on premium payments. There are four options available to the policyholder: (1) to relinquish the policy for its CASH SURRENDER VALUE; (2) to take an EXTENDED TERM OPTION instead of the cash surrender value; (3) to take *reduced paid-up insurance* instead of the cash surrender value; and (4) to borrow from the insurer, using the cash value as COLLATERAL.

nonforfeiture extended term benefit The right of a policyholder having a life insurance policy with CASH value to continue full COVERAGE for a period, as determined by the table in the POLICY, without paying additional PREMIUMS.

nonforfeiture options A LIFE INSURANCE provision preventing the EQUITY of an INSURED from being forfeited. There are four benefits a POLICYHOLDER can select under the option: CASH SURRENDER VALUE, EXTENDED TERM INSURANCE, LOAN VALUE, and PAID UP INSURANCE. If the policyholder does not select an option, the policy will have a DEFAULT option, often extended term insurance.

nonforfeiture right *See* NONFORFEITURE EXTENDED TERM BENEFIT.

nonforfeiture table A CASH VALUE LIFE INSURANCE policy table listing the insured's options to take the policy as extended TERM INSURANCE, as cash, or as reduced paid-up life insurance. *See also* NONFORFEITURE CLAUSE.

no-fault A legal concept whereby the parties affected do not have to prove fault or no-fault in an action. No-fault takes a constructive view by seeking to redress the harm caused rather than to determine fault or blame for an action.
divorce: A concept used in certain states allowing a marriage to be terminated by proclaiming it to be irretrievably broken because of irreconcilable differences. Thus, it is not incumbent upon the parties to determine who is at fault.
insurance: A concept widely used in automobile INSURANCE when the law permits an aggrieved party in a traffic accident to recover all expenses from insurance without determining fault in the accident. Often, there are restrictions on the right of third parties to sue in order to discourage frivolous suits.

noninstallment credit A type of consumer credit that includes SINGLE PAYMENT LOANS and OPEN-ENDED CREDIT.

nonmonetary benefits Personnel benefits, provided by an organization, that cannot be converted into CASH or have taxable value. Such benefits include HEALTH, DISABILITY, and LIFE INSURANCE.

nonparticipating life insurance policy A LIFE INSURANCE policy that does not pay DIVIDENDS.

nonparticipating policies *See* NONPARTICIPATING LIFE INSURANCE POLICY.

nonparticipating preferred stock PREFERRED STOCK paying only stipulated DIVIDENDS with no possibility of increases because of an increase in CORPORATE profits. Nonparticipating preferred STOCKHOLDERS do *not* receive a proportionate share in excess dividends of the company over stated rates.

nonqualified deferred compensation plan
An employee deferred compensation plan, not enjoying the federal tax advantages of a QUALI-FIED DEFERRED COMPENSATION PLAN, in which employers receive a federal tax deduction for contributions paid into the plan on behalf of the employees. While not having a TAX DEDUCTION can be a serious disadvantage for an employer providing a deferred compensation plan, there are advantages:
1. Provisions that would otherwise be declared discriminatory are allowed.
2. Benefits do not have to be allocated to all employees, only to those whom the employer deems to have sufficient merit. The net result could be a lower cost plan than a QUALIFIED DEFERRED COMPENSATION PLAN.

nonrefund annuity Or, *straight life* or *pure annuity*. An annuity whose payments are guaranteed for the life of the annuitant, with no refund to anyone at death.

nonrefund annuities A form of ANNUITY not providing for a refund of the PREMIUMS plus INTEREST to BENEFICIARIES if the ANNUITANT dies during the accumulation period.

nontaxable gross income *See* EXEMPT IN-COME.

nonvoting stock An EQUITY SECURITY that does not give the holder the right to vote in company matters, such as electing the board of directors. PREFERRED STOCK is typically nonvoting. Some companies have different classes of common stock to restrict voting. For example, class "A" may be controlled by management and be voting while class "B" may be nonvoting.

normal retirement The age at which one is normally eligible to RETIRE. Under federal law the RETIREMENT AGE has been increased from 65

to 70. Employees who RETIRE may be entitled to a PENSION, as provided under the provisions of the EMPLOYMENT RETIREMENT INCOME SECURITY ACT of 1974, as well as to SOCIAL SECURITY retirement benefits.

normal retirement age *See* NORMAL RETIRE-MENT.

normal return The usual income earned on an asset at the customary interest rate. This normal return rate can be the risk-free interest rate (such as rates on TREASURY BILLS, NOTES, or BONDS) plus an add-on for the associated RISK.

normal trading unit The standard size of an order for a given security. For example, stocks typically have a trading unit of 100 shares, called a ROUND LOT. Stock units of fewer than 100 shares are termed ODD LOTS.

not rated (NR) An indication that a SECURITY has not been rated by one of the securities rating agencies such as Moody's or Standard & Poor's. It carries no positive or negative INVESTMENT connotations.

note A legally transferable DEBT INSTRUMENT by which the issuer resolves to pay the PAYEE within a specified period of time. Notes normally pay a stated rate of INTEREST dependent upon the MAR-KET RATE OF INTEREST.

An individual may sign his or her note payable promising to pay money to another party, such as a BANK, or CREDITOR, at a future date. The payment consists of PRINCIPAL and interest. For example, a $10,000, one-year, 10% note will require a payment at maturity of $11,000 ($10,000 principal + $1,000 interest). The $1,000 equals $10,000 × 10%.

Governmental notes normally have a MATURI-TY of from two to ten years, whereas municipal notes commonly have shorter term maturities ranging from one to four years with two-year maturities being the most common. Often notes are issued on the basis of the full faith and credit of the issuer carrying no COLLATERAL.

collateral note: A note by which the promise to

pay is secured by a pledge of property such as SECURITIES, REAL ESTATE or other ASSETS.

demand note: A note payable on demand by the payee rather than on a specific MATURITY date.

joint note: A note by which two or more individuals are *mutually indebted* for payment.

mortgage note: See MORTGAGE LOAN.

secured note: See COLLATERAL NOTE (above).

time note: As opposed to a demand note, a note payable at a definite time in the future.

unsecured note: A note of indebtedness not pledging any COLLATERAL or security to guarantee payment.

not-held order (NH) A SECURITIES trading order directive to a BROKER either for a LIMIT or MARKET ORDER giving the broker time and price latitude in executing the transaction. In effect, it allows the broker to back away from the crowd until he or she feels conditions are more favorable for the TRADE.

In a not-held order, the client agrees not to hold the broker accountable for fulfilling the order within a particular time period.

notice of cancellation clause

1. A notice, normally in writing, in which notice of termination is given by one person to another. A notice of cancellation is given pursuant to a cancellation provision in a contract to forestall future liability.

2. In INSURANCE, a notice given between an INSURER and a reinsurer or an insurer and an INSURED of the termination of a contract or policy at the time of renewal, or, in the latter case, for lack of PREMIUM payments.

A notice of cancellation can also be issued for a current POLICY when a renegotiation of its features and agreements is desired.

not-sufficient-funds check (NSF) Or, *bounced check*. Notification by a BANK to a DRAWEE that a

CHECK cannot be negotiated because the DRAWER'S ACCOUNT does not have sufficient funds to cover it. Often a bad CHECK processing fee will be charged to both the drawee and to the drawer by the respective banks.

In preparing one's BANK reconciliation, one deducts the NSF check from the book BALANCE.

novation Jointly agreeing to provide an equivalent legal obligation, liability, or DEBT for a prior one. Parties to the contract can also be substituted.

A novation requires a valid prior contract, mutual agreement of all the parties to the CONTRACT, and the cancellation of the original contract or discharge of the original parties prior to the substitution of a new contractual agreement and/or parties to it, respectively.

The new contract can have the original parties. Substituted parties can have the original or a new contract as long as the major requirements for a novation are met.

N-ratio method A formula for estimating the ANNUAL PERCENTAGE RATE (APR) on an ADD-ON LOAN.

null and void In law, something that is not allowable or binding and as such, is not legally enforceable. An example is a provision in a written agreement that is unlawful.

numismatic coin A coin having value and INTEREST to a numismatist because of its rarity or special characteristics. A NUMISMATIST will collect, evaluate, and trade such coins.

numismatist One who appraises and collects coins having unique characteristics including rarity, quality, and historical importance. *See also* NUMISMATIC COIN.

O

obligation

1. An indebtedness, such as owing money to a bank. Typically, the obligation is in the form of a written promise.

2. A duty to perform some act, such as a commitment to support a family.

occasional disbursements Payment of money on an irregular basis for settling obligations including DIVIDENDS, EXPENSE reimbursements, and payments of current expenses.

occupational hazard Workplace perils, including the incidence of disease and accident, that are an inextricable part of the performance of work-related duties. For example, medical personnel risk contracting disease when working in a hospital environment. The lives of policemen are at risk when the officers perform their duties.

occupational pension A PENSION PLAN, available to the employees in a workplace, to which the employer and the employees may jointly contribute. The terms and circumstances of the pension determine the employees' ability to quit prior to actual retirement age without losing vested rights.
See also PENSION PLAN; EMPLOYMENT RETIREMENT INCOME SECURITY ACT (ERISA); NONCONTRIBUTORY PENSION PLAN; PORTABILITY.

odd lot Any exception to the standard trading unit. For example, a standard unit of stock is 100 shares, called ROUND LOT. Any amount other than 100 shares or multiples thereof would be an odd lot. An example of an odd lot is 25 shares. The commission rate on an odd-lot transaction typically includes an odd-lot differential, usually one-eighth of a point. The commission rate on an odd-lot transaction is relatively higher than on a round-lot transaction.

odd-lot broker *See* ODD-LOT DEALER.

odd-lot dealer The role of today's odd-lot dealers has evolved from the time when they used to assemble odd lots of stock and sell them to member brokers for retail sale to their clients. Today, the NEW YORK STOCK EXCHANGE provides this service free to its member brokers.

The odd-lot retail INVESTOR does pay a higher COMMISSION for an odd-lot purchase to the BROKER. While commission rates can vary, a typical odd lot commission would be 12 1/2 cents or one-eighth of a point. Thus, buying 40 shares of a STOCK trading at $12 per share would cost $12 1/8 per SHARE for an odd-lot purchase.

odd-lot theory A theory that the timing of the small INVESTOR buying or selling small ODD-LOT shares of STOCK is usually wrong and therefore contraindicative of MARKET movements. Thus, when a measurable increase in ODD-LOT buying occurs, the market is positioned for a downward CORRECTION. Conversely, a measurable increase in odd-lot selling is interpreted to mean that the market is positioned for an upward reversal.

However, research has not validated odd-lot theory, showing instead that the timing of odd-lot buyers is fairly accurate, and rather closely matches the performance of the market. Thus, odd-lot theory is out of favor today, and no longer given credence.

off board

1. A trade occurring in the OVER-THE-COUNTER MARKET or an execution of a LISTED SECURITY not consummated on a national stock exchange.

2. A block of stock traded among clients of a brokerage house, or between the client and the brokerage firm itself, with the latter purchasing or disposing of securities it holds.

offer

1. Or, *asked price*. The price for which one is willing to sell a security. The BID AND ASKED prices for OVER-THE-COUNTER securities are published in newspapers.

2. A proposal to perform some activity or to pay some money. Once an offer is accepted, a contract exists.

3. To offer a good or service for sale.

offer price

1. The price for which an item may be purchased. For example, a prospective seller may be offering his or her house for sale at $250,000.

2. The price at which a new secondary issue of securities is placed on sale to investors. For example, if a new issue of ABC stock is priced at $50 a share, the offer price is $50.

3. The price per share of a MUTUAL FUND listed in the newspapers. This price is based on the NET ASSET VALUE (NAV) (if a no-load mutual fund) or NAV and a sales charge (if a LOAD mutual fund).

offer wanted (OW)   A notice given by an investor that he or she is waiting for an offer from a prospective seller of a stock or bond. The abbreviation OW may appear in the PINK SHEETS for stocks and YELLOW SHEETS for corporate bonds that are exchanged in the over-the-counter market.

offering date   The first day a stock or bond issue will be available for purchase by the public.

off-floor order   An order to purchase or sell a security originating outside the exchange. These orders represent client orders starting with brokers, rather than orders of floor members (on-floor orders) for their accounts. Off-floor orders must be transacted prior to on-floor ones.

old age, survivors disability and health insurance (OASDHI)   Or, *Social Security*. A U.S. government Social Security insurance program established in 1935 and providing not only retirement benefits but also payments for survivors, DISABILITY INCOME for workers and their dependents, and health-care benefits for low-income and elderly families and individuals.

omitted dividend   A regularly scheduled DIVIDEND that was not voted to be declared by a company's board of directors. Often, when this occurs, the company is seeking to conserve cash assets by avoiding the payment of the dividend. The unexpected announcement of an omitted DIVIDEND will have a depressing affect on the price of the company's STOCK as it is an indication of financial difficulty; it also makes the stock less attractive as an INVESTMENT vehicle.

on account

1. A purchase made on credit.

2. A partial payment of a debt.

on line

1. The active state of computer equipment, the central processing unit, disk drives, printers, and processing data.

2. The active state of linking computers at remote distance via telephone lines. The computers are transferring data to each other.

on-line data base   Information transmitted by telephone, microwaves, or other means that may be accessed with a modem and displayed on a monitor or as a printout. To take advantage of a data base, typically stored on a mainframe, one needs a personal computer, telecommunications software, a modem, and a telephone. A data base may consist of information on tax laws and regulations, investment information, financial data on companies, and other information. For a listing of on-line data bases, reference may be made to *The Computer Phone Book: Directory of On-Line Systems* published by New American Library.

open

banking: To start a bank account.
finance: Balance still owed.
investments:

1. To set up a brokerage account.

2. A buy or sell order for securities that has not yet been executed.

open account

1. An account having a balance, as when a consumer still owes a department store money for purchases.

2. A credit relationship between seller and buyer.

open buy order In SECURITIES, any unexecuted buy order. The term open buy order is often used synonymously to mean an order that is GOOD-TILL-CANCELED (GTC). Technically, however, the order could also be a DAY ORDER.
See also GOOD-TILL-CANCELED ORDER (GTC).

open contract A futures contract that has not yet been closed out. The contract is closed when either it is sold or when the commodities are received.

open-end account *See* OPEN-END CREDIT.

open-end car lease An automobile LEASE in which an additional open payment is required after the return of the vehicle to allow for any change in its condition that would affect its value.
See also OPEN-END LEASE.

open-end credit A practice commonly found with CREDIT CARD and REVOLVING CHARGE accounts by which initial CREDIT LIMITS are established upon the opening of the ACCOUNT, but no DEBT is actually incurred. Each additional purchase represents an extension of credit. Partial monthly payments of any debt incurred for multiple purchases are permitted with no fixed date being established to pay the BALANCE.

open-end (mutual) funds A mutual fund from which an investor buys shares and to which the investor resells these shares. This type of fund offers to sell and redeem shares on a continual basis for an indefinite time period. Shares are purchased at NET ASSET VALUE (NAV) plus commission (if any) and redeemed at NAV less a service charge (if any).

open-end investment companies *See* OPEN-END (MUTUAL) FUNDS.

open-end investment trust *See* INVESTMENT TRUST; OPEN-END (MUTUAL) FUNDS.

open-end lease A LEASE agreement providing for a final additional payment on the return of the property to the LESSOR, adjusting for any change in its value.

open-end mortgage The borrower may obtain additional financing from the lender according to the mortgage agreement that usually specifies a maximum amount that can be borrowed.
See also CLOSED-END MORTGAGE.

open interest The total amount of exercisable CONTRACTS that were purchased in the FUTURES and OPTIONS MARKETS. Until such time as the futures or options either expire or are EXERCISED, they will remain on the records of the clearing house as open interest.

open listing An agreement that allows a REAL ESTATE AGENT as well as the homeowner or other agents to attempt simultaneously to sell the home.

open order Any order that has not been fulfilled.
business: The equivalent of a standing order.
securities: Any valid buy or sell order that has not been executed. While an open order can be just a DAY ORDER, often the term is used to mean GOOD-TILL-CANCELED (GTC).

open outcry A trading practice in the commodity exchange by which dealers stand in a "pit" on the trading floor and yell out bid and offer prices for commodities.

opening escrow The situation in which the DEPOSIT a buyer gives for the purchase of a property is delivered to the escrow agent, who is to hold it on behalf of the seller.

opening transaction In investments, the purchase of a CALL or PUT OPTION creating the future right to buy or sell a STOCK. In an opening call transaction the purchaser creates the right to buy a stock, while in an opening put transaction the purchaser creates the right to sell a stock.

operating in the red A vernacular term describing a business sustaining a loss from current operations. The INCOME STATEMENT shows an imbalance between EXPENSES and revenues. *See also* OPERATING LOSS.

operating loss A loss incurred by a business. Gross expenses exceed gross sales.

opportunity cost The cost of giving up one financial option for another. For example, the opportunity cost of investing in a risky business venture is the risk-free return of, say, 8% on a TREASURY BILL.

option
1. The right to buy or sell something within a fixed period of time. For example, in REAL ESTATE a purchaser enters into a CONTRACT in which he puts $20,000 into an ESCROW ACCOUNT for the purpose of buying a $200,000 piece of property within six months. Thus, he has an option to buy the property at a fixed price within a certain period of time.
2. In the SECURITIES industry, an option is a FUTURE CONTRACT or STOCK contract to buy or sell either a COMMODITY or stock at a specified price, the STRIKING PRICE, before an expiration date.
3. In INSURANCE, the choice given to a LIFE INSURANCE policyowner of the terms of a death benefit. Or, OPTIONAL MODES OF SETTLEMENT.
See also CALL OPTION; FUTURES CONTRACT; PUT OPTION.

option account An ACCOUNT established in a BROKERAGE FIRM allowing a client to buy and sell STOCK OPTIONS. In order to establish the account, the client must first complete an OPTION AGREEMENT. This agreement is used by the BROKERAGE FIRM to determine that the client qualifies for the firm's financial ability limitations.
See also OPTION AGREEMENT.

option agreement Or, *option account agreement form*. A form required to be completed by clients of a BROKERAGE FIRM in order to obtain an OPTION ACCOUNT. In addition to obtaining financial information to determine the client's financial qualifications, prior investing experience is also sought as well as the client's agreement to comply with the requirements of the Option Clearing Corporation and of the exchange on which the option is traded.

option charge account *See* REVOLVING CHARGE ACCOUNT.

option holder An individual who has purchased and still retains a CALL or PUT option.

option mutual fund A MUTUAL FUND that purchases and/or sells options to enhance the worth of the fund's shares. An aggressive or conservative approach may be practiced. An aggressive option growth fund may buy CALLS and PUTS in selected stocks that are expected to change in price significantly either upward or downward. If such significant price change materializes, substantial returns will be earned. However, if the fund manager is wrong, the entire premium will be lost since the options will expire. On the other hand, a conservative option income fund may profit from the premium obtained by selling calls and put options on securities included in the fund's investment portfolio.

option premium The excess of the STRIKING PRICE of a CALL or PUT OPTION over the price at which the underlying SECURITY is trading. For example, if XYZ stock is trading at $52 per share, and the 50 call option, expiring in July, is selling at $6 per call, then the option premium equals the price of the call minus (the price of the underlying security minus striking price). Thus, the option premium would be $4 = [$6 − ($52-$50)].
See also OPTION PRICE.

option price The MARKET PRICE at which a STOCK OPTION is selling. All option prices are for a single option on one SHARE of STOCK, but all option contracts are sold in ROUND LOTS of 100. For example, if the option price is $4, the price of the option contract is $400.

The option price is the difference between the STRIKING PRICE of a CALL or PUT OPTION and the price at which the underlying security is trading plus any PREMIUM, unless the option is trading at a DISCOUNT prior to its expiration.
See also OPTION PREMIUM.

option spread Any combination of numerous option investing strategies in which STOCK OPTIONS for the same underlying SECURITY, often using two different time periods, are HEDGED against each other to reduce RISK while still taking advantage of price movements in the underlying security. Properly used, option spreads can be very effective in reducing risk and exploiting profit opportunities; however, the COMMISSION costs associated with an option spread can be substantial. Examples of option spreads include butterfly, HORIZONTAL, DIAGONAL, sandwich, and VERTICAL.

option strategy Any of a series of OPTION tactics by which an INVESTOR seeks to increase INVESTMENT return while reducing the RISK. These tactics include HEDGING stock investments by WRITING COVERED CALL OPTIONS; buying PUT OPTIONS to offset risk in the purchase of the underlying SECURITY; buying put options to offset short sales of the underlying security; buying CALL or put options to take advantage of anticipated short-term trading opportunities; developing option SPREAD strategies; and selling NAKED OPTIONS.
See also OPTION SPREAD.

option writing A situation in which the writer of a CALL agrees to sell shares at the strike price paid for the call option. Call option writers do the opposite of what buyers do. An option is written because the writer believes that a price increase in the stock will be less than what the call purchaser anticipates. The writer may even expect a flat or decreasing price in the security. Option writers receive the option premium less

related transaction costs. If the option is not exercised, the writer earns the price paid for it. If the option is exercised, the writer incurs a loss, which may be significant.

optional dividend A dividend of a company giving the recipient an option as to the type of dividend to be received, typically in cash and/or shares.

optionally renewable A contract that may be renewed at the option of the insurer, such as in health insurance. At the expiration date of the contract, the insurer will decide whether or not to renew.

oral contract A contract that is not in writing or signed by the parties. In most cases, oral contracts are legally enforceable except for those related to the sale of real estate.

order An oral or written directive to perform some positive or negative action that may be legally applied.
law: A directive, mandate, or command from a court or administrative agency.
negotiable instruments: A request by the PAYEE to the maker stating "Pay to the order of Mary Doe".
securities: A client's buy or sell order to a BROKER. Most orders are verbal orders, which is why it is important for the broker to know his or her client.

There are four categories of security orders: LIMIT ORDER, MARKET ORDER, STOP ORDER, and TIME ORDER. In addition, there are two time orders: a DAY ORDER and a GOOD-TILL-CANCELED (GTC) ORDER.

order ticket A form completed by a SECURITIES BROKER for a client; it shows the client's name, account number, number of SHARES to buy or sell, the name of the security, the trading exchange, and the kind of order (MARKET ORDER, LIMIT ORDER, GOOD-TILL-CANCELED (GTC), STOP ORDER, DAY ORDER, etc.). The order is passed on to the floor of the EXCHANGE where it will be executed by a floor BROKER, who will indicate the price at which the TRADE was completed by writing it on the ticket.

ordinary annuity An INSURANCE CONTRACT designed to pay an income to the annuitant on a monthly, quarterly, or semiannual basis. While ANNUITIES do have DEATH BENEFITS, they differ from LIFE INSURANCE in that they are intended to provide INCOME for the ANNUITANT during his or her lifetime rather than simply provide a lump-sum distribution to the beneficiaries on the insured's death.

There are a variety of methods for paying for an annuity during the ACCUMULATION PERIOD including LUMP-SUM PAYMENTS. There are also a variety of ways a benefit can be distributed to an annuitant during the LIQUIDATION PERIOD. *See also* DEFERRED GROUP ANNUITY; GUARANTEED MINIMUM ANNUITY; GUARANTEED PERIOD ANNUITY; JOINT AND LAST SURVIVORSHIP ANNUITY; LIFE ANNUITY; LIFE ANNUITY WITH NO REFUND (straight life); PERIOD CERTAIN; NONREFUND ANNUITY; QUALIFYING ANNUITY; RETIREMENT ANNUITY.

ordinary income INCOME from the usual activities of an individual or business as distinguished from CAPITAL GAINS. Such income includes WAGES, SALARIES, fees, COMMISSIONS, TIPS, BONUSES, prizes and awards, director's fees, earned INTEREST, and others. Subsequent to current tax law, long-term and short-term capital gains are also treated as ordinary income for TAX purposes.

ordinary interest INTEREST based on a 360-day year rather than a 365-day year. The former is termed SIMPLE INTEREST while the latter is termed EXACT INTEREST. The difference between the two forms of interest can be substantial when calculated on large sums of MONEY.

ordinary life A type of LIFE INSURANCE contract in which coverage and premium payments continue for the life of the insured.

organized market A number of merchants who conduct themselves based on specified rules in buying and selling goods and/or services.

organized securities exchange An institution in which LISTED SECURITIES such as STOCK are traded by exchange members on a floor organized according to different types of securities. The largest and most prestigious example is the NEW YORK STOCK EXCHANGE.

organized stock exchange *See* ORGANIZED SECURITIES EXCHANGE.

original issue discount (OID) Discount from PAR VALUE when a BOND is first issued. The most extreme version of an original issue discount (OID) is a ZERO COUPON BOND, which is issued at a substantial discount from its maturity value. No interest is paid to the holder of the bond while held; rather, the bond is paid in full at maturity. The gain is the difference between the purchase price and the maturity value.

original maturity The time period for a debt security from the date of issue until the due date. For example, a bond dated January 1, 19X1, and maturing January 1, 19X5, has an original maturity of four years.

other insurance clause A provision in an insurance policy indicating the degree of coverage in case another insurance policy covers the same insured risk. An example is two health insurance policies held by the same individual.

other people's money (OPM) The use of borrowed funds by individuals to increase the return on an invested capital. Examples are a MORTGAGE to buy REAL ESTATE and buying STOCK on MARGIN.
See also FINANCIAL LEVERAGE; LEVERAGE.

outlay A cash expenditure, such as the initial cash paid to buy a car.

out-of-favor industry or stock An industry or stock that is not at the current time attractive to investors. As a result, the stock price of companies in the industry languishes. An industry such as hotels may be unpopular, for example, because of a recession restricting spending.

out of line A stock that is priced excessively high or low relative to similar stocks in the market. Such a determination may be based on the PRICE-EARNINGS RATIOS. If all other similar companies had price-earnings ratios of 12, while company XYZ had a price-earnings ratio of 20, the company is probably overpriced.

out-of-the-money A CALL or PUT OPTION whose STRIKING PRICE exceeds the MARKET PRICE of the STOCK in either direction. For example, if the market price of a stock is $26, a person buying or selling a $30 call option or a $20 put option is making an out-of-the-money option transaction.
See also IN THE MONEY.

outstanding
1. The balance due on an item still remains, such as a claim filed with the insurance company that is still unpaid.
2. A prominent or distinguished accomplishment, such as earning an MBA.

outstanding check A CHECK issued by the maker but not yet cleared by the BANK. In preparing the BANK RECONCILIATION, the amount of the check must be deducted from the BANK BALANCE.

outstanding deposit Or, *deposit-in-transit*. A CREDIT issued to an ACCOUNT by a DEPOSITOR, but which has not yet cleared the BANK. An example is a CHECK received by the depositor from a customer but which was deposited in the "after-hours depository" of the bank. In preparing the BANK RECONCILIATION, the deposit-in-transit is added to the BANK BALANCE.

over age 55 home sale exemption The Internal Revenue Code (IRC Sections 1034 and 121) allowing an individual over the age of 55 to sell a principal residence at a gain and exclude once in a lifetime up to $125,000 of the gain from taxation. The exclusion is allowed regardless of whether the taxpayer purchases another home. The individual must have used the property as a principal residence for three of the last five years. For example, Naomi, over age 55, sells her principal residence, in which she has lived for the last three years, at a $175,000 gain. She may exclude $125,000 of the gain from taxation. The rest of the gain is a taxable capital gain.
See also 1034 EXCHANGE (ROLLOVER).

overbought
in general: Description of the condition that occurs when an individual or a firm buys too much or takes too large a position in a particular item causing a surplus to exist. At this point, efforts, including a sale, will be made to reduce inventory.
securities: Descriptive of the state occurring in the STOCK MARKET when SECURITY prices, as measured by the DJIA, other market INDEXES, as well as the average PRICE EARNINGS RATIOS of the companies, have reached or exceeded the RESISTANCE LEVEL. At this point, the downside risk will exceed the upside potential and prices could fall in the short term.
See also OVERSOLD; RESISTANCE LEVEL.

overdraft
check: A CHECK written by the MAKER exceeding the BALANCE in the ACCOUNT. Such a check will be rejected by the bank because of NOT-SUFFICIENT-FUNDS (NSF).
overdraft loan: A previously approved LINE OF CREDIT allowing an individual to borrow money, up to the approved CREDIT LIMIT, by using his or her CHECKING ACCOUNT. INTEREST is charged only on the funds actually borrowed in the overdraft account for as long as the amount is outstanding.
See also BOUNCED CHECK.

overdraft protection *See* OVERDRAFT.

overextension
banking: The extension of more CREDIT to an individual or company than can reasonably be expected to be repaid.
business: The condition of a business that has overly expanded itself and is having financial and management difficulties because of it.
financial: The situation of a person who is excessively in DEBT beyond his or her ability to

pay. An example is the result of using CHARGE ACCOUNTS beyond one's financial limits.

physical labor: An individual's doing more physically than he or she can realistically handle.

securities: The situation of an individual whose STOCK MARGIN purchases exceed his or her financial resources to repay.

oversold

securities: Descriptive of a situation in which the prices of the STOCK MARKET, as measured by the DJIA and other indexes, have fallen to or below the SUPPORT LEVEL. At such a time, prices become unreasonably depressed in terms of the average PRICE EARNINGS RATIOS of many companies. In this scenario, the upside potential exceeds the downside risk, presenting a buying opportunity.

See also OVERBOUGHT.

overspending Descriptive of an individual who is spending more money or incurring more debt than he or she has income to cover.

oversubscribed Term used to describe the UNDERWRITING of a SECURITY issue when there are more buyers than SHARES available. In such an event, when the issue is made public, the price would normally rise rapidly as those not having the opportunity to buy shares at the initial offering will now bid the MARKET PRICE up in an effort to obtain shares.

On occasion, when an oversubscribed condition exists early in the initial offering of a security, it may be possible to issue additional shares to satisfy demand.

See also HOT ISSUE.

over-the-counter (OTC) market Not a specific institution but rather a way of trading securities; a forum where unlisted securities are traded. TRADERS (dealers) use a telecommunications network called the NATIONAL ASSOCIATION OF SECURITY DEALERS AUTOMATED QUOTATION SYSTEM (NASDAQ) for transactions in these securities. Each over-the-counter trader makes a market in particular securities by offering to buy or sell them at specified prices. The BID PRICE is the maximum price the dealer offers for a security. The ASKED PRICE is the lowest price at which the dealer will sell the security. The dealer's profit is the spread between the bid price and asked price.

overwithholding Descriptive of the situation in which a taxpayer has too much INCOME TAX deducted from his or her SALARY or other INCOME. The net result is that the taxpayer qualifies for a TAX REFUND from the INTERNAL REVENUE SERVICE and possibly, from a state income tax authority as well, at the end of the taxable year. This situation is normally remedied by increasing the number of DEPENDENTS declared on a W-4 IRS form, which will reduce the income tax withheld from the salary.

See also WITHHOLDING TAX.

owners' equity The interest of the owners in the assets of the business represented by capital investments and accumulated earnings less any dividends.

ownership rights under life insurance The rights of the insured as provided for in the policy. The policyholder may exercise all privileges and receive all benefits as per the terms of the insurance policy.

P

package life insurance A LIFE INSURANCE contract that combines basic types of life insurance such as TERM, WHOLE LIFE, and ENDOWMENT.

package mortgage A mortgage on both the purchased real estate and specified personal property of a durable nature (e.g., appliances, furniture). All of the financing is treated as one mortgage to be repaid.

paid up Descriptive of a situation in which all payments have been made. An example is a life insurance policy for which all the premiums have been paid.

paper profit or loss
securities: An UNREALIZED PROFIT OR LOSS of a security compared with its original acquisition price. A paper profit occurs when the MARKET PRICE of a SECURITY exceeds the original purchase price, while an unrealized loss occurs when the MARKET PRICE of a security declines from the initial purchase price. Such profits or losses have no tax effect except upon the actual sale of the security when it becomes a realized profit or loss.

par value The dollar amount arbitrarily assigned each share of stock in the company's charter and printed on the STOCK CERTIFICATE. It is a NOMINAL or FACE VALUE of a COMMON STOCK. For PREFERRED STOCKS and BONDS, the value on which the issuer promises to pay DIVIDENDS.

parking The practice of putting money in a relatively RISK-free INVESTMENT, paying a MARKET RATE of interest, while waiting for a buying opportunity to occur in another market such as securities or real estate. Parking usually occurs when the INVESTOR believes the downside potential of a particular market exceeds the upside

potential. The ASSETS are then realized by the investor and are parked in a secure investment medium, such as a MONEY MARKET FUND.

partial delivery A situation in which a broker does not deliver the entire amount of a security or commodity bought. An example is an agreement to deliver 50,000 shares, fulfilled only partially by the delivery of 40,000 shares.

partial disability Physical or psychological conditions that prevent an insured from performing part of his or her typical job functions.

partial release A stipulation in a MORTGAGE that permits some of the secured property to be relieved as COLLATERAL when specified conditions occur.

partial taking Acquisition of part of property or property rights when condemnation occurs. The owner must be fairly compensated.

participating dividends The DIVIDEND of a rarely issued form of PREFERRED STOCK that participates, along with common stock, in any additional dividend payments. There are two types of participating dividends.

In a partial participating dividend, the preferred STOCKHOLDERS participate above the preferred rate on a pro rata basis with common stockholders up to an amount stated on the stock certificate. For example, on a 5% preferred stock issue, the participation may be up to 8%, limiting the additional participation to 3%.

In a fully participating dividend, preferred SHAREHOLDERS receive the preferred dividend and they participate fully in any pro rata SHARE with common stockholders in any additional dividends.

The right of a preferred stockholder to receive a participating dividend is stated in the PROSPECTUS and on the certificate. Various states

have restrictions governing participating dividends, and regulations of the state having jurisdiction may affect any distributions.
See also PARTICIPATING PREFERRED STOCK.

participating insurance   INSURANCE that pays DIVIDENDS to the policyholder. A portion of the PREMIUM is returned to the policyholder as a dividend.

participating policies   A LIFE INSURANCE POLICY that pays its owners DIVIDENDS. Dividends can be paid in a variety of ways:

1. Paid in CASH.
2. Applied to reduce policy premiums.
3. Used to purchase additional PAID-UP INSURANCE.
4. Placed in an interest-bearing account with the insurance company.
5. Applied to the premium of an annual TERM INSURANCE policy.

participating policy dividend   Or, *participating insurance*. A life insurance policy that pays its owner dividends. The dividends may be received in cash or reinvested by the insurance company to earn interest, reduce the premium payment, or purchase additional insurance.

participating preferred stock   A rarely issued type of PREFERRED STOCK. Besides receiving the usual stated dividend, preferred stockholders "participate" with common stockholders in any extra dividends paid. For example, a 5% fully participating preferred stock receives its 5% preference rate plus a pro rata share of excess dividends, based on the total par value of the common stock and preferred stock, after common stockholders have received their matching 5% of par value of the common stock.

participation certificate   A certificate evidencing equity in a pool of funds or in other instruments, such as an interest in notes. Typically, principal and interest payments go to the certificate holders each month.

participation or coinsurance clause   Or, *coinsurance clause*. A provision in HEALTH INSUR-ANCE policies specifying that the company will pay some portion (80% to 90%) of the amount of the covered loss in excess of the DEDUCTIBLE.

partnership   A form of business organization created by two or more individuals who contribute capital and effort. Partnerships are easily created at low cost and have few governmental restrictions, but they have some disadvantages: (1) the partners have unlimited financial liability, (2) the partnership can be dissolved upon the withdrawal of one of the partners for any reason, and (3) these organizations have limited ability to raise large amounts of capital.

Within partnerships there are two types of partners: a GENERAL PARTNER, who takes an active management role in the partnership, and a LIMITED PARTNER, who only contributes money, with his or her LIABILITY being restricted to the amount of the original INVESTMENT.

passbook   A small book issued by BANKS to DEPOSITORS who maintain SAVINGS ACCOUNTS. The passbook has the name of the depositor and the depositor's signature as well as a complete record of all the transactions in the ACCOUNT including DEPOSITS, withdrawals, and INTEREST. In order for any transaction to occur, banks normally require the depositor to show the passbook for verification as well as for recording the transaction.

passbook savings accounts   A common form of savings in which the depositor's current account balance, including credited interest, is shown in a small booklet.

passed dividend   A customarily scheduled DIVIDEND that the corporation elects not to pay. A passed dividend is not deemed an obligation of the company except in the case of a CUMULATIVE PREFERRED STOCK DIVIDEND. A corporation may choose to omit a dividend because of financial exigency when the money is required for other obligations. The act of omitting the dividend is termed "passing the dividend."

Normally, a passed dividend will deleteriously affect the price of the stock since it may be interpreted as a sign of financial weakness. On occasion, however, the price of the stock may actually rise since investors may feel management is acting responsibly.

pass-through securities   SECURITIES backed by a pool of MORTGAGES. The PRINCIPAL and interest payments made monthly on the mortgages in this pool are passed through to the investors who purchased the mortgage-backed security. Examples of pass-through securities are the mortgage-backed securities guaranteed by the GNMA and FREDDIE MAC SECURITIES. The Freddie Mac securities do not carry a federal guarantee.
See also MORTGAGE-BACKED SECURITIES.

password
in general: Any word or phrase that permits an activity to occur. For example, a sentry at a gatepost may ask for the password from an individual seeking entry. If the individual cannot state the password, he or she is denied entrance.
computers: A word or phrase required to gain access to a telecommunications network, data base, or other secure computer system. Passwords are widely used to prevent unauthorized access to vital data and information. Persons purposely bypassing computer password systems are termed "computer hackers."

past-due balance method   A method of computing finance charges whereby a customer who pays the account in full within a specified period of time, such as 30 days from the BILLING DATE, is relieved of FINANCE CHARGES. This method is used to stimulate customers to repay their accounts fully. For example, assume that the monthly interest rate is 1.5%, which represents an annual rate of 18%. The previous balance is $400 and the payment was made on the 15th day of the month. Since the payment was made prior to that specified date, the finance charge would be zero.
See also ADJUSTED BALANCE METHOD; AVERAGE DAILY BALANCE METHOD; PREVIOUS BALANCE METHOD.

pawnbroker   An individual who often lends small amounts of money, at a stated rate of INTEREST, and requires the DEPOSIT of personal property as COLLATERAL. If the LOAN is not repaid, the collateral becomes the personal property of the pawnbroker.
See also PAWN SHOP.

pawn shop   A store where a PAWNBROKER carries on his or her trade. A pawnbroker will lend money to an individual on the basis of the value of an item, such as a piece of jewelry, which must be surrendered to the pawnbroker for COLLATERAL. If the conditions of the loan are not met, the pawnbroker has the right of ownership of the "pawned" item.
See also PAWNBROKER.

payable   Descriptive of an amount owed to another party. A payable item is one that is unpaid, whether or not due. The failure to satisfy a payable on the due date may result in an interest charge. An example is money owed by an individual to a retail store on a purchase of merchandise.

pay-as-you-go basis
1. A method of paying income taxes whereby the employer deducts a portion of income each pay period and remits it to the INTERNAL REVENUE SERVICE.
2. Paying for a service as you use it.

pay-as-you-go pension plan   A pension plan in which the firm pays its retired workers their pensions from its current operating budget.

payback period   The number of years necessary to recover the initial investment. The payback period equals

$$\frac{\text{Initial Investment}}{\text{Annual Cash Inflow}}$$

Assume an investment of $10,000 in a security that will pay $2,000 a year for 8 years. The payback period is

$$\$10,000/\$2,000 = 5 \text{ years}$$

The payback period should be as short as possible as the money recouped can be invested for a return. Also, a shorter payback period means less risk associated with getting the investment money back.

payee The person to whom payment is made through a BILL, CASH, CHECK, NOTE, or PROMISSORY NOTE.
See also PAYER.

payer The person obligated to make a payment to a PAYEE.

paying agent An individual selected by a PAYER to make payments to designated PAYEES.

payment date The date on or before payment must be made in order to comply with a contractual obligation.
See also DUE DATE.

payment in kind A form of payment made without MONEY as the original obligation must be satisfied with comparable goods. For example, if an individual borrows a can of paint, then a payment in kind would be another can, preferably new, of comparable paint. This method differs from BARTER in that a payment in kind is made not with different goods but with the same type of goods or material.

A payment in kind replaces one good with another comparable one.

payment plan A plan specifying the dates and amounts of payments to be made under a financing agreement.

payoff
1. Complete satisfaction of a DEBT.
2. An unethical or illegal payment made to obtain otherwise unobtainable goods or favors. Examples of a payoff would be a BRIBE or a KICKBACK.

payout In investments, the annual percentage of corporate net income paid out as dividends to common stockholders.

payout ratio The dividends per share divided by the earnings per share. For example, if a company pays out dividends per share of $2 and earnings per share is $10, the payout ratio is 20%. In general, stockholders prefer companies with higher payout ratios.

payroll withholding The amount taken out of an employee's salary for taxes and other items (e.g., union dues) to be remitted by the employer to other parties (e.g., Internal Revenue Service, union).

pay up The action of an investor who delayed buying a desired stock until its price began to rise and must now pay a higher price for it.

pecuniary exchange A trade involving dollars as the exchange basis.

pecuniary legacy A provision in a will that passes money to a particular party.

penalty clause A provision in a contract stating a dollar amount or rate a party to the contract must pay for failure to comply with the terms. An example is the penalty charged by a bank for the early withdrawal of funds from a CERTIFICATE OF DEPOSIT. Another example is the penalty assessed for a late mortgage payment.

penny stocks Low-priced, often highly SPECULATIVE STOCKS, which typically sell for $1 or less per share. All penny stocks are traded in the OVER-THE-COUNTER (OTC) market. Because of the highly speculative nature of these stocks, the SEC requires the broker to do two things to protect investors: (1) provide written proof that a high-risk penny-stock investment is suitable for an investor, and (2) obtain consent in writing from new investors in penny stocks.

Pension Benefit Guarantee Corporation (PBGC) A federal government corporation established by a provision of the EMPLOYEE RETIREMENT INCOME SECURITY ACT OF 1974 (ERISA). This organization guarantees to eligible workers certain benefits payable to them even if their employer's PENSION PLAN has insufficient assets to fulfill its commitments. Payment is financed through premiums paid by insured plans.

pension fund Resources set aside periodically by the employer and/or employee that earn a return so the accumulated principal and interest will be adequate to satisfy the employee's retirement goals. Pension contributions are typically paid to a trustee, such as an insurance company, who directly pays the employees at retirement. Retirement payments come from pension fund assets.

pension plan A legal agreement in which the employer agrees to provide retirement benefits to employees. Plans vary among employers. The employee may or may not contribute to the fund depending on the terms of the agreement. The deposited pension monies accumulate a return (dividends, interest income) over time. At retirement, the individual typically receives the funds in an annuity. The amounts received from the employer's contributions or originally non-taxed employee contributions are subject to income tax when withdrawn. A self-employed individual may have his or her own pension plan.
See also DEFINED BENEFIT PENSION PLAN; DEFINED CONTRIBUTION PENSION PLAN; KEOGH PENSION PLAN; INDIVIDUAL RETIREMENT ACCOUNT.

pension plan funding: group deposit administration annuity A pension plan funding in which employer contributions are deposited to earn interest. At employee retirement, an IMMEDIATE ANNUITY is bought for the employee. The benefit is computed by a formula.

pension plan funding: group immediate participation guaranteed (IPG) contract annuity A modified version of the PENSION PLAN FUNDING: GROUP DEPOSIT ADMINISTRATION ANNUITY under which the employer participates in the investment and expense experience of the plan. The investments may do well or poorly. Employer contributions earn interest. At retirement, an *immediate* annuity is purchased for the employee. The amount of benefit to be received will depend upon the benefit formula, investment experience, expenses, and mortality figures.

pension plan funding: group permanent contract An insurance policy whose value equals the benefits to be paid to plan participants (employees) at the normal retirement age. It is based on the following assumptions: (1) the rate of earnings remains the same until retirement; (2) the contributions made are adequate to meet potential benefits. As employee wages increase, the contribution is similarly increased.

pension plan funding: individual contract pension plan An employee retirement plan in which the benefit is tied to current earnings, assuming they will remain the same until the normal retirement age. As employee wages increase, additional contracts are bought. The retirement benefits will depend on the benefit formula and the UNDERWRITER'S investment experience.

people planning
1. Career planning for an individual based upon his or her aptitudes, education skills, and personality. For example, a person may be best suited to become an attorney because of excellent analytical ability, aggressive personality, and oral communication skills.
2. Estate planning that gives major emphasis to the satisfaction of human needs, including the financial and psychological needs of others. Dependents with health problems, for example, are considered because they may be unable to manage funds themselves.

per capita Per person. For example, the per capita INCOME of the United States is arrived at by dividing the entire population by the total personal income of everyone in the country including children and others who do not earn any INCOME at all.

percent of monthly gross income rule A rule of thumb that a lender uses to determine a borrower's housing affordability. The rule says that a borrower's monthly mortgage payment, PROPERTY TAXES, and INSURANCE should not exceed 25% of his or her family's monthly GROSS INCOME (or about 35% for a FEDERAL HOUSING

ADMINISTRATION (FHA) or VETERANS ADMINISTRATION (VA) MORTGAGE.) For example, if a borrower and spouse have a gross income of $60,000 ($5,000 a month), under the above rule, their monthly mortgage payment, property taxes, and insurance should not exceed 25% of $5,000, or $1,250

See also HOUSING AFFORDABILITY INDEX; 35-PERCENT RULE.

percentage order An order placed with a broker to buy or sell a given number of shares after a certain volume of these shares has been executed, typically for one trading day. It may take the form of a MARKET ORDER or LIMIT ORDER.

per diem Per day. The term is used most frequently in connection with payment by the day for work done. As an example, an accountant may work on a PER DIEM basis for a CPA firm.

per stirpes A form of distribution that occurs when an individual dies INTESTATE. Under a per stirpes distribution, the ESTATE is divided by the children of the deceased and by their children. For example, if a wife dies intestate, having survived her husband, and there were four children resulting from the union, one of whom predeceased his mother after having two children of his own, the estate would be divided in such a way that the three surviving children would each receive one-fourth of the estate, while the two children of the deceased fourth child would each receive one-eighth of the estate.

performance (go-go) fund A MUTUAL FUND that emphasizes performance as measured by the total return earned on the shareholders' investments. The investment strategies of the fund are highly speculative.

performance stock Or, *growth stock*. A stock with solid growth potential that is expected to outperform in price the average security in the short term. These stocks typically pay few or no dividends in order to reinvest the earnings for future growth. A performance stock may include a speculative security.

peril In insurance, a condition or situation that may result in future damages or loss. There may be exposure to harm or injury. An individual is sometimes warned to "proceed at your own risk."

period certain annuity An ANNUITY that guarantees payments to the ANNUITANT—or a beneficiary if the annuitant should die early—for a fixed time period.

periodic payment plan A plan to accumulate funds in a MUTUAL FUND by making periodic investments on a regular basis (e.g., monthly, quarterly) over a specified period of time (e.g., 5 years). The participants benefit from DOLLAR COST AVERAGING.

periodic purchase deferred contract An annuity contract providing for constant dollar amount payments, referred to as premiums, on a periodic basis (e.g., monthly). The annuitant specifies when payments are to start. The agreement can be either variable or fixed.

permanent life insurance *See* WHOLE LIFE INSURANCE.

perpetual annuity A contract, sold by insurance companies, that pay a monthly income to the BENEFICIARY indefinitely.

perpetual bond
1. A BOND not having a maturity date. The bond may be redeemed by the investor only when the issuing company is liquidated. The bond pays interest indefinitely.
2. A bond with such a long life that it is considered PERPETUAL.

perpetual warrant A WARRANT without an expiration date to purchase a given number of shares of stock at a specified price.

perpetuity An ANNUITY that goes on indefinitely. An example of a perpetuity is PREFERRED STOCK that yields a constant dollar DIVIDEND indefinitely.

perquisite (perk) A FRINGE BENEFIT given to an employee in addition to salary. Examples are medical and dental benefits, pension contributions, and use of company cars.

personal and dependency exemption In taxation, a deduction allowed per person in computing taxable income. However, no exemption is allowed for an individual who can be claimed as a dependent on another taxpayer's return. The number of exemptions appears on IRS Form 1040, line 6.

personal article floater (PAF) policy An insurance policy providing blanket comprehensive coverage for virtually all of the insured's personal property.

personal assets Or, *personal estate.*

1. All the personal property and other ASSETS an individual has in his or her ESTATE.

2. All of one's property used exclusively for personal purposes.

personal auto policy (PAP) An auto insurance policy designed for an individual driver. It is somewhat more limited in coverage than the family auto policy.

personal exemption In INCOME TAX, the amount an individual can exclude from personal INCOME. In 1991, the personal exemption was $2,150 per individual. Additional taxpayer exemptions can be claimed for being over the age of 65, blindness, and having additional qualified dependents.

personal financial planning A process for arriving at comprehensive solutions to an individual's personal, business, and financial problems and concerns. It therefore involves the development and implementation of total, coordinated plans for the achievement of one's overall financial objectives. Each person will have different financial objectives depending on individual circumstances, goals, attitudes, and needs but the total objectives of most people can be classified as follows:

1. Protection against financial loss from personal risks such as death, disability, or unemployment
2. Capital accumulation for emergencies
3. Provision for retirement income
4. Reduction of taxes
5. ESTATE PLANNING
6. Investment and property management

Personal financial planning covers a wide variety of financial services and products:

1. TAX PLANNING and management
2. INVESTMENTS
3. INSURANCE
4. RETIREMENT PLANNING
5. Estate planning

Our economic growth, the tax structure, and the changes that have taken place in our social framework have created complexity in financial planning. The following events should be noted:

- Increasingly complex tax laws
- A complex economy and proliferation of available financial products
- Difficulty of saving for retirement
- Higher income tax brackets for most middle-class individuals
- Inflationary pressures creating artificial increases in income and losses in PURCHASING POWER

Most people are not trained to deal with these complex factors. FINANCIAL PLANNING has emerged as an important new profession in recent years. Personal financial planning can help find ways to ensure a client's secure financial future.

personal financial planning software Computer software that helps the user arrive at comprehensive solutions for an individual's personal finance, business, and financial problems and concerns. The software can assist in examining income and expenses, comparing actual to budget expenditures, monitoring assets and debts, analyzing goals, and investment, tax, and retirement planning. Examples of popular software are *Dollars and Sense, Financial Independence,* and *Managing Your Money.*

See also PERSONAL FINANCIAL PLANNING; MONEY MANAGEMENT SOFTWARE.

personal financial statements Personal financial statements prepared for an individual or family to show financial health. Some uses of the statements include computation of net worth, obtaining credit, retirement planning, estate planning, and tax planning.

In the balance sheet, assets are reflected at their estimated current values and are listed in the order of liquidity (maturity). Current value may be determined based on recent transactions of similar items and appraisals. In determining current value of assets, a deduction should be made for relevant selling costs.

Investments should be shown by major category, such as real estate. Significant investments in a sole proprietorship or partnership should be segregated. For example, a significant interest in a closely held business should be shown separately from the equity investment in other companies. If assets are jointly owned, only the individual's beneficial interest should be reported.

Asset valuation guidelines exist. Marketable securities, including stocks and bonds, should be recorded at current quoted market prices. If a stock is not traded on the financial statement date, the bid price should preferably be used. Precious metals should be shown at current value. Life insurance should be reported at cash surrender value after subtracting any loans against it. The current balance in pension plans should be listed. Also included are the current value of vested benefits in company profit-sharing plans. The investment in a closely held business can be valued by a qualified appraiser. Real estate should be valued at anticipated selling price using a licensed appraiser's report. Personal property should be valued at appraised value derived from a specialist's opinion or reference to a guide indicating valuation of personal items (e.g., blue book for auto values). A great deal of time need not be spent estimating the value of household items, since an approximation is typically adequate. A listing of assets may take the following form:

asset description current value percentage of total assets

Liabilities are reported at current value by payment date, without distinction between current and noncurrent. Personal, investment, and business liabilities should be listed separately. The current balance of the mortgage should be listed. Loans for business or investment purposes, including margin accounts, should be listed.

Income taxes are estimated on the difference between assets and liabilities. Taxes are based *as if* assets have been sold. In making tax estimates, the effect of prior year's unpaid tax obligations and the current year's estimates should be considered. Also note withholding tax payments.

Example: You own XYZ stock that was bought six years ago for $8,000. The stock is presently worth $17,000. You are in the 28% tax bracket. If you sold the stock today, there would be a $9,000 gain, which would result in $2,520 in taxes. The $2,520 should be included in the "provision for estimated taxes on the difference between carrying amounts and tax bases of assets and liabilities." As the $2,520 constitutes an amount of taxes that would be payable upon sale of the stock, it should be presented as a credit in the personal balance sheet because it reduces net worth.

An illustrative personal balance sheet follows:

YOUR PERSONAL BALANCE SHEET
DECEMBER 31, 19XX

Assets	
Cash	$5,000
Interest and dividends receivable	200
Marketable securities	10,000
Interest in closely held company	6,000
Cash surrender value of life insurance	1,000
Real estate	100,000
Personal property	30,000
Total Assets	$152,200

Liabilities

Credit cards	$6,000
Income taxes payable	2,520
Loans payable	10,000
Mortgage payable	60,000
Total Liabilities	$78,520
Estimated taxes on the differences between assets and liabilities	30,000
Total Liabilities and Tax Provision	$108,520
Net Worth	$43,680

personal identification number A number used by a customer to identify himself or herself to an AUTOMATIC TELLER MACHINE (ATM).

personal inflation rate The rise in prices for goods and services used by an individual based on his or her spending needs. This is distinguished from a general inflation rate experienced by all consumers, such as the CONSUMER PRICE INDEX.

personal injury protection insurance (PIP) A type of AUTOMOBILE INSURANCE coverage providing for personal injury protection in states with no-fault auto insurance. It includes medical expense and loss of income reimbursement without regard to fault of the driver.

personal insurance INSURANCE covering life or health risks for individuals.

personal liability
1. The amount one individual owes to another.
2. A legal exposure of one's personal ASSETS to the financial claims of another. For example, a sole proprietor has personal liability exposure for the business he or she is conducting for which personal liability insurance should be purchased.

personal limitations The personal constraints an individual has that may inhibit accomplishment of financial goals. For example, one may be restricted by education or health in becoming a millionaire.

personal property *See* PERSONAL ASSETS.

personal savings The earnings a person makes less his or her personal expenditures. Personal savings are invested, for example, in bank accounts, mutual funds, and stocks.

personal spending style The spending tastes of an individual. This varies, as people differ in habits, income, age, and other characteristics. Some prefer to live lavishly while others are modest in their expenditures.

physical damage insurance An INSURANCE POLICY covering the POLICYOWNER for any RISK that can result in physical damage to the INSURED object. For example, a comprehensive automobile INSURANCE POLICY normally covers physical damage to the automobile.
See also HOMEOWNER'S INSURANCE POLICY; PERSONAL AUTO POLICY (PAP); PROPERTY DAMAGE LIABILITY INSURANCE.

pickup bond A bond, with a high interest rate, that is nearing its callable date. In all probability, such a bond will be called since the issuer will want to issue new debt at the lower prevailing interest rates. An example is some of the high-yield municipal bonds, issued by New York City during the financial crisis, that were called.

pink sheets Pink sheets of paper giving daily price quotes on all OVER-THE-COUNTER stocks not shown in the NATIONAL ASSOCIATION OF SECURITIES DEALERS AUTOMATED QUOTATION SYSTEM (NASDAQ). The pink sheets are printed by the National Quotations Bureau, giving the last bid and asked prices of the stock as well as its trading symbol. A list of BROKERS who are the marketmakers in the STOCK is also given. These brokers can be contacted by STOCKBROKERS for further information, including the BOOK SIZE.

PITI Short for "PRINCIPAL, INTEREST, TAXES, AND INSURANCE," the components of many monthly mortgage loan payments.

placement
1. The sale of a new issue of securities to the public or in private.

2. Obtaining a job.

See also PLACEMENT AGENCY.

placement agency A business that places prospective employees with an employer for a fee. An example is Robert Half.

plaintiff An individual bringing a legal action against a defendant. The plaintiff seeks relief from the court against a defendant.

plan document A formal, written, legal statement, often contained in a booklet, stating the provisions of an employee benefit insurance program.

plan participants The employees covered by an insurance or pension plan.

plan sponsor The group offering an insurance or pension program, such as an employer or labor union.

planning An individual deciding upon what has to be accomplished to reach personal goals in an efficient and effective way by proper allocation of his or her talents and time. For example, an individual will have to plan saving and spending properly to have a desired amount at retirement.

play on gold An investment in gold made indirectly by buying the common stock of companies mining gold or investing in a closed-end mutual fund that buys shares in gold mining companies. Changes in the market prices of gold mining stocks are closely correlated to changes in the price of gold.

pledging An individual giving assets to a creditor as COLLATERAL for debt. Although the individual retains title, the creditor has physical possession of the property. When the debt is paid, the creditor releases the property to the debtor.

pocket money MONEY found in one's pocket. A small amount of money an individual has allotted for personal purposes including personal pleasures. Pocket money is not critical to the financial well-being of the individual, and is not considered a vital ASSET.

point
securities:
1. In the case of shares of STOCK, a point means $1. For example, if Xerox shares rise 2 points, each share has risen $2.
2. In the case of BONDS, a point means $10, since a bond is quoted as a percentage of $1,000. A bond that rises 2 points gains 2% of $1,000 or $20 in value.
3. In the case of MARKET AVERAGES, the word point means merely that and no more. It is not equivalent to any fixed sum of money.
banking: A loan service fee; each point equals 1% of the amount of the total MORTGAGE LOAN, which must be paid in full when a home is bought. It is a one-time, immediate charge that increases the effective cost of borrowing. Example: $50,000 × .01 = $500. Costs can be added to the mortgage and paid over the lifetime of the contract.

point-and-figure chart A chart used in technical security analysis using Xs to mark an upward movement in the price of security and a series of Os to mark downward price movements. A point-and-figure chart is not time bound and is used solely to mark price movements in a security for the purpose of understanding a basic price pattern over time.

point of sale (POS) terminal A computer-controlled price scanner that reads bar codes imprinted on goods. The POS is linked to a data base containing all the prices corresponding to the bar codes on the goods being scanned; these prices are entered in a cash register. The POS facilitates reading and registering prices, increasing accuracy, maintaining inventory levels, triggering reorders at predetermined inventory levels, and maintaining an accurate record of all transactions.

points
mortgage: An additional cost a LENDER adds to the basic MORTGAGE charges. Each point repre-

sents 1% of the face value of the mortgage loan. Points are charged for governmentally backed FHA and VA loans as well as private loans. The points are charges the lender receives "up front." Essentially, each point the lender charges is the same as deducting an equivalent percentage point from the face value of the MORTGAGE itself, although the mortgagor is still responsible for the entire mortgage. Thus, the mortgage is DISCOUNTED by the mortgagee.

The effect of a 10-point charge on a 30-year, $60,000 conventional mortgage is illustrated below.

Points are competitive among mortgagees, and potential mortgagors should do comparison shopping to obtain the best rate. Points tend to increase when there is a high demand for mortgage money.

In mortgages, points are considered INTEREST, as they are a percentage of the face value of the mortgage. Therefore, under most interpretations of the INTERNAL REVENUE SERVICE Tax Law, they are considered TAX DEDUCTIBLE for the homeowner if they are charged in conjunction with the purchase of a principal residence.

bonds: In BONDS, one point represents 1% in the FACE VALUE price of a $1,000 BOND. Thus, a point change would represent $10. Bond prices are quoted in points. A bond price of 80 is $800, and a five-point increase would be $50 for a total of $850.

stocks: In STOCKS, a point is a change of $1.00 in the market price of a stock. If a stock declines two points, it is a decline of $2.00 in MARKET VALUE per SHARE.

policy
procedures: A specific course of predetermined procedures. Policies are rules and regulations to be followed in certain specific events. For example, a parent may develop a policy that a child can watch television only after all homework is finished.
insurance: In INSURANCE, a written agreement that defines COVERAGE against specified perils and the limits of that coverage.

policy adjustment
procedures: Any change in a set of procedures to accommodate new or unexpected developments. For example, a small business owner may change the policy of a business to conform to a new government regulation requiring greater disclosure to the consumer.
insurance: An adjustment in the terms of an INSURANCE POLICY to adjust for new COVERAGES or INSUREDS. For example, an insured may seek additional coverage that will require an adjustment in both the coverage and the premium.

policy limit In INSURANCE, the limit of COVERAGE of a policy.

policy loan In INSURANCE, the amount a POLICYHOLDER of a LIFE INSURANCE POLICY can borrow at INTEREST against the CASH SURRENDER VALUE. If the interest is not paid, it is deducted from the cash surrender value of the policy. If the policyowner dies the DEATH BENEFIT is adjusted by any outstanding LOANS or unpaid interest payments. If the cash value of the POLICY is exhausted through loans, the policy ceases.

The POLICYOWNER may repay the interest or the loan at any time, or may continue the loan,

MORTGAGE PAYMENTS + POINTS

Principal	Interest Rate	Years	Monthly Payment	Total Payments	Total Interest
$60,000.00	10.00%	30	$526.54	$189,555.46	$129,555.46
10 Points				$6,000.00	
Total Payments + Points				$195,555.46	

as long as the interest and the loan do not exceed the cash value of the life insurance policy.

The amount of MONEY available to the policyowner depends on the length of time the policy has been held and its cash surrender value. More recent life insurance policies charge MARKET RATES OF INTEREST for their loans; however, earlier policies often charged below market interest rates on their loans.

policyholder/policyowner   An individual who owns an INSURANCE POLICY.

portability   In pensions, the ability of a PENSION holder to transfer the pension benefit credits from one employer to another.

portfolio   A holding of various investment vehicles to reduce risk by DIVERSIFICATION. A portfolio may contain BONDS, PREFERRED STOCKS, COMMON STOCKS of various types of businesses, and other investment instruments.
See also ASSET ALLOCATION.

portfolio diversification   The process of selecting alternative investment instruments that have dissimilar RISK-RETURN characteristics. This concept provides a lower but acceptable overall potential return.
See also ASSET ALLOCATION; PORTFOLIO.

portfolio manager   A professional responsible for the management of a PORTFOLIO of various investment vehicles on behalf of an individual or institutional investor. A portfolio manager may work for a MUTUAL FUND, PENSION FUND, PROFIT-SHARING PLAN, bank trust department, or insurance company, as well as private investors. For a fee, the manager has the FIDUCIARY RESPONSIBILITY to manage the investment assets prudently and make sure the funds grow as much as possible for a given amount of RISK.

position
employment: The job one holds in an employment situation. Positions carry with them responsibilities, compensation, and benefits.
securities: The number of SHARES or BONDS purchased in a SECURITY. For example, the number of shares will determine the EQUITY ownership one has in a particular company and any voting rights to which the SHAREHOLDER might be entitled.

positive carry   Or, *positive spread*. A situation in which the interest cost to borrow money for investment is less than the rate of return on that investment. For example, if a 12% loan is taken out in order to buy a bond yielding 15%, there is a positive carry.
See also NEGATIVE LEVERAGE; POSITIVE LEVERAGE.

positive leverage   When borrowed funds cost less than the return earned on those funds. It is using other people's money to make money.
See also LEVERAGE; LEVERAGE IN REAL ESTATE INVESTING.

positive yield curve   A condition in which the interest rates on long-term debt securities are higher than the interest rates on short-term debt securities of similar quality. This is typical, as an investor usually receives a higher interest rate when investing in long-term debt securities because of the longer time period involved, which results in greater uncertainty and risk. For example, the yield curve is positive when the interest rate on 30-year Treasury bonds is higher than the interest rate on 6-month Treasury bills.
See also NEGATIVE YIELD CURVE.

possession by adverse possession   A means of acquiring TITLE to REAL ESTATE whereby an occupant has been in actual, open, exclusive, and continuous occupancy of property under a claim of right for a period required by law. For example, Ms. Smith acquired title to the property where she lived, although she had no official DEED, because she had lived there all her life and the actual owner was unknown.

postdated check   A CHECK made out for a date sometime in the future. This check cannot be cashed prior to the date indicated. Postdated checks are often made to provide for the delivery of future funds intended to cover the check.

postponing income   Request of an employer or client to postpone sending a payment for services until a later date, often done to postpone the payment of taxes until a later year. For example, a consultant may ask a client to send in a check in January 19X8 for services performed in October 19X7. In this way, the consultant may not have to pay tax on that income until April 15, 19X9, when the 19X8 tax return must be filed—unless the individual files a 1040 ES, which is paid quarterly. NOTE: Most individuals are on a cash basis so income is recognized when cash is received even though the services were performed in a prior year.

power of acceptance An offeree's ability to create a binding contract by agreeing to the terms of an offer and giving appropriate consideration. Consideration may take the form of making a down payment or agreeing to render future services.

power of appointment Authority given to an individual to sell or otherwise dispose of the property of another, or of an interest therein.

power of attorney A legally executed and witnessed document giving another the power to act as one's attorney or agent in handling all personal affairs. The power may be general or specific. The power of attorney is revoked upon the death of the principal.

power of invasion A provision in a trust agreement permitting the TRUSTEE or BENEFICIARY the right to sell part of the estate principal and make payment therefrom to the BENEFICIARY.

preauthorized payment
banking: An automatic transfer of funds, usually done electronically, to the lenders to make payment on a loan to a third party. A contractual agreement specifies the amount to be debited and the date the funds are to be transferred. Payments to third party creditors may also be made by preauthorized check.
employment: A payment that has been approved in advance. For example, an employer may have already given permission to an employee to incur business-related expenses for

which he or she will automatically be reimbursed.

precious metals Valuable commodities, such as gold and silver, representing a private store of value. Precious metals are a liquid asset, have international markets, and serve as inflation hedges, but they may experience instability in price. The prices usually rise in difficult times and decline in stable ones. There is no periodic tax, such as with real estate. Tax is paid when the precious metals are sold at a gain. The disadvantages to ownership of precious metals are the high transaction cost, high storage costs, and lack of periodic income.

precompute An INSTALLMENT LENDING practice in which either the total annual interest is subtracted from the maturity value of the loan to determine the proceeds to be received, or the total annual interest is added to the amount to be paid back in equal installments. In either instance, the effective interest rate exceeds the stated interest rate. The effective interest rate must be disclosed to the borrower under the "truth-in-lending" statutes.

preemptive right The right of a current stockholder to maintain his or her percentage ownership interest in the firm by buying new shares on a proportionate basis before they are issued to the public. In some cases, the new shares may be bought at a lower price than the prevailing market price. Further, brokerage commissions are avoided. For example, if a person owns 1% of a company's shares and there is a new issue of 10,000 shares, that individual is permitted to buy 100 shares.

preexisting condition In insurance, a condition already in existence at the date an insurance policy is issued and that is typically excluded from coverage under that policy. However, some policies may waive exclusion from coverage of that item after a period of time has elapsed. For example, a medical insurance policy may exclude coverage for a preexisting thyroid problem.

preferred provider organization (PPO) A group of medical providers (doctors, hospitals, etc.) who contract with a HEALTH INSURANCE company to provide services at a discount to policyholders if the policyholders choose to be served by PPO members.

preferred stock A HYBRID SECURITY that possesses features of both COMMON STOCK and a corporate BOND. It is like COMMON STOCK in the following ways:

- It represents EQUITY ownership and is issued without stated maturity dates.
- It pays DIVIDENDS.

Preferred stock is also like a corporate bond in some ways:

- It provides for prior claims on earnings and assets.
- Its dividend is fixed for the life of the issue.
- It can carry CALL and CONVERTIBLE features and SINKING FUND provisions.

If preferred stocks are listed on the organized exchanges, they are reported in the same sections as common stocks in newspapers. The symbol "pf" appears after the name of the corporation, designating the issue as preferred. Preferred stocks are read the same way as common stock quotations. The issues are listed in MOODY'S *Bond Record* and rated by STANDARD & POOR'S and Moody's.
See also PREFERRED STOCK RATINGS.

preferred stock fund A MUTUAL FUND that invests in PREFERRED STOCK with the emphasis on income rather than growth.

preferred stock ratings Like BOND RATINGS, ratings given by STANDARD & POOR'S and MOODY'S for the investment quality of PREFERRED STOCKS. S&P uses basically the same rating system as they do with bonds, except that triple A ratings are not given to preferred stocks. Moody's uses a slightly different system, which is given below. These ratings are intended to provide an indication of the quality of the issue and are based largely on an assessment of the firm's ability to pay preferred dividends in a prompt and timely fashion. Note, however, that preferred stock ratings should not be compared with bond ratings as they are not equivalent.

MOODY'S PREFERRED STOCK RATING SYSTEM

Rating Symbol	Definition
aaa	Top quality
aa	High grade
a	Upper-medium grade
baa	Lower-medium grade
ba	Speculative type
b	Little assurance of future dividends
caa	Likely to be already in arrears

See also BOND RATINGS.

preliminary prospectus Or, *red herring.* The initial document, prepared by an UNDERWRITER for a new issue of securities, that is read by potential investors. Although financial data are provided about the company, they are not in as much detail as will be provided in the final prospectus. Information in the preliminary prospectus may also be changed when the final prospectus is issued.

premium
1. The purchase price of a BOND or preferred issue higher than the PAR or FACE VALUE.
2. Purchasing or selling price of an OPTION contract.
3. The periodic fee paid for INSURANCE protection.
4. Promotion item given away in a marketing campaign.
5. Extra payment made for incentive purposes.
6. Amount in excess of MARKET VALUE of an entity in a TENDER OFFER.

premium adjustment endorsement A clause in an insurance contract stating that the initial premium' may be modified during the insured period or when coverage elapses based on the actual loss experience of the insured.

premium loan Money borrowed against the cash value of a life insurance policy to pay the premium due.

premium mode The specified timing of premium payments, such as monthly.

premium pay Extra compensation to an employee for working at undesirable times or in unfavorable working conditions.

prenuptial contract An agreement entered into by those contemplating marriage. The intention and purpose of a prenuptial contract is to secure all property and possessions of either or both parties to the proposed marriage for themselves or their heirs. For example, Donald Trump and his wife signed several prenuptial contracts in an effort to secure his possessions.

prepaid interest
interest that an individual has paid prior to its being actually incurred. An example is one year's interest that a BORROWER agrees to pay in advance to a bank on a loan. This is a rare occurrence. In a personal BALANCE SHEET, prepaid interest is shown as an ASSET.

prepayment Payment made prior to the receipt of merchandise or services. The payment of an obligation prior to its maturity date. INSURANCE POLICIES often have a prepayment feature for their COVERAGE.
See also DUE DATE.

prepayment fee A charge imposed on the remaining PRINCIPAL, often found in MORTGAGES, when a DEBT or other obligation is paid in advance of its due date. By illustration, Sam Smith gets a $75,000 mortgage at 10% to purchase a home having a 5% prepayment fee. If he pays the MORTGAGE immediately, he will have to pay $3,750 ($75,000 × 5%) as a prepayment fee.

prepayment of loan clause A clause that allows a lender to charge the borrower a penalty for repaying a loan before its due date (prepaying).
See also CALL FEATURE.

prepayment penalty A penalty charge levied by a lender when a borrower repays a loan before a specified time.

prepayment privilege A provision in a financing agreement that allows the debtor to pay more than the required monthly amount and to pay the loan off early without PREPAYMENT PENALTY.
See also PREPAYMENT OF LOAN CLAUSE.

prepayment terms The terms of CREDIT specifying conditions that apply when a loan is repaid prior to the maturity date.

present value The current worth of a future sum or stream—ANNUITY or mixed—of dollars discounted at a specified rate. The process of finding present value is the inverse of finding FUTURE VALUE (the COMPOUNDING process).
See also TIME VALUE OF MONEY.

present value analysis A method of valuing securities such as STOCKS, BONDS, and REAL ESTATE that determines the discounted PRESENT VALUE of an anticipated stream of earnings, including DIVIDENDS, interest income, rental income, and future CAPITAL GAINS.
See also DISCOUNTED CASH FLOW; TIME VALUE OF MONEY.

present value method *See* PRESENT VALUE ANALYSIS.

present value tables Precalculated tables that provide the PRESENT VALUES of $1 or an ANNUITY of $1 for various periods and at various discount rates. They are found in Appendix A, Table 3 and Table 4, respectively.
See also TIME VALUE OF MONEY.

preshopping research Before buying merchandise, an individual compares different products and prices among stores so as to make the best purchase decision.

presumptive disability The assumption of total disability when an insured loses hearing, sight, speech, or a limb. If such occurs to an insured under a disability insurance policy, the insurer typically assumes the person is disabled, even if he or she goes back to work. Depending upon the policy, the insurer may pay periodic monthly payments or a lump-sum amount.

pretax earnings The NET INCOME of a company or individual prior to the payment of TAXES. NET INCOME is gross earnings less expenses.

preventive maintenance Any type of maintenance procedures performed on an object for the purpose of preventing future repairs and providing for a longer useful life. For example, most automobile manufacturers recommend changing the oil in a car after every three to five thousand miles of use.

previous balance method A CREDIT CARD billing method that bases interest charges on the amount owed on the final billing date of the previous month with no payments or credits deducted. This is the most expensive for the customer because interest is computed on the outstanding balance at the beginning of the period.

For example, assume that the monthly interest rate is 1.5%, which represents an annual rate of 18%. The previous balance is $400 and the payment was made on the 15th day of the month. The finance charges under this method are computed as shown below:

$$\$400 \times 1.5\% = \$6.00$$

See also ADJUSTED BALANCE METHOD; AVERAGE DAILY BALANCE METHOD; PAST DUE BALANCE METHOD.

price adjustment Any change made in the price of a service or good to compensate for some modification. For example, a piece of merchandise that has been used as a display item, and which has been handled by consumers, may have a price adjustment made to it for wear and tear. Here, the consumer may get a bargain.

price charge
in general: The amount of money charged or paid for a good or service. Normally, prices are charged in CASH; however, in BARTER systems the price can be charged in equivalent units.
accounting: The amount of MONEY paid for a good or service charged to a specific ACCOUNT.

price gap In securities, a price gap is the difference between the opening price of a STOCK and its previous closing price. For example, if a stock closed at the end of a trading day at $25 per share and opened the next day at $30 per share, there would be a $5 price gap. A price gap is considered significant for TECHNICAL ANALYSIS because it signifies an OVERBOUGHT or OVERSOLD condition.

price indices Various price indices that are used to measure living costs, price-level changes, and INFLATION.
consumer price index (CPI): The CPI measures the cost of a fixed bundle of goods (some 400 consumer goods and services) representative of the purchases of the typical working-class urban family. The fixed basket is divided into the following categories: food and beverages, housing, apparel, transportation, medical care, entertainment, and other. Generally referred to as a "cost-of-living index," it is published by the Bureau of Labor Statistics of the U.S. Department of Labor. The CPI is widely used for escalation clauses. The last base year for calculating the CPI index was 1982–1984 at which time it was assigned 100.
producer price index (PPI): Like the CPI, the PPI is a measure of the cost of a given basket of goods priced in wholesale markets, including raw materials, semifinished goods, and finished goods. The PPI is published monthly by the Bureau of Labor Statistics of the Department of Commerce. The PPI signals changes in the general price level, or the CPI, some time before they actually materialize. (Since the PPI does not include services, caution should be exercised when the principal cause of inflation is service prices). For this reason, the PPI and especially some of its subindices, such as the index of sensitive materials, serve as certain

leading indicators that are closely watched by policy makers.

GNP deflator (implicit price index): The GNP deflator is a weighted average of the price indices used to deflate the components of GNP. Thus, it reflects price changes for goods and services bought by consumers, businesses, and governments. The GNP deflator is found by dividing current GNP in a given year by constant (real) GNP. Because it covers a broader group of goods and services than the CPI and PPI, the GNP deflator is a very widely used price index that is frequently used to measure inflation. The GNP deflator, unlike the CPI and PPI, is available only quarterly—not monthly. It is also published by the U.S. Department of Commerce. *See also* ECONOMIC INDICATORS; INDEXATION; INDEX OF LEADING INDICATORS.

price range In investments, the high and low price of a security over a time period. In newspaper quotations, the high and low price is stated for the past year. Generally, the INVESTOR has a better chance for price APPRECIATION when the security is purchased near the bottom of its price range than the top. However, INVESTMENT fundamentals such as the company's earnings and overall economic and MARKET conditions have to be assessed as well.

price spread

1. In investments, the variation between the BID and ASKED PRICES of a security. Generally, those securities trading with heavy volume have narrow spreads, whereas those with relatively low trading volume have wider price spreads.

2. The instantaneous buying and selling of OPTIONS for the identical security but at varying striking prices. By purchasing the option with the lower strike price, the investor can COLLATERALIZE that by selling the option on the same security at the higher STRIKE PRICE.

primary beneficiary

insurance: The individual identified as the principal BENEFICIARY(ies) of an INSURANCE POLICY. Secondary beneficiaries may also be nominated in the event the primary beneficiary(ies) predecease the POLICYHOLDER.

pension: The person or persons designated as the principal beneficiary(ies) to a PENSION PLAN. Secondary beneficiaries may also be nominated in the event the primary beneficiary(ies) predecease the pension holder.

trust: The individual(s) designated to receive the immediate benefits of a TRUST at the time of a DISTRIBUTION. Secondary beneficiaries may also be nominated in the event the primary beneficiary(ies) predecease the trust distribution. *See also* PER STIRPES.

primary market A market that trades new issues of securities, as distinguished from the SECONDARY MARKET, where securities of old issues are traded. The term also applies to auctions of government securities such as Treasury bills. *See also* FOURTH MARKET; THIRD MARKET.

prime interest rate The interest rate charged by banks on short-term commercial loans to their most financially sound borrowers. It is the lowest possible interest rate charged by banks to corporate borrowers. Commercial loans are often at an interest rate of prime plus a spread.

principal

1. The face amount of a FINANCIAL INSTRUMENT such as a NOTE or BOND. For example, a $10,000, 9% one-year bond has a CAPITAL portion of $10,000 and an INTEREST portion of $900.

2. An amount put at RISK in an INVESTMENT.

3. An individual for whom another serves as an AGENT.

4. In a transaction, the primary person bearing full financial liability.

5. The owner of a business.

6. An associate in a professional PARTNERSHIP.

7. A DEALER in a security who makes transactions for his or her own ACCOUNT.

principal amount The sum upon which INTEREST computations may be made in a debt or

business INVESTMENT. The FACE VALUE of a NOTE or BOND.
See also PRINCIPAL.

principal (on an annuity) The amount paid by an ANNUITANT or person buying the annuity during the accumulation period.

principle of indemnity An insurance rule stating that an insured may not be reimbursed for loss at an amount above the fair market value of the loss incurred.

prior preferred stock Or, *preference preferred shares.* PREFERRED STOCK coming before other issues of preferred stock in payment of dividends and distribution in bankruptcy.

private limited partnership An unregistered partnership with the Securities and Exchange Commission that cannot have more than 35 limited partners. This partnership may hold real estate, oil and gas properties, and other ventures. Some are structured to emphasize income and capital appreciation while others are directed toward obtaining tax breaks.

private mortgage insurance (PMI) INSURANCE for lenders that insures them against loss on certain mortgages, in case of default. There are typically low DOWN PAYMENTS. It is a policy that a home buyer can get from a private lender to qualify for a down payment of less than 20%. In such a case, the borrower pays the PREMIUMS.

private offering When securities are issued for the first time by the company itself, thus bypassing an INVESTMENT BANKER. Such an offering may be made directly to current shareholders, executives, or large institutions (e.g., insurance companies, banks).

private placement The issuing of equity and debt securities directly to either one or a few large investors by a company or other entity. The large investors may be financial institutions such as insurance companies, commercial banks, and pension plans. Advantages to the issuing company of a private placement are smaller flotation cost, avoidance of SEC filing requirements, and faster acquisition of funds. The disadvantages of a private placement are limited market and possible restrictions placed on the company by institutions.

privileged communication A confidential relationship between parties that legally permits the recipient of the information to withhold disclosure of it. An example is communications between attorney and client. There is no such common law relationship between CPA and client. However, some states have passed laws recognizing this relationship.

probability The possibility that something will occur or has occurred. For example, the probability of an employee's getting a raise of 10% or more may be 75%.

probate A judicial procedure to test the authenticity and validity of an ESTATE, WILL, GUARDIANSHIP, or TRUST agreement.

probate estate *See* PROBATE.

proceeds
transaction: The funds received in a sale, LOAN, SECURITY offering, or any other financial transaction.
insurance: The net amount received from a LIFE INSURANCE policy.

producer price index (PPI) A measure of the cost of a given basket of goods priced in wholesale markets, including raw materials, semifinished goods, and finished goods. The PPI is published monthly by the Bureau of Labor Statistics of the Department of Commerce.
See also PRICE INDICES.

productivity The measured relationship between the quantity of output and the input. For example, labor productivity is the output of employees expressed in terms of the quantity produced per labor hour.

professional corporation A company established by professionals, including medical doctors, accountants, attorneys, and architects.

Although a professional corporation still has unlimited liability for malpractice, there are certain tax advantages to being treated as an S Corporation. A key tax benefit is the avoidance of double taxation since only personal tax is paid (not corporate tax) on the income. The professional corporation files Form 1120-S, which passes the income and the resulting tax onto the individual's Form 1040. Another important benefit is that greater contributions can be made to a pension plan.

professional liability insurance　An insurance policy taken out by a professional for malpractice coverage. The policy covers legal fees and possible damages. Medical doctors, accountants, and attorneys typically take out such policies.

profit-sharing plan　A plan instituted by a company in which employees receive a stipulated percentage of the profits of the firm. The terms of profit-sharing plans differ widely; however, there is usually a stated amount above which profit-sharing proceeds will be distributed, based on a predetermined formula.

In those periods when the company does not produce a qualified profit for the profit-sharing plan, there are no DISTRIBUTIONS to employees. The basic intent is provide an incentive to improve productivity as well as loyalty to the firm.

profit taking　In COMMODITY and SECURITY trading, the action of traders to realize profits. Profit taking is a depressant to MARKET prices.

program
n:　An organized system for completing objectives. For example, a company may develop and use a management development program for developing and improving its managerial staff.
v:　To arrange, classify, categorize, or systematize any area of concern, such as entertainment, music, management strategy, and governmental actions.
computers:　To produce a sequence of software instructions to be executed by the central processing unit of a computer to accomplish a particular objective action.

program trading　The term used to describe the use of computer software to generate security trading decisions. The software has built-in guidelines that instantaneously trigger buy and sell orders when differences in the prices of the securities are great enough to produce profit. Program trading is used by institutional investors, who place buy and sell orders in large blocks of ten thousand or more units. This type of large trade tends to have a significant impact on the prices of securities in the market. Sometimes, the program trading orders from a number of firms reach the trading floors. This impact can be seen most readily during what is called TRIPLE WITCHING HOUR. The triple witching hour occurs four times annually in the hour prior to the moment (4:15 P.M. EST, on the third Friday of March, June, September, and December) when STOCK OPTIONS, STOCK INDEX OPTIONS, and STOCK INDEX FUTURES all expire at once. During this hour, the DOW-JONES INDUSTRIAL AVERAGE and other indices have been known to change drastically. For example, there may be a drop of 2% to 5%, respectively, a steep decline in so short a time period. Fortunately, the market usually recovers within a week or so—but if an individual wanted to sell during one of these drops he or she could take an anticipated loss. For the small investor, it might be best to stay out of the market on the days immediately before the triple witching hour. On the other hand, the speculative investor might choose this as an opportune time to act.

progressive tax　A TAX designed to have higher rates for those in higher income brackets. The FEDERAL INCOME TAX is a form of a progressive tax. Thus, the 1990 federal income tax rate is as follows for a taxpayer whose filing status is single:

　15% on taxable income not exceeding $19,450
　28% on income more than $19,450 but not exceeding $47,050

33% on income more than $47,050 but not exceeding $97,620

In a progressive tax, the higher one's TAXABLE INCOME, the higher the PERCENTAGE OF TAXATION one will pay.

progressive tax rate structure *See* PROGRESSIVE TAX.

promissory note A written promise to pay a certain stated sum to an individual at a stated time, usually including INTEREST payments. If the NOTE promises to make payment on demand, then it is negotiable. It is also negotiable if it is a bearer PROMISSORY NOTE and it has matured.

The person who signs the note and promises to pay is the PAYOR, while the person to whom the note is assigned is the PAYEE.

proof of loss The supporting documentation of loss the insured must present to the insurance company to receive reimbursement under the policy. For example, life insurance proceeds will be paid only upon presentation to the insurance company of a death certificate. Loss reimbursement from an auto accident will be paid only upon presentation of a paid repair bill.

property damage liability insurance An INSURANCE policy that promises to pay all the legal obligations of the insured resulting from negligence in which damage to the property has been caused.

property damage liability losses Losses resulting from damage to or destruction of property.

property depreciation insurance Insurance coverage that provides for the replacement of damaged property, based on REPLACEMENT COST. Thus, the accumulated depreciation is not deducted in determining reimbursement under the policy.

property exposures The susceptibility of the property to damage or deterioration because of surrounding conditions. For example, a home on the water is vulnerable to flood damage.

property insurance INSURANCE that provides protection against losses resulting from the damage to or destruction of property (such as auto and home) or possessions. It is wise to carry such insurance to protect family assets and future income from a catastrophic event.

property inventory A listing of all ASSETS an individual owns, their cost, and their current MARKET VALUE. Individuals should maintain a current property inventory, including photographs, of all their personal ASSETS to provide documentation for insurance reimbursement for possible fire and theft losses. Such an inventory would also provide support of loss for tax purposes.

property management The operation of property as a business, such as managing an apartment building.

property owner An individual having the rights of ownership to specific property whether it is personal or real, tangible or intangible. For example, an author of a published work may retain royalty rights to any sales revenues resulting from the publisher's book sales.

property owner association agreement In REAL ESTATE, a contractual agreement of a group of property owners, often CONDOMINIUM owners, detailing their joint ownership duties and rights. Normally, the property owner association agreement permits members to approve new owners before a sale transaction can be completed, and provides the right to assess each association property owner for agreed upon building improvements or other expenses. For example, if the swimming pool in a condominium development develops a major leak requiring $100,000 in repairs and there are 50 property owner association members, the property owner's association will assess each association member $2,000 ($100,000/50) for the needed repairs.

property report In REAL ESTATE, a report required by the Interstate Land Sale Act for the sale of SUBDIVISIONS having 50 or more lots. It is filed with the Federal Department of Housing and Urban Development's Office of Interstate Land Sales Registration.

property tax   A TAX assessed on real property. A property tax is determined by its land use classification, ranging from rural farmland to heavy industry, improvements made on the property, its ASSESSED VALUATION, and the MILLAGE RATE.

The property tax is levied by various governmental jurisdictions including state governments (rarely used), county and local governments, special districts and authorities, and independent school districts.

Often the property tax is included in the property owner's monthly mortgage payment and therefore is an added cost to the monthly carrying charges for the property.

proportional tax   Or, *flat rate tax*.
income: A fixed-rate TAX based on INCOME irrespective of the amount of income.
property: A fixed-rate tax based on real or tangible property regardless of value.

prorating clause of disability insurance
Allows the insurer to increase the premiums if the insured changes to a more risky occupation.

prospectus   A circular, required by the Securities Act of 1933, that describes SECURITIES being offered for sale. Its purpose is FULL DISCLOSURE, especially of any adverse prospects for the issuer. It discloses facts regarding the issuer's operations, including the experience of its management, its financial status, any anticipated legal matters that could affect the company, and potential risks of investing in the corporation.

protective covenants
in general: A formal written, signed, and delivered agreement between two or more people to perform, or not perform, one or more specific actions.
deed covenant: In REAL ESTATE, an affirmation in a DEED that certain actions, or improvements, shall or shall not occur on a specific piece of property. Normally, such covenants provide for the use of the property, such as residential; control architectural and design standards; control the number of people living in a specific area; and prohibit certain practices, including the sale of alcoholic beverages. For example, a covenant may appear in a property deed that no dwelling shall be constructed having fewer than 3,500 square feet of living space on a property size less than two acres.
finance: An agreement, often in the form of an INDENTURE, restricting certain financial transactions. For example, a COVENANT may be agreed to in a LOAN agreement that an individual may not borrow any more money from another source against a specific piece of COLLATERALIZED property.

proxy   An authorization given by a stockholder of a company to another to vote for him or her at an election (e.g., board of directors) or for a corporate resolution. The transfer is restricted in duration and typically is only for a specific occasion.

proxy statement   A report, included by direction of the SECURITIES AND EXCHANGE COMMISSION with a PROXY solicitation, presenting to the STOCKHOLDERS information about to be voted on as well as giving the names and background of those individuals seeking election to a company's board of directors or other ruling body.

prudent investment   *See* PRUDENT MAN RULE.

prudent man rule   An investment norm. In some states, the law requires that a FIDUCIARY, such as a TRUSTEE, may invest the fund's money only in a list of securities, called the LEGAL LIST, designated by the municipality. A reasonable degree of safety and return is expected.

public debt   DEBT contracted by governments. Debt occurs when federal, state, or local public expenditures exceed revenues obtained from taxation. The federal public debt is, by far, the single largest public debt in the United States. As of 1990, the U.S. national debt exceeded three trillion dollars with INTEREST costs exceeding $175,000,000.

An individual may invest in federal, state, or local debt and typically obtain TAX-EXEMPT interest. For example, interest earned on U.S. Treasury securities is not taxed on the New York state tax return. Interest earned by a New York resident on New York municipal bonds is "triple tax free" from federal, state, and local taxation.

public limited partnership A LIMITED PARTNERSHIP registered with the Securities and Exchange Commission and available as an investment to the public through brokerage firms. Limited partnerships may be in real estate, oil and gas, and similar ventures.

public offering

1. Offering SECURITIES to investors at large after registration details have been filed with the SEC.

2. The sale of a LIMITED PARTNERSHIP. It is registered with the SEC and required to meet specified SEC restrictions.

public syndicate

in general: A group of two or more individuals or companies joining together for the purpose of implementing a project that is beyond their respective individual financial capabilities. A syndication agreement is agreed to whereby all profits or losses will be proportionately shared.

finance: A group of BANKS and/or UNDERWRITERS who join together for the purpose of underwriting a new public SECURITY offering. Upon the successful completion of the security offering, the public syndicate is disbanded.

real estate: A method of selling property whereby a syndicate sponsor, the syndicator, raises capital to purchase and/or develop property by selling SHARES to INVESTORS.

insurance: Groups of INSURERS join together to pool their financial resources to underwrite a risk larger than their respective individual financial abilities. This is more common among reinsurers than standard underwriters. Syndicate members agree on proportional shares of PREMIUMS, losses, EXPENSES, and profits.

puffery Exaggerated claims regarding the qualities of a property or an investment. Puffery is often used by a salesperson to convince a potential buyer to make a purchase. Puffery could be grounds for a misrepresentation lawsuit.

punitive damages Or, *exemplary damages.* Damages, awarded by a court of law to a plaintiff in an action, over and above the actual financial loss incurred by the plaintiff. Such damages are awarded by the court when wrong done by the defendant in the action was judged to be the result of malice, fraud, violence, or evil intent.

The concept of punitive damages is to set an example by punishing the defendant.

purchase agreement *See* CONTRACT OF SALE.

purchase and sale agreement (P&S) Any contract entered into in which there is a buyer and a seller who agree to exchange one thing for another.

purchase contract *See* CONTRACT OF SALE.

purchase loan CREDIT extended to a consumer to make a purchase. Purchase loans require the payment of INTEREST.
See also CONSUMER CREDIT; CONSUMER FINANCE COMPANY; CREDIT CARD; LOAN: MORTGAGE.

purchase-money mortgage A form of seller financing. It is a MORTGAGE LOAN from a seller in place of cash for the acquisition of REAL ESTATE. *See also* CREATIVE FINANCING.

purchasing power

1. The dollar amount of products and services an income can buy after adjusting for INFLATION. Purchasing power can be measured by comparing a price index (such as the CONSUMER PRICE INDEX) for a given base period to the one of the present period.

2. The amount of credit available to an investor in his or her margin account to buy more securities. For example, an investor with purchasing power of $10,000 in his or her brokerage

account can purchase $20,000 worth of securities under the 50% MARGIN REQUIREMENT.

purchasing power risk A RISK resulting from possible changes in price levels in the economy that can have a significant effect on the prices of securities.

pure play A securities term applying to a firm that has basically a single line of business. An investor finding that line of business attractive would be inclined to invest in the company. For example, Grumman Corporation would represent a pure play for a defense contractor. Merck and Company would constitute a pure play in pharmaceuticals.

pure risk Uncontrollable external RISKS to an individual from natural hazards relating to accidents, death, earthquakes, fire, weather, and related events. The occurrence of such events can have a serious negative impact on a business or individual, with serious emotional, financial, and physical consequences. Many pure risks and their losses are INSURABLE.

put The option to sell a given security at a strike (exercise) price within a specified time period. Each put is for 100 shares. A premium must be paid for the purchase of the option. Contracts on listed puts have standardized dates for periods of three, six, and nine months, although as these contracts approach expiration, they may be purchased with a significantly shorter life.

Assume the market price of a stock is $45 per share. A put is bought at an exercise price of $45. The cost of the put is $4, or a total of $400 ($4 × 100 shares). When the market price of the stock reaches $30, the put is exercised, realizing a profit of $15 per share, or a total of $1,500.

put bond A form of a BOND in which the purchaser has the option of redeeming the BOND back to the issuer prior to the MATURITY DATE and receiving the full FACE VALUE of the bond. The terms of such redemption vary; however, a redemption of a PUT BOND may be exercised only once during the life of the bond or at stated intervals. Because of the early redemption privilege, put bonds normally command a market PREMIUM.

put option
bonds: A BONDHOLDER's right to CASH in a BOND prior to maturity.
options: An OPTION to sell an underlying SECURITY at a stated price, the STRIKING PRICE, by a specified time, the EXPIRATION DATE. The absolute value of a put option is equal to the difference between its striking price and the underlying MARKET PRICE of the security. The market price of a put option is the difference between the striking price of a CALL or put option and the price at which the underlying security is trading plus any PREMIUM, unless the option is trading at a DISCOUNT prior to its expiration.

For example, a STOCK has a market price of $35. An INVESTOR acquires a put to sell 100 shares of stock at $35 per share. The cost of the put is $300 ($3 × 100 shares). At the EXPIRATION DATE of the put, the price of the stock drops to $15 a share. The investor therefore realizes a gain of $2,000 ($20 × 100 shares). The net gain before brokerage COMMISSIONS is $1,700 ($2,000 − $300).

Put options are purchased if the investor feels a security is going to drop in price or as a method of HEDGING a security investment against market RISK.
See also OPTION PREMIUM; OPTION PRICE.

pyramiding
in general: A method of building ASSETS by making extensive use of LEVERAGE. An example is buying real estate properties with low down payments.
business: A method of acquiring the assets of other corporations by leveraging one's original assets. A more recent variation of this methodology is the leveraged buyout or LBO. In principle, little or no original COLLATERAL is needed. All that is needed is CREDIT.

fraud: A method of escalating values built on fabricated assets. The most famous of these schemes occurred during the 1920s, perpetrated by Charles Ponzi, in which DIVIDENDS were paid to early INVESTORS out of the payments received from later investors. When no new investors joined the investment scheme, it collapsed.

securities: Using MARGIN BUYING to acquire conrol over a large number of SECURITIES. Using this strategy, the investor can earn huge returns on a relatively small investment, but has an equally large risk of loss if the market goes down.

qualification period In INSURANCE, an interim period of time during which the INSURED does not qualify for benefits in order to protect the INSURER from possible fraud or deception. While the qualification period exists, the INSURED will not obtain insured reimbursement for any harm that occurs. A qualification period is found in HEALTH INSURANCE and PENSION PLANS and must be stated in the policy.

qualified endorsement A signature on the back of a negotiable document such as a check transferring the funds to another party and including wording to restrict the endorser's legal obligation. For example, by writing "without endorsement," the endorser is not liable if the instrument is unpaid.

qualified pension plan *See* QUALIFIED PLAN OR TRUST.

qualified plan or trust A tax-deferred pension contribution plan under the 1954 INTERNAL REVENUE SERVICE rules by which the employer and employee contribute to a PENSION PLAN and shelter the employee's INCOME from TAXATION during the accumulation period of the plan. The employer's contribution is considered, within specified limits, an expense. The employee is not deemed to have received income until withdrawals occur at retirement. The purpose is to accumulate savings that will then be paid out and taxed upon RETIREMENT when the employee is probably earning a lower income and thus paying lower INCOME TAX rates.

qualified stock option plan Or, *incentive stock option*. An optional STOCK PURCHASE PLAN provided by public CORPORATIONS to their employees to buy the company's STOCK at below market prices during a specified option period. If the MARKET PRICE of the STOCK drops below the OPTION price, the option is canceled.

Under current tax law, if the stock price should decline below the market price, the company may offer a new stock option price to its employees. There is a $100,000 limit on the amount of stock that can be EXERCISED through a qualified stock option plan in any one year.

qualified terminable interest property (Q-TIP) trust A TRUST whereby all INCOME from the trust will go to the surviving spouse during his or her lifetime. The trust prohibits the transfer of the ASSETS to anyone else, but does provide for the surviving spouse to WILL the remaining assets to certain parties designated by the deceased spouse.

The basic strategy in a Q-TIP Trust is to designate only that portion of an estate's assets as direct property for the surviving spouse, permitting a pass-through of the remaining assets of the trust, upon the death of the surviving spouse, to other heirs, usually the children. The intent is to avoid ESTATE TAXES while giving the surviving spouse full enjoyment of all the income derived from the trust's ASSETS.

qualifying annuity An ANNUITY designed to be a part of a QUALIFIED PENSION PLAN; its PREMIUMS and earnings are TAX DEFERRED until the ANNUITANT retires.

quality of life   The conditions under which an individual lives. The quality of life is determined by several factors including proper housing, good diet, adequate exercise, being fit and healthy. One's level of INCOME is an important determinant of the quality of life one will enjoy.

quality-of-products legislation   Or, *lemon laws*. Legislation to protect consumers from the purchase of products of inferior quality. Most so-called lemon laws are state laws. The state of New York was one of the first to pass and implement such a law. It is directed primarily at automobile dealerships that do not repair newly purchased automobiles within the first five attempts at getting the repair done. After the fifth attempt, the law provides that the consumer must have a full REFUND for the price of the vehicle.

quality stock fund   A MUTUAL FUND that invests only in the stock of companies with a track record of strong performance.

quarters of coverage for social security   In order to qualify to receive SOCIAL SECURITY retirement benefits, an individual must have been paying into the system for forty quarters or ten years. Individuals born prior to the year 1933 may be required to have worked fewer quarters; however, this is being phased out, and all others will be required to contribute to the system for forty quarters. Total benefits are directly affected by total contributions and the age at which one retires. Retiring prior to age 65 will result in fewer benefits.

quasi-contract   A legal duty prescribed by law, rather than from a contract, that is directed at preventing the exploitation of one party over another. Its purpose is to assure fairness and justice. For example, if in repairing a malfunctioning motor in a refrigerator, the repairman also notices and repairs another related defective part in the cooling system, the repairman must be compensated for repairing the second part even though only the motor was contracted for. There is an implied quasi-contract to repair related parts to the motor so the unit will operate.

quid pro quo
in general: From the Latin meaning something in exchange for something else. Giving or performing something in exchange for something done for or received by an individual. For example, an individual expedites an order for another in return for getting first choice in selecting a desired item.
securities: A business arrangement whereby a SECURITIES firm will give business, usually in the form of TRADES, to another firm in exchange for receiving a service such as research. This type of a business arrangement is also termed SOFT DOLLARS.

quitclaim deed   A DEED that conveys whatever present right, title, or interest the grantor may have. It does not warrant that the grantor actually has any particular title or interest in the property. It is customarily used to clear some CLOUD ON THE TITLE such as deed restrictions that are no longer enforceable, or an unused easement. In addition, it frequently is used by a spouse to convey his or her half of COMMUNITY OR JOINT TENANCY PROPERTY to the other spouse. *See also* WARRANTY DEED.

quotation   Or, *quote*. The highest BID to buy and the lowest offer to sell a security in a given market at a given time. For example, if you ask your broker for a quotation on a stock, he or she may say, for example, "26 ¼ to 26 ½." This means that $26.25 was the highest price any buyer wanted to pay (bid) at the time the quotation was given on the exchange and that $26.50 was the lowest price at which any holder of the stock offered to sell.

quoted price   The price at which the last purchase and sale of a specific SECURITY or COMMODITY was made. *See also* QUOTATION.

R

rally A sharp upward MARKET PRICE movement in a STOCK or the STOCK MARKET accompanied by an increase in trading volume. The rally has only short-term significance unless it is followed on the subsequent trading days by a continuation of the upward movement, which is termed a confirmation.

random walk theory A theory of STOCK MARKET price movements suggesting that the prices of STOCKS are random and that it is futile to try to predict future prices based upon past price movements. Individual stock prices are affected by a whole range of random events including overall direction of the STOCK MARKET, government rulings, changes in earnings, new product releases, competitive developments, INTEREST RATES, the MONEY SUPPLY, and the rate of unemployment.

range In SECURITIES, a range is the upper and lower trading limits of a security's or MARKET'S PRICE movements over a period of time. Newspaper quotations state the high and low price range of a security for the past year. There is great technical significance when a STOCK or the overall MARKET BREAKS OUT of a particular trading range, whether it is higher or lower.

rate cap A ceiling on the interest rate to be charged on a loan. For example, a variable rate mortgage may provide that the maximum interest rate to be charged may not exceed 15%.

rate of return *See* YIELD.

rating
credit: A process used by the lender to decide on the soundness of making a loan. It systematically assigns ranks to individuals or businesses in terms of their financial soundness. The lower the rating, the higher the interest rate.

See also CREDIT RATING; CREDIT SCORING.
securities: Evaluation of investment grade and credit risk of a security as derived by rating services, such as MOODY'S, FITCH INVESTORS SERVICE, and STANDARD & POOR'S.
See also BOND RATINGS; PREFERRED STOCK RATINGS.
insurance:
1. A valuation of insurance risks, using such methods as probability theory and mortality rates, so as to establish the premium rates for varying rating categories.
2. Annual ratings of financial stability and claim service given to insurance companies by A. M. Best Company.
See also BEST'S RATINGS.

rational investment choice A selection of an investment that is reasonable and expected based on the position and needs of an investor. For example, a logical investment for a retired person depending upon a fixed annual income may be a high-quality utility stock known for a stable dividend payment.

raw land Unimproved property. Such property has no utilities, sewers, streets, or structures and often has to be cleared.

reaction A decline in the market price of securities occurring subsequent to a period of advancing prices. The cause may be unfavorable economic news, political unrest, or just profit taking.

real assets Tangible assets having physical substance that one can touch (e.g., REAL ESTATE, COLLECTIBLES, and PRECIOUS METALS).

real estate Or, *real property*. Something permanently affixed or attached to the land, such as buildings, walls, fences, and shrubs. It is contrasted from PERSONAL PROPERTY, which is movable.

real estate agent Salesperson or BROKER who sells real estate for his or her principal on a commission basis.
See also REAL ESTATE BROKER.

real estate appraisal To estimate the value of real estate. There are three approaches to real estate appraisal. The first is the MARKET COMPARISON APPROACH, which values property based on recent sales of similar properties. The second is the COST APPROACH, which adds together the cost of the individual components, that is, land value plus current construction costs minus depreciation. The third method is the INCOME APPROACH, which considers only the amount of net income the property can reasonably generate plus any anticipated price increase or decrease.

real estate broker A BROKER who finds a buyer or seller of property for a principal on a commission basis. He or she may act as a loan broker in arranging loans on real property.
See also BROKER (REAL ESTATE).

real estate investment company A CORPORATION that sells its shares and uses the proceeds to make REAL ESTATE investments.
See also REAL ESTATE INVESTMENT TRUSTS (REITS).

real estate investment trusts (REITs) CORPORATIONS that operate much like CLOSED-END MUTUAL FUNDS, investing shareholders' money in diversified real estate or mortgage portfolios instead of STOCKS or BONDS. Their shares trade on the major stock exchanges or over the counter.

By law, REITs must distribute 95% of their net earnings to shareholders, and in turn they are exempt from corporate taxes on income or gains. Since REIT earnings are not taxed before they are distributed, the investor receives a larger percentage of the profits than with stocks. REIT yields are high, ranging between 5½% to 10½%.

types of REITs

There are three types of REITs: EQUITY REITs invest primarily in INCOME-PRODUCING PROPERTIES; MORTGAGE REITs lend funds to developers or builders; and hybrid REITs do both. Experts feel that equity REITs are the safest.

basics about REITs

Where to Buy	Stockbrokers
Pluses	Dividend income with competitive yields
	Potential appreciation in price
	A liquid investment in an illiquid area
	Means of PORTFOLIO DIVERSIFICATION and participation in a variety of real estate with minimal cash outlay
Minuses	Possible glut in real estate or weakening demand
	Market risk: possible decline in share price
Safety	Low
Liquidity	Very high: shares traded on major exchanges or over the counter and therefore sold at any time
Taxes	Income subject to tax upon sale

how to select a REIT

Before buying any REIT, be sure to read the latest ANNUAL REPORT, *The Value Line Investment Survey, Audit Investment's Newsletter,* or *Realty Stock Review.* Check the following points.

- Track record: determine how long the REIT has been in business and how solid its dividend record is
- Debt level: make sure that the unsecured debt level is low
- Cash flow: make sure that operating cash flow covers the dividend
- Adequate diversification: beware of REITs investing in only one type of property
- Property location: beware of geographically depressed areas
- Type of property: learn whether it invests in nursing homes, some apartment buildings, shopping centers, presently favored; "seasoned" properties preferred

- Aggressive management: avoid REITs that do not upgrade properties
- Earnings: monitor earnings regularly; be prepared to sell when the market or property location weakens

real estate owned (REO) Real property repossessed by a lender by means of FORECLOSURE and retained in inventory.

real estate property tax The dominant form of PROPERTY TAXES paid by the owner of real estate. It is typically collected by the county and distributed among other governmental bodies to finance schools and other services. The tax is normally based on the ASSESSED VALUE of the property. The assessed value varies by states.

real estate settlement procedures act (RES-PA) A federal act that deals with procedures to be followed in certain types of real estate CLOSINGS. Its purpose is to regulate and standardize real estate settlement practices when "federally related" first mortgage loans are made on one- to four-family residences, condominiums, and co-operatives.

real estate syndicate A group of investors who pool their money to buy high-priced real estate.
See also SYNDICATES.

real gain or loss REAL INCOME or RETURN discounted for inflation. Real gain or loss represents real purchasing power. This is computed by dividing the amount of money received by a cost of living index such as the CONSUMER PRICE INDEX.

real income Income measured in constant prices relative to some base period. It is the income adjusted for changes in purchasing power caused by inflation. Real wages is an example of real income.
See also PURCHASING POWER; REAL GAIN OR LOSS; REAL RETURN ON INVESTMENT.

real interest rate RATE OF INTEREST that is adjusted for INFLATION.

real property Land and all property attached to land, such as buildings, trees, and fences.

real return on investment The YIELD after subtracting the effects of INFLATION. It is the return on investment expressed in real PURCHASING POWER.

realize The conversion of a financial or real asset into cash. For example, an investor may decide to sell stock, and realize a gain or loss in so doing. Prior to actual sale, any gain or loss is unrealized.

realized profit or loss A profit or loss achieved as the result of a sale. Realized profits and losses have tax consequences. A realized profit is fully taxable less any costs and other realized losses. Unlike a PAPER PROFIT, a realized profit or loss is an actual profit or loss.

realized yield An investor may trade in and out of a BOND long before it matures. He or she obviously needs a measure of RETURN to evaluate the investment appeal of any bonds he or she intends to buy and sell. Realized yield is used for this purpose. This measure is simply a variation of YIELD TO MATURITY, as only two variables are changed in the yield to maturity formula. The future price is used in place of PAR VALUE ($1,000), and the length of HOLDING PERIOD is substituted for the number of years to MATURITY.

Assume that a BONDHOLDER anticipates holding the bond for only three years and has estimated that interest rates will change in the future so that the price of the bond will move to about $925 from its present level of $877.70. Thus, the investor will buy the bond today at a MARKET PRICE of $877.70 and sell the issue three years later at a price of $925. The realized yield is shown below:

$$\text{Realized yield} = \frac{\$80 + (\$925 - \$877.70)/3}{(\$925 + \$877.70)/2}$$

$$= \frac{\$80 + \$15.77}{\$901.35} = \frac{\$95.77}{\$901.35}$$

$$= 10.63\%$$

See also BOND YIELD; YIELD TO CALL: YIELD TO MATURITY (YTM).

realtor   An active member of a local real estate board affiliated with the National Association of Real Estate Boards.
See also BROKER (REAL ESTATE); REAL ESTATE AGENT.

reasonable man doctrine   A general concept describing an individual who is prudent, mature, and responsible. For example, an individual may avoid excessive RISK by balancing INVESTMENTS through DIVERSIFICATION.
See also PRUDENT MAN RULE.

rebate
1. An abatement, reimbursement, or allotment. A REFUND of the MONEY paid for an item or service often as a promotion.
2. A return of a portion of a LOAN or DEBT if it is paid prior to the DUE DATE.
3. A surplus tax payment that is returned.
4. A KICKBACK of a charge, often illegal, for the performance of a particular service or provision of a wanted good or item.

recapture
in general: Return of an INVESTMENT or payments made through a contractual agreement or by a DEPRECIATION provision.
real estate: The return by owners of a property investment usually through a depreciation allowance.
possession: A provision in a contract allowing the previous owner of an ASSET to take it back under certain conditions. For example, if an individual sells a business to someone on an INSTALLMENT PURCHASE AGREEMENT and the buyer does not make the payments, the previous owner could recapture the business by taking possession of it.

receipts
1. A written document affirming that a payment has been made for an item or service. Such a receipt normally states the name of the person, the date of the transaction, an itemization of the purchase, and the amount. Receipts should always be retained to authenticate a purchase. They may be needed for many reasons, including a loss for INSURANCE purposes, as well as documentation for a TAX DEDUCTION.
2. MONIES actually received. For example, the receipts obtained at the end of a business day by an owner of a retail store.

receiver   A court-appointed individual who takes possession, but not the TITLE, to a business during a BANKRUPTCY procedure, termed a RECEIVERSHIP or a FORECLOSURE proceeding. The receiver has the responsibility of managing the affairs of the business prudently including collecting all monies, paying bills, and otherwise conducting the normal business activities.

The receiver operates under the guidance of the court and may attempt to return the business back to a solvent position; however, a receiver may recommend LIQUIDATION if the continued operation of the business is no longer tenable.

recession   A lower phase of a BUSINESS CYCLE, in which the economy's output (GNP), income, corporate profits, and employment are declining, coupled with a declining rate of business investment and consumer spending. Two to three successive quarterly declines in GNP is usually the sign of recession. Economists, however, have never made clear the distinction between recession and depression. It is the old rule of thumb that if your neighbor loses his job, it is a recession; if you lose yours, it is a depression.
See also BUSINESS CYCLE; DEPRESSION.

reciprocal arrangement   An agreement that one party will do something if another performs some agreed upon action. As an example, individual A agrees to buy a car from individual B if the latter first buys furniture from the former.

record
in general: Written evidence attesting to the

fact of the occurrence of activities, transactions, and other events.

computer: A data record stored in the computer containing categorized information for a single event or observation. A collection of data records is termed a data file.

criminology: Evidence of an individual's previous arrests and convictions.

record date *See* DATE OF RECORD; PAYMENT DATE.

recordkeeping The process of maintaining records. For example, a BOOKKEEPER keeps the records for a business by entering TRANSACTIONS into a journal and then posting from the journal to the ledger. An individual keeps his or her own financial records such as recording deposits and issued CHECKS in the CHECKBOOK.

recourse An individual's right to recover from another payment for something done or incurred. For example, if a person performs services or incurs a cost on behalf of another, that person has a legal right to collect payment.

Under NEGOTIABLE INSTRUMENTS law, recourse gives one the right to collect from a writer or endorser of a negotiable instrument (e.g., check).

recourse loan

1. A loan for which the guarantor is responsible if the borrower fails to pay.

2. A loan to a LIMITED PARTNERSHIP in which the lender has a right to the general assets of the partnership if the collateralized assets are insufficient in amount.

recovery

1. In a legal action, a court award won by a plaintiff against a defendant for wrongdoing.

2. In securities or commodities, a period of increasing prices after a drop in prices.

3. In insurance, money that an insurance company obtains due to reinsurance.

4. An expansion (prosperity) phase in the business or economic cycle.

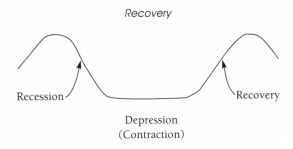

recurring clause The time period in a medical insurance policy that must elapse between a prior illness and a current one in order for the current one to be treated as a separate illness eligible for a new set of benefits.

red bread An expense category, called "adjustments," that is created to allow flexibility in budgeting. Its purpose is to cover deficit spending in other expense categories.

red herring A slang term for a preliminary PROSPECTUS that outlines the important features of a new security issue. It does not contain selling price information or offering date. It is so named because it is stamped in red ink telling the reader that the document is not an official offer to sell the securities.
See also PRELIMINARY PROSPECTUS.

redeemable security A security that can be called prior to its maturity date, such as a CALLABLE BOND.

redemption (exit) fees Fees that a MUTUAL FUND charges when an investor sells his or her share of a fund. These fees can range from a flat $5 to 2% of the amount withdrawn. The redemption fee may decline on a sliding basis depending on how long the funds were invested. For example, 3% after one year, 2% after two years, 1% after three years, and no fee thereafter.
See also MUTUAL FUNDS.

redemption price

1. The price at which a BOND may be redeemed before maturity, at the option of the

issuer. Redemption value also applies to the price the company must pay to call in certain types of preferred stock.
See also CALL PRICE.

2. The price per share the MUTUAL FUND shareholder receives when he or she cashes in the shares. The value of the shares depends on the MARKET VALUE of the fund's PORTFOLIO of securities at the time.

redress INDEMNIFICATION, restitution, reparation, or COMPENSATION for some incurred harm or wrong. Any form of EQUITABLE relief.
See also RECOVERY.

referee In arbitration, the third party who decides on the finding in a dispute between two parties. The complaining parties agree in advance to accept the referee's decision. The decision of the arbitrator is legally enforceable.

refinance A revised schedule of debt payments, including a MORTGAGE. Creditors may be willing to refinance a person's debts if he or she cannot meet the original payments or if interest rates have fallen since a borrower took out a loan. Whether refinancing is worthwhile depends on the costs of refinancing and the time required to recoup those costs through low mortgage payments. The costs of refinancing are the CLOSING COSTS.

To get a rough estimate of the closing costs, take the costs of refinancing (3% to 6% of the outstanding principal) and multiply it by the amount of the loan.

Example: Assume that refinancing is $75,000. A 14% mortgage involves closing fees of $3,750, and the new interest rate is 10%. At the new rate of 10%, the monthly payment on a 30-year fixed loan would be $658. That is a savings of $231 from the monthly payment of $889 required on a 14% loan. Dividing the total refinancing cost of $3,750 by $231 gives a recovery period of about 16 months. The accompanying table illustrates the monthly and yearly savings from refinancing to a 10%, 30-year, fixed-rate mortgage for $75,000.

SAVINGS FROM REFINANCING

Present Mortgage Rate	Current Monthly Payment	Monthly Payment at 10%	Monthly Savings at 10%	Annual Savings at 10%
12.0%	$771	$658	$113	$1,356
12.5	800	658	142	1,704
13.0	830	658	172	2,064
13.5	859	658	201	2,412
14.0	889	658	231	2,772
15.0	948	658	290	3,480

reflex rally In investments, increasing prices in securities that is consistent with the general rising price movement but represents an adjustment to securities that have been excessively sold in the market.

reformation A correction to a legally enforceable agreement because of a mutual mistake in the original contract. The initial contract did not represent the intent of the parties. Note that if one party was mistaken, reformation is not possible unless the person's error was caused from the other party's fraud.

refund Amount paid back or credit given due to an overcollection or the return of merchandise. Examples are a tax return for the overpayment of taxes during the year and a cash refund given for clothing returned to the store that was originally bought for cash.

refund annuity A type of annuity returning premiums plus interest to a beneficiary if the annuitant dies during the accumulation period. This coverage is more expensive than a straight life (pure) annuity.
See also NONREFUND ANNUITY.

regional stock exchanges Organized securities exchanges other than the NEW YORK STOCK EXCHANGE (NYSE) and the AMERICAN STOCK EXCHANGE (AMEX) that deal primarily in securities having a local or regional flavor.

registered bond A BOND on whose face the identity of the BONDHOLDER is registered; the bondholder's name is also listed with the issuing company, governmental jurisdiction, or REGISTRAR. An endorsement must be made by the registered owner to transfer the bond. A check for the PRINCIPAL and INTEREST will normally be mailed only to the listed bondholder. In some cases, the bond is recorded and not the interest coupons. In this case, the bearer of the COUPON will receive payment.

registered certificate Any CERTIFICATE of a SECURITY registered in the owner's name by the REGISTRAR and in the records of the company or jurisdiction. Examples include REGISTERED BONDS and registered STOCK. In the United States, most securities have registered certificates.
See also REGISTERED SECURITY.

registered check A CHECK issued by a BANK after the MAKER deposits the MONEY. The name of the PAYOR is placed on the check and the bank inserts its name and the amount of the check. The check is assigned a special number. A registered check becomes an obligation of the bank. The bank charges a fee for the service.

A registered check is also termed a CASHIER'S CHECK, MONEY ORDER, or BANK DRAFT.

registered homeownership savings plans (RHOSPs) A tax-deferred Canadian savings plan designed for future homeowners. Investors can place up to $1,000 annually into the plan for a lifetime maximum of $10,000.

registered representative (RR) Or, *account executive; customer's broker; stock broker.* An employee who is registered and licensed with the SECURITIES AND EXCHANGE COMMISSION as well as with the appropriate STOCK EXCHANGES with which the employee buys and sells client securities. A registered representative has the responsibility of conforming to the rulings of the Securities and Exchange Commission and the appropriate stock exchanges as well as to the policies of the BROKERAGE FIRM representing his or her client's best interests.

registered retirement savings plans (RRSPs) A Canadian tax shelter that allows investors to set aside a portion of their income for retirement.

registered security A SECURITY registered in the owner's name and listed on the records of the issuing company or jurisdiction as well as with the REGISTRAR. An example would be a REGISTERED BOND. A BEARER BOND and a BEARER STOCK are unregistered securities.

registrar
in general: Person responsible for keeping and securing official records. For example, a college registrar maintains official student records and transcripts.
real estate: The individual holding official REAL ESTATE records including DEEDS, MORTGAGES, and surveys. This is often the clerk of the governmental jurisdiction, for example, the county or town clerk.
securities: The trustee for all new issue BOND and STOCK CERTIFICATE records. Often this function is accomplished by a BANK. The registrar maintains the CORPORATION'S or jurisdiction's security register and takes possession of transferred security certificates from the TRANSFER AGENT as well as newly issued certificates. A function of the registrar is to substantiate the uniformity between old and new security registration numbers.

registration
in general: The process of recording all official information regarding a transaction.
securities: A required review and approval of all pertinent information relating to the issuance of a security by the SECURITIES AND EXCHANGE COMMISSION. Such information must include a complete financial analysis of a company, its MARKET prospects, and management and operational information.

registration statement
1. A statement issued to the SECURITIES AND EXCHANGE COMMISSION or other appropriate regulatory body by a company issuing new securi-

ties. The filing includes financial statements and other related financial information concerning the new issue. The SEC must approve the formal document prior to the securities being publicly issued.

2. A filing with the SEC by the various stock exchanges.

regressive tax A TAX having a higher incidence on and consuming a larger amount of the INCOME of the lower-income portion of the population. A SALES TAX consumes a larger percentage of the lower-income population's income as a larger proportion of their income is used for CONSUMPTION expenditures.

regular passbook savings account A savings account that permits frequent deposit or withdrawal of funds, recorded in a small book held by the depositor. The interest rate is lower than that on a CERTIFICATE OF DEPOSIT.

regular-way settlement In investments, the transfer of the certificate and payment therefore by the fifth business day subsequent to when the transaction occurred. There are instances when the settlement must be made by the next business day, as with calls and puts.

regulated investment company A MUTUAL FUND that satisfies the Internal Revenue Service's Regulation M to pass on dividends, interest, and capital gains to investors so as to get around double taxation. The only tax is paid by the individual when filing Form 1040. Note that even though the shareholder reinvests the income in the mutual fund, he or she still must pay tax on the monies. The mutual fund does *not* pay tax on these income sources.

In order to qualify for this tax benefit, the fund must (1) distribute a minimum of 90% of its earnings to shareholders; (2) not use in excess of 5% of its money to invest in one business entity; and (3) not retain in excess of 10% of the voting shares of another company.

regulation Q The Federal Reserve Bank's regulation that sets deposit interest rate ceilings and regulates advertising of interest on SAVINGS ACCOUNTS. This regulation applies to all commercial banks. It was first instituted in the Banking Act of 1933.

regulation T The Federal Reserve Bank's regulation governing the amount of CREDIT that may be advanced by BROKERS and DEALERS to customers for the purchase of securities.
See also INITIAL MARGIN; MARGIN BUYING; MAINTENANCE MARGIN REQUIREMENT.

regulation Z The Federal Reserve Bank's rule that regulates consumer and mortgage credit transactions. A lender must specify the ANNUAL PERCENTAGE RATE (APR) of the loan and other key information in consumer and mortgage credit contracts.

rehabilitation The restoration of an item or part to a workable condition. An example is repairing a neglected home to good condition.

rehabilitation clause A provision in a health insurance policy that provides financial aid to a disabled policyholder who is receiving vocational rehabilitation.

rehabilitation coverage A clause in a medical insurance policy providing that the insured disabled person must undertake vocational rehabilitation. Related expenses are reimbursed under the policy.

reimbursement
1. An individual making payment to another to cover out-of-pocket costs. An example is an employer's reimbursing the employee for his or her costs (e.g., auto expenses, taxi fare, office supplies). Many employers reimburse employees for education expenses.
2. In insurance, payment of benefits by an insurer to an insured in conformity with the provisions of the insurance policy for covered losses.

reinstatement
insurance: the restitution of a POLICY that has lapsed because of nonpayment of PREMIUMS.

Normally, the reinstatement period for a LIFE INSURANCE policy is three years; however, evidence of continued insurability is often required. Such evidence normally requires the applicant to pass a physical examination. Reinstatement also requires that all past PREMIUMS be paid in full; as the INSURED has now aged, there would be a higher premium if reinstatement did not occur.

securities: The restoration of a PASSED DIVIDEND. If the security is CUMULATIVE PREFERRED STOCK, all the passed dividends must be paid in full before the current year's dividend is paid.

reinstatement clause In INSURANCE, a clause in the POLICY stating that in the event a policy lapses because of PREMIUM nonpayment, all unpaid premiums will have to be paid and any additional requirements must be met before REINSTATEMENT can occur.

reinvestment privilege The right of a shareholder to reinvest the income received from a MUTUAL FUND (including dividends, interest, and capital gains) back into the mutual fund. By exercising this privilege, the shareholder can buy additional shares without a sales charge.

reinvestment rate The rate of return earned by reinvesting the interest from a FIXED INCOME SECURITY. The reinvestment rate on a coupon bond will change depending upon prevailing interest rates. However, the imputed reinvestment rate on a ZERO COUPON BOND is the same because there are no interest payments. The principal and interest are payable at maturity.

rejection
investments: A broker's or client's refusal to accept a delivery of a security in connection with a trade because of something lacking or being inappropriate. An example may be the failure to include an ENDORSEMENT.
insurance: An insurance company declines to issue a policy due to the applicant's poor health.
credit: A creditor's refusal to give credit to the applicant due to his or her poor financial condition.

relative strength In investments, comparing the performance of a company's stock relative to other stocks in the population or industry for a specified time frame. When strength is *positive,* superior performance exists. However, when strength is *negative,* poor or marginal performance exists.

release
in general: Voluntarily to quit, abandon, or give up any further legal right against another. For example, exercising a PREPAYMENT OF LOAN CLAUSE would release the BORROWER from any further financial loan obligations.
real estate: To free REAL ESTATE from a MORTGAGE by paying the mortgage. When a mortgage is paid in its entirety, often a confirming release of record is issued, legally attesting to the retirement of the DEBT.
finance: The creditor's forgiveness of the debtor's obligation.

release clause In a MORTGAGE, a clause that permits part of the collateral to be released from any further lien obligations upon the borrower's making a specified payment. For example, an individual may obtain a BLANKET MORTGAGE for a piece of REAL ESTATE containing several structures. The mortgage may have a release clause in it permitting individual structures to be released from any further mortgage obligations when the mortgagor receives an indicated payment from the mortgagee, either through sale of the structure or by making the payment.

remainder The remaining interest in an ESTATE after all expenses have been paid. For example, if a business is willed to A for life with the remainder to B upon A's death, B has a remainder interest.

remaining monthly balance The remaining portion of DEBT paid on a monthly basis. A CREDIT service charge is computed on the outstanding BALANCE of the buyer's account on a monthly basis. For example, an individual having a CHARGE ACCOUNT pays only a portion of the bill, whereupon he or she is charged INTEREST on the remaining monthly BALANCE.

remedial loan society A pawnshop operated by a nonprofit entity that lends money at reasonable rates.

remit A payment of money by one party to another for a good or service. Payment can be made by CASH, CHECK, or an ELECTRONIC FUNDS TRANSFER SYSTEM.

renegotiated rate mortgage (RRM) A mortgage that provides a borrower with a FIXED-RATE MORTGAGE that expires at a predetermined time, such as in three, four, or five years. This allows the lender and borrower to renegotiate the mortgage rate periodically. The unpaid balance of the mortgage comes due in a BALLOON PAYMENT, but can be refinanced at prevailing interest rates. This mortgage was authorized in 1980 by the FEDERAL HOME LOAN BANK BOARD for federal savings and loan associations.

renewable term A contract that can be renewed at its expiration for another specified time period. An example may be a bank loan or insurance policy.

renewable term life insurance An option of a LIFE INSURANCE policy that allows the insured to renew the insurance for a specified time period for a definite number of times.

renewal By rolling over or substituting an item that is shortly going to end, such as extending the due date on a loan. Renewal of a loan is typically accomplished by canceling a maturing note and making a new one. Another example is renewal of the insured's auto insurance policy by the company.

renewal option The right of a party to renew a contract, if desired. For example, the tenant may have the right to renew a lease for a given amount and term.

rent The payment from the TENANT to the landlord for the right to use property such as an APARTMENT.

rent controls A governmental policy setting the maximum amount of RENT landlords can charge TENANTS. The purpose of rent control is to prevent rent gouging during a housing shortage. If a tenant feels the LANDLORD is violating the rent control law by overcharging, he or she may contact the appropriate rental control agency. While rent control is effective in controlling housing rental rates, it also has the effect of discouraging private INVESTMENT in additional rental housing as it limits potential profit.

rental agency A business that leases property for a fee. An example is a car rental firm.

rental contract An agreement to lease property for a specified amount and term stipulating the terms and conditions for use. An example is the contract between landlord and tenant.

REO *See* REAL ESTATE OWNED.

repairs Expenses that are necessary to maintain property in good working order. Examples are electrical and plumbing.

replacement cost
in general: The cost of replacing one item with another for the purpose of providing the same function with the same useful life.
insurance: The cost of replacing an INSURED'S property with comparable property less the cost of DEPRECIATION (fair wear and tear). In this context, replacement cost is equivalent to the current cash value of an insured item. The purpose is to restore the insured's property without suffering a financial loss or enjoying a profit.
real estate: The cost of replacing an existing structure with another exact replica. The current construction costs of replacing buildings and homes built years ago are substantially more than the original construction costs.

replacement cost coverage A special endorsement available with homeowners' and tenants' insurance policies that replaces property with comparable acquisitions at today's prices, generally up to a specified maximum reimbursement.

repossession The reacquisition of COLLATERAL by the lender when the borrower defaults on the loan.

repudiation The refusal of a person to honor A DEBT or meet the terms of a contractual or other legal obligation. Only a governmental entity could, for example, repudiate a debt without precipitating legal recovery procedures.

repurchase agreement (REPO) The temporary sale of SECURITIES (such as U.S. TREASURY or GOVERNMENT AGENCY SECURITIES, BANKERS' AC-CEPTANCES, CERTIFICATES OF DEPOSIT, COMMERCIAL PAPER and other MARKETABLE SECURITIES) to the investor (lender) accompanied by an agreement to repurchase them at some point in the near future. There is a provision for interest to be paid to the investor at the end of the transaction. Theoretically, the funds borrowed are collateralized by securities.

rescind The act of canceling, nullifying, abrogating, or dishonoring a contractual obligation. The TRUTH-IN-LENDING ACT provides the right of RECISSION whereby an individual can annul a CONTRACT without penalties, including the refund of any deposits within three business days.

Other types of contracts may also be rescinded when they are improperly executed. For example, a minor under the legal age may rescind a contract with no penalties since children cannot make legal CONTRACTS.
See also RESCISSION.

rescission The unmaking or undoing of a legal contract either with the consent of both parties or by one party exercising the right of recission, citing sufficient legal grounds. The grounds could include FRAUD or participation in the contract by a minor who, because of age, does not have the authority to enter into a contractual obligation.
See also RESCIND.

reserve Funds put away by an individual to meet a particular contingency. An example is money one puts aside when buying a new house in the event unexpected repairs are needed.

reserve requirements Cash reserves required by the Federal Reserve for its financial member institutions.

reset bonds A BOND that provides investors with insurance against falling bond prices. It does this by guaranteeing that at some point the interest rate will be increased to maintain the original value of the bond. Such an increase could be necessary if market interest rates are rising or if there are concerns about the issuer's financial strength. However, the investor must beware that risk still exists because a financially troubled company may not be able to satisfy the terms of its reset provisions.

resident manager An individual who supervises the operation of apartments while living in one of the apartments. Some duties include showing vacant apartments to prospective tenants and making sure the apartments are well kept.

residential broker A REAL ESTATE BROKER who lists and sells houses or condominiums, as distinguished from a COMMERCIAL BROKER who deals in business property.

residential lot Subdivided acreage with utilities (including water, electricity, and sewerage) typically located within or adjacent to established communities.

residential mortgage A MORTGAGE for residential property.

residential property An owner-occupied property; includes not only the single-family dwelling but almost any type of structure designed for habitation—condominiums, cooperatives, town houses, "plexes"—where the owner can live in one but rents the others.

residential service contract An insurance contract or home warranty, typically for one year, covering electrical, plumbing, and other features of the home.

residential unit A property designed for residential living—such as a house, DUPLEX, APARTMENT, MOBILE HOME, or CONDOMINIUM.

residual disability benefits INSURANCE COV-
ERAGE for a residual disability that leaves the
insured only partial ability to perform actions or
duties formerly performed. The benefits are
normally guaranteed for the unused portion of
the DISABILITY POLICY up to the age of 65.
Assuming at least a 25% loss in current earnings,
the residual benefits equal the percentage of loss
times the monthly benefit for total disability.

The computation for a monthly residual disability benefit is as follows:

$$\frac{\text{Loss of monthly income}}{\text{Previous monthly income}} \times \frac{\text{Monthly benefit for}}{\text{total disability}}$$

residual maturity The time period from the
current day to the due date of a financial
instrument. For example, a bond dated January
1, 19X1, but issued January 1, 19X2, and maturing on January 1, 19X5, has a residual maturity
of three years.

residuary estate The remaining portion of an
ESTATE after all expenses, obligations, and DISTRI-
BUTIONS have been made. The residuary estate is
equal to the gross estate less all DEBTS, CHARGES,
and other LEGACIES.

resistance level The price at which a particular security or the overall market tends to stop
increasing. TECHNICAL ANALYSTS are encouraged
when the market price of a stock rises above the
resistance line since it may indicate that new
highs will be reached. The diagram shown below
demonstrates this concept.
See also SUPPORT LEVEL.

restrictive covenant
1. Language in a LOAN agreement by which
the borrower agrees to do certain things but
refrain from others. An example of an affirmative convenant is a borrower's agreeing to maintain proper insurance. An example of a negative
covenant is a prohibition against the borrower's
selling assets.
2. A provision in a BOND agreement protecting BONDHOLDER interests, such as the debtor's
promising to maintain timely payments of principal and interest.
3. A provision in a contract that denies or
limits the full rights of the purchaser or lessor
to the property. For example, a landlord may
stipulate in the lease that the tenant may not
put up paneling unless written permission is
obtained.

restrictive endorsement A signature on the
back of a check transferring the amount to
another party, but limiting the check for a single
purpose. An example is the wording "for deposit
only" thus preventing the check from being
cashed.
See also BLANK ENDORSEMENT; SPECIAL ENDORSE-
MENT.

Resistance Level

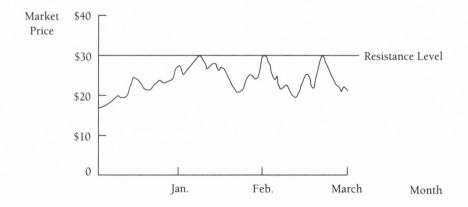

Restrictive Endorsement

For deposit only
L. Jones

resume A summary of the education, experience, interests, and so on of an individual applying for a job or for some other reason (e.g., promotion).

retail house A brokerage firm whose clientele is mainly individuals rather than institutions.

retail installment contract and security agreement (conditional sales contract) Or, *a conditional sales contract*. A written agreement between creditor and borrower that permits the borrower to receive goods and services at the time of the purchase but allows the creditor to retain TITLE to the merchandise until payment is completed.

retail investor In the STOCK and BOND markets, a retail INVESTOR is a customer of a BROKERAGE FIRM typically buying small amounts of SECURITIES for his or her own account and paying full COMMISSION costs. In recent years, the role of the retail INVESTOR has steadily diminished as institutional investors are responsible for an increasing amount of MARKET volume. Further, many small investors are putting their money into MUTUAL FUNDS.

retail price The price retail customers pay for services and items. Wholesale distributors sell goods and services at wholesale prices to retail businesses. The retail price includes the wholesale price plus the retailer's markup or profit margin.

retired bond A BOND for which the DEBT has been fully paid at or before maturity, nullifying the debt. The satisfaction of the debt may be accomplished by actual payment or by CONVERSION into stock as in a CONVERTIBLE BOND.

retirement
employment: Leaving one's place of employment and no longer working on an active basis. The federal RETIREMENT AGE is now 70. People who retire live on FIXED INCOME from pensions, investments, and Social Security retirement benefits.
debt: The satisfaction of a DEBT through either actual payment or CONVERSION into a form of EQUITY as in a CONVERTIBLE BOND.
fixed assets: The removal of an ASSET from active operation upon reaching the end of its useful life or through its sale. For example, steam locomotives were retired by railroads upon the introduction of diesel locomotives.

retirement age The age at which one ends employment and is entitled to receive RETIREMENT BENEFITS. The federal RETIREMENT AGE is now 70. Employees covered under the SOCIAL SECURITY ACT can receive full Social Security retirement benefits at the age of 65. In the United States, there is no mandatory retirement age.

retirement and pension planning The process of considering explicitly an individual's future needs for retirement and an examination of how present resources may be allocated to serve those needs. A FINANCIAL ADVISER such as a FINANCIAL PLANNER, a CPA, or a LIFE INSURANCE agent may be called upon to advise one on the type of retirement plan necessary to meet particular needs.

The first step in retirement planning is to develop retirement goals. Once they have been set, specific savings plans aimed at achieving them should be developed. It is essential for financial security in old age for one to provide some income to accomplish retirement goals. The means of saving for retirement are Social Security, employer retirement and PENSION PLANS, ANNUITIES, and individual retirement and savings plans. An easy way to plan for retirement is to state retirement income objectives as a percentage of present earnings. For example, if one desires a retirement income of 70% of his or her final take-home pay, the amount necessary to fund this need can be determined.

types of pension and retirement plans

Two major sources of retirement income are company-sponsored pension plans and individual retirement plans. They are summarized below:

> *Company-sponsored pension plans*
> Qualified company retirement plans
> Profit sharing plans
> 401(K) salary reduction plans
> Tax-sheltered annuities (TSA)
> Employee stock ownership plans (ESOP)
> Simplified employee pension plan (SEP)
> *Individual retirement plans*
> Individual retirement accounts (IRAs)
> Keoghs
> Annuities

qualified company retirement plans: The IRS permits a corporate employer to make contributions to a retirement plan that is qualified. Qualified means that it meets a number of specific criteria in order to deduct from taxable income contributions to the plan. The investment income of the plan is allowed to accumulate untaxed.

profit-sharing plans: A profit-sharing plan is a type of DEFINED CONTRIBUTION PLAN. Unlike other qualified plans, employees may not have to wait until retirement to receive distributions. Since the company must contribute only when it earns a profit, the amount of benefit at retirement is highly uncertain.

401(k) salary reduction plans: In addition to, or in place of, a QUALIFIED PENSION PLAN or PROFIT-SHARING PLAN, one may set up a 401(K) salary reduction plan, which defers a portion of his or her salary for retirement. This is like building a nest egg for the future by taking a cut in pay. Tax savings more than offset a paper cut (on paper) since employees end up with more take-home pay and more retirement income.

Example: An individual saves 10% of his or her $40,000-a-year salary in a 401(K) plan. He

or she is married with two children, the only wage-earner in the family, and does not itemize deductions. How will the individual fare with a 401(K) plan and without one?

TAKE-HOME PAY

	With 401(K) Plan	Without 401(K) Plan
Base pay	$40,000	$40,000
Salary reduction	4,000	None
Taxable income	$36,000	$40,000
Federal and FICA taxes	8,159	9,279
Savings after taxes	None	4,000
Take-home pay	$27,841	$26,721

Extra take-home pay under 401(K) $1,120

Retirement income will grow faster inside a tax-sheltered plan, such as 401(K), than outside one. This is because the interest earned will go untaxed and keep compounding.

tax-sheltered annuities (TSA): If one is an employee of a nonprofit institution, he or she is eligible for a TSA. A TSA is similar to the 401(K), but one may withdraw the funds at any age for any reason without tax penalty. Ordinary taxes must be paid on all withdrawals.

employee stock ownership plans (ESOP): ESOP is a stock-bonus plan. The contributions made by the employer are tax deductible.

simplified employee pension (SEP): SEP is a plan in which an employer makes annual contributions on the employee's behalf to an individual retirement account set up by the employee.

If one does not have a company retirement plan, or would like to supplement a company plan through additional private savings, the benefits of tax deferral can also be attained through individual-oriented investments, such as INDIVIDUAL RETIREMENT ACCOUNTS (IRAs), KEOGHS, and ANNUITIES.

individual retirement accounts (IRAs)

The IRA is a retirement savings plan that individuals set up themselves. The IRA is a qualified individual retirement plan in which contributions not only grow tax free but are also either tax deductible or not included in their income. Under the TAX REFORM ACT OF 1986, however, a person who is covered by an employer's retirement plan, or who files a joint return with a spouse who is covered by such a plan, may be entitled to only a partial deduction or no deduction at all, depending on the ADJUSTED GROSS INCOME (AGI). The DEDUCTION begins to decrease when the taxpayer's income rises above a certain level and is eliminated altogether when it reaches a higher level. The deduction is reduced or eliminated entirely depending on filing status and income as shown in the table below.

If a person is not covered by an employee retirement plan, he or she can still take a full IRA deduction of up to $2,000, or 100% of compensation, whichever is less.

keoghs

A self-employed person may set up a Keogh plan. Keogh contributions are tax sheltered and their earnings are tax deferred. The overall federal limit on annual contributions is 25% of annual compensation or $30,000, whichever is less.

annuities

An annuity is a SAVINGS ACCOUNT with an insurance company or other investment company. A person makes either a lump-sum deposit or periodic payments to the company and at retirement, he or she "annuitizes"—receives regular payments for a specified time period (usually a certain number of years or for the rest of life). All the payments build up tax free and are taxed only when withdrawn at retirement, a time when an individual is usually in a lower tax bracket. Annuities pay off at retirement; life insurance pays off at death.

Annuities come in two basic varieties: fixed and variable.

fixed rate annuities: In a fixed annuity, the insurance company guarantees principal plus a minimum rate of interest. If one has little tolerance for risk, the fixed annuity is an ideal investment. In buying a fixed annuity, be aware of two interest rates. One is the minimum guaranteed rate, which applies for the duration of the contract. The other is the "current" rate of interest, which reflects market conditions.

variable annuities: In a variable annuity, the company does not provide the same guarantee as for fixed annuities. The company invests in COMMON STOCKS, corporate BONDS, or MONEY MARKET instruments, and the investment value fluctuates with the performance of these investments. Note that with a variable annuity, a policyholder bears the risk of the investment options. An advantage is that most companies allow the investor to switch to another fund within the variable variety.

Annuities can be for everybody. For young people, the vehicles are an excellent forced savings plan. For older people, they are tax-favored investments that can guarantee an income for life. There are, however, some pitfalls:

- Penalties for early withdrawals of money imposed by the IRS and insurance company
- Surrender charges if a policyholder decides to cash in the contract early
- The so-called nonqualified annuities, which are annuities with the tax-deferral feature but which are paid for with after-tax dollars. Qualified annuities, on the other hand, are used to fund such vehicles as INDIVIDUAL RETIREMENT ACCOUNTS (IRAs) and PENSION PLANS. In a qualified annuity, the contribu-

If filing status is	Deduction is reduced if AGI is within range of	Deduction is eliminated if AGI is
Single, or Head of Household	$25,000 – $35,000	$35,000 or more
Married–joint return, or Qualifying widow(er)	$40,000 – $50,000	$50,000 or more
Married–separate return	$0 – $10,000	$10,000 or more

tions not only grow tax free but are also either tax deductible or not included in one's income.

Unlike pension plans and IRAs, there are no limitations on the amount to be contributed to an annuity.

retirement annuity An ANNUITY, DEFERRED ANNUITY, or DEFERRED GROUP ANNUITY for which the payment date commences at the age of retirement. Under this plan all PAYMENTS, including PREPAYMENTS and INTEREST, less any pension plan CHARGES, accumulate for the payment of the retirement annuity for the retiree. The ANNUITY ACCUMULATION acts as a form of LIFE INSURANCE in the event of the ANNUITANT'S death.

retirement fund Sum of money INVESTED by an employee, often with matching employer contributions, in a fund for the purpose of providing an income to the employee upon retirement. The INVESTMENT of such funds by PENSION FUND managers has become a major factor in the STOCK MARKET. Retirement funds are regulated by the EMPLOYMENT RETIREMENT SECURITIES ACT OF 1974 (ERISA).

retirement goal An objective that an individual strives to attain at retirement, such as having $1,000,000 when he or she leaves work at age 65.

retirement income INCOME a retired employee receives from a RETIREMENT ANNUITY, RETIREMENT FUND, SOCIAL SECURITY, and other INVESTMENTS. This income is often referred to as FIXED INCOME; however, the income may in fact vary depending upon the continuing investment returns of the RETIREMENT FUND and the COST OF LIVING ADJUSTMENTS (COLA) of SOCIAL SECURITY.

retirement plan A plan provided by the employer and/or employee to PAY RETIREMENT BENEFITS when the employee RETIRES. The plan normally consists of developing various financial OPTIONS in the RETIREMENT FUND such as the extent of the CONTRIBUTION to the plan, choice of beneficiaries, and payment options.

In addition to financial considerations, RETIREMENT PLANNING also includes considerations of housing arrangements, possible relocation, and a possible second career.

retroactive contract A CONTRACT in which the provisions and possible remunerative considerations extend back to a certain period of time. For example, an employee contract may specify that employees hired within the past two years may have a stipulated pay increase retroactive to the date they were employed.

retroactive pay *See* RETROACTIVE CONTRACT.

return The reward for investing. The investor must compare the EXPECTED RETURN for a given investment with the risk involved. The return on an investment consists of the following sources of income:

1. Periodic cash payments, called CURRENT INCOME.
2. Appreciation (or depreciation) in market value, called CAPITAL GAINS (or losses).

Current income, which is received on a periodic basis, may take the form of interest, dividends, rent, and the like. Capital gains or losses represent changes in market value. A capital gain is the amount by which the proceeds from the sale of an investment exceed its original purchase price. If the investment is sold for less than its purchase price, then the difference is a capital loss.

See also BOND YIELD; HOLDING PERIOD RETURN (HPR); YIELD.

revenue bond A BOND, often used in state and local government finance, for which the INTEREST and PRINCIPAL payments are to be made by certain specified revenues. For example, a bridge and tunnel authority revenue BOND may pledge the toll revenues of specified bridges and tunnels to make the INTEREST and principal payments of the bond.

Governmental revenue bonds may have additional TAX revenue pledges as well, depending on the terms and conditions of the bond itself.

reversal

1. A change in direction, as when stock or commodity prices begin to fall after they have risen.

2. A change in direction in the price of a FUTURES CONTRACT. See illustrative chart below.

reverse annuity mortgage (RAM) A MORT-GAGE that allows a borrower to receive monthly receipts against the EQUITY in his or her home. It is designed for older people who own their homes and need additional funds to meet current living expenses but do not want to sell their homes. At the end of the payment term, often 10 or 15 years, the mortgage on the borrower's home equals a predetermined amount so that the value of the equity is reduced by the amount.

reverse discrimination A situation in which an employer favors minorities at the expense of others, such as in hiring and promotion. This may arise from a quota that has not been approved as an AFFIRMATIVE ACTION policy.

reverse leverage Or, *negative leverage*. The interest rate on debt is higher than the rate of return generated from investing the borrowed funds. This magnifies losses.
See also POSITIVE LEVERAGE.

reverse mortgage Mortgage used by older homeowners in need of extra monthly income; they can use the resources of their home by taking out a reverse mortgage. Homeowners who are cash poor but house rich with a minimal or no mortgage put their homes up as collateral. They receive periodic payments from the lender for either a fixed term or for life. The loan is repaid, including accrued interest, in a lump sum either at the end of a fixed term or when the borrower moves, sells, or dies. A reverse mortgage does not affect one's eligibility for Medicare or Social Security. Since reverse mortgages involve high application fees, they are costly in the short term and typically should not be used if the borrower expects to move within three or four years. A listing of lenders may be obtained from the National Center for Home Equity Conversion, 348 West Main Street, Marshall, MN 56258.

reverse stock split A decision by the board of directors of a public company to reduce the total number of SHARES outstanding by some specified amount. The individual STOCKHOLDERS will retain the same EQUITY in the company, but since the total amount of shares of STOCK outstanding is reduced, the per share MARKET VALUE will be increased. By illustration, a company with 100,000 shares has a 50% reverse split resulting in new total outstanding shares of 50,000 (100,000 × 50%). A reverse stock split is often

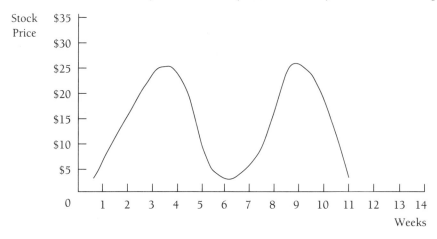

Reversal

used by a company when the market value of its shares drops to a level considered unacceptable by the management of the company.

reversion Or, *estate in reversion*. A vested interest or ESTATE in which an individual has a fixed interest sometime in the future. The remnant left in an estate by a GRANTOR of the estate through the operation of law. For example, if a grantor is required by the INTERNAL REVENUE SERVICE to pay a large sum of MONEY as a form of back TAXES, the portion remaining reverts to the estate for future distribution to the BENEFICIARIES.

reversionary interest A property interest an individual has that is currently possessed by another. Upon the termination of the possession, the property reverts to the grantor. For example, the INCOME derived from an ESTATE is given to the wife of A for her lifetime. Upon her demise, the income returns to the estate whereupon the children will then share the INCOME.

reversionary trust A property interest in a TRUST that will take effect after the termination of an intervening INTEREST is satisfied. For example, the INCOME from a trust is given to a benefactor's wife, and upon her death, the income will revert to the trust to be used as the trust directors see fit.

reversionary value The estimated value of property after a certain period of time has elapsed.

revocable trust An arrangement that deeds income-generating assets to heirs. The grantor may change the terms of the TRUST, if desired. The grantor also has the right to terminate the trust. It is different from an irrevocable trust because assets may be transferred permanently while the grantor is alive; thus, it avoids estate taxes.
See also IRREVOCABLE TRUST.

revolving account Any CHARGE ACCOUNT for which the user has the option to pay the bill in full or spread repayment over several months.

revolving charge account A type of CREDIT that allows the user to continue to purchase goods as long as he or she does not exceed the CREDIT LIMIT established or let the account become delinquent by not making specified minimum payments.

revolving credit An ACCOUNT on which new loans are made as old loans are paid off, as in a retail store CREDIT ACCOUNT.
See also OPEN-END CREDIT.

revolving credit account *See* REVOLVING CHARGE ACCOUNT.

revolving fund A fund that is automatically replenished to its original amount as money from it is used. An example is an employee's petty cash fund for miscellaneous expenses.

ride sharing A form of *car pooling* in which individuals sharing a common interest such as commuting to work elect to share one car and divide the expenses rather than drive individual cars. The government encourages ride sharing since it conserves energy, reduces environmental pollutants, and reduces traffic congestion.

rider A written modification to an insurance policy that changes its provisions. The rider may update the policy, and add or delete specified coverage.

right *See* SUBSCRIPTION RIGHT.

right of action The privilege to initiate legal action. In some cases, this right can be exercised only after other prescribed actions stated in the written agreement have been exercised. For example, the contract may stipulate that arbitration should be used to settle differences. If the arbitrator's decision is not acceptable to a party, he or she may then proceed in a court action.

right of courtesy The husband's legal right, upon the death of his wife, to a life estate in all lands his wife owned.

right of dower A LIFE ESTATE right of a widow on the death of her husband, should he die intestate, to all his lands and possessions for her and her children's support. In the event she dissents from his will, the widow is entitled to one-third of all the ASSETS of her husband's ESTATE.

The right of dower has been abolished in almost all states and substantially altered in others.

right of election The right of a surviving spouse to take a specified portion of the PROBATE estate regardless of what the WILL provides.

right of first refusal A right of a person to be offered something before it is offered to others. For example, a tenant whose apartment is going to be converted to a cooperative has the first right of refusal before the unit may be sold to others. The existing tenant is often given a lower insider price.

right of redemption

1. The right to recover property taken away by FORECLOSURE by paying the lender the principal balance and interest due plus the lender's foreclosure costs.

2. The right of a debtor in BANKRUPTCY to recover PERSONAL PROPERTY under lien by making payment to the creditor.

right of rescission The right of a borrower to cancel, within three business days, a credit contract in which his or her principal place or residence is used as security. This right does not apply to first mortgage loans.

right of return A buyer's option to return unsatisfactory goods to the seller for credit within a prescribed time period.

right of subrogation The substitution of one person or CORPORATION for another when the substituted person or corporation has the same rights and duties as the original party or parties. An INSURANCE COMPANY can subrogate for the INSURED when the insured is being sued and defend against the plaintiff in an action.

right of survivorship The survival right of an individual to the property of another when an INTEREST was involved. This right is implicit in a JOINT TENANCY or a TENANCY BY THE ENTIRETY.

rights offering Or, *rights issue*. A limited time right granted to current STOCKHOLDERS to buy additional shares of stock at a reduced price. Rights can also be traded on a market basis proportionate to the price of the underlying STOCK. For example, a right might be offered to current STOCKHOLDERS to purchase one new share of common stock for every two already owned at 75% of the MARKET PRICE.

rising bottoms A term used by TECHNICAL

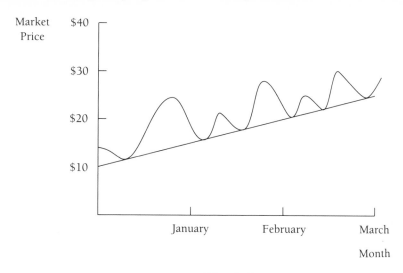

Rising Bottoms

ANALYSTS to depict an increasing trend in the low prices of a security or commodity. On a chart, the daily lows in prices move in an upward direction. In rising bottoms, there is evidence of high support levels. If this situation is combined with ascending tops, a bullish indication exists. See illustrative chart on page 267.

risk

1. Variability about income, returns, or other financial variable.
2. Possibility of losing value.
3. A peril insured against.

Among the commonly encountered types of risk are the following:

risk of principal: The chance that invested capital will lose its value.

liquidity risk: The possibility that an asset may not be sold on short notice for its market value. If an investment must be sold at a high discount, it is said to have a substantial amount of liquidity risk.

default risk: The risk that a borrower will be unable to make interest payments or principal repayments on debt. For example, there is a great amount of default risk inherent in the bonds of a company experiencing financial difficulty.

market risk: Refers to changes in a stock's price that result from changes in the stock market as a whole, regardless of the fundamental change in a firm's earning power, as prices of all stocks are correlated to some degree with broad swings in the stock market.

interest rate risk: Refers to the fluctuations in the value of an asset as the interest rates and conditions of the money and capital markets change. Interest rate risk relates to fixed income securities such as bonds. For example, if interest rates rise (fall), bond prices fall (rise).

purchasing power risk: Relates to the possibility that an investor will receive a lesser amount of purchasing power than was originally invested. Bonds are most affected by this risk as the issuer will be paying back in cheaper dollars during an inflationary period.

systematic and unsystematic risk: The portion of a security's risk, called unsystematic risk, that can be controlled through DIVERSIFICATION. This type of risk is unique to a given security. Business, liquidity, and default risks fall in this category. Nondiversifiable risk, more commonly referred to as systematic risk, results from forces outside the firm's control and are therefore not unique to the given security. Purchasing power, interest rate, and market risks fall into this category. This type of risk is measured by the BETA coefficient.

exchange risk: The chance of loss on foreign currency exchange.

actuarial risk: The risk an insurance company covers in exchange for premiums, such as the risk of the insured's premature death.

risk averse Opposed to RISK. It is a subjective attitude against risk taking. An investor not willing to take risk may place his or her funds into U.S. Treasury bills.

risk management The analysis of and planning for potential RISKS and their subsequent losses. The objective of risk management is to try to minimize the financial consequence of random losses.

See also INSURANCE PROGRAMS; INVESTMENT PLANNING.

risk measures Quantitative measures of RISK. They attempt to assess the degree of variation or uncertainty about earnings or return. There are several measures, including the standard deviation, coefficient of variation, and BETA. The STANDARD DEVIATION is a statistical measure of dispersion of the probability distribution of possible returns. The smaller the deviation, the tighter the distribution, and thus, the lower the riskiness of the investment.

One must be careful in using the standard deviation to compare risks as it is only an absolute measure of dispersion (risk) and does not consider the dispersion of outcomes in relationship to an expected return. In comparisons of securities with differing expected returns, the COEFFICIENT OF VARIATION is commonly used. The coefficient of variation (CV) is computed simply by dividing the standard deviation for a security by its expected value. The higher the coefficient, the more risky the security. Beta measures a stock's or mutual fund's volatility relative to the general market.

risk neutral An adjective describing an individual who neither fears nor enjoys RISK but views it in an objective, rational manner with a view toward its control when beneficial.

risk premium The amount by which the required return on an asset or security exceeds the risk-free rate, such as the T-bill rate. The risk premium is the additional return required to compensate an investor for assuming a given level of RISK. The higher this premium, the more risky the security, and vice versa.

risk reduction An attempt to minimize risk by taking some action, such as diversifying one's investment portfolio or obtaining proper insurance coverage.

risk retension *See* SELF-INSURANCE.

risk-return trade-off A concept that is integral to personal finance. All personal financial and investment decisions involve some sort of balance between RISK and RETURN. The investor must compare the EXPECTED RETURN from a given investment with the risk associated with it. Generally speaking, the higher the risk undertaken, the more ample the return, and conversely, the lower the risk, the more modest the return. In the case of investing in stock, the investor would demand a higher return from a speculative stock to compensate for the higher level of risk.

The proper assessment and balance of the various risk-return trade-offs is part of creating a sound personal financial and investment plan.

risk taker A person who is not fearful of uncertainty and may even enjoy risky, speculative situations. He or she is a person who will take a chance or gamble in hopes of winning.

Return versus Risk

Risk–Return Function

Expected Return

Risk–free Rate

Risk

risk transfer An individual transferring a given risk to another, such as taking out fire and theft insurance policies so the insurance company will bear much of the risk of loss.

roll up Selling one option position and buying another having a higher strike price.

rollover

investment: Moving funds from one INVESTMENT to another without actually receiving the cash value of the original investment. For example, if an individual owns a $10,000 TREASURY NOTE or CERTIFICATE OF DEPOSIT, upon its maturity the original investment can be rolled over into a new $10,000 Treasury note or certificate of deposit without receiving the cash value of the original note or certificate. An INVESTOR may sell a security and roll over the proceeds into the same security thereby establishing a new cost basis for the security.
See THIRTY-DAY WASH SALE.

loans: A method of extending the terms of a loan. Rather than calling the PRINCIPAL of the LOAN, a BANK may just grant a new LOAN at a renegotiated INTEREST RATE. This has happened with international loans when the country borrowing the MONEY was unable to pay the principal of the loan. Another example is to rollover a BALLOON LOAN into a new loan rather than calling for the BALLOON PAYMENT.

rollover loan

1. A delay in making a principal payment on a loan that a bank permits a debtor because of a reason such as current financial difficulties.

2. The extension of a loan at the end of the term at the prevailing market interest rate.

3. A mortgage loan in which the amortization of principal is long-term based but the interest rate is based on the short term.

rollover mortgage A MORTGAGE in which the rate of interest is fixed but the whole loan is negotiated, or rolled over, after a fixed time period.

round lot Or, *even lot*. A unit of trading on a securities exchange. For example, a round lot on the New York Stock Exchange is 100 shares of stock or one $1,000 face-value bond (although brokers may have their own higher round lot requirements in the case of bonds). Inactive stocks have a ten-share round lot.

round-lot orders The generally accepted trading unit of shares of STOCK. This is usually 100 shares although some inactive SECURITIES have a round lot of ten shares. As institutional investors increasingly dominate the trading environment, 500 shares is becoming an institutional round-lot order.

round trip

1. The process and time interval of buying and selling a security.

2. When the investor buys back a stock that he or she has shorted in the market. This is done to cover the short position.

row house A single-family unit attached to other units by common walls.

rubber check *See* BOUNCED CHECK; NOT-SUFFI-CIENT-FUNDS (NSF) CHECK.

rule An established regulation or guide for conduct, procedure, or usage. An example is a state requirement for motorists to have automobile insurance or for an investor to put up 50% cash on the purchase of a stock in a margin account.

rule of 72 and rule of 69 A rule of thumb method used to determine how many years it takes to double investment money. Under this method, dividing the number 72 by the fixed rate of return equals the number of years it takes for annual earnings from the investment to double. That is,

$$72/r \text{ (in percent)}$$

Example 1: Richard bought a piece of property yielding an annual return of 25%. The investment will double in less than three years.

$$72/25 = 2.88 \text{ years.}$$

The rule of 69, which is very similar to the rule of 72, states that an amount of money invested at r% per period will double in

$$69/r \text{ (in percent)} + .35 \text{ periods.}$$

Example 2: Using the same data from the previous example,

$$69/25 + .35 = 2.76 + .35 = 3.11 \text{ years}$$

rule of 78 Or, *the rule of the sum of the digits*. A method that banks use to develop a LOAN AMORTIZATION schedule. It results in a borrower's paying more interest in the beginning of a loan when he or she has the use of more of the money, and less interest as the debt is reduced. Therefore, it is important to know how much interest can be saved by prepaying the loan after a certain month and how much of the loan is still owed.

Example: Mary borrows $3,180 ($3,000 principal and $180 interest) for 12 months, so her equal monthly payment is $265 ($3,180/12). She wants to know how much interest she saves by prepaying the loan after six payments. Mary might guess $90 ($180 × 6/12), reasoning that interest is charged uniformly each month, but she would be wrong. Here is how the rule of 78 works.

1. First, add up all the digits for the number of payments scheduled to be made, in this case the sum of the digits 1 through 12 (1+2+3 . . . +12 = 78).

Generally, you can find the sum of the digits (SD) using the following formula:

$$SD = n(n+1)/2 = 12(12+1)/2 = (12)(13)/2$$
$$= 156/2 = 78$$

where n = the number of months. (The sum of the digits for a four-year [48 months] loan is 1,176 [(48)(48+1)/2 = (48)(49)/2 = 1,176]). (See Loan Amortization Schedule below.)

2. In the first month, before making any payments, Mary has the use of the entire amount borrowed. She thus pays 12/78ths (or 15.39%) of the total interest in the first payment. In the second month, she pays 11/78ths (14.10%); in the third, 10/78ths (12.82%); and so on down to the last payment, 1/78ths (1.28%). Thus, the first month's total payment of $265 contains $27.69 (15.39% × $180) in interest and $237.31 ($265 − $27.69) in principal. The 12th and last payment of $265 contains $2.30 (1.28% × $180) in interest and $262.70 in principal.

3. In order to find out how much interest is saved by prepaying after the sixth payment,

Mary merely adds up the digits for the remaining six payments. Thus, using the above formula, 6(6+1)/2 = 21. This means that 21/78ths of the interest, or $48.46 (21/78 × $180), will be saved.

4. To calculate the amount of principal still owed, subtract the total amount of interest already paid, $131.54 ($180 − $48.46), from the total amount of payments made, $1,590 (6 × $265), giving $1,458.46. Then subtract this from the original $3,000 principal, giving $1,541.54 still owed.

5. Does it pay to pay off after the sixth payment? It depends on how much return Mary can get from investing elsewhere. In this example, she needed $1,541.54 to pay off the loan to save $48.46 in interest. For loans of longer maturities, the same rules apply, though the actual sum of the digits will be different. Thus, for a 48-month loan, the borrower would pay 48/1176ths of the total interest in the first month, 47/1176ths in the second month and so on.

LOAN AMORTIZATION SCHEDULE
Based on a loan of $3,180 ($3,000 principal and $180 interest)

Payment Number	Fraction (Percent) Earned by Lender	Monthly Payment	Interest	Principal
1	12/78 (15.39%)	$265	$27.69*	$237.31**
2	11/78 (14.10%)	265	25.39	239.61
3	10/78 (12.82%)	265	23.08	241.92
4	9/78 (11.54%)	265	20.77	244.23
5	8/78 (10.26%)	265	18.46	246.54
6	7/78 (8.97%)	265	16.15	248.85
7	6/78 (7.69%)	265	13.85	251.15
8	5/78 (6.41%)	265	11.54	253.46
9	4/78 (5.13%)	265	9.23	255.77
10	3/78 (3.85%)	265	6.92	258.08
11	2/78 (2.56%)	265	4.62	260.38
12	1/78 (1.28%)	265	2.30	262.70
78	78/78 (100%)	$3,180	$180.00	$3,000.00

*$27.69 = $180.00 × 12/78 (15.39%)
**$237.31 = $265 − $27.69

S

safe deposit box A secured lock box available for rent in banks and used as storage place for keeping valuables such as jewelry, contracts, STOCK CERTIFICATES, TITLES, and other special documents.

safekeeping The protection of an item by storing it in a safe place. Money, documents, and valuables may be retained in a secure location to guard against theft or destruction. Examples are keeping important papers in a safe deposit box and retaining securities in a vault.

safety Condition of protecting oneself or one's assets against loss. For example, when the stock market is deemed to be excessively risky, investors may make a "flight to safety" by withdrawing funds and investing in U.S. government securities. Many individuals put most of their money in the bank because of the safety associated with the $100,000 federal deposit insurance. Assets are also protected through insurance such as homeowner's insurance.

salary A regular form of compensation an employee receives from an employer. Salaries are normally paid on a weekly, biweekly, or monthly basis depending on the pattern the employer establishes. Salaries normally include employee benefits such as HEALTH INSURANCE and SOCIAL SECURITY benefits. TAXES and other expenses are deducted from salaries.
See also SALARY DEDUCTIONS.

salary deductions Or, *payroll deductions.* Mandatory and agreed-to deductions made from the payroll of an employee. Mandatory payroll deductions include SOCIAL SECURITY taxes, HEALTH INSURANCE, federal and applicable local and state withholding TAXES. Voluntary deductions include PENSION contributions, union dues, and any specially elected INSURANCE deductions.

The amount remaining after deductions is TAKE-HOME PAY.

salary freeze An immobilization of SALARY increases by management normally due to tight BUDGETARY restrictions. During a period of a salary freeze, all salaries remain at current levels until the salary freeze is lifted or modified. For example, in 1990, Greyhound Dial Corporation froze the salaries of Greyhound employees because of financial difficulties resulting from a prolonged strike.

salary incentive An additional amount of money paid to an employee in order to promote additional performance, productivity, or sales. For example, if a salesperson's sales exceed a certain level, the employee will receive a salary incentive. Salary incentives normally are paid in CASH; however, in-kind salary incentives include special vacations or the use of a resort.

salary reduction loan *See* 401(K) PLAN.

salary review An appraisal by an employer of an employee's performance over a period of time, usually yearly, to determine whether an adjustment should be made to the employee's salary. Often, the reasons for the employer's decision are given to the employee.

sales charge A fee assessed to invest or buy something. For example, a MUTUAL FUND may charge a 3% sales commission on funds invested. The sales charge is deducted immediately and reduces the net investment into the fund. If $1,000 is invested and the sales charge is 3%, the net funds invested by the shareholder into the fund amount to only $970 (97% × $1,000). Often, the sales charge declines with an increasing investment.

sales contract An agreement between the seller and buyer specifying the terms of sale.

sales finance agency (company) A financial institution that purchases contracts from retailers of certain types of merchandise—typically more expensive items such as automobiles, furniture, and appliances—after which the credit user whose contract is purchased usually makes payments to the sales finance company.

sales returns and allowances A credit given to a customer because of returned merchandise or defective goods not suitable to customer needs.

sales tax A state or local tax based on a percentage of the selling price of a good or service that the buyer pays. The seller collects the tax and remits it to the sales tax agency. For example, if goods having a selling price of $5,000 are bought and the sales tax is 8%, the amount of sales tax is $40 ($5,000 × 8%). Thus, the total purchase price is $5,040. The sales tax, if any, varies among states. The sales tax is not deductible on an individual's tax return.

Sallie Mae *See* STUDENT LOAN MARKETING ASSOCIATION SECURITIES.

sandwich lease A lease by which the lessee becomes a lessor by SUBLETTING the property to another. Often, the sandwich leaseholder does not own or use the property.

saucer A pattern in a technical chart showing that the price of an equity or debt security has bottomed out and is now rising. On the other hand, an inverse saucer shows that the price of the security has topped out and is declining. See illustrative chart below depicting a saucer.

savings Funds set aside, commonly in interest-bearing form, to accomplish financial or investment goals.

savings account A BANK ACCOUNT established by a DEPOSITOR for the purpose of putting aside money for future spending goals. Such accounts can be established in either a commercial or SAVINGS BANK; however, in certain states where commercial banks are not permitted to open a SAVINGS ACCOUNT, a SPECIAL INTEREST ACCOUNT can be opened. Savings accounts normally earn a competitive rate of interest and are insured by the FEDERAL DEPOSIT INSURANCE CORPORATION

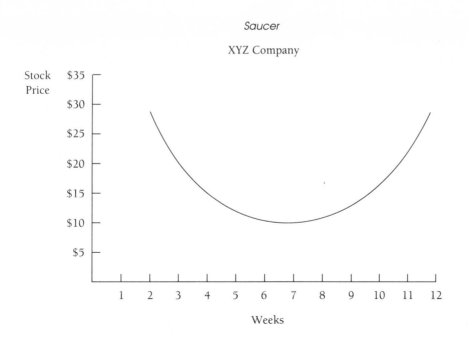

Saucer

XYZ Company

up to $100,000. There are two types of SAVINGS ACCOUNTS: a PASSBOOK ACCOUNT and a STATEMENT SAVINGS ACCOUNT.

savings accumulation plan An arrangement whereby an investor makes scheduled purchases of a specified dollar amount of shares in a MUTUAL FUND.

savings and loan association A FINANCIAL INSTITUTION that channels the savings of its depositors primarily into mortgage and home improvement loans. It specializes in originating, servicing, and holding mortgage loans.

savings bank *See* SAVINGS AND LOAN ASSOCIATION; MUTUAL SAVINGS BANK.

savings bond *See* U.S. SAVINGS BOND.

savings certificate A CERTIFICATE evidencing a savings deposit in a FINANCIAL INSTITUTION such as a SAVINGS AND LOAN ASSOCIATION, a MUTUAL SAVINGS BANK, or a COMMERCIAL BANK.

savings deposit Cash balances that may be kept in depository institutions such as COMMERCIAL BANKS, SAVINGS AND LOAN ASSOCIATIONS, MUTUAL SAVINGS BANKS, or CREDIT UNIONS.

savings element The accumulation in the cash value of life insurance. In the beginning years, it represents the excess of premiums paid over the real cost of protection. If the policyholder cancels the policy, he or she will receive its cash value on that date. Hence, a life insurance policy does have a savings element to it in the form of the increasing cash value.

savings illusion Even though an individual accumulates savings in an account that earns interest, one has to consider what the savings will really be worth after considering inflation. For example, if the interest rate on a bank account is 6% and the inflation rate is 5%, the savings have increased by only 1%, taking into account the change in the purchasing power of the dollar. Also, the depositor will be taxed based on interest income at the 6% rate. Hence, one has to consider what is really left after inflation and taxes.

savings investment A type of investment in which the saver expects virtually no risk for either the PRINCIPAL or the interest.

savings rate The percentage of savings of the income earned by an individual.

savings ratio The ratio of savings to income after taxes (disposable income). A high ratio is desirable, as the individual is building up his or her savings for needed future expenditures.

scab An employee who continues to work during a strike. Often, scabs are new employees hired to replace striking workers. Being a scab worker has an element of risk to personal safety from resentful striking employees. For example, a scab driving a Greyhound bus was killed in the bus during a strike against the company.

schedule of estimated expenditures A list of budgeted CASH expenditures an individual anticipates he or she will have to pay for a prescribed period of time. Examples of estimated EXPENDITURES are for food, clothing, and entertainment. This schedule aids in personal planning so the individual can project how much INCOME he or she needs or what costs have to be cut.

schedule of estimated income A listing of expected revenue sources for a prescribed time period. Forecast income includes salaries, interest income, dividend income, gifts, and so on. This forecast helps an individual plan how much he or she can spend based upon the source and amounts of estimated income.

scheduled payment A payment due at a particular time. Each of the installments in a credit agreement is specified as to amount and DUE DATE.

scholarship The amount received by an individual to attend an educational institution or program. The amount received as a qualified scholarship by an individual who is a candidate for a degree at a recognized educational institution is excluded from taxable income.

screen (stocks) The process of looking at stocks that satisfy the investor's needs and goals. The investor determines which stocks meet his or her established criteria. To expedite matters, stocks may be screened through a software program applied to a data base of securities. For example, an investor may screen stocks to select for further analysis only those that have price-earnings ratios of 5 or lower coupled with a five-year annualized growth rate in market price per share of at least 10%.

scrip

1. A document giving the receiver the ability to obtain cash, other assets, or stock of the company. The scrip may be exercisable currently or at a stated later date. An example is scrip representing FRACTIONAL SHARES arising from a stock split.

2. A written promise issued by a government to exchange at a subsequent date real currency for the document.

3. A coupon given by a corporation to its staff in purchasing company goods.

scrip dividend Or, *liability dividend*. A dividend in the form of notes payable when the company has a cash problem. The cash payment for the dividend will occur in the future and include an element of both principal and interest.

seasonality A fluctuation in business or economic conditions that occurs on a regular basis. It may be caused by such factors as weather and vacations. An example is the sales volume of the toy industry in November and December, the months in which it records its highest sales. Seasonality affects individuals, such as an accountant who is extremely busy during tax season.

seasoned issue A security of a financially sound and mature company that should perform well in good times and hold its own in bad times. Typically, a seasoned issue will experience stability in price and provide good liquidity in the secondary market. As a result, it is attractive to investors.

seat Membership on a securities or commodities exchange. There are required rules for entry. You have to have a seat in order to trade. The price for a seat changes depending upon market conditions. During bad financial times, the price will drop. There are about 1,400 seats on the New York Stock Exchange.

second death insurance A life insurance policy paying a death benefit only when the second of two insureds dies. If one dies, there is no benefit.

second deed of trust (mortgage) A DEED OF TRUST or MORTGAGE in REAL ESTATE in which the lender subordinates his or her loan to another lender whose priority is first in the event of nonpayment by the borrower.

second injury fund An insurance fund established by most states to encourage companies to hire handicapped people. If a handicapped employee suffers a later work-related injury or disease causing total disability, the employer is liable only for worker's compensation on the second injury or disease. The fund covers the difference between the benefit for total disability and that for the second injury.

second mortgage A mortgage debt with a subordinated claim to that of the first mortgage. However, a second mortgage is senior to subsequent liens. A second mortgage may be used to reduce the amount of a cash down payment or in refinancing to raise cash for some purpose (e.g., home improvement, investment in a business). The interest rate on the second mortgage is higher because of the increased risk. The second mortgage typically has a repayment term significantly shorter than the first mortgage with a fixed amortization schedule. There may also be a balloon payment. By illustration, a home costs $200,000 and a first mortgage is taken out for 70%, totaling $140,000. Thus, a $60,000 down payment is needed. If a second mortgage is available for $40,000, then the required cash down payment will be $20,000.

secondary distribution Or, *secondary offering*. The redistribution of a block of previously issued shares. The sale is generally handled through an underwriting company or SYNDICATE and the shares are usually offered at a fixed price, which is related to the current MARKET PRICE of the securities. The securities may be listed or unlisted. There are certain block dispositions requiring SEC sanction.

secondary market The market in which previously issued securities are traded between investors. It is equivalent to a used-car market. *See also* PRIMARY MARKET.

secondary party An individual obligated to pay a debt if the debtor does not pay the creditor. For example, John receives a check from a debtor (Howard). However, John signs the check and gives it to Cathy to whom he owes money. John is secondarily liable on the check, so that if the check is dishonored by Howard, Cathy can look to John for payment.

secret warranty A warranty about which customers are not notified. For example, if a defect in an auto manufacturer's car is found in a later year, the auto manufacturer may not formally notify its purchasers. However, in an issue of *Consumer Reports,* the problem is reported on and those owning the car are advised that the auto manufacturer will fix the problem free of charge if notified. Note that the auto manufacturer did not formally notify its customers. A situation such as this occurred with one of the authors' General Motors Oldsmobile cars in 1989 when the auto dealer fixed the defect.

Section 403(b) plan An INDIVIDUAL RETIREMENT PLAN specified in the INTERNAL REVENUE CODE (IRC) Section 403 (b) in which employees of certain nonprofit organizations may set aside funds, thus deferring current taxation until retirement.

Sections I and II (homeowner's policy) Sections of a HOMEOWNER'S POLICY. Section I applies to the home, contents, and accompanying structures. Section II provides comprehensive coverage for personal liability and the medical pay-ments and property damage incurred by persons other than the insured.

sector A grouping of stocks in a particular category, typically within one industry. For example, the sector that the investor may concentrate on is analysis of pharmaceutical sales.

sector (mutual) fund Or, *specialized fund.* A MUTUAL FUND that invests in one or two fields or industries (sectors). These funds are risky in that they rise and fall depending on how the individual fields or industries do. An example is Prudential Bache Utility Fund.

secured bond A bond that is secured by a pledge of assets or other COLLATERAL that can be sold, if required, to obtain payment. The nature of the lien is specified in the indenture.

secured loan A LOAN requiring that certain assets be pledged as COLLATERAL to secure the debt. Examples of collateral might be one's home or automobile.

securities Financial instruments of issuers that provide investors with ownership rights and return in the form typically of periodic payments (dividends, interest) and appreciation (or decline) in market price. Examples of securities are stocks, bonds, and options.

Securities and Exchange Commission A federal independent regulatory agency, established by the Securities Act of 1933 and the Securities Exchange Act of 1934, whose major objective is to regulate the SECURITIES markets to protect the INVESTOR against fraudulent trading practices, insider trading, and other types of deceit to which an investor could be susceptible. One of the methods the SEC uses to promote the public interest is demanding full public disclosure of all SECURITIES trading on the exchanges as well as requiring the registration of all interstate securities. As with most independent regulatory agencies, the SEC has a hearing body to consider complaints brought before it and can render quasi-judicial administrative rulings that have the force of law.

The SEC has the authority to regulate all national securities exchanges and related parties, including INVESTMENT COMPANIES, INVESTMENT ADVISERS AND COUNSELORS, and OVER-THE-COUNTER BROKERS and DEALERS, as well as all other aspects of the securities industry. In addition to the 1933 and 1934 securities acts, responsibilities of the SEC include the Public Utility Holding Company Act of 1935, the Trust Indenture Act of 1939, the Investment Company Act of 1940, and the Investment Advisers Act of 1940.

securities exchanges Privately owned and operated SECURITY MARKETS regulated by the SECURITIES AND EXCHANGE COMMISSION as well as their own boards of governors. The security exchanges include the NEW YORK STOCK EXCHANGE, the AMERICAN STOCK EXCHANGE, and the OVER-THE-COUNTER STOCK EXCHANGE. Regional STOCK EXCHANGES include the Philadelphia Stock Exchange, the Boston Regional Stock Exchange, the Midwest Regional Stock Exchange, and the Pacific Regional Stock Exchange.

The largest stock exchange in terms of capitalization and daily trading volume is the New York Stock Exchange. In addition to these domestic stock exchanges, there are numerous international stock exchanges such as the Tokyo, Toronto, and London Stock Exchanges.

Securities Investors Protection Corporation (SIPC) A nonprofit entity formed by the Securities Protection Act of 1970 promulgating financial safeguards for INVESTORS. Licensed brokers and dealers with the SECURITIES AND EXCHANGE COMMISSION are required to be participants of SIPC.

Acting much like the FDIC, SIPC will protect investors' ASSETS in the event of a DEALER'S financial failure. Under the terms of the act, SIPC will insure INVESTORS accounts up to $500,000, only $100,000 of which can be cash assets.

SIPC has a seven person board of governors that implements policies and procedures as well as overseeing its normal functions.

securities market indices Indices that measure the value of a number of securities chosen as a sample to reflect the behavior of the general market of investments.
See also MARKET INDICES AND AVERAGES.

securities markets The markets in which financial assets such as STOCKS, BONDS, and other financial instruments are traded.
See also FINANCIAL INSTITUTIONS AND MARKETS.

security
1. A certificate of ownership in a company (e.g., stock), an evidence of a debtor's obligation (e.g., bond), or other ownership rights.
2. COLLATERAL issued to support a borrowing. An example is a house that serves as security for the mortgage.
3. Means of protecting property from unauthorized access or use, such as posting a security guard in an apartment building.

security agreement A legal contract in which the installment lender has control over the item being financed. Assets and/or property are pledged as collateral. The agreement describes the property and its location so it may be identified easily by the lender. If the borrower defaults, the lender may sell the assigned collateral. There may be loan covenants contained in the agreement, such as a requirement that the borrower have adequate insurance coverage for the assets pledged.

security analysis Various kinds of analyses, such as of the economy of the securities markets, of the industry of concern, and of the firm on which the security is issued, that help in the evaluation of the quality and general desirability of a security investment.
See FINANCIAL ANALYSIS; FUNDAMENTAL ANALYSIS; TECHNICAL ANALYSIS.

security deposit An amount paid in advance to a landlord to pay for refurbishing the unit beyond what would be expected from normal wear and tear. It is similar to a DAMAGE DEPOSIT, but additional restrictions that may apply should be listed in the LEASE. The security deposit may be refunded upon the expiration of the lease provided the premises are in good condition.

security interest A creditor's control over property. When a loan is secured with COLLATERAL, security interest gives the creditor the right to go to court to obtain possession of the property in the event the borrower defaults. Generally the creditor can sell the property, apply the amount received (less expenses) to the balance owed, and sue the customer for any remaining amount due. State laws vary regarding creditors' rights and obligations in this area.

security rating An appraisal of the investment and credit risk of a security issued by a company or governmental agency. Security ratings are given by such commercial rating services as Standard & Poor's and Moody's.

seek a market The action of a seller looking for a buyer, or vice versa.

self-amortizing mortgage A mortgage that will be paid off through periodic principal and interest payments.

self-employed income The net taxable income of a self-employed person, reported on Schedule C of IRS Form 1040. Examples of self-employed income are consulting income and earnings from services provided to clients. The self-employed individual pays a higher Social Security tax than a regular employee.

self-employed retirement plan *See* KEOGH PENSION PLAN

self-employment tax Tax to which a self-employed individual is subject, the objective being to provide him or her with Social Security benefits. The tax is assessed on the individual's self-employed income. This tax is paid by adding an amount to the income tax computed on Form 1040. The self-employment tax is computed on Schedule SE of Form 1040.

self-insurance Funds set aside by an individual as protection against a possible loss. Funds may be deposited in a lump sum or periodically. Self-insurance is more suitable for minimal possible losses that may occur on a more regular basis. The objective is to eliminate unneeded insurance premiums. However, by not taking out insurance, the individual is at greater risk. Self-insurance is not advisable for potentially huge losses such as a fire loss on one's home.

seller financing Arrangements under which the seller of a home agrees to lend the buyer some or all of the purchase price.
See also CREATIVE FINANCING.

sell order An order by an investor to a BROKER to sell a particular SECURITY. A sell order may be a LIMIT ORDER, MARKET ORDER, a DAY ORDER, or a GOOD-TILL-CANCELED ORDER (GTC). The broker is obligated to obey the customer's order and try to get an orderly execution through the FLOOR BROKER.

sell out
1. Liquidation of inventory by a retail store before going out of business. The consumer may get some very good values.
2. An order given by a seller to sell a security. When the initial investor does not pay for the security when due, the defaulting buyer is legally liable for the seller's losses resulting from the failure to honor the commitment.
3. A broker's liquidation of stocks to satisfy an unmet margin call.
See also MARGIN CALL.

seller's market A market in which the seller has the advantage because demand for the product, property, or security exceeds supply. In addition, the seller has a strong influence over the terms of sale. This will drive up the price.
See also BUYERS'S MARKET.

selling against the box A SHORT SALE undertaken to protect a profit in a stock and to defer tax liability to another year. For example, an investor owns 100 shares of ABC Company, which has gone up and which he thinks may decline. Consequently, he sells the 100 shares "short" and keeps them. If ABC Company stock declines, the profit on his short sale is exactly offset by the loss in the market value of the stock he owns. If ABC Company stock advances, the loss on his short sale is offset by the gain in the market value of the stock he has retained.

selling charge *See* LOAD.

selling climax A condition in the securities markets in which a sudden selling surge develops, accompanied by high volume, resulting in investor panic. Prices drop precipitously. Such a selling surge is technically significant, indicating the bottom of a market's selling pressure. This event implies that a rally is soon to develop. See illustrative chart below.

selling group Or, *syndicate*. A group responsible for disposing of recently issued securities that may be bought by individual and corporate investors. There is an allocation of securities to be sold by DEALERS and BROKERS. The members of the group are typically compensated through sales commissions rather than receiving an underwriting fee.

selling short *See* SHORT SELLING (SALE).

senior debenture A form of unsecured DEBT issued by large, well-established CORPORATIONS having precedence, in the event of the liquidation of a company's assets, over other DEBENTURES.

senior debts Any form of DEBT, including BONDS, DEBENTURES, MORTGAGES, and NOTES PAYABLE, having a precedent claim, in the event of LIQUIDATION, on an entity's capital structure. These claims must be satisfied prior to the satisfaction of any other debt demand.

senior mortgage bond A MORTGAGE BOND having a precedent claim on any ASSETS and earnings, in the event of a CORPORATION LIQUIDATION, over any other MORTGAGES with subordinate LIENS.

sensitive market A market that may quickly be affected by new developments. As a result, prices of securities will be significantly swayed by positive or negative news. This type of market is more risky because of the greater uncertainty surrounding price movements.

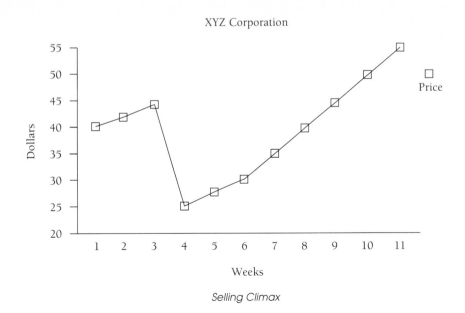

XYZ Corporation

Selling Climax

sentiment indicators Measures to appraise optimistic or pessimistic views of the market by investors. Many TECHNICAL ANALYSTS make recommendations that are opposite of what the sentiment indicators point to. This is one contrary opinion approach. For example, when most investors are BEARISH, the market is probably going to go up.

separable property Property wholly owned by one spouse, which belonged to the spouse before marriage or was received as a gift or an inheritance. This property legally belongs to that spouse and cannot be taken away in a debt action or for estate valuation.

separate return A tax return filed by a married couple who opt to report separately their own incomes, itemized deductions, exemptions, and tax credits. The overall tax is usually higher compared to joint tax returns when separate returns are filed.
See also JOINT TAX RETURN; MARITAL TAX RATE.

serial bond A BOND that matures in installments over time rather than at one MATURITY DATE.

serial redemption The retirement of a SERIAL BOND at a scheduled maturity date.

Series E bond A U.S. SAVINGS BOND issued from 1941 to 1979. It was then replaced by SERIES EE and SERIES HH BONDS.

Series EE savings bond A U.S. government bond purchased for 50% of its face value. It pays no periodic interest, since the interest accumulates between the purchase price and the bond's maturity value. For example, a Series EE bond can be purchased for $100 and redeemed at maturity for $200. Series EE bonds can be purchased in denominations from $25 to $5,000, with a maximum purchase limit of $15,000 annually. Early redemption is penalized with a lower interest rate than that stated on the bond. When held for at least five years, Series EE bonds earn market-based interest or a guaranteed minimum, whichever is higher. Bonds held for less than five years earn a lower rate of return. The market-based rate, announced each May and November, is 85% of the market average on five-year Treasury securities.

Example: George Lee decided to invest $5,000 in a Series EE savings bond for his retirement. If the interest averages 8% after 10 years, how much will he have after 10 years? (assume a semiannual interest accrual).

The future value of $1 (Appendix A, Table 1 factor) for 20 periods at a semiannual rate of 4% is 2.191. The amount George will have after 10 years equals $10,955 ($5,000 × 2.191).
Advantages
- Both Series EE and SERIES HH interest income are exempt from state and local taxes. Federal income taxes can be deferred on Series EE bonds until they are redeemed. It can be deferred even beyond this point by rolling over the EE bonds into Series HH bonds.
- There are no service charges when one purchases or redeems savings bonds, as there are with many other investments.
- The bonds offer safety and complete security backed by the U.S. government.
Disadvantages
- Lack of liquidity
- Relatively lower yield
U.S. savings bonds can be purchased at most banks and other financial institutions or through payroll deduction plans. They can be replaced if lost, stolen, or destroyed. Bonds of both series must be held at least six months before they can be redeemed.

Series HH savings bond A U.S. government bond issued only in exchange for SERIES E and EE SAVINGS BONDS. It is purchased at face value and pays interest semiannually until maturity five years later. Early redemption will be penalized at slightly less than face value. The bond can be redeemed after six months and has a maturity period of ten years.
See also SERIES EE SAVINGS BOND.

service adjustment The change in service years credited to an employee in computing PENSION and other FRINGE BENEFITS.

service bureau A service business that makes its facilities available to outsiders at a fee. An example is a service offering computer use. Because of economies of scale, the user will incur a lower cost from using the service than by doing it himself or herself.

service contract An agreement bought by an owner of a product to have that product repaired as necessary. This contract may be taken out with the vendor or a third party. Examples are service contracts on household appliances and television sets. A service contract gives the owner peace of mind, knowing the item will be fixed at a predetermined fee if problems occur; however, such a contract is generally more costly than paying for the repairs out of pocket as they occur.

service credit In computation of fringe benefits (e.g., pension plan), the credit given to an employee for the number of years he or she has worked.

service department A department within a retail store providing services to customers, such as wrapping merchandise, reviewing credit applications, and handling merchandise returns.

service life It is how long an owner anticipates to use an asset. The service life of property may be shorter than its economic life. By illustration, five years may be the length of time an owner expects to drive a car.

service of process The delivery of a notice or document in a suit to the opposite party to effectuate a charge against him or her with receipt of the charge and to subject that person to its legal effect. The service of process gives a defendant reasonable notice of the proceedings against him or her to afford ample opportunity to appear and be heard.

services offered policyholders Various administrative and risk management services that may be purchased by the insured. Examples of additional services that may be taken out include loss control and claims adjustment.

servicing

1. The periodic, routine maintenance of household items and other assets (e.g., cars).

2. The handling of an account, as an insurance account handled by an insurance broker.

settlement

in general: A resolution of differences between two or more people resolving the claims of all concerned. Such a settlement is reached after a negotiation period between all the participants has occurred. For example, a claim settlement by an insured is achieved with his or her INSURANCE company after a period of proposals and counterproposals has occurred.

securities: Fulfilling a SECURITIES transaction through the delivery of a proper security certificate including the requisite payment. This occurs in a REGULAR-WAY DELIVERY not later than five business days. The settlement for security options is one business day.

settlement date

securities: the delivery date when the necessary SECURITY CERTIFICATES and the receipt of payment have occurred. In REGULAR-WAY DELIVERY, the settlement date is not later than five business days following the TRADE DATE (security transaction). In security options, the settlement date is not later than one business day after the transaction.

real estate: Upon a purchase, the date when the title for a parcel of land and its improvements has been transferred.

settlement options The options available to the LIFE INSURANCE BENEFICIARY and/or the insured concerning the form of payment of the DEATH BENEFIT of a life insurance policy: over fixed periods, in fixed amounts, interest only, or as income for life.

several but joint agreement An arrangement in which members of an underwriting syndicate of a new issue agree to sell shares allocated to them as well as any shares not sold by the other group members.
See also SEVERALLY BUT NOT JOINTLY.

severally but not jointly A type of agreement in an underwriting of a new issue whereby group members contract to buy a specified percentage of the new issue (severally), but do not have joint liability for shares not sold by other syndicate members.
See also SEVERAL BUT JOINT AGREEMENT.

severalty An individual's sole ownership of REAL PROPERTY.

severance damages The amount awarded by a governmental unit when an individual's property is condemned for the inconvenience of moving.

severance pay Employer compensation to an employee who has been laid off. It is supposed to help bridge the gap of the income lost while the former employee is looking for a new job. For example, a laid-off executive may receive one month's pay.

shakeout
business: A condition in which businesses, often in the same industry, experience a significant loss of profitability through a combination of increased competition and lower product demand. In a business shakeout, some businesses often fail.
securities: A situation in which a MARKET suddenly experiences rapidly falling prices, accompanied by high volume, until it reaches a new TRADING RANGE.

share One unit of ownership interest in a company, MUTUAL FUND, LIMITED PARTNERSHIP, or other. In the case of ownership in a company, a stock certificate is issued including the company's name, stockholder's name, number of shares, and such information. For example, the owner of 200 shares of a company's common stock that has 10,000 shares outstanding has a 2% equity interest.

share account A CREDIT UNION SAVINGS ACCOUNT.

share broker A discount BROKER whose commission is significantly less than that of a full-service broker. The share broker's commission is based on the number and the price of shares traded.
See also VALUE BROKER.

share draft An instrument much like a CHECK, used by CREDIT UNIONS to process withdrawals from an interest-bearing share account.

share draft account A CREDIT UNION CHECKING ACCOUNT. It is much like a NEGOTIABLE ORDER OF WITHDRAWAL (NOW) account. Interest is paid on the balance. A minimum balance is required. If the balance falls below a minimum, a service charge is assessed.

shared appreciation mortgage (SAM) A MORTGAGE in which the borrower pays a lower rate of interest in return for agreeing to share a portion of the price APPRECIATION with the lender.

shared driving In automobile insurance, a factor on which the insurance company bases its premium—those within a family who share use of the automobile. For example, the insurance company views younger drivers as greater insurable risks than parents.

shared equity mortgage (SEM) Or, *equity participation mortgage.* A MORTGAGE in which the borrower pays a lower rate of interest in return for granting a share of the EQUITY in the price APPRECIATION with an outside investor. The outside investor either provides some of the money needed to buy the house or agrees to help make monthly payments. The investor may also receive valuable annual tax write-offs. For example, Norman obtains a SEM from a mortgage lender. The lender provides one-third of the necessary down payment. Norman makes loan payments. At resale, the lender gets one-third of the proceeds after repayment of the balance of the loan.

shareholder In SECURITIES, an investor owning STOCK in a company.

shareholder report A report issued to shareholders of a company, MUTUAL FUND, or other entity revealing the status, financial performance, and other relevant information about the entity.

short

1. A stock is sold by an investor who does not have title to it. The seller anticipates a drop in price and at that time will buy the stock back. A profit is realized between the higher selling price and the lower purchase price. To sell short, an individual must have a brokerage account.

2. Having insufficient funds to complete a purchase.

short bond   A BOND with a near-term maturity, typically one year or less.

short coupon   An interest payment on a bond that is due sooner than the customary six-month period. A short coupon payment takes place when the initial date of the bond is less than six months from the first date interest is due.

short covering   In securities, the act of buying back borrowed securities sold SHORT in the market. This process is completed by a *short seller* either to lock in a profit, prevent a loss in a rising market, or to close out a HEDGE position.

short hedge   A transaction that reduces or eliminates the risk of a drop in the price of a security or commodity without involving ownership. An example is buying a PUT OPTION on a stock owned.

short interest   The total open interest in SHARES sold SHORT in a particular SECURITY MARKET. The total number of shares sold short on the NEW YORK STOCK EXCHANGE is published monthly. The number of shares sold SHORT gives an indication of INVESTOR sentiment. A large SHORT-INTEREST RATIO is bullish in that these investors would have to COVER their positions if the MARKET began to rise. Conversely, a small SHORT-INTEREST RATIO is BEARISH, as it indicates that investors are fully invested.
See also SHORT-INTEREST RATIO; SHORT-INTEREST THEORY; SHORT POSITION.

short-interest ratio   The ratio of the number of SHARES sold SHORT to the total average daily trading volume of a STOCK.
See also SHORT INTEREST; SHORT-INTEREST THEORY; SHORT POSITION.

short-interest theory   A theory predicting upward price movements of SECURITIES based on the SHORT-INTEREST RATIO. A rule-of-thumb measure states that the SHORT-INTEREST RATIO is BULLISH if it exceeds 1½ to 2 times the average daily volume of a security.

However, with the advent of the COVERED CALL WRITING strategy, INVESTORS tend to borrow STOCK after being exercised by a stock purchaser, significantly distorting the effectiveness of classic short interest theory.
See also SHORT INTEREST; SHORT POSITION.

short position   The act of borrowing a SECURITY from a BROKERAGE firm in order to sell it in the open MARKET. The INVESTOR is either HEDGING a LONG POSITION in a SECURITY or speculating that the price of a security is about to decline, whereupon he or she would profit by COVERING the short position through repurchasing the security at a lower price than it was sold SHORT. Assume an INVESTOR sells SHORT 100 SHARES of a stock for a total of $3,500. The BROKER borrows the shares and holds the proceeds of the short sale to secure the LOAN and satisfy MARGIN REQUIREMENTS. Later, the investor buys the stock at $20 per share, repays the 100 shares, earning a per-share profit of $15, for a total of $1,500.
See also SHORT INTEREST; SHORT-INTEREST RATIO; SHORT-INTEREST THEORY.

short-run financial goals   Monetary and financial goals that are established for one or two years.

short selling (sale)   A trading technique in which one sells a security he or she does not own (by borrowing it from a broker) and later buying a like amount of the same security. This technique is used to make a profit from a fall in stock price. The rationale behind short selling goes as follows. The simplest way to make money in the stock market is to buy a stock at a low price and sell it later at a higher one. In a short-selling situation, investors are reversing the sequence; they are selling high, promising to buy back the stock later at what they hope will be a lower price. If the stock price falls, they make money. If it rises and they have to buy back their stocks for more than they sold them for, they lose money.

An investor who wants to sell short has to set up a margin account with a STOCKBROKER and comply with rules established by the federal government, the SEC, and the BROKERAGE HOUSE. The reason for this requirement is that the government and the brokerage house want to ensure that the investor will be able to buy back the stock if the price rises suddenly. Thus, the Federal Reserve requires that an investor have in his or her account cash or securities worth at least 50% of the market value of the stock he wants to sell short. Another requirement is that a stock can be sold short only when the stock price has risen (UP TICK). Thus an investor cannot sell short a listed stock that drops steadily from $50 to $30. Stocks traded over the counter, on the other hand, may be sold short any time. The short-seller normally pays no interest charge. He or she must, however, keep the proceeds from the sale in his or her brokerage account. The brokerage firm invests that money in short-term securities and keeps the interest. The firm also gets its normal commission.

Since selling short can be extremely risky, the investor is advised to use some strategies. Following are three of the most common short-selling strategies:

1. Go short because you think the stock price is going to decline.

2. Go short if you want to postpone making a gain and paying taxes on it from one year to the next. Let us suppose, for example, that the 100 shares of Apple Company you bought at $10 are now selling at $35 and you would like to sell the stock and take your profit. If you sell now, you will have to pay income taxes on the gain by

next April 15. If you want to postpone the gain until the following year you can tell your broker to short your Apple Company stock against the box. Then the broker will keep the STOCK CERTIFICATE in his or her vault (or box) and sell it short. Because you both own the stock and have sold it short, you are hedged against increases or decreases in the price of Apple stock. For example, if Apple Company stock rises to $50 a share by the time you sell it in January, you will have an additional $15 a share gain on the stock you own but a $15 a share loss on the stock you sell short. If, on the other hand, Apple Company stock falls back to $10, you will have no gain in the stock you originally purchased but a $25 a share gain in the stock you sold short.

3. Go short to protect yourself if you own the stock but for some reason cannot sell. If, for example, you buy stock through a payroll purchase plan at the end of each quarter but do not get the certificates until several weeks later, it may make sense to sell your shares short to lock in the gain.

short squeeze When securities or commodities futures begin to increase in price and investors who had a short sale are forced to cover their short position or possibly incur significant losses. If this is done by many short-sellers, the action is referred to as a short squeeze. For example, if a commodity futures trading is stopped because the price has reached an up limit, the short seller is prevented from closing out his or her short sale by purchasing the futures contract because it has gone "limit up."

short term

1. Descriptive of an asset or investment that will be converted into cash within one year or less.

2. Descriptive of a liability that is payable within one year or less.

3. For long-term bonds, a period of about four years.

short-term capital gain or loss The profit or loss from selling an INVESTMENT that is held one

year or less. Short-term profits are considered ORDINARY INCOME, while short-term losses are deducted from CURRENT INCOME. Short-term gains or losses do not qualify for any special tax treatment.
See also SHORT-TERM GAIN OR LOSS.

short-term debt   Or, *current liabilities*. DEBTS or other LIABILITIES payable within one year. Examples are ACCOUNTS payable, short-term LOANS payable, and accrued expenses bills, such as telephone and electricity charges. The portion of long-term DEBT payable within one year is also considered short-term debt. An example is the current year payment on a five-year note payable.

short-term gain or loss   Any business or financial gain or loss that occurs within one year. Short-term gains or losses do not receive any special tax consideration.
See also SHORT-TERM CAPITAL GAIN OR LOSS.

short-term goals or objectives   Any goal or objective that is reached within one year. For example, an individual may plan on earning more money in the current year than last year. An individual may have as a near-term goal buying a new car.

short-term investment   Any INVESTMENT intended to be held for one year or less. Examples are a three-month TREASURY BILL, a six-month CERTIFICATE OF DEPOSIT, and a STOCK or BOND that will be sold within the year.
See also SHORT-TERM CAPITAL GAIN OR LOSS; SHORT-TERM GAIN OR LOSS.

short-term investor   An individual who invests in a security or commodity with the intent of holding it for one year or less.

short-term municipal bond fund   A type of MONEY MARKET FUND that invests in short-term MUNICIPAL BONDS and offers LIQUIDITY with tax-free interest.

sick leave   The amount of days accumulated for possible illness based on the service period with the employer. The employee will be paid for the days he or she is sick. For example, an employer may give one sick-leave day per month to employees. Thus, 12 sick-leave days are earned per year. The employer may place a limit of 180 on total sick-leave days that can be accrued so the employee will not accumulate more. Some employers give retired people payment for all or part of their accumulated sick-leave days.

sickness policy   An insurance policy that covers a specific disease, such as cancer.

side-by-side trading   The exchange of a stock and an option on it on the identical exchange.

sideways market   In SECURITIES, a MARKET in which the prices do not fluctuate significantly. In such a market, there are no major price changes. The market may be considered to be in a period of consolidation.

sight draft   An order signed by the drawer requesting the drawee to pay the amount due the payee upon demand. In many instances, the drawer and payee are the same. A sight draft may be used when the seller of goods wishes to retain control of the goods being shipped to an importer or exporter because of credit reasons or to retain title.

signature card   A card required by BANKS to be kept on file for the purpose of identifying and confirming a DEPOSITOR'S signature for withdrawals, CHECK cashing, or other documentary authorization. The DEPOSITOR signs the card and the bank retains it on file.

signature loan   An unsecured personal loan. Requires only a borrower's signature, if supported by satisfactory CREDIT HISTORY, employment, and income.

silent partner   A PARTNER in a PARTNERSHIP who provides funds but has no direct operational management role. A silent partner shares the net income equally with other GENERAL PARTNERS. While a silent partner is often unknown, he or she has equal liability with the partnership.

simple interest The interest charge computed on the original principal. It is compared with COMPOUND INTEREST, which is applied to the original principal and accumulated interest. The simple interest on a $50,000, 10% loan is $5,000.

simple interest method The method in which interest is charged only on the actual loan balance outstanding. For example, Jerry wants to find the monthly payment required on a $1,000, 12%, 12-month loan. From Table 6, Appendix A (Monthly Installment Loan Payments), he would find a value of $88.85. This is the monthly payment it will take him to pay off the $1,000 loan in 12 months.
See also ADD-ON METHOD; ANNUAL PERCENTAGE RATE (APR); RULE OF 78.

simple rate of return Or, *accounting* or *unadjusted rate of return*. The return obtained by dividing the expected future annual net income by the required investment. Sometimes the average investment rather than the original initial investment is used as the required investment; this is called the AVERAGE RATE OF RETURN.
Example: Consider the following investment:

Initial investment	$6,500
Estimated life	20 years
Expected annual net income	$675

The simple rate of return is $675/$6,500 = 10.4%. Using the average investment, which is usually assumed to be one-half the original investment, the average rate of return will be doubled as follows:

$$\$675/1/2(\$6,500) = \$675/\$3,250 = 20.8\%$$

simple trust A TRUST that is legally obligated to distribute all of its income currently.

simple yield Return on a bond equal to the nominal dollar interest divided by the market value. It is an approximate, simplified rate earned by the bondholder. Assume a $1,000, 7%, 10-year bond is issued at 96% of face value. The simple yield equals

$$\frac{\text{Nominal interest}}{\text{Market value}} = \frac{7\% \times \$1,000}{96\% \times \$1,000} = \frac{\$70}{\$960} = 7.3\%$$

simplified employee pension/individual retirement A type of INDIVIDUAL RETIREMENT ACCOUNT that any employer can offer to employees. Employers can contribute to SIMPLIFIED EMPLOYER PENSION (SEP) accounts.

simplified employer pension plan (sep) A PENSION PLAN whereby an employer makes annual contributions on the employee's behalf to an INDIVIDUAL RETIREMENT ACCOUNT (IRA) set up by the employee.

simultaneous destruction A condition under which all of one's property is subject to loss at the same time due to a common PERIL such as an earthquake or flood.

single family dwelling Any house or other dwelling designed and zoned for only one-family use. Other dwellings may be attached to a single family dwelling but do not share the same plumbing, heating, or electrical system. Single family dwellings include detached housing, CONDOMINIUMS, COOPERATIVES, and TOWNHOUSES.

single life annuity An ANNUITY that covers the life of a single ANNUITANT.

single limit automobile liability An automobile LIABILITY POLICY that specifies the maximum amount paid per accident as a single lump sum rather than in terms of separate per-individual and per-accident limits for bodily injury and property damage.

single payment loan A loan requiring that the borrower repay principal and interest in a single sum at the end of the loan period or with periodic interest payments.

single premium annuity contract An ANNUITY purchased with a LUMP-SUM payment, often just prior to retirement.

single premium deferred annuity (SPDA) A tax-deferred investment in which the investor makes one payment to another insurance company or mutual fund. The value of the ANNUITY declines over time based on the terms of the contract. Tax is paid only when withdrawals are made, generally when the taxpayer is older and in a lower tax bracket. There is no limitation on the single premium amount to be contributed.

single premium life insurance An INSURANCE policy that requires only one premium payment. *See also* SINGLE PREMIUM WHOLE LIFE (SPWL) INSURANCE

single premium whole life (SPWL) insurance WHOLE LIFE INSURANCE that requires only one PREMIUM payment. It is a policy with a low-risk investment flavor. For a minimum amount of $5,000, paid once, a policyholder gets a paid-up insurance policy. His or her money is invested at a guaranteed rate of interest, for one year or longer. SPWL has the following features:

1. CASH VALUE earns interest immediately at competitive rates
2. The owner may borrow interest earned annually after the first year. Borrowings up to the amount that the policy has earned will be treated as taxable income.
3. The owner may take out a loan for up to 90% of the principal at lower rates.
4. The owner receives permanent LIFE INSURANCE coverage.
5. Withdrawals and loans are not subject to tax.
6. The policy allows tax-deferred accumulation of cash values.
7. Tax-free death benefits are given to named beneficiaries.

Minuses of SPWL include the following:

1. There are usually surrender charges if the money is taken out.
2. The interest rate is generally guaranteed for only one year and could drop.

When shopping for SPWL, it is advisable to get answers to the following questions:

1. What is the "net interest" rate at which the cash value will grow? The net interest rate is the YIELD after subtracting costs of the insurance and administrative expenses.
2. What is the surrender charge?
3. Are there any loan-processing fees? What is the loan interest rate?
4. Is there a bail-out plan that enables one to cash in the policy without penalty if interest rates drop below the initial rate?

single-state municipal bond fund A bond fund that invests solely in the municipal bonds of a particular state. For example, the bond fund may invest only in New York municipal bonds. The main reason the fund invests in one state, such as New York, is that interest earned on municipal bonds of the state in which the investor resides is tax-free to that investor. Thus, the New York resident would get "triple tax-free interest."

sinking fund A fund established for periodic payments, aimed at amortizing a financial obligation such as a BOND. The funds can be invested in income-producing securities. The objective is to accumulate PRINCIPAL and investment income sufficient to retire the obligation at its MATURITY. *See also* TIME VALUE OF MONEY.

skip-payment privilege

1. A provision in a loan agreement permitting the debtor to miss a payment, provided the lender receives advance notification.
2. A right granted to a credit cardholder to defer payment on a purchase to a later month without charge. An example is a department store's allowing a customer to charge a purchase in December 19X1 for holiday shopping but not pay for it until March 19X2.

sleeper

1. An investment, such as a stock, that suddenly is a favorite and substantially increases in price.
2. A security having strong future growth possibilities but at the present time shows little vacillation in price.

slump A short-term fall-off in price, volume, or performance. Examples are a drop in economic activity (e.g., recession), a temporary downward trend in the price of a security, and a decline in employee performance. A slump is not viewed as critical because a rebound in activity or performance is expected.

small business According to the SMALL BUSINESS ADMINISTRATION, a term applied to retail firms that have an annual sales volume of less than $1 million, and manufacturing firms with fewer than 250 employees. A small enterprise has the following characteristics: relatively small size in a particular industry, localized scope of operations, modest activity, personal involvement of its owner or owners in operations, and comparatively limited initial investment of capital. A small business is often family owned.

small business administration (SBA) A federal agency set up in 1953 to provide financing through LOANS or other guarantees for small businesses. The SBA also established a program called the Minority Enterprise Small Business Investment Corporation (MESBIC), which provides direct and guaranteed loans to minority entrepreneurs. Under this program, all private minority INVESTMENTS are matched by federal funds.

Additional legislation authorized the SBA to contribute to the VENTURE CAPITAL requirements of START-UP companies by licensing and funding small business investment companies (SBICs) to maintain a loan for rehabilitation of property damaged by natural disaster (floods, hurricanes, etc.) and to provide LOANS, counseling, and training for small business owners.

The SBA derives all of its funding from congressional appropriations.

small claims court A special court designed to provide swift, inexpensive, and informal settlement of normally small financial claims between parties. Typically, the parties represent themselves. An owner of a retail store might sue a customer for nonpayment of a bill in this court.

small investor Or, *retail investor*. A person who purchases small amounts of stocks or bonds, typically in ODD-LOT amounts.

small loan act State law restricting the terms under which small loans may be made and the interest that may be charged for them.

snowballing Description of a situation or activity that quickly accelerates with increasing momentum. An example is a surge in financial problems experienced by a worker who is unemployed for a long period of time.

social insurance A required benefit program in which employees are eligible for benefits as a matter of right. The purpose is to provide a minimum standard of living for lower paid employees. A governmental agency administers the plan.

Social Security The federal SOCIAL SECURITY Act passed in 1935 to provide supplemental RETIREMENT insurance benefits to its beneficiaries as supervised by the Social Security Administration. Employees and employers pay an equal share of the Social Security TAX, up to a maximum level of annual INCOME, which is then pooled in Social Security TRUST funds. Upon retirement, the employee can qualify for supplemental Social Security income depending upon the number of years worked, amounts paid into the fund, and retirement age.

The Social Security Administration also administers Aid to Families with Dependent Children (AFDC); Unemployment Insurance; Medicare; Public Assistance to the Aged, Blind, and Disabled; Veterans' Compensation and Pensions; MEDICAID; the Food Stamp program; Student Aid; Housing Subsidies and Public Housing; and Nutritional Programs for Children.

Social Security disability income insurance INSURANCE providing benefits to help replace the lost income of eligible disabled workers during a period of DISABILITY that is expected to last 12 full months or until the worker's death.

Social Security integration The coordination of a private pension plan with SOCIAL SECURITY benefits.

Social Security survivors' benefits Payments by the SOCIAL SECURITY ADMINISTRATION to the family of the deceased; the level of benefits is based on the amount of SOCIAL SECURITY TAXES paid by the deceased.

Social Security tax A TAX on INCOME paid equally by the employer and the employee up to a certain maximum level of income that has increased over time. The TAX is CREDITED to the individual employee's Social Security account identified by an individually assigned SOCIAL SECURITY number.

soft dollars A financial arrangement in which services are exchanged for certain HARD DOLLAR transactions. For example, a BROKERAGE FIRM may agree to provide free institutional security research to an INVESTMENT ADVISER who performs a certain level of SECURITY trades for his or her clients with the brokerage firm.

soft spot A minor weakness in something, such as a weakness in a stock or industry even though the overall market is doing quite well.

sole ownership *See* SOLE PROPRIETORSHIP.

sole proprietor life and health insurance A life and health policy for the owner of a sole proprietorship.

sole proprietorship A business or other financial venture in which a single person is the managing owner bearing full financial liability for the enterprise.

solvency ratio The ratio of an individual's net worth (assets minus liabilities) divided by total assets. The higher the ratio, the more financially strong the person is.

Sotheby's Art Index A weighted price INDEX of over 400 individual collectibles grouped into 12 "market baskets" that include paintings, ceramics, and furniture. It was developed by Jeremy Ecstein, a statistician with Sotheby's in London and appears in *Barron's*.

source record The basic supporting documentation for a transaction entered into by a person. Examples of source documents are purchase invoices and telephone bills.

speculation home A SINGLE FAMILY DWELLING built for profit by a commercial building contractor in the belief that a buyer will be found for the structure. The builder and the financier assume full financial responsibility for the dwelling in the event that it is not sold.

special bid A means of purchasing a significant number of shares directly on the exchange. The broker receives his or her fee directly from the bidder. The bid price cannot be below the last trading price.

special endorsement A signature on the back of a check by which the endorsee transfers the amount to another party by specifically writing the payee's name on the check.

special offering A securities issuance approved by the SECURITIES AND EXCHANGE COMMISSION for a large block of shares that were sold at a prior time by the business. However, it is restricted to New York Stock Exchange members and occurs during normal trading hours. The selling member sets a fixed price, typically based on the current market price. The seller pays all commissions. The buyers are member firms that may purchase for clients or for their own accounts.

special savings account A savings account giving a slightly higher interest rate than a passbook account but in exchange mandates that the saver keep a certain minimum balance and/or maintain the balance for a specified time period. An example is a CERTIFICATE OF DEPOSIT.

special situation

1. A temporarily *undervalued* security with above average-future potential. Examples are a company that will probably be taken over, or is ready to announce an important new patented product. Fidelity Investors has a mutual fund called "special situations" that searches out such stocks.

2. A stock that vacillates sharply in price for

the day, possibly resulting in a distorted effect on a stock market average. An example is a rumored takeover candidate.

special tax bond

1. A municipal revenue bond that will be paid from excise taxes, such as those on liquor and tobacco. However, the municipality does not guarantee the repayment of the bond out of ordinary income taxes. Interest earned is tax exempt to the recipient.

2. A special assessment bond repaid from taxes imposed on a specific locality receiving direct benefits from public works paid for from the proceeds of the bond. An example is a bond issued for the sole purpose of constructing sewers. The homeowners in the locality are assessed taxes to pay for the bonds at maturity. Special assessment bonds are typically not backed by the general obligation of the municipality.

special warranty deed   A DEED to property in which the grantor limits the title warranty to the grantee. A grantor does not warrant a title defect to the property arising from a circumstance prior to the time of his or her ownership.

specialist

in general: An individual who develops and is recognized for an area of expertise within a business, profession, or any other field of interest.

securities: An individual member of a STOCK or COMMODITY exchange representing one or more SECURITIES to FLOOR BROKERS for a portion of their commission. It is the specialist's responsibility to maintain an orderly trading market. The specialist executes LIMIT ORDERS as well as buying or selling securities when prices begin to fluctuate rapidly. Such a trading environment could become disorderly without the specialist's market management. All specialists operate under the governance of their respective market's rules.

specialist block purchase or sale   In SECURITIES, a large block of stock the MARKET SPECIALIST may acquire or sell under special rules. For example, it may be that a TRUST FUND desires to LIQUIDATE a million shares of STOCK at one time. Under normal market conditions, this BLOCK of stock is too large for any one buyer. The specialist may arrange to buy the stock from the trust fund at a discount from the current market price by arranging to sell the block in smaller ROUND LOTS to other buyers at a negotiated price.

The specialist normally performs a block purchase or sale through negotiated prices after BROKERAGE FIRMS are notified of the pending transaction through the wire service.

specialist broker   *See* SPECIALIST.

specialized (mutual) fund   Or, *specialty fund; sector fund.* A MUTUAL FUND whose stock portfolio tends to be concentrated in STOCKS of companies in specific industries (such as energy, gold mining, BANKING, INSURANCE, or others) or locations.

specialty fund   *See* SPECIALIZED (MUTUAL) FUND.

specific insurance   A single insurance policy for only one type of property at a single location. An example is a person's specifically insuring his or her expensive, unique bar.

specific legacy   A BEQUEST of a specific item, such as a rare painting.

specific lien   A LIEN on a particular property, such as a person's car used as security for a loan.

specific performance   A situation in which a party guilty of breaching a contract is required by the court to complete his or her duties under that contract. Specific performance is dictated only if the subject matter of the contract is unique and money damages will not suffice. An example that would require specific performance is one's failure to deliver a specific piece of property.

speculation   Investing CAPITAL in any type of property or SECURITY with the anticipation of making a fast, significant, short-term profit through price change. Speculation often involves a high degree of RISK.

speculative bond A low-grade BOND, often either in default or pending DEFAULT, which an INVESTOR buys expecting an improvement in its fundamentals to increase its price and assure the payment of its INTEREST and PRINCIPAL. An example is a JUNK BOND, in default, that an investor buys with the expectation that the underlying CORPORATION'S financial condition will improve to the point that it will be able to resume payment of its interest payments, thus increasing the bond's market value. In such a situation, the investor will receive all interest in arrears as well as having CAPITAL APPRECIATION.

speculative day traders In SECURITIES, TRADERS who buy a security in the belief it will make an intraday price movement sufficient to return a profit. Such traders are often termed "tape watchers."

speculative investment An investment involving considerable RISK of loss but the chance of large gain.

speculative risk A RISK that exists when there is a possibility of either a loss or a gain. Examples include starting a business, making an investment, or gambling at a casino. INSURANCE is not designed to cover a speculative risk.

speculative stock A STOCK purchased by an investor who is willing to bear a greater amount of investment RISK in the hope of receiving large capital APPRECIATION. It is a stock considered to be risky and characterized by wide price fluctuations. PENNY STOCKS are considered speculative.

speculator *See* SPECULATION.

spendthrift trust clause Or, *spendthrift trust, spendthrift clause.* A trust, or a clause in a TRUST, preventing an individual BENEFICIARY from receiving all that he or she is entitled to in order to protect the ASSETS of the trust from the beneficiary's irresponsible spending.

split In SECURITIES, the equitable distribution of a STOCK DIVIDEND having the net effect of increasing the number of a company's outstanding shares. This action will result in the proportionate lowering of the market value of the individual shares. For example, if the MARKET PRICE of a stock is $100 and the company issues a two-for-one stock SPLIT, each SHAREHOLDER will receive an additional share of STOCK for every one he or she owns and the market price of the stock will drop to $50.

split commission Commission divided between the BROKER who executes a trade and the one who referred the business to him or her (e.g., financial planner). The referral may be, for example, a stock or real estate purchase.

split dollar life insurance An insurance policy whose premiums, rights, and death proceeds are split between parties (e.g., employer and employee, husband and wife, parent and child). The employer pays part of the premiums at a minimum equal to the increase in CASH VALUE. The employee may pay the balance of the premium, or it may be paid in full by the employer. If the increase in cash value equals or exceeds the yearly premium, the employer pays the entire premium.

split estate trust A TRUST established to receive the estate property in different segments, typically to reduce estate taxes.

split-funded pension plan A qualified pension plan in which both a TRUST FUND and an insurance contract are used to fund the plan.

split limits coverage Insurance coverage stating limits of liability for different kinds of claims resulting from a loss. Coverage may be split (limited) per individual, per event, between property damage and bodily injury, or other ways. Property damage liability may specify a limit per accident. For example, a policy providing limits of $200,000/$300,000/$50,000 would give a maximum of $200,000 for bodily injury coverage per person, $300,000 total bodily injury coverage per accident, and $50,000 total property damage liability coverage per accident.

split offering A new municipal bond issue consisting of both regular TERM BONDS and SERIAL BONDS.

split order A large securities transaction that is broken down into parts to be executed over a reasonable time period. This is to avoid causing a sudden, drastic change in the price of the security.

split rating Different ratings assigned to the identical security by two rating services. For example, a rating given by Moody's Investors Service and a different rating by Standard & Poor's on the same security.

split shift A work shift interrupted by an unpaid, temporarily stopped time period. An example is a bus driver's working in the morning and evening transporting passengers to Atlantic City, New Jersey, but being off during the afternoon when the passengers are at the casinos.

spousal IRA An individual's retirement account for a nonworking spouse.

spread
1. The difference between the BID and ASK prices of a security.
2. The difference between the purchase price paid by an INVESTMENT BANKING firm and expected resale price of a new issue of securities.
3. The difference in YIELD between various grades of securities at comparable maturity dates.

spread order In listed OPTIONS trading, a spread order is used by a customer to determine the gross CREDIT or DEBIT to his or her ACCOUNT when completing two or more simultaneous option transactions with the same underlying STOCK. For example, a client wishes to roll over three COVERED call options on 300 shares of the underlying stock XYZ, selling at 52, to a more distant EXPIRATION DATE. He tells the BROKER to buy back three January 50 XYZ calls and sell three July 50 XYZ calls with a 3½ point spread

credited to the customer. It is the responsibility of the FLOOR BROKER to manage this TRADE in order to reach a 3½ point credit per CALL to the customer:

Buy 3 January 50 striking price XYZ Call Options
Sell 3 July 50 striking price Call Options
Gross Credit 3½ points per Call Option
$350.00 × 3 = $1,050.00

The actual price at which the January 50 CALL OPTIONS were bought and the July 50 call options were sold is immaterial as long as 3½ points per call is credited to the customer.

spreading The use of OPTION TRADING on the same underlying SECURITY when the client buys and sells options at different STRIKING PRICES and EXPIRATION DATES in the expectation that certain changes in the MARKET PRICE of the STOCK will result in option profits.
See also ALLIGATOR SPREAD; DIAGONAL SPREAD; HORIZONTAL SPREAD; OPTION SPREAD; SPREAD ORDER.

squeeze
1. A tight-money period when it is difficult to get loans; if a loan can be obtained, interest rates are high.
2. A situation in which a good or service is in very limited supply and therefore its price dramatically rises.
See also SHORT SQUEEZE.

stagflation The incidence of rising prices during a slowdown in business activity.
See also INFLATION; RECESSION.

staggering maturities Bonds held by an investor that mature on different dates to reduce the risk of nonpayment in poor economic times, as well as to lower the risk that the bonds will have to be renewed at unusually low interest rates. A bond investor may diversify by buying short-term, intermediate-term, and long-term bonds. A change in interest rates has a greater effect on the price of long-term bonds since they are locked into a fixed interest rate for a long-term period. If prevailing market interest rates increase, for example, the price of long-term bonds will fall much faster than the price of short-term bonds.

Standard & Poor's Index A set of very popular measures of SECURITIES MARKET performance.
See MARKET INDICES AND AVERAGES; STANDARD & POOR'S 500 STOCK COMPOSITE.

Standard & Poor's 500 Stock Composite (S & P 500) The 500 Stock Composite Index calculated by Standard & Poor's. It differs from the DOW-JONES INDUSTRIAL AVERAGE (DJIA) in several important ways. First, it is a value-weighted, rather than price-weighted, index. This means that the index considers not only the price of a stock but also the number of shares outstanding. That is, it is based on the aggregate market value of the stock: price times number of shares. An advantage of the index over the DJIA is that STOCK SPLITS and STOCK DIVIDENDS do not affect the index value. A disadvantage is that large capitalization stocks—those with a large number of shares outstanding—heavily influence the index value. The S & P 500 actually consists of four separate indexes: the 400 industrials, the 40 utilities, the 20 transportation, and the 40 financial.
See also MARKET INDICES AND AVERAGES.

standard deduction The amount a taxpayer who does not itemize his or her federal tax deductions can deduct in determining TAXABLE INCOME. In 1990 the standard deduction for a married couple filing jointly was $5,450, and the standard deduction for a single taxpayer was $3,250.

standard marital trust A TRUST expressly created within a WILL whereby either surviving spouse is the principal BENEFICIARY. A TRUSTEE is established for the purpose of administering the trust and it is structured to take full advantage of the marital INCOME TAX DEDUCTIONS.

standard of living
nationally: The degree of prosperity enjoyed in a country. Measures of the standard of living include diet, housing conditions, quality of med-

ical care, educational system, transportation and communication systems, and others.
personally: The quality of life enjoyed by an individual. This is determined by the amount of DISPOSABLE INCOME, housing conditions, clothing, education, personal automobile, and similar measures.

state taxes TAXES levied by a state. State taxes include sales taxes, INCOME TAXES, use taxes, EXCISE TAXES, and personal property taxes, among others. The TAX RATES vary among states. Further, some states do not assess certain types of taxes. Excessive state taxation is controlled by all 50 states competing with one another for industry and jobs.

stated interest rate Or, *coupon, nominal rate,* or *face interest rate.*
1. A fixed interest rate printed on the BOND CERTIFICATE. The interest rate is applied to the face value of the bond. For example, a $1,000 face value bond with a 8% coupon will pay $80 per year ($1,000 × 8%).
2. The interest rate announced for a savings account, as distinguished from the EFFECTIVE INTEREST RATE, which includes compounded interests.

statement
accounting: A formal accounting of a CHARGE for a good or service. For example, a utility bill presents a statement of charges for the consumer.
personal: A verbal or written assertion.
legal: An allegation or declaration of factual matters.

statement of cash flows
1. An individual's preparation of cash receipts and cash payments that allows the person to see where cash is coming from and where cash is being used. The statement may be prepared on a yearly, quarterly, monthly, or other basis. It helps the person keep track of cash sources and spending habits.
An illustrative statement follows:

Cash balance—1/1		$160,000
Cash receipts:		
Wages	$40,000	
Interest and dividend income	5,000	
Gifts	2,000	
Sale of furniture	1,000	
Total cash receipts		48,000
Cash available		$208,000
Cash payments:		
Rent	6,000	
Utilities	3,000	
Entertainment	5,000	
Purchase of a car	13,000	
Food	9,000	
Transportation	4,000	
Taxes	6,000	
Total cash payments		46,000
Cash balance—12/31		$162,000

2. A required statement prepared by a company in its annual report showing cash flow from operating, investing, and financing activities. The statement shows the cash receipts and cash payments of the company and can be analyzed by the investor to appraise the firm's liquidity posture. Cash is defined in this statement as cash plus short-term marketable securities having a maturity of three months or less.

statement of earnings See INCOME STATEMENT.

statute of limitations A statutory time limitation for assessing or prosecuting for an infringement, improper act, or civil or criminal offense. Notification or proceedings must be brought prior to the EXPIRATION DATE of the applicable federal, state, or local statute of limitations. For example, except for tax fraud, the INTERNAL REVENUE SERVICE must assess INCOME TAXES within THREE years after the tax return was filed. In the case where income is underreported by 25% or more, the statute of limitations is six years. Most states allow up to SIX years to file a claim for violation of a written contract and five years for civil (tort) liability claims.

step-up trust A type of LIVING TRUST in which the trustee steps up to take the grantor's place in everyday operations and decision making.

sticker price The retail price of an item as stated on an affixed manufacturer's itemized statement of charges. The sticker price gives a complete itemization of the individual components. For example, a new car has its price affixed to the window of the car, giving a complete itemization of the various components of the car. Typically, the buyer can purchase the automobile for a lower price.
See also STICKER SHOCK.

sticker shock A generic term originating with the price of new cars. Consumers went into a state of disbelief upon reading the high STICKER PRICE of new cars.

stock SHARES of CAPITAL of a publicly traded CORPORATION. The two types of stock include COMMON STOCK and PREFERRED STOCK. Stock is traded in a STOCK EXCHANGE.
See also CUMULATIVE PREFERRED STOCK; GLAMOUR STOCK; LETTER STOCK; NONCUMULATIVE PREFERRED STOCK; NONPARTICIPATING PREFERRED STOCK.

stock ahead In SECURITIES, a term used to describe a queue of STOCK waiting to be either purchased or sold at LIMIT prices. The SPECIALIST maintains the stock book having the pending purchase and sale orders. As the orders are matched up, the transactions are completed. They are done on a first-come-first-served basis.

stock appreciation right (SAR) An employer award giving employees a right to receive cash and/or stock. The right is worth the excess of market price of shares above the option price when the rights are exercised.

stock bonus plan A plan in which employer contributions are given for the benefit of employees to receive the employer's stock. The limit an employer may deduct for taxes in any one year is 15% of compensation. The plan may be a form of compensation or recognition for good employee performance.

stock certificate A CERTIFICATE verifying an individual's ownership of SHARES in a publicly held CORPORATION. The stock certificate is a legal obligation of the CORPORATION and states the number of shares the individual owns, the name of the company, the serial number of the stock certificate, and the PAR VALUE of the stock.

A PREFERRED STOCK certificate will also state the DIVIDEND payable to the stockholder and whether it is CUMULATIVE.

Stock certificates must be presented at the time of sale. If the STOCKHOLDER maintains a MARGIN ACCOUNT, the stock certificate is kept by the BROKERAGE FIRM in the STREET NAME.

stock commission   The amount charged by the BROKERAGE FIRM for buying or selling STOCK. Stock commissions are determined by the number of shares being transacted and the price of the stock. Brokerage houses do offer competitive rates and the INVESTOR can do comparison shopping for the best rate.

stock company   A company fully owned by shareholders as evidenced by stock certificates. The stockholders have limited liability for the company's debts. They share in profits and losses.

stock dividend   Additional SHARES issued to INVESTORS as a DIVIDEND. A stock dividend may be given when the cash position of the company is inadequate and/or when the company wants to promote more trading by reducing the MARKET PRICE of stock. Assume an individual owns 100 shares of ABC Company common stock. If a 10% stock dividend is declared, the individual will receive 10 more shares for a total of 110 shares. Because a stock dividend results in more shares outstanding, the market price per share will drop proportionately.

Since stock dividends increase the shares outstanding of the corporation, applicable OPTION prices must be adjusted to reflect the new shares.

stock exchange   A marketplace in which buyers and sellers are brought together to trade securities, such as the NEW YORK STOCK EXCHANGE (NYSE).

stock exchange indices   See MARKET (STOCK) INDEXES AND AVERAGES.

stock index futures   A contract to buy or sell a broad stock market index. An example is the Standard & Poor's 100 Stock Index. Stock index futures allow the investor to buy and sell the "market as a whole" instead of a particular security. An investor expecting a bull market but unsure which stock will increase might buy (long) a STOCK INDEX FUTURE. Another investor may hedge his or her portfolio against loss in a bear market by selling a stock index future.

stock indices and averages   See MARKET (STOCK) INDEXES AND AVERAGES.

stock insurance company   An insurance company owned by stockholders that receives the firm's profits in the form of stockholder dividends. However, policyholders' interests come before those of stockholders.

stock limit order   See LIMIT ORDER.

stock market   A MARKET in which SECURITIES are TRADED. All stock markets are ruled by boards of governors. Securities traded include COMMON STOCK, convertibles, PREFERRED STOCK, RIGHTS, and WARRANTS. The principal stock markets in the United States are the NEW YORK STOCK EXCHANGE, the AMERICAN STOCK EXCHANGE, and the NATIONAL OVER-THE-COUNTER MARKET.

stock option   The right to buy or sell a stock at a particular price within a given time period. A stock option enables one to speculate in stocks with a minimal investment. There is great potential for return. However, the entire investment may be lost if the stock does not move sufficiently in the right direction. Stock options can also be used to hedge one's position in other securities.
See also CALL; PUT.

stock option plan   A plan giving the holder the right to buy a certain number of shares of stock at a certain price by a specified date. Stock option plans are typically used to compensate corporate officers and other employees for their services. Typically, a STOCK OPTION may not be exercised until the employee has worked a specified number of years (e.g., three years) after the date the option is granted. The value of the compensation of the stock option is measured by the quoted market price of the stock less the option price to the employee. Assume an employee has the option to buy 2,000 shares at an option price of $10 having a current market price of $15. The value of the compensation of the stock option is $10,000 (2,000 shares × $5).

stock order   An instruction given to a broker to buy or sell a stock. Most stock orders are verbal instructions.

stock power   A legal document that transfers ownership of a REGISTERED SECURITY. This form is attached to the STOCK CERTIFICATE when the security is sold or pledged as COLLATERAL. The POWER OF ATTORNEY grants the owner's permission to a TRANSFER AGENT to transfer ownership to another party.

stock purchase plan   An employee benefit designed to facilitate the purchase of a company's STOCK often at a price lower than the market or at a reduced commission cost. These plans often include an employer's payment toward the acquisition of the stock. The plans are continual over time and companies often offer to reinvest the DIVIDENDS in more stock accumulation.

An EMPLOYEE STOCK OWNERSHIP PLAN (ESOP) is another form of a stock purchase plan in which the employees eventually have ownership control of the company.

stock rating   Evaluations of STOCKS based on the company's financial health and management quality. Stocks are rated by such services as Fitch's Investor Service, Moody's, and Standard & Poor's. Stocks having higher ratings include many of the BLUE-CHIP stocks and the FORTUNE 500 COMPANIES.

stock right   Or, *preemptive right*. A privilege giving a current stockholder the first right to buy shares in a new offering below the market price, thus maintaining the stockholder's proportionate ownership interest. Assume an investor owns 1% of Company ABC. If the company issues 10,000 additional shares, the investor may receive a stock rights offering—an opportunity to buy 1%, or 100 shares, of the new issue. The right enables the investor to buy new common stock at a subscription price for a short time, typically no more than several weeks. The subscription price (exercise price) is typically lower than the public offering price of the stock. A single right is the privilege applicable to the holder of one old share of capital stock to purchase a certain number of shares of new capital stock.

stock split   *See* SPLIT.

stock symbol   Or, *trading symbol*. The abbreviation assigned to a company's STOCK by the respective STOCK EXCHANGE where it trades. Stocks trading on the NEW YORK STOCK EXCHANGE have two or three letters, for example, IBM. Stocks trading on the AMERICAN STOCK EXCHANGE have three or four symbols, while stocks trading OVER-THE-COUNTER have four or five symbols.

stock transfer agent   An agent selected by a company to keep the records of its issued equity and debt securities. The agent lists the names of new owners of the securities, issues new certificates to buyers, cancels old certificates of sellers, and replaces lost certificates. A fee is assessed when replacement certificates are needed because of theft or loss. The agent prepares a list of all stockholders and the shares owned so dividends may be properly paid. The transfer agent makes sure that an overissuance of certificates does not occur. Although a transfer agent is typically an outside party, often a commercial bank, the issuing company may act as its own transfer agent.

stock types
1. The different kinds of stocks, such as PRE-

FERRED STOCK and COMMON STOCK. In addition, a stock type may come in different classes such as "class A" and "class B," with the distinction applying to voting rights.

2. The characteristics of alternative investment objectives considered when one buys stocks, such as growth stocks, income-producing stocks, speculative stocks, and blue chips.

stock warrants A warrant, cheap in price, giving one the right to buy "X" shares at "X" price sometime in the future. If the warrant is not converted at maturity, the price goes to zero. A warrant may or may not be in a one-to-one ratio with the stock already owned. It is usually good for several years. In fact, there are perpetual warrants with no maturity date. Warrants may be given as sweeteners for a preferred stock issue or a bond issue to increase marketability or lower the interest rate on a bond. Warrants are generally detachable from the bond and have a market of their own. They pay no dividends and do not have voting rights. The warrant enables the investor to take part indirectly in price appreciation.

stockbroker An employee of a STOCK BROKERAGE FIRM who is licensed with the SECURITIES AND EXCHANGE COMMISSION and the STOCK exchanges where he or she trades securities for customers. Stockbrokers normally work on a SALARY plus COMMISSION basis derived from the amount of commissions generated from SECURITY purchases and sales. Stockbrokers are also termed ACCOUNT EXECUTIVES or REGISTERED REPRESENTATIVES.

stockholder of record Stockholders whose names are registered in the books of the issuing company. One must be a stockholder prior to the DATE OF RECORD in order to qualify to receive the DIVIDEND. For example, a company's board of directors declares a dividend on its COMMON STOCK of $.25 per SHARE on May 5 to the stockholders of record on May 25 to be paid on June 25. The stockholders of record as of May 25 will receive a $.25 dividend per share on June 25, the DATE OF PAYMENT. Stockholders of record

are entitled to the full rights of all stockholders including voting on PROXY issues, participating in annual meetings, and receiving all publicly issued STOCKHOLDERS' REPORTS.

stockholder's report A report issued to all stockholders giving the financial results of the company as well as discussing pertinent business and corporate developments. The stockholder's report consists of an ANNUAL REPORT, quarterly reports, and special stockholder reports. The annual stockholder's report normally has a CERTIFIED PUBLIC ACCOUNTANT'S statement regarding the firm's financial status. It gives extensive attention to the accomplishments of the firm over the past year and discusses current and future business concerns.

stockholder/shareholder A term describing those individuals or organizations owning an interest in a publicly held corporation by owning shares of STOCK issued by the company. The shares of ownership are certified by STOCK CERTIFICATES in the owners' names. A stockholder/shareholder has limited LIABILITY and is not legally responsible for corporate liabilities while still enjoying full corporate ownership privileges and rights. Stockholders share in the financial success of the company in the form of DIVIDENDS and APPRECIATION in the MARKET PRICE of the stock.

stop-limit order An investor's order to his or her broker to buy or sell a security at a given price or better but only after a specified stop price occurs. In effect, it is a combined stop order and limit order. For example, one may instruct his or her broker to "buy 100 shares of ABC Company 30 STOP 31 LIMIT." This means that if the market price reaches $30, the broker places a limit order to be executed at $31 or lower. The investor takes the chance of losing a buying opportunity if the limit price or better never occurs.

stop-loss order An instruction to a broker to buy or sell a stock when it increases to or falls below a specified price. Assume an investor owns ABC Company stock having a current market price of $20 per share. The stop-loss order is to sell this stock if it drops to $15 per share. By selling the shares at a predetermined price, the investor is insulated from further stock price declines.

stop payment   In banking, instructions issued by a DEPOSITOR to prevent payment on an issued CHECK. The most common reason for stopping payment is in the case of a misplaced, lost, or stolen check as well as a disagreement with the PAYEE. The customer can request a stop payment by telephone; however, BANKS do require written confirmation for their own justification of a stop payment. Complete information of the CHECK in question must be provided, including the name of the payee, the amount of the check, the number and date of the check. Banks normally charge a processing fee for a stop payment. Banks will not accept a check having a stop payment order.

stop-loss protection
securities: A STOP LIMIT order that is triggered when a SECURITY'S price falls below the STOP PRICE whereupon the order becomes a MARKET ORDER to sell. The purpose of stop-loss protection is to preserve a profit or prevent a loss.
reinsurance: Protection for a reinsurance company against a maximum level of losses from an INSURANCE COMPANY when losses exceed a certain percentage of the PREMIUM.
See STOP PRICE.

stopped stock   In SECURITIES, a commitment by a SPECIALIST to a member of the STOCK EXCHANGE that a stock order will be transacted at the highest offer price within a specified time with the assurance that the SPECIALIST'S price is guaranteed. The EXCHANGE member may seek a better price; however, if this is not possible, the stopped stock order will be executed.

stop price   The price stated by a customer to his or her BROKER at which a STOP ORDER translates into a MARKET ORDER.
See also STOP-LOSS PROTECTION.

storage charge   A fee charged to store items owned by an individual. An example is the charge made by a warehouse that stores the property of an individual who needs temporary space while moving from one residence to another.

straddle   The combination of a CALL and PUT on the same stock with identical strike prices and expiration dates. It is used to take advantage of significant fluctuation in stock price. A significant price movement on one side will cover the cost of obtaining the options.

straight bankruptcy   *See* BANKRUPTCY; CHAPTER 7.

straight life (pure) annuity   An ANNUITY that pays a fixed amount every month until the ANNUITANT'S death, with no refund to any other person.
See also NONREFUND ANNUITY.

straight loan   An unsecured loan given by a lender to a borrower. COLLATERAL is not necessary because of the creditworthiness of the borrower.

straight term   An insurance policy for a specified number of years in which the coverage continues unchanged.

straight term life insurance   LIFE INSURANCE that has a fixed amount of benefits and is issued for a fixed time period.

straight time   The typical hourly rate for an employee multiplied by the hours worked. Compensation is based on time and not productive output. The employee is not paid overtime.

strap   The individual's purchase of an option contract combining two calls and one put on the same security. This contract can be purchased at a lower cost than the three options bought separately. The calls and put have similar features, such as exercise prices and maturities.

strategy   An individual's planning of goals that he or she wants to achieve by a certain date. Examples of goals are desired net worth, retirement age, and career success. The person plans how the objectives are to be accomplished.

street An abbreviated term for Wall Street, referring to the financial district in New York City. If one hears that the street recommends ABC Company stock, it means that investment analysts favor that company.

street broker A broker dealing with over-the-counter securities rather than those listed on an exchange.

street name An individual's stock or bond certificate being kept in the broker's name for safekeeping by the broker or other nominee. If a margin account exists, the securities must be in "street name" as collateral for the unpaid margin account. The transfer of securities upon sale is easier when the stock is registered in the broker's name than in the customer's. The client gives his or her authorization for transactions in that security. Monthly brokerage statements are received outlining activities for the month. The holding of securities in street name hastens the execution and transfer of securities transactions.

street smarts Intelligence gained from field experience rather than from formal education.

strike price Or, *striking price; exercise price.* The price at which a CALL OPTION or a PUT OPTION can be exercised, normally at a price set close to the market price of the stock at the time the option is issued. It is the exercise price for an OPTION.

strip

1. The individual's purchase of an option contract combining two puts and one call on the same security. The puts and call have similar features, such as strike prices and maturities.

2. The purchase of stock with the major aim of collecting dividends.

3. A practice of a brokerage firm of distinguishing between the principal and coupon interest of a bond, which are then issued individually in the form of a zero coupon security.

stripped bond A BOND divided into its PRINCIPAL and interest payments, which are then sold separately as a ZERO-COUPON BOND.

strong market A situation in which the market prices of securities are increasing with high volume. The demand exceeds the supply for securities.
See also WEAK MARKET.

Student Loan Marketing Association (Sallie Mae) securities Purchases by the Student Loan Marketing Association (Sallie Mae) of loans made by FINANCIAL INSTITUTIONS under a variety of federal and state loan programs. Sallie Mae securities are not guaranteed, but are generally insured by the federal government and its agencies. These securities include floating rate and fixed rate obligations with maturities of five years or more as well as discount notes with maturities from a few days to 360 days.

Subchapter S corporation Or, *tax-option corporations; small business corporations.* A form of corporation whose stockholders are taxed as partners. To qualify as an S corporation, a corporation cannot have more than 35 shareholders; it cannot have any nonresident foreigners as shareholders; it cannot have more than one class of stock; and it must properly elect Subchapter S status. The S corporation can distribute its income directly to shareholders and avoid the corporate income tax while enjoying the other advantages of the corporate form.

sublease A lease transferred from a lessee to another lessee. The new lessee is referred to as the sublessee (subtenant).

sublessor The original lessee of rented premises who then leases the property to a subtenant.

subletting The action by which a lessee leases the property to another lessee.

subordinated debenture An unsecured BOND that is given a secondary claim (with respect to both earnings and assets) to that of holders of senior DEBENTURES.

subordination clause A clause that permits a MORTGAGE recorded at a later date to take priority over an existing mortgage.

subrent The action by which a lessee rents his or her apartment to another.

subrogation rights Rights that allow an INSURER to take action against a negligent third party (and that party's insurance company) to obtain reimbursement for payments made to an insured.

subscriber One who agrees to the terms of a SUBSCRIPTION at the SUBSCRIPTION PRICE.

subscription
1. An arrangement to buy newly issued securities.
2. A pledge to contribute money to a charity.
3. The price paid to receive reading matter on a periodic basis, such as a periodical or magazine.

subscription price The price that a current stockholder must pay to buy common shares in connection with a rights or warrant offering.

subscription right The right of current stockholders to purchase a new issue of stock before it goes public, typically below the PUBLIC OFFERING price. The right usually has a two-to-four-week life, and may be transferred. In most instances, one share of ownership gives the stockholder one right. However, the number of rights necessary to purchase a new share may vary. In exercising the right, the stockholder delivers the necessary number of rights plus the payment for the new shares.

substitution
securities:
1. The exchange of securities. For example, a security analyst recommends replacing one stock in an industry by another in that same industry.
2. The replacement of a different security of the same value for another security serving as COLLATERAL in a MARGIN ACCOUNT.

law:
1. Replacement of one party to a contract by another.
banking:
1. Replacement of the original collateral by another collateral.

subtenant An individual who leases rented premises from the original lessee. The sublease is for a period not exceeding the original lease term.

suicide clause A LIFE INSURANCE clause that voids the contract if an insured commits suicide within a specified period of time (such as within two years) after the issuance of the policy.

sunk costs Costs incurred some time in the past that will affect any decision made now or in the future. Sunk costs are irrelevant to future decisions. An example is the price an owner paid for a business 20 years ago; it is immaterial in a decision of whether he or she should sell that business today and buy a new business.

super money market funds MONEY MARKET MUTUAL FUNDS that are characterized by the following: (1) they offer yields usually 1% higher than most other money market funds, (2) they waive all or part of their management fees, and (3) they impose some limitations on check-writing privileges.

super NOW account A government-insured NEGOTIABLE ORDER OF WITHDRAWAL (NOW) account issued by financial institutions that may pay a free market rate of interest and offer unlimited check-writing privileges. Minimum balances are required. If the ACCOUNT BALANCE falls below the minimum deposit required, the interest rate drops to a PASSBOOK SAVINGS rate.

supplemental agreement An agreement that modifies a prior one and includes additional provisions.

supplemental health insurance A form of HEALTH INSURANCE designed to fill the gap in coverage of the standard health insurance plans or provide reimbursement in addition to that provided by the standard plans.

supplemental security income A federal SO-CIAL SECURITY program administered by the Social Security Administration that provides limited monetary benefits for the blind, disabled, and indigent.

support level The price at which a particular security or the whole market stops decreasing. For a stock to go below the support line is a very bearish sign. The price falls because supply exceeds demand. A support level is typically identified by TECHNICAL ANALYSTS as the price at which a security or entire market bottomed in the past. When a stock is moving downward to the support line, the term "testing the market" is used and the stock should rebound after it reaches the support level. See illustrative diagram below.
See also RESISTANCE LEVEL.

surcharge An add-on charge. If you buy an item for $50, an additional charge of 10% will automatically be added, resulting in a total cost of $55 ($50 + $5). Another example is a tax of 2% based on the original computed tax of

$3,000, resulting in a total tax of $3,060 ($3,000 + $60).

surgical expense insurance HEALTH INSURANCE coverage for the cost of surgery.

surgical insurance A form of HEALTH INSURANCE that pays for surgical procedures.

surplus A positive balance resulting when two groups of numbers offset each other. For example, total assets less total liabilities equals net worth. Revenue less expenses equals net income.
See also DEFICIT.

surrender The termination of a lease or insurance policy by mutual agreement of the parties.

surrender life insurance The right of a policyholder to cancel a life insurance policy in order to receive its CASH SURRENDER VALUE.

surrender value In LIFE INSURANCE, the CASH VALUE of a cash life insurance policy. Surrender occurs when a cash POLICYHOLDER realizes a policy's cash value through relinquishing the policy.

surtax A TAX imposed on a tax. Normally, a surtax is imposed when certain limits are ex-

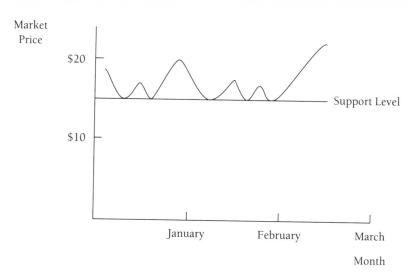

Support Level

ceeded. For example, a 20% individual INCOME TAX on $100,000 is $20,000. A 10% surtax on the individual income tax would be an additional $2,000 ($20,000 × 10%).

surviving spouse In a marriage, the spouse surviving the other spouse's death. The term is important in ESTATES, LIFE INSURANCE, TRUSTS, and WILLS.

survivorship The continued living of one or more persons after the death of another party. Survivorship is important in determining the BENEFICIARIES in ESTATES, LIFE INSURANCE, TRUSTS, and WILLS.
See also RIGHT OF SURVIVORSHIP.

survivorship account An account, as at a bank, to whose balance the surviving party is entitled upon the death of the other party named in the account. It is a type of JOINT TENANCY common in husband and wife accounts.

survivorship benefit (on an annuity) The portion of the premiums and interest that have not been returned to the ANNUITANT prior to his or her death.

suspended trading A temporary stop in the trading of a given security. Trading may be stopped to correct an imbalance of buy and sell orders, in anticipation of a major announcement, or because of sudden investigation of the company by a regulatory agency.

swap The selling of one security and buying of another security for the purpose of improving overall YIELD with little or no market or credit RISK. There are two primary types of swaps: (1) EXTENSION SWAPS, in which the investor tries to determine whether extending the maturity of an instrument would improve overall return, based on yield curve analysis, and (2) YIELD SPREAD SWAPS or QUALITY SWAPS, in which the investor relies on the differences in YIELD SPREADS between the various investments to enhance total yield.

sweat equity The EQUITY in property created by the investment of work in it by the buyer or holder, which directly increases the value of the asset.

sweetener An attractive feature added to the issuance of a security to prompt readier purchase of it. An example is the CONVERSION FEATURE added to a PREFERRED STOCK or BOND.

swing loan *See* BRIDGE LOAN.

swing shift A work shift from midafternoon until midnight, or until the midnight shift.

switching
1. The sale of one security (stock, bond) and the purchase of another security. For example, the investor may decide to sell a stock with little perceived potential and replace it with one that appears to be on the move.
2. The substitution of one property for another, such as the sale of a real estate investment for a similar one at a different "preferred" location.

switching (exchange) privilege The transfer of money from one mutual fund to another. This transfer may be between funds of the same family or with a different family. The switching between funds is based on the shareholder's perception of changing opportunities or problems with a particular segment of investments. Also, the shareholder's obligations may change. For example, an investor may move funds out of JUNK BONDS into a MONEY MARKET FUND if he or she feels the "junk bond" market is about to collapse. If a transfer is made in a load fund, a sales charge will be levied. However, a transfer made in a no-load fund is free.

syndicates
securities: A group of INVESTMENT BANKERS brought together for the purpose of underwriting and distributing a new issue of securities or a large block of an outstanding issue.
real estate: A LIMITED PARTNERSHIP that invests in various types of real estate and is professionally managed. It is registered with the SEC and includes a great number of LIMITED PARTNERS.

systematic investment plan A plan in which the shareholder makes specified deposits each period to a savings or investment account, such as a mutual fund.

systematic withdrawal plan A plan permitting the mutual fund shareholder to receive given amounts each period.

T

take a position

1. An investor's purchase of a security, often with the intention of keeping it for a long time. If an investor buys 5% or more of a company's stock, he or she must file information with the Securities and Exchange Commission, respective stock exchange, and the company itself.

2. The broker/dealer's retaining securities in inventory. The intent may be to hold them for the long term or short term.

takedown

1. An INVESTMENT BANKER's proportionate share of a new or secondary securities issue that is to be distributed to the public.

2. The price that securities are allocated among underwriters.

take-home pay In SALARIES, the amount of MONEY left after all DEDUCTIONS have been taken. For example, if an individual has a $1,000 salary and has $200 taken out for INCOME TAX, $55 for SOCIAL SECURITY taxes, $45 for medical benefits, and $60 for a PENSION PLAN, the take-home pay would be: $1,000 − ($200 + $55 + $45 + $60) = $640.

takeover The acquisition of the ASSETS of one CORPORATION by another. This might be done through a LEVERAGED BUYOUT or through a straight purchase. It can be done through a hostile takeover in which the TAKEOVER TARGET is an unwitting victim of the takeover or a friendly merger in which negotiations occur between the acquirer and the TAKEOVER TARGET.

A takeover results in the merging of the assets of the two corporations.

takeover target A company that becomes the candidate for a TAKEOVER attempt by another firm. In a hostile takeover the takeover target is totally surprised by the TAKEOVER, whereas in a friendly merger the takeover target participates in TAKEOVER negotiations prior to its occurrence.

take-up

1. In investments, an investor who remits the balance due on a MARGIN ACCOUNT, so as to obtain complete ownership.

2. An UNDERWRITER who directly sells stocks or bonds to the public.

taking delivery

1. The acceptance of goods delivered by a shipper or carrier. Typically, the recipient must sign a receipt.

2. The acceptance of a security certificate or commodity that has been bought or transferred.

tangible assets *See* TANGIBLE PROPERTY.

tangible property Tangible items of real and personal property that generally have a long life, such as housing and other REAL ESTATE, automobiles, jewelry, cash, and other physical assets.

tax A mandatory charge imposed by government on individuals and companies for the purpose of realizing REVENUES. There are several types of taxes. The most common include INCOME TAXES, PROPERTY TAXES, SALES TAXES, SURTAXES, and use taxes. These can be further classified into PROGRESSIVE and REGRESSIVE taxes.

tax audit An AUDIT by the INTERNAL REVENUE SERVICE or other governmental unit to ensure an individual's compliance with the TAX laws. A tax audit may be on selected items (e.g., contributions, interest) or of the entire tax return. A tax audit usually occurs when what is reported by a taxpayer appears unreasonable.

tax avoidance The payment of the least amount of tax LEGALLY possible. Tax avoidance is accomplished by using TAX SHELTERS, having TAX EXEMPTIONS, and ESTATE PLANNING. TAX EVASION is an illegal method of avoiding the payment of taxes.

tax base The collective value of property, income, and other taxable activity or assets subject to tax. Tax revenues are computed at the tax base times the tax rate. For property taxation, the tax base is the total assessed value of all taxable property less exemptions.

tax basis
1. The price of a security purchased, including all relevant costs, such as brokerage fees. This becomes the cost for tax purposes.
2. The cost basis of property, such as a home owned for tax purposes.

Example: A home was initially bought for $80,000. Capital improvements to it (e.g., roof, electric system) cost $40,000. The house was later sold for $200,000. The gain on the sale of the house was

Selling price	$200,000
Less cost basis	120,000
Gain subject to tax	$80,000

tax bracket The tax rate an individual falls into based upon his or her TAXABLE INCOME. The tax rate is applied to every dollar of taxable income over the base amount for that bracket. Under current tax law, the tax brackets are 15%, 28%, and 31%.

tax credit A reduction in taxes payable to the Internal Revenue Service, state, or local government. The tax credit is more beneficial to the taxpayer relative to an itemized deduction because it reduces taxes on a dollar-for-dollar basis. An example of a tax credit is for child care.

For example, if the computed tax based on taxable income is $12,000 and there is a $500 tax credit, the tax payable after the credit is $11,500.

tax deductible An expense allowed as a deduction on the tax return. Examples are charitable contributions, interest on a mortgage, and property taxes. Some items are deductible only over a specified amount. For example, under current tax law, medical payments must exceed 7.5% of ADJUSTED GROSS INCOME to be tax deductible.

tax-deductible expenditure record A record of expenses incurred that are tax deductible. The record includes the date, amount, and reason for the expenditure. For example, in order to claim automobile expenses as a business deduction, a log must be kept. The tax deduction for promotion and entertainment must be supported by detailed records including the name of the party entertained and why. Without adequate records and supporting documentation, the Internal Revenue Service may disallow the deduction on an audit.

tax deed A DEED granted by the government to an individual buying the property for unpaid taxes.

tax deferral A feature available in certain INVESTMENTS, including TAX DEFERRED ANNUITIES, in which the payment of taxes on income occurs only after the benefit is received. Other examples of tax-deferred investments include INDIVIDUAL RETIREMENT ACCOUNTS (IRA), KEOGH PLANS, Series EE and HH U.S. savings bonds, stock purchase or DIVIDEND REINVESTMENT PLANS, and UNIVERSAL, VARIABLE, or WHOLE LIFE INSURANCE POLICIES.

tax effect The impact on taxes of a taxable revenue or expense item. For example, interest on a mortgage of $1,000 will result in a tax savings of $280 at the 28% tax bracket. The net of tax effect is $720 ($1,000 − $280).

tax election The selection of an option with regard to the tax treatment of specific situations or transactions. An example is the decision of a married couple to file separately rather than prepare a joint tax return.

tax-equivalent yield The YIELD on a tax-free MUNICIPAL BOND on an equivalent before-tax yield basis. The formula used to equate interest on tax-free municipals to other taxable investments is shown below:

$$\text{Tax-equivalent yield} = \text{Tax-exempt yield}/(1 - \text{tax rate})$$

If an individual has a MARGINAL TAX RATE of 28% and is evaluating a municipal bond paying 10% interest, the equivalent before-tax bond yield on a taxable investment is

$$10\%/(1 - .28) = 13.9\%$$

Thus, he or she could choose between a taxable investment paying 13.9% and a tax-exempt bond paying 10% as their yields are the same.
See also BOND YIELD; YIELD.

tax evasion Or, *tax fraud.* An illegal practice of avoiding the payment of taxes. Tax evasion methods include unreported INCOME, fraudulently claiming tax exemptions, and overstating deductions. Tax FRAUD is a criminal offense.

tax exempt A tax-free status granted to certain organizations and governmental entities. Most registered charitable organizations and TAX-EXEMPT BONDS are free from taxation from other governmental entities. However, governmental entities can, if they so choose, tax the INTEREST on their own SECURITIES. For example, interest paid on federal government securities is taxable by the federal government, but not by state or local governments. Normally, most state and local government jurisdictions do not tax the interest payments on their own securities as an incentive for individuals living in the jurisdiction to purchase them. However, outside states and jurisdictions can and often do tax other state and local government security INTEREST payments.
See also GENERAL OBLIGATION BOND; INDUSTRIAL REVENUE BOND.

tax-exempt bonds BONDS issued by state and local governments that are exempt from federal income tax. In addition to state governments, these bonds may be issued by any legally constituted unit of local government including cities, counties, villages, townships, and special districts. Most units of state and local governments do not tax their own TAX-EXEMPT BONDS, but they do tax those of outside states and their jurisdiction's tax-exempt bonds. This is done to attract local investors and discourage competition from other states.

Within a state, a jurisdiction's bonds are exempt from all state and local as well as federal taxes. They are, therefore, TRIPLE TAX EXEMPT.

TAX-EXEMPT INCOME is equivalent to higher taxable income. For example, for an individual in the 33% TAX BRACKET, receiving 7% tax-free INCOME is equivalent to 10.45% (7%/.67) INTEREST on a taxable CERTIFICATE OF DEPOSIT. However, any CAPITAL GAINS earned on the sale of a TAX-EXEMPT BOND is taxable at standard TAX RATES.
See also TAX-EXEMPT SECURITIES.

tax-exempt income INCOME that is EXEMPT from federal, state, and local taxation. Such income is derived from TAX-EXEMPT SECURITIES, including TAX-EXEMPT BONDS, as well as grants such as scholarships that are used to pay the costs of tuition and individual welfare payments.

tax-exempt securities Any SECURITY producing TAX-EXEMPT INCOME. TAX-EXEMPT BONDS are an example of a tax-exempt security.

tax-free exchange *See* 1031 TAX-FREE EXCHANGE.

tax liability A legally incurred obligation to pay certain TAXES as the result of owning property or earning INCOME. For example, a REAL ESTATE owner will have a liability to pay PROPERTY TAXES.

tax lien A DEBT attached against property for failure to pay taxes. A governmental jurisdiction can order a TAX SALE of property for the failure to pay property taxes. A tax lien can be removed by paying the TAXES that are owed.

tax loss A tax benefit provided to individuals for applying losses to CAPITAL GAINS. Individuals may carry over losses for an unlimited number of years to offset capital gains. For example, if a taxpayer has a net CAPITAL loss for the year on STOCK transactions of $5,000, he or she can only deduct a maximum of $3,000 in the current year. The remaining capital loss of $2,000 is carried forward to future years. Capital losses are reported on Schedule D of Form 1040.

tax planning A methodical analysis of various tax options and implications for individuals, leading to the development of an overall tax-reduction strategy for current and future tax periods. Considerations involved in tax planning include knowing the timing of asset maturities and sales, determining the appropriate filing status, understanding the tax implications of INVESTMENT decisions, knowing when to receive INCOME and pay expenditures, determining the method of receiving retirement funds, and deciding the appropriate timing and size of gifts as well as to whom they should be donated. ESTATE PLANNING is critical for tax planning.

tax planning software Computer software specifically designed to help in TAX PLANNING. Tax-planning software provides *what-if* spreadsheet capabilities with which the impact of various TAX strategies can be calculated. Examples of tax-planning applications are timing the sale of a security, ascertaining how many years to take out funds at retirement from a PENSION PLAN, and deciding on the timing of investments.

For example, Aardvark/McGraw-Hill Tax Proposal Analyzer appraises the effect of tax reform on tax obligations, INVESTMENT strategies, and RETIREMENT PLANNING. TAX LIABILITY is computed using present and proposed TAX RATES.

tax preparation services A business that prepares individual tax returns for a fee. The tax returns may be done manually or electronically. Professionals trained in tax preparation include certified public accountants, attorneys, and others with adequate tax training. An example of a tax service is H & R Block.

tax rate The tax to be paid based on a percentage of taxable income. The tax rate typically changes as the unit of the tax base changes. The tax rate depends on whether a joint, head of household, or single filer return is prepared. For example, the minimum tax rate for a single individual might be stated as 15% on taxable income of $19,450 or less.

tax-rate schedule The schedule used to compute tax on a given taxable income. The marginal tax rate usually increases as the taxable income rises. For example, for tax returns filed on a joint basis, the tax rates might be

15%	0 – $32,450
28%	$32,451 – $78,400
33%	$78,401 – $162,770

tax refund A refund of taxes from overpayment. Overpayment of taxes usually occurs because of mistakes, overestimating INCOME in a given period of time, not claiming sufficient EXEMPTIONS, or a change in TAX RATES.

tax return A form used for reporting INCOME to the government. Federal individual income taxes are reported on Forms 1040, 1040A, or 1040EZ. State and local governments requiring INCOME TAXES have their own forms normally modeled after the federal tax return forms.

tax schedules Supplemental tax forms used for deductions as well as to report INCOME and compute taxes. For the federal INCOME TAX, tax schedules include Schedule A, Itemized Deductions, Schedule B, INTEREST and DIVIDEND Income, Schedule D, Capital Gains and Losses, Schedule E, Supplemental Income and Loss, Schedule C, Profit or Loss From Business, Schedule SE, SOCIAL SECURITY Self-Employment Tax, and Tax Rate Schedules.

tax service companies Companies specializing in the preparation of individual INCOME TAX returns. The best known of these companies is H & R Block.

tax shelter Any legal methodology or device an individual can use to reduce his or her TAX LIABILITY legally. Tax shelters function by providing CREDIT or DEDUCTIONS to INCOME. Most tax shelters were eliminated under the TAX REFORM ACT OF 1986.

tax-sheltered annuities (TSA) A federal program that permits certain employers of nonprofit organizations to place up to a stated percentage of an employee's salary into a qualified pension program. This income is free from current income taxes, and the investment income accumulates tax deferred.
See also RETIREMENT AND PENSION PLANNING.

tax-sheltered college education fund A fund in which money can be accumulated tax free and used to pay future college education expenses of a child.

tax-sheltered (qualified) retirement plan A financial plan approved by the IRS for special tax advantages that reduce taxes and increase RETIREMENT BENEFITS.
See also RETIREMENT AND PENSION PLANNING.

tax shield Tax deductions that result in the payment of lower taxes. The tax shield equals the deduction times the tax rate. For example, assume interest on a mortgage is $2,000 and the tax rate is 28%; the tax shield (savings) is $2,000 × .28 = $560. The individual saves $560 annually in taxes from the interest deduction. The higher the deduction, the greater the tax shield.

tax software Software designed to be used on a personal computer to facilitate the preparation and printing of federal and state INCOME TAX returns. TAX PLANNING modules using TEMPLATES are also included for CORPORATIONS, PARTNERSHIPS, individuals, and ESTATES and TRUSTS. The software is completely integrated allowing all separately completed TAX SCHEDULES to be summarized and totaled in the final return.

tax table A printed table accompanying the TAX RETURN for computing taxes payable based on taxable INCOME. If the income exceeds $50,000 the taxpayer must use a tax rate schedule that provides a percentage calculation of taxable income based on filing status.

tax write-off An item that is deductible for tax purposes. An example is the depreciation on a self-employed taxpayer's computer and car used for business purposes, deducted as a business expense on Schedule C of Form 1040.

taxable estate The portion of an ESTATE remaining after all expenses have been paid for funerals, administrative costs, the satisfaction of DEBTS, TAXES, loss, transfers to a surviving spouse, and other contributions. The taxable estate is the portion that is subject to the federal unified transfer tax at death. An estate is taxed by the federal government and most state governments. The estate, not the recipients, pays the tax. At the present time, there is a $600,000 federal exclusion on property transfer by the deceased person. No estate tax exists for property going from one spouse to another.

taxable event An occurrence that has a tax consequence. For example, the sale of a home, at a gain, by a 35-year-old individual who does not move into a new home within two years is subject to tax. Another example is a casualty loss that may be tax deductible.

taxable gift *See* GIFT TAX.

taxable income ADJUSTED GROSS INCOME (AGI) less itemized deductions and personal exemptions. Taxable income is the basis for determining the tax owed by reference to the tax tables (taxable income of $50,000 or less) or tax rate schedules (taxable income of more than $50,000).

technical analysis An approach to forecasting stock prices based on historical volume and price patterns. It uses charts (e.g., line chart, bar chart, point-and-figure chart) to depict trends in the overall market as well as specific securities.

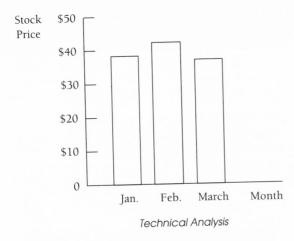

Technical Analysis

Technical analysts feel that the market can be predicted in terms of direction and magnitude. Stock prices move with the market because they adjust to various demand and supply forces. A pattern is uncovered in terms of stock price changes, volume, and other market data. Based on chart data, technical analysts recommend securities and the timing of buys and sells.

Some possible indicators of market and stock performance include TRADING VOLUME, MARKET BREADTH, BARRON'S CONFIDENCE INDEX, MUTUAL FUND cash position, SHORT POSITION, ODD-LOT THEORY, and the Index of BEARISH Sentiment. See sample company chart.

technical correction In SECURITIES, a short-term correction in a STOCK or the overall STOCK MARKET from an OVERBOUGHT condition. INVESTORS seek to lock in profits by selling their securities.

technical rebound In SECURITIES, a technical buying surge occurring in an OVERSOLD stock or STOCK MARKET. INVESTORS see the possibility of short-term profits by buying securities forcing SHORT sellers to COVER their positions.

technical theory The belief that securities prices are solely the result of the forces of supply and demand.
See also TECHNICAL ANALYSIS.

telecommunications The transmission of messages by computer, fax, telephone, telegram, or television. Modern technological developments have ushered in an age of telecommunications in which faxed messages and computer telecommunication networks make a whole world of data and information instantly available. The majority of telecommunications use a telephone line or radio waves; however, satellite transmission is assuming greater importance in this function.

Computer telecommunications allows the transmission of machine readable data as well as executable programs to any other computer, using a modem and a serial port on the computer. This enables one to do extensive data analysis as quickly as the data are developed and transmitted. For example, a Lotus Development Corporation product, SIGNAL, provides a PC user the ability to monitor STOCK transactions in real time, capturing the data into a spreadsheet for instant analysis.

telephone switching An essential computerized device that automatically selects telephone transmission circuits for the transmission of telephone messages. It permits extremely rapid connections to be made through a network of telephone connections.

teller In banking, an individual employed for the purpose of performing customer transactions. AUTOMATIC TELLER MACHINES (ATMs) are playing an increasingly important role in expediting BANK transactions for customers.

template In personal computers, a worksheet that includes formulas for a given application with the data. It is a blank worksheet on which data are saved and filled in as required for future personal finance applications. Templates are guides for preparing the spreadsheet. They are predefined files, including cell formulas and row or column labels for specific applications. In effect, they are worksheet models designed to solve specific types of problems. Templates allow for the referencing of cells and formulations of interrelated formulas and functions. They are used to analyze similar transactions. An example is a template indicating the effect of a change in sales on expenses.

temporary investment

1. An INVESTMENT intended to be held for less than one year.

2. A short-term investment made until another investment possibility is realized. For example, if an INVESTOR believes the downside RISK exceeds the upside potential in the STOCK MARKET, he or she may put the investment CAPITAL in a relatively risk-free investment, such as a MONEY MARKET FUND, where interest on the capital will be paid until the investor perceives that the upside potential in the STOCK MARKET exceeds the downside risk, whereupon the MONEY will be reinvested in the STOCK MARKET.

temporary life annuity An ANNUITY provided for in an insurance contract stipulating that benefits continue for a specified time period only if the annuitant survives.

1040 Form 1040 is issued by the United States INTERNAL REVENUE SERVICE for individual INCOME TAX returns. Anyone who earns INCOME above certain minimum requirements, depending upon age and marital status, must file an annual return. While many supplemental INCOME TAX SCHEDULES are available, the standard 1040 comes with many schedules and forms, including Schedule A (itemized deductions), Schedule B (INTEREST and DIVIDEND INCOME), Schedule C (business profit or loss), Schedule D (capital gains and losses), Schedule E (supplemental income and loss), Schedule SE (Social Security self-employment TAX), Form 2441 (child and dependent care EXPENSES), and Form 4562 (DEPRECIATION and amortization). TAXES are paid on a person's WAGES, INCOME, COMMISSIONS, profits, and passive income, that is, INTEREST and DIVIDEND INCOME.

Penalties are assessed if no TAX return is filed or for outright fraud.

1040 EZ A simplified individual income tax return form. It may be used by a taxpayer who

(1) has single filing status, (2) is under 65 years old, (3) is not blind, (4) claims no dependents, (5) has taxable income below $50,000, (6) has income only from wages, tips, and taxable interest income below $400, and (7) is not liable for supplemental Medicare premiums. The taxpayer may not take adjustments to gross income, itemized deductions, or tax credits on Form 1040 EZ. The "single" column of the tax table is used to find the tax that is entered on Line 7 of the form.

10-K report Annual filing with the SECURITIES AND EXCHANGE COMMISSION for publicly traded companies. Financial statements and supporting information are furnished. Form 10-K typically includes more financial information than that contained in the annual report. Included are the audited basic financial statements consisting of the balance sheet, income statement, and statement of cash flows. Examples of disclosures are sales, operating income, segmental sales by major product line for the last five years, and general business information.

10-Q report A quarterly filing with the Securities and Exchange Commission by publicly traded companies. It contains interim financial statements and related disclosures and may cover one particular quarter or be cumulative. It should present comparative figures for the same period of the previous year. The statements may or may not be audited. Form 10-Q is less comprehensive than Form 10-K.

1031 tax-free exchange The Internal Revenue Code (IRC Section 1031) provision that deals with tax-free exchanges of certain property. Property owners may sell "like-kind" properties and defer tax charges on the sale's profits by meeting the requirements for an IRC "1031 exchange." Specifically included for exchange are properties used or held for rental income, for business purposes, as investment property (e.g., vacant land held for profit, ground leases), or as a vacation home. An owner of these qualifying like-kind properties must adhere exactly to the following time constraints: first, the seller must *identify*, in writing, the prospective replacement property within 45 days after ESCROW on the old property, and second, the seller must take TITLE to the new property either within 180 days of the old property's close of escrow or by the DUE DATE of the seller's next tax return, including extensions, whichever is earlier. For example, under Section 1031, Lynne trades her appreciated land for Bob's fourplex. EQUITIES are the same. Lynne's adjusted tax basis in the land becomes her adjusted tax basis in the apartment.

1034 exchange (rollover) The Internal Revenue Code (IRC Section 1034) dealing with sale of personal residences. Generally, there is no recognized gain or loss on the sale of a personal residence, provided another one is purchased within 24 months before or after the sale of the old residence, a 48-month period. Also, the new one must cost at least as much as the ADJUSTED SALES PRICE of the old one (sales price, less expenses of sale, less fixing-up expenses). For example, under Section 1034, Kim can defer tax on the $30,000 gain on the home she sold for $235,000 by buying a new one that costs more. *See also* OVER AGE 55 HOME SALE EXEMPTION.

tenancy
1. The time period a TENANT may occupy premises; it may be a fixed term lease (e.g., 3 years) or a period tenancy (e.g., month to month).
2. The right or interest to possess REAL ESTATE, whether by TITLE or by LEASE.
See also JOINT TENANCY; TENANCY IN COMMON.

tenancy at will Occupancy that may be terminated by either the landlord or tenant at their discretion. The agreement may be oral or in writing.

tenancy by the entirety A form of ownership by husband and wife, recognized in certain states, in which the rights of the deceased spouse automatically pass to the survivor. It is the same as JOINT TENANCY, except that one spouse cannot dispose of his or her share without permission of the other spouse.

tenancy in common
real estate: Ownership of property by any two or more persons in undivided interests (not necessarily equal) without the right of survivorship. If one tenant dies, his or her share is transferred to the estate rather than to the other common tenants. An example of this arrangement is partners in real property.
securities: Ownership of a BROKERAGE ACCOUNT by at least two individuals, each having a separable equity.
See also JOINT TENANCY; TENANCY BY THE ENTIRETY.

tenancy in severalty The ownership of property by one person. For example, Bruce owns land as a tenant in severalty. He enjoys the absence of cotenants.

tenant
1. The person renting a residential unit.
2. A business renting commercial space.

tenants in common *See* TENANCY IN COMMON.

tenants' union A group of rental occupants who have banded together.

tender
1. To present something of worth for another's acceptance. For example, making a bid at a public auction.
2. An offer to buy back a bond payable by the issuing company.
See also TENDER OFFER.

tender offer A bid to purchase stock of a company at a given price, typically at an amount greater than the current market price. The purpose is to obtain voting control of a TARGET COMPANY. The tender offer may be submitted directly to the company's board of directors, or to the stockholders. If a prospective acquiring company buys 5% or more of the voting common stock of a target company, disclosures must be made to the Securities and Exchange Commission, target company, and relevant stock exchange.

tenure

property: The right and obligations of using and holding property.

employment: The right of holding responsibly a position of employment. For example, the job status of a university professor who has earned tenure.

term

1. A specified number of years.

2. The length of time an agreement or policy is effective, such as a three-year lease, a one-year insurance policy, and a two-year loan.

3. A condition set forth in an agreement. Examples are that the tenant must not have a dog in the apartment, and the annual interest rate on a loan is 12%.

4. A period of time a person is to serve, such as a four-year term as an elected official.

term bond A BOND that matures on one date. Typically, there may be a sinking fund established to retire the bond at maturity. It is, however, possible that the bond indenture may permit early extinguishment of the issue at the option of the company.

term certificate A CERTIFICATE OF DEPOSIT with a long maturity date, typically ranging from one year to ten years.

term life insurance A form of LIFE INSURANCE that covers the INSURED only for a given period of years, such as 5, 10, 20, or until a given age, such as 65, and does not provide for the accumulation of any cash values. Term insurance comes in several varieties:

level term: The face amount (the amount of coverage) remains fixed for the life of the contract.

declining, decreasing, or reducing term: The face amount periodically drops according to a fixed schedule over 10, 15, or more years.

convertible term: The policy can be converted into a CASH VALUE policy with no need to meet

medical standards at the time of conversion. Most insurance companies offer policies that are both convertible and renewable up to specified ages or for a fixed period.

term loan

1. A loan that requires only interest payments until the last day of its term, at which time the full payment is due. It involves a BALLOON PAYMENT.

See also STRAIGHT LOAN.

2. Intermediate- to long-term (typically, 2 to 10 years) secured loan granted to a business by a COMMERCIAL BANK, INSURANCE company, or commercial finance company, usually to finance capital equipment or provide working capital. The loan is amortized over a fixed period.

termination The end of an agreement, as when an insurance company decides to cancel the insurance policy.

termination benefit Money paid to an employee let go by the employer. Such payment may be made in a LUMP-SUM or ANNUITY form.

termination insurance Employee protection of pension benefits under the provisions of the Pension Benefit Guaranty Corporation in the event the pension plan is terminated.

testament Or, *will.* The disposition of personal property. Common usage uses the terms WILL, testament, and LAST WILL AND TESTAMENT interchangeably.

testamentary capacity Having the intellectual capability of understanding the nature of the terms and conditions of a will and their implications. A TESTATOR must have the ability to comprehend his or her estate and its eventual disposition and effects in order to validate a will.

testamentary intention Understanding and interpreting the purpose of a TESTATOR in his or her WILL. The disposition of the testator's ESTATE must be clear and unambiguous or it could be challenged in court. For example, understanding the testamentary intentions of Howard Hughes in his WILL was a crucial issue in determining the eventual disposition of the Hughes estate.

testamentary trust A TRUST created by a WILL taking effect upon the death of the donor, also termed settlor. It empowers a trust administrator to implement the terms of the testamentary trust.

testate An individual who dies leaving a WILL for determining the distribution of the ESTATE.

testator/testatrix A man or woman, respectively, who makes a WILL.

thin market A market in which there are comparatively few bids to buy or offers to sell, or both. The term applies to a single stock or to the entire STOCK MARKET. In a thin market, buying or selling a few shares of stock can affect its price disproportionately in either direction. Price volatility is therefore generally greater than in markets with more liquidity.

thinly held stock A company's stock owned by only a few investors. As a result, significiant variability in price may take place on low activity and it is difficult to sell large blocks of the stock.

third market Trading in the OVER-THE-COUNTER MARKET of securities listed on an exchange. The trades are executed between institutional investors who buy and sell securities to one another. By trading a significant number of securities, they are able to save commissions and avoid the disturbing price effects that can occur otherwise.

third party
in general: An individual who is not directly involved in an act but may have an interest in it. For example, an individual witnesses A striking B and is later subpoenaed into court to testify to what he or she witnessed. Another example would be a BENEFICIARY to a TRUST held by the BANK for a client.
insurance: An individual autonomous from the INSURED and the insurer. A policy is purchased by the insured from an INSURANCE COMPANY for LIABILITY COVERAGE INDEMNIFYING an action brought by a third party.

third party check A negotiated check that is not payable to the writer. The third party is the payee, who can then get credit for the check in his or her bank account by endorsing the back of the check. There can also be a double-endorsed check. After endorsing the back of the check, the payee passes the check to another who can then cash it. The Uniform Commercial Code (UCC) allows transfer of a check to a new owner any number of times.

thirty-day account An account in which purchases must be paid in full within 30 days.

thirty-day charge account *See* THIRTY-DAY ACCOUNT.

thirty-day wash sale A rule by the INTERNAL REVENUE SERVICE stating that losses on a STOCK may not be recognized if the same stock is repurchased within 30 days from the date of the sale.
See also WASH SALE.

35-percent rule A rule that a lender uses to determine a borrower's housing affordability. The rule says that a borrower can afford no more than 35% of monthly take-home pay. For example, a borrower's gross annual income is $33,000 per year and take-home pay is $2,095 per month. At 35% he or she could afford a monthly payment of $733. Using this amount, the mortgage rate (variable or fixed), the mortgage term, and a mortgage payment schedule, the lender can determine how much the person can qualify for. Assuming an interest rate of 13% and a 30-year term, he or she could borrow $66,260. (From Table 5, Appendix A, the monthly payment for a $10,000 mortgage loan is $110.62. Hence, $733/$110.62 = 6.626, 6.626 × $10,000 = $66,260.)
See also HOUSING AFFORDABILITY INDEX; PERCENT OF MONTHLY GROSS INCOME RULE.

threshold The exemptions and deductions a taxpayer is permitted so that income is only subject to tax above this amount.

thrift institution A depository institution, including SAVINGS AND LOAN ASSOCIATIONS and MUTUAL SAVINGS BANKS. If organized as a mutual association, depositors are shareholders. They offer savings accounts and make home mortgage loans.

tick An upward or downward movement in a stock's trading price. The term undoubtedly is derived from the time when STOCK trades were reported on a TICKER TAPE. Careful observation of the ticks on a stock gives an indication of INVESTOR sentiment.

ticker A real-time telegraphic INSTRUMENT reporting current trades on the various STOCK EXCHANGES as well as current news developments. The trades and events reported on the ticker have importance for the brokerage industry and the news media.

ticker symbol *See* STOCK SYMBOL.

ticker tape The tape instrument that displays the stock symbols, prices, and volume of security transactions around the world within minutes after each trade on the floor.

tight market A market in which the spreads between the BID and ASKED price of a security are very small. This is a sign that the security is in abundant supply and being actively traded.

tight money
1. Fewer funds available to borrowers from lending institutions and creditors. This is a situation in which credit is difficult to obtain.
2. A reduction in the dollars available for individual spending because of a decrease in the money supply.

time deposit A fixed-term SAVINGS DEPOSIT or CERTIFICATE OF DEPOSIT that must be on DEPOSIT for a certain period of time before the holder can withdraw it without paying an EARLY WITHDRAWAL PENALTY.

time draft A draft that is negotiable only after a specified date. A time draft differs from a SIGHT DRAFT that is payable upon presentation and delivery.

time limit
1. The period of time within which an insured must file a claim for reimbursement under an insurance policy. For example, Group Health Incorporated requires that a claim for health care be filed no later than March 31 of the year following the year in which medical services were provided.
2. The time period within which an insurer must contest coverage for a preexisting condition or misrepresentation. For example, most states give insurers three years to contest misrepresentations.
3. A limitation placed on the period of time one has to reply to something. Examples are a prospective employee's having 60 days to reply to a job offer, and a tenant having 30 days to decide whether to renew a lease.

time loan A loan with a fixed term, such 90 or 120 days. It is typically a DISCOUNT LOAN in which the interest is deducted up front from the loan amount.

time sharing
1. The division of ownership in real estate property over a designated time period. An example is a co-owned vacation apartment, used by co-owners at different times during the year.
2. The use of a terminal to access a mainframe computer in a multi-user environment. The user can download information, upload information, send and receive electronic mail, and use computer programs.

time spread An investor purchases and sells a CALL and a PUT with the identical exercise price but with different expiration dates. The objective is to try to gain from the difference in OPTION PREMIUMS.

time value of money The concept that states that money is worth different sums at different time periods. In other words, one dollar today is worth more than one dollar tomorrow. Time value of money is a critical consideration in financial and investment decisions. For example, COMPOUND INTEREST (future value) calculations are needed to determine future earnings resulting from an investment in financial assets such as STOCKS and BONDS. DISCOUNTING, or calculating PRESENT VALUE, which is inversely related to compounding, is used to determine today's value of future cash flows associated with investments in fixed assets such as real estate. There are plenty of applications of time value of money in PERSONAL FINANCIAL PLANNING. The concepts, calculations, and applications of future values and present values are presented below.

future values—compounding

A dollar in hand today is worth more than a dollar to be received tomorrow because of the interest it could earn in an investment such as a savings account. Compounding interest means that interest earns interest. For the discussion of the concepts of compounding and time value, the following definitions are used:

F_n = future value = the amount of money at the end of year n

P = principal = annual interest rate

n = number of years

Then,

F_1 = the amount of money at the end of year 1 = principal and interest = $P + iP = P(1+i)$

F_2 = the amount of money at the end of year 2 = $F_1(1+i) = P(1+i)(1+i) = P(1+i)^2$

The future value of an investment compounded annually at rate i for n years is $F_n = P(1+i)^n = P. T_1(i,n)$ where $T_1(i,n)$ is the future value of $1 found in Table 1, Appendix A (future value of $1).

Example 1: Paul Nani places $1,000 in a savings account earning 8% interest compounded annually. How much money will he have in the account at the end of 4 years?

$$F_n = P(1+i)^n$$
$$F_4 = \$1,000 (1 + 0.08)^4$$

From Table 1, the T_1 value for 4 years at 8% is 1.361.

Therefore,

$$F_4 = \$1,000 (1.36) = \$1,361$$

Example 2: Steve Hahn invested a large sum of money in the stock of Sigma Corporation. The company paid a $3 dividend per share. The dividend is expected to increase by 20% per year for the next three years. He wishes to project the dividends for years one through three.

$F_n \quad P(1+i)^n$
$F_1 = \$3(1+0.2)^1 = \$3 (1.200) = \$3.60$
$F_2 = \$3(1+0.2)^2 = \$3 (1.440) = \$4.32$
$F_3 = \$3(1+0.2)^3 = \$3 (1.728) = \$5.18$

future value of an annuity

An ANNUITY is defined as a series of payments (or receipts) of a fixed amount for a specified number of periods. Each payment is assumed to occur at the end of the period. The future value of an annuity is a compound annuity that involves depositing or investing an equal sum of money at the end of each year for a certain number of years and allowing it to grow. Let

S = the future value on an n-year annuity

A = the amount of an annuity

Then

$$S = A \ T_2(i,n)$$

where $T_2(i,n)$ provides the future value for an n-year annuity of $1 compounded at i%; it can be found in Table 2, Appendix A (Future Value of an Annuity of $1).

Example 3: Lisa Clarke wishes to determine the sum of money she will have in her savings account at the end of 6 years by depositing $1,000 at the end of each year for the next 6 years. The annual interest rate is 8%. The $T_2(8\%, 6$ years) is given in Table 2 as 7.336. Therefore,

$$S = \$1,000 \ T_2(8,6) = \$1,000 (7.336) = \$7,336$$

present value—discounting

Present value is the present worth of future sums of money. The process of calculating present values, or discounting, is actually the opposite of finding the compounded future value. In connection with present value calculations, the interest rate i is called the discount rate.

Recall that

$$F_n = P (1+i)^n$$

Therefore,

$$P = \frac{F_n}{(1+i)^n} = \left[F_n \frac{1}{(1+i)^n} \right] = F_n T_3(i,n)$$

where $T_3(i,n)$ provides the present value $1 and is given in Table 3, Appendix A (Present Value of $1).

Example 4: John Jaffe has been given an opportunity to receive $20,000 6 years from now. If he can earn 10% on his investments, what is the most he should pay for this opportunity? To answer this question, one must compute the present value of $20,000 to be received 6 years from now at a 10% rate of discount. F_6 is $20,000, i is 10% and n is 6 years. $T_3(10,6)$ from Table 3 is 0.565.

$$P = \$2,000 \left[\frac{1}{(1+0.1)^6} \right] = \$20,000\ T_3(10,6)$$
$$= \$20,000(0.565)$$
$$= \$11,300$$

This means that for John Jaffe, who can earn 10% on his investment, receiving $11,300 now or $20,000 six years from now would be the same since the amounts are time equivalent. In other words, he could invest $11,300 today at 10% and have $20,000 in 6 years.

present value of mixed streams of cash flows

The present value of a series of mixed payments (or receipts) is the sum of the present value of each individual payment. We know that the present value of each individual payment is the payment times the appropriate T_3.

Example 5: Bonnie Brown has been offered an opportunity to receive the following mixed stream of revenue over the next 3 years:

Year	Revenue
1	$1,000
2	$2,000
3	$500

If she must earn a minimum of 6% on her investment, what is the most she should pay today? The present value of this series of mixed streams of revenue is as follows:

Year	Revenue ($)	×	$T_3(i,n)$	=	Present Value
1	1,000		0.943		$943
2	2,000		0.890		1,780
3	500		0.840		420
					$3,143

present value of an annuity

Interest received from BONDS, PENSION FUNDS, and insurance obligations all involve annuities. To compare these financial instruments, we need to know the present value of each. The present value of an annuity can be found by using the following equation:

$$A = T_4(i,n)$$

where $T_4(i,n)$ is the present value of an annuity of $1 discounted at i percent for n years and is found in Table 4, Appendix A (Present Value of an Annuity of $1).

Example 6: Assume that the revenues in Example 5 form an annuity of $1,000 for 3 years. Then the present value is

$$\$1,000\ T_4(6,3) = \$1,000\ (2.673) = \$2,673$$

APPLICATIONS OF FUTURE VALUES AND PRESENT VALUES

Future and present values have numerous applications in personal finance and investments, which are covered throughout the dictionary. Three of these applications are presented below.

deposits to accumulate a future sum (or sinking fund)

An individual might wish to find the annual deposit (or payment) that is necessary to accumulate a future sum. To find this future amount (or sinking fund) we can use the formula for finding the future value of an annuity.

$$S = A \times T_2$$

Solving for A, we obtain:

$$\text{Sinking fund amount} = A = \frac{S}{T_2}$$

Example 7: Karen Black wishes to determine the equal annual end-of-year deposits required to accumulate $5,000 at the end of 5 years when her son enters college. The interest rate is 10%. (Note that $T_2(10,5) = 6.105$ [from Table 2].) The annual deposit is

$$A = \frac{5,000}{6.105} = \$819$$

In other words, if she deposits $819 at the end of each year for 5 years at 10% interest, she will have accumulated $5,000 at the end of the fifth year.

amortized loans

If a loan is to be repaid in equal periodic amounts, it is said to be an amortized loan. Examples include auto loans, mortgage loans, and most commercial loans. The periodic payment can easily be computed as follows:

$$P = A \times T_4$$

Solve for A as shown:

$$\text{Amount of loan} = A = \frac{P}{T_4}$$

Example 8: Kim Naomi has a 40-month auto loan of $5,000 at a 12% annual interest rate. She wants to find out the monthly loan payment amount.

Note that $i = 12\%/12$ months $= 1\%$ and $T_4(1,40) = 32.8347$ (from Table 4, Appendix A). Therefore,

$$A = \frac{\$5,000}{32.835} = \$152.28$$

So, to repay the principal and interest on a $5,000, 12%, 40-month loan, Kim Naomi has to pay $152.28 a month for the next 40 months.

rates of growth

In personal finance, it is sometimes necessary to calculate rate of growth, associated with a stream of income.

Example 9: Assume that your income was $25,000 in 19X1, and 10 years later it had increased to $37,000. The compound annual rate of growth of your income can be computed as follows:

$$F_n = P \times T_1$$

Solving this for T_1,

$$T_1(i,n) = \frac{F_n}{P}$$

$$T_1 = \frac{\$37,000}{\$25,000} = 1.48$$

Table 1, Appendix A, shows that T_1 of 1.48 at 10 years is at $i = 4\%$. Your income grew at an annual rate of 4%.

Note that many financial calculators are available that contain preprogrammed formulas and perform many present value and future applications. They include Radio Shack EC5500, Hewlett-Packard 10B, Sharp EL733, and Texas Instruments BA35.

time-limit-on-certain defense clause Or, IN-CONTESTABILITY CLAUSE. A period, usually two years, after which an insurer may not raise defenses against the payment of losses on HEALTH INSURANCE policies.
See also INCONTESTABILITY CLAUSE.

timing A good time to do something to achieve an optimal benefit. An example is selecting a suitable time to invest in stocks before they rise, or entering into a lease transaction before rental rates rise. The choice of the right time for an action is based on judgment.

tip

1. In investments, a recommendation to buy or sell a security or commodity based on accurate or inaccurate information. Typically, the term refers to INSIDE INFORMATION, which cannot be used legally as the data have not yet been made public. A transaction entered into based on a tip may prove profitable or unprofitable, depending on the reliability of the information supplied.

2. Or, *gratuity*. Extra compensation given for satisfactory services provided, such as leaving a tip for the waiter.

title The legal right of an ownership interest in a property. It is evidence of ownership and lawful possession.

title abstract *See* TITLE.

title check An investigation to determine who legally has the TITLE to property. For example, when a house is sold, the attorney for the buyer will do a title search to assure that the seller owns the house.

title insurance INSURANCE required of home buyers by lenders, to protect against loss due to defective TITLES. The policies are written by a title insurance company.

title search An inquiry of the history of the property to determine whether there are any restrictions or defects on the TITLE including MORTGAGES, ENCUMBRANCES, and all LIENS.

tombstone A term given to a financial advertisement, normally placed by INVESTMENT BANKERS, in the financial section of a newspaper or other publication stating the financial terms of a pending security offering. The tombstone will name the lead underwriter at the top of the list of secondary UNDERWRITERS, ranked by order of their participation in the offering.

The word "tombstone" comes from the black border appearing around the advertisement giving it a very somber appearance.

top-down approach to investing The investor first analyzes economic trends, then selects a suitable industry, and finally invests in an attractive company in that industry. The company selected should perform well based on the economic trend. For example, if the economy is growing rapidly, the investor may find the home construction industry to be attractive, and then decide to buy stock in Kaufman and Broad Home Corporation because it offers growth prospects.

top/peak In investments, the highest price a security went to over a stated time frame. After the peak was reached, the market price of the security fell.

topping out The action of a SECURITY or STOCK MARKET that has experienced a sharp increase in price followed by a progressively slower increase in value over a subsequent period. This gradual slowing in price appreciation is an important technical sell indicator.

topping up clause A provision in a loan contract in which securities are pledged. The borrower must give the creditor a specified amount of securities as COLLATERAL. In case the market price of the securities drops, additional securities must be pledged. If the debtor cannot oblige, the loan becomes immediately payable.

tort liability A legal obligation arising from a civil wrong or injury for which a judicial remedy can occur. A tort liability arises as a result of any combination of a direct violation of an individual's rights, the transgression of a public obligation resulting in damage to an individual, or a private wrongdoing to another individual. For example, if an individual is struck and injured by a municipal bus as he or she is legally crossing the street, this would be a direct violation of and a wrongdoing to the individual. This is a violation of the municipality's obligation to preserve and protect the safety and welfare of the public. The injured individual may sue the municipality for damages.

total cost A sum of all related costs for a transaction or an item or service. For example, the total cost to paint a house could include the number of gallons of paint involved, additional materials needed such as new shutters, and the number of hours of labor at an hourly rate required to complete the job. The sum of all of these items would be the total cost.

total disability An injury or illness that prevents a worker from performing the duties of any occupation for which he or she is suited through experience, education, or training.

total return The RETURN received on an investment over a specified period of time. It is composed of two basic elements—the CURRENT

YIELD such as dividend, interest, and rental income, and CAPITAL GAINS OR LOSSES. It is usually expressed as an annual percentage.
See also HOLDING PERIOD RETURN; RETURN; YIELD.

total volume The total shares or contracts of an equity security, debt security, commodity future, or other security traded for the day. This may also refer to the aggregate trades on the national and regional stock exchanges for stocks for the day. The total volume for over-the-counter stocks is indicated by the NASDAQ index. In the case of options, this may be the volume of trades transacted.

Totten trust A TRUST that is typically a SAVINGS ACCOUNT opened at a financial institution where money is deposited in trust for a beneficiary while the grantor maintains control over the account, including the power of withdrawal.

towing and labor coverage In automobile insurance, COVERAGE for towing and related labor charges for an automobile POLICYHOLDER.

townhouse An attached dwelling in a multiple housing complex having at least two floors and often having a garage. Such dwellings are often found in CONDOMINIUM and COOPERATIVE APARTMENT developments.

trade
1. The exchange of securities or commodities taking place on organized exchanges (e.g., stock exchange, commodity exchange) or informally (e.g., over-the-counter market).
2. The exchange of goods and services. An exchange usually requires the payment of money and/or financial instruments. A barter arrangement is also possible.
3. An occupation, profession, or business. A trade usually refers to a skilled occupation such as the plumbing trade.
4. Those who merchandise, sell, or manufacture a particular product line.

trade against the wind A rule of a stock exchange requiring a specialist in a given stock to sell stock out of personal inventory to level out price vacillations.

trade association An organization representing the interests of companies in the industry.

trade date The date on which a SECURITY transaction occurred. REGULAR-WAY DELIVERY is five days after the trade date.

trader One who buys and sells for his or her own account for short-term profit. It may be also a BROKER who buys and sells in the OVER-THE-COUNTER MARKET.

trading index An index of the market performance of stocks taking into account price changes and volume.

trading on equity Or, *financial leverage*. The use of borrowed funds to magnify RETURN. Trading profitably on the equity, also known as positive (favorable) financial leverage, means that the borrowed funds generate a higher rate of return than the interest rate paid for the use of the funds. The excess accrues to the benefit of the owner because it magnifies, or increases, his or her earnings.
See also LEVERAGE.

trading pattern In SECURITIES, an observed regularity in the way a security trades. A trading pattern will contribute to the establishment of a TRADING RANGE. For a security to break out of an established trading pattern is technically significant.

trading post A position on the floor of the stock exchange where buy-and-sell orders for securities take place. These posts must be manned only by members of the stock exchange. At the post, the specialist in the security carries out his or her activities. The floor brokers having orders for the security congregate around the post. On the New York Stock Exchange, there are 22 trading posts.

trading profit Short-term profits earned by buying and selling STOCKS and COMMODITIES.

Individuals seeking trading profits are not long-term INVESTORS and may be DAY traders.

trading range A period of time during which SECURITY prices are confined to a defined price range. How long this period of time exists depends on MARKET conditions, and the trading range is not inviolable. However, a significant break out of the trading range has important technical implications. It may mark a new range at a different price level.

trading unit The number of shares, bonds, or other securities typically used for trading on the exchanges.

trading volume The total sales of SECURITIES generated in a given period of time. Trading volume is a very strong technical indicator of a new direction in a MARKET. For example, high volume accompanying a significant market price rise is technical confirmation of the market's direction; light volume accompanying this MARKET PRICE rise would give a technical signal to INVESTORS to be cautious about the significance of the rise. In the latter case, there is no confirmation of the market price movement.

transaction
in general: The sale, purchase, or transfer of any service or good.
securities: The purchase or sale of a specified number of SECURITIES at a certain price.
See also TRANSACTION COST.

transaction cost The cost of making a specific SECURITY or REAL ESTATE TRANSACTION. Real estate transaction costs include survey costs, MORTGAGE POINTS, MORTGAGE origination fees, recording fees, state transfer taxes, SURVEY costs, TITLE INSURANCE, and TITLE SEARCH fees.

transcribe
1. The transfer of an amount from one financial record to another. An example is transferring an amount from a bill to the checkbook.
2. To transform audio information into a typed copy.

transfer
1. Moving something from one location to another, such as withdrawing savings from one bank account and putting the money into another bank account offering a higher interest rate.
2. The switching of ownership to property. An example is the delivery of a stock certificate from the seller's broker to the buyer's broker so that there may be a legal transfer of ownership.
3. A change of ownership recorded on the books, such as a transfer agent's listing the name of the new owner of a bond.

transfer agent *See* STOCK TRANSFER AGENT.

transfer payments
government finance: MONEY transferred directly to people. Transfer payments would include disability payments, SOCIAL SECURITY retirement payments, unemployment compensation, veterans' benefits, and welfare payments.
current accounts: Disbursements of INTEREST and DIVIDENDS to foreign entities and governments as recorded in the balance of payments.

transfer tax In SECURITIES, a TAX charged by the federal and/or state government on a TRADE transaction an INVESTOR makes based on the amount of the execution. The cost is incurred by the INVESTOR and is at a low rate. There is no transfer tax on BONDS.

travel and entertainment account A separate account through which the employer agrees to reimburse employees, often salespeople, for expenses incurred in traveling and entertaining in the performance of their duties. In many cases, the employees use separate credit cards to charge for travel and entertainment so specific records may be kept for tax purposes.

travel and entertainment expense A tax deduction allowed as a business expense. The taxpayer is permitted to deduct 80% of the expense. For example, if travel and entertainment comes to $300, a $240 deduction is allowed. However, transportation expenses to and from the business meal are 100% deductible. To be deductible, a business meal must be *directly related* to the active conduct of the taxpayer's trade or business. *Unreimbursed* employee expenses for business travel and entertainment become miscellaneous ITEMIZED DEDUCTIONS subject to a 2% of ADJUSTED GROSS INCOME "floor."

traveler's check A check designed to assist in financial transactions for those traveling to distant locations. Traveler's checks come in various denominations ranging from $10 to $100 and having two signature authorization areas. The traveler signs the first area when he or she initially obtains the checks; to facilitate authentication of the signature, the traveler signs the check again when it is about to be negotiated.

The advantage of traveler's checks is that if lost, they can be reissued no matter where the individual is. Traveler's checks are issued at BANKS; the denominated amount of the check must be paid for as well as any imposed BANK service fee.

American Express developed the concept of traveler's checks.

treasuries Debt obligations issued and backed by the FULL CREDIT AND FAITH of the U.S. government. Depending on their denominations and maturities, they are classified into the three types: TREASURY BILLS, TREASURY NOTES, and TREASURY BONDS. The income earned on Treasuries is exempt from state and local taxes.

Treasury bill (T-bill) A short-term obligation of the U.S. government that may be purchased for a minimum of $10,000, but at a discount, with maturities of three months, six months, or one year. T-bills are perhaps the safest investment, 100% guaranteed by the U.S. government. They are available through banks or other financial institutions for a small fee or through Federal Reserve offices. Although T-bills cannot be cashed early, they are usually fairly easy to sell as there is an active SECONDARY MARKET.

The interest is exempt from state and local taxes. T-bills are sold at a discount to FACE VALUE.

Example: A one-year T-bill is bought at a STATED INTEREST RATE of 8.5%. The amount of discount is $850 (8.5% × $10,000). The price the buyer will pay is $9,150 ($10,000 − $850). The yield then is $850. The EFFECTIVE ANNUAL YIELD is 9.29% ($850/$9,150).

Treasury bond
1. A federal treasury security that matures in over ten years, initially selling for FACE VALUE, and paying a fixed rate of interest semiannually throughout its life. It is issued in minimum denominations of $1,000.
2. A BOND issued by a company and later repurchased.

Treasury issues *See* TREASURIES.

Treasury note A U.S. government security that can be bought in $1,000 and $10,000 denominations, with a maturity of one to ten years and a semiannual fixed interest rate slightly higher than that of a TREASURY BILL. Like Treasury bills, they are liquid, marketable, and virtually risk free.

treasury stock Stocks that were issued by a company and later bought back. Treasury shares may be reissued or canceled. Treasury stocks receive no dividend and carry no voting rights. The treasury stock may be used for various purposes, such as a stock bonus plan for key employees or as payment in acquiring another company.

trend The direction of movement in prices and/or volume of securities or commodities. The trend may be increasing, decreasing, or moving sideways. Other examples of trends are the historical movement in interest rates and inflation.

trend line In a chart or diagram, there is a line that connects the points. The line may go between the minimum and maximum points. The trend line shows direction. This can be helpful, for example, in predicting the future prices of commodities based on historical movements.

triple net leases A LEASE that requires tenants

to pay all utilities, INSURANCE, TAXES, and maintenance costs.

triple witching hour *See* PROGRAM TRADING.

truncation A reduction in processing steps to lower operating costs. An example is check truncation used by some banks. The bank does not return the canceled checks to the depositor but retains the checks or prepares a mirofilm record of them in a file. The depositor may request a copy of the canceled check for a minimal or no fee.

trust An agreement in which the trustee takes title to the property (referred to as the corpus) owned by the grantor (donor) to protect or conserve it for either the grantor or the trust's beneficiary. The trust is established by the grantor. The trustee is usually given authority to invest the property for a return. Trusts may be revocable or irrevocable.
See also IRREVOCABLE TRUST; REVOCABLE TRUST.

trust account An account that is held in trust for another person. For example, upon the death of the depositor, a bank account would belong to the individual the account is in trust for.

trust company
   1. An entity that serves as a trustee, fiduciary, or agent of funds for people. The funds may be in trust for children, an estate, or others. The trust company performs a custodial function. The trust may also invest funds held in conformity with state law. Many trust functions are conducted by commercial banks.
   2. A trust company may also serve as a fiscal agent for a company, paying dividends and bond interest.

trust deed *See* DEED OF TRUST.

trust fund A fund set up as a stipulation of a TRUST giving financial management authority to a TRUSTEE. The trustee has responsibility for distributing funds to the BENEFICIARIES as well as for paying all DEBTS for the trust. Depending on the terms of the trust, the MONIES may also be invested by the trustee.

trust fund pension plan A pension plan in which the employer contributions go to a trustee, who is then responsible for investing the funds and paying benefits to retirees.

trustee
in general: An individual or entity holding property in TRUST for a BENEFICIARY. Trustees have the duty of managing the assets in the best interests of the beneficiaries. A trustee violating the terms of a trust can face serious civil charges.
joint trustees: Two or more individuals being entrusted with property for one or more beneficiaries.
judicial trustee: A trustee appointed by a court for the purpose of administering the terms of a trust.
testamentary trustee: A trustee appointed by a will for the purpose of administering a TRUST created by the WILL. The executor of the will is separate from the testamentary TRUSTEE who is charged with the responsibility of administering the terms of the established trust.
See also TRUSTEE IN BANKRUPTCY.

trustee account *See* TRUST FUND.

trustee in bankruptcy An individual chosen by a judge or creditors of a bankrupt person to handle matters including the sale of the bankrupt's assets, management of the funds from the sale of those assets, payment of expenses, and distribution of the remaining funds to creditors. The trustee is typically compensated with a specified percentage of the value of what is liquidated.

Truth-in-Lending Act (TILA) Or, *Consumer Credit Protection Act of 1969; Regulation Z.* A major federal law designed to protect credit purchasers. The most important provision is the requirement that both the dollar amount of finance charges and the ANNUAL PERCENTAGE RATE (APR) charged must be disclosed before credit is extended.
See also REGULATION Z.

turkey A bad investment or business arrangement. Examples are a stock that suddenly falls significantly or a computer that develops many mechanical problems after purchase.

turnaround property A run-down property that can be fixed up and sold for a profit.

turnover The volume of business in a security or the entire market. For example, if turnover on the NEW YORK STOCK EXCHANGE is reported at 3,000,000 shares on a particular day, 3,000,000 shares changed hands. ODD-LOT turnover is tabulated separately and ordinarily is not included in reported volume.

12B–1 fees Fees of a MUTUAL FUND that cover advertising and marketing costs but do nothing to improve the performance of the fund. Their main purpose is to bring new customers to the fund and ultimately more money for the fund's management to invest.

two-class common stock A business that issues two types of common stock. For example, class A may have voting rights while class B may not. A stockholder cannot automatically transfer between the different types of common stock.

two-dollar broker Or, *independent broker*. A member of a stock exchange handling another broker's transactions. The other broker may not be a member of the exchange, absent from the exchange floor, or preoccupied with other matters. The ''two-dollar'' term is used because many years ago these brokers used to receive $2 for each 100-share transaction. Of course, the fees are much higher today depending on the dollar value of the transaction.

U

umbrella personal liability policy A supplemental LIABILITY INSURANCE policy that provides excess liability coverage after the liability coverage from other policies is consumed. It reimburses for losses incurred because of the negligence of the INSURED beyond the basic limits of other insurance contracts.

uncovered *See* NAKED.

uncovered option *See* NAKED OPTION.

underinsurance The failure to carry sufficient insurance. For example, the INSURED may fail to purchase coverage equal to the replacement cost of the property.

underlying futures contract An option is underlied by a futures contract. An example is a futures option on a commodity. When the option is transacted, delivery is made in the related futures contract.

underlying security

1. The common stock that must be delivered if the conversion option of a bond or preferred stock, warrant, or right is exercised.

2. The stock that is the basis for a call or put option. As an example, if a call is written on General Motors, the applicable shares of General Motors must be delivered if the option is exercised.

3. A stock or bond backed by a third entity, as when the bond of a subsidiary is guaranteed by the parent company.

undervalued Property, SECURITIES, or any other ASSET that is valued at less than its MARKET VALUE. For example, a STOCK may be selling on the market for less than its BOOK VALUE, which would indicate it is a BARGAIN since the REPLACEMENT COST of its assets is higher than its equity evaluation. Such a stock may become a TAKEOVER TARGET.

underwriting Acceptance of risk in return for payment.

1. In investments, in a new securities issue, the underwriter (investment banker) may carry out the underwriting function by buying securities at a set price from the issuer (e.g., company, government), hoping to sell them at a higher price to the public. The difference is the spread, or profit. If the underwriter is unable to sell the new issue bought, a loss will be incurred. *See also* UNDERWRITING SECURITIES.

2. In insurance, the process of reviewing and accepting or rejecting an insurance risk for a premium. If the item is to be insured, an appropriate insurance premium must be determined. The objective of underwriting is to diversify the risk among many insureds in an equitable manner.

3. In banking, a detailed credit analysis before a loan is granted based on the person's financial background, employment history, and other factors.

underwriting securities The process of selling a new security issue, typically carried out by investment banking firms. The underwriter may purchase the securities at a lower price from the issuer than the price at which he or she resells them to the public, thereby making a profit from the spread. The investment banker may assume the risk of the new issue if it cannot be resold. *See also* UNDERWRITING.

underwriting syndicate A group of investment banking firms that accepts responsibility for selling a new security issue. The UNDERWRITERS pool the risk and assure successful distribution of the issue. Most arrangements are divided syndicates in which the liability of the members is limited to their individual participations. *See also* INVESTMENT BANKER.

unearned income

income tax: Passive INCOME received from sources other than working, such as DIVIDEND and INTEREST payments. EARNED INCOME would be income received from WAGES or SALARY or business income.

accounting: Income received for products or services but not earned. For example, a retainer paid an attorney for future legal services.

unemployment The state of being out of work. To be considered unemployed by the Department of Labor, an individual must satisfy three conditions: he or she (1) must have been previously employed; (2) must be actively seeking employment; and (3) cannot be unemployed longer than 26 weeks, after which unemployment benefits expire.

Unemployed individuals are entitled to receive unemployment benefits from the state unemployment COMPENSATION division of the Department of Labor.

unencumbered A property that is clear of creditor liens. If cash is paid, as for a house, the home is owned free and clear. After an individual pays off a car loan, the car becomes unencumbered property. Unencumbered property may be sold or conveyed to another party. A MARGIN ACCOUNT for stock is encumbered.

unfunded pension plan A "pay as you go" PENSION PLAN. It allows the employer to make payments to retirees from CURRENT INCOME.

unified estate and gift tax A federal tax charged on the net value of an estate and on gifts above a certain amount. The transferrer is liable for gift taxes. However, if the transferrer for some reason does not pay them, the transferree will be held liable for payment.

unified tax credit A credit deducted from the taxpayer's estate or gift tax liability. However, the amount of the unified credit available at death will be reduced to the extent that any portion of the credit is used to offset GIFT TAXES on lifetime transfers. The unified tax credit for estates left by one who dies is currently $192,800, which is equivalent to an exemption of $600,000.

uniform commercial code (UCC) A legal code drafted by the National Conference of Commissioners of Uniform State Laws. It was adopted by all states except Louisiana. It includes all forms of commercial transactions including, BANK DEPOSITS, BANKRUPTCY, COMMERCIAL PAPER, LETTERS OF CREDIT, uncertified CHECKS, and WARRANTIES.

Uniform Gift to Minors Act (UGMA) A uniform act establishing rules for transferring and administering ASSETS to a minor. A CUSTODIAN is designated to act on the behalf of the minor, making all related INVESTMENT decisions including buying and selling ASSETS for the minor. All earned INCOME is TAXED to the minor. The custodianship ends when the child reaches the age of majority.

uniform probate code A uniform act simplifying and clarifying the law concerning the affairs of decedents, missing persons, protected persons, minors, and incapacitated persons. It facilitates discovering and making known the intent of a DECEDENT in distributing his or her property as well as expediting the LIQUIDATION of the ESTATE and subsequent distributions.

Another intent of the law is to ensure that INHERITANCE TAXES are paid. It also provides a safeguard against possible inequities whereby some BENEFICIARIES may receive a large share of an ESTATE as NONPROBATE PROPERTY without sharing in the TAX LIABILITY.

uniform residential landlord and tenant act An act designed, in part, to provide protection to persons who rent premises as their residence. The act constitutes a basic revision of landlord-tenant law whereby the landlord-tenant CONTRACTUAL relationship is recognized. The obligations of the parties are interdependent. The act deals, in part, with the nature and duration of the landlord-tenant relationship, tenants' rights, and LANDLORD and TENANT obligations.

It was approved by the National Conference of Commissioners on Uniform State Laws in 1972. It has been adopted by at least 13 states.

uniform settlement statement A uniform code providing, in part, that for goods accepted or a finance LEASE agreed to, when these do not conform to assurances given by the provider or lessor, the goods may be returned for a refund or the lease can be revoked or rejected. However, if imperfections or nonconformance were known prior to the acceptance, it cannot be revoked. In the case of a finance lease, the lessor makes certain WARRANTIES to the lessee.

Other sections of the act provide that a lessee must notify a lessor of any imperfections in order to seek relief or there shall be no remedy. The act also provides for relief through the litigation process.

unilateral contract An agreement in which one party agrees to do or not do something in return for the *actual* performance of another person.

uninsured motorist coverage *See* UNINSURED MOTORIST INSURANCE.

uninsured motorist endorsement *See* UNINSURED MOTORIST INSURANCE.

uninsured motorist insurance AUTOMOBILE INSURANCE that provides reimbursement to the owner of a vehicle for losses caused by an uninsured motorist. Its objective is to protect the insured driver and passengers from bodily injury losses and, in some states, property damage losses resulting from an auto accident caused by an uninsured motorist.

unissued stock Authorized shares that have not yet been issued. If 300,000 shares are authorized and 175,000 are issued, 125,000 shares remain unissued.

unit benefit plan A pension plan in which periodic retirement income is credited to an employee based on his or her service years. The increment may be based on a percentage of salary or a flat dollar amount. When the employee retires, the percentage of salary is multiplied by the service years. The resulting percentage is applied to the employee's average earnings. For example, if an employee retires with 25 years of service, a final average salary of

$80,000, and a percentage compensation of 2%, the annual retirement benefit equals

$$25\% \times \$80,000 \times .02 = \$40,000$$

unit investment trust A CLOSED-END investment company in which the proceeds from the sale of original shares are invested in a fixed portfolio of taxable or tax-exempt bonds and held until maturity. Like a MUTUAL FUND, a unit investment trust offers to small investors the advantages of a large, professionally selected and diversified PORTFOLIO. Unlike a mutual fund, however, its portfolio is fixed; once structured, it is not actively managed. Unit investment trusts are also available for MONEY MARKET securities, corporate BONDS of different grades; MORTGAGE-BACKED SECURITIES; PREFERRED STOCKS; utility COMMON STOCKS; and other investments. Unit trusts are most suitable for people who need a fixed income and a guaranteed return of capital. They disband and pay off investors after the majority of their investments have been redeemed.
See also INVESTMENT COMPANY; INVESTMENT TRUST.

unit of trading *See* TRADING UNIT.

unit price The price of one unit. As an example, the price to buy one chair is $65.

unit trust *See* UNIT INVESTMENT TRUST.

united states government securities Securities issued by the U.S. government, such as treasury bonds, notes, and bills. Since these securities are backed by the guarantee of the U.S. government, they are of low risk.

universal life insurance A variation of WHOLE LIFE INSURANCE that combines investment features with TERM LIFE INSURANCE. The savings yields are substantially higher than for whole life. It provides both the pure death protection and CASH VALUE buildup of whole life insurance but with variability in the FACE AMOUNT, DEATH BENEFIT, rate of cash value accumulation, PREMIUMS, and RATE OF RETURN. Premiums and cover-

age may be adjusted periodically. If the insured cannot make a premium payment, he or she can use the money from the cash value to cover it. As with regular whole life, the insured can borrow against the cash value, usually at below-market interest rates. He or she can cash in the insurance policy at any time and collect all or most of the savings.
See also INSURANCE PROGRAMS

unlimited liability In a sole proprietorship or a general partnership the owners' liability is *not* restricted to the capital investments. Thus, if the business goes bankrupt, the owner risks his or her personal assets to meet creditor claims. In a corporation, however, the stockholder has limited liability up to the amount of his or her investment.

unlimited marital deduction The absence of ESTATE TAX regardless of the amount transferred if a deceased spouse leaves his or her ESTATE to the other spouse.

unlisted An item that is not listed on a book of records. If it is unlisted, it may be unavailable to third parties. An example is an unlisted telephone number that the telephone company will not give out to the public.

unlisted security A stock or bond not bought or sold on an organized exchange, such as the New York Stock Exchange, but rather traded as an over-the-counter security.

unlisted trading A transacting of securities not posted on a stock exchange, but executed on that exchange as a courtesy to its members. To do this, the exchange must apply formerly for permission to the Securities and Exchange Commission and provide the necessary information to investors. Although the New York Stock Exchange does not permit unlisted trading, some other organized exchanges, such as the American Stock Exchange, do.

unloading The sale of securities, commodities, or property to avoid additional losses after a decline in price. An example is sale of a stock that is falling in price and for which the future outlook is dim.

unmargined account In SECURITIES, a CASH ACCOUNT. A securities account in which no MONEY is borrowed from the BROKER.

unpaid dividend A dividend that has been declared but has not yet been incurred. A declared dividend is a legal obligation of the company. For example, if a dividend is declared on January 15 payable on April 1, it is unpaid prior to April 1.

unrealized profit and loss *See* PAPER PROFIT AND LOSS.

unrecorded deed The transfer of a property DEED from one party to another without publicly recording it. The recording of a deed in a public office provides constructive notice of the act of the sale and helps to prevent possible FRAUD.

unsecured bond A BOND that has no COLLATERAL as security for the debt and is backed only by the good faith and reputation of the issuer.

unsecured loan A LOAN for which no COLLATERAL is required.
See also SIGNATURE LOAN.

unsecured note A CREDIT note in which a lender's only security is the borrower's personal financial situation and CREDIT HISTORY.

unwind a trade The reversal of a security transaction by offsetting it with another transaction. As an example, after a person buys 100 shares of a particular stock, he or she has second thoughts and decides to sell them.

up reversal A drastic temporary increase in the prices of securities or commodities following an overall downward trend in price.
See also DOWN REVERSAL.

up tick Or, *plus tick*. A term used to designate a price higher than that on the preceding transaction in the stock. A stock may be sold short only on an UP TICK, or on a ZERO-PLUS TICK. Zero-plus tick is a term used for a transaction at the same price as the preceding trade but higher than the preceding different price. Conversely, DOWN TICK, or MINUS TICK, is a term used to designate a transaction made at a price lower than the preceding trade. A ZERO-MINUS TICK is a transaction made at the same price as the preceding sale but lower than the preceding different price. A plus sign, or a minus sign, is displayed throughout the day next to the last price of each company's stock traded at each trading post on the floor of the NEW YORK STOCK EXCHANGE (NYSE).

upload In TELECOMMUNICATIONS, the transmission of binary programs or data from one computer to another. Uploading requires a computer, serial RS 232 port, modem, and access to a telephone line. Uploading is done with microcomputers through a series of data translation protocols such as ASCII, Compuserve B, Kermit, XModem, and YModem. The opposite of uploading is DOWNLOADING, which is to receive binary programs or data from another computer.

For example, it is possible to upload one's income tax return to the INTERNAL REVENUE SERVICE to facilitate an income tax refund.

upside potential An estimate of the possible comparative appreciation of value in an individual SECURITY or broad MARKET. In FUNDAMENTAL ANALYSIS, one would consider several factors in evaluating the upside potential in the value of SECURITIES, including the current PRICE-EARNINGS RATIO, BOOK VALUE, BUSINESS CYCLE, and industry outlook. In technical analysis, other factors would be considered, including the current chart formation of the individual SECURITY, volume, and new highs and lows. The opposite of upside potential is DOWNSIDE RISK, which is an estimate of the possible comparative DEPRECIATION of an individual security or broad market.

INVESTORS always evaluate individual securities and the broad market in terms of the upside potential versus the DOWNSIDE RISK. Thus, there is an eternal struggle between the BULLS and the BEARS.

upside trend In SECURITIES, a comparatively long-lasting trend in upward price movement of an individual security or the broad market. Upside trends are never even, and they are often punctuated by downside REVERSALS. The length of the upside trend in comparison to other periods of price REVERSALS is very significant for TECHNICAL ANALYSIS.
See also UPSWING.

upswing In SECURITIES, a period of upward price movement in a security or the broad MARKET after recent price REVERSALS. Longer-lasting upswings are termed an UPSIDE TREND.

uptrend *See* UPSIDE TREND.

U.S. savings bond A BOND issued in various denominations and maturities by the U.S. Treasury to assist in financing federal government operations. These bonds are backed by the FULL FAITH AND CREDIT of the U.S. government.
See also U.S. SERIES EE BONDS; U.S. SERIES HH BONDS.

U.S. Series HH bonds *See* SERIES HH.

U.S. Series EE bonds *See* SERIES EE.

U.S. Treasury note *See* TREASURY NOTE.

usual, customary, and reasonable charges (UCR) The established limits for reimbursement under an insurance policy. A medical insurance plan will reimburse the insured for a doctor's full charge provided it is a reasonable amount based on similar charges by other physicians in the area. If the charge is excessive, reimbursement will be based on the customary charge. For example, if a doctor charges a patient $125 and the insurance company deems the usual charge to be $100, the insurance reimbursement will be based on the $100 charge.

usury laws State laws that govern legal interest-rate maximums that can be charged by lenders for different types of loans.

utility
1. The satisfaction of a specified want. Each person has his or her own utility preferences as to what is important personally. For example, one person may be risk adverse while another is a risk seeker.
2. A type of software providing a specific function.
3. A service provided to operate daily functions, such as electricity.

V

VA loan guarantees Home LOANS guaranteed by the VETERANS ADMINISTRATION. The program was initiated by the Servicemen's Readjustment Act of 1944 as amended. The Veterans Administration issues a 60% *loan guaranty* for a sum not to exceed $27,500. The MORTGAGED home must be a principal residence. VA loans are granted with no down payment to qualified veterans.

valid will A WILL that has satisfied legal requirements and is enforceable by law.

valuable papers (records) insurance Insurance coverage for important papers destroyed or damaged. The insurance reimbursement is limited to an amount not exceeding the actual cash value of the loss, or the amount needed to repair or replace the damaged or destroyed papers. The policy requires that the insured have the papers kept secured under lock and key.

valuables Items of significant value such as gold jewelry. They are typically easy to carry. Specific insurance coverage is typically required, as for an expensive diamond ring.

value

1. What an item is worth in terms of dollars. Examples are what a person's home or car could sell for. In insurance policies, there are typically two measures of value for an insured item: "going market price" and current replacement cost.

2. The perceived personal importance of something to an individual that makes it desirable or useful to that person. For example, one individual will find an artistic painting to be of great pleasure while another person will not derive any psychic enjoyment from such a painting.

value broker A DISCOUNT BROKER whose commission is significantly less than that of a full-service broker. The value broker bases the commission on a percentage of the dollar amount of a transaction. Hence, it is cost efficient to use this broker for trades of low-priced securities. *See also* SHARE BROKER.

value line investment survey An investment advisory service that ranks the quality of hundreds of companies. The service predicts which stocks will perform the best and worst over the next year. The service looks at stocks in terms of timeliness, safety, risk, and similar features. The ranking system goes from 1 (highest rank) to 5 (lowest rank).

valued approach In health insurance, the payment to an insured of amounts stated in the policy. Such amounts do not necessarily have a direct relationship to the actual costs incurred.

valued payment plan of health insurance Agreement by the insurance company to pay the insured a fixed amount of money if the insured event occurs.

valued policy An insurance policy under which the contract amount of the policy must be paid if the property is destroyed.

vandalism and malicious mischief insurance Insurance coverage typically written as an endorsement to a standard fire policy applying to loss from intentional acts of vandals. This coverage is particularly recommended for those who are not occupying the premises during parts of the day.

van pooling A form of commuter pooling for which a van or large suburban-type truck is used to carry commuters to and from their places of employment in one centralized area. Various arrangements are used, such as having a private company offer the service or having the van owned jointly by the commuters, in which case all expenses are shared.

Van pooling is convenient and reasonable, and it provides an opportunity for informal socializing.

variable annuity An ANNUITY that pays the ANNUITANT varying amounts according to the performance of the insurance company's investments. With a variable annuity, the annuitant bears the RISK of the investment options. *See also* RETIREMENT AND PENSION PLANNING; SINGLE PREMIUM DEFERRED ANNUITY (SPDA).

variable cost Or, *variable expenditure*. Direct charges or costs varying according to the degree of usage or external factors such as gasoline expense based on mileage driven and utility bills.

in total: Costs that vary in direct proportion to activity changes. Examples include WAGES paid in proportion to the total hours worked.

per unit: The unit rate is the same with the costs varying only in terms of the volume of use.

variable expense *See* VARIABLE COST.

variable interest rate An interest rate on a CREDIT CARD or other instrument that moves up or down monthly according to changes in an INDEX of the lender's cost of funds.

variable life insurance A type of CASH VALUE LIFE INSURANCE that allows the policyholder to choose the investments made with his or her CASH VALUE accumulations and to share in the gains and losses of those investments. Like UNIVERSAL LIFE INSURANCE, variable life insurance

promises higher investment yields than traditional whole life. It is similar to WHOLE LIFE INSURANCE except that the policyholder can specify how the PREMIUMS are to be invested. Since the insured decides where his or her money is invested and bears the risk of those investments, variable life is considered a SECURITY by the government and is the only kind of life insurance sold by PROSPECTUS.
See also INSURANCE PROGRAMS; WHOLE LIFE INSURANCE.

variable rate certificate A CERTIFICATE OF DEPOSIT that has a varying rate of interest depending on such factors as market conditions (e.g., prime interest rate) and factors to which the rate of interest is tied (e.g., stock market index). The rate of interest moves upward and downward over time. For example, a 90-day certificate of deposit may be adjusted quarterly.

variable rate mortgage (VRM) A MORTGAGE for which interest rates are not fixed. The rate applicable to the mortgage goes up or down, depending on the movement of an outside INDEX such as the rate paid on U.S. TREASURY SECURITIES or the cost of funds.

variable-universal life insurance *See* VARIABLE LIFE INSURANCE.

variance The difference between actual and budgeted expenditures. For example, if an individual's budgeted costs for the month are $8,000 and actual costs are $9,500, there is an unfavorable variance of $1,500. The reasons for the overspending should be evaluated and any appropriate corrective action taken. Perhaps the reason for the overspending was an exorbitant amount of entertainment.

vendor's lien Or, *purchase money mortgage.* A seller's claim to property held by a buyer as security for some debt or charge.

vested The rights of an individual to benefits from employment, such as pension, sick leave, and vacation. Pension benefits are vested when the employee has worked a specified number of years. The person may then leave the employer for another one and still collect the accumulated amount at retirement. For example, an employee might be 100% vested after five years of service.

vested interest An individual's current or future interest in something, financial or otherwise. For example, an employee is dependent upon or has a vested interest in the financial survival of his or her employer.

Veterans Administration (VA) A federal government agency that helps veterans of the armed forces obtain housing. For example, it guarantees a HOME LOAN for up to a specified dollar amount or percentage of the loan balance, whichever is less.

Veterans Administration (VA) hospitals Hospitals that provide health care to veterans of the armed forces.

Veterans Administration (VA) mortgage A mortgage given to an eligible veteran or to a surviving spouse guaranteed by the pledge of the Veterans Administration to the financial institution. Generally, a veteran who has served more than 120 days of active duty in the armed forces is eligible for a home loan with no or minimal down payment. Interest rates on VA mortgages are set by the Veterans Administration.

vicarious liability The liability imputed to an individual by the actions of another. The law provides that the other should be held legally accountable for the wrong committed by someone else. By illustration, Joe, driving a delivery truck for ACE Department Store, hits a pedestrian. In conformity with the doctrine of respondent superior, the ACE Department Store is vicariously liable for the pedestrian's injuries.

videotext Data transmitted over a telephone line between a computer and a television screen. The system is interactive. An example is a bank transaction made or an order placed for merchandise.

violation Any abuse, disobedience, lawbreaking, transgression, or wrongdoing that occurs. A violation may result in some form of punishment or legal action.

VISA A CREDIT CARD issued by BANKS with credit charges including INTEREST on the unpaid balance and possible annual fees. The CREDIT CARD is billed monthly and members can pay only a minimal monthly charge. All VISA credit cards have an individual CREDIT LIMIT that is determined by the issuer.
See also BANK CARD.

vocational guidance CAREER PLANNING and counseling for individuals seeking a livelihood through pursuing an occupation or profession. Those providing vocational guidance are termed vocational guidance counselors or career counselors.

vocational rehabilitation Updated vocational training for those displaced by skill obsolescence or having been out of the work force for an extended period. An example is training in computerized application design (CAD) for a displaced draftsman.

voidable Descriptive of a contract that may be annulled by a party to it because of some illegality (e.g., fraud), incompetence, or the existence of some provision to rescind it.

volatile market In SECURITIES, a MARKET characterized by rapid and unpredictable short-term price movements.

volatility Extreme sensitivity to environmental conditions, causing erratic and unstable short-term changes. A volatile STOCK MARKET is easily influenced by news developments causing it unpredictably to reverse direction in violent short-term swings.

voluntary accumulation plan A plan in which a mutual fund investor buys shares in it on a recurring basis. The shareholder decides when to make the deposit and how much to invest.

voluntary bankruptcy BANKRUPTCY declared by any insolvent individual or business. It is different from INVOLUNTARY BANKRUPTCY, which is applied for by the creditors.
See BANKRUPTCY; CHAPTER 7; CHAPTER 11; CHAPTER 13.

voluntary conveyance
1. When property is transferred without consideration given, such as a gift.
2. When the debtor relieves himself or herself from the liability, such as giving a finance company the car that served as the collateral for the loan.

voluntary deductible employee contribution plan A pension plan allowing an employee to contribute by electing to have money deducted from each paycheck. Some pension plans (e.g., 401[K]) allow employees to contribute before-tax dollars while others require after-tax dollar contributions.

voluntary liquidation The approved liquidation of a company by its shareholders, such as that due to severe financial problems.

voluntary unemployment Condition in which a person chooses to be unemployed. Reasons could be that the only work available is considered by the person to be unsuitable because of his or her background or prior salary.

voting right The right to vote in person or by mail, such as a common stockholder's right to vote by PROXY for a company's board of directors.

voting stock Stock in a company that provides the shareholder with the right to vote in corporate affairs. COMMON STOCK typically carries voting rights.

W

W-2 form A tax form sent by the employer to the employee listing for the year wages earned, federal and state income tax withheld, Social Security tax withheld, and other information. This form provides information to be used in preparing federal, state, and local tax returns, and copies of the W-2 must be attached to the returns when filed.

W-4 form A form prepared by the employee and given to the employer containing needed information for the employer's determination of the amount to be withheld for taxes each pay period. Information on the form includes the number of exemptions, Social Security number, and similar data.

wage Compensation received by an employee from the employer for work performed.

wage assignment A LOAN clause that allows the lender to collect a certain portion of a borrower's wages from his or her employer if the borrower fails to make payment of the loan contract according to terms or has defaulted on the loan. It is prohibited by law in some states.

wage earner An employee who works for a SALARY.

wage garnishment A court order that requires a borrower's employer to pay a lender a regular sum in order to reduce a debt. It is a legal action taken only after a credit user has defaulted. The CONSUMER CREDIT PROTECTION ACT limits the amount of disposable income subject to garnishment and prohibits the dismissal of an employee for garnishment of any one indebtedness.

wage scale The SALARY progression established by a firm for its employees. Normally, the wage scale is based on factors that include seniority, importance of the task, hours worked, and comparable industry wages. The wage scale can be a major objective in COLLECTIVE BARGAINING.

wage spiral A period of rapidly rising WAGES seemingly having no end in sight. A wage spiral often results during a high INFLATION period when WAGE EARNERS seek to keep pace with the increase in prices by steadily forcing wages to increase.

waiting period Or, *elimination period*. A provision of DISABILITY INCOME INSURANCE that requires the insured to wait a specified length of time after DISABILITY before payment begins.

waiver of premium A clause or an option in an insurance policy that provides for automatic payment of premiums should the policyholder be ill or disabled. This option may be included in an insurance policy or be purchased separately. With this option, the insurer waives premiums if the insured becomes permanently disabled. All policy benefits remain in force during the waiver period.

waiver of premium clause *See* WAIVER OF PREMIUM.

waiver of premium option *See* WAIVER OF PREMIUM.

wallflower A stock that is no longer in vogue with investors; as a result it usually experiences a low price-earnings multiple.

Wall Street A street in lower New York City surrounded by the entire financial district. Both the NEW YORK STOCK EXCHANGE and the AMERICAN STOCK EXCHANGE are located there. Wall Street has become the sign of capitalism throughout the world.

want A need or desire for a good or service.

warrant An assurance of a product's quality or as to the good title of property.
See also STOCK WARRANTS.

warranty An assurance by a seller to a buyer to satisfy for a stated period of time deficiencies in the quality or performance of items such as an automobile or appliance. Typically, there is no additional charge for correcting deficiencies during the warranty period.
See also EXPRESS WARRANTY; IMPLIED WARRANTY.

warranty deed The DEED that guarantees that the title is free of any legal claims including ENCUMBRANCES. It contains EXPRESS WARRANTIES of TITLE and quiet possession.
See also QUITCLAIM DEED.

warranty of habitability An implied assurance from a landlord to a prospective tenant that an apartment is safe and void of health problems.

warranty of merchantability An assurance that purchased goods are suitable and appropriate for use as intended.

wash sale
1. The sale of a security for which no loss is recognized for tax purposes because within 30 days preceding or after the disposal date the investor bought a substantially identical security.
2. The MANIPULATION of stock prices upward when two or more parties buy the stock from each other at higher prices. The objective is to give the false implication of market activity in a security so that unsuspecting investors become interested in it, driving up the price further. The manipulator then sells the security at the INFLATED price.

watch list
banking: A closely monitored list, established by the government, of BANKS in danger of failing.
securities: A list of SECURITIES a BROKERAGE FIRM or INDIVIDUAL STOCKBROKER may single out to observe, either because of unique INVESTMENT characteristics, such as being possible TAKEOVER candidates, or for other INVESTOR interest.

water damage insurance Insurance coverage for water damage caused by leaks or overflows in plumbing, heating, refrigeration, air conditioning, or other system within the home. Damage could also be caused by rain or snow that penetrates the interior of the house, as from broken windows or open doors. There may be a separate policy or coverage may be contained in a standard property insurance policy.

watered stock Capital stock issued in exchange for assets having fair market values below the par or stated value. As a result, assets are recorded at overstated values. If the board of directors acted in bad faith, this practice is illegal.

weak market In SECURITIES, a STOCK MARKET characterized by low volume and listless trading. A weak market often has a wide gap between the BID AND ASKED prices. An INVESTMENT saying is that one should "never TRADE in a weak MARKET."

wealth An accumulation of ASSETS that an individual or other entity has developed over a period of time, often a lifetime in the case of an individual.

when issued A conditional transaction of an authorized security but that has not yet been issued. The purchase is on a contingent standing until the issue is completed and the trade occurs. "When issued" status may be a couple of weeks. An example is a new issue of stocks or bonds that are traded on a "when, as, and if issued" basis. In the financial newspapers, "WI" is placed next to the price of the security.

whipsaw In investments, a significantly favorable or negative event resulting from the movement in price of a security. The investor is caught in unstable price movements and experiences losses on his or her trades. Examples are buying a stock just before it drops resulting in a loss, and selling a stock just before it rises.

white knight A slang term for an individual or company that saves a corporation from an unfriendly takeover by taking it over himself or herself. The result is that the targeted corporation is rescued from the unwanted bidder's control.

white sheets In investments, sheets published daily by the National Quotation Bureau providing information on OVER-THE-COUNTER securities, including data on prices (bid and asked prices) and dealers in the stock.
See also YELLOW SHEETS; PINK SHEETS.

whole life insurance A CASH VALUE LIFE INSURANCE policy that provides level protection for a fixed premium for the lifetime of the insured and includes a savings feature. The policy remains in force as long as the insured continues to pay the insurance premiums. The premiums remain level and fixed. It has loan privileges, optional riders, and surrender and exchange rights.
See also INSURANCE PROGRAMS.

wholesale banking Banking that deals in a significant volume of transactions typically with large depositors such as major corporations. There may also be dealings with other financial institutions. This is in contrast to RETAIL BANKING, which applies to regular smaller accounts of people and small businesses.

wide opening An unusually large difference between the bid and asked prices of a security at the start of a trading session.

will A written document specifying that a person, called a testator, is disposing of his or her property, upon death, to the parties named. The will may also specify other conditions that have to be met before the property may be fully disposed of. To be enforceable, the will must be signed and witnessed.

withdrawal plan A plan available through most MUTUAL FUNDS whereby fund holders can withdraw income or CAPITAL GAINS on a systematic basis.

withholding allowance The amount withheld from the employee's paycheck by the employer for remission to federal and state taxing agencies. The amount withheld depends upon the employee's wages and the number of exemptions claimed.

withholding tax A deduction from the employee's salary made by the employer for the payment of federal, state, and local taxes. It is paid to the applicable taxing bodies. For example, the employer may remit the withholding tax directly to the Internal Revenue Service or deposit the funds into a specified bank on a periodic basis as dictated by the IRS.

worker's compensation insurance An insurance program paid for by the employer and designed to compensate the worker for job-related injuries or illness, without regard to a finding of negligence of either party.

working control Or, *effective control*. The important influence of an individual on something. Examples are the decisive influence of a senior vice president on the employing company's decision making, and majority ownership by a stockholder of a closely held company.

wraparound annuity An ANNUITY contract in which the investor has latitude in selecting the investments (e.g., stocks to bonds, money market to stocks) made by the sponsor. By putting funds into an investment and receiving an annuity, the investor defers payment of taxes on the income generated from the investment. To accumulate tax-free annuity earnings the insurance company must both legally own the invested monies and manage the portfolio.

wraparound mortgage (trust deed) Or, *all inclusive trust deed* (AITD). A MORTGAGE (TRUST DEED) that encompasses existing mortgages and is subordinate (junior) to them. The existing mortgages stay on the property and the new mortgage wraps around them. The existing mortgage loan generally carries lower interest rates than the one on the new mortgage loan.

This loan arrangement is a form of SELLER FINANCING.
See also CREATIVE FINANCING.

writ A court order requiring the named individual to act or not act on something mentioned. An example is an order to a husband to make alimony payments to his wife.

writer of options An INVESTOR who sells COVERED OPTIONS on underlying SECURITIES in an attempt to maximize an investment return.

Y

year-end bonus A bonus given by an employer to employees at the end of the year. It is typically based on the employee's performance for the period and how well the employer's business has done. In the securities industry, a year-end bonus is typical.

year-end dividend A corporate dividend paid to investors at period-end. It is based on the firm's profitability for the year, and is typically in the form of an *additional* dividend.

year-end review An evaluation made at the end of the year based on performance or experience. Examples are an employer's review of an employee's work performance, and an insurance company's appraisal of an insured driver's auto accident and traffic summons experience.

year to date (YTD) The period of time from the beginning of the calendar year to the present.

yellow sheets A daily issue of the National Quotation Bureau that lists the bid and asked quotes and dealers in over-the-counter corporate bonds. The sheets are in yellow.
See also PINK SHEETS; WHITE SHEETS.

yield (rate of return) Or, *return*.
in general: The income earned on an investment, usually expressed as a percentage of the MARKET PRICE.
stocks: Percentage return earned on a common stock or preferred stock in dividends. It is computed by dividing the total of DIVIDENDS paid in the preceding 12 months by the CURRENT MARKET PRICE. For example, a STOCK with a current market value of $40 a share, which has paid $2 in dividends in the preceding 12 months, is said to return 5% ($2/$40). If an investor paid $20 for the stock five years earlier, the stock would be returning 10% on the original investment.
See also DIVIDEND YIELD.
bonds: The CURRENT YIELD or YIELD TO MATURITY (YTM).
See also BOND YIELD; REALIZED YIELD; YIELD TO CALL.
loans: Money earned on a loan, which is determined by multiplying the ANNUAL PERCENTAGE RATE (APR) by the term of the loan.

yield spread The difference between the YIELDS received on two different type BONDS with different ratings. In times of economic uncertainty, the yield spread increases because investors demand higher premiums on risky issues to compensate for the increased chance of DEFAULT.
See also BOND RATINGS.

yield to call A YIELD on a BOND to be called. Not all bonds are held to maturity. If the bond may be called prior to maturity, the YIELD-TO-MATURITY (YTM) formula will have the CALL PRICE in place of the par value of $1,000. For example, a 20-year bond was initially issued at a 13.5% coupon rate, and after two years, rates dropped. The bond is currently selling for $1,180, the yield to maturity on the bond is 11.15%, and the bond can be called in five years after issue at $1,090. Thus if an investor buys the bond two years after issue, the bond may be called back after three more years at $1,090. .Then the yield to call is

$$\frac{\$135 + (\$1,090 - \$1,180)/3}{(\$1,090 + \$1,180)/2} = \frac{\$135 + (-\$90/3)}{\$1,135}$$

$$= \frac{\$105}{\$1,135} = 9.25\%$$

Note that the yield-to-call figure of 9.25% is 190 basis points less than the yield to maturity of 11.15%. Clearly, the investor needs to be aware of the differential because a lower return is earned.

See also BOND YIELD.

yield to maturity (YTM) The annual RATE OF RETURN that a bondholder purchasing a BOND today and holding it to MATURITY would receive on the investment. It is the EFFECTIVE RATE OF RETURN on a bond calculated from its MARKET PRICE, FACE VALUE, COUPON RATE, and time remaining to maturity.

The exact way of calculating this measure is the same as the one for the INTERNAL RATE OF RETURN. But the approximate method is

$$\text{Yield} = \frac{I + (\$1,000 - V)/n}{(\$1,000 + V)/2}$$

where V = the market value of the bond
  I = dollars of interest paid per year
  n = number of years to maturity
For example, the YTM of a 10-year, 8% coupon, $1,000 par value bond at a price of $877.60 is

$$\text{Yield} = \frac{\$80 + (\$1,000 - \$877.60)/10}{(\$1,000 + \$877.60)/2}$$

$$= \frac{\$80 + \$12.24}{\$938.80} = \frac{\$92.24}{\$938.80}$$

$$= \$9.8\%$$

See also BOND YIELD.

yo-yo stock A STOCK characterized by highly volatile MARKET prices. Its trading price goes up and down like a yo-yo.

yuppie An acronym describing a young upwardly mobile professional pursuing instant gratification and high SALARY through often rash career advancement measures while living an ostentatious life-style often beyond his or her financial means. Yuppies characterized the fast-moving period of time during the 1980s.

Z

Z score A score produced by E. Altman's BANKRUPTCY prediction model used to forecast corporate bankruptcy. The Z score equals

$$Z = 1.2 \times X1 + 1.4 \times X2 + 3.3 \times X3$$
$$+ 0.6 \times X4 + 0.999 \times X5$$

where $X1$ = working capital/total assets, $X2$ = retained earnings/total assets, $X3$ = earnings before interest and taxes/total assets, $X4$ = market value of equity/book value of debt, and $X5$ = sales/total assets. The Z score, also called ZETA SCORE, is known to be about 90% accurate in forecasting business failure one year in ad-

vance and about 80% accurate in forecasting bankruptcy two years in advance.

zero-coupon bond Or, *original issue discount (OID) bond.* A bond bought at a deep DISCOUNT. The interest instead of being paid out directly is added to the principal semiannually and both the principal and the accumulated interest are paid at MATURITY. Although a fixed rate is implicit in the discount and the specific maturity, these bonds are not fixed income securities in the traditional sense because they provide for no periodic income. Although the interest on the bond is paid at maturity, accrued interest is taxable yearly as ordinary income. Zero-coupon bonds have two basic advantages over regular coupon-bearing bonds: (1) a relatively small investment is required to buy these bonds, and (2) a specific YIELD is assured throughout the term of the investment. Many investors are interested in an investment that accumulates and compounds interest automatically rather than paying interest regularly. This eliminates the need for reinvestment of periodic interest income, perhaps at lower rates than the initial investment.

See also COUPON BOND; DEEP DISCOUNT BOND.

zero-sum game An investment situation in which the total wealth of all TRADERS remains the same. Total gains of winners exactly equal the total losses of losers and thus the trading simply redistributes the wealth among the traders.

zone of employment The physical area within which injuries to the workers are covered by workers' compensation. It refers to the place of employment as well as to entrances and exits that are the responsibility of the employer.

zoning laws Local government ordinances originating from state police powers governing real estate development including structural and design requirements. Zoning ordinances normally define (1) various usage classifications ranging from agricultural to heavy industry; (2) building restrictions including minimum-square-footage building requirements as well as prohibitions; (3) the establishment of a zoning board of appeals to hear petitions for nonconforming uses; and (4) violation penalties and procedures.

Appendixes

Appendix A: Tables

TABLE 1
THE FUTURE VALUE OF $1.00
(COMPOUNDED AMOUNT OF $1.00)
$(1 + i)^n = T_1 (i, n)$

Periods	4%	6%	8%	10%	12%	14%	20%
1	1.040	1.060	1.080	1.100	1.120	1.140	1.200
2	1.082	1.124	1.166	1.210	1.254	1.300	1.440
3	1.125	1.191	1.260	1.331	1.405	1.482	1.728
4	1.170	1.263	1.361	1.464	1.574	1.689	2.074
5	1.217	1.338	1.469	1.611	1.762	1.925	2.488
6	1.265	1.419	1.587	1.772	1.974	2.195	2.986
7	1.316	1.504	1.714	1.949	2.211	2.502	3.583
8	1.369	1.594	1.851	2.144	2.476	2.853	4.300
9	1.423	1.690	1.999	2.359	2.773	3.252	5.160
10	1.480	1.791	2.159	2.594	3.106	3.707	6.192
11	1.540	1.898	2.332	2.853	3.479	4.226	7.430
12	1.601	2.012	2.518	3.139	3.896	4.818	8.916
13	1.665	2.133	2.720	3.452	4.364	5.492	10.699
14	1.732	2.261	2.937	3.798	4.887	6.261	12.839
15	1.801	2.397	3.172	4.177	5.474	7.138	15.407
16	1.873	2.540	3.426	4.595	6.130	8.137	18.488
17	1.948	2.693	3.700	5.055	6.866	9.277	22.186
18	2.026	2.854	3.996	5.560	7.690	10.575	26.623
19	2.107	3.026	4.316	6.116	8.613	12.056	31.948
20	2.191	3.207	4.661	6.728	9.646	13.743	38.338
30	3.243	5.744	10.063	17.450	29.960	50.950	237.380
40	4.801	10.286	21.725	45.260	93.051	188.880	1469.800

TABLE 2
THE FUTURE VALUE OF AN ANNUITY OF $1.00*
(COMPOUNDED AMOUNT OF AN ANNUITY OF $1.00)

$$\frac{(1 + i)^n - 1}{i} = T_2 \,(i, \, n)$$

Periods	4%	6%	8%	10%	12%	14%	20%
1	1.000	1.000	1.000	1.000	1.000	1.000	1.000
2	2.040	2.060	2.080	2.100	2.120	2.140	2.200
3	3.122	3.184	3.246	3.310	3.374	3.440	3.640
4	4.247	4.375	4.506	4.641	4.779	4.921	5.368
5	5.416	5.637	5.867	6.105	6.353	6.610	7.442
6	6.633	6.975	7.336	7.716	8.115	8.536	9.930
7	7.898	8.394	8.923	9.487	10.089	10.730	12.916
8	9.214	9.898	10.637	11.436	12.300	13.233	16.499
9	10.583	11.491	12.488	13.580	14.776	16.085	20.799
10	12.006	13.181	14.487	15.938	17.549	19.337	25.959
11	13.486	14.972	16.646	18.531	20.655	23.045	32.150
12	15.026	16.870	18.977	21.385	24.133	27.271	39.580
13	16.627	18.882	21.495	24.523	28.029	32.089	48.497
14	18.292	21.015	24.215	27.976	32.393	37.581	59.196
15	20.024	23.276	27.152	31.773	37.280	43.842	72.035
16	21.825	25.673	30.324	35.950	42.753	50.980	87.442
17	23.698	28.213	33.750	40.546	48.884	59.118	105.930
18	25.645	30.906	37.450	45.600	55.750	68.394	128.120
19	27.671	33.760	41.446	51.160	63.440	78.969	154.740
20	29.778	36.778	45.762	57.276	75.052	91.025	186.690
30	56.085	79.058	113.283	164.496	241.330	356.790	1181.900
40	95.026	154.762	259.057	442.597	767.090	1342.000	7343.900

*Payments (or receipts) at the *end* of each period.

TABLE 3
PRESENT VALUE OF $1.00

$$\frac{1}{(1 + i)^n} = T_3 (i, n)$$

Periods	4%	6%	8%	10%	12%	14%	16%	18%	20%	22%	24%	26%	28%	30%	40%
1	.962	.943	.926	.909	.893	.877	.862	.847	.833	.820	.806	.794	.781	.769	.714
2	.925	.890	.857	.826	.797	.769	.743	.718	.694	.672	.650	.630	.610	.592	.510
3	.889	.840	.794	.751	.712	.675	.641	.609	.579	.551	.524	.500	.477	.455	.364
4	.855	.792	.735	.683	.636	.592	.552	.516	.482	.451	.423	.397	.373	.350	.260
5	.822	.747	.681	.621	.567	.519	.476	.437	.402	.370	.341	.315	.291	.269	.186
6	.790	.705	.630	.564	.507	.456	.410	.370	.335	.303	.275	.250	.227	.207	.133
7	.760	.665	.583	.513	.452	.400	.354	.314	.279	.249	.222	.198	.178	.159	.095
8	.731	.627	.540	.467	.404	.351	.305	.266	.233	.204	.179	.157	.139	.123	.068
9	.703	.592	.500	.424	.361	.308	.263	.225	.194	.167	.144	.125	.108	.094	.048
10	.676	.558	.463	.386	.322	.270	.227	.191	.162	.137	.116	.099	.085	.073	.035
11	.650	.527	.429	.350	.287	.237	.195	.162	.135	.112	.094	.079	.066	.056	.025
12	.625	.497	.397	.319	.257	.208	.168	.137	.112	.092	.076	.062	.052	.043	.018
13	.601	.469	.368	.290	.229	.182	.145	.116	.093	.075	.061	.050	.040	.033	.013
14	.577	.442	.340	.263	.205	.160	.125	.099	.078	.062	.049	.039	.032	.025	.009
15	.555	.417	.315	.239	.183	.140	.108	.084	.065	.051	.040	.031	.025	.020	.006
16	.534	.394	.292	.218	.163	.123	.093	.071	.054	.042	.032	.025	.019	.015	.005
17	.513	.371	.270	.198	.146	.108	.080	.060	.045	.034	.026	.020	.015	.012	.003
18	.494	.350	.250	.180	.130	.095	.069	.051	.038	.028	.021	.016	.012	.009	.002
19	.475	.331	.232	.164	.116	.083	.060	.043	.031	.023	.017	.012	.009	.007	.002
20	.456	.312	.215	.149	.104	.073	.051	.037	.026	.019	.014	.010	.007	.005	.001
21	.439	.294	.199	.135	.093	.064	.044	.031	.022	.015	.011	.008	.006	.004	.001
22	.422	.278	.184	.123	.083	.056	.038	.026	.018	.013	.009	.006	.004	.003	.001
23	.406	.262	.170	.112	.074	.049	.033	.022	.015	.010	.007	.005	.003	.002	
24	.390	.247	.158	.102	.066	.043	.028	.019	.013	.008	.006	.004	.003	.002	
25	.375	.233	.146	.092	.059	.038	.024	.016	.010	.007	.005	.003	.002	.001	
26	.361	.220	.135	.084	.053	.033	.021	.014	.009	.006	.004	.002	.002	.001	
27	.347	.207	.125	.076	.047	.029	.018	.011	.007	.005	.003	.002	.001	.001	
28	.333	.196	.116	.069	.042	.026	.016	.010	.006	.004	.002	.002	.001	.001	
29	.321	.185	.107	.063	.037	.022	.014	.008	.005	.003	.002	.001	.001	.001	
30	.308	.174	.099	.057	.033	.020	.012	.007	.004	.003	.002	.001	.001		
40	.208	.097	.046	.022	.011	.005	.003	.001	.001						

TABLE 4
PRESENT VALUE OF AN ANNUITY OF $1.00*

$$\frac{1}{i}\left[1 - \frac{1}{(1 + i)^n} \right] = T_4 \, (i, n)$$

Periods	4%	6%	8%	10%	12%	14%	16%	18%
1	0.962	0.943	0.926	0.909	0.893	0.877	0.862	0.847
2	1.886	1.833	1.783	1.736	1.690	1.647	1.605	1.566
3	2.775	2.673	2.577	2.487	2.402	2.322	2.246	2.174
4	3.630	3.465	3.312	3.170	3.037	2.914	2.798	2.690
5	4.452	4.212	3.993	3.791	3.605	3.433	3.274	3.127
6	5.242	4.917	4.623	4.355	4.111	3.889	3.685	3.498
7	6.002	5.582	5.206	4.868	4.564	4.288	4.039	3.812
8	6.733	6.210	5.747	5.335	4.968	4.639	4.344	4.078
9	7.435	6.802	6.247	5.759	5.328	4.946	4.607	4.303
10	8.111	7.360	6.710	6.145	5.650	5.216	4.833	4.494
11	8.760	7.887	7.139	6.495	5.938	5.453	5.029	4.656
12	9.385	8.384	7.536	6.814	6.194	5.660	5.197	4.793
13	9.986	8.853	7.904	7.103	6.424	5.842	5.342	4.910
14	10.563	9.295	8.244	7.367	6.628	6.002	5.468	5.008
15	11.118	9.712	8.559	7.606	6.811	6.142	5.575	5.092
16	11.652	10.106	8.851	7.824	6.974	6.265	5.669	5.162
17	12.166	10.477	9.122	8.022	7.120	6.373	5.749	5.222
18	12.659	10.828	9.372	8.201	7.250	6.467	5.818	5.273
19	13.134	11.158	9.604	8.365	7.366	6.550	5.877	5.316
20	13.590	11.470	9.818	8.514	7.469	6.623	5.929	5.353
21	14.029	11.764	10.017	8.649	7.562	6.687	5.973	5.384
22	14.451	12.042	10.201	8.772	7.645	6.743	6.011	5.410
23	14.857	12.303	10.371	8.883	7.718	6.792	6.044	5.432
24	15.247	12.550	10.529	8.985	7.784	6.835	6.073	5.451
25	15.622	12.783	10.675	9.077	7.843	6.873	6.097	5.467
26	15.983	13.003	10.810	9.161	7.896	6.906	6.118	5.480
27	16.330	13.211	10.935	9.237	7.943	6.935	6.136	5.492
28	16.663	13.406	11.051	9.307	7.984	6.961	6.152	5.502
29	16.984	13.591	11.158	9.370	8.022	6.983	6.166	5.510
30	17.292	13.765	11.258	9.427	8.055	7.003	6.177	5.517
40	19.793	15.046	11.925	9.779	8.244	7.105	6.234	5.548

*Payments (or receipts) at the *end* of each period.

20%	22%	24%	25%	26%	28%	30%	40%
0.833	0.820	0.806	0.800	0.794	0.781	0.769	0.714
1.528	1.492	1.457	1.440	1.424	1.392	1.361	1.224
2.106	2.042	1.981	1.952	1.923	1.868	1.816	1.589
2.589	2.494	2.404	2.362	2.320	2.241	2.166	1.849
2.991	2.864	2.745	2.689	2.635	2.532	2.436	2.035
3.326	3.167	3.020	2.951	2.885	2.759	2.643	2.168
3.605	3.416	3.242	3.161	3.083	2.937	2.802	2.263
3.837	3.619	3.421	3.329	3.241	3.076	2.925	2.331
4.031	3.786	3.566	3.463	3.366	3.184	3.019	2.379
4.192	3.923	3.682	3.571	3.465	3.269	3.092	2.414
4.327	4.035	3.776	3.656	3.544	3.335	3.147	2.438
4.439	4.127	3.851	3.725	3.606	3.387	3.190	2.456
4.533	4.203	3.912	3.780	3.656	3.427	3.223	2.468
4.611	4.265	3.962	3.824	3.695	3.459	3.249	2.477
4.675	4.315	4.001	3.859	3.726	3.483	3.268	2.484
4.730	4.357	4.033	3.887	3.751	3.503	3.283	2.489
4.775	4.391	4.059	3.910	3.771	3.518	3.295	2.492
4.812	4.419	4.080	3.928	3.786	3.529	3.304	2.494
4.844	4.442	4.097	3.942	3.799	3.539	3.311	2.496
4.870	4.460	4.110	3.954	3.808	3.546	3.316	2.497
4.891	4.476	4.121	3.963	3.816	3.551	3.320	2.498
4.909	4.488	4.130	3.970	3.822	3.556	3.323	2.498
4.925	4.499	4.137	3.976	3.827	3.559	3.325	2.499
4.937	4.507	4.143	3.981	3.831	3.562	3.327	2.499
4.948	4.514	4.147	3.985	3.834	3.564	3.329	2.499
4.956	4.520	4.151	3.988	3.837	3.566	3.330	2.500
4.964	4.524	4.154	3.990	3.839	3.567	3.331	2.500
4.970	4.528	4.157	3.992	3.840	3.568	3.331	2.500
4.975	4.531	4.159	3.994	3.841	3.569	3.332	2.500
4.979	4.534	4.160	3.995	3.842	3.569	3.332	2.500
4.997	4.544	4.166	3.999	3.846	3.571	3.333	2.500

TABLE 5
A TABLE OF MONTHLY MORTGAGE PAYMENTS
(MONTHLY PAYMENTS NECESSARY TO REPAY A $10,000 LOAN)

Rate of Interest	Loan Term				
	10 years	15 years	20 years	25 years	30 years
7½%	$118.71	$92.71	$80.56	$73.90	$69.93
8	121.33	95.57	83.65	77.19	73.38
8½	123.99	98.48	86.79	80.53	76.90
9	126.68	101.43	89.98	83.92	80.47
9½	129.40	104.43	93.22	87.37	84.09
10	132.16	107.47	96.51	90.88	87.76
10½	134.94	110.54	99.84	94.42	91.48
11	137.76	113.66	103.22	98.02	95.24
11½	140.60	116.82	106.65	101.65	99.03
12	143.48	120.02	110.11	105.33	102.86
12½	146.38	123.26	113.62	109.04	106.73
13	149.32	126.53	117.16	112.79	110.62
13½	152.28	129.84	120.74	116.57	114.55
14	155.27	133.18	124.36	120.38	118.49
14½	158.29	136.56	128.00	124.22	122.46
15	161.34	139.96	131.68	128.09	126.45

TABLE 6
A TABLE OF MONTHLY INSTALLMENT LOAN PAYMENTS
(TO REPAY A $1,000 SIMPLE INTEREST LOAN)

Rate of Interest	Loan Term						
	6 months	12 months	18 months	24 months	36 months	48 months	60 months
7½%	$170.33	$86.76	$58.92	$45.00	$31.11	$24.18	$20.05
8	170.58	86.99	59.15	45.23	31.34	24.42	20.28
8½	170.82	87.22	59.37	45.46	31.57	24.65	20.52
9	171.07	87.46	59.60	45.69	31.80	24.89	20.76
9½	171.32	87.69	59.83	45.92	32.04	25.13	21.01
10	171.56	87.92	60.06	46.15	32.27	25.37	21.25
10½	171.81	88.15	60.29	46.38	32.51	25.61	21.50
11	172.05	88.50	60.64	46.73	32.86	25.97	21.87
11½	172.30	88.62	60.76	46.85	32.98	26.09	22.00
12	172.55	88.85	60.99	47.08	33.22	26.34	22.25
12½	172.80	89.09	61.22	47.31	33.46	26.58	22.50
13	173.04	89.32	61.45	47.55	33.70	26.83	22.76
14	173.54	89.79	61.92	48.02	34.18	27.33	23.27
15	174.03	90.26	62.39	48.49	34.67	27.84	23.79
16	174.53	90.74	62.86	48.97	35.16	28.35	24.32
17	175.03	91.21	63.34	49.45	35.66	28.86	24.86
18	175.53	91.68	63.81	49.93	36.16	29.38	25.40

Appendix B: Sources of Consumer Help

CORPORATE CONSUMER CONTACTS

Many companies have consumer affairs or customer relations departments to answer questions or to help resolve consumer complaints. If you cannot resolve a complaint where you made the purchase, then contact the company's headquarters.

For the addresses and telephone numbers of more than 600 companies, see the "Corporate Consumer Contacts" section of the most recent publication of the *Consumer's Resource Handbook,* Office of the Special Adviser to the President for Consumer Affairs, The White House, Washington, DC, and the United States Office of Consumer Affairs.

CONSUMER CREDIT COUNSELING SERVICES

Counseling services provide assistance to individuals having difficulty budgeting their money and/or meeting necessary monthly expenses. Many organizations, including credit unions, family service centers, and religious organizations, offer some type of free or low-cost credit counseling.

The CONSUMER CREDIT COUNSELING SERVICE (CCCS) is one nonprofit organization that provides money management techniques, debt payment plans, and education programs. Counselors take into consideration the needs of the client as well as the needs of the creditor when working out a debt repayment plan. You can find the CCCS office nearest you by contacting the National Foundation for Consumer Credit, Inc., 8701 Georgia Avenue, Suite 507, Silver Spring, MD 20910 (301/589-5600).

SOURCE: Adapted from the Office of the Special Adviser to the President for Consumer Affairs, *Consumer's Resource Handbook* (Washington, DC: The White House and the United States Office of Consumer Affairs, 1990), pp. 4–7.

CONSUMER INFORMATION CATALOG

The *Consumer Information Catalog* lists more than 200 free or low-cost federal booklets on a variety of topics, many of which may be helpful in addressing consumer complaints or problems. Topics include careers and education, child care, federal benefits, financial planning, gardening, health, housing, small business, travel, hobbies, and cars. This free catalog is published quarterly by the Consumer Information Center and may be ordered from Catalog, Consumer Information Center, Pueblo, CO 81009.

STATE, COUNTY, AND CITY GOVERNMENT CONSUMER OFFICES

City and county consumer offices can be helpful because they are easy to contact and are familiar with local businesses and laws. If there is no local consumer office in your area, contact your state's consumer office. State consumer offices are set up differently across the nation. Some states have a separate department of consumer affairs, while others have a consumer affairs office as part of the governor's office or attorney general's office. These offices will help or refer you to the proper agency.

If you have a consumer problem with a business outside the state where you live, you should contact the consumer office in the state where you made the purchase. When you contact any local or state consumer office, be sure to have handy copies of your sales receipts, other sales documents, and all correspondence with the company. A list of state government consumer protection offices is given in Appendix F.

Many states also have special commissions and agencies that handle consumer questions and complaints about banks, insurance, utilities, vocational and rehabilitation services, and weights and measures. A list of state utility commissions is provided in Appendix G. Additional information can be found in the *Consumer's Resource Handbook,* Office of the Special Adviser to the President for Consumer Affairs, The White House, Washington, DC and the United States Office of Consumer Affairs.

SELECTED FEDERAL AGENCIES

Many federal agencies have enforcement and/or complaint handling duties for products and services used by the general public. Others act for the benefit of the public but do not resolve individual consumer problems.

Agencies also have fact sheets, booklets, and other information that may be helpful in making purchase decisions and dealing with consumer problems. If you need help in deciding where to go with your consumer problem, consult Appendix E, "Selected Federal Agencies." The agencies listed here respond to consumer questions and complaints. Additionally, of course, you can consult the nearest federal information center (FIC) listed in Appendix D.

LEGAL AID OFFICES

Legal Aid offices help individuals who cannot afford to hire private lawyers. There are more than 1,000 of these offices around the country, staffed by lawyers, paralegals, and law students. All offer free legal services to those who qualify.

Funding is provided by a variety of sources, including federal, state, and local governments and private donations. Many law schools nationwide conduct clinics in which law students assist practicing lawyers with these cases as part of their training.

These offices generally offer legal assistance with problems such as landlord-tenant relations, credit, utilities, family issues (such as divorce and adoption), Social Security, welfare, unemployment, and workmen's compensation. Each Legal Aid office has its own board of directors that determines the priorities of the office and the kinds of cases handled. If the Legal Aid office in your area does not handle your type of case, it should be able to refer you to other local, state, or national organizations that can provide advice or help. Check the telephone directory or call your local consumer protection office to find the address and telephone number of the Legal Aid office near you.

LEGAL SERVICES CORPORATION

The Legal Services Corporation (LSC) was created by Congress in 1974. There are LSC offices in all 50 states, Puerto Rico, the Virgin Islands, Guam, and Micronesia. Check the telephone directory for the LSC office nearest you or call the Federal Information Center (FIC) listed in Appendix D. If you wish to buy a full directory of all LSC programs, write or call:

Public Affairs
Legal Services Corporation
400 Virginia Avenue, S.W.
Washington, DC 20024–2751
(202) 863–4089

PRIVATE LAWYERS

If you need help finding a lawyer, check with the Lawyer Referral Service of your state, city, or county bar association listed in local telephone directories.

Complaints about a lawyer should be referred to your state, county, or city bar association.

SMALL CLAIMS COURTS

Small claims courts were established to resolve disputes involving claims for small debts and accounts. While the maximum amounts that can be claimed or awarded differ from state to state, court procedures generally are simple, inexpensive, quick, and informal. Court fees are small, and you often get your filing fee back if you win your case. Generally, you will not need a lawyer. In fact, in some states, lawyers are not permitted. If you live in a state permitting lawyers and the party you are suing brings one, do not be intimidated. The court is informal and most judges make allowances for consumers who appear without lawyers.

Remember, even though the court is informal, the ruling must be followed, just like any other court.

If the party bringing the suit wins the case, the party who loses will often follow the court's decision without additional legal action. Sometimes, however, losing parties will not obey the decision. In these cases, the winning party may go back to court and ask for the order to be "enforced." Depending on the local laws, the court may, for example, order property to be taken by law enforcement officials and sold. The winning party will get the money from the sale up to the amount they are owed. Or, if the person who owes the money receives a salary, the court may order the employer to *garnish* or deduct money from each paycheck and give it to the winner of the lawsuit.

Check your local telephone book under your municipal, county, or state government headings for small claims court offices. When you contact the court, ask the court clerk how to use the small claims court. To understand the process better, attend a small claims court session before taking your case to court.

TRADE ASSOCIATIONS AND OTHER DISPUTE RESOLUTION PROGRAMS

There are nearly 40,000 trade and professional associations in the United States representing a variety of interests (including banks, insurance companies, and clothing manufacturers) and professionals (such as accountants, lawyers, doctors, and therapists).

Some of these associations and their members have established programs to help consumers with complaints not resolved at the point of purchase. If you have a problem with a company and cannot get it resolved, ask if the company is a member of an association.

These programs are usually called alternative dispute resolution programs. Generally, there are three types of programs: arbitration, conciliation, and mediation. All three methods of dispute resolution vary. Ask for a copy of the rules of the program before you file your case. Generally, the decisions of the arbitrators are binding and must be accepted by both the customer and the business. However, in other forms of dispute resolution, only the business is required to accept the decision. In some programs, decisions are not binding on either party.

Trade associations have various consumer functions, which are described in the

National Trade & Professional Associations of the United States. Check your local library for this book and related sources of help.

For a very complete listing of trade associations and other resolution programs see the *Consumer's Resource Handbooks,* Office of the Special Adviser to the President for Consumer Affairs, The White House, Washington, DC, and the United States Office of Consumer Affairs.

ADDITIONAL SOURCES OF HELP

Libraries   Local libraries can be a good source of help. Many libraries have specially designated business sections specializing in the collection of business-related materials. Consult your local telephone book to find their addresses and telephone numbers.

Certain libraries have been designated as government depositories by federal and/or state governments for storing governmental publications including census materials, hearings, and special reports. Governmental depositories can be a gold mine of information for the public. Some university and other private libraries allow the public to use their reference materials.

Media Programs   Many local newspapers and radio and television stations throughout the United States have "Action Line" or "Hot Line" services. These programs may be able to help consumers resolve their problems because of their influence in communities. Some action lines select only the most severe or newsworthy problems or those occurring most frequently. In any event, they are selective and cannot be relied upon universally.

To find these services, check with your local newspapers, radio and television stations, or your local library.

Occupational and Professional Licensing Boards   Many state agencies license or register members of various professions including doctors, lawyers, nurses, accountants, pharmacists, funeral directors, plumbers, electricians, car repair shops, employment agencies, collection agencies, beauticians, and television and radio repair shops.

In addition to setting licensing standards, these boards also set rules and regulations; prepare and give examinations; issue, deny, or revoke licenses; bring disciplinary actions; and handle consumer complaints.

Many boards have referral services or consumer education materials to help you select a professional. If you have a complaint and contact a licensing agency, the agency will contact the professional on your behalf. If necessary, they may conduct an investigation and take disciplinary action against the professional. This action may include probation license suspension, or license revocation.

To locate the local office of an occupational or professional licensing board, check your local telephone directory under the headings of Licensing Boards or Professional Associations, or look for the name of the individual agency. If there is no local office, contact the state consumer office.

Appendix C: Consumer Tips

This section contains helpful information for consumers seeking to be better informed. It contains information about airline travel, buying a used car, car repair, child care, choosing a school, choosing a job training program, paying for job training or college, credit cards, home improvements, long distance telephone service, the right to privacy, tips for shopping by mail, and related suggestions.

AIRLINE TRAVEL

1. When making an airline reservation, always ask about fees or penalties for changing or canceling a reservation or a paid ticket. There may be a variety of ticket prices with varying penalties and conditions. Choose the one that best fits your needs.

2. Read the disclosure statement on the back of your ticket. It explains your rights and responsibilities as a passenger, in addition to the airline's liability for overbooking seats and for losing or damaging luggage.

3. When flights are overbooked, airline representatives are required to ask for volunteers to give up their reservations in exchange for a payment of the airline's choosing. If you volunteer, be sure to get any compensation arrangement in writing.

4. If you are "bumped" or involuntarily reassigned to a later flight, the airline must provide a written statement of your rights and entitled compensation. The complete rules for compensation are available at all airport ticket counters and boarding locations.

BUYING A USED CAR

1. Look for and read the "buyer's guide," which must be displayed in the window of all used cars sold by dealers. The buyer's guide explains who must pay for repairs after purchase. It will tell you if there is a warranty on the car, what the warranty covers, and whether a service contract is available.

SOURCE: Adapted from the Office of the Special Adviser to the President for Consumer Affairs, *Consumer's Resource Handbook* (Washington, DC: The White House and the United States Office of Consumer Affairs, 1990).

350

2. Comparison shop for price, condition, warranty, and mileage for the model(s) you are interested in buying. Also compare available interest rates and other terms of financing agreements.

3. To estimate the total cost of the car, add in any interest rates for financing, the cost of a service contract (if any), and any service or repair expenses you will be likely to pay.

4. Before buying the car, you might want to consider having a mechanic inspect it.

5. Check the reliability of the dealer with your state or local consumer protection agency. Also check the local Better Business Bureau to learn whether a large number of complaints against the dealer have been filed.

6. When purchasing a used car from someone other than a dealer, get a bill of sale, the proper title and registration, and copies of all financial transactions.

CAR REPAIR

1. Before having your car repaired, check the shop's complaint record with your state or local consumer protection office or local Better Business Bureau.

2. Describe the problems you are having with the car as completely as possible. Tell the mechanic exactly what you want done.

3. Before you leave the car, make sure the work order reflects what you want done.

4. Ask for a written estimate before any major repair work is done. Make sure the work order says that you must approve any additional repair work.

5. If additional work is done without your permission, you do not have to pay for the unapproved work, and you have the right to have your bill adjusted.

6. Ask to inspect and/or keep all replaced parts.

7. Keep copies of all work orders and receipts and get all warranties in writing.

8. Many states have "lemon" laws for new cars that have recurring problems. Contact your local or state consumer protection office for more details.

SELECTING CHILD CARE

Choosing child care is an important issue for parents. Here are some questions parents may want to ask when looking for child care:

1. What are the licensing laws for day-care providers in your city, county, or state? Your local consumer protection office is a good place to check for this information.

2. Do care givers have references? What about special training in child development and education? How many children does each adult look after?

3. Is the home or center clean? Is there enough space inside and outside for the children to play? Is the playground fenced?

4. If the center is large, do visitors and children sign in and out? What are the safety precautions in case of fire or other emergencies?

5. What about sick children? Do they stay home? What if a child needs medical help?

6. How does the staff discipline children? How much of each day is filled with planned activities? Are activities geared to children's ages and development?

7. What are the fees for half-days, overtime, or sick children?

8. Are childrens' pictures or projects displayed and changed often?

9. Do care givers tell you what your child did that day and how he or she is progressing?

After your child is in a program, you may wish to ask:

1. Does your child talk happily about the program?

2. Do you know new employees? Do they talk to your child?

For further information:

The Department of Labor's Women's Bureau Work and Family Clearinghouse provides information about child or elder care. Call (202) 523–4486.

CHOOSING A SCHOOL

Education is probably the best investment anyone can make in one's future. However, educational choices are extremely complex and expensive. The following tips are intended to help with the process of choosing a school.

CHOOSING A SCHOOL FOR A CHILD

1. Education is a large industry. There are many types of schools, including schools for musicians, librarians, chefs; there are public schools, private schools, and other types.

2. Every child has different educational needs. The challenge is to match the needs and abilities of the child with the educational strengths of a particular school.

3. All parents should become involved with their child's educational process. Visit the school often. Get to know the curriculum of the school, its teachers, and its administrators. Volunteer for the PTA and related organizations.

4. Public schools are either organized into independent school districts having their own taxing authority, or they are a part of a dependent school district where their budgets depend on the governmental jurisdiction of which they are a part. Request a copy of your school's budget. Attend and participate in school board meetings.

5. The U.S. Department of Education has published a booklet, "Choosing a School for Your Child." Free copies may be ordered by writing *Choosing a School,* Consumer Information Center, Pueblo, CO 81009.

CHOOSING A JOB-TRAINING PROGRAM

1. If you are seeking a job-training program, avoid scams by checking with your local consumer protection office or Better Business Bureau before you enroll.

2. Before going back to school, check to learn whether local employers or others offer similar training free or through tuition reimbursement.

3. Be certain the skills the school teaches will be useful to you and are currently being used in the workplace.

4. If you must learn how to use equipment, does the school have enough equipment so that every student can practice using it? Is it of state-of-the-art quality?

5. How many recent students graduated? How many found jobs in their fields? Did the school help them find jobs, and how long did it take? How do current and past students feel about the school's program?

6. Will the program improve your math, reading, and thinking skills? Will it teach you how to keep learning after graduation?

7. Does the program include on-the-job training? Do teachers work with industry and update their skills regularly?

8. Do you have to take out a loan to pay for the program? Who pays back the loan if the school does not deliver on its promises?

PAYING FOR JOB TRAINING OR COLLEGE

There are several sources of financial aid, including scholarships, fellowships, grants, and loans. Only loans have to be repaid by the student. The U.S. Department of Education oversees federal financial aid programs for job training or college.

1. Check your local library for information about financial aid for education. Also check with individual schools about their financial aid programs.

2. Federal financial aid is administered by the U.S. Department of Education. However, student loans must be repaid, and the Department of Education has adopted stiff penalties for those failing to repay their loans.

3. Many states have financial aid programs available for students. Contact your state's department of education for further information.

CREDIT CARDS

1. Keep a list of your credit card numbers, expiration dates, and the phone number of each card issue in a safe place.

2. Credit card issuers offer a wide variety of terms (annual percentage rate, methods of calculating the balance subject to the finance charge, minimum monthly payments, and actual membership fees). Comparison shop for a credit card to determine its suitability.

3. When you use your credit card, watch your card after giving it to a clerk. Take your card back promptly after the clerk records the transaction; be sure you are given your card.

4. Tear up the carbons when you take your credit card receipt.

5. Never sign a blank receipt. Draw a line through any blank spaces above the total when you sign receipts.

6. Open credit card bills promptly and compare them with your receipts to check for unauthorized charges and billing errors.

7. Write the card issuer promptly to report any questionable charges. Written inquiries should not be included with your payment. Instead, check the billing statement for the correct address for billing questions. The inquiry must be in writing and must be sent within 60 days to guarantee your rights under the Fair Credit Billing Act.

8. Never give your credit card number over the telephone unless you made the call. Never put your card number on a postcard or on the outside of an envelope.

9. Sign new cards as soon as they arrive. Cut up and throw away expired cards. Cut up and return unwanted cards to the issuer.

10. If any of your credit cards are missing or stolen, report the loss as soon as possible to the card issuer. Check your credit card statement for a telephone number for reporting stolen credit cards. Follow up your phone calls with a letter to each card issuer. The letter should contain your card number, the date the card was missing, and the date you called in the loss.

11. If you report the loss before a credit card is used, the issuer cannot hold you responsible for any subsequent unauthorized charges. If a thief uses your card before you report it missing, the most you will owe for unauthorized charges on each card is $50.

HOME IMPROVEMENTS

1. Compare costs by getting more than one estimate. Each estimate should be based on the same building specifications, materials and time frame.

2. Before choosing a contractor, check with state, county, or local consumer protection agencies to learn whether a large number of complaints have been filed against the contractor.

3. Check with your local housing authority to learn whether licensing and/or bonding are required of contractors in your area. If so, ask to see the contractor's license and bonding papers.

4. Be sure the written contract includes the contractor's full name, address, phone number, and professional license number (where required). The contract should also include a thorough description of the work to be done, the grade and quality of the materials to be used, the agreed-upon starting and completion date, the total costs, payment schedule, warranty, how debris will be removed, and any other relevant information. Never sign a partially blank contract. Fill in or draw a line through any blank space.

5. Most contractors have liability and compensation insurance to protect the customer from a lawsuit in the event of an accident. Ask to see a copy of the insurance certificate.

6. If the work requires a building permit, the contractor should apply for it in his or her name. This action avoids financial responsibility in the event the work does not pass inspection and needs to be redone.

7. When you sign a nonemergency home improvement contract in your home and in the presence of a contractor (or contractor's representative), you usually have three business days in which to cancel the contract. You must be told about your cancellation rights and be provided with cancellation forms. If you decide to cancel, it is recommended that you send a notice of cancellation by telegram or certified mail, return receipt requested.

8. For a large remodeling involving many subcontractors and a substantial financial commitment, it is wise to protect yourself from liens against your home in the event the contractor does not pay subcontractors or suppliers. Add a release-of-lien clause to the contract or place your payments in an escrow account until the work is completed.

9. If you cannot pay for a project without a loan, add a clause to your contract stating it is valid only if financing is obtained.

10. Thoroughly inspect the contractor's work before making final payment or signing a completion certificate. It is often advisable to supervise the work in progress to determine whether it conforms to contractual obligations.

LONG DISTANCE TELEPHONE SERVICE

1. To compare long distance telephone carriers, think about when, how often, and where you use long distance service. Then compare the charges, restrictions, and procedures for making calls.

2. Not all carriers provide service to all areas. Make sure the one you choose provides service to the areas you call most often.

3. Each long distance carrier may have a different billing system. Some give credit for uncompleted calls, wrong numbers, or calls that are unanswered.

4. Ask about one-time-only and regular charges. Is there a subscription fee, monthly service fee, or a monthly minimum charge?

5. Judge the quality of a carrier's performance (transmission capability, service, billing, and crediting). A trial period may help you decide whether the quality of phone service is adequate. Before signing up, be sure you understand the terms of the carrier's cancellation policy and the costs involved in switching to another carrier.

6. Many companies now provide operator services, including directory assistance and collect calls for telephones in hotels, airports, and other public places. When you dial the operator, ask which carrier is providing the service and how much you will be billed. If you prefer a different service, you may have to dial a separate access number. Check with your long distance company to learn whether it provides operator services and how to use them.

THE RIGHT TO PRIVACY

The following are ways the consumer can protect the privacy of his or her credit, medical, and insurance records:

1. When filling out an application for credit, insurance, or a job, ask how the information you are providing will be used. Who will have access to it? Will your mailing address be sold to other companies? How long is the information kept? How often is it updated?

2. The Direct Marketing Association (DMA) operates the Mail Preference Service and the Telephone Preference Service. If you wish to have your name removed from nationally-based advertising lists, write to the following:

Direct Marketing Association
6 East 43rd Street
New York, NY 10017

3. Credit bureaus keep records about how you pay your bills, how much credit you have, and other information. For a small fee, you can find out what is in your credit record and the names of the companies that have asked for information about you. If you are turned down for credit, there is no cost to learn what is in your credit report. The creditor will tell you which credit bureau to write or call.

4. If you find a mistake in your credit report, the credit bureau must check it and correct it for you. Any negative information that cannot be proved also must be removed. However, correct information about late payments can stay on your record for seven years. More severe credit problems such as bankruptcies can stay on your record for up to ten years. You can also add to your file your own 100-word explanation for a credit problem.

TIPS FOR SHOPPING BY MAIL, BY TELEPHONE, AND BY TELEVISION

This is the age of convenience, and consumers have a wide variety of methods for making purchases, including shopping by television.

Things to Consider 1. Be suspicious of exaggerated product claims or very low prices and read product descriptions very carefully—sometimes pictures of products are misleading.

2. If you have any doubts about the company, check with the U.S. Postal Service, your state or local consumer protection agency, or the Better Business Bureau before ordering.

3. Ask about the firm's return policy. If it is not stated, ask before you order. For example, does the company pay charges for shipping and return? Is a warranty or guarantee available? Does the company sometimes substitute comparable goods for the product you want to order?

4. Keep a complete record of your order including the company's name, address, and telephone number; the price of the items ordered; any handling or other charges; the date you mailed (or telephoned) in the order; and your method of payment. Keep copies of canceled checks and/or statements.

5. If you order by mail, your order should be shipped within 30 days after the

company receives your complete order, unless another period is agreed upon when placing the order or is stated in an advertisement. If your order is delayed, a notice of delay should be sent to you within the promised shipping period along with an option to cancel the order.

6. If you buy a product through a television shopping program, check the cost of the same item sold by other sources, including local stores, catalogs, and others.

7. If you want to buy a product based on a telephone call from the company, ask for the name, address, and phone number where you can reach the caller after considering the offer.

8. Never give your credit card or social security number over the telephone as proof of your identity.

9. Postal regulations allow you to write a check payable to the sender, rather than the delivery company, for cash on delivery (COD) orders. If, after examining the merchandise, you feel there has been misrepresentation or fraud, you can stop payment on the check and file a complaint with the U.S. Postal Inspector's Office (see Appendix E, "Selected Federal Agencies," for the address).

10. You can have a charge removed from your bill if you did not receive the goods or services or if your order was obtained through misrepresentation or fraud. You must notify the credit card company in writing, at the billing inquiries/disputes address, within 60 days after the charge first appeared on your bill.

Appendix D: Federal Information Centers

Federal Information Centers (FICs) can help you find information about federal government services, programs, and regulations. FICs can also tell you which federal agency to contact for help with problems.

Alabama

Birmingham (205) 322-8591
Mobile (205) 438-1421

Alaska

Anchorage (907) 271-2898

Arizona

Phoenix (602) 261-3313

Arkansas

Little Rock (501) 378-6177

California

Los Angeles (213) 894-3800
San Diego (619) 557-6030
San Francisco
(415) 556-6600
Santa Ana (714) 836-2386

Colorado

Colorado Springs
(303) 471-9491
Denver (303) 844-6575

Connecticut

Hartford (203) 527-2617
New Haven (203) 624-4720

Florida

Ft. Lauderdale
(305) 522-8531
Jacksonville (904) 354-4756
Miami (305) 536-4155
Orlando (407) 422-1800
St. Petersburg
(813) 893-3495
Tampa (813) 229-7911
West Palm Beach
(407) 833-7566

SOURCE: The Office of the Special Adviser to the President for Consumer Affairs, "Federal Information Centers," *Consumer's Resource Handbook* (Washington, DC: The White House and the United States Office of Consumer Affairs, 1990), p. 77.

Georgia

Atlanta (404) 331-6891

Hawaii

Honolulu (808) 541-1365

Illinois

Chicago (312) 353-4242

Indiana

Gary (219) 883-4110
Indianapolis (317) 226-7373

Iowa

From all points in Iowa
1 (800) 532-1556

Kansas

From all points in Kansas
1 (800) 432-2934

Kentucky

Louisville (502) 582-6261

Louisiana

New Orleans
(504) 589-6696

Maryland

Baltimore (301) 962-4980

Massachusetts

Boston (617) 565-8121

Michigan

Detroit (313) 226-7016
Grand Rapids
(616) 732-2739

Minnesota

Minneapolis (612) 370-3333

Missouri

St. Louis (314) 539-2106
From elsewhere in Missouri
1 (800) 392-7711

Nebraska

Omaha (402) 221-3353
From elsewhere in Nebraska
1 (800) 642-8383

New Jersey

Newark (201) 645-3600
Trenton (609) 396-4400

New Mexico

Albuquerque
(505) 766-3091

New York

Albany (518) 463-4421
Buffalo (716) 846-4010
New York (212) 264-4464

Rochester (716) 546-5075
Syracuse (315) 476-8545

North Carolina

Charlotte (704) 376-3600

Ohio

Akron (216) 375-5638
Cincinnati (513) 684-2801
Cleveland (216) 522-4040
Columbus (614) 221-1014
Dayton (513) 223-7377
Toledo (419) 241-3223

Oklahoma

Oklahoma City
(405) 231-4868
Tulsa (918) 584-4193

Oregon

Portland (503) 326-2222

Pennsylvania

Philadelphia (215) 597-7042
Pittsburgh (412) 644-3456

Rhode Island

Providence (401) 331-5565

Tennessee

Chattanooga (615) 265-8231
Memphis (901) 521-3285
Nashville (615) 242-5056

Texas

Austin (512) 472-5494
Dallas (214) 767-8585
Fort Worth (817) 334-3624
Houston (713) 653-3025
San Antonio (512) 224-4471

Utah

Salt Lake City
(801) 524-5353

Virginia

Norfolk (804) 441-3101
Richmond (804) 643-4920
Roanoke (703) 982-8591

Washington

Seattle (206) 442-0570
Tacoma (206) 383-7970

Wisconsin

Milwaukee (414) 271-2273

Appendix E: Selected Federal Agencies

The Federal government agencies listed in this appendix can help answer consumer questions and resolve complaints. Some of these agencies have regional, district, or local offices. The symbol TDD after certain telephone numbers indicates it has a telecommunications device for the deaf.

Commission on Civil Rights

Look in your telephone directory under "U.S. Government, Civil Rights Commission." If it does not appear, call the nearest FIC (see Appendix D) or contact:

COMMISSION ON CIVIL RIGHTS
1121 Vermont Avenue, N.W.
Washington, DC 20425
1 (800) 552-6843
(voice/TDD complaint referral)
(202) 376-8521
(voice in DC complaint referral)
(202) 376-8116
(TDD in DC complaint referral)

Commodity Futures Trading Commission (CFTC)

2033 K Street, N.W.
Washington, DC 20581

(202) 254-3067
(complaints only)
(202) 254-8630
(information)

Consumer Information Center (CIC)

Pueblo, CO 81009

Consumer Product Safety Commission (CPSC)

To report a hazardous product or a product-related injury, or to inquire about product recalls, call or write:

PRODUCT SAFETY HOTLINE
Consumer Product Safety Commission
Washington, DC 20207
1 (800) 638-CPSC
1 (800) 638-8270

SOURCE: The Office of the Special Adviser to the President for Consumer Affairs, "Selected Federal Agencies," *Consumer's Resource Handbook* (Washington, DC: The White House and the United States Office of Consumer Affairs, 1990), pp. 78–83.

(TDD)
1 (800) 492-8104
(TDD in MD)

Department of Agriculture (USDA)

AGRICULTURAL MARKETING SERVICE
Department of Agriculture
Washington, DC 20250
(202) 447-8998

FARMERS HOME ADMINISTRATION
Department of Agriculture
Washington, DC 20250

FOOD AND NUTRITION SERVICE
Department of Agriculture
3101 Park Center Drive
Alexandria, VA 22302
(703) 756-3276

HUMAN NUTRITION INFORMATION
SERVICE
Department of Agriculture
Federal Building
Rooms 360 and 364
6505 Belcrest Road
Hyattsville, MD 20782
(301) 436-8617, 7725

INSPECTOR GENERAL'S HOTLINE
Office of the Inspector General
Department of Agriculture
P.O. Box 23399
Washington, DC 20026
(202) 472-1388
1 (800) 424-9121

MEAT AND POULTRY HOTLINE, FOOD
SAFETY AND INSPECTION SERVICE
Department of Agriculture
Washington, DC 20250
(202) 447-3333
(voice/TDD)

1 (800) 535-4555
(voice/TDD)

OFFICE OF THE CONSUMER ADVISER
Department of Agriculture
Washington, DC 20250
(202) 382-9681

Department of Commerce

BUREAU OF THE CENSUS
Customer Services
Data User Services Division
Department of Commerce
Washington, DC 20233
(301) 763-4100

CONSTITUENT AFFAIRS
National Weather Service
Department of Commerce
Washington, DC 20901
(301) 427-7258

NATIONAL INSTITUTE OF STANDARDS AND
TECHNOLOGY
Office of Weights and Measures
Department of Commerce
Washington, DC 20234
(301) 975-4004

NATIONAL MARINE FISHERIES SERVICE
Office of Trade and Industry Services
Department of Commerce
1335 East-West Highway
Silver Spring, MD 20910
(301) 427-2355
(inspection and safety)
(301) 427-2358
(nutrition information)

OFFICE OF CONSUMER AFFAIRS
Department of Commerce
Room 5718
Washington, DC 20230
(202) 377-5001

OFFICE OF METRIC PROGRAMS
Department of Commerce
Room H4082
Washington, DC 20230
(202) 377-0944

PATENT AND TRADEMARK OFFICE
Department of Commerce
Washington, DC 20231
(703) 557-3341

Department of Defense

OFFICE OF NATIONAL OMBUDSMAN
National Committee for Employer Support of
the Guard and Reserve
Suite 414
1111 20th Street, N.W.
Washington, DC 20036-3407
(202) 653-0852
1 (800) 336-4590
Provides assistance with employer/employee
problems for members of the Guard and Reserve and their employers.

Department of Education

CONSUMER AFFAIRS STAFF
Department of Education
Washington, DC 20202
(202) 732-3679

FEDERAL STUDENT FINANCIAL AID
PROGRAM
Department of Education
P.O. Box 84
Washington, DC 20044
1 (800) 333-INFO
Provides information about federal student fi-
nancial aid programs for students, parents, and
educators. Answers questions on student eligi-

bility; provides help in completing financial
aid applications, and provides help with student loan problems.

INSPECTOR GENERAL'S HOTLINE
Department of Education
P.O. Box 23458
Washington, DC 20026
(202) 755-2770
1 (800) MIS-USED
Audits and investigates to prevent and detect
fraud, waste, and abuse of department funds.
Persons may call anonymously to report possi-
ble violations of laws, rules, or regulations.

OFFICE OF PUBLIC AFFAIRS
Department of Education
Washington, DC 20202
(202) 732-4564

Department of Energy

For information about conservation and renewable energy:

NATIONAL APPROPRIATE TECHNOLOGY
ASSISTANCE SERVICE
Department of Energy
P.O. Box 2525
Butte, MT 59702-2525
1 (800) 428-1718
(toll free in MT)
1 (800) 428-2525
(toll free outside MT)

CONSERVATION AND RENEWABLE ENERGY
INQUIRY AND REFERRAL SERVICE
Department of Energy
P.O. Box 8900
Silver Spring, MD 20907
1 (800) 523-2929

DIVISION OF CONSUMER AFFAIRS
Department of Energy
Washington, DC 20585

OFFICE OF CONSERVATION AND
RENEWABLE ENERGY
Weatherization Assistance Inquiries:
Department of Energy
Washington, DC 20585
(202) 586-2204

Department of Health and Human Services (HHS)

AIDS HOTLINE
Acquired Immune Deficiency Syndrome
1 (800) 342-AIDS

CANCER HOTLINE
1 (800) 4-CANCER
During daytime hours, callers in California,
Florida, Georgia, Illinois, Northern New Jersey, New York, and Texas may ask for
Spanish-speaking staff members.
1-(800) 638-6070
(toll free in AK)
808-524-1234 (Oahu, Hawaii; call collect from
neighboring islands)

CONSUMER AFFAIRS AND INFORMATION
STAFF
Food and Drug Administration
Department of Health and Human Services
5600 Fishers Lane
Room 16-85
Rockville, MD 20857
(301) 443-3170

FOOD AND DRUG ADMINISTRATION (FDA)
Look in your telephone directory under "U.S.
Government, Health and Human Services Department, Food and Drug Administration." If it
does not appear, call the FIC nearest you (see
Appendix D) or contact:

HEALTH CARE FINANCING
ADMINISTRATION
Department of Health and Human Services
6325 Security Boulevard

Baltimore, MD 21207
(301) 966-3000

HEALTH STANDARDS AND QUALITY
BUREAU
Health Care Financing Administration
Department of Health and Human Services
6325 Security Boulevard
Baltimore, MD 21207
(301) 966-0841

HILL-BURTON FREE HOSPITAL CARE
HOTLINE
1 (800) 492-0359
(toll free in MD)
1 (800) 368-5779
(toll free outside MD)

NATIONAL CENTER ON CHILD ABUSE AND
NEGLECT
Department of Health and Human Services
P.O. Box 1182
Washington, DC 20013
(202) 245-0586

NATIONAL HEALTH INFORMATION CENTER
Department of Health and Human Services
P.O. Box 1133
Washington, DC 20013
(301) 565-4167
1 (800) 336-4797

NATIONAL RUNAWAY SWITCHBOARD
1 (800) 621-4000

OFFICE OF CHILD SUPPORT
ENFORCEMENT
Department of Health and Human Services
Washington, DC 20201
(202) 252-5377

OFFICE FOR CIVIL RIGHTS
Department of Health and Human Services
Washington, DC 20201
(202) 245-6671
(202) 472-2916 (TDD)

OFFICE OF PREPAID HEALTH CARE
Department of Health and Human Services
Washington, DC 20201
(202) 245-8036

PRESIDENT'S COUNCIL ON PHYSICAL
FITNESS AND SPORTS
Department of Health and Human Services
450 5th Street, N.W.
Washington, DC 20001

SECOND SURGICAL OPINION PROGRAM
Department of Health and Human Services
Washington, DC 20201
1 (800) 492-6803
(toll free in MD)
1 (800) 838-6833
(toll free outside MD)

SOCIAL SECURITY ADMINISTRATION
1 (800) 2345-SSA
In Guam and U.S. Territories, look in the telephone book under "U.S. Government."

Department of Housing and Urban Development (HUD)

INTERSTATE LAND SALES REGISTRATION
DIVISION
Department of Housing and Urban Development
Room 6278
Washington, DC 20410
(202) 755-0502

MANUFACTURED HOUSING AND
CONSTRUCTION STANDARDS DIVISION
Department of Housing and Urban Development
Room 9156
Washington, DC 20410
(202) 755-6920

OFFICE OF FAIR HOUSING AND EQUAL
OPPORTUNITY
Department of Housing and Urban Development

Room 5100
Washington, DC 20410
(202) 755-7252
1 (800) 424-8590

OFFICE OF SINGLE FAMILY HOUSING
Department of Housing and Urban Development
Room 9266
Washington, DC 20410
(202) 755-3046

OFFICE OF URBAN REHABILITATION
Department of Housing and Urban Development
Room 7168
Washington, DC 20410
(202) 755-5685

TITLE I INSURANCE DIVISION
Department of Housing and Urban Development
Room 9158
Washington, DC 20410
(202) 755-6680

Department of the Interior

BUREAU OF INDIAN AFFAIRS
Department of the Interior
Washington, DC 20240
(202) 343-4072

BUREAU OF LAND MANAGEMENT
Department of the Interior
Washington, DC 20240
(202) 343-5717

CONSUMER AFFAIRS ADMINISTRATOR
Office of the Secretary
Department of the Interior
Washington, DC 20240
(202) 343-5521

NATIONAL PARK SERVICE
Department of the Interior
Washington, DC 20240
(202) 343-4917

UNITED STATES FISH AND WILDLIFE
SERVICE
Department of the Interior
Washington, DC 20240
(703) 358-2156

UNITED STATES GEOLOGICAL SURVEY
Department of the Interior
12201 Sunrise Valley Drive
Reston, VA 22092
(703) 648-4427

Department of Justice

ANTITRUST DIVISION
Department of Justice
Washington, DC 20530
(202) 633-3543

Civil Rights Division

Look in your telephone directory under "U.S.
Government, Justice Department, Civil Rights
Division." If it does not appear, call the near-
est FIC (see Appendix D) or contact:

CIVIL RIGHTS DIVISION
Department of Justice
Washington, DC 20530
(202) 633-3847
(202) 633-2608 (TDD)

Drug Enforcement Administration (DEA)

Look in your telephone directory under "U.S.
Government, Justice Department, Drug Enforcement Administration." If it does not appear, call the nearest FIC (see Appendix D) or
contact:

DRUG ENFORCEMENT ADMINISTRATION
Department of Justice
Washington, DC 20537
(202) 633-1000

Federal Bureau of Investigation (FBI)

Look in your telephone directory under "U.S.
Government, Justice Department, Federal Bureau of Investigation." You may also contact:

FEDERAL BUREAU OF INVESTIGATION
Department of Justice
Washington, DC 20535
(202) 324-3000

Immigration and Naturalization Service
(INS)

Look in your telephone directory under "U.S.
Government, Justice Department, Immigration
and Naturalization Service." If it does not appear, call the nearest FIC (see Appendix D) or
contact:

IMMIGRATION AND NATURALIZATION
SERVICE
Department of Justice
4420 North Fairfax Drive
Arlington, VA 22203
(703) 235-4055

Department of Labor

COORDINATOR OF CONSUMER AFFAIRS
Department of Labor
Washington, DC 20210
(202) 523-6060

EMPLOYMENT STANDARDS
ADMINISTRATION
Office of Information and Consumer Affairs
Department of Labor
Washington, DC 20210
(202) 523-8743

MINE SAFETY AND HEALTH
ADMINISTRATION
Office of Information and Public Affairs
Department of Labor
Ballston Towers #3
Arlington, VA 22203
(703) 235-1452

OCCUPATIONAL SAFETY AND HEALTH
ADMINISTRATION
Office of Information and Public Affairs
Department of Labor
Washington, DC 20210
(202) 523-8151

WOMEN'S BUREAU, THE WORK AND
FAMILY CLEARINGHOUSE
Division of Information and Publications
Department of Labor
Washington, DC 20210
(202) 523-6652
Employers may contact this office for information about dependent care (child and/or elder care) policies.

Department of State

OVERSEAS CITIZEN SERVICES
Department of State
Washington, DC 20520
(202) 647-3666
(non-emergencies)
(202) 647-5225
(emergencies)

PASSPORT SERVICES
Department of State
1425 K Street, N.W.
Washington, DC 20524
(202) 647-0518

VISA SERVICES
Department of State
Washington, DC 20520
(202) 647-0510

Department of Transportation (DOT)

Air Safety

FEDERAL AVIATION ADMINISTRATION (FAA)
Community and Consumer Liaison Division,
FAA
Department of Transportation
Washington, DC 20591
(202) 267-3479, 8592
1 (800) FAA-SURE
(toll free except in DC)

Airline Passenger Complaints

OFFICE OF INTERGOVERNMENTAL AND
CONSUMER AFFAIRS
Department of Transportation
Washington, DC 20590
(202) 366-2220

Auto Safety Hotline

NATIONAL HIGHWAY TRAFFIC SAFETY
ADMINISTRATION (NHTSA)
Department of Transportation
Washington, DC 20690
(202) 366-0123
(202) 755-8919
1 (800) 424-9393
1 (800) 424-9153
(toll free TDD)

Boating Safety Classes

UNITED STATES COAST GUARD, OFFICE
OF BOATING, PUBLIC AND CONSUMER
AFFAIRS
Department of Transportation
Washington, DC 20593
(202) 267-0972

Boating Safety Hotline

UNITED STATES COAST GUARD
Department of Transportation
Washington, DC 20593
(202) 267-0780
1 (800) 368-5647

Oil and Chemical Spills

NATIONAL RESPONSE CENTER
United States Coast Guard Headquarters, G-TGC-2
Department of Transportation
Washington, DC 20593
(202) 267-2675
1 (800) 424-8802

Department of the Treasury

BUREAU OF ALCOHOL, TOBACCO AND FIREARMS
Look in your telephone directory under "U.S. Government, Treasury Department, Bureau of Alcohol, Tobacco and Firearms." If it does not appear, call the nearest FIC (see Appendix D) or contact:

BUREAU OF ALCOHOL, TOBACCO AND FIREARMS
Department of the Treasury
Room 6213
1200 Pennsylvania Avenue, N.W.
Washington, DC 20226
(202) 789-3175
To report lost or stolen explosives, or to report explosions or bombings, call:
(202) 789-3000
1 (800) 424-9555
(toll free outside DC)

BUREAU OF THE PUBLIC DEBT
Consumer Affairs
Office of the Commissioner
Department of the Treasury
E Street Building
Washington, DC 20239-0001
(202) 376-4300

COMPTROLLER OF THE CURRENCY
The Comptroller of the Currency handles complaints about national banks, *i.e.*, banks that have the world "National" in their names or the initials "N.A." after their names.
For assistance, look in your telephone directory under "U.S. Government, Treasury Department, Comptroller of the Currency." If it does not appear, call the nearest FIC (see Appendix D) or contact:

COMPTROLLER OF THE CURRENCY
Director, Consumer Activities
Department of the Treasury
490 L'Enfant Plaza, S.W.
Washington, DC 20219
(202) 287-4265

INTERNAL REVENUE SERVICE (IRS)
Look in your telephone directory under "U.S. Government, Treasury Department, Internal Revenue Service." If it does not appear, call the nearest FIC (see Appendix D).

OFFICE OF THRIFT SUPERVISION
(formerly Federal Home Loan Bank Board)
The Office of Thrift Supervision handles complaints about Savings and Loan Associations and Savings Banks.

For assistance contact:

OFFICE OF THRIFT SUPERVISION
Consumer Affairs
1700 G Street, N.W.
Washington, DC 20552
(202) 906-6237
1 (800) 842-6929
(toll free except in DC)

UNITED STATES CUSTOMS SERVICE
Look in your telephone directory under "U.S. Government, Treasury Department, U.S. Customs Service." If it does not appear, call the nearest FIC (see Appendix D).
To report fraudulent import practices call U.S. Customs Service's **Fraud Hotline**: 1 (800) USA-FAKE
To report drug smuggling activity call U.S. Customs Service's **Narcotics Hotline**: 1 (800) BE-ALERT

UNITED STATES MINT
Consumer Affairs Division
Department of the Treasury
10001 Aerospace Road
Lanham, MD 20706
(301) 436-7400

UNITED STATES SAVINGS BONDS DIVISION
Office of Public Affairs
Department of the Treasury
1111 20th Street, N.W.
Room 302
Washington, DC 20226
(202) 634-5389
1 (800) US-BONDS

Environmental Protection Agency (EPA)

ASBESTOS ACTION PROGRAM
(202) 382-3949

CHEMICAL EMERGENCY PREPAREDNESS
PROGRAM (CEPP) HOTLINE
Environmental Protection Agency
Washington, DC 20460
(202) 479-2449
1 (800) 535-0202
(toll free except in AK and DC)

INSPECTOR GENERAL'S WHISTLE BLOWER
HOTLINE
(202) 382-4977
1 (800) 424-4000

NATIONAL PESTICIDES TELECOMMUNI-
CATIONS NETWORK (NPTN)
(806) 743-3091
1 (800) 858-PEST
(toll free outside TX)

OFFICE OF PUBLIC AFFAIRS
Environmental Protection Agency
Washington, DC 20460
(202) 382-4361

PUBLIC INFORMATION CENTER (PIC)
Environmental Protection Agency
Washington, DC 20460

RESOURCE CONSERVATION AND RECOVERY
ACT (RCRA)/SUPERFUND HOTLINE
Environmental Protection Agency
Washington, DC 20460
(202) 382-3000
1 (800) 424-9348
(toll free outside DC)

SAFE DRINKING WATER HOTLINE
(202) 382-5533
1 (800) 428-4791
(toll free outside DC)

TOXIC SUBSTANCES CONTROL ACT
ASSISTANCE INFORMATION SERVICE
Environmental Protection Agency
Washington, DC 20024
(202) 554-1404

Equal Employment Opportunity Commission

Look in your telephone directory under "U.S.
Government, Equal Employment Opportunity
Commission." If it does not appear, call the
nearest FIC (see Appendix D) or contact:

OFFICE OF PROGRAM OPERATIONS
Equal Employment Opportunity Commission
1801 L Street, N.W.
Washington, DC 20507
(202) 663-4801

Federal Communications Commission (FCC)

Complaints about Telephone Systems

COMMON CARRIER BUREAU
Informal Complaints Branch
Federal Communications Commission
2025 M Street, N.W.
Room 6202

Washington, DC 20554
(202) 632-7553
(202) 832-6999 (TDD)

General Information

CONSUMER ASSISTANCE AND SMALL
BUSINESS OFFICE
Federal Communications Commission
1919 M Street, N.W.
Room 254
Washington, DC 20554
(202) 632-7000
(202) 832-8999 (TDD)

Complaints about Radio or Television

MASS MEDIA BUREAU
Complaints and Investigations
Federal Communications Commission
2025 M Street, N.W.
Room 8210
Washington, DC 20554
(202) 632-7048

Federal Deposit Insurance Corporation (FDIC)

The FDIC handles complaints about FDIC-insured banks that are not members of the Federal Reserve System. For assistance, look in your telephone directory under "U.S. Government, Federal Deposit Insurance Corporation." If it does not appear, call the nearest FIC (see Appendix D) or contact:

OFFICE OF CONSUMER AFFAIRS
Federal Deposit Insurance Corporation
550 17th Street, N.W.
(F130)
Washington, DC 20429
(202) 898-3536
(202) 898-3535 (TDD)
1 (800) 424-5488
(toll free outside DC)

Federal Emergency Management Agency

Look in your telephone directory under "U.S. Government, Federal Emergency Management Agency." If it does not appear, call the nearest FIC (see Appendix D) or contact:

EMERGENCY PREPAREDNESS AND
RESPONSE
Office of the External Affairs Directorate
Federal Emergency Management Agency
Washington, DC 20472
(202) 646-4000

OFFICE OF DISASTER ASSISTANCE
PROGRAMS
Federal Emergency Management Agency
Washington, DC 20472
(202) 646-3615

Federal Maritime Commission

OFFICE OF INFORMAL INQUIRIES AND
COMPLAINTS
1100 L Street, N.W.
Washington, DC 20573
(202) 523-5807

Federal Reserve System

The Board of Governors handles consumer complaints about state banks and trust companies that are members of the Federal Reserve System. For assistance, look in your telephone directory under "U.S. Government, Federal Reserve System, Board of Governors" or "Federal Reserve Bank." If it does not appear, call the nearest FIC (see Appendix D) or contact:

BOARD OF GOVERNORS OF THE FEDERAL
RESERVE SYSTEM
Division of Consumer and Community Affairs
Washington, DC 20551
(202) 452-3946

Federal Trade Commission (FTC)

Look in your telephone directory under "U.S. Government, Federal Trade Commission." If it does not appear, call the nearest FIC (see Appendix D) or contact:

CORRESPONDENCE BRANCH
Federal Trade Commission
Washington, DC 20580
(202) 326-2222
(publications)

General Services Administration (GSA)

Government Publications

PUBLICATIONS SERVICE SECTION
Government Printing Office
Washington, DC 20402
(202) 275-3050

Subscriptions to Government Periodicals:

SUBSCRIPTION RESEARCH SECTION
Government Printing Office
Washington, DC 20402
(202) 275-3054

Interstate Commerce Commission (ICC)

OFFICE OF COMPLIANCE AND CONSUMER ASSISTANCE
Washington, DC 20423
(202) 275-7148

National Archives and Records Administration

REFERENCE SERVICES BRANCH
National Archives and Records Administration
Washington, DC 20408
(202) 523-3220
(202) 523-0774 (TDD)

FEDERAL REGISTER
National Archives and Records Administration
Washington, DC 20408
(202) 523-5240
(202) 523-0774 (TDD)

PUBLICATIONS SERVICES
National Archives and Records Administration
Washington, DC 20408
(202) 523-3181
(202) 523-0774 (TDD)

National Credit Union Administration

Look in your telephone directory under "U.S. Government, National Credit Union Administration." If it does not appear, call the nearest FIC (see Appendix D) or contact:

NATIONAL CREDIT UNION ADMINISTRATION
1776 G Street N.W.
Washington, DC 20456
(202) 682-9600

National Labor Relations Board

OFFICE OF THE EXECUTIVE SECRETARY
1717 Pennsylvania Ave., N.W.
Room 701
Washington, DC 20570
(202) 254-9430

Nuclear Regulatory Commission (NRC)

OFFICE OF GOVERNMENTAL AND PUBLIC AFFAIRS
Washington, DC 20555
(301) 492-0240

Pension Benefit Guaranty Corporation

2020 K Street, N.W.
Washington, DC 20006

(202) 778-8800
(202) 778-8859 (TDD)

Postal Rate Commission

OFFICE OF THE CONSUMER ADVOCATE
Postal Rate Commission
Washington, DC 20268
(202) 789-6830

President's Committee on Employment of People with Disabilities

1111 20th Street, N.W.
Suite 636
Washington, DC 20036-3470
(202) 653-5044
(202) 653-5050 (TDD)

Railroad Retirement Board

844 Rush Street
Chicago, IL 60611
(312) 751-4500

Securities and Exchange Commission (SEC)

OFFICE OF CONSUMER AFFAIRS AND
INFORMATION SERVICE
450 5th Street, N.W.
(Mail Stop 2-6)
Washington, DC 20549
(202) 272-7440
(investor complaints)
(202) 272-7450
(filings by corporations and other regulated entities)
(202) 272-5624
(SEC information Line—general topics and sources of assistance)

Small Business Administration (SBA)

OFFICE OF CONSUMER AFFAIRS
1441 L Street, N.W.

Washington, DC 20416
(202) 653-6170

Tennessee Valley Authority (TVA)

COMMUNITY RELATIONS DEPARTMENT
400 West Summit Hill Drive
Knoxville, TN 37902
(615) 632-8000

United States Postal Service (USPS)

If you experience difficulty when ordering merchandise or conducting business transactions through the mail, or suspect that you have been the victim of a mail fraud or misrepresentation scheme, contact your postmaster or local Postal Inspector. Look in your telephone directory under "U.S. Government, Postal Service U.S." for these local listings. If they do not appear, contact:

CHIEF POSTAL INSPECTOR
United States Postal Service
Washington, DC 20260-2100
(202) 268-4267
For consumer convenience, all post offices and letter carriers have postage-free Consumer Service Cards available for reporting mail problems and submitting comments and suggestions. If the problem cannot be resolved using the Consumer Service Card or through direct contact with the local post office, write or call:

CONSUMER ADVOCATE
United States Postal Service
Washington, DC 20260-6720
(202) 268-2284

Department of Veterans Affairs (VA)

For information about VA medical care or benefits, write, call or visit the nearest VA facility. Your telephone directory will list a VA Medical

Center or Regional Office under "U.S. Government, Department of Veterans Affairs" or under "U.S. Government, Veterans Administration." Policy issues may be addressed:

For burials and memorials:

NATIONAL CEMETERY SYSTEM (40H)
Department of Veterans Affairs
810 Vermont Avenue, N.W.
Washington, DC 20420
(202) 233-5012

For medical matters:

VETERANS HEALTH SERVICES AND
RESEARCH ADMINISTRATION (101C)
Department of Veterans Affairs
810 Vermont Avenue, N.W.
Washington, DC 20420
(202) 233-3975

For other benefits:

VETERANS BENEFITS ADMINISTRATION (27)
Department of Veterans Affairs
810 Vermont Avenue, N.W.
Washington, DC 20420
(202) 233-2567

For other information:

DEPUTY ASSISTANT SECRETARY FOR
VETERANS LIAISON
Department of Veterans Affairs
810 Vermont Avenue, N.W.
Washington, DC 20420
(202) 233-3113

Appendix F: State Government Consumer Protection Offices

State consumer protection offices can help you with consumer questions or problems. They are a good source of information because many of them enforce consumer protection and fraud laws. State consumer protection offices can help you resolve consumer complaints, and they often provide consumer education information.

If you want to file a complaint, call your local consumer protection office to learn what you need to do.

This list is arranged alphabetically by state. Many states have county and city government consumer protection offices. Consult your telephone book under consumer protection offices for the appropriate governmental listing. The symbol TDD after certain telephone numbers indicates it has a telecommunications device for the deaf.

ALABAMA

Director
Consumer Protection Division
Office of Attorney General
11 South Union Street
Montgomery, AL 36130
(205) 261-7334
1 (800) 392-5658
(toll free in AL)

ALASKA

Chief
Consumer Protection Section

Office of Attorney General
1031 West Fourth Avenue
Suite 110-B
Anchorage, AK 99501
(907) 456-8588

AMERICAN SAMOA

Director
Consumer Protection Bureau
P.O. Box 7
Pago Pago, AS 96799
011 (684) 633-4163
011 (684) 663-4164

Source: The Office of the Special Adviser to the President for Consumer Affairs, "State, County, and City Government Consumer Protection Offices," *Consumer's Resource Handbook* (Washington, DC: The White House and the United States Office of Consumer Affairs, 1990), pp. 48–59.

ARIZONA

Chief Counsel
Financial Fraud Division
Office of Attorney General
1275 West Washington Street
Phoenix, AZ 85007
(602) 542-3702
(fraud only)
1 (800) 352-8431

Assistant Attorney General
Financial Fraud Division
Office of Attorney General
402 West Congress Street, Suite 315
Tucson, AZ 85701
(602) 628-5501

ARKANSAS

Director
Consumer Protection Division
Office of Attorney General
200 Tower Building
4th & Center Streets
Little Rock, AR 72201
(501) 682-2007
(voice/TDD)
1 (800) 482-8982
(voice/TDD in AR)

CALIFORNIA

Director
California Department of Consumer Affairs
1020 "N" Street
Sacramento, CA 95814
(916) 445-0660 (complaint assistance)
(916) 445-1254 (consumer information)
(916) 522-1700 (TDD)

COLORADO

Chief
Consumer Protection Unit

Office of Attorney General
1525 Sherman Street
3rd Floor
Denver, CO 80203
(303) 866-5167

Consumer and Food Specialist
Department of Agriculture
1525 Sherman Street
4th Floor
Denver, CO 80203

CONNECTICUT

Commissioner
Department of Consumer Protection
State Office Building
165 Capitol Avenue
Hartford, CT 06106
(203) 566-4999
1 (800) 842-2649
(toll free in CT)

Assistant Attorney General
Antitrust/Consumer Protection
Office of Attorney General
110 Sherman Street
Hartford, CT 06105
(203) 566-5374

DELAWARE

Director
Division of Consumer Affairs
Department of Community Affairs
820 North French Street, 4th Floor
Wilmington, DE 19801
(302) 571-3250

Deputy-in-Charge
Economic Crime/Consumer Rights Division
Office of Attorney General
820 North French Street
Wilmington, DE 19801
(302) 571-3849

DISTRICT OF COLUMBIA

Director
Department of Consumer and Regulatory
Affairs
614 H Street, N.W.
Washington, DC 20001
(202) 727-7000

FLORIDA

Director
Department of Agriculture and Consumer
Services
Division of Consumer Services
218 Mayo Building
Tallahassee, FL 32399
(904) 488-2226
1 (800) 342-2176 (toll free TDD in FL)
1 (800) 327-3382
(toll free information and education in FL)
1 (800) 321-5366
(toll free lemon law in FL)

Chief
Consumer Litigation Section
Consumer Protection Division
Office of Attorney General
401 N.W. Second Avenue, Suite 921 N
Miami, FL 33128
(305) 377-5619

GEORGIA

Administrator
Governor's Office of Consumer Affairs
2 Martin Luther King, Jr., Drive, S.W.
Plaza Level–East Tower
Atlanta, GA 30334
(404) 656-7000, 3790
1 (800) 282-5808 (toll free in GA)

HAWAII

Director
Office of Consumer Protection
Department of Commerce and Consumer
Affairs
828 Fort Street Mall
P.O. Box 3767
Honolulu, HI 96812-3767
(808) 548-2560
(administration and legal—in HI)
(808) 548-2540
(complaints and investigation—in HI)

Investigator
Office of Consumer Protection
Department of Commerce and Consumer
Affairs
75 Aupuni Street
Hilo, HI 96720
(808) 961-7433

Investigator
Office of Consumer Protection
Department of Commerce and Consumer
Affairs
3060 Eiwa Street
Lihue, HI 96766
(808) 245-4365

Investigator
Office of Consumer Protection
Department of Commerce and Consumer
Affairs
54 High Street
P.O. Box 1098
Wailuku, HI 96793
(808) 244-4387

ILLINOIS

Director
Governor's Office of Citizens Assistance
201 West Monroe Street
Springfield, IL 62706
(217) 782-0244
1 (800) 642-3112 (toll free in IL)

Chief
Consumer Protection Division
Office of Attorney General

100 West Randolph
12th Floor
Chicago, IL 60601
(312) 917-3580
(312) 793-2852 (TDD)

Director
Department of Citizen Rights
100 West Randolph
13th Floor
Chicago, IL 60601
(312) 917-3289
(312) 917-7123 (TDD)

INDIANA

Chief Counsel and Director
Consumer Protection Division
Office of Attorney General
219 State House
Indianapolis, IN 46204
(317) 232-6330
1 (800) 382-5516 (toll free in IN)

IOWA

Iowa Citizens' Aide/Ombudsman
215 E. 7th Street
Capitol Complex
Des Moines, IA 50319
(515) 281-3592
(515) 242-5065 (TDD)
1 (800) 358-5510 (toll free in IA)

Assistant Attorney General
Consumer Protection Division
Office of Attorney General
1300 East Walnut Street
2nd Floor
Des Moines, IA 50319
(515) 281-5926

KANSAS

Deputy Attorney General
Consumer Protection Division

Office of Attorney General
Kansas Judicial Center
Topeka, KS 66612
(913) 296-3751
1 (800) 432-2310 (toll free in KS)

KENTUCKY

Director
Consumer Protection Division
Office of Attorney General
209 Saint Clair Street
Frankfort, KY 40601
(502) 564-2200
1 (800) 432-9257 (toll free in KY)

Administrator
Consumer Protection Division
Office of Attorney General
107 S. 4th Street
Louisville, KY 40202
(502) 588-3262
1 (800) 432-9257 (toll free in KY)

LOUISIANA

Chief
Consumer Protection Section
Office of Attorney General
State Capitol Building
P.O. Box 94005
Baton Rouge, LA 70804
(504) 342-7013

Assistant Commissioner
Office of Agro-Consumer Services
Department of Agriculture
325 Loyola Avenue
Room 317
New Orleans, LA 70112
(504) 568-5472

MAINE

Superintendent
Bureau of Consumer Credit Protection

State House State No. 35
Augusta, ME 04333
(207) 289-3716 (9 A.M.–1 P.M.)

MARYLAND

Chief
Consumer Protection Division
Office of Attorney General
Seven North Calvert Street
Baltimore, MD 212022
(301) 528-8662
(9 A.M.–2 P.M.)
(202) 470-7534
(Washington, D.C. metro area)
(301) 576-6372
(voice/TDD in Baltimore area)
1 (800) 492-2114, then dial 870-892
(toll free in MD)

Consumer Specialist
Eastern Shore Branch Office
Consumer Protection Division
Office of Attorney General
State Office Complex
Route 50 and Cypress Street
Salisbury, MD 21801
(301) 543-6620

Director
Western Maryland Branch Office
Consumer Protection Division
Office of Attorney General
138 East Antietam Street
Suite 210
Hagerstown, MD 21740
(301) 791-4780

MASSACHUSETTS

Chief
Consumer Protection Division
Department of Attorney General
131 Tremont Street
Boston, MA 02111
(617) 727-8400
(information and referral only)

Secretary
Executive Office of Consumer Affairs and
Business Regulation
One Ashburton Place
Room 1411
Boston, MA 02108
(information and referral only)

Assistant Attorney General
Consumer Protection Division
Department of Attorney General
436 Dwight Street
Springfield, MA 01103
(413) 784-1240

MICHIGAN

Assistant Attorney General
Consumer Protection Division
Office of Attorney General
670 Law Building
Lansing, MI 48913
(517) 373-1140

Executive Director
Michigan Consumers Council
414 Hollister Building
106 West Allegan Street
Lansing, MI 48933
(517) 373-0947
(517) 373-0701 (TDD)

Director
Bureau of Automotive Regulation
Michigan Department of State
Lansing, MI 48918
(517) 373-7858
1 (800) 292-4204 (toll free in MI)

MINNESOTA

Director
Office of Consumer Services
Office of Attorney General
117 University Avenue
St. Paul, MN 55155
(612) 296-2331

Complaint Mediator
Consumer Services Division
Office of Attorney General
320 West Second Street
Duluth, MN 55802
(218) 723-4891

MISSISSIPPI

Special Assistant Attorney General
Chief, Consumer Protection Division
Office of Attorney General
P.O. Box 220
Jackson, MS 39205
(601) 354-6018

Director
Regulatory Services
Department of Agriculture and Commerce
500 Greymont Avenue
P.O. Box 1609
Jackson, MS 39215
(601) 354-7063

Consumer Counselor
Gulf Coast Regional Office of the Attorney
General
P.O. Box 1411
Biloxi, MS 39533
(601) 436-6000

MISSOURI

Director
Department of Economic Development
P.O. Box 1157
Jefferson City, MO 65102
(314) 751-4962

Chief Counsel
Trade Offense Division
Office of Attorney General
P.O. Box 899
Jefferson City, MO 65102
(314) 751-2616
1 (800) 392-8222 (toll free in MO)

MONTANA

Consumer Affairs Unit
Department of Commerce
1424 Ninth Avenue
Helena, MT 59620
(406) 444-4312

NEBRASKA

Assistant Attorney General
Consumer Protection Division
Department of Justice
2115 State Capitol
P.O. Box 98920
Lincoln, NE 68509
(402) 471-4723

NEVADA

Commissioner of Consumer Affairs
Department of Commerce
State Mail Room Complex
Las Vegas, NV 89158
(702) 486-4150

Consumer Services Officer
Consumer Affairs Division
Department of Commerce
201 Nye Building
Capitol Complex
Carson City, NV 86710
(702) 885-4340

NEW HAMPSHIRE

Chief
Consumer Protection and Antitrust Division
Office of Attorney General
State House Annex
Concord, NH 03301
(603) 271-3641

NEW JERSEY

Director
Division of Consumer Affairs
1100 Raymond Boulevard
Room 316
Newark, NJ 07102
(201) 648-4010

Assistant Attorney General
Division of Law
Office of Attorney General
1100 Raymond Boulevard
Room 316
Newark, NJ 07102
(201) 648-4730

Commissioner
Department of the Public Advocate
CN850 Justice Complex
Trenton, NJ 08625
(609) 292-7087
1 (800) 792-8600 (toll free in NJ)

NEW MEXICO

Director
Consumer and Economic Crime Division
Office of Attorney General
P.O. Drawer 1508
Santa Fe, NM 87504
(505) 872-6910
1 (800) 432-2070 (toll free in NM)

NEW YORK

Chairperson and Executive Director
New York State
Consumer Protection Board
99 Washington Avenue
Albany, NY 12210
(518) 474-8583

Assistant Attorney General
Bureau of Consumer Frauds and Protection

Office of Attorney General
State Capitol
Albany, NY 12224
(518) 474-5481

Chairperson and Executive Director
New York State
Consumer Protection Board
250 Broadway, 17th Floor
New York, NY 10007-2593
(212) 587-4908

Assistant Attorney General
Bureau of Consumer Frauds and Protection
Office of Attorney General
120 Broadway
New York, NY 10271
(212) 341-2300

NORTH CAROLINA

Special Deputy Attorney General
Consumer Protection Section
Office of Attorney General
Department of Justice Building
P.O. Box 629
Raleigh, NC 27602
(919) 733-7741

NORTH DAKOTA

Office of Attorney General
600 E. Boulevard
Bismarck, ND 58505
(701) 224-2210
1 (800) 472-2600 (toll free in ND)

Director
Consumer Fraud Division
Office of Attorney General
600 East Boulevard
Bismarck, ND 58505
(701) 224-3404
1 (800) 472-2600 (toll free in ND)

OHIO

Consumer Frauds and Crimes Section
Office of Attorney General
300 East Broad Street
State Office Tower
25th Floor
Columbus, OH 43266-0410
(614) 466-4986 (complaints)
1 (800) 282-0515 (toll free in OH)
(614) 466-1393 (TDD)

Consumers' Counsel
77 South High Street
15th Floor
Columbus, OH 43266
(614) 466-9605
(voice/TDD)
1 (800) 282-9448 (toll free in OH)

OKLAHOMA

Assistant Attorney General for Consumer
Affairs
Office of Attorney General
112 State Capitol Building
Oklahoma City, OK 73105
(405) 521-3921

Administrator
Department of Consumer Credit
4545 Lincoln Boulevard, Suite 104
Oklahoma City, OK 73105
(405) 521-3653

OREGON

Financial Fraud Section
Department of Justice
Justice Building
Salem, OR 97310
(503) 378-4320

PENNSYLVANIA

Director
Bureau of Consumer Protection

Office of Attorney General
Strawberry Square
14th Floor
Harrisburg, PA 17120
(717) 787-9707
1 (800) 441-2555 (toll free in PA)

Consumer Advocate
Office of Consumer Advocate–Utilities
Office of Attorney General
Strawberry Square
14th Floor
Harrisburg, PA 17120
(717) 783-5048 (utilities only)

Deputy Attorney General
Bureau of Consumer Protection
Office of Attorney General
27 North Seventh Street
Allentown, PA 18101
(215) 821-6690

Deputy Attorney General
Bureau of Consumer Protection
Office of Attorney General
919 State Street
Room 203
Erie, PA 16501
(814) 871-4371

Attorney in Charge
Bureau of Consumer Protection
Office of Attorney General
Strawberry Square
14th Floor
Harrisburg, PA 17120
(717) 787-7109

Bureau of Consumer Protection
Office of the Attorney General
IGA Building Route 219 North
P.O. Box 716
Ebensbury, PA 15931
(814) 949-7900

Deputy Attorney General
Bureau of Consumer Protection
Office of Attorney General
1009 State Office Building

1400 West Spring Garden Street
Philadelphia, PA 19130
(215) 560-2414

Deputy Attorney General
Bureau of Consumer Protection
Office of Attorney General
Manor Building
4th Floor
564 Forbes Avenue
Pittsburgh, PA 15219
(412) 565-5135

Deputy Attorney General
Bureau of Consumer Protection
Office of Attorney General
State Office Building
Room 358
100 Lackawanna Avenue
Scranton, PA 18503
(717) 963-4913

PUERTO RICO

Department of Consumer Affairs
Minillas Station
P.O. Box 41059
Santurce, PR 00940
(809) 722-7555

Secretary
Department of Justice
P.O. Box 192
Old San Juan, PR 00902
(809) 721-2900

RHODE ISLAND

Director
Consumer Protection Division
Department of Attorney General
72 Pine Street
Providence, RI 02903
(401) 277-2104
(401) 274-4400 ext. 354
(voice/TDD)
1 (800) 852-7776 (toll free in RI)

Executive Director
Rhode Island Consumers' Council
365 Broadway
Providence, RI 02909
(401) 277-2764

SOUTH CAROLINA

Assistant Attorney General
Consumer Fraud and Antitrust Section
Office of Attorney General
P.O. Box 11549
Columbia, SC 29211
(803) 734-3970

Administrator
Department of Consumer Affairs
P.O. Box 5757
Columbia, SC 29250
(803) 734-9452
(803) 734-9455 (TDD)
1 (800) 922-1594 (toll free in SC)

State Ombudsman
Office of Executive Policy and Program
1205 Pendleton Street, Room 308
Columbia, SC 29201
(803) 734-0457

SOUTH DAKOTA

Assistant Attorney General
Division of Consumer Affairs
Office of Attorney General
State Capitol Building
Pierre, SD 57501
(605) 773-4400

TENNESSEE

Deputy Attorney General
Antitrust and Consumer Protection Division
Office of Attorney General
450 James Robertson Parkway
Nashville, TN 37219

(615) 741-4737
1 (800) 342-8385 (toll free in TN)

TEXAS

Assistant Attorney General and Chief
Consumer Protection Division
Office of Attorney General
Capitol Station
P.O. Box 12548
Austin, TX 78711
(512) 463-2070

Public Counsel
Office of Consumer Protection
State Board of Insurance
One Republic Plaza
333 Guadalupe
Box 44
Austin, TX 75202
(214) 742-8944

Assistant Attorney General
Consumer Protection Division
Office of Attorney General
6090 Surety Drive, Rm. 260
El Paso, TX 79905

Assistant Attorney General
Consumer Protection Division
Office of Attorney General
1019 Congress Street, Suite 1550
Houston, TX 77002
(713) 223-5886

Assistant Attorney General
Consumer Protection Division
Office of Attorney General
1208 14th Street, Suite 801
Lubbock, TX 79401
(806) 747-5238

Assistant Attorney General
Consumer Protection Division
Office of Attorney General
3600 North 23rd Street, Suite 305
McAllen, TX 78501
(512) 682-4547

Assistant Attorney General
Consumer Protection Division
Office of Attorney General
200 Main Plaza, Suite 400
San Antonio, TX 78205
(512) 225-4191

UTAH

Division of Consumer Protection
Department of Commerce
160 East 3rd South
P.O. Box 45802
Salt Lake City, UT 84145
(801) 530-6601

Assistant Attorney General for Consumer
Affairs
Office of Attorney General
115 State Capitol
Salt Lake City, UT 84114
(801) 538-1331

VERMONT

Assistant Attorney General and Chief
Public Protection Division
Office of Attorney General
109 State Street
Montpelier, VT 05602
(802) 828-3171

Supervisor
Consumer Assurance Section
Department of Agriculture
116 State Street
Montpelier, VT 05602
(802) 828-2436

VIRGIN ISLANDS

Commissioner
Department of Licensing and Consumer Affairs
Property and Procurement Building
Subbase #1, Rm. 205
St. Thomas, VI 00801
(809) 774-3130

VIRGINIA

Senior Assistant Attorney General
Antitrust and Consumer Litigation Section
Office of Attorney General
Supreme Court Building
101 North Eighth Street
Richmond, VA 23219
(804) 786-2116
1 (800) 451-1525 (toll free in VA)

Director
Office of Consumer Affairs
Department of Agriculture and Consumer Services
Room 101
Washington Building
1100 Bank Street
Richmond, VA 23219
(804) 786-2042
1 (800) 552-9963 (toll free in VA)

Investigator
Northern Virginia Branch
Office of Consumer Affairs
Department of Agriculture and Consumer Services
100 North Washington St., Suite 412
Falls Church, VA 22046
(703) 532-1613

WASHINGTON

Investigator
Consumer and Business Fair Practices Division
Office of Attorney General
North 122 Capitol Way
Olympia, WA 98501
(206) 753-6210

Assistant Attorney General and Chief
Consumer and Business Fair Practices Division
Office of Attorney General
710 2nd Avenue, Suite 1300
Seattle, WA 98104
(206) 464-7744
1 (800) 551-4636 (toll free in WA)

Chief
Consumer and Business Fair Practices Division
Office of Attorney General
West 1116 Riverside Avenue
Spokane, WA 99201
(509) 456-3123

Contact Person
Consumer and Business Fair Practices Division
Office of Attorney General
1019 Pacific Avenue
3rd Floor
Tacoma, WA 98402
(206) 593-2904

Appendix G: State Utility Commissions

State utility commissions regulate consumer service and rates for gas, electricity, and a variety of other services within your state. These include rates for moving household goods and for telephone services. In some states, the utility commission regulates water and transportation rates. Rates for those utilities and services provided between states are regulated by the federal government.

Many utility commissions handle consumer complaints. Sometimes, if a number of complaints are received about the same utility matter, they will conduct investigations.

If you have a consumer question or complaint about a utility matter, write or call the commission in your state. The symbol TDD after certain telephone numbers indicates it has a telecommunications device for the deaf.

ALABAMA

President
Public Service Commission
P.O. Box 991
Montgomery, AL 36101
(205) 261-5207
1 (800) 392-8050
(toll free in AL)

ALASKA

Chairman
Public Utilities Commission
420 "L" Street, Suite 100

Anchorage, AK 99501
(907) 276-6222

ARIZONA

Chairman
Corporation Commission
1200 West Washington Street
Phoenix, AZ 85007
(602) 542-3935
(602) 255-2105 (TDD)

ARKANSAS

Chairman
Public Service Commission

SOURCE: The Office of the Special Adviser to the President for Consumer Affairs, "State Utility Commissions," *Consumer's Resource Handbook* (Washington, D.C.: The White House and the United States Office of Consumer Affairs, 1990), pp. 67–8.

1000 Center Street
Little Rock, AR 72202
(501) 682-1453
1 (800) 482-1164
(toll free in AR)

CALIFORNIA

President
Public Utilities Commission
505 Van Ness Avenue
Room 5207
San Francisco, CA 94102
(415) 557-2444
(415) 557-0798 (TDD)

COLORADO

Chairman
Public Utilities Commission
1580 Logan Street
Logan Tower–Office Level 2
Denver, CO 80203
(303) 894-2021
1 (800) 888-0170
(toll free in CO)

CONNECTICUT

Chairperson
Department of Public Utility Control
1 Central Park Plaza
New Britain, CT 06051
(203) 827-1553
1 (800) 382-4586
(toll free in CT)

DELAWARE

Chairman
Public Service Commission
1560 South DuPont Highway
P.O. Box 457
Dover, DE 19903
(302) 736-4247

1 (800) 282-8574
(toll free in DE)

DISTRICT OF COLUMBIA

Chairperson
Public Service Commission
450 Fifth Street, N.W.
Washington, DC 20001
(202) 626-5110

FLORIDA

Chairman
Public Service Commission
101 East Gaines Street
Tallahassee, FL 32399-0850
(904) 488-7001
1 (800) 342-3552
(toll free in FL)

GEORGIA

Chairman
Public Service Commission
Atlanta, GA 30334
(404) 656-4556
1 (800) 282-5813
(toll free in GA)

HAWAII

Chairman
Public Utilities Commission
465 South King Street
Room 103
Honolulu, HI 96813
(808) 548-3990

IDAHO

President
Public Utilities Commission

State House
Boise, ID 83720
(208) 334-3427

ILLINOIS

Chairman
Commerce Commission
527 East Capitol Avenue
P.O. Box 19280
Springfield, IL 62794
(217) 782-7295
(217) 782-7434 (TDD)

INDIANA

Chairman
Utility Regulatory Commission
913 State Office Building
Indianapolis, IN 46204
(317) 232-5979

IOWA

Chairman
State Utilities Board
Lucas State Office Bldg.
Des Moines, IA 50319

KANSAS

Chairman
State Corporation Commission
Docking State Office Building
Topeka, KS 66612
(913) 296-3324
1 (800) 662-0027
(toll free in KS)

KENTUCKY

Chairman
Public Service Commission

730 Schenkel Lane
P.O. Box 615
Frankfort, KY 40602
(502) 564-3940

LOUISIANA

Chairman
Public Service Commission
One American Place
Suite 1630
P.O. Box 9115
Baton Rouge, LA 70825
(504) 342-4404
1 (800) 228-9368
(toll free in LA)

MAINE

Chairman
Public Utilities Commission
State House State 18
Augusta, ME 04333
(207) 289-3831
1 (800) 452-4699
(toll free in ME)

MARYLAND

Chairman
Public Service Commission
231 East Baltimore Street
Baltimore, MD 21202
(301) 333-6000
1 (800) 492-0474
(toll free in MD)

MASSACHUSETTS

Chairman
Department of Public Utilities
100 Cambridge Street
12th Floor
Boston, MA 02202
(617) 727-3500

MICHIGAN

Chairperson
Public Service Commission
6545 Mercantile Way
P.O. Box 30221
Lansing, MI 48909
(517) 334-6445
1 (800) 292-9555
(toll free in MI)
1 (800) 443-8926
(toll free TDD in MI)

MINNESOTA

Chairman
Public Utilities Commission
780 American Center Building
160 East Kellogg Boulevard
St. Paul, MN 55101
(812) 296-7124
(812) 287-1200 (TDD)
1 (800) 852-8747
(toll free in MN)

MISSISSIPPI

Chairman
Public Service Commission
P.O. Box 1174
Jackson, MS 39215
(601) 961-5400

MISSOURI

Chairman
Public Service Commission
P.O. Box 360
Jefferson City, MO 65102
(314) 751-3234
1 (800) 392-4211
(toll free in MO)

MONTANA

Chairman
Public Service Commission
2701 Prospect Avenue
Helena, MT 59620
(406) 444-6199

NEBRASKA

Chairman
Public Service Commission
300 The Atrium
1200 "N" Street
P.O. Box 94927
Lincoln, NE 68509
(402) 471-3101

NEVADA

Chairman
Public Service Commission
727 Fairview Drive
Carson City, NV 89710
(702) 687-6000

NEW HAMPSHIRE

Chairman
Public Utilities Commission
8 Old Suncook Road
Building O. 1
Concord, NH 03301
(603) 271-2431
1 (800) 852-3793
(toll free in NH)

NEW JERSEY

President
Board of Public Utilities
Two Gateway Center
Newark, NJ 07102

(201) 648-2027
(201) 648-7983 (TDD)
1 (800) 824-0241
(toll free in NJ)

NEW MEXICO

Chairman
Public Service Commission
P.O. Box 2205
Santa Fe, NM 87504
(505) 827-6940

NEW YORK

Chairman
Public Service Commission
3 Empire State Plaza
Albany, NY 12223
(518) 474-7080
1 (800) 342-3377
(toll free in NY—complaints)
1 (800) 342-3355
(toll free in NY)
(emergency service cutoff
7:30 A.M.–7:30 P.M. Monday–Friday)

NORTH CAROLINA

Chairman
Utilities Commission
P.O. Box 29510-0510
Raleigh, NC 27626
(919) 733-4249

NORTH DAKOTA

President
Public Service Commission
State Capitol Building
Bismarck, ND 58505
(701) 224-2400

1 (800) 932-2400
(toll free in ND)

OHIO

Chairman
Public Utilities Commission
180 East Broad Street
Columbus, OH 43266-0573
(614) 466-3016
(614) 466-8180 (TDD)
1 (800) 282-0198
(toll free in OH)

OKLAHOMA

Chairman
Corporation Commission
Jim Thorpe Office Building
Oklahoma City, OK 73105
(405) 521-2264
1 (800) 522-8154
(toll free in OK)

OREGON

Chairman
Public Utilities Commission
300 Labor and Industries Bldg.
Salem, OR 97310
(503) 378-6611
1 (800) 522-2404
(toll free in OR)

PENNSYLVANIA

Chairman
Public Utility Commission
P.O. Box 3265
Harrisburg, PA 17120
(717) 783-1740
1 (800) 782-1110
(toll free in PA)

PUERTO RICO

Chairman
Public Service Commission
Call Box 870
Hato Rey, PR 00919-0870
(809) 751-5050

RHODE ISLAND

Chairman
Public Utilities Commission
100 Orange Street
Providence, RI 02903
(401) 277-3500
(voice/TDD)
1 (800) 342-1000
(toll free in RI)

SOUTH CAROLINA

Chairman
Public Service Commission
P.O. Drawer 11649
Columbia, SC 29211
(803) 737-5100
1 (800) 922-1531
(toll free in SC)

SOUTH DAKOTA

Chairman
Public Utilities Commission
500 East Capitol Avenue
Pierre, SD 57501
(605) 773-3201

TENNESSEE

Chairman
Public Service Commission
460 James Robertson Parkway

Nashville, TN 37219
(615) 741-2904
1 (800) 342-8359
(toll free voice/TDD in TN)

TEXAS

Chairman
Public Utility Commission
7800 Shoal Creek Boulevard
Suite 400 N
Austin, TX 78757
(512) 458-0100
(512) 458-0221 (TDD)

UTAH

Chairman
Public Service Commission
160 East 300 South
P.O. Box 45585
Salt Lake City, UT 84115
(801) 530-6716

VERMONT

Chairman
Public Service Board
120 State Street
State Office Building
Montpelier, VT 05602
(802) 828-2358
1 (800) 622-4496
(toll free in VT)

VIRGIN ISLANDS

Chairman
Public Services Commission
P.O. Box 40
Charlotte Amalie
St. Thomas, VI 00804
(809) 776-1291

VIRGINIA

Chairman
State Corporation Commission
P.O. Box 1197
Richmond, VA 23209
(804) 786-3608
1 (800) 552-7945
(toll free in VA)

WASHINGTON

Chairman
Utilities and Transportation Commission
1300 Evergreen Park Dr., South
Olympia, WA 98504
(206) 753-6423
1 (800) 562-6150
(toll free in WA)

WEST VIRGINIA

Chairman
Public Service Commission

P.O. Box 812
Charleston, WV 25323
(304) 340-0300
1 (800) 344-5113
(toll free in WV)

WISCONSIN

Chairman
Public Service Commission
4802 Sheboygan Avenue
P.O. Box 7854
Madison, WI 53707
(608) 266-2001

WYOMING

Chairman
Public Service Commission
700 West 21st Street
Cheyenne, WY 82002
(307) 777-7427